Documents of
AMERICAN
BROADCASTING

Documents of

AMERICAN

BROADCASTING

Second Edition

Edited by **FRANK J. KAHN**

Herbert H. Lehman College
City University of New York

Prentice-Hall, Inc., Englewood Cliffs, New Jersey

ISBN: 0-13-216986-X

Library of Congress Catalog Card Number: 72-12050

10 9 8 7 6 5 4 3 2 1

PRENTICE-HALL INTERNATIONAL, INC., *London*
PRENTICE-HALL OF AUSTRALIA, PTY. LTD., *Sydney*
PRENTICE-HALL OF CANADA, LTD., *Toronto*
PRENTICE-HALL OF INDIA PRIVATE LIMITED, *New Delhi*
PRENTICE-HALL OF JAPAN, INC., *Tokyo*

For Abs and J-P

PREFACE

The germinal idea for this book occurred to me shortly after I began to teach. As an instructor of broadcasting I considered it advisable for my students to read certain laws, decisions, reports, and other documents in their original form. Although several texts referred to such materials, and some included extracts or, in all too few instances, a complete document or two, there existed no collection of primary sources in broadcasting. Thus, I either duplicated certain documents for classroom distribution, referred students to law books they were untrained to use, or, as was most often the case, dropped the idea because of the difficulty of gaining access to such sources. Other instructors shared the same problem of inconvenient accessibility.

This second edition of *Documents of American Broadcasting* should continue to serve the obvious need for a collection of primary reference sources in the field of broadcasting. The unusually eventful years following publication of the first edition have produced significant changes in radio and television. One quarter of the nearly sixty documents in this expanded and revised edition were generated while the first edition was in print, and the entirely new Part Five, "The Public's Interest," would not have been justified only five years ago. Several documents carried over from the earlier version have undergone modifications which are reflected in this current edition. Major sections of the former edition's treatment of educational broadcasting are now incorporated in Part One. Regrettably, some documents had to be dropped altogether in this edition for reasons of pertinence and precedence.

Documents of American Broadcasting can be used as a primary text in upper-class and graduate level courses such as "Issues in Mass Communication," "History of Broadcasting,""Radio-TV Law," or "Freedom of Speech in the Mass Media." It is also intended to serve as a supplementary text and reference work for a variety of non-studio broadcasting courses, especially in the fields of management, programming, and journalism. In addition, the book should be helpful to professional broadcasters, though it is no substitute for legal counsel or a well-stocked law library.

Undoubtedly, had this work been edited by someone else its contents would have been somewhat different. The selections are functions of my particular orientation to broadcasting and broadcasting education, as well as the era during which the selections were made. The bibliographic entries in the lists of "Related Reading" have been chosen on the basis of their ease of access and their historical or contemporary significance.

Individual documents have been grouped into five sections. Many of them become doubly valuable when read in conjunction with selections in other sections. For example, the "Network" case which appears in Part Four, "Regulation of Competition," is also highly relevant to Part Two, "Freedom of Expression: Regulation of Programming," since the decision has much to say regarding freedom of speech in broadcasting. Similarly, Part Five's *Citizens Communications Center* decision relates to the *Policy Statement on Comparative Broadcast Hearings* in Part Four. Readers are urged not to misconstrue an organizational convenience as didactic necessity.

I have endeavored to include as much of each document as readers are likely to find useful. Most documents appear in their entirety, including concurrences and dissents that provoke thought and illuminate issues. Because of their value as research aids, explanations of the main text, and intimations of what the future holds for public policy regarding broadcasting, I have excised none of the frequently lengthy footnotes that accompany legal opinions. While some documents have been edited so as to minimize the redundant and irrelevant, if I have erred on the side of plenitude the reader can rectify this by skipping over what he deems of little consequence.

Variant footnote styles and forms of legal citation have not been brought into conformity. Such an attempt at consistency would modify documents whose formal and substantive integrity it is this book's intention to preserve.

I am indebted to Giraud Chester, Bob Crawford, Frank P. Fogarty, Eugene S. Foster, Garnet R. Garrison, Lawrence Myers, Jr., Charles A. Siepmann, and Edgar E. Willis, all of whom commented on the concept, contents, and organization of this book's first edition, and all of whom gave advice that tested and often improved my original conception. I am also most grateful to the many broadcast educators throughout the country who were kind enough to tell me what they thought was most urgently needed in this second edition. Space permits only the barest listing of this edition's benefactors, but Edward F. Douglass must be singled out for his unstinting contributions and encouragement. Special thanks are due Barry Cole, who provided me with information and documents that official FCC channels sometimes failed to produce, and Stockton Helffrich, who enabled this volume to incorporate recent revisions of the Television Code of the National Association of Broadcasters. I, of course, am solely responsible for any of this work's shortcomings.

F. J. K.

March, 1973

CONTENTS

Part Three
FREEDOM OF EXPRESSION:
BROADCAST JOURNALISM   359

INTRODUCTION

Broadcasting in the United States has progressed from its fumbling, almost accidental beginnings to accepted institutional status. Today radio and television are properly regarded as popular entertainment media, as well as powerful social, economic, educational, journalistic, and political instruments in America.

The basic system of U.S. broadcasting is an amalgam of commercial free enterprise and limited governmental regulation. This structure is augmented by a similarly regulated noncommercial, educational system. Yet, the present organization of the broadcast media in this country did not simply "happen." Rather, it is the product of particular American values and needs, as well as the result of unique democratic methods of applying values to implement needs.

The documents in this volume cast light on shifting values and needs and are fundamental to a full understanding of the development, operation, and significance of broadcasting in America. They have been selected and arranged so as to focus on the history and recurrent issues in the field. The editor's interpretation of the documents has been minimized in order that the reader may analyze and judge the materials for himself. For those who wish to consider these documents in a broader context, the following current surveys are recommended:

> Chester, Giraud, Garnet R. Garrison, and Edgar E. Willis. *Television and Radio*, 4th ed. New York: Appleton-Century-Crofts, 1971.
>
> Head, Sydney W. *Broadcasting in America*, 2nd ed. Boston: Houghton Mifflin, 1972.

The best general history of American broadcasting is Erik Barnouw's fine trilogy, subtitled *A History of Broadcasting in the United States:*

> *A Tower in Babel* (Vol. I, to 1933). New York: Oxford University Press, 1966.
>
> *The Golden Web* (Vol. II, 1933—1953). New York: Oxford University Press, 1968.
>
> *The Image Empire* (Vol. III, from 1953). New York: Oxford University Press, 1970.

Three works that treat mass communication law from different and complementary perspectives are:

Emery, Walter B. *Broadcasting and Government: Responsibilities and Regulations*, revised ed. East Lansing, Mich.: Michigan State University Press, 1971.

Gillmor, Donald M., and Jerome A. Barron. *Mass Communication Law: Cases and Comment*. St. Paul, Minn.: West Publishing Co., 1969. (A 1971 supplement is available.)

Nelson, Harold L., and Dwight L. Teeter, Jr. *Law of Mass Communications: Freedom and Control of Print and Broadcast Media*. Mineola, N.Y.: Foundation Press, 1969.

More specific bibliographic entries appear at the end of each of this book's five parts.

A NOTE ON LEGAL CITATION

Since legal citation may pose some problem for those unfamiliar with legal research, an explanation is necessary for readers who wish to explore sources cited throughout this text.

Judicial and quasi-judicial citations follow the form **36 FCC 147**. The italicized name of the case precedes and the year of the decision (in parentheses) follows as additional aids to locating decisions. The complete citation for the above example is: *In re Pacifica Foundation*, 36 FCC 147 (1964). "FCC" means the decision is found in *Federal Communications Commission Reports*. The number immediately preceding "FCC" indicates the volume (36) in which the decision is located, while the number directly following "FCC" denotes the page (147) on which the decision begins. An entry such as **33 FCC 250, 255** refers to page 255 of a decision that begins on page 250 of volume 33 of *Federal Communications Commission Reports*.

The following sources and their abbreviations are the most frequently encountered in broadcast law citations :

Appeals Cases, District of Columbia	App. D.C.
Code of Federal Regulations (FCC rules)	C.F.R.
Federal Communications Commission (or *Federal Radio Commission) Annual Report*	FCC (or FRC) Ann. Rep.
Federal Communications Commission Reports	FCC
Federal Register	Fed. Reg.
Federal Reporter	F.
Federal Supplement	F.Supp.
Opinions of the Attorney General	Ops. Att'y Gen.
Radio Regulation (Pike and Fischer)	R.R.
United States Supreme Court Reports	U.S.

A citation followed by the notation "2d," e.g., **62 F.2d 850**, means that the decision is found in the second series of the indicated source. *Federal*

Communications Commission Reports, Federal Reporter, and P̶i̶k̶e̶ and F̶i̶s̶c̶h̶e̶r̶'s *Radio Regulation* are presently in their second series.

FCC 63-734 and similar entries refer to mimeographed notices issued by the Federal Communications Commission. The numbers before the hyphen are the last two digits of the year of the notice, while the numbers after the hyphen specify the sequence of notices in a given year. Accordingly, the above example refers to the 734th notice published by the FCC in 1963.

Federal laws are found in *United States Code* (U.S.C.), *United States Code Annotated* (U.S.C.A.), and *Statutes at Large* (Stat.). The *Congressional Record* contains transcripts of debates on the floor of the Senate and House of Representatives. Congressional reports and messages are compiled in Senate and House serial sets. Records of hearings before congressional committees are published separately by the Government Printing Office.

For further guidance concerning legal notation consult the latest edition of *A Uniform System of Citation* published by the Harvard Law Review Association, Cambridge, Massachusetts. Any good law dictionary (*Black's,* for example) will serve to define legal terms.

Documents of
AMERICAN
BROADCASTING

PART ONE

DEVELOPMENT OF
BROADCAST REGULATION

The growth of communications law generally parallels the startling evolution of communications technology. Since technological development usually precedes the regulation of its utilization and social effects, broadcast law has never quite kept pace with scientific invention and innovation in the field. Broadcasting first assumed its familiar form as a network distributed, advertiser supported, mass medium under the inadequate provisions of the Radio Act of 1912. Similarly, developments such as cable television and Pay-TV were never contemplated in the Communications Act of 1934.

Congress enacted effective broadcast legislation in 1927 only when it became painfully apparent that the absence of such regulation would result in the misuse of a precious national resource — the radio spectrum. Unable to oversee the fine points of broadcast regulation itself, the Congress established an expert body (first the Federal Radio Commission, then the Federal Communications Commission) to act as its regulatory delegate. The basic Congressional mandate was that broadcasting must serve the public interest; the definition and application of that criterion were left to the Commission, which was entrusted with broad discretionary powers.

In recent years the regulatory structure has been modified

so as to foster the development of a dual system of American broadcasting. On one hand is the commercial sector which accounts for about 90 percent of all broadcasting stations. Commercial radio and television stations supply the most popular programs and are supported by advertising revenues. On the other hand is the noncommercial sector, dubbed "Public Broadcasting," which provides instructional, cultural, and minority interest programming, supported by private grants and increasing amounts of federal funds. Both areas are intended to serve the public interest; neither seems entirely capable of doing so alone. The continuing development of this dualism reaffirms the validity of trial-and-error democratic processes as the recognized miscalculations of the past encourage struggles toward a more perfect future.

Whatever criticisms may be made regarding the formulation and administration of broadcast law in the United States, it is clear that American broadcasting could never have achieved its amazing accomplishments without the regulatory scheme that took shape in the last half century. Both the prescriptive and proscriptive provisions of our laws serve to lend credence to the contention that America's unique amalgam of private enterprise and the public interest in broadcasting is consistent with public policy as enunciated by the people's elected representatives and their appointees. Whether broadcasting shaped the law or the law shaped broadcasting then becomes as unanswerable a question as the familiar one about chickens and eggs.

1

THE U.S. CONSTITUTION

1787–1868

Broadcast regulation springs from that source of all Federal law, the Constitution. The commerce clause was subsequently interpreted by the Supreme Court to include the regulation of interstate communication, of which broadcasting is an example. The First Amendment to the Constitution is echoed by Section 29 of the Radio Act of 1927 and Section 326 of the Communications Act of 1934.

Article I, Section 8. The Congress shall have Power ... To regulate Commerce with foreign Nations, and among the several States, and with the Indian Tribes; ... To promote the Progress of Science and useful Arts, by securing for limited Times to Authors and Inventors the exclusive Right to their respective Writings and Discoveries ...

First Amendment. Congress shall make no law respecting an establishment of religion, or prohibiting the free exercise thereof; or abridging the freedom of speech, or of the press; or the right of the people peaceably to assemble, and to petition the government for a redress of grievances.

Fifth Amendment. No person shall ... be deprived of life, liberty, or property, without due process of law; nor shall private property be taken for public use, without just compensation.

Sixth Amendment. In all criminal prosecutions, the accused shall enjoy the right to a speedy and public trial, by an impartial jury of the State and district wherein the crime shall have been committed, which district shall have been previously ascertained by law, and to be informed of the nature and cause of the accusation; to be confronted with the witnesses against him; to have

3

compulsory process for obtaining witnesses in his favor, and to have the Assistance of Counsel for his defence.

Fourteenth Amendment. Sec. 1. . . . No State shall make or enforce any law which shall abridge the privileges or immunities of citizens of the United States; nor shall any State deprive any person of life, liberty, or property, without due process of law; nor deny to any person within its jurisdiction the equal protection of the laws. . . .

2

THE WIRELESS SHIP ACT
OF 1910

Public Law 262, 61st Congress
June 24, 1910

This first American radio law, enacted ten years before the advent of broadcasting, was limited to the use of radio as a lifesaving device at sea.

Be it enacted by the Senate and House of Representatives of the United States of America in Congress assembled, That from and after the first day of July, nineteen hundred and eleven, it shall be unlawful for any ocean-going steamer of the United States, or of any foreign country, carrying passengers and carrying fifty or more persons, including passengers and crew, to leave or attempt to leave any port of the United States unless such steamer shall be equipped with an efficient apparatus for radio-communication, in good working order, in charge of a person skilled in the use of such apparatus, which apparatus shall be capable of transmitting and receiving messages over a distance of at least one hundred miles, night or day: *Provided,* That the provisions of this act shall not apply to steamers plying only between ports less than two hundred miles apart.

Sec. 2.   That for the purpose of this act apparatus for radio-communication shall not be deemed to be efficient unless the company installing it shall contract in writing to exchange, and shall, in fact, exchange, as far as may be physically practicable, to be determined by the master of the vessel, messages with shore or ship stations using other systems of radio-communication.

Sec. 3.   That the master or other person being in charge of any such vessel which leaves or attempts to leave any port of the United States in violation of any of the provisions of this act shall, upon conviction, be fined in a sum not more than five thousand dollars, and any such fine shall be a lien upon such vessel, and such vessel may be libeled therefor in any district court of the United

[handwritten margin notes: "no ship can leave w/out radio equip." and "leaving w/out equip. violation"]

5

States within the jurisdiction of which such vessel shall arrive or depart, and the leaving or attempting to leave each and every port of the United States shall constitute a separate offense.

Sec. 4.   That the Secretary of Commerce and Labor shall make such regulations as may be necessary to secure the proper execution of this act by collectors of customs and other officers of the Government.

3

THE RADIO ACT
OF 1912

Public Law 264, 62d Congress
August 13, 1912

This first comprehensive piece of radio legislation made it illegal to operate a radio station without a license from the Secretary of Commerce but failed to provide sufficient discretionary standards for the effective regulation of broadcasting, which was still not envisioned at the time of enactment.

Be it enacted by the Senate and House of Representatives of the United States of America in Congress assembled, That a person, company, or corporation within the jurisdiction of the United States shall not use or operate any apparatus for radio communication as a means of commercial intercourse among the several States, or with foreign nations, or upon any vessel of the United States engaged in interstate or foreign commerce, or for the transmission of radiograms or signals the effect of which extends beyond the jurisdiction of the State or Territory in which the same are made, or where interference would be caused thereby with the receipt of messages or signals from beyond the jurisdiction of the said State or Territory, except under and in accordance with a license, revocable for cause, in that behalf granted by the Secretary of Commerce and Labor upon application therefor; but nothing in this Act shall be construed to apply to the transmission and exchange of radiograms or signals between points situated in the same State: *Provided,* That the effect thereof shall not extend beyond the jurisdiction of the said State or interfere with the reception of radiograms or signals from beyond said jurisdiction; and a license shall not be required for the transmission or exchange of radiograms or signals by or on behalf of the Government of the United States, but every Government station on land or sea shall have special call letters designated and published in the list of radio stations of the United States by the Department of Commerce and Labor. Any person, company, or corporation that shall use or operate any apparatus for radio communication in violation of this section, or knowingly aid or abet another person, company, or corporation in so doing, shall be deemed guilty of a misdemeanor, and on conviction thereof shall be punished by a fine not exceeding five hundred dollars, and the apparatus or device so unlawfully used and operated may be adjudged forfeited to the United States.

Sec. 2.   That every such license shall be in such form as the Secretary of Commerce and Labor shall determine and shall contain the restrictions, pursuant to this Act, on and subject to which the license is granted; that every such license shall be issued only to citizens of the United States or Porto Rico or to a company incorporated under the laws of some State or Territory or of the United States or Porto Rico, and shall specify the ownership and location of the station in which said apparatus shall be used and other particulars for its identification and to enable its range to be estimated; shall state the purpose of the station, and, in case of a station in actual operation at the date of passage of this Act, shall contain the statement that satisfactory proof has been furnished that it was actually operating on the above-mentioned date; shall state the wave length or the wave lengths authorized for use by the station for the prevention of interference and the hours for which the station is licensed for work; and shall not be construed to authorize the use of any apparatus for radio communication in any other station than that specified. Every such license shall be subject to the regulations contained herein, and such regulations as may be established from time to time by authority of this act or subsequent acts and treaties of the United States. Every such license shall provide that the President of the United States in time of war or public peril or disaster may cause the closing of any station for radio communication and the removal therefrom of all radio apparatus, or may authorize the use or control of any such station or apparatus by any department of the Government, upon just compensation to the owners.

Sec. 3.   That every such apparatus shall at all times while in use and operation as aforesaid be in charge or under the supervision of a person or persons licensed for that purpose by the Secretary of Commerce and Labor. Every person so licensed who in the operation of any radio apparatus shall fail to observe and obey regulations contained in or made pursuant to this act or subsequent acts or treaties of the United States, or any one of them, or who shall fail to enforce obedience thereto by an unlicensed person while serving under his supervision, in addition to the punishments and penalties herein prescribed, may suffer the suspension of the said license for a period to be fixed by the Secretary of Commerce and Labor not exceeding one year. It shall be unlawful to employ any unlicensed person or for any unlicensed person to serve in charge or in supervision of the use and operation of such apparatus, and any person violating this provision shall be guilty of a misdemeanor, and on conviction thereof shall be punished by a fine of not more than one hundred dollars or imprisonment for not more than two months; or both, in the discretion of the court, for each and every such offense: *Provided*, That in case of emergency the Secretary of Commerce and Labor may authorize a collector of customs to issue a temporary permit, in lieu of a license, to the operator on a vessel subject to the radio ship act of June twenty-fourth, nineteen hundred and ten.

Sec. 4.   That for the purpose of preventing or minimizing interference with communication between stations in which such apparatus is operated, to facilitate radio communication, and to further the prompt receipt of distress signals, said private and commercial stations shall be subject to the regulations of this section. These regulations shall be enforced by the Secretary of Commerce and Labor through the collectors of customs and other officers of the Government as other regulations herein provided for.

The Secretary of Commerce and Labor may, in his discretion, waive the provisions of any or all of these regulations when no interference of the character above mentioned can ensue.

The Secretary of Commerce and Labor may grant special temporary licenses to stations actually engaged in conducting experiments for the development of the science of radio communication, or the apparatus pertaining thereto, to carry on special tests, using any amount of power or any wave lengths, at such hours and under such conditions as will insure the least interference with the sending or receipt of commercial or Government radiograms, of distress signals and radiograms, or with the work of other stations.

In these regulations the naval and military stations shall be understood to be stations on land.

REGULATIONS

Normal wave length

First.   Every station shall be required to designate a certain definite wave length as the normal sending and receiving wave length of the station. This wave length shall not exceed six hundred meters or it shall exceed one thousand six hundred meters. Every coastal station open to general public service shall at all times be ready to receive messages of such wave lengths as are required by the Berlin convention. Every ship station, except as hereinafter provided, and every coast station open to general public service shall be prepared to use two sending wave lengths, one of three hundred meters and one of six hundred meters, as required by the international convention in force: *Provided*, That the Secretary of Commerce and Labor may, in his discretion, change the limit of wave length reservation made by regulations first and second to accord with any international agreement to which the United States is a party.

Other wave lengths

Second.   In addition to the normal sending wave length all stations, except as provided hereinafter in these regulations, may use other sending wave lengths: *Provided*, That they do not exceed six hundred meters or that they do exceed one thousand six hundred meters: *Provided further*, That the character of the waves emitted conforms to the requirements of regulations third and fourth following.

Use of a "pure wave"

Third.   At all stations if the sending apparatus, to be referred to hereinafter as the "transmitter," is of such a character that the energy is radiated in two or more wave lengths, more or less sharply defined, as indicated by a sensitive wave meter, the energy in no one of the lesser waves shall exceed ten per centum of that in the greatest.

Use of a "sharp wave"

Fourth.   At all stations the logarithmic decreement per complete oscillation in the wave trains emitted by the transmitter shall not exceed two-tenths, except when sending distress signals or signals and messages relating thereto.

Use of "standard distress wave"

Fifth.   Every station on shipboard shall be prepared to send distress calls on the normal wave length designated by the international convention in force, except on vessels of small tonnage unable to have plants insuring that wave length.

Signal of distress

Sixth.   The distress call used shall be the international signal of distress
· · · — — — · · ·

Use of "broad interfering wave" for distress signals

Seventh. When sending distress signals, the transmitter of a station on shipboard may be tuned in such a manner as to create a maximum of interference with a maximum of radiation.

Distance requirements for distress signals

Eighth. Every station on shipboard, wherever practicable, shall be prepared to send distress signals of the character specified in regulations fifth and sixth with sufficient power to enable them to be received by day over sea a distance of one hundred nautical miles by a shipboard station equipped with apparatus for both sending and receiving equal in all essential particulars to that of the station first mentioned.

"Right of way" for distress signals

Ninth. All stations are required to give absolute priority to signals and radiograms relating to ships in distress; to cease all sending on hearing a distress signal; and, except when engaged in answering or aiding the ship in distress, to refrain from sending until all signals and radiograms relating thereto are completed.

Reduced power for ships near a government station

Tenth. No station on shipboard, when within fifteen nautical miles of a naval or military station, shall use a transformer input exceeding one kilowatt, nor, when within five nautical miles of such a station, a transformer input exceeding one-half kilowatt, except for sending signals of distress, or signals or radiograms relating thereto.

Intercommunication

Eleventh. Each shore station open to general public service between the coast and vessels at sea shall be bound to exchange radiograms with any similar shore station and with any ship station without distinction of the radio system adopted by such stations, respectively, and each station on shipboard shall be bound to exchange radiograms with any other station on shipboard without distinction of the radio systems adopted by each station, respectively.

It shall be the duty of each such shore station, during the hours it is in operation, to listen in at intervals of not less than fifteen minutes and for a period not less than two minutes, with the receiver tuned to receive messages of three hundred-meter wave lengths.

Division of time

Twelfth.   At important seaports and at all other places where naval or military and private commercial shore stations operate in such close proximity that interference with the work of naval and military stations can not be avoided by the enforcement of the regulations contained in the foregoing regulations concerning wave lengths and character of signals emitted, such private or commercial shore stations as do interfere with the reception of signals by the naval and military stations concerned shall not use their transmitters during the first fifteen minutes of each hour, local standard time. The Secretary of Commerce and Labor may, on the recommendation of the department concerned, designate the station or stations which may be required to observe this division of time.

Government stations to observe division of time

Thirteenth.   The naval or military stations for which the above-mentioned division of time may be established shall transmit signals or radiograms only during the first fifteen minutes of each hour, local standard time, except in case of signals or radiograms relating to vessels in distress, as hereinbefore provided.

Use of unnecessary power

Fourteenth.   In all circumstances, except in case of signals or radiograms relating to vessels in distress, all stations shall use the minimum amount of energy necessary to carry out any communication desired.

General restrictions on private stations

Fifteenth.   No private or commercial station not engaged in the transaction of bona fide commercial business by radio communication or in experimentation in connection with the development and manufacture of radio apparatus for commercial purposes shall use a transmitting wave length exceeding two hundred meters, or a transformer input exceeding one kilowatt, except by special authority of the Secretary of Commerce and Labor contained in the license of the station: *Provided*, That the owner or operator of a station of the character mentioned in this regulation shall not be liable for a violation of the requirements of the third or fourth regulations to the penalties of one hundred dollars or twenty-five dollars, respectively, provided in this section unless the person maintaining or operating such station shall have been notified in writing that the said transmitter has been found, upon tests conducted by the Government, to be so adjusted as to violate the third and fourth regulations, and opportunity has been given to said owner or operator to adjust said transmitter in conformity with said regulations.

Special restrictions in the vicinities of government stations

Sixteenth.   No station of the character mentioned in regulation fifteenth situated within five nautical miles of a naval or military station shall use a transmitting wave length exceeding two hundred meters or a transformer input exceeding one-half kilowatt.

Ship stations to communicate with nearest shore stations

Seventeenth.   In general, the shipboard stations shall transmit their radiograms to the nearest shore station. A sender on board a vessel shall, however, have the right to designate the shore station through which he desires to have his radiograms transmitted. If this can not be done, the wishes of the sender are to be complied with only if the transmission can be effected without interfering with the service of other stations.

Limitations for future installations in vicinities of government stations

Eighteenth.   No station on shore not in actual operation at the date of the passage of this act shall be licensed for the transaction of commercial business by radio communication within fifteen nautical miles of the following naval or military stations, to wit: Arlington, Virginia; Key West, Florida; San Juan, Porto Rico; North Head and Tatoosh Island, Washington; San Diego, California; and those established or which may be established in Alaska and in the Canal Zone; and the head of the department having control of such Government stations shall, so far as is consistent with the transaction of governmental business, arrange for the transmission and receipt of commercial radiograms under the provisions of the Berlin convention of nineteen hundred and six and future international conventions or treaties to which the United States may be a party, at each of the stations above referred to, and shall fix the rates therefor, subject to control of such rates by Congress. At such stations and wherever and whenever shore stations open for general public business between the coast and vessels at sea under the provisions of the Berlin convention of nineteen hundred and six and future international conventions and treaties to which the United States may be a party shall not be so established as to insure a constant service day and night without interruption, and in all localities wherever or whenever such service shall not be maintained by a commercial shore station within one hundred nautical miles of a naval radio station, the Secretary of the Navy shall, so far as is consistent with the transaction of Government business, open naval radio stations to the general public business described above, and shall fix rates for such service, subject to control of such rates by Congress. The receipts from such radiograms shall be covered into the Treasury as miscellaneous receipts.

Secrecy of messages

Nineteenth.   No person or persons engaged in or having knowledge of the operation of any station or stations shall divulge or publish the contents of any messages transmitted or received by such station, except to the person or persons to whom the same may be directed, or their authorized agent, or to another station employed to forward such message to its destination, unless legally required so to do by the court of competent jurisdiction or other competent authority. Any person guilty of divulging or publishing any message, except as herein provided, shall, on conviction thereof, be punishable by a fine of not more than two hundred and fifty dollars or imprisonment for a period of not exceeding three months, or both fine and imprisonment, in the discretion of the court.

Penalties

For violation of any of these regulations, subject to which a license under sections one and two of this act may be issued, the owner of the apparatus shall be liable to a penalty of one hundred dollars, which may be reduced or remitted by the Secretary of Commerce and Labor, and for repeated violations of any of such regulations the license may be revoked.

For violation of any of these regulations, except as provided in regulation nineteenth, subject to which a license under section three of this act may be issued, the operator shall be subject to a penalty of twenty-five dollars, which may be reduced or remitted by the Secretary of Commerce and Labor, and for repeated violations of any such regulations, the license shall be suspended or revoked.

Sec. 5. That every license granted under the provisions of this act for the operation or use of apparatus for radio communication shall prescribe that the operator thereof shall not willfully or maliciously interfere with any other radio communication. Such interference shall be deemed a misdemeanor, and upon conviction thereof the owner or operator, or both, shall be punishable by a fine of not to exceed five hundred dollars or imprisonment for not to exceed one year, or both.

Sec. 6. That the expression "radio communication" as used in this act means any system of electrical communication by telegraphy or telephony without the aid of any wire connecting the points from and at which the radiograms, signals, or other communications are sent or received.

Sec. 7. That a person, company, or corporation within the jurisdiction of the United States shall not knowingly utter or transmit, or cause to be uttered or transmitted, any false or fraudulent distress signal or call or false or fraudulent signal, call, or other radiogram of any kind. The penalty for so uttering or transmitting a false or fraudulent distress signal or call shall be a fine of not more than two thousand five hundred dollars or imprisonment for not more than five years, or both, in the discretion of the court, for each and every such offense, and the penalty for so uttering or transmitting, or causing to be uttered or transmitted, any other false or fraudulent signal, call, or other radiogram shall be a fine of not more than one thousand dollars or imprisonment for not more than two years, or both, in the discretion of the court, for each and every such offense.

Sec. 8. That a person, company, or corporation shall not use or operate any apparatus for radio communication on a foreign ship in territorial waters of the United States otherwise than in accordance with the provisions of sections four and seven of this act and so much of section five as imposes a penalty for interference. Save as aforesaid, nothing in this act shall apply to apparatus for radio communication on any foreign ship.

Sec. 9. That the trial of any offense under this act shall be in the district in which it is committed, or if the offense is committed upon the high seas or out of the jurisdiction of any particular State or district the trial shall be in the district where the offender may be found or into which he shall be first brought.

Sec. 10.   That this act shall not apply to the Philippine Islands.

Sec. 11.   That this act shall take effect and be in force on and after four months from its passage.

4

BREAKDOWN OF THE ACT
OF 1912

Broadcasting in the United States began in 1920, when station KDKA in Pittsburgh, Pennsylvania, reported the Harding-Cox election returns to a widely dispersed audience. By early 1923 some 576 stations were licensed for broadcasting. The public's investment in receiving apparatus had increased by leaps and bounds as more stations came on the air.

Secretary of Commerce Herbert Hoover valiantly tried to minimize interference problems under the Act of 1912. The three legal decisions, below, vitiated the discretionary powers the Secretary had been exercising, and pointed out the need for more effective broadcast legislation.

1920 - beg. of commercial radio.

A

HOOVER v.

INTERCITY RADIO CO., INC.*

286 F. 1003 (D.C. Cir.)
February 5, 1923

Van Orsdel, Associate Justice.

This appeal is from an order of the Supreme Court of the District of Columbia, directing the issuance of a writ of mandamus requiring appellant, Secretary of Commerce, to issue to plaintiff company, a license to operate a radio station in the city of New York.

The plaintiff alleged that it has been engaged in the business of wireless telegraphy between New York and other cities of the United States since January 16, 1920, under licenses issued from time to time by defendant, pursuant to the Act of Congress approved August 13, 1912, 37 Stat. 302 (Comp. St. § 10100–10109). It was further alleged that the last license expired on November 12, 1921; that defendant refused to grant plaintiff a new license for the operation of its station; that appellee, in all respects, complied with the requirements of the act of Congress and of the regulations contained therein; and that the duty imposed upon defendant of granting licenses is purely a ministerial one.

Defendant answered, admitting the refusal of the license, but defending on the ground that he had been unable to ascertain a wave length for use by plaintiff, which would not interfere with government and private stations, and that under the provisions of the act of Congress the issuance or refusal of a license is a matter wholly within his discretion.

Section 1 of the act (Comp. St. § 10100) forbids the operation of radio apparatus, where interferences would be caused with receipt of messages or signals from beyond the jurisdiction of the state or territory in which it is situated, "except under and in accordance with a license, revocable for cause, in that behalf granted by the Secretary of Commerce and Labor upon application therefor." The license shall be in form prescribed by the Secretary, containing the restrictions pursuant to the act "on and subject to which the license is granted." Section 2 (Comp. St. § 10101). The license also "shall state the wave length or the wave lengths authorized for use by the station for the prevention of interference and the hours for which the station is licensed for work." The license is further made subject to the regulations of the act and such regulations as may be made by the authority of the act.

The Secretary of Commerce is given authority, for the purpose of preventing or minimizing interference with communication between stations, to enforce the regulations established by the act through the collectors of customs and other officers of the government, with power, however, in his discretion, to waive the provisions of the regulations when no interference obtains.

The act further provides as follows:

All stations are required to give absolute priority to signals and radiograms relating to ships in distress; to cease all sending on hearing a distress signal; and, except when engaged in answering or aiding the ship in distress, to refrain from sending until all signals and radiograms relating thereto are completed. Section 4 (Comp. St. § 10103).

Private or commercial shore stations, so situated that their operation interferes with naval and military stations, are forbidden to "use their transmitters during the first fifteen minutes of each hour, local standard time," during which time the military and naval stations shall transmit signals or radiograms, "except in case of signals or radiograms relating to vessels in distress." The Secretary is forbidden to license private or commercial stations to adopt a wave length between 600 meters and 1,600 meters, the wave lengths between these figures being reserved for governmental agencies. Penalties are prescribed for violations of the act.

Congress seems to have legislated on the subject of radio telegraphy with reference to the undeveloped state of the art. Interference in operation is conceded; hence the act undertakes to prescribe regulations by which the interference may be minimized rather than prevented. It regulates the preferences to be accorded distress signals and government business. It specifically subjects private and commercial stations to the regulations prescribed by the act, the enforcement of which is imposed upon the Secretary of Commerce, acting "through the collectors of customs and other officers of the government." Indeed, the impossibility of totally eliminating interference was recognized internationally by the London Convention which resulted in the Treaty of July 8, 1913 (38 Stat. 1672).

Complete control of the whole subject was reserved by Congress in the provision of section 2 (Comp. St. § 10101) that "such license shall be subject to the regulations contained herein, and such regulations as may be established from time to time by authority of this act or subsequent acts or treaties of the United States," and the further provision that "such license shall provide that the President of the United States in time of war or public peril or disaster may cause the closing of any station for radio communication and the removal therefrom of all radio apparatus, or may authorize the use or control of any such station or apparatus by any department of the government, upon just compensation to the owners."

We are in accord with the construction placed upon the act by the Attorney General on October 24, 1912 (29 Op. Atty. Gen. 579), in response to an inquiry from the Secretary of Commerce and Labor, as follows:

The language of the act, the nature of the subject-matter regulated, as well as the general scope of the statute, negative the idea that Congress intended to repose any such discretion in you in the matter of licenses. It is apparent from the act as a whole that Congress determined thereby to put the subject of radio communication under federal supervision, so far as it was interstate or foreign in its nature. It is also apparent therefrom that that supervision and control is taken by Congress upon itself, and that the Secretary of Commerce and Labor is only authorized to deal with the matter as provided in the act, and is given no general regulative power in respect thereto. The act prescribes the conditions under which the licensees shall operate, containing a set of regulations, with penalties for their violation.

That Congress intended to fully regulate the business of radio telegraphy, without leaving it to the discretion of an executive officer, is apparent from the report of the House committee in recommending the passage of the bill to the House of Representatives, as follows:

The first section of the bill defines its scope within the commerce clause of the Constitution, and requires all wireless stations, ship and shore, public and private, to be licensed by the Secretary of Commerce and Labor. This section does not give the head of that department discretionary power over the issue of licenses, but in fact provides for an enumeration of the wireless stations of the United States and on vessels under the American flag. The license system proposed is substantially the same as that in use for the documenting upward of 25,000 merchant vessels.

It was further stated by the chairman of the committee on commerce in the Senate, when the bill was under consideration, that "it is compulsory with the Secretary of Commerce and Labor that upon application these licenses shall be issued."

While committee reports are not binding upon the courts in interpreting statutes, they are indicative of the legislative intention, and will be followed when the statements so made accord with the reasonable interpretation to be drawn from the language of the act itself.

We are not unmindful of the strict rule forbidding interference with the exercise of official discretion by the extraordinary processes of the courts. The rule that mandamus will not lie to control the action of an official of the executive department, in the exercise of discretionary power, is too well settled to require discussion. But where the duty imposed is purely ministerial, and there is no discretion reposed in the officer, the courts will not hesitate to require the performance of the duty as prescribed.

In the present case the duty of naming a wave length is mandatory upon the Secretary. The only discretionary act is in selecting a wave length, within the limitations prescribed in the statute, which, in his judgment, will result in the least possible interference. The issuing of a license is not dependent upon the fixing of a wave length. It is a restriction entering into the license. The wave length named by the Secretary merely measures the extent of the privilege granted to the licensee.

It logically follows that the duty of issuing licenses to persons or corporations coming within the classification designated in the act reposes no discretion whatever in the Secretary of Commerce. The duty is mandatory; hence the courts will not hesitate to require its performance.

The judgment is affirmed, with costs.

B

UNITED STATES v. ZENITH

RADIO CORPORATION et al.*

U.S. sued bec of Sec. of C decisions

12 F.2d 614 (N.D. Ill.)
April 16, 1926

Wilkerson, District Judge.

The information charges violations of section 1 of the Act of August 13, 1912, c. 287 (37 Stat. 302 [Comp. St. § 10100]).

The first count alleges that on December 19, 1925, defendant Zenith Radio Corporation used and operated certain apparatus for radio communication, as a means of commercial intercourse among several states of the United States, to wit, from Mt. Prospect, Ill., to Seattle, Wash.; which apparatus was so used and operated not under and in accordance with a license such as described in the act; and that defendant McDonald aided, abetted, and procured the commission of the offense. The second, third, and fourth counts charge offenses on other dates in the same language as count 1.

The fifth, sixth, seventh, and eighth counts are the same as the first four

*Reprinted with the permission of West Publishing Company ©1926.

counts, except that it is charged that the corporation "used and operated certain apparatus for radio communication for the transmission of radiograms and signals, the effect of which then and there extended beyond the jurisdiction of the state in which the same were then and there made."

Section 1 of the act in question prohibits the use of apparatus for radio communication as a means of commercial intercourse among the several states, or with foreign nations, or upon any vessel of the United States engaged in interstate or foreign commerce, or for the transmission of radiograms or signals the effect of which extends beyond the jurisdiction of the state or territory in which the same are made, or where interference would be caused thereby with the receipt of messages or signals from beyond the jurisdiction of said state or territory, except under and in accordance with a license, revocable for cause, granted by the Secretary of Commerce upon application therefor. It is provided:

Any person, company, or corporation that shall use or operate any apparatus for radio communication in violation of this section, or knowingly aid or abet another person, company, or corporation in so doing, shall be deemed guilty of a misdemeanor. . . .

Section 2 of the act (Comp. St. § 10101) provides:

Every such license shall be in such form as the Secretary of Commerce (and Labor) shall determine and shall contain the restrictions, pursuant to this act, on and subject to which the license is granted; every such license shall be issued only to citizens of the United States or Porto Rico or to a company incorporated under the laws of some state or territory or of the United States or Porto Rico, and shall specify the ownership and location of the station in which said apparatus shall be used and other particulars for its identification and to enable its range to be estimated; shall state the purpose of the station, and, in case of a station in actual operation at the date of passage of this act, shall contain the statement that satisfactory proof has been furnished that it was actually operating on the above-mentioned date; shall state the wave length or the wave lengths authorized for use by the station for the prevention of interference and the hours for which the station is licensed for work; and shall not be construed to authorize the use of any apparatus for radio communication in any other station than that specified. Every such license shall be subject to the regulations contained herein and such regulations as may be established from time to time by authority of this act or subsequent acts and treaties of the United States. Every such license shall provide that the President of the United States in time of war or public peril or disaster may cause the closing of any station for radio communication and the removal therefrom of all radio apparatus, or may authorize the use or control of any such station or apparatus by any department of the government, upon just compensation to the owners.

Section 4 of the act (Comp. St. § 10103) provides:

For the purpose of preventing or minimizing interference with communication between stations in which such apparatus is operated, to facilitate radio communication, and to further the prompt receipt of distress signals, said private and commercial stations shall be subject to the regulations of the section. These regulations shall be enforced by the Secretary of Commerce (and Labor) through the collectors of customs and other officers of the government as other regulations herein provided for.

The Secretary of Commerce (and Labor) may, in his discretion, waive the provisions of any or all of these regulations when no interference of the character above mentioned can ensue.

Among the regulations prescribed in section 4 are the following:

Normal wave length

First. Every station shall be required to designate a certain definite wave length as the normal sending and receiving wave length of the station. This wave length shall not exceed six hundred meters or it shall exceed one thousand six hundred meters. Every coastal station open to general public service shall at all times be ready to receive messages of such wave lengths as are required by the Berlin convention. Every ship station, except as hereinafter provided, and every coast station open to general public service shall be prepared to use two sending wave lengths, one of three hundred meters and one of six hundred meters, as required by the international convention in force: Provided, that the Secretary of Commerce (and Labor) may, in his discretion, change the limit of wave length reservation made by regulations first and second to accord with any international agreement to which the United States is a party.

Other wave lengths

Second. In addition to the normal sending wave length all stations, except as provided hereinafter in these regulations, may use other sending wave lengths: Provided, that they do not exceed six hundred meters or that they do exceed one thousand six hundred meters: Provided further, that the character of the waves emitted conforms to the requirements of regulations third and fourth following. . . .

Division of time

Twelfth. At important seaports and at all other places where naval or military and private or commercial shore stations operate in such close proximity that interference with the work of naval and military stations cannot be avoided by the enforcement of the regulations contained in the foregoing regulations concerning wave lengths and character of signals emitted, such private or commercial shore stations as do interfere with the reception of signals by the naval and military stations concerned shall not use their transmitters during the first fifteen minutes of each hour, local standard time. The Secretary of Commerce (and Labor) may, on the recommendation of the department concerned, designate the station or stations which may be required to observe this division of time. . . .

General restrictions on private stations

Fifteenth.   No private or commercial station not engaged in the transaction of bona fide commercial business by radio communication or in experimentation in connection with the development and manufacture of radio apparatus for commercial purposes shall use a transmitting wave length exceeding two hundred meters, or a transformer input exceeding one kilowatt, except by special authority of the Secretary of Commerce (and Labor) contained in the license of the station: Provided, that the owner or operator of a station of the character mentioned in this regulation shall not be liable for a violation of the requirements of the third or fourth regulations to the penalties of one hundred dollars or twenty-five dollars, respectively, provided in this section unless the person maintaining or operating such station shall have been notified in writing that the said transmitter has been found, upon tests conducted by the government, to be so adjusted as to violate the said third and fourth regulations, and opportunity has been given to said owner or operator to adjust said transmitter in conformity with said regulations. . . .

Penalties

For violation of any of these regulations, subject to which a license under sections one and two of this act may be issued, the owner of the apparatus shall be liable to a penalty of one hundred dollars, which may be reduced or remitted by the Secretary of Commerce (and Labor), and for repeated violations of any of such regulations, the license may be revoked.

For violation of any of these regulations, except as provided in regulation nineteenth, subject to which a license under section three of this act may be issued, the operator shall be subject to a penalty of twenty-five dollars, which may be reduced or remitted by the Secretary of Commerce (and Labor), and for repeated violations of any such regulations, the license shall be suspended or revoked.

The Secretary of Commerce granted a license on September 21, 1925, to defendant corporation, and that license was in effect at the times of the alleged offenses charged in the information. . . .

Among the provisions of the license, the following are to be noted particularly:

This station to be operated only on Thursday nights from 10 to 12 p.m., Central Standard time, and then only when the use of this period is not desired by the General Electric Company's Denver station. This license is also issued conditionally upon the avoidance of interference with other stations.

In view of special conditions the station is authorized to use for communication exclusively with stations licensed by the United States the following additional wave lengths under 600 or over 1,600 meters: Meters, 332.4.

The material facts are not in dispute. It is agreed that defendant corporation, on the dates charged in the information, operated its station on a wave length and at times which were not authorized.

The broad provisions of section 1 of the act prohibit the use of the radio apparatus except *under and in accordance* with a license granted by the Secretary of Commerce. The use of the apparatus in violation of this provision is made a misdemeanor, punishable by fine up to $500 and forfeiture of the apparatus.

Section 2 of the act provides that the license shall contain the restrictions, *pursuant to the act*, on and subject to which the license is granted. It is provided in section 2 that the license "shall state the wave length or the wave lengths authorized for use by the station for the prevention of interference and the hours for which the station is licensed for work." It is further provided: "Every such license shall be subject to the regulations contained herein and such regulations as may be established from time to time by authority of this act or subsequent acts and treaties of the United States."

There is no express grant of power in the act to the Secretary of Commerce to establish regulations. The regulations subject to which the license is granted are contained in the fourth section of the act.

The fifteenth regulation prohibits a private or commercial station not engaged in the transaction of bona fide commercial business by radio communication or in experimentation in connection with the development and manufacture of radio apparatus for commercial purposes from using a wave length exceeding 200 meters except by special authority of the Secretary of Commerce. Defendant's license authorizes the use of a wave length of 332.4 meters on Thursday night from 10 to 12 p.m. *when the use of this period is not desired by the General Electric Company's Denver Station.*

Each of the acts of the defendant, relied upon by the United States as the basis of prosecution, is within the prohibition of the fifteenth regulation. Each count of the information covers broadcasting on a wave length of 329.5 meters at a time not covered by the authority in the license. Section 4 contains a special provision for penalties for violations of the regulations as follows:

For violation of any of these regulations, subject to which a license under sections one and two of this act may be issued, the owner of the apparatus shall be liable to a penalty of one hundred dollars, which may be reduced or remitted by the Secretary of Commerce, . . . and for repeated violations . . . the license may be revoked.

Does the operation of the station upon any wave length at any other time than from 10 to 12 p.m. on Thursday constitute a violation of section 1? The license provides:

This station to be operated only on Thursday nights from 10 to 12 p.m. Central Standard time and then only when the use of this period is not desired by the General Electric Company's Denver Station.

The provision in section 2 as to stating in the license the hours for which the station is licensed must be read and interpreted in its relation to the entire act.

The Secretary of Commerce is required to issue the license subject to the regulations in the act. The Congress has withheld from him the power to prescribe additional regulations. If there is a conflict between a provision in the license and the regulations established by Congress, the latter must control. Division of time is covered by the twelfth regulation. The provision in section 2 as to hours appears, in view of the references in that section to the regulations, to refer to the regulation as to the division of time. At least, the statute is ambiguous in this respect, and, while it should be given a reasonable construction, ambiguities are not to be solved so as to embrace offenses not clearly within the law. Krichman v. U.S., 256 U.S. 363, 367, 41 S. Ct. 514, 65 L. Ed. 992.

Furthermore, we must remember, in considering an act of Congress, that a construction which might render it unconstitutional is to be avoided. A statute must be construed, if fairly possible, so as to avoid not only the conclusion that it is unconstitutional but grave doubts upon that score. U.S. v. Standard Brewery, 251 U.S. 210, 220, 40 St. Ct. 139, 64 L. Ed. 229; U.S. v. Jin Fuey Moy, 241 U.S. 394, 401, 36 S. Ct. 658, 60 L. Ed. 1061, Ann. Cas. 1917D, 854.

If section 2 is construed to give to the Secretary of Commerce power to restrict the operation of a station as the United States contends is done by this license, what is the test or standard established by Congress, by which the discretion of the Secretary is to be controlled? In other words, what rule has Congress laid down for his guidance in determining division of time between the defendant and the General Electric Company? U.S. v. Grimaud, 220 U.S. 506, 519, 31 S. Ct. 480, 55 L. Ed. 563; Union Bridge Co. v. U.S., 204 U.S. 364, 27 S. Ct. 367, 51 L. Ed. 523; Field v. Clark, 143 U.S. 649, 692, 12 S. Ct. 495, 36 L. Ed. 294. No language is more worthy of frequent and thoughtful consideration than these words of Mr. Justice Matthews, speaking for the Supreme Court in Yick Wo v. Hopkins, 118 U.S. 356, 369, 6 S. Ct. 1064, 1071 (30 L. Ed. 220):

When we consider the nature and the theory of our institutions of government, the principles upon which they are supposed to rest, and review the history of their development, we are constrained to conclude that they do not mean to leave room for the play and action of purely personal and arbitrary power.

Congress cannot delegate its power to make a law, but it can make a law to delegate a power to determine some fact cr state of facts upon which the law makes or intends to make its own action depend. Has Congress prescribed the rule or standard which is to control the Secretary of Commerce in the exercise of his discretion with the degree of certainty required in criminal statutes? It is axiomatic that statutes creating and defining crimes cannot be extended by intendment, and that no act, however wrongful, can be punished under such a statute, unless clearly within its terms. There can be no constructive offenses, and, before a man can be punished, his case must be plainly and unmistakably within the statute. U.S. v. Weitzel, 246 U.S. 533, 543, 38 S. Ct. 381, 62 L. Ed. 872; U.S. v. Harris, 177 U.S. 305, 310, 20 S. Ct. 609, 44 L. Ed. 780; Todd v. U.S., 158 U.S. 278, 282, 15 S. Ct. 889, 39 L. Ed. 982.

If we view the acts of the defendant corporation as violations of the fifteenth regulation, and admit for the present purpose the validity of that regulation, do they constitute a violation of section 1 also because the restrictions imposed under the regulation are included in the license? It is elementary that where there is, in an act, a specific provision relating to a particular subject, that provision must govern in respect to the subject as against general provisions in the act, although the latter, standing alone, would be broad enough to include the subject to which the more particular provision relates. Endlich, Interpretation of Statutes, § 216; Swiss National Insurance Co. v. Miller, 53 App. D.C. 173, 289 F. 571, 576; Washington v. Miller, 235 U.S. 422, 428, 35 S. Ct. 119, 59 L. Ed. 295; U.S. v. Nix, 189 U.S. 199, 205, 23 S. Ct. 495, 47 L. Ed. 775; Townsend v. Little, 109 U.S. 504, 519, 3 S. Ct. 357, 27 L. Ed. 1012. This rule is particularly applicable to criminal statutes in which the specific provisions relating to particular subjects carry smaller penalties than the general provision. Congress, when it inserted the regulations in the statute, provided especially for their violation. That provision should control, in my opinion, against the general, indefinite, and ambiguous provisions of sections 1 and 2.

My conclusion is that, under the rules applicable to criminal statutes, sections 1 and 2 cannot be construed to cover the acts of the defendant upon which this prosecution is based. Other questions have been argued which it is unnecessary to decide.

Reference has been made to the rule of practical construction. It is sufficient to say that administrative rulings cannot add to the terms of an act of Congress and make conduct criminal which such laws leave untouched. U.S. v. Standard Brewery, 251 U.S. 210, 220, 40 S. Ct. 139, 64 L. Ed. 229.

Finding for defendants.

C

ATTORNEY GENERAL'S

OPINION

35 Ops. Att'y Gen. 126

July 8, 1926

Department of Justice

July 8, 1926.

Sir: Receipt is acknowledged of your letter of June 4, 1926, in which you ask for a definition of your powers and duties with respect to the regulation of radio broadcasting under the Act of August 13, 1912, c. 287 (37 Stat. 302). Specifically, you request my opinion upon the following five questions:

(1) Does the 1912 Act require broadcasting stations to obtain licenses, and is the operation of such a station without a license an offense under that Act?

(2) Has the Secretary of Commerce authority under the 1912 Act to assign wave lengths and times of operation and limit the power of stations?

(3) Has a station, whose license stipulates a wave length for its use, the right to use any other wave length, and if it does operate on a different wave length, is it in violation of the law and does it become subject to the penalties of the Act?

(4) If a station, whose license stipulates a period during which only the station may operate and limits its power, transmits at different times, or with excessive power, is it in violation of the Act and does it become subject to the penalties of the Act?

(5) Has the Secretary of Commerce power to fix the duration of the licenses which he issues or should they be indeterminate, continuing in effect until revoked or until Congress otherwise provides?

With respect to the first question, my answer to both its parts is in the affirmative. Section 1 of the Act of 1912 provides—

That a person, company, or corporation within the jurisdiction of the United States shall not use or operate any apparatus for radio communication as a means of commercial intercourse among the several States, or with foreign nations, or upon any vessel of the United States engaged in interstate or foreign commerce, or for the transmission of radiograms or signals the effect of which extends beyond the jurisdiction of the State or Territory in which the same are made, or where interference would be caused thereby with the receipt of messages or signals from beyond the jurisdiction of the said State or Territory, except under and in accordance with a license, revocable for cause, in that behalf granted by the Secretary of Commerce (and Labor) upon application therefor; but nothing in this Act shall be construed to apply to the transmission and exchange of radiograms or signals between points situated in the same State: *Provided*, That the effect thereof shall not extend beyond the jurisdiction of the said State or interfere with the reception of radiograms or signals from beyond said jurisdiction. . . .

Violation of this section is declared to be a misdemeanor.

There is no doubt whatever that radio communication is a proper subject for Federal regulation under the commerce clause of the Constitution. *Pensacola Telegraph Company* v. *Western Union Telegraph Company*, 96 U.S. 1, 9, 24 Op. 100. And it may be noticed in passing that even purely intrastate transmission of radio waves may fall within the scope of Federal power when it disturbs the air in such a manner as to interfere with interstate communication, a situation recognized and provided for in the Act. Cf. *Minnesota Rate Cases*, 230 U.S. 352.

While the Act of 1912 was originally drafted to apply primarily to wireless telegraphy, its language is broad enough to cover wireless telephony as well; and this was clearly the intention of its framers (62nd Cong., 2nd Sess., S. Rept. 698). Whether the transmission is for profit is immaterial so far as the commerce clause is concerned. *American Express Company* v. *United States*, 212 U.S. 522; *Caminetti* v. *United States*, 242 U.S. 470.

For these reasons I am of the opinion that broadcasting is within the terms of the 1912 Act; that a license must be obtained before a broadcasting station may be lawfully operated; and that the penalties of section 1 of the Act may be imposed upon any person or corporation who operates such a station without a license.

Your second question involves three separate problems:

(a)   The assignment of wave lengths.
(b)   The assignment of hours of operation.
(c)   The limitation of power.

(a)   As to the assignment of wave lengths, section 2 of the Act provides—

That every such license shall be in such form as the Secretary of Commerce (and Labor) shall determine and shall contain the restrictions, pursuant to this Act, on and subject to which the license is granted; . . . shall state the wave length or the wave lengths authorized for use by the station for the prevention of interference and the hours for which the station is licensed for work. . . . Every such license shall be subject to the regulations contained herein and such regulations as may be established from time to time by authority of this Act or subsequent Acts and treaties of the United States.

The power to make general regulations is nowhere granted by specific language to the Secretary. On the contrary, it seems clear from section 4 of the Act that Congress intended to cover the entire field itself, and that, with minor exceptions, Congress left very little to the discretion of any administrative officer. This fact is made additionally plain by the reports which accompanied the Act in both Houses. 62d Cong. 2d Sess., S. Rept. 698; *ibid.*, H.R. Rept. 582. Cf. 29 Op. 579.

The first regulation in section 4 provides that the station shall be required to designate a definite wave length, outside of the band between 600 and 1,600 meters (reserved for Government stations), and that ship stations shall be prepared to use 300 and 600 meters.

The second regulation provides that in addition to the normal sending wave length, all stations, except as otherwise provided in the regulations, may use "other sending wave lengths," again excluding the band from 600 to 1,600 meters.

These two regulations constitute a direct legislative regulation of the use of wave lengths. They preclude the possibility of administrative discretion in the same field. In *Hoover* v. *Intercity Radio Company*, 286 Fed. 1003, it was held that it was mandatory upon the Secretary under the Act to grant licenses to all applicants complying with its provisions. The court added in that case these remarks:

In the present case the duty of naming a wave length is mandatory upon the Secretary. The only discretionary act is in selecting a wave length, within the limitations prescribed in the statute, which, in his judgment, will result in the least possible interference. The issuing of a license is not dependent upon the fixing of a wave length. It is a restriction entering into the license. The wave length named by the Secretary merely measures the extent of the privilege granted to the licensee.

You have advised me that following this decision you have assumed that you had discretionary authority in assigning wave lengths for the use of particular stations, and have made such assignments to the individual broadcasting stations.

However, in my opinion, these remarks of the Court of Appeals are to be construed as applying only to the *normal* sending and receiving wave length which every station is required to designate under the first regulation. But under the second regulation, any station is at liberty to use "other wave lengths" at will, provided only that they do not trespass upon the band from 600 to 1,600 meters. This conclusion appears to be in accord with the opinion of the District Court for the Northern District of Illinois in the case . . . of *United States* v. *Zenith Radio Corporation*.

But it is suggested that under the fifteenth regulation broadcasting stations may not, without special authority from the Secretary, use wave lengths over 200 meters or power exceeding one kilowatt. This regulation is applicable only to "private and commercial stations not engaged in the transaction of bona fide commercial business by radio communication." I am of opinion that broadcasting is "the transaction of bona fide commercial business" (*Witmark* v. *Bamberger*, 291 Fed. 776; *Remick* v. *American Automobile Accessories Co.*, 298 Fed. 628), and that it is conducted "by radio communication." Broadcasting stations, therefore, do not fall within the scope of the fifteenth regulation; and the Secretary is without power to impose on them the restrictions provided therein.

From the foregoing consideration I am forced to conclude that you have no general authority under the Act to assign wave lengths to broadcasting stations, except for the purpose of designating normal wave lengths under regulation 1.

(b)   As to the assignment of hours of operation:

The second section of the Act, already quoted, provides that the license shall state "the hours for which the station is licensed for work." By the twelfth and thirteenth regulations the Secretary, on the recommendation of the Department concerned, may designate stations which must refrain from operating during the first 15 minutes of each hour — a period to be reserved in designated localities for Government stations. These two regulations are the only ones in which a division of time is mentioned; and it is to them that the second section of the Act refers. I therefore conclude that you have no general authority to fix the times at which broadcasting stations may operate, apart from the limitations of regulations 12 and 13.

(c)   As to the limitation of power:

The only provisions concerning this are to be found in regulation 14, which requires all stations to use "the minimum amount of energy necessary to carry out any communication desired." It does not appear that the Secretary is given power to determine in advance what this minimum amount shall be for every case; and I therefore conclude that you have no authority to insert such a determination as a part of any license.

What I have said above with respect to your second question necessarily serves also as an answer to your third. While a station may not lawfully operate without a license, yet under the decision in the *Intercity Co.* case and under 29 Op. 579 you are required to issue such a license on request. And while a normal wave length must be designated under regulation 1, any station is free to operate on other wave lengths under regulation 2.

The same considerations cover your fourth question. Since the Act confers upon you no general authority to fix hours of operation or to limit power, any station may with impunity operate at hours and with powers other than those fixed in its license, subject only to regulations 12 and 13 and to the penalties against malicious interference contained in section 5.

With respect to your fifth question, I can find no authority in the Act for the issuance of licenses of limited duration.

It is apparent from the answers contained in this opinion that the present legislation is inadequate to cover the art of broadcasting, which has been almost entirely developed since the passage of the 1912 Act. If the present situation requires control, I can only suggest that it be sought in new legislation, carefully adapted to meet the needs of both the present and the future.

Respectfully,

William J. Donovan,
Acting Attorney General.

To the Secretary of Commerce.

5

PRESIDENT COOLIDGE'S

MESSAGE TO CONGRESS

H. R. Doc. 483, 69th Congress, 2d Session

December 7, 1926

During the period subsequent to the Attorney General's Opinion of July 8, 1926, chaos ruled the airwaves. Stations switched their frequencies and their power at will, as Secretary Hoover abandoned his attempts to minimize interference. In short order 200 new stations crowded on the air. Broadcast reception was jumbled and sporadic.

President Coolidge, in the following excerpt from his Congressional message, recommended that new radio legislation be enacted.

RADIO LEGISLATION

The Department of Commerce has for some years urgently presented the necessity for further legislation in order to protect radio listeners from interference between broadcasting stations and to carry out other regulatory functions. Both branches of Congress at the last session passed enactments intended to effect such regulation, but the two bills yet remain to be brought into agreement and final passage.

Due to decisions of the courts, the authority of the department under the law of 1912 has broken down; many more stations have been operating than can be accommodated within the limited number of wave lengths available; further stations are in course of construction; many stations have departed from the scheme of allocation set down by the department, and the whole service of this most important public function has drifted into such chaos as seems likely, if not remedied, to destroy its great value. I most urgently recommend that this legislation should be speedily enacted.

I do not believe it is desirable to set up further independent agencies in the

Government. Rather I believe it advisable to entrust the important functions of deciding who shall exercise the privilege of radio transmission and under what conditions, the assigning of wave lengths and determination of power, to a board to be assembled whenever action on such questions becomes necessary. There should be right of appeal to the courts from the decisions of such board. The administration of the decisions of the board and the other features of regulation and promotion of radio in the public interest, together with scientific research, should remain in the Department of Commerce. Such an arrangement makes for more expert, more efficient, and more economical administration than an independent agency or board, whose duties, after initial stages, require but little attention, in which administrative functions are confused with semijudicial functions and from which of necessity there must be greatly increased personnel and expenditure.

6

SENATE JOINT
RESOLUTION 125

Public Resolution 47, 69th Congress
December 8, 1926

On March 15, 1926, the House of Representatives passed a radio bill introduced by Congressman Wallace White, Jr., and based on recommendations of the Fourth National Radio Conference. On July 2, 1926, the Senate passed a similar bill introduced by Senator Clarence Dill. Senate-House conferees reported one day later that they could not reconcile the differences in the two versions prior to the session's end. They suggested passage of a Senate Joint Resolution that would preserve the status quo of all radio by limiting licensing periods and by requiring licensees to sign a waiver of claim to ownership of frequencies. This Resolution, although swiftly passed by the Senate and House, was delayed by the impending close of the session. The Resolution was thus not signed by the President until December 8, 1926.

Resolved by the Senate and House of Representatives of the United States of America in Congress assembled, That until otherwise provided by law, no original license for the operation of any radio broadcasting station and no renewal of a license of an existing broadcasting station, shall be granted for longer periods than ninety days and no original license for the operation of any other class of radio station and no renewal of the license for an existing station of any other class than a broadcasting station, shall be granted for longer periods than two years; and that no original radio license or the renewal of an existing license shall be granted after the date of the passage of this resolution unless the applicant therefor shall execute in writing a waiver of any right or of any claim to any right, as against the United States, to any wave length or to the use of the ether in radio transmission because of previous license to use the same or because of the use thereof.

7

THE RADIO ACT

OF 1927

Public Law 632, 69th Congress
February 23, 1927

The Senate-House conferees presented their compromise bill on January 27, 1927. It was passed by the House on January 29; the Senate approved it on February 18. Five days later President Coolidge signed the Radio Act of 1927 into law.

The five-member Federal Radio Commission, created as a temporary body by the Act, remained in power from year to year through various acts of Congress until the 1927 Act was supplanted by the Communications Act of 1934, which gave rise to a permanent body.

The 1927 Act established "public interest, convenience, and necessity," a phrase borrowed from public utility legislation, as the discretionary licensing standard. This and other features of the Act were substantially re-enacted in the 1934 law. The Radio Act of 1927 may, therefore, be regarded as the basis of current broadcast regulation.

Be it enacted by the Senate and House of Representatives of the United States of America in Congress assembled, That this Act is intended to regulate all forms of interstate and foreign radio transmissions and communications within the United States, its Territories and possessions; to maintain the control of the United States over all the channels of interstate and foreign radio transmission; and to provide for the use of such channels, but not the ownership thereof, by individuals, firms, or corporations, for limited periods of time, under licenses granted by Federal authority, and no such license shall be construed to create any right, beyond the terms, conditions, and periods of the license. That no person, firm, company, or corporation shall use or operate any apparatus for the transmission of energy or communications or signals by radio (a) from one place in any Territory or possession of the United States or in the District of Columbia to another place in the same Territory, possession, or District; or (b) from any State, Territory, or possession of the United States, or from the District of Columbia to any other State, Territory, or possession of the United States; or (c) from any place in any State, Territory, or possession of the United States, or in the District of Columbia, to any place in any foreign country or to any vessel; or (d) within any State when the effects of such use extend beyond the borders of said State, or when interference is caused by such use or operation with the transmission of such energy, communications, or signals from within said State to any place beyond its borders, or from any place beyond its borders to any place within said State, or with the transmission or reception of such energy, communications, or signals from and/or to places beyond the borders of said State; or (e) upon any vessel of the United States; or (f) upon any aircraft or other mobile stations within the United States, except under and in accordance with this Act and with a license in that behalf granted under the provisions of this Act.

Sec. 2.   For the purposes of this Act, the United States is divided into five zones, as follows: The first zone shall embrace the States of Maine, New Hampshire, Vermont, Massachusetts, Connecticut, Rhode Island, New York, New Jersey, Delaware, Maryland, the District of Columbia, Porto Rico, and the Virgin Islands; the second zone shall embrace the States of Pennsylvania, Virginia, West Virginia, Ohio, Michigan, and Kentucky; the third zone shall embrace the States of North Carolina, South Carolina, Georgia, Florida, Alabama, Tennessee, Mississippi, Arkansas, Louisiana, Texas, and Oklahoma; the fourth zone shall embrace the States of Indiana, Illinois, Wisconsin, Minnesota, North Dakota, South Dakota, Iowa, Nebraska, Kansas, and Missouri; and the fifth zone shall embrace the States of Montana, Idaho, Wyoming, Colorado, New Mexico, Arizona, Utah, Nevada, Washington, Oregon, California, the Territory of Hawaii, and Alaska.

Sec. 3.   That a commission is hereby created and established to be known as the Federal Radio Commission, hereinafter referred to as the commission, which shall be composed of five commissioners appointed by the President, by and with the advice and consent of the Senate, and one of whom the President shall designate as chairman: *Provided*, That chairmen thereafter elected shall be chosen by the commission itself.

Each member of the commission shall be a citizen of the United States and an actual resident citizen of a State within the zone from which appointed at the time of said appointment. Not more than one commissioner shall be appointed from any zone. No member of the commission shall be financially interested in the manufacture or sale of radio apparatus or in the transmission or operation of radiotelegraphy, radiotelephony, or radio broadcasting. Not more than three commissioners shall be members of the same political party.

The first commissioners shall be appointed for the terms of two, three, four, five, and six years, respectively, from the date of the taking effect of this Act, the term of each to be designated by the President, but their successors shall be appointed for terms of six years, except that any person chosen to fill a vacancy shall be appointed only for the unexpired term of the commissioner whom he shall succeed.

The first meeting of the commission shall be held in the city of Washington at such time and place as the chairman of the commission may fix. The commission shall convene thereafter at such times and places as a majority of the commission may determine, or upon call of the chairman thereof.

The commission may appoint a secretary, and such clerks, special counsel, experts, examiners, and other employees as it may from time to time find necessary for the proper performance of its duties and as from time to time may be appropriated for by Congress.

The commission shall have an official seal and shall annually make a full report of its operations to the Congress.

The members of the commission shall receive a compensation of $10,000 for the first year of their service, said year to date from the first meeting of said commission, and thereafter a compensation of $30 per day for each day's attendance upon sessions of the commission or while engaged upon work of the commission and while traveling to and from such sessions, and also their necessary traveling expenses.

Sec. 4.   Except as otherwise provided in this Act, the commission, from time to time, as public convenience, interest, or necessity requires, shall—

(a)   Classify radio stations;

(b)   Prescribe the nature of the service to be rendered by each class of licensed stations and each station within any class;

(c)   Assign bands of frequencies or wave lengths to the various classes of stations, and assign frequencies or wave lengths for each individual station and determine the power which each station shall use and the time during which it may operate;

(d)   Determine the location of classes of stations or individual stations;

(e)   Regulate the kind of apparatus to be used with respect to its external effects and the purity and sharpness of the emissions from each station and from the apparatus therein;

(f)   Make such regulations not inconsistent with law as it may deem necessary to prevent interference between stations and to carry out the provisions of this Act: *Provided, however*, That changes in the wave lengths, authorized power, in the character of emitted signals, or in the times of operation of any station, shall not be made without the consent of the station licensee unless, in the judgment of the commission, such changes will promote public convenience or interest or will serve public necessity or the provisions of this Act will be more fully complied with;

(g)   Have authority to establish areas or zones to be served by any station;

(h)   Have authority to make special regulations applicable to radio stations engaged in chain broadcasting;

(i)   Have authority to make general rules and regulations requiring stations to keep such records of programs, transmissions of energy, communications, or signals as it may deem desirable;

(j)   Have authority to exclude from the requirements of any regulations in whole or in part any radio station upon railroad rolling stock, or to modify such regulations in its discretion;

(k)   Have authority to hold hearings, summon witnesses, administer oaths, compel the production of books, documents, and papers and to make such investigations as may be necessary in the performance of its duties. The commission may make such expenditures (including expenditures for rent and personal services at the seat of government and elsewhere, for law books, periodicals, and books of reference, and for printing and binding) as may be necessary for the execution of the functions vested in the commission and, as from time to time may be appropriated for by Congress. All expenditures of the commission shall be allowed and paid upon the presentation of itemized vouchers therefor approved by the chairman.

Sec. 5.   From and after one year after the first meeting of the commission created by this Act, all the powers and authority vested in the commission under the terms of this Act, except as to the revocation of licenses, shall be vested in and exercised by the Secretary of Commerce; except that thereafter the commission shall have power and jurisdiction to act upon and determine any and all matters brought before it under the terms of this section.

It shall also be the duty of the Secretary of Commerce—

(A)   For and during a period of one year from the first meeting of the commission created by this Act, to immediately refer to the commission all applications for station licenses or for the renewal or modification of existing station licenses.

(B)   From and after one year from the first meeting of the commission created by this Act, to refer to the commission for its action any application for a station license or for the renewal or modification of any existing station license as to the granting of which dispute, controversy, or conflict arises or against the granting of which protest is filed within ten days after the date of filing said application by any party in interest and any application as to which such reference is requested by the applicant at the time of filing said application.

(C)   To prescribe the qualifications of station operators, to classify them according to the duties to be performed, to fix the forms of such licenses, and to issue them to such persons as he finds qualified.

(D)   To suspend the license of any operator for a period not exceeding two years upon proof sufficient to satisfy him that the licensee (a) has violated any provision of any Act or treaty binding on the United States which the Secretary of Commerce or the commission is authorized by this Act to administer or by any regulation made by the commission or the Secretary of

Commerce under any such Act or treaty; or (b) has failed to carry out the lawful orders of the master of the vessel on which he is employed; or (c) has willfully damaged or permitted radio apparatus to be damaged; or (d) has transmitted superfluous radio communications or signals or radio communications containing profane or obscene words or language; or (e) has willfully or maliciously interfered with any other radio communications or signals.

(E)   To inspect all transmitting apparatus to ascertain whether in construction and operation it conforms to the requirements of this Act, the rules and regulations of the licensing authority, and the license under which it is constructed or operated.

(F)   To report to the commission from time to time any violations of this Act, the rules, regulations, or orders of the commission, or of the terms or conditions of any license.

(G)   To designate call letters of all stations.

(H)   To cause to be published such call letters and such other announcements and data as in his judgment may be required for the efficient operation of radio stations subject to the jurisdiction of the United States and for the proper enforcement of this Act.

The Secretary may refer to the commission at any time any matter the determination of which is vested in him by the terms of this Act.

Any person, firm, company, or corporation, any State or political division thereof aggrieved or whose interests are adversely affected by any decision, determination, or regulation of the Secretary of Commerce may appeal therefrom to the commission by filing with the Secretary of Commerce notice of such appeal within thirty days after such decision or determination or promulgation of such regulation. All papers, documents, and other records pertaining to such application on file with the Secretary shall thereupon be transferred by him to the commission. The commission shall hear such appeal de novo under such rules and regulations as it may determine.

Decisions by the commission as to matters so appealed and as to all other matters over which it has jurisdiction shall be final, subject to the right of appeal herein given.

No station license shall be granted by the commission or the Secretary of Commerce until the applicant therefor shall have signed a waiver of any claim to the use of any particular frequency or wave length or of the ether as against the regulatory power of the United States because of the previous use of the same, whether by license or otherwise.

Sec. 6.   Radio stations belonging to and operated by the United States shall not be subject to the provisions of sections 1, 4, and 5 of this Act. All such Government stations shall use such frequencies or wave lengths as shall be assigned to each or to each class by the President. All such stations, except stations on board naval and other Government vessels while at sea or beyond the limits of the continental United States, when transmitting any radio communication or signal other than a communication or signal relating to

Government business shall conform to such rules and regulations designed to prevent interference with other radio stations and the rights of others as the licensing authority may prescribe. Upon proclamation by the President that there exists war or a threat of war or a state of public peril or disaster or other national emergency, or in order to preserve the neutrality of the United States, the President may suspend or amend, for such time as he may see fit, the rules and regulations applicable to any or all stations within the jurisdiction of the United States as prescribed by the licensing authority, and may cause the closing of any station for radio communication and the removal therefrom of its apparatus and equipment, or he may authorize the use or control of any such station and/or its apparatus and equipment by any department of the Government under such regulations as he may prescribe, upon just compensation to the owners. Radio stations on board vessels of the United States Shipping Board or the United States Shipping Board Emergency Fleet Corporation or the Inland and Coastwise Waterways Service shall be subject to the provisions of this Act.

Sec. 7.   The President shall ascertain the just compensation for such use or control and certify the amount ascertained to Congress for appropriation and payment to the person entitled thereto. If the amount so certified is unsatisfactory to the person entitled thereto, such person shall be paid only 75 per centum of the amount and shall be entitled to sue the United States to recover such further sum as added to such payment of 75 per centum which will make such amount as will be just compensation for the use and control. Such suit shall be brought in the manner provided by paragraph 20 of section 24, or by section 145 of the Judicial Code, as amended.

Sec. 8.   All stations owned and operated by the United States, except mobile stations of the Army of the United States, and all other stations on land and sea, shall have special call letters designated by the Secretary of Commerce.

Section 1 of this Act shall not apply to any person, firm, company, or corporation sending radio communications or signals on a foreign ship while the same is within the jurisdiction of the United States, but such communications or signals shall be transmitted only in accordance with such regulations designed to prevent interference as may be promulgated under the authority of this Act.

Sec. 9.   The licensing authority, if public convenience, interest, or necessity will be served thereby, subject to the limitations of this Act, shall grant to any applicant therefor a station license provided for by this Act.

In considering applications for licenses and renewals of licenses, when and in so far as there is a demand for the same, the licensing authority shall make such a distribution of licenses, bands of frequency of wave lengths, periods of time for operation, and of power among the different States and communities as to give fair, efficient, and equitable radio service to each of the same.

No license granted for the operation of a broadcasting station shall be for a longer term than three years and no license so granted for any other class of station shall be for a longer term than five years, and any license granted may be revoked as hereinafter provided. Upon the expiration of any license, upon application therefor, a renewal of such license may be granted from time to time for a term of not to exceed three years in the case of broadcasting licenses and not to exceed five years in the case of other licenses.

No renewal of an existing station license shall be granted more than thirty days prior to the expiration of the original license.

Sec. 10.   The licensing authority may grant station licenses only upon written application therefor addressed to it. All applications shall be filed with the Secretary of Commerce. All such applications shall set forth such facts as the licensing authority by regulation may prescribe as to the citizenship, character, and financial, technical, and other qualifications of the applicant to operate the station; the ownership and location of the proposed station and of the stations, if any, with which it is proposed to communicate; the frequencies or wave lengths and the power desired to be used; the hours of the day or other periods of time during which it is proposed to operate the station; the purposes for which the station is to be used; and such other information as it may require. The licensing authority at any time after the filing of such original application and during the term of any such license may require from an applicant or licensee further written statements of fact to enable it to determine whether such original application should be granted or denied or such license revoked. Such application and/or such statement of fact shall be signed by the applicant and/or licensee under oath or affirmation.

The licensing authority in granting any license for a station intended or used for commercial communication between the United States or any Territory or possession, continental or insular, subject to the jurisdiction of the United States, and any foreign country, may impose any terms, conditions, or restrictions authorized to be imposed with respect to submarine-cable licenses by section 2 of an Act entitled "An Act relating to the landing and the operation of submarine cables in the United States," approved May 24, 1921.

Sec. 11.   If upon examination of any application for a station license or for the renewal or modification of a station license the licensing authority shall determine that public interest, convenience, or necessity would be served by the granting thereof, it shall authorize the issuance, renewal, or modification thereof in accordance with said finding. In the event the licensing authority upon examination of any such application does not reach such decision with respect thereto, it shall notify the applicant thereof, shall fix and give notice of a time and place for hearing thereon, and shall afford such applicant an opportunity to be heard under such rules and regulations as it may prescribe.

Such station licenses as the licensing authority may grant shall be in such general form as it may prescribe, but each license shall contain, in addition to other provisions, a statement of the following conditions to which such license shall be subject:

(A)   The station license shall not vest in the licensee any right to operate the station nor any right in the use of the frequencies or wave length designated in the license beyond the term thereof nor in any other manner than authorized therein.

(B)   Neither the license nor the right granted thereunder shall be assigned or otherwise transferred in violation of this Act.

(C)   Every license issued under this Act shall be subject in terms to the right of use or control conferred by section 6 hereof.

In cases of emergency arising during the period of one year from and after the first meeting of the commission created hereby, or on applications filed during said time for temporary changes in terms of licenses when the commission is not in session and prompt action is deemed necessary, the Secretary of Commerce shall have authority to exercise the powers and duties of the commission, except as to revocation of licenses, but all such exercise of powers shall be promptly reported to the members of the commission, and any action by the Secretary authorized under this paragraph shall continue in force and have effect only until such time as the commission shall act thereon.

Sec. 12.   The station license required hereby shall not be granted to, or after the granting thereof such license shall not be transferred in any manner, either voluntarily or involuntarily, to (a) any alien or the representative of any alien; (b) to any foreign government, or the representative thereof; (c) to any company, corporation, or association organized under the laws of any foreign government; (d) to any company, corporation, or association of which any officer or director is an alien, or of which more than one-fifth of the capital stock may be voted by aliens or their representatives or by a foreign government or representative thereof, or by any company, corporation, or association organized under the laws of a foreign country.

The station license required hereby, the frequencies or wave length or lengths authorized to be used by the licensee, and the rights therein granted shall not be transferred, assigned, or in any manner, either voluntarily or involuntarily, disposed of to any person, firm, company, or corporation without the consent in writing of the licensing authority.

Sec. 13.   The licensing authority is hereby directed to refuse a station license and/or the permit hereinafter required for the construction of a station to any person, firm, company, or corporation, or any subsidiary thereof, which has been finally adjudged guilty by a Federal court of unlawfully monopolizing or attempting unlawfully to monopolize, after this Act takes effect, radio communication, directly or indirectly, through the control of the manufacture or sale of radio apparatus, through exclusive traffic arrangements, or by any other means or to have been using unfair methods of competition. The granting of a license shall not estop the United States or any person aggrieved from proceeding against such person, firm, company, or corporation for violating the law against unfair methods of competition or for a violation of the law against unlawful restraints and monopolies and/or combinations, contracts, or agreements in restraint of trade, or from instituting proceedings for the dissolution of such firm, company, or corporation.

Sec. 14.   Any station license shall be revocable by the commission for false statements either in the application or in the statement of fact which may be required by section 10 hereof, or because of conditions revealed by such statements of fact as may be required from time to time which would warrant the licensing authority in refusing to grant a license on an original application, or for failure to operate substantially as set forth in the license, for violation of or failure to observe any of the restrictions and conditions of this Act, or of any regulation of the licensing authority authorized by this Act or by a treaty ratified by the United States, or whenever the Interstate Commerce Commission, or any other Federal body in the exercise of authority conferred upon it by law, shall find and shall certify to the commission that any licensee bound so to do, has failed to provide reasonable facilities for the transmission of radio communications, or that any licensee has made any unjust and unreasonable charge, or has been guilty of any discrimination, either as to charge or as to service or has made or prescribed any unjust and unreasonable classification, regulation, or practice with respect to the transmission of radio communications or service: *Provided*, That no such order of revocation shall take effect until thirty days' notice in writing thereof, stating the cause for the proposed revocation, has been given to the parties known by the commission to be interested in such license. Any person in interest aggrieved by said order may make written application to the commission at any time within said thirty days for a hearing upon such order, and upon the filing of such written application said order of revocation shall stand suspended until the conclusion of the hearing herein directed. Notice in writing of said hearing shall be given by the commission to all the parties known to it to be interested in such license twenty days prior to the time of said hearing. Said hearing shall be conducted under such rules and in such manner as the commission may prescribe. Upon the conclusion hereof the commission may affirm, modify, or revoke said orders of revocation.

Sec. 15.   All laws of the United States relating to unlawful restraints and monopolies and to combinations, contracts, or agreements in restraint of trade are hereby declared to be applicable to the manufacture and sale of and to trade in radio apparatus and devices entering into or affecting interstate or foreign commerce and to interstate or foreign radio communications. Whenever in any suit, action, or proceeding, civil or criminal, brought under the provisions of any of said laws or in any proceeding brought to enforce or to review findings and orders of the Federal Trade Commission or other governmental agency in respect of any matters as to which said commission or other governmental agency is by law authorized to act, any licensee shall be found guilty of the violation of the provisions of such laws or any of them, the court, in addition to the penalties imposed by said laws, may adjudge, order, and/or decree that the license of such licensee shall, as of the date the decree or judgment becomes finally effective or as of such other date as the said decree shall fix, be revoked and that all rights under such license shall thereupon cease: *Provided, however*, That such licensee shall have the same right of appeal or review as is provided by law in respect of other decrees and judgments of said court.

Sec. 16.   Any applicant for a construction permit, for a station license, or for the renewal or modification of an existing station license whose application is refused by the licensing authority shall have the right to appeal from said decision to the Court of Appeals of the District of Columbia; and any licensee whose license is revoked by the commission shall have the right to appeal from such decision of revocation to said Court of Appeals of the District of Columbia or to the district court of the United States in which the apparatus licensed is operated, by filing with said court, within twenty days after the decision complained of is effective, notice in writing of said appeal and of the reasons therefor.

The licensing authority from whose decision an appeal is taken shall be notified of said appeal by service upon it, prior to the filing thereof, of a certified copy of said appeal and of the reasons therefor. Within twenty days after the filing of said appeal the licensing authority shall file with the court the originals or certified copies of all papers and evidence presented to it upon the original application for a permit or license or in the hearing upon said order of revocation, and also a like copy of its decision thereon and a full statement in writing of the facts and the grounds for its decision as found and given by it. Within twenty days after the filing of said statement by the licensing authority either party may give notice to the court of his desire to adduce additional evidence. Said notice shall be in the form of a verified petition stating the nature and character of said additional evidence, and the court may thereupon order such evidence to be taken in such manner and upon such terms and conditions as it may deem proper.

At the earliest convenient time the court shall hear, review, and determine the appeal upon said record and evidence, and may alter or revise the decision appealed from and enter such judgment as to it may seem just. The revision by the court shall be confined to the points set forth in the reasons of appeal.

Sec. 17.   After the passage of this Act no person, firm, company, or corporation now or hereafter directly or indirectly through any subsidiary, associated, or affiliated person, firm, company, corporation, or agent, or otherwise, in the business of transmitting and/or receiving for hire energy, communications, or signals by radio in accordance with the terms of the license issued under this Act, shall by purchase, lease, construction, or otherwise, directly or indirectly, acquire, own, control, or operate any cable or wire telegraph or telephone line or system between any place in any State, Territory, or possession of the United States or in the District of Columbia, and any place in any foreign country, or shall acquire, own, or control any part of the stock or other capital share of any interest in the physical property and/or other assets of any such cable, wire, telegraph, or telephone line or system, if in either case the purpose is and/or the effect thereof may be to substantially lessen competition or to restrain commerce between any place in any State, Territory, or possession of the United States or in the District of Columbia and any place in any foreign country, or unlawfully to create monopoly in any line of commerce; nor shall any person, firm, company, or corporation now or hereafter engaged directly or indirectly through any subsidiary, associated, or affiliated person, company, corporation, or agent, or otherwise, in the business of transmitting and/or receiving for hire messages by any cable, wire, telegraph, or telephone line or system (a) between any place in any State, Territory, or possession of the United States or in the District of Columbia, and any place in any other State, Territory, or possession of the United States; or (b) between any place in any State, Territory, or possession of the United States, or the District of Columbia, and any place in any foreign country, by purchase, lease, construction, or otherwise, directly or indirectly acquire, own, control, or operate any station or the apparatus therein, or any system for transmitting and/or receiving radio communications or signals between any place in any State, Territory, or possession of the United States or in the District of Columbia, and any place in any foreign country, or shall acquire, own, or control any part of the stock or other capital share or any interest in the physical property and/or other assets of any such radio station, apparatus, or system, if in either case the purpose is and/or the effect thereof may be to substantially lessen competition or to restrain commerce between any place in any State, Territory, or possession of the United States or in the District of Columbia, and any place in any foreign country, or unlawfully to create monopoly in any line of commerce.

Sec. 18.   If any licensee shall permit any person who is a legally qualified candidate for any public office to use a broadcasting station, he shall afford equal opportunities to all other such candidates for that office in the use of such broadcasting station, and the licensing authority shall make rules and regulations to carry this provision into effect: *Provided*, That such licensee shall have no power of censorship over the material broadcast under the provisions of this paragraph. No obligation is hereby imposed upon any licensee to allow the use of its station by any such candidate.

Sec. 19.   All matter broadcast by any radio station for which service, money, or any other valuable consideration is directly or indirectly paid, or promised to or charged or accepted by, the station so broadcasting, from any person, firm, company, or corporation, shall, at the time the same is so broadcast, be announced as paid for or furnished, as the case may be, by such person, firm, company, or corporation.

Sec. 20.   The actual operation of all transmitting apparatus in any radio station for which a station license is required by this Act shall be carried on only by a person holding an operator's license issued hereunder. No person shall operate any such apparatus in such station except under and in accordance with an operator's license issued to him by the Secretary of Commerce.

Sec. 21.   No license shall be issued under the authority of this Act for the operation of any station the construction of which is begun or is continued after this Act takes effect, unless a permit for its construction has been granted by the licensing authority upon written application therefor. The licensing authority may grant such permit if public convenience, interest, or necessity will be served by the construction of the station. This application shall set forth such facts as the licensing authority by regulation may prescribe as to the citizenship, character, and the financial, technical, and other ability of the applicant to construct and operate the station, the ownership and location of the proposed station and of the station or stations with which it is proposed to communicate, the frequencies and wave length or wave lengths desired to be used, the hours of the day or other periods of time during which it is proposed to operate the station, the purpose for which the station is to be used, the type of transmitting apparatus to be used, the power to be used, the date upon which the station is expected to be completed and in operation, and such other information as the licensing authority may require. Such application shall be signed by the applicant under oath or affirmation.

Such permit for construction shall show specifically the earliest and latest dates between which the actual operation of such station is expected to begin, and shall provide that said permit will be automatically forfeited if the station is not ready for operation within the time specified or within such further time as the licensing authority may allow, unless prevented by causes not under the control of the grantee. The rights under any such permit shall not be assigned or otherwise transferred to any person, firm, company, or corporation without the approval of the licensing authority. A permit for construction shall not be required for Government stations, amateur stations, or stations upon mobile vessels, railroad rolling stock, or aircraft. Upon the completion of any station for the construction or continued construction for which a permit has been granted, and upon it being made to appear to the licensing authority that all the terms, conditions, and obligations set forth in the application and permit have been fully met, and that no cause or circumstance arising or first coming to the knowledge of the licensing authority since the granting of the permit would, in the judgment of the licensing authority, make the operation of such station against the public interest, the licensing authority shall issue a license to the lawful holder of said permit for the operation of said station. Said license shall conform generally to the terms of said permit.

Sec. 22.   The licensing authority is authorized to designate from time to time radio stations the communications or signals of which, in its opinion, are liable to interfere with the transmission or with respect thereto which the Commission may by order require, to keep a licensed radio operator listening in on the wave lengths designated for signals of distress and radio communications relating thereto during the entire period the transmitter of such station is in operation.

Sec. 23.   Every radio station on shipboard shall be equipped to transmit radio communications or signals of distress on the frequency or wave length specified by the licensing authority, with apparatus capable of transmitting and receiving messages over a distance of at least one hundred miles by day or night. When sending radio communications or signals of distress and radio communications relating thereto the transmitting set may be adjusted in such a manner as to produce a maximum of radiation irrespective of the amount of interference which may thus be caused.

All radio stations, including Government stations and stations on board foreign vessels when within the territorial waters of the United States, shall give absolute priority to radio communications or signals relating to ships in distress; shall cease all sending on frequencies or wave lengths which will interfere with hearing a radio communication or signal of distress, and, except when engaged in answering or aiding the ship in distress, shall refrain from sending any radio communications or signals until there is assurance that no interference will be caused with the radio communications or signals relating thereto, and shall assist the vessel in distress, so far as possible, by complying with its instructions.

Sec. 24.   Every shore station open to general public service between the coast and vessels at sea shall be bound to exchange radio communications or signals with any ship station without distinction as to radio systems or instruments adopted by such stations, respectively, and each station on shipboard shall be bound to exchange radio communications or signals with any other station on shipboard without distinction as to radio systems or instruments adopted by each station.

Sec. 25.   At all places where Government and private or commercial radio stations on land operate in such close proximity that interference with the work of Government stations can not be avoided when they are operating simultaneously such private or commercial stations as do interfere with the transmission or reception of radio communications or signals by the Government stations concerned shall not use their transmitters during the first fifteen minutes of each hour, local standard time.

The Government stations for which the above-mentioned division of time is established shall transmit radio communications or signals only during the first fifteen minutes of each hour, local standard time, except in case of signals or radio communications relating to vessels in distress and vessel requests for information as to course, location, or compass direction.

Sec. 26.   In all circumstances, except in case of radio communications or signals relating to vessels in distress, all radio stations, including those owned and operated by the United States, shall use the minimum amount of power necessary to carry out the communication desired.

Sec. 27.   No person receiving or assisting in receiving any radio communication shall divulge or publish the contents, substance, purport, effect, or meaning thereof except through authorized channels of transmission or reception to any person other than the addressee, his agent, or attorney, or to a telephone, telegraph, cable, or radio station employed or authorized to forward such radio communication to its destination, or to proper accounting or distributing officers of the various communicating centers over which the radio communication may be passed, or to the master of a ship under whom he is serving, or in response to a subpoena issued by a court of competent jurisdiction, or on demand of other lawful authority; and no person not being authorized by the sender shall intercept any message and divulge or publish the contents, substance, purport, effect, or meaning of such intercepted message to any person; and no person not being entitled thereto shall receive or assist in receiving any radio communication and use the same or any information therein contained for his own benefit or for the benefit of another not entitled thereto; and no person having received such intercepted radio communication or having become acquainted with the contents, substance, purport, effect, or meaning of the same or any part thereof, knowing that such information was so obtained, shall divulge or publish the contents, substance, purport, effect, or meaning of the same or any part thereof, or use the same or any information therein contained for his own benefit or for the benefit of another not entitled thereto: *Provided,* That this section shall not apply to the receiving, divulging, publishing, or utilizing the contents of any radio communication broadcasted or transmitted by amateurs or others for the use of the general public or relating to ships in distress.

Sec. 28. No person, firm, company, or corporation within the jurisdiction of the United States shall knowingly utter or transmit, or cause to be uttered or transmitted, any false or fraudulent signal of distress, or communication relating thereto, nor shall any broadcasting station rebroadcast the program or any part thereof of another broadcasting station without the express authority of the originating station.

Sec. 29. Nothing in this Act shall be understood or construed to give the licensing authority the power of censorship over the radio communications or signals transmitted by any radio station, and no regulation or condition shall be promulgated or fixed by the licensing authority which shall interfere with the right of free speech by means of radio communications. No person within the jurisdiction of the United States shall utter any obscene, indecent, or profane language by means of radio communication.

Sec. 30. The Secretary of the Navy is hereby authorized unless restrained by international agreement, under the terms and conditions and at rates prescribed by him, which rates shall be just and reasonable, and which, upon complaint, shall be subject to review and revision by the Interstate Commerce Commission, to use all radio stations and apparatus, wherever located, owned by the United States and under the control of the Navy Department (a) for the reception and transmission of press messages offered by any newspaper published in the United States, its Territories or possessions, or published by citizens of the United States in foreign countries, or by any press association of the United States, and (b) for the reception and transmission of private commercial messages between ships, between ship and shore, between localities in Alaska and between Alaska and the continental United States: *Provided,* That the rates fixed for the reception and transmission of all such messages, other than press messages between the Pacific coast of the United States, Hawaii, Alaska, the Philippine Islands, and the Orient, and between the United States and the Virgin Islands, shall not be less than the rates charged by privately owned and operated stations for like messages and service: *Provided further*, That the right to use such stations for any of the purposes named in this section shall terminate and cease as between any countries or localities or between any locality and privately operated ships whenever privately owned and operated stations are capable of meeting the normal communication requirements between such countries or localities or between any locality and privately operated ships, and the licensing authority shall have notified the Secretary of the Navy thereof.

Sec. 31. The expression "radio communication" or "radio communications" wherever used in this Act means any intelligence, message, signal, power, pictures, or communication of any nature transferred by electrical energy from one point to another without the aid of any wire connecting the points from and at which the electrical energy is sent or received and any system by means of which such transfer of energy is effected.

Sec. 32. Any person, firm, company, or corporation failing or refusing to observe or violating any rule, regulation, restriction, or condition made or imposed by the licensing authority under the authority of this Act or of any international radio convention or treaty ratified or adhered to by the United States, in addition to any other penalties provided by law, upon conviction thereof by a court of competent jurisdiction, shall be punished by a fine of not more than $500 for each and every offense.

Sec. 33. Any person, firm, company, or corporation who shall violate any provision of this Act, or shall knowingly make any false oath or affirmation in any affidavit required or authorized by this Act, or shall knowingly swear falsely to a material matter in any hearing authorized by this Act, upon conviction thereof in any court of competent jurisdiction shall be punished by a fine of not more than $5,000 or by imprisonment for a term of not more than five years or both for each and every such offense.

Sec. 34. The trial of any offense under this Act shall be in the district in which it is committed; or if the offense is committed upon the high seas, or out of the jurisdiction of any particular State or district, the trial shall be in the district where the offender may be found or into which he shall be first brought.

Sec. 35. This Act shall not apply to the Philippine Islands or to the Canal Zone. In international radio matters the Philippine Islands and the Canal Zone shall be represented by the Secretary of State.

Sec. 36. The licensing authority is authorized to designate any officer or employee of any other department of the Government on duty in any Territory or possession of the United States other than the Philippine Islands and the Canal Zone, to render therein such services in connection with the administration of the radio laws of the United States as such authority may prescribe: *Provided*, That such designation shall be approved by the head of the department in which such person is employed.

Sec. 37. The unexpended balance of the moneys appropriated in the item for "wireless communication laws," under the caption "Bureau of Navigation" in

Title III of the Act entitled "An Act making appropriations for the Departments of State and Justice and for the judiciary, and for the Departments of Commerce and Labor, for the fiscal year ending June 30, 1927, and for other purposes," approved April 29, 1926, and the appropriation for the same purposes for the fiscal year ending June 30, 1928, shall be available both for expenditures incurred in the administration of this Act and for expenditures for the purposes specified in such items. There is hereby authorized to be appropriated for each fiscal year such sums as may be necessary for the administration of this Act and for the purposes specified in such item.

Sec. 38.   If any provision of this Act or the application thereof to any person, firm, company, or corporation, or to any circumstances, is held invalid, the remainder of the Act and the application of such provision to other persons, firms, companies, or corporations, or to other circumstances, shall not be affected thereby.

Sec. 39.   The Act entitled "An Act to regulate radio communication," approved August 13, 1912, the joint resolution to authorize the operation of Government-owned radio stations for the general public, and for other purposes, approved June 5, 1920, as amended, and the joint resolution entitled "Joint resolution limiting the time for which licenses for radio transmission may be granted, and for other purposes," approved December 8, 1926, are hereby repealed.

Such repeal, however, shall not affect any act done or any right accrued or any suit or proceeding had or commenced in any civil cause prior to said repeal, but all liabilities under said laws shall continue and may be enforced in the same manner as if committed; and all penalties, forfeitures, or liabilities incurred prior to taking effect hereof, under any law embraced in, changed, modified, or repealed by this Act, may be prosecuted and punished in the same manner and with the same effect as if this Act had not been passed.

Nothing in this section shall be construed as authorizing any person now using or operating any apparatus for the transmission of radio energy or radio communications or signals to continue such use except under and in accordance with this Act and with a license granted in accordance with the authority hereinbefore conferred.

Sec. 40.   This Act shall take effect and be in force upon its passage and approval, except that for and during a period of sixty days after such approval no holder of a license or an extension thereof issued by the Secretary of Commerce under said Act of August 13, 1912, shall be subject to the penalties provided herein for operating a station without the license herein required.

Sec. 41.   This Act may be referred to and cited as the Radio Act of 1927.

8

PRESIDENT ROOSEVELT'S
MESSAGE TO CONGRESS

S. Doc. 144, 73d Congress, 2d Session
February 26, 1934

Various proposals to unify and consolidate Federal regulation of interstate communications media had been considered since 1929. President Roosevelt made the following legislative recommendation after an Interdepartmental Committee conducted a study of the problem. Congress responded with the Communications Act of 1934.

To the Congress:

I have long felt that for the sake of clarity and effectiveness the relationship of the Federal Government to certain services known as utilities should be divided into three fields: Transportation, power, and communications. The problems of transportation are vested in the Interstate Commerce Commission, and the problems of power, its development, transmission, and distribution, in the Federal Power Commission.

In the field of communications, however, there is today no single Government agency charged with broad authority.

The Congress has vested certain authority over certain forms of communications in the Interstate Commerce Commission, and there is in addition the agency known as the Federal Radio Commission.

I recommend that the Congress create a new agency to be known as the Federal Communications Commission, such agency to be vested with the authority now lying in the Federal Radio Commission and with such authority over communications as now lies with the Interstate Commerce Commission — the services affected to be all of those which rely on wires, cables, or radio as a medium of transmission.

It is my thought that a new commission such as I suggest might well be organized this year by transferring the present authority for the control of communications of the Radio Commission and the Interstate Commerce Commission. The new body should, in addition, be given full power to investigate and study the business of existing companies and make recommendations to the Congress for additional legislation at the next session.

Franklin D. Roosevelt

The White House
February 26, 1934

9
THE COMMUNICATIONS ACT
OF 1934

Public Law 416, 73d Congress
June 19, 1934 (Amended to January, 1969)

This Act is the statute through which Congress currently exercises its jurisdiction over interstate communication by wire and radio. Although the Act has been frequently amended, the substance of the broadcasting provisions of the 1934 version, based largely on the Radio Act of 1927, has remained intact.

Only those sections most relevant to broadcasting appear in this edited version. Title II, which deals with "Common Carriers," is completely omitted. Sections 312 and 315 reflect 1972 legislative changes.

TITLE I
GENERAL PROVISIONS

Purposes of Act: Creation of Federal Communications Commission

Sec. 1. For the purpose of regulating interstate and foreign commerce in communication by wire and radio so as to make available, so far as possible, to all the people of the United States a rapid, efficient, Nation-wide, and world-wide wire and radio communication service with adequate facilities at reasonable charges, for the purpose of the national defense, for the purpose of promoting safety of life and property through the use of wire and radio communication, and for the purpose of securing a more effective execution of this policy by centralizing authority heretofore granted by law to several agencies and by granting additional authority with respect to interstate and foreign commerce in wire and radio communication, there is hereby created a commission to be known as the "Federal Communications Commission," which shall be constituted as hereinafter provided, and which shall execute and enforce the provisions of this Act.

Application of Act

Sec. 2.   (a)   The provisions of this Act shall apply to all interstate and foreign communication by wire or radio and all interstate and foreign transmission of energy by radio, which originates and/or is received within the United States, and to all persons engaged within the United States in such communication or such transmission of energy by radio, and to the licensing and regulating of all radio stations as hereinafter provided; but it shall not apply to persons engaged in wire or radio communication or transmission in the Canal Zone, or to wire or radio communication or transmission wholly within the Canal Zone.

(b)   Subject to the provisions of section 301, nothing in this Act shall be construed to apply or to give the Commission jurisdiction with respect to (1) charges, classifications, practices, services, facilities, or regulations for or in connection with intrastate communication service by wire or radio of any carrier, or (2) any carrier engaged in interstate or foreign communication solely through physical connection with the facilities of another carrier not directly or indirectly controlling or controlled by, or under direct or indirect common control with such carrier, or (3) any carrier engaged in interstate or foreign communication solely through connection by radio, or by wire and radio, with facilities, located in an adjoining State or in Canada or Mexico (where they adjoin the State in which the carrier is doing business), of another carrier not directly or indirectly controlling or controlled by, or under direct or indirect common control with such carrier, or (4) any carrier to which clause (2) or clause (3) would be applicable except for furnishing interstate mobile radio communication service or radio communication service to mobile stations on land vehicles in Canada or Mexico; except that sections 201 through 205 of this Act, both inclusive, shall, except as otherwise provided therein, apply to carriers described in clauses (2), (3), and (4).

Definitions

Sec. 3.   For the purposes of this Act, unless the context otherwise requires—

(a)   "Wire communication" or "communication by wire" means the transmission of writing, signs, signals, pictures, and sounds of all kinds by aid of wire, cable, or other like connection between the points of origin and reception of such transmission, including all instrumentalities, facilities, apparatus, and services (among other things, the receipt, forwarding, and delivery of communications) incidental to such transmission.

(b) "Radio communication" or "communication by radio" means the transmission by radio of writing, signs, signals, pictures, and sounds of all kinds, including all instrumentalities, facilities, apparatus, and services (among other things, the receipt, forwarding, and delivery of communications) incidental to such transmission.

(c) "Licensee" means the holder of a radio station license granted or continued in force under authority of this Act.

(d) "Transmission of energy by radio" or "radio transmission of energy" includes both such transmission and all instrumentalities, facilities, and services incidental to such transmission.

(e) "Interstate communication" or "interstate transmission" means communication or transmission (1) from any State, Territory, or possession of the United States (other than the Canal Zone), or the District of Columbia, to any other State, Territory, or possession of the United States (other than the Canal Zone), or the District of Columbia, (2) from or to the United States to or from the Canal Zone, insofar as such communication of transmission takes place within the United States, or (3) between points within the United States but through a foreign country; but shall not, with respect to the provisions of title II of this Act (other than section 223 thereof), include wire or radio communication between points in the same State, Territory, or possession of the United States, or the District of Columbia, through any place outside thereof, if such communication is regulated by a State commission.

(f) "Foreign communication" or "foreign transmission" means communication or transmission from or to any place in the United States to or from a foreign country, or between a station in the United States and a mobile station located outside the United States.

(g) "United States" means the several States and Territories, the District of Columbia, and the possessions of the United States, but does not include the Canal Zone.

(h) "Common carrier" or "carrier" means any person engaged as a common carrier for hire, in interstate or foreign communication by wire or radio or in interstate or foreign radio transmission of energy, except where reference is made to common carriers not subject to this Act; but a person engaged in radio broadcasting shall not, insofar as such person is so engaged, be deemed a common carrier. *amateur not a comm-cat's.*

(i) "Person" includes an individual, partnership, association, joint-stock company, trust, or corporation.

(j) "Corporation" includes any corporation, joint-stock company, or association.

(k) "Radio station" or "station" means a station equipped to engage in radio communication or radio transmission of energy.

(l) "Mobile station" means a radio-communication station capable of being moved and which ordinarily does move.

(m) "Land station" means a station, other than a mobile station, used for radio communication with mobile stations.

(n) "Mobile service" means the radio-communication service carried on between mobile stations and land stations, and by mobile stations communicating among themselves.

(o) "Broadcasting" means the dissemination of radio communications intended to be received by the public, directly or by the intermediary of relay stations.

(p) "Chain broadcasting" means simultaneous broadcasting of an identical program by two or more connected stations.

(q) "Amateur station" means a radio station operated by a duly authorized person interested in radio technique solely with a personal aim and without pecuniary interest. . . .

(cc) "Station license," "radio station license," or "license" means that instrument of authorization required by this Act or the rules and regulations of the Commission made pursuant to this Act, for the use or operation of apparatus for transmission of energy, or communications, or signals by radio by whatever name the instrument may be designated by the Commission.

(dd) "Broadcast station," "broadcasting station," or "radio broadcast station" means a radio station equipped to engage in broadcasting as herein defined.

(ee) "Construction permit" or "permit for construction" means that instrument of authorization required by this Act or the rules and regulations of the Commission made pursuant to this Act for the construction of a station, or the installation of apparatus, for the transmission of energy, or communications, or signals by radio, by whatever name the instrument may be designated by the Commission. . . .

Provisions relating to the Commission

Sec. 4. (a) The Federal Communications Commission (in this Act referred to as the "Commission") shall be composed of seven commissioners appointed by the President, by and with the advice and consent of the Senate, one of whom the President shall designate as chairman.

(b) Each member of the Commission shall be a citizen of the United States. No member of the Commission or person in its employ shall be financially interested in the manufacture or sale of radio apparatus or of apparatus for wire or radio communication; in communication by wire or radio or in radio transmission of energy; in any company furnishing services or such apparatus to any company engaged in communication by wire or radio or to any company manufacturing or selling apparatus used for communication by wire or radio; or in any company owning stocks, bonds, or other securities of any such company; nor be in the employ of or hold any official relation to any person subject to any of the provisions of this Act, nor own stocks, bonds, or other securities of any corporation subject to any of the provisions of this Act. Such commissioners shall not engage in any other business, vocation, profession, or employment. Any such commissioner serving as such after one year from the date of enactment of the Communications Act Amendments, 1952, shall not for a period of one year following the termination of his service as a commissioner represent any person before the Commission in a professional capacity, except that this restriction shall not apply to any commissioner who has served the full term for which he was appointed. Not more than four members of the Commission shall be members of the same political party.

(c)   The Commissioners first appointed under this Act shall continue in office for the terms of one, two, three, four, five, six, and seven years, respectively, from the date of the taking effect of this Act, the term of each to be designated by the President, but their successors shall be appointed for terms of seven years and until their successors are appointed and have qualified, except that they shall not continue to serve beyond the expiration of the next session of Congress subsequent to the expiration of said fixed term of office; except that any person chosen to fill a vacancy shall be appointed only for the unexpired term of the Commissioner whom he succeeds. No vacancy in the Commission shall impair the right of the remaining commissioners to exercise all the powers of the Commission.

(d)   Each commissioner shall receive an annual salary of $20,000, payable in monthly installments, and the chairman during the period of his service as chairman, shall receive an annual salary of $20,500.*

(e)   The principal office of the Commission shall be in the District of Columbia, where its general sessions shall be held; but whenever the convenience of the public or of the parties may be promoted or delay or expense prevented thereby, the Commission may hold special sessions in any part of the United States.

(f)   (1)   The Commission shall have authority, subject to the provisions of the civil-service laws and the Classification Act of 1949, as amended, to appoint such officers, engineers, accountants, attorneys, inspectors, examiners, and other employees as are necessary in the exercise of its functions.

(2)   Without regard to the civil-service laws, but subject to the Classification Act of 1949, each commissioner may appoint a legal assistant, an engineering assistant, and a secretary, each of whom shall perform such duties as such commissioner shall direct. In addition, the chairman of the Commission may appoint, without regard to the civil-service laws, but subject to the Classification Act of 1949, an administrative assistant who shall perform such duties as the chairman shall direct.

(3)   The Commission shall fix a reasonable rate of extra compen-

*Commissioners currently receive $38,000 annually; the Chairman receives $40,000. [Ed.]

sation for overtime services of engineers in charge and radio engineers of the Field Engineering and Monitoring Bureau of the Federal Communications Commission, who may be required to remain on duty between the hours of 5 o'clock postmeridian and 8 o'clock antemeridian or on Sundays or holidays to perform services in connection with the inspection of ship radio equipment and apparatus for the purposes of part II of title III of this Act or the Great Lakes Agreement, on the basis of one-half day's additional pay for each two hours or fraction thereof of at least one hour that the overtime extends beyond 5 o'clock postmeridian (but not to exceed two and one-half days' pay for the full period from 5 o'clock postmeridian to 8 o'clock antemeridian) and two additional days' pay for Sunday or holiday duty. The said extra compensation for overtime services shall be paid by the master, owner, or agent of such vessel to the local United States collector of customs or his representative, who shall deposit such collection into the Treasury of the United States to an appropriately designated receipt account: *Provided*, That the amounts of such collections received by the said collector of customs or his representatives shall be covered into the Treasury as miscellaneous receipts; and the payments of such extra compensation to the several employees entitled thereto shall be made from the annual appropriations for salaries and expenses of the Commission: *Provided further*, That to the extent that the annual appropriations which are hereby authorized to be made from the general fund of the Treasury are insufficient, there are hereby authorized to be appropriated from the general fund of the Treasury such additional amounts as may be necessary to the extent that the amounts of such receipts are in excess of the amounts appropriated: *Provided further*, That such extra compensation shall be paid if such field employees have been ordered to report for duty and have so reported whether the actual inspection of the radio equipment or apparatus takes place or not: *And provided further*, That in those ports where customary working hours are other than those hereinabove mentioned, the engineers in charge are vested with authority to regulate the hours of such employees so as to agree with prevailing working hours in said ports where inspections are to be made, but nothing contained in this proviso shall be construed in any manner to alter the length of a working day for the engineers in charge and radio engineers or the overtime pay herein fixed.

(g) The Commission may make such expenditures (including expenditures for rent and personal services at the seat of government and elsewhere, for office supplies, law books, periodicals, and books of reference, for printing and binding, for land for use as sites for radio monitoring stations and related facilities, including living quarters where necessary in remote areas, for the construction of such stations and facilities, and for the improvement, furnishing, equipping, and repairing of such stations and facilities and of laboratories and other related facilities (including construction of minor subsidiary buildings and structures not exceeding $25,000 in any one instance) used in connection with technical research activities), as may be necessary for the execution of the functions vested in the Commission and as from time to time may be appropriated for by Congress. All expenditures of the Commission, including all necessary expenses for transportation incurred by the commissioners or by their employees, under their orders, in making any investigation or upon any official business in any other places than in the city of Washington, shall be allowed and paid on the presentation of itemized vouchers therefor approved by the chairman of the Commission or by such other members or officer thereof as may be designated by the Commission for that purpose.

(h)   Four members of the Commission shall constitute a quorum thereof. The Commission shall have an official seal which shall be judicially noticed.

(i)   The Commission may perform any and all acts, make such rules and regulations, and issue such orders, not inconsistent with this Act, as may be necessary in the execution of its functions.

(j)   The Commission may conduct its proceedings in such manner as will best conduce to the proper dispatch of business and to the ends of justice. No commissioner shall participate in any hearing or proceeding in which he has a pecuniary interest. Any party may appear before the Commission and be heard in person or by attorney. Every vote and official act of the Commission shall be entered of record, and its proceedings shall be public upon the request of any party interested. The Commission is authorized to withhold publication of records or proceedings containing secret information affecting the national defense.

(k)   The Commission shall make an annual report to Congress, copies of which shall be distributed as are other reports transmitted to Congress. Such reports shall contain—

(1)   such information and data collected by the Commission as may be considered of value in the determination of questions connected with the regulation of interstate and foreign wire and radio communication and radio transmission of energy;

(2)   such information and data concerning the functioning of the Commission as will be of value to Congress in appraising the amount and character of the work and accomplishments of the Commission and the adequacy of its staff and equipment: *Provided*, That the first and second annual reports following the date of enactment of the Communications Act Amendments, 1952, shall set forth in detail the number and caption of pending applications requesting approval of transfer of control or assignment of a broadcasting station license, or construction permits for new broadcasting stations, or for increases in power, or for changes of frequency of existing broadcasting stations at the beginning and end of the period covered by such reports;*

(4)   an itemized statement of all funds expended during the preceding year by the Commission, of the sources of such funds, and of the

*Subparagraph (3) was repealed by Public Law 86-533, approved June 29, 1960. [Ed.]

authority in this Act or elsewhere under which such expenditures were made; and

(5)   specific recommendations to Congress as to additional legislation which the Commission deems necessary or desirable, including all legislative proposals submitted for approval to the Director of the Bureau of the Budget.

(l)   All reports of investigations made by the Commission shall be entered of record, and a copy thereof shall be furnished to the party who may have complained, and to any common carrier or licensee that may have been complained of.

(m)   The Commission shall provide for the publication of its reports and decisions in such form and manner as may be best adapted for public information and use, and such authorized publications shall be competent evidence of the reports and decisions of the Commission therein contained in all courts of the United States and of the several States without any further proof or authentication thereof.

(n)   Rates of compensation of persons appointed under this section shall be subject to the reduction applicable to officers and employees of the Federal Government generally.

(o)   For the purpose of obtaining maximum effectiveness from the use of radio and wire communications in connection with safety of life and property, the Commission shall investigate and study all phases of the problem and the best methods of obtaining the cooperation and coordination of these systems.

Organization and functioning of the Commission

Sec. 5.   (a)   The member of the Commission designated by the President as chairman shall be the chief executive officer of the Commission. It shall be his duty to preside at all meetings and sessions of the Commission, to represent the Commission in all matters relating to legislation and legislative reports, except that any commissioner may present his own or minority views or supplemental reports, to represent the Commission in all matters requiring conferences or communications with other governmental officers, departments or agencies, and generally to coordinate and organize the work of the Commission in such manner as to promote prompt and efficient disposition of all matters within the jurisdiction of the Commission. In the case of a vacancy in the office of the chairman of the Commission, or the absence or inability of the chairman to serve, the Commission may temporarily designate one of its members to act as chairman until the cause or circumstance requiring such designation shall have been eliminated or corrected.

(b)   Within six months after the enactment of the Communications Act Amendments, 1952, and from time to time thereafter as the Commission may find necessary, the Commission shall organize its staff into (1) integrated bureaus, to function on the basis of the Commission's principal workload operations, and (2) such other divisional organizations as the Commission may deem necessary. Each such integrated bureau shall include such legal, engineering, accounting, administrative, clerical, and other personnel as the Commission may determine to be necessary to perform its functions.*

(d)   (1)   When necessary to the proper functioning of the Commission and the prompt and orderly conduct of its business, the Commission may, by published rule or by order, delegate any of its functions (except functions granted to the Commission by this paragraph and by paragraphs (4), (5), and (6) of this subsection) to a panel of commissioners, an individual commissioner, an employee board, or an individual employee, including functions with respect to hearing, determining, ordering, certifying, reporting, or otherwise acting as to any work, business, or matter; except that in delegating review functions to employees in cases of adjudication (as defined in the Administrative Procedure Act), the delegation in any such case may be made only to an employee board consisting of three or more employees referred to in paragraph (8). Any such rule or order may be adopted, amended, or rescinded only by a vote of a majority of the members of the Commission then holding office. Nothing in this paragraph shall authorize the Commission to provide for the conduct, by any person or persons other than persons referred to in clauses (2) and (3) of section 7(a) of the Administrative Procedure Act, of any hearing to which such section 7(a) applies.

(2)   As used in this subsection (d) the term "order, decision, report, or action" does not include an initial, tentative, or recommended decision to which exceptions may be filed as provided in section 409(b).

(3)   Any order, decision, report, or action made or taken pursuant to any such delegation, unless reviewed as provided in paragraph (4), shall have the same force and effect, and shall be made, evidenced, and enforced in the same manner, as orders, decisions, reports, or other actions of the Commission.

(4)   Any person aggrieved by any such order, decision, report or action may file an application for review by the Commission within such time and in such manner as the Commission shall prescribe, and every such application shall be passed upon by the Commission. The Commission, on its own initiative, may review in whole or in part, at such time and in such manner as it shall determine, any order, decision, report, or action made or taken pursuant to any delegation under paragraph (1).

(5)   In passing upon applications for review, the Commission may grant, in whole or in part, or deny such applications without specifying any

*Subsection 5(c) was repealed by Public Law 87-192, approved August 31, 1961. [Ed.]

reasons therefor. No such application for review shall rely on questions of fact or law upon which the panel of commissioners, individual commissioner, employee board, or individual employee has been afforded no opportunity to pass.

(6)   If the Commission grants the application for review, it may affirm, modify, or set aside the order, decision, report, or action, or it may order a rehearing upon such order, decision, report, or action in accordance with section 405.

(7)   The filing of an application for review under this subsection shall be a condition precedent to judicial review of any order, decision, report, or action made or taken pursuant to a delegation under paragraph (1). The time within which a petition for review must be filed in a proceeding to which section 402(a) applies, or within which an appeal must be taken under section 402(b), shall be computed from the date upon which public notice is given of orders disposing of all applications for review filed in any case.

(8)   The employees to whom the Commission may delegate review functions in any case of adjudication (as defined in the Administrative Procedure Act) shall be qualified, by reason of their training, experience, and competence, to perform such review functions, and shall perform no duties inconsistent with such review functions. Such employees shall be in a grade classification or salary level commensurate with their important duties, and in no event less than the grade classification or salary level of the employee or employees whose actions are to be reviewed. In the performance of such review functions such employees shall be assigned to cases in rotation so far as practicable and shall not be responsible to or subject to the supervision or direction of any officer, employee, or agent engaged in the performance of investigative or prosecuting functions for any agency.

(9)   The secretary and seal of the Commission shall be the secretary and seal of each panel of the Commission, each individual commissioner, and each employee board or individual employee exercising functions delegated pursuant to paragraph (1) of this subsection.

(e)   Meetings of the Commission shall be held at regular intervals, not less frequently than once each calendar month, at which times the functioning of the Commission and the handling of its work load shall be reviewed and such orders shall be entered and other action taken as may be necessary or appropriate to expedite the prompt and orderly conduct of the business of the Commission with the objective of rendering a final decision (1) within three months from the date of filing in all original application, renewal, and transfer cases in which it will not be necessary to hold a hearing, and (2) within six months from the final date of the hearing in all hearing cases; and the Commission shall promptly report to the Congress each such case which has been pending before it more than such three- or six-month period, respectively, stating the reasons therefor.

TITLE III
PROVISIONS RELATING TO RADIO

PART I – GENERAL PROVISIONS

License for radio communication or transmission of energy

Sec. 301. It is the purpose of this Act, among other things, to maintain the control of the United States over all the channels of interstate and foreign radio transmission; and to provide for the use of such channels, but not the ownership thereof, by persons for limited periods of time, under licenses granted by Federal authority, and no such license shall be construed to create any right, beyond the terms, conditions, and periods of the license. No person shall use or operate any apparatus for the transmission of energy or communications or signals by radio (a) from one place in any Territory or possession of the United States or in the District of Columbia to another place in the same Territory, possession, or district; or (b) from any State, Territory, or possession of the United States, or from the District of Columbia to any other State, Territory, or possession of the United States; or (c) from any place in any State, Territory, or possession of the United States, or in the District of Columbia, to any place in any foreign country or to any vessel; or (d) within any State when the effects of such use extend beyond the borders of said State, or when interference is caused by such use or operation with the transmission of such energy, communications, or signals from within said State to any place beyond its borders, or from any place beyond its borders to any place within said State, or with the transmission or reception of such energy, communications, or signals from and/or to places beyond the borders of said State; or (e) upon any vessel or aircraft of the United States; or (f) upon any other mobile stations within the jurisdiction of the United States, except under and in accordance with this Act and with a license in that behalf granted under the provisions of this Act.

Sec. 302. (a) The Commission may, consistent with the public interest, convenience, and necessity, make reasonable regulations governing the interference potential of devices which in their operation are capable of emitting radio frequency energy by radiation, conduction, or other means in sufficient degree to cause harmful interference to radio communications. Such regulations shall be applicable to the manufacture, import, sale, offer for sale, shipment, or use of such devices.

(b) No person shall manufacture, import, sell, offer for sale, ship, or use devices which fail to comply with regulations promulgated pursuant to this section.

(c) The provisions of this section shall not be applicable to carriers transporting such devices without trading in them, to devices manufactured solely for export, to the manufacture, assembly, or installation of devices for its own use by a public utility engaged in providing electric service, or to devices for use by the Government of the United States or any agency thereof. Devices for use by the Government of the United States or any agency thereof shall be developed, procured, or otherwise acquired, including offshore procurement, under United States Government criteria, standards, or specifications designed to achieve the common objective of reducing interference to radio reception, taking into account the unique needs of national defense and security.

General powers of the Commission

Sec. 303.   Except as otherwise provided in this Act, the Commission from time to time, as public convenience, interest, or necessity requires shall—

(a) Classify radio stations;

(b)   Prescribe the nature of the service to be rendered by each class of licensed stations and each station within any class;

(c)   Assign bands of frequencies to the various classes of stations, and assign frequencies for each individual station and determine the power which each station shall use and the time during which it may operate;

(d)   Determine the location of classes of stations or individual stations;

(e)   Regulate the kind of apparatus to be used with respect to its external effects and the purity and sharpness of the emissions from each station and from the apparatus therein;

(f)   Make such regulations not inconsistent with law as it may deem necessary to prevent interference between stations and to carry out the provisions of this Act: *Provided, however*, that changes in the frequencies, authorized power, or in the times of operation of any station, shall not be made without the consent of the station licensee unless, after a public hearing, the Commission shall determine that such changes will promote public convenience or interest or will serve public necessity, or the provisions of this Act will be more fully complied with;

(g)   Study new uses for radio, provide for experimental uses of frequencies, and generally encourage the larger and more effective use of radio in the public interest;

(h)   Have authority to establish areas or zones to be served by any station;

(i)   Have authority to make special regulations applicable to radio stations engaged in chain broadcasting;

(j)   Have authority to make general rules and regulations requiring stations to keep such records of programs, transmissions of energy, communications, or signals as it may deem desirable;

(k)   Have authority to exclude from the requirements of any regulations in whole or in part any radio station upon railroad rolling stock, or to modify such regulations in its discretion;

(l)   (1)   Have authority to prescribe the qualifications of station operators, to classify them according to the duties to be performed, to fix the forms of such licenses, and to issue them to such citizens or nationals of the United States, or citizens of the Trust Territory of the Pacific Islands presenting valid identity certificates issued by the high Commissioner of such Territory, as the Commission finds qualified, except that in issuing licenses for the operation of radio stations on aircraft the Commission may, if it finds that the public interest will be served thereby, waive the requirement of citizenship in the case of persons holding United States pilot certificates or in the case of persons holding foreign aircraft pilot certificates which are valid in the United States on the basis of reciprocal agreements entered into with foreign governments;

(2)   Notwithstanding section 301 of this Act and paragraph (1) of this subsection, the Commission may issue authorizations, under such conditions and terms as it may prescribe, to permit an alien licensed by his government as an amateur radio operator to operate his amateur radio station licensed by his government in the United States, its possessions, and the Commonwealth of Puerto Rico provided there is in effect a bilateral agreement between the United States and the alien's government for such operation on a reciprocal basis by United States amateur radio operators: *Provided*, That when an application for an authorization is received by the Commission, it shall notify the appropriate agencies of the Government of such fact, and such agencies shall forthwith furnish to the Commission such information in their possession as bears upon the compatibility of the request with the national security: *And provided further*, That the requested authorization may then be granted unless the Commission shall determine that information received from such agencies necessitates denial of the request. Other provisions of this Act and of the Administrative Procedure Act shall not be applicable to any request or application for or modification, suspension, or cancellation of any such authorization.

(m)   (1)   Have authority to suspend the license of any operator upon proof sufficient to satisfy the Commission that the licensee—

(A)   Has violated any provision of any Act, treaty, or convention binding on the United States, which the Commission is authorized to administer, or any regulation made by the Commission under any such Act, treaty, or convention; or

(B)   Has failed to carry out a lawful order of the master or person lawfully in charge of the ship or aircraft on which he is employed; or

(C)   Has willfully damaged or permitted radio apparatus or installations to be damaged; or

(D)   Has transmitted superfluous radio communications or signals or communications containing profane or obscene words, language, or meaning, or has knowingly transmitted—

           (1)   False or deceptive signals or communications, or

           (2)   A call signal or letter which has not been assigned by proper authority to the station he is operating; or

           (E)   Has willfully or maliciously interfered with any other radio communications or signals; or

           (F)   Has obtained or attempted to obtain, or has assisted another to obtain or attempt to obtain, an operator's license by fraudulent means.

           (2)   No order of suspension of any operator's license shall take effect until fifteen days' notice in writing thereof, stating the cause for the proposed suspension, has been given to the operator licensee who may make written application to the Commission at any time within said fifteen days for a hearing upon such order. The notice to the operator licensee shall not be effective until actually received by him, and from that time he shall have fifteen days in which to mail the said application. In the event that physical conditions prevent mailing of the application at the expiration of the fifteen-day period, the application shall then be mailed as soon as possible thereafter, accompanied by a satisfactory explanation of the delay. Upon receipt by the Commission of such application for hearing, said order of suspension shall be held in abeyance until the conclusion of the hearing which shall be conducted under such rules as the Commission may prescribe. Upon the conclusion of said hearing the Commission may affirm, modify, or revoke said order of suspension.

    (n)   Have authority to inspect all radio installations associated with stations required to be licensed by any Act or which are subject to the provisions of any Act, treaty, or convention binding on the United States, to ascertain whether in construction, installation, and operation they conform to the requirements of the rules and regulations of the Commission, the provisions of any Act, the terms of any treaty or convention binding on the United States, and the conditions of the license or other instrument of authorization under which they are constructed, installed, or operated.

    (o)   Have authority to designate call letters of all stations;

    (p)   Have authority to cause to be published such call letters and such other announcements and data as in the judgment of the Commission may be required for the efficient operation of radio stations subject to the jurisdiction of the United States and for the proper enforcement of this Act;

    (q)   Have authority to require the painting and/or illumination of radio towers if and when in its judgment such towers constitute, or there is a reasonable possibility that they may constitute, a menace to air navigation. The permittee or licensee shall maintain the painting and/or illumination of the tower as prescribed by the Commission pursuant to this section. In the event that the tower ceases to be licensed by the Commission for the transmission of radio energy, the owner of the tower shall maintain the prescribed painting and/or illumination of such tower until it is dismantled, and the Commission may require the owner to dismantle and remove the tower when the Administrator of the Federal Aviation Agency determines that there is a reasonable possibility that it may constitute a menace to air navigation.

(r) Make such rules and regulations and prescribe such restrictions and conditions, not inconsistent with law, as may be necessary to carry out the provisions of this Act, or any international radio or wire communications treaty or convention, or regulations annexed thereto, including any treaty or convention insofar as it relates to the use of radio, to which the United States is or may hereafter become a party.

(s) Have authority to require that apparatus designed to receive television pictures broadcast simultaneously with sound be capable of adequately receiving all frequencies allocated by the Commission to television broadcasting when such apparatus is shipped in interstate commerce, or is imported from any foreign country into the United States, for sale or resale to the public.

Waiver by licensee

Sec. 304. No station license shall be granted by the Commission until the applicant therefor shall have signed a waiver of any claim to the use of any particular frequency or of the ether as against the regulatory power of the United States because of the previous use of the same, whether by license or otherwise.

Government-owned stations

Sec. 305. (a) Radio stations belonging to and operated by the United States shall not be subject to the provisions of sections 301 and 303 of this Act. All such Government stations shall use such frequencies as shall be assigned to each or to each class by the President. All such stations, except stations on board naval and other Government vessels while at sea or beyond the limits of the continental United States, when transmitting any radio communication or signal other than a communication or signal relating to Government business, shall conform to such rules and regulations designed to prevent interference with other radio stations and the rights of others as the Commission may prescribe.

(b) Radio stations on board vessels of the United States Maritime Commission or the Inland and Coastwise Waterways Service shall be subject to the provisions of this title.

(c) All stations owned and operated by the United States, except mobile stations of the Army of the United States, and all other stations on land and sea, shall have special call letters designated by the Commission.

(d)   The provisions of sections 301 and 303 of this Act notwithstanding, the President may, provided he determines it to be consistent with and in the interest of national security, authorize a foreign government, under such terms and conditions as he may prescribe, to construct and operate at the seat of government of the United States a low-power radio station in the fixed service at or near the site of the embassy or legation of such foreign government for transmission of its messages to points outside the United States, but only (1) where he determines that the authorization would be consistent with the national interest of the United States and (2) where such foreign government has provided reciprocal privileges to the United States to construct and operate radio stations within territories subject to its jurisdiction. Foreign government stations authorized pursuant to the provisions of this subsection shall conform to such rules and regulations as the President may prescribe. The authorization of such stations, and the renewal, modification, suspension, revocation, or other termination of such authority shall be in accordance with such procedures as may be established by the President and shall not be subject to the other provisions of this Act or of the Administrative Procedure Act.

Foreign ships

Sec. 306.   Section 301 of this Act shall not apply to any person sending radio communications or signals on a foreign ship while the same is within the jurisdiction of the United States, but such communications or signals shall be transmitted only in accordance with such regulations designed to prevent interference as may be promulgated under the authority of this Act.

Allocation of facilities; Terms of licenses

Sec. 307.   (a)   The Commission, if public convenience, interest, or necessity will be served thereby, subject to the limitations of this Act, shall grant to any applicant therefor a station license provided for by this Act.

(b)   In considering applications for licenses, and modifications and renewals thereof, when and insofar as there is demand for the same, the Commission shall make such distribution of licenses, frequencies, hours of operation, and of power among the several States and communities as to provide a fair, efficient, and equitable distribution of radio service to each of the same.

(c)   The Commission shall study the proposal that Congress by statute allocate fixed percentages of radio broadcasting facilities to particular types or kinds of non-profit radio programs or to persons identified with particular types or kinds of non-profit activities, and shall report to Congress, not later than

February 1, 1935, its recommendations together with the reasons for the same.

(d)   No license granted for the operation of a broadcasting station shall be for a longer term than three years and no license so granted for any other class of station shall be for a longer term than five years, and any license granted may be revoked as hereinafter provided. Upon the expiration of any license, upon application therefor, a renewal of such license may be granted from time to time for a term of not to exceed three years in the case of broadcasting licenses, and not to exceed five years in the case of other licenses, if the Commission finds that public interest, convenience, and necessity would be served thereby. In order to expedite action on applications for renewal of broadcasting station licenses and in order to avoid needless expense to applicants for such renewals, the Commission shall not require any such applicant to file any information which previously has been furnished to the Commission or which is not directly material to the considerations that affect the granting or denial of such application, but the Commission may require any new or additional facts it deems necessary to make its findings. Pending any hearing and final decision on such an application and the disposition of any petition for rehearing pursuant to section 405, the Commission shall continue such license in effect. Consistently with the foregoing provisions of this subsection, the Commission may by rule prescribe the period or periods for which licenses shall be granted and renewed for particular classes of stations, but the Commission may not adopt or follow any rule which would preclude it, in any case involving a station of a particular class, from granting or renewing a license for a shorter period than that prescribed for stations of such class if, in its judgment, public interest, convenience, or necessity would be served by such action.

(e)   No renewal of an existing station license in the broadcast or the common carrier services shall be granted more than thirty days prior to the expiration of the original license.

Applications for licenses;
Conditions in license for foreign communication

Sec. 308.   (a)   The Commission may grant construction permits and station licenses, or modifications or renewals thereof, only upon written application therefor received by it: *Provided*, That (1) in cases of emergency found by the Commission involving danger to life or property or due to damage to equipment, or (2) during a national emergency proclaimed by the President or declared by the Congress and during the continuance of any war in which the United States is engaged and when such action is necessary for the national defense or security or otherwise in furtherance of the war effort, or (3) in cases of emergency where the Commission finds, in the nonbroadcast services, that it would not be feasible to secure renewal applications from existing licensees or otherwise to follow normal licensing procedure, the Commission may grant construction permits and station licenses, or modifications or renewals thereof, during the emergency so found by the Commission or during the continuance of any such national emergency or war, in such manner and upon such terms and conditions as the Commission shall by regulation prescribe, and without the filing of a formal application, but no authorization so granted shall continue in effect beyond the period of the emergency or war requiring it: *Provided further*, That the Commission may issue by cable, telegraph, or radio a permit for the operation of a station on a vessel of the United States at sea, effective in lieu of a license until said vessel shall return to a port of the continental United States.

(b) All applications for station licenses, or modifications or renewals thereof, shall set forth such facts as the Commission by regulation may prescribe as to the citizenship, character, and financial, technical, and other qualifications of the applicant to operate the station; the ownership and location of the proposed station and of the stations, if any, with which it is proposed to communicate; the frequencies and the power desired to be used; the hours of the day or other periods of time during which it is proposed to operate the station; the purposes for which the station is to be used; and such other information as it may require. The Commission, at any time after the filing of such original application and during the term of any such license, may require from an applicant or licensee further written statements of fact to enable it to determine whether such original application should be granted or denied or such license revoked. Such application and/or such statement of fact shall be signed by the applicant and/or licensee.

(c) The Commission in granting any license for a station intended or used for commercial communication between the United States or any Territory or possession, continental or insular, subject to the jurisdiction of the United States, and any foreign country, may impose any terms, conditions, or restrictions authorized to be imposed with respect to submarine-cable licenses by section 2 of an Act entitled "An Act relating to the landing and the operation of submarine cables in the United States," approved May 24, 1921.

Action upon applications; Form of and conditions attached to licenses

Sec. 309. (a) Subject to the provisions of this section, the Commission shall determine, in the case of each application filed with it to which section 308 applies, whether the public interest, convenience, and necessity will be served by the granting of such application, and, if the Commission, upon examination of such application and upon consideration of such other matters as the Commission may officially notice, shall find that public interest, convenience, and necessity would be served by the granting thereof, it shall grant such application.

(b)   Except as provided in subsection (c) of this section, no such application—

(1)   for an instrument of authorization in the case of a station in the broadcasting or common carrier services, or

(2)   for an instrument of authorization in the case of a station in any of the following categories:

(A)   fixed point-to-point microwave stations (exclusive of control and relay stations used as integral parts of mobile radio systems),

(B)   industrial radio positioning stations for which frequencies are assigned on an exclusive basis,

(C)   aeronautical en route stations,

(D)   aeronautical advisory stations,

(E)   airdrome control stations,

(F)   aeronautical fixed stations, and

(G)   such other stations or classes of stations, not in the broadcasting or common carrier services, as the Commission shall by rule prescribe,

shall be granted by the Commission earlier than thirty days following issuance of public notice by the Commission of the acceptance for filing of such application or of any substantial amendment thereof.

(c)   Subsection (b) of this section shall not apply—

(1)   to any minor amendment of an application to which such subsection is applicable, or

(2)   to any application for—

(A)   a minor change in the facilities of an authorized station,

(B)   consent to an involuntary assignment or transfer under section 310(b) or to an assignment or transfer thereunder which does not involve a substantial change in ownership or control,

(C)   a license under section 319(c) or, pending application for or grant of such license, any special or temporary authorization to permit interim operation to facilitate completion of authorized construction or to provide substantially the same service as would be authorized by such license,

(D)   extension of time to complete construction of authorized facilities,

(E)   an authorization of facilities for remote pickups, studio links and similar facilities for use in the operation of a broadcast station,

(F)   authorizations pursuant to section 325(b) where the programs to be transmitted are special events not of a continuing nature,

(G)   a special temporary authorization for nonbroadcast operation not to exceed thirty days where no application for regular operation is contemplated to be filed or not to exceed sixty days pending the filing of an application for such regular operation, or

(H)   an authorization under any of the proviso clauses of section 308(a).

(d)   (1)   Any party in interest may file with the Commission a petition to deny any application (whether as originally filed or as amended) to which subsection (b) of this section applies at any time prior to the day of Commission grant thereof without hearing or the day of formal designation thereof for hearing; except that with respect to any classification of applications, the Commission from time to time by rule may specify a shorter period (no less than thirty days following the issuance of public notice by the Commission of the acceptance for filing of such application or of any substantial amendment thereof), which shorter period shall be reasonably related to the time when the applications would normally be reached for processing. The petitioner shall serve a copy of such petition on the applicant. The petition shall contain specific allegations of fact sufficient to show that the petitioner is a party in interest and that a grant of the application would be prima facie inconsistent with subsection (a). Such allegations of fact shall, except for those of which official notice may be taken, be supported by affidavit of a person or persons with personal knowledge thereof. The applicant shall be given the opportunity to file a reply in which allegations of fact or denials thereof shall similarly be supported by affidavit.

(2)   If the Commission finds on the basis of the application, the pleadings filed, or other matters which it may officially notice that there are no substantial and material questions of fact and that a grant of the application would be consistent with subsection (a), it shall make the grant, deny the petition, and issue a concise statement of the reasons for denying the petition, which statement shall dispose of all substantial issues raised by the petition. If a substantial and material question of fact is presented or if the Commission for any reason is unable to find that grant of the application would be consistent with subsection (a), it shall proceed as provided in subsection (e).

(e)   If, in the case of any application to which subsection (a) of this section applies, a substantial and material question of fact is presented or the Commission for any reason is unable to make the finding specified in such subsection, it shall formally designate the application for hearing on the ground or reasons then obtaining and shall forthwith notify the applicant and all other known parties in interest of such action and the grounds and reasons therefor, specifying with particularity the matters and things in issue but not including issues or requirements phrased generally. When the Commission has so designated an application for hearing, the parties in interest, if any, who are not notified by the Commission of such action may acquire the status of a party to the proceeding thereon by filing a petition for intervention showing the basis for their interest not more than thirty days after publication of the hearing issues or any substantial amendment thereto in the Federal Register. Any hearing subsequently held upon such application shall be a full hearing in which the applicant and all other parties in interest shall be permitted to participate. The burden of proceeding with the introduction of evidence and the burden of proof shall be upon the applicant, except that with respect to any issue presented by a petition to deny or a petition to enlarge the issues, such burdens shall be as determined by the Commission.

(f) When an application subject to subsection (b) has been filed, the Commission, notwithstanding the requirements of such subsection, may, if the grant of such application is otherwise authorized by law and if it finds that there are extraordinary circumstances requiring emergency operations in the public interest and that delay in the institution of such emergency operations would seriously prejudice the public interest, grant a temporary authorization, accompanied by a statement of its reasons therefor, to permit such emergency operations for a period not exceeding ninety days, and upon making like findings may extend such temporary authorization for one additional period not to exceed ninety days. When any such grant of a temporary authorization is made, the Commission shall give expeditious treatment to any timely filed petition to deny such application and to any petition for rehearing of such grant filed under section 405.

(g) The Commission is authorized to adopt reasonable classifications of applications and amendments in order to effectuate the purposes of this section.

(h) Such station licenses as the Commission may grant shall be in such general form as it may prescribe, but each license shall contain, in addition to other provisions, a statement of the following conditions to which such license shall be subject: (1) The station license shall not vest in the licensee any right to operate the station nor any right in the use of the frequencies designated in the license beyond the term thereof nor in any other manner than authorized therein; (2) neither the license nor the right granted thereunder shall be assigned or otherwise transferred in violation of this Act; (3) every license issued under this Act shall be subject in terms to the right of use or control conferred by section 606 of this Act.

Limitation on holding and transfer of licenses

Sec. 310. (a) The station license required hereby shall not be granted to or held by—

(1) Any alien or the representative of any alien;

(2) Any foreign government or the representative thereof;

(3) Any corporation organized under the laws of any foreign government;

(4) Any corporation of which any officer or director is an alien or

of which more than one-fifth of the capital stock is owned of record or voted by aliens or their representatives or by a foreign government or representative thereof or by any corporation organized under the laws of a foreign country;

(5)   Any corporation directly or indirectly controlled by any other corporation of which any officer or more than one-fourth of the directors are aliens, or of which more than one-fourth of the capital stock is owned of record or voted after June 1, 1935, by aliens, their representative, or by a foreign government or representative thereof, or by any corporation organized under the laws of a foreign country, if the Commission finds that the public interest will be served by the refusal or the revocation of such license.

Nothing in this subsection shall prevent the licensing of radio apparatus on board any vessel, aircraft, or other mobile station of the United States when the installation and use of such apparatus is required by Act of Congress or any treaty to which the United States is a party.

Notwithstanding paragraph (1) of this subsection, a license for a radio station on an aircraft may be granted to and held by a person who is an alien or a representative of an alien if such person holds a United States pilot certificate or a foreign aircraft pilot certificate which is valid in the United States on the basis of reciprocal agreements entered into with foreign governments.

Notwithstanding section 301 of this Act and paragraphs (1) and (2) of this subsection, the Commission may issue authorizations, under such conditions and terms as it may prescribe, to permit an alien licensed by his government as an amateur radio operator to operate his amateur radio station licensed by his government in the United States, its possessions, and the Commonwealth of Puerto Rico provided there is in effect a bilateral agreement between the United States and the alien's government for such operation on a reciprocal basis by United States amateur radio operators: *Provided*, That when an application for an authorization is received by the Commission, it shall notify the appropriate agencies of the Government of such fact, and such agencies shall forthwith furnish to the Commission such information in their possession as bears upon the compatibility of the request with the national security: *And provided further*, That the requested authorization may then be granted unless the Commission shall determine that information received from such agencies necessitates denial of the request. Other provisions of this Act and of the Administrative Procedure Act shall not be applicable to any request or application for or modification, suspension, or cancellation of any such authorization.

(b)   No construction permit or station license, or any rights thereunder, shall be transferred, assigned, or disposed of in any manner, voluntarily or involuntarily, directly or indirectly, or by transfer of control of any corporation holding such permit or license, to any person except upon application to the Commission and upon finding by the Commission that the public interest, convenience, and necessity will be served thereby. Any such application shall be disposed of as if the proposed transferee or assignee were making application under section 308 for the permit or license in question; but in acting thereon the Commission may not consider whether the public interest, convenience, and necessity might be served by the transfer, assignment, or disposal of the permit or license to a person other than the proposed transferee or assignee.

Special requirements with respect to certain applications in the broadcasting service

Sec. 311.   (a)   When there is filed with the Commission any application to which section 309(b)(1) applies, for an instrument of authorization for a station in the broadcasting service, the applicant—

(1)   shall give notice of such filing in the principal area which is served or is to be served by the station; and

(2)   if the application is formally designated for hearing in accordance with section 309, shall give notice of such hearing in such area at least ten days before commencement of such hearing.

The Commission shall by rule prescribe the form and content of the notices to be given in compliance with this subsection, and the manner and frequency with which such notices shall be given.

(b)   Hearings referred to in subsection (a) may be held at such places as the Commission shall determine to be appropriate, and in making such determination in any case the Commission shall consider whether the public interest, convenience, or necessity will be served by conducting the hearing at a place in, or in the vicinity of, the principal area to be served by the station involved.

(c)   (1)   If there are pending before the Commission two or more applications for a permit for construction of a broadcasting station, only one of which can be granted, it shall be unlawful, without approval of the Commission, for the applicants or any of them to effectuate an agreement whereby one or more of such applicants withdraws his or their application or applications.

(2)   The request for Commission approval in any such case shall be made in writing jointly by all the parties to the agreement. Such request shall contain or be accompanied by full information with respect to the agreement, set forth in such detail, form, and manner as the Commission shall by rule require.

(3)   The Commission shall approve the agreement only if it determines that the agreement is consistent with the public interest, convenience, or necessity. If the agreement does not contemplate a merger, but contemplates the making of any direct or indirect payment to any party thereto in consideration of his withdrawal of his application, the Commission may determine the agreement to be consistent with the public interest, convenience,

or necessity only if the amount or value of such payment, as determined by the Commission, is not in excess of the aggregate amount determined by the Commission to have been legitimately and prudently expended and to be expended by such applicant in connection with preparing, filing, and advocating the granting of his application.

(4)   For the purposes of this subsection an application shall be deemed to be "pending" before the Commission from the time such application is filed with the Commission until an order of the Commission granting or denying it is no longer subject to rehearing by the Commission or to review by any court.

Administrative sanctions

Sec. 312.*   (a)   The Commission may revoke any station license or construction permit—

(1)   for false statements knowingly made either in the application or in any statement of fact which may be required pursuant to section 308;

(2)   because of conditions coming to the attention of the Commission which would warrant it in refusing to grant a license or permit on an original application;

(3)   for willful or repeated failure to operate substantially as set forth in the license;

(4)   for willful or repeated violation of, or willful or repeated failure to observe any provision of this Act or any rule or regulation of the Commission authorized by this Act or by a treaty ratified by the United States;

(5)   for violation of or failure to observe any final cease and desist order issued by the Commission under this section;

(6)   for violation of section 1304, 1343, or 1464 of title 18 of the United States Code; or

(7)   for willful or repeated failure to allow reasonable access to or to permit purchase of reasonable amounts of time for the use of a broadcasting station by a legally qualified candidate for Federal elective office on behalf of his candidacy.

(b)   Where any person (1) has failed to operate substantially as set forth in a license, (2) has violated or failed to observe any of the provisions of this Act, or section 1304, 1343, or 1464 of title 18 of the United States Code, or (3) has violated or failed to observe any rule or regulation of the Commission authorized by this Act or by a treaty ratified by the United States, the Commission may order such person to cease and desist from such action.

*This section has been amended to comply with the Campaign Communications Reform Act (Title I of the Federal Election Campaign Act of 1971), Public Law 92-225, approved February 7, 1972. [Ed.]

(c)   Before revoking a license or permit pursuant to subsection (a), or issuing a cease and desist order pursuant to subsection (b), the Commission shall serve upon the licensee, permittee, or person involved an order to show cause why an order of revocation or a cease and desist order should not be issued. Any such order to show cause shall contain a statement of the matters with respect to which the Commission is inquiring and shall call upon said licensee, permittee, or person to appear before the Commission at a time and place stated in the order, but in no event less than thirty days after the receipt of such order, and give evidence upon the matter specified therein; except that where safety of life or property is involved, the Commission may provide in the order for a shorter period. If after hearing, or a waiver thereof, the Commission determines that an order of revocation or a cease and desist order should issue, it shall issue such order, which shall include a statement of the findings of the Commission and the grounds and reasons therefor and specify the effective date of the order, and shall cause the same to be served on said licensee, permittee, or person.

(d)   In any case where a hearing is conducted pursuant to the provisions of this section, both the burden of proceeding with the introduction of evidence and the burden of proof shall be upon the Commission.

(e)   The provisions of section 9(b) of the Administrative Procedure Act which apply with respect to the institution of any proceeding for the revocation of a license or permit shall apply also with respect to the institution, under this section, of any proceeding for the issuance of a cease and desist order.

Application of antitrust laws; Refusal of licenses and permits in certain cases

Sec. 313.   (a)   All laws of the United States relating to unlawful restraints and monopolies and to combinations, contracts, or agreements in restraint of trade are hereby declared to be applicable to the manufacture and sale of and to trade in radio apparatus and devices entering into or affecting interstate or foreign commerce and to interstate or foreign radio communications. Whenever in any suit, action, or proceeding, civil or criminal, brought under the provisions of any of said laws or in any proceedings brought to enforce or to review findings and orders of the Federal Trade Commission or other governmental agency in respect of any matters as to which said Commission or other governmental agency is by law authorized to act, any licensee shall be found guilty of the violation of the provisions of such laws or any of them, the court, in addition to the penalties imposed by said laws, may adjudge, order, and/or decree that the license of such licensee shall, as of the date the decree or judgment becomes finally effective or as of such other date as the said decree shall fix, be revoked and that all rights under such license shall thereupon cease: *Provided, however,* That such licensee shall have the same right of appeal or review, as is provided by law in respect of other decrees and judgments of said court.

(b)   The Commission is hereby directed to refuse a station license and/or the permit hereinafter required for the construction of a station to any person (or to any person directly or indirectly controlled by such person) whose license has been revoked by a court under this section.

Preservation of competition in commerce

Sec. 314.   After the effective date of this Act no person engaged directly, or indirectly through any person directly or indirectly controlling or controlled by, or under direct or indirect common control with, such person, or through an agent, or otherwise, in the business of transmitting and/or receiving for hire energy, communications, or signals by radio in accordance with the terms of the license issued under this Act, shall by purchase, lease, construction, or otherwise, directly or indirectly, acquire, own, control, or operate any cable or wire telegraph or telephone line or system between any place in any State, Territory, or possession of the United States or in the District of Columbia, and any place in any foreign country, or shall acquire, own, or control any part of the stock or other capital share or any interest in the physical property and/or other assets of any such cable, wire, telegraph, or telephone line or system, if in either case the purpose is and/or the effect thereof may be to substantially lessen competition or to restrain commerce between any place in any State, Territory, or possession of the United States, or in the District of Columbia, and any place in any foreign country, or unlawfully to create monopoly in any line of commerce; nor shall any person engaged directly, or indirectly through any person directly or indirectly controlling or controlled by, or under direct or indirect common control with, such person, or through an agent, or otherwise, in the business of transmitting and/or receiving for hire messages by any cable, wire, telegraph, or telephone line or system (a) between any place in any State, Territory, or possession of the United States, or in the District of Columbia, and any place in any other State, Territory, or possession of the United States; or (b) between any place in any State, Territory, or possession of the United States, or the District of Columbia, and any place in any foreign country, by purchase, lease, construction, or otherwise, directly or indirectly acquire, own, control, or operate any station or the apparatus therein, or any system for transmitting and/or receiving radio communications or signals between any place in any State, Territory, or possession of the United States, or in the District of Columbia, and any place in any foreign country, or shall acquire, own, or control any part of the stock or other capital share of any interest in the physical property and/or other assets of any such radio station, apparatus, or system, if in either case, the purpose is and/or the effect thereof may be to substantially lessen competition or to restrain commerce between any place in any State, Territory, or possession of the United States, or in the District of Columbia, and any place in any foreign country, or unlawfully to create monopoly in any line of commerce.

Facilities for candidates for public office

Sec. 315.* [(a) If any licensee shall permit any person who is a legally qualified candidate for any public office to use a broadcasting station, he shall afford equal opportunities to all other such candidates for that office in the use of such broadcasting station: *Provided*, That such licensee shall have no power of censorship over the material broadcast under the provisions of this section. No obligation is imposed under this subsection upon any licensee to allow the use of its station by any such candidate. Appearance by a legally qualified candidate on any

(1) bona fide newscast,

(2) bona fide news interview,

(3) bona fide news documentary (if the appearance of the candidate is incidental to the presentation of the subject or subjects covered by the news documentary), or

(4) on-the-spot coverage of bona fide news events (including but not limited to political conventions and activities incidental thereto),

shall not be deemed to be use of a broadcasting station within the meaning of this subsection] Nothing in the foregoing sentence shall be construed as relieving broadcasters, in connection with the presentation of newscasts, news interviews, news documentaries, and on-the-spot coverage of news events, from the obligation imposed upon them under this Act to operate in the public interest and to afford reasonable opportunity for the discussion of conflicting views on issues of public importance.

(b) The charges made for the use of any broadcasting station by any person who is a legally qualified candidate for any public office in connection with his campaign for nomination for election, or election, to such office shall not exceed—

(1) during the forty-five days preceding the date of a primary or primary runoff election and during the sixty days preceding the date of a general or special election in which such person is a candidate, the lowest unit charge of the station for the same class and amount of time for the same period; and

(2) at any other time, the charges made for comparable use of such station by other users thereof.

*This section has been amended to comply with the Campaign Communications Reform Act (Title I of the Federal Election Campaign Act of 1971), Public Law 92-225, approved February 7, 1972. [Ed.]

(c)   No station licensee may make any charge for the use of such station by or on behalf of any legally qualified candidate for Federal elective office (or for nomination to such office) unless such candidate (or a person specifically authorized by such candidate in writing to do so) certifies to such licensee in writing that the payment of such charge will not violate any limitation specified in paragraph (1), (2), or (3) of section 104(a) of the Campaign Communications Reform Act, whichever paragraph is applicable.

(d)   If a State by law and expressly—

(1)   has provided that a primary or other election for any office of such State or of a political subdivision thereof is subject to this subsection,

(2)   has specified a limitation upon total expenditures for the use of broadcasting stations on behalf of the candidacy of each legally qualified candidate in such election,

(3)   has provided in any such law an unequivocal expression of intent to be bound by the provisions of this subsection, and

(4)   has stipulated that the amount of such limitation shall not exceed the amount which would be determined for such election under section 104(a) (1) (B) or 104(a) (2) (B) (whichever is applicable) of the Campaign Communications Reform Act had such election been an election for a Federal elective office or nomination thereto;

then no station licensee may make any charge for the use of such station by or on behalf of any legally qualified candidate in such election unless such candidate (or a person specifically authorized by such candidate in writing to do so) certifies to such licensee in writing that the payment of such charge will not violate such State limitation.

(e)   Whoever willfully and knowingly violates the provisions of subsection (c) or (d) of this section shall be punished by a fine not to exceed $5,000 or imprisonment for a period not to exceed five years, or both. The provisions of sections 501 through 503 of this Act shall not apply to violations of either such subsection.

(f)   (1)   For the purposes of this section:

(A)   The term "broadcasting station" includes a community antenna television system.

(B)   The terms "licensee" and "station licensee" when used with respect to a community antenna television system, means the operator of such system.

(C)   The term "Federal elective office" means the office of President of the United States, or of Senator or Representative in, or Resident Commissioner or Delegate to, the Congress of the United States.

(2)   For purposes of subsections (c) and (d), the term "legally qualified candidate" means any person who (A) meets the qualifications prescribed by the applicable laws to hold the office for which he is a candidate

and (B) is eligible under applicable State law to be voted for by the electorate directly or by means of delegates or electors.

(g)   The Commission shall prescribe appropriate rules and regulations to carry out the provisions of this section.

Modification by Commission of construction permits or licenses

Sec. 316.   (a)   Any station license or construction permit may be modified by the Commission either for a limited time or for the duration of the term thereof, if in the judgment of the Commission such action will promote the public interest, convenience, and necessity, or the provisions of this Act or of any treaty ratified by the United States will be more fully complied with. No such order of modification shall become final until the holder of the license or permit shall have been notified in writing of the proposed action and the grounds and reasons therefor, and shall have been given reasonable opportunity, in no event less than thirty days, to show cause by public hearing, if requested, why such order of modification should not issue: *Provided*, That where safety of life or property is involved, the Commission may by order provide for a shorter period of notice.

(b)   In any case where a hearing is conducted pursuant to the provisions of this section, both the burden of proceeding with the introduction of evidence and the burden of proof shall be upon the Commission.

Announcement with respect to certain matter broadcast

Sec. 317.   (a)   (1)   All matter broadcast by any radio station for which any money, service or other valuable consideration is directly or indirectly paid, or promised to or charged or accepted by, the station so broadcasting, from any person, shall, at the time the same is so broadcast, be announced as paid for or furnished, as the case may be, by such person: *Provided*, That "service or other valuable consideration" shall not include any service or property furnished without charge or at a nominal charge for use on, or in connection with, a broadcast unless it is so furnished in consideration for an identification in a broadcast of any person, product, service, trademark, or brand name beyond an identification which is reasonably related to the use of such service or property on the broadcast.

(2)   Nothing in this section shall preclude the Commission from requiring that an appropriate announcement shall be made at the time of the broadcast in the case of any political program or any program involving the discussion of any controversial issue for which any films, records, transcriptions, talent, scripts, or other material or service of any kind have been furnished,

without charge or at a nominal charge, directly or indirectly, as an inducement to the broadcast of such program.

(b)   In any case where a report has been made to a radio station, as required by section 508 of this Act, of circumstances which would have required an announcement under this section had the consideration been received by such radio station, an appropriate announcement shall be made by such radio station.

(c)   The licensee of each radio station shall exercise reasonable diligence to obtain from its employees, and from other persons with whom it deals directly in connection with any program or program matter for broadcast, information to enable such licensee to make the announcement required by this section.

(d)   The Commission may waive the requirement of an announcement as provided in this section in any case or class of cases with respect to which it determines that the public interest, convenience, or necessity does not require the broadcasting of such announcement.

(e)   The Commission shall prescribe appropriate rules and regulations to carry out the provisions of this section.

Operation of transmitting apparatus

Sec. 318.   The actual operation of all transmitting apparatus in any radio station for which a station license is required by this Act shall be carried on only by a person holding an operator's license issued hereunder, and no person shall operate any such apparatus in such station except under and in accordance with an operator's license issued to him by the Commission: *Provided, however,* That the Commission if it shall find that the public interest, convenience, or necessity will be served thereby may waive or modify the foregoing provisions of this section for the operation of any station except (1) stations for which licensed operators are required by international agreement, (2) stations for which licensed operators are required for safety purposes, (3) stations engaged in broadcasting (other than those engaged solely in the function of rebroadcasting the signals of television broadcast stations) and (4) stations operated as common carriers on frequencies below thirty thousand kilocycles: *Provided further,* That the Commission shall have power to make special regulations governing the granting of licenses for the use of automatic radio devices and for the operation of such devices.

Construction permits

Sec. 319.   (a)   No license shall be issued under the authority of this Act for the operation of any station the construction of which is begun or is continued after this Act takes effect, unless a permit for its construction has been granted by the Commission. The application for a construction permit shall set forth such facts as the Commission by regulation may prescribe as to the citizenship, character, and the financial, technical, and other ability of the applicant to construct and operate the station, the ownership and location of the proposed station and of the station or stations with which it is proposed to communicate, the frequencies desired to be used, the hours of the day or other periods of time during which it is proposed to operate the station, the purpose for which the station is to be used, the type of transmitting apparatus to be used, the power to be used, the date upon which the station is expected to be completed and in operation, and such other information as the Commission may require. Such application shall be signed by the applicant.

(b)   Such permit for construction shall show specifically the earliest and latest dates between which the actual operation of such station is expected to begin, and shall provide that said permit will be automatically forfeited if the station is not ready for operation within the time specified or within such further time as the Commission may allow, unless prevented by causes not under the control of the grantee.

(c)   Upon the completion of any station for the construction or continued construction of which a permit has been granted, and upon it being made to appear to the Commission that all the terms, conditions, and obligations set forth in the application and permit have been fully met, and that no cause or circumstance arising or first coming to the knowledge of the Commission since the granting of the permit would, in the judgment of the Commission, make the operation of such station against the public interest, the Commission shall issue a license to the lawful holder of said permit for the operation of said station. Said license shall conform generally to the terms of said permit. The provisions of section 309(a), (b), (c), (d), (e), (f), and (g) shall not apply with respect to any station license the issuance of which is provided for and governed by the provisions of this subsection.

(d)   A permit for construction shall not be required for Government stations, amateur stations, or mobile stations. With respect to stations or classes of stations other than Government stations, amateur stations, mobile stations, and broadcasting stations, the Commission may waive the requirement of a permit for construction if it finds that the public interest, convenience, or necessity would be served thereby: *Provided, however*, That such waiver shall apply only to stations whose construction is begun subsequent to the effective date of the waiver. If the Commission finds that the public interest, convenience, and necessity would be served thereby, it may waive the requirement of a permit for construction of a station that is engaged solely in rebroadcasting television signals if such station was constructed on or before the date of enactment of this sentence.

False distress signals; Rebroadcasting; Studios of foreign stations

Sec. 325. (a) No person within the jurisdiction of the United States shall knowingly utter or transmit, or cause to be uttered or transmitted, any false or fraudulent signal of distress, or communication relating thereto, nor shall any broadcasting station rebroadcast the program or any part thereof of another broadcasting station without the express authority of the originating station.

(b) No person shall be permitted to locate, use, or maintain a radio broadcast studio or other place or apparatus from which or whereby sound waves are converted into electrical energy, or mechanical or physical reproduction of sound waves produced, and caused to be transmitted or delivered to a radio station in a foreign country for the purpose of being broadcast from any radio station there having a power output of sufficient intensity and/or being so located geographically that its emissions may be received consistently in the United States, without first obtaining a permit from the Commission upon proper application therefor.

(c) Such application shall contain such information as the Commission may by regulation prescribe, and the granting or refusal thereof shall be subject to the requirements of section 309 hereof with respect to applications for station licenses or renewal or modification thereof, and the license or permission so granted shall be revocable for false statements in the application so required or when the Commission, after hearings, shall find its continuation no longer in the public interest.

Censorship; Indecent language

Sec. 326. Nothing in this Act shall be understood or construed to give the Commission the power of censorship over the radio communications or signals transmitted by any radio station, and no regulation or condition shall be promulgated or fixed by the Commission which shall interfere with the right of free speech by means of radio communication.

Prohibition against shipment of certain television receivers

Sec. 330. (a) No person shall ship in interstate commerce, or import from any foreign country into the United States, for sale or resale to the public, apparatus described in paragraph (s) of section 303 unless it complies with rules prescribed by the Commission pursuant to the authority granted by that paragraph: *Provided*, That this section shall not apply to carriers transporting such apparatus without trading in it.

(b)   For the purposes of this section and section 303(s)—

(1)   The term "interstate commerce" means (A) commerce between any State, the District of Columbia, the Commonwealth of Puerto Rico, or any possession of the United States and any place outside thereof which is within the United States, (B) commerce between points in the same State, the District of Columbia, the Commonwealth of Puerto Rico, or any possession of the United States but through any place outside thereof, or (C) commerce wholly within the District of Columbia or any possession of the United States.

(2)   The term "United States" means the several States, the District of Columbia, the Commonwealth of Puerto Rico, and the possessions of the United States, but does not include the Canal Zone.*

PART IV – GRANTS FOR NONCOMMERCIAL EDUCATIONAL BROADCASTING FACILITIES: CORPORATION FOR PUBLIC BROADCASTING

SUBPART A
GRANTS FOR FACILITIES

Declaration of purpose

Sec. 390.   The purpose of this subpart is to assist (through matching grants) in the construction of noncommercial educational television or radio broadcasting facilities.

Authorization of appropriations

Sec. 391.   There are authorized to be appropriated for the fiscal year ending June 30, 1963, and each of the four succeeding fiscal years such sums, not exceeding $32,000,000 in the aggregate, as may be necessary to carry out the purposes of section 390. There are also authorized to be appropriated for carrying out the purposes of such section, $10,500,000 for the fiscal year ending June 30, 1968, $12,500,000 for the fiscal year ending June 30, 1969, and

*Parts II and III of Title III relating to maritime uses of radio are omitted. [Ed.]

$15,000,000 for the fiscal year ending June 30, 1970. Sums appropriated pursuant to this section shall remain available for payment of grants for projects for which applications, approved under section 392, have been submitted under such section prior to July 1, 1971.

Grants for construction

Sec. 392.   (a)   For each project for the construction of noncommercial educational television or radio broadcasting facilities there shall be submitted to the Secretary an application for a grant containing such information with respect to such project as the Secretary may by regulation require, including the total cost of such project and the amount of the Federal grant requested for such project, and providing assurance satisfactory to the Secretary—

(1)   that the applicant is (A) an agency or officer responsible for the supervision of public elementary or secondary education or public higher education within that State, or within a political subdivision thereof, (B) in the case of a project for television facilities, the State noncommercial educational television agency or, in the case of a project for radio facilities, the State educational radio agency, (C) a college or university deriving its support in whole or in part from tax revenues, (D) (i) in the case of a project for television facilities, a nonprofit foundation, corporation, or association which is organized primarily to engage in or encourage noncommercial educational television broadcasting and is eligible to receive a license from the Federal Communications Commission for a noncommercial educational television broadcasting station pursuant to the rules and regulations of the Commission in effect on April 12, 1962, or (ii) in the case of a project for radio facilities, a nonprofit foundation, corporation, or association which is organized primarily to engage in or encourage noncommercial educational radio broadcasting and is eligible to receive a license from the Federal Communications Commission; or meets the requirements of clause (i) and is also organized to engage in or encourage such radio broadcasting and is eligible for such a license for such a radio station, or (E) a municipality which owns and operates a broadcasting facility transmitting only noncommercial programs;

(2)   that the operation of such educational broadcasting facilities will be under the control of the applicant or a person qualified under paragraph (1) to be such an applicant;

(3)   that necessary funds to construct, operate, and maintain such educational broadcasting facilities will be available when needed;

(4)   that such broadcasting facilities will be used only for educational purposes; and

(5)   that, in the case of an application with respect to radio broadcasting facilities, there has been comprehensive planning for educational

broadcasting facilities and services in the area the applicant proposes to serve and the applicant has participated in such planning, and the applicant will make the most efficient use of the frequency assignment.

(b)   The total of the grants made under this part from the appropriation for any fiscal year for the construction of noncommercial educational television broadcasting facilities and noncommercial educational radio broadcasting facilities in any State may not exceed 8½ per centum of such appropriation.

Notice to State educational television and radio agencies

(c)   (1)   In order to assure proper coordination of construction of noncommercial educational television broadcasting facilities within each State which has established a State educational television agency, each applicant for a grant under this section for a project for construction of such facilities in such State, other than such agency, shall notify such agency of each application for such a grant which is submitted by it to the Secretary, and the Secretary shall advise such agency with respect to the disposition of each such application.

(2)   In order to assure proper coordination of construction of noncommercial educational radio broadcasting facilities within each State which has established a State educational radio agency, each applicant for a grant under this section for a project for construction of such facilities in such State, other than such agency, shall notify such agency of each application for such a grant which is submitted by it to the Secretary, and the Secretary shall advise such agency with respect to the disposition of each such application.

(d)   The Secretary shall base his determinations of whether to approve applications for grants under this section and the amount of such grants on criteria set forth in regulations and designed to achieve (1) prompt and effective use of all noncommercial educational television channels remaining available, (2) equitable geographical distribution of noncommercial educational television broadcasting facilities or noncommercial educational radio broadcasting facilities, as the case may be, throughout the States, and (3) provision of noncommercial educational television broadcasting facilities or noncommercial educational radio broadcasting facilities, as the case may be, which will serve the greatest number of persons and serve them in as many areas as possible, and which are adaptable to the broadest educational uses.

(e)   Upon approving any application under this section with respect to any project, the Secretary shall make a grant to the applicant in the amount determined by him, but not exceeding 75 per centum of the amount determined by the Secretary to be the reasonable and necessary cost of such project. The Secretary shall pay such amount from the sum available therefor, in advance or by way or reimbursement, and in such installments consistent with construction progress, as he may determine.

(f)   If, within ten years after completion of any project for construction of educational television or radio broadcasting facilities with respect to which a grant has been made under this section—

> (1)   the applicant or other owner of such facilities ceases to be an agency, officer, institution, foundation, corporation, or association described in subsection (a)(1) of this section, or
>
> (2)   such facilities cease to be used for noncommercial educational television purposes or noncommercial educational radio purposes, as the case may be (unless the Secretary determines, in accordance with regulations, that there is good cause for releasing the applicant or other owner from the obligation so to do),

the United States shall be entitled to recover from the applicant or other owner of such facilities the amount bearing the same ratio to the then value (as determined by agreement of the parties or by action brought in the United States district court for the district in which such facilities are situated) of such facilities, as the amount of the Federal participation bore to the cost of construction of such facilities.

Records

Sec. 393. (a) Each recipient of assistance under this subpart shall keep such records as may be reasonably necessary to enable the Secretary to carry out his functions under this subpart, including records which fully disclose the amount and the disposition by such recipient of the proceeds of such assistance, the total cost of the project or undertaking in connection with which such assistance is given or used, and the amount and nature of that portion of the cost of the project or undertaking supplied by other sources, and such other records as will facilitate an effective audit.

(b)   The Secretary and the Comptroller General of the United States, or any of their duly authorized representatives, shall have access for the purpose of audit and examination to any books, documents, papers, and records of the recipient that are pertinent to assistance received under this subpart.

Rules and regulations

Sec. 394.   The Secretary is authorized to make such rules and regulations as may be necessary to carry out this subpart, including regulations relating to the order of priority in approving applications for projects under section 392 or to determining the amounts of grants for such projects.

Provision of assistance by
Federal Communications Commission

Sec. 395.   The Federal Communications Commission is authorized to provide such assistance in carrying out the provisions of this subpart as may be requested by the Secretary. The Secretary shall provide for consultation and close cooperation with the Federal Communications Commission in the administration of his functions under this subpart which are of interest to or affect the functions of the Commission.

SUBPART B
CORPORATION FOR PUBLIC BROADCASTING

Congressional declaration of policy

Sec. 396.   (a)   The Congress hereby finds and declares—

(1) that it is in the public interest to encourage the growth and development of noncommercial educational radio and television broadcasting, including the use of such media for instructional purposes;

(2)   that expansion and development of noncommercial educational radio and television broadcasting and of diversity of its programing depend on freedom, imagination, and initiative on both the local and national levels;

(3)   that the encouragement and support of noncommercial educational radio and television broadcasting, while matters of importance for private and local development, are also of appropriate and important concern to the Federal Government;

(4)   that it furthers the general welfare to encourage noncommercial educational radio and television broadcast programing which will be responsive to the interests of people both in particular localities and throughout the United States, and which will constitute an expression of diversity and excellence;

(5)   that it is necessary and appropriate for the Federal Government to complement, assist, and support a national policy that will most effectively make noncommercial educational radio and television service available to all the citizens of the United States;

(6)   that a private corporation should be created to facilitate the development of educational radio and television broadcasting and to afford

maximum protection to such broadcasting from extraneous interference and control.

Corporation established

(b)   There is authorized to be established a nonprofit corporation, to be known as the "Corporation for Public Broadcasting," which will not be an agency or establishment of the United States Government. The Corporation shall be subject to the provisions of this section, and, to the extent consistent with this section, to the District of Columbia Nonprofit Corporation Act.

Board of Directors

(c)   (1)   The Corporation shall have a Board of Directors (hereinafter in this section referred to as the "Board"), consisting of fifteen members appointed by the President, by and with the advice and consent of the Senate. Not more than eight members of the Board may be members of the same political party.

(2)   The members of the Board (A) shall be selected from among citizens of the United States (not regular fulltime employees of the United States) who are eminent in such fields as education, cultural and civic affairs, or the arts, including radio and television; (B) shall be selected so as to provide as nearly as practicable a broad representation of various regions of the country, various professions and occupations, and various kinds of talent and experience appropriate to the functions and responsibilities of the Corporation.

(3)   The members of the initial Board of Directors shall serve as incorporators and shall take whatever actions are necessary to establish the Corporation under the District of Columbia Nonprofit Corporation Act.

(4)   The term of office of each member of the Board shall be six years; except that (A) any member appointed to fill a vacancy occurring prior to the expiration of the term for which his predecessor was appointed shall be appointed for the remainder of such term; and (B) the terms of office of members first taking office shall begin on the date of incorporation and shall expire, as designated at the time of their appointment, five at the end of two years, five at the end of four years, and five at the end of six years. No member shall be eligible to serve in excess of two consecutive terms of six years each. Notwithstanding the preceding provisions of this paragraph, a member whose term has expired may serve until his successor has qualified.

(5)   Any vacancy in the Board shall not affect its power, but shall be filled in the manner in which the original appointments were made.

Election of Chairman; compensation

(d) (1) The President shall designate one of the members first appointed to the Board as Chairman; thereafter the members of the Board shall annually elect one of their number as Chairman. The members of the Board shall also elect one or more of them as a Vice Chairman or Vice Chairmen.

(2) The members of the Board shall not, by reason of such membership, be deemed to be employees of the United States. They shall, while attending meetings of the Board or while engaged in duties related to such meetings or in other activities of the Board pursuant to this subpart be entitled to receive compensation at the rate of $100 per day including travel time, and while away from their homes or regular places of business they may be allowed travel expenses, including per diem in lieu of subsistence, equal to that authorized by law (5 U.S.C. 5703) for persons in the Government service employed intermittently.

Officers and employees

(e) (1) The Corporation shall have a President, and such other officers as may be named and appointed by the Board for terms and at rates of compensation fixed by the Board. No individual other than a citizen of the United States may be an officer of the Corporation. No officer of the Corporation, other than the Chairman and any Vice Chairman, may receive any salary or other compensation from any source other than the Corporation during the period of his employment by the Corporation. All officers shall serve at the pleasure of the Board.

(2) Except as provided in the second sentence of subsection (c)(1) of this section, no political test or qualification shall be used in selecting, appointing, promoting, or taking other personnel actions with respect to officers, agents, and employees of the Corporation.

Nonprofit and nonpolitical nature of the Corporation

(f) (1) The Corporation shall have no power to issue any shares of stock, or to declare or pay any dividends.

(2) No part of the income or assets of the Corporation shall inure to the benefit of any director, officer, employee, or any other individual except as salary or reasonable compensation for services.

(3) The Corporation may not contribute to or otherwise support any political party or candidate for elective public office.

Purposes and activities of the Corporation

(g) (1) In order to achieve the objectives and to carry out the purposes of this subpart, as set out in subsection (a), the Corporation is authorized to—

(A) facilitate the full development of educational broadcasting in which programs of high quality, obtained from diverse sources, will be made available to noncommercial educational television or radio broadcast stations, with strict adherence to objectivity and balance in all programs or series of programs of a controversial nature;

(B) assist in the establishment and development of one or more systems of interconnection to be used for the distribution of educational television or radio programs so that all noncommercial educational television or radio broadcast stations that wish to may broadcast the programs at times chosen by the stations;

(C) assist in the establishment and development of one or more systems of noncommercial educational television or radio broadcast stations throughout the United States;

(D) carry out its purposes and functions and engage in its activities in ways that will most effectively assure the maximum freedom of the noncommercial educational television or radio broadcast systems and local stations from interference with or control of program content or other activities.

(2) Included in the activities of the Corporation authorized for accomplishment of the purposes set forth in subsection (a) of this section, are, among others not specifically named—

(A) to obtain grants from and to make contracts with individuals and with private, State, and Federal agencies, organizations, and institutions;

(B) to contract with or make grants to program production entities, individuals, and selected noncommercial educational broadcast stations for the production of, and otherwise to procure, educational television or radio programs for national or regional distribution to noncommercial educational broadcast stations;

(C) to make payments to existing and new noncommercial educational broadcast stations to aid in financing local educational television or radio programing costs of such stations, particularly innovative approaches thereto, and other costs of operation of such stations;

(D) to establish and maintain a library and archives of noncommercial educational television or radio programs and related materials and develop public awareness of and disseminate information about noncommercial educational television or radio broadcasting by various means, including the publication of a journal;

(E) to arrange, by grant or contract with appropriate public or private agencies, organizations, or institutions, for interconnection facilities suitable for distribution and transmission of educational television or radio programs to noncommercial educational broadcast stations;

(F) to hire or accept the voluntary services of consultants, experts, advisory boards, and panels to aid the Corporation in carrying out the purposes of this section;

(G) to encourage the creation of new noncommercial educational broadcast stations in order to enhance such service on a local, State, regional, and national basis;

(H) conduct (directly or through grants or contracts) research, demonstrations, or training in matters related to noncommercial educational television or radio broadcasting.

(3) To carry out the foregoing purposes and engage in the foregoing activities, the Corporation shall have the usual powers conferred upon a nonprofit corporation by the District of Columbia Nonprofit Corporation Act, except that the Corporation may not own or operate any television or radio broadcast station, system, or network, community antenna television system, or interconnection or program production facility.

Authorization for free or reduced rate interconnection service

(h) Nothing in the Communications Act of 1934, as amended, or in any other provision of law shall be construed to prevent United States communications common carriers from rendering free or reduced rate communications interconnection services for noncommercial educational television or radio services, subject to such rules and regulations as the Federal Communications Commission may prescribe.

Report to Congress

(i) The Corporation shall submit an annual report for the preceding fiscal year ending June 30 to the President for transmittal to the Congress on or before the 31st day of December of each year. The report shall include a comprehensive and detailed report of the Corporation's operations, activities, financial condition, and accomplishments under this section and may include such recommendations as the Corporation deems appropriate.

Right to repeal, alter, or amend

(j)   The right to repeal, alter, or amend this section at any time is expressly reserved.

Financing

(k)   (1)   There are authorized to be appropriated for expenses of the Corporation for the fiscal year ending June 30, 1969, the sum of $9,000,000, to remain available until expended.

(2)   Notwithstanding the preceding provisions of this section, no grant or contract pursuant to this section may provide for payment from the appropriation for the fiscal year ending June 30, 1969, for any one project or to any one station of more than $250,000.

Records and audit

(l)   (1)   (A)   The accounts of the Corporation shall be audited annually in accordance with generally accepted auditing standards by independent certified public accountants or independent licensed public accountants certified or licensed by a regulatory authority of a State or other political subdivision of the United States. The audits shall be conducted at the place or places where the accounts of the Corporation are normally kept. All books, accounts, financial records, reports, files, and all other papers, things, or property belonging to or in use by the Corporation and necessary to facilitate the audits shall be made available to the person or persons conducting the audits; and full facilities for verifying transactions with the balances or securities held by depositories, fiscal agents and custodians shall be afforded to such person or persons.

(B)   The report of each such independent audit shall be included in the annual report required by subsection (i) of this section. The audit report shall set forth the scope of the audit and include such statements as are necessary to present fairly the Corporation's assets and liabilities, surplus or deficit, with an analysis of the changes therein during the year, supplemented in reasonable detail by a statement of the Corporation's income and expenses during the year, and a statement of the sources and application of funds, together with the independent auditor's opinion of those statements.

(2)   (A)   The financial transactions of the Corporation for any fiscal year during which Federal funds are available to finance any portion of its operations may be audited by the General Accounting Office in accordance with the principles and procedures applicable to commercial corporate transactions and under such rules and regulations as may be prescribed by the Comptroller General of the United States. Any such audit shall be conducted at the place or places where accounts of the Corporation are normally kept. The representative of the General Accounting Office shall have access to all books, accounts, records, reports, files, and all other papers, things, or property belonging to or in use by the Corporation pertaining to its financial transactions and necessary to facilitate the audit, and they shall be afforded full facilities for verifying transactions with the balances or securities held by depositories, fiscal agents, and custodians. All such books, accounts, records, reports, files, papers and property of the Corporation shall remain in possession and custody of the Corporation.

(B)   A report of each such audit shall be made by the Comptroller General to the Congress. The report to the Congress shall contain such comments and information as the Comptroller General may deem necessary to inform Congress of the financial operations and condition of the Corporation, together with such recommendations with respect thereto as he may deem advisable. The report shall also show specifically any program, expenditure, or other financial transaction or undertaking observed in the course of the audit, which, in the opinion of the Comptroller General, has been carried on or made without authority of law. A copy of each report shall be furnished to the President, to the Secretary, and to the Corporation at the time submitted to the Congress.

(3)   (A)   Each recipient of assistance by grant or contract, other than a fixed price contract awarded pursuant to competitive bidding procedures, under this section shall keep such records as may be reasonably necessary to fully disclose the amount and the disposition by such recipient of the proceeds of such assistance, the total cost of the project or undertaking in connection with which such assistance is given or used, and the amount and nature of that portion of the cost of the project or undertaking supplied by other sources, and such other records as will facilitate an effective audit.

(B)   The Corporation or any of its duly authorized representatives, shall have access for the purpose of audit and examination to any books, documents, papers, and records of the recipient that are pertinent to assistance received under this section. The Comptroller General of the United States or any of his duly authorized representatives shall also have access thereto for such purpose during any fiscal year for which Federal Funds are available to the Corporation.

SUBPART C
GENERAL

Definitions

Sec. 397.   For the purposes of this part—

(1)   The term "State" includes the District of Columbia, the Commonwealth of Puerto Rico, the Virgin Islands, Guam, American Samoa, and the Trust Territory of the Pacific Islands.

(2)   The term "construction," as applied to educational television broadcasting facilities, or educational radio broadcasting facilities means the acquisition and installation of transmission apparatus (including towers, microwave equipment, boosters, translators, repeaters, mobile equipment, and video-recording equipment) necessary for television broadcasting or radio broadcasting, as the case may be, including apparatus which may incidentally be used for transmitting closed circuit television programs, but does not include the construction or repair of structures to house such apparatus. In the case of apparatus the acquisition and installation of which is so included, such term also includes planning therefor.

(3)   The term "Secretary" means the Secretary of Health, Education, and Welfare.

(4)   The terms "State educational television agency" and "State educational radio agency" mean, with respect to television broadcasting and radio broadcasting, respectively, (A) a board or commission established by State law for the purpose of promoting such broadcasting within a State, (B) a board or commission appointed by the Governor of a State for such purpose if such appointment is not inconsistent with State law, or (C) a State officer or agency responsible for the supervision of public elementary or secondary education or public higher education within the State which has been designated by the Governor to assume responsibility for the promotion of such broadcasting; and, in the case of the District of Columbia, the term "Governor" means the Board of Commissioners of the District of Columbia and, in the case of the Trust Territory of the Pacific Islands, means the High Commissioner thereof.

(5)   The term "nonprofit" as applied to any foundation, corporation, or association, means a foundation, corporation, or association, no part of the net earnings of which inures, or may lawfully inure, to the benefit of any private shareholder or individual.

(6)   The term "Corporation" means the Corporation authorized to be established by subpart B of this part.

(7)   The term "noncommercial educational broadcast station" means a

television or radio broadcast station, which (A) under the rules and regulations of the Federal Communications Commission in effect on the date of enactment of the Public Broadcasting Act of 1967, is eligible to be licensed or is licensed by the Commission as a noncommercial educational radio or television broadcast station and which is owned and operated by a public agency or nonprofit private foundation, corporation, or association or (B) is owned and operated by a municipality and which transmits only noncommercial programs for educational purposes.

(8)   The term "interconnection" means the use of microwave equipment, boosters, translators, repeaters, communication space satellites, or other apparatus or equipment for the transmission and distribution of television or radio programs to noncommercial educational television or radio broadcast stations.

(9)   The term "educational television or radio programs" means programs which are primarily designed for educational or cultural purposes.

Federal interference or control prohibited

Sec. 398.   Nothing contained in this part shall be deemed (1) to amend any other provision of, or requirement under this Act; or (2) to authorize any department, agency, officer, or employee of the United States to exercise any direction, supervision, or control over educational television or radio broadcasting, or over the Corporation or any of its grantees or contractors, or over the charter or bylaws of the Corporation, or over the curriculum, program of instruction, or personnel of any educational institution, school system, or educational broadcasting station or system.

Editorializing and support of
political candidates prohibited

Sec. 399.   No noncommercial educational broadcasting station may engage in editorializing or may support or oppose any candidate for political office.

TITLE IV
PROCEDURAL AND ADMINISTRATIVE PROVISIONS

Jurisdiction to enforce Act and orders of Commission

Sec. 401.   (a)   The district courts of the United States shall have jurisdiction, upon application of the Attorney General of the United States at the request of the Commission, alleging a failure to comply with or a violation of any of the provisions of this Act by any person, to issue a writ or writs of mandamus commanding such person to comply with the provisions of this Act.

(b)   If any person fails or neglects to obey any order of the Commission other than for the payment of money, while the same is in effect, the Commission or any party injured thereby, or the United States, by its Attorney General, may apply to the appropriate district court of the United States for the enforcement of such order. If, after hearing, that court determines that the order was regularly made and duly served, and that the person is in disobedience of the same, the court shall enforce obedience to such order by a writ of injunction or other proper process, mandatory or otherwise, to restrain such person or the officers, agents, or representatives of such person, from further disobedience of such order, or to enjoin upon it or them obedience to the same.

(c)   Upon the request of the Commission it shall be the duty of any district attorney of the United States to whom the Commission may apply to institute in the proper court and to prosecute under the direction of the Attorney General of the United States all necessary proceedings for the enforcement of the provisions of this Act and for the punishment of all violations thereof, and the costs and expenses of such prosecutions shall be paid out of the appropriations for the expenses of the courts of the United States.

(d)   The provisions of the Expediting Act, approved February 11, 1903, as amended, and of section 238(1) of the Judicial Code, as amended, shall be held to apply to any suit in equity arising under Title II of this Act, wherein the United States is complainant.

Proceedings to enjoin, set aside, annul, or
suspend orders of the Commission

Sec. 402.   (a)   Any proceeding to enjoin, set aside, annul, or suspend any order of the Commission under this Act (except those appealable under subsection (b) of this section) shall be brought as provided by and in the manner prescribed in Public Law 901, Eighty-first Congress, approved December 29, 1950.

(b)   Appeals may be taken from decisions and orders of the Commission to the United States Court of Appeals for the District of Columbia in any of the following cases:

(1)   By any applicant for a construction permit or station license, whose application is denied by the Commission.

(2)   By any applicant for the renewal or modification of any such instrument of authorization whose application is denied by the Commission.

(3)   By any party to an application for authority to transfer, assign, or dispose of any such instrument of authorization, or any rights thereunder, whose application is denied by the Commission.

(4)   By any applicant for the permit required by section 325 of this Act whose application has been denied by the Commission, or by any permittee under said section whose permit has been revoked by the Commission.

(5)   By the holder of any construction permit or station license which has been modified or revoked by the Commission.

(6)   By any other person who is aggrieved or whose interests are adversely affected by any order of the Commission granting or denying any application described in paragraphs (1), (2), (3), and (4) hereof.

(7)   By any person upon whom an order to cease and desist has been served under section 312 of this Act.

(8)   By any radio operator whose license has been suspended by the Commission.

(c)   Such appeal shall be taken by filing a notice of appeal with the court within thirty days from the date upon which public notice is given of the decision or order complained of. Such notice of appeal shall contain a concise statement of the nature of the proceedings as to which the appeal is taken; a concise statement of the reasons on which the applicant intends to rely, separately stated and numbered; and proof of service of a true copy of said notice and statement upon the Commission. Upon filing of such notice, the court shall have jurisdiction of the proceedings and of the questions determined therein and shall have power, by order, directed to the Commission or any other party to the appeal, to grant such temporary relief as it may deem just and proper. Orders granting temporary relief may be either affirmative or negative in their scope and application so as to permit either the maintenance of the status quo in the matter in which the appeal is taken or the restoration of a position or status terminated or adversely affected by the order appealed from and shall, unless otherwise ordered by the court, be effective pending hearing and determination of said appeal and compliance by the Commission with the final judgment of the court rendered in said appeal.

(d)   Upon the filing of any such notice of appeal the Commission shall, not later than five days after the date of service upon it, notify each person shown by the records of the Commission to be interested in said appeal of the filing and pendency of the same and shall thereafter permit any such person to inspect and make copies of said notice and statement of reasons therefor at the office of the Commission in the city of Washington. Within thirty days after the filing of an appeal, the Commission shall file with the court the record upon which the order complained of was entered, as provided in Section 2112 of Title 28, United States Code.

(e)   Within thirty days after the filing of any such appeal any interested person may intervene and participate in the proceedings had upon said appeal by filing with the court a notice of intention to intervene and a verified statement showing the nature of the interest of such party, together with proof of service of true copies of said notice and statement, both upon appellant and upon the

all public

Commission. Any person who would be aggrieved or whose interest would be adversely affected by a reversal or modification of the order of the Commission complained of shall be considered an interested party.

(f)   The record and briefs upon which any such appeal shall be heard and determined by the court shall contain such information and material, and shall be prepared within such time and in such manner as the court may by rule prescribe.

(g)   At the earliest convenient time the court shall hear and determine the appeal upon the record before it in the manner prescribed by section 10(e) of the Administrative Procedure Act.

(h)   In the event that the court shall render a decision and enter an order reversing the order of the Commission, it shall remand the case to the Commission to carry out the judgment of the court and it shall be the duty of the Commission, in the absence of the proceedings to review such judgment, to forthwith give effect thereto, and unless otherwise ordered by the court, to do so upon the basis of the proceedings already had and the record upon which said appeal was heard and determined.

(i)   The court may, in its discretion, enter judgment for costs in favor of or against an appellant, or other interested parties intervening in said appeal, but not against the Commission, depending upon the nature of the issues involved upon said appeal and the outcome thereof.

(j)   The court's judgment shall be final, subject, however, to review by the Supreme Court of the United States upon writ of certiorari on petition therefor under section 1254 of title 28 of the United States Code, by the appellant, by the Commission, or by any interested party intervening in the appeal, or by certification by the court pursuant to the provisions of that section.

Inquiry by Commission on its own motion

Sec. 403.   The Commission shall have full authority and power at any time to institute an inquiry, on its own motion, in any case and as to any matter or thing concerning which complaint is authorized to be made, to or before the Commission by any provision of this Act, or concerning which any question may arise under any of the provisions of this Act, or relating to the enforcement of any of the provisions of this Act. The Commission shall have the same powers and authority to proceed with any inquiry instituted on its own motion as though it had been appealed to by complaint or petition under any of the provisions of this Act, including the power to make and enforce any order or orders in the case, or relating to the matter or thing concerning which the inquiry is had, excepting orders for the payment of money.

Reports of investigations

Sec. 404.   Whenever an investigation shall be made by the Commission it shall be its duty to make a report in writing in respect thereto, which shall state the conclusions of the Commission, together with its decision, order, or requirements in the premises; and in case damages are awarded such report shall include the findings of fact on which the award is made.

Rehearings

Sec. 405.   After an order, decision, report, or action has been made or taken in any proceeding by the Commission, or by any designated authority within the Commission pursuant to a delegation under section 5(d)(1), any party thereto, or any other person aggrieved or whose interests are adversely affected thereby, may petition for rehearing only to the authority making or taking the order, decision, report, or action; and it shall be lawful for such authority, whether it be the Commission or other authority designated under section 5(d)(1), in its discretion, to grant such a rehearing if sufficient reason therefor be made to appear. A petition for rehearing must be filed within thirty days from the date upon which public notice is given of the order, decision, report, or action complained of. No such application shall excuse any person from complying with or obeying any order, decision, report, or action of the Commission, or operate in any manner to stay or postpone the enforcement thereof, without the special order of the Commission. The filing of a petition for rehearing shall not be a condition precedent to judicial review of any such order, decision, report, or action, except where the party seeking such review (1) was not a party to the proceedings resulting in such order, decision, report, or action, or (2) relies on questions of fact or law upon which the Commission, or designated authority within the Commission, has been afforded no opportunity to pass. The Commission, or designated authority within the Commission, shall enter an order, with a concise statement of the reasons therefor, denying a petition for rehearing or granting such petition, in whole or in part, and ordering such further proceedings as may be appropriate: *Provided*, That in any case where such petition relates to an instrument of authorization granted without a hearing, the Commission, or designated authority within the Commission, shall take such action within ninety days of the filing of such petition. Rehearings shall be governed by such general rules as the Commission may establish, except that no evidence other than newly discovered evidence, evidence which has become available only since the original taking of evidence, or evidence which the Commission or designated authority within the Commission believes should have been taken in the original proceeding shall be taken on any rehearing. The time within which a petition for review must be filed in a proceeding to which section 402(a) applies, or within which an appeal must be taken under section 402(b) in any case, shall be computed from the date upon which public notice is given of orders disposing of all petitions for rehearing filed with the Commission in such proceeding or case, but any order, decision, report, or action made or taken after such rehearing reversing, changing, or modifying the original order shall be subject to the same provisions with respect to rehearing as an original order.

TITLE V
PENAL PROVISIONS — FORFEITURES

General penalty

Sec. 501. Any person who willfully and knowingly does or causes or suffers to be done any act, matter, or thing, in this Act prohibited or declared to be unlawful, or who willfully or knowingly omits or fails to do any act, matter, or thing in this Act required to be done, or willfully and knowingly causes or suffers such omission or failure, shall, upon conviction thereof, be punished for such offense, for which no penalty (other than a forfeiture) is provided in this Act, by a fine of not more than $10,000 or by imprisonment for a term not exceeding one year, or both; except that any person, having been once convicted of an offense punishable under this section, who is subsequently convicted of violating any provision of this Act punishable under this section, shall be punished by a fine of not more than $10,000 or by imprisonment for a term not exceeding two years, or both.

Sec. 502. Any person who willfully and knowingly violates any rule, regulation, restriction, or condition made or imposed by the Commission under authority of this Act, or any rule, regulation, restriction, or condition made or imposed by any international radio or wire communications treaty or convention, or regulations annexed thereto, to which the United States is or may hereafter become a party, shall, in addition to any other penalties provided by law, be punished, upon conviction thereof, by a fine of not more than $500 for each and every day during which such offense occurs.

Sec. 503. (a) Any person who shall deliver messages for interstate or foreign transmission to any carrier, or for whom, as sender or receiver, any such carrier shall transmit any interstate or foreign wire or radio communication, who shall knowingly by employee, agent, officer, or otherwise, directly or indirectly, by or through any means or device whatsoever, receive or accept from such common carrier any sum of money or any other valuable consideration as a rebate or offset against the regular charges for transmission of such messages as fixed by the schedules of charges provided for in this Act, shall in addition to any other penalty provided by this Act forfeit to the United States a sum of money three times the amount of money so received or accepted and three times the value of any other consideration so received or accepted, to be ascertained by the trial court; and in the trial of said action all such rebates or other considerations so received or accepted, for a period of six years prior to the commencement of the action, may be included therein, and the amount recovered shall be three times the total amount of money, or three times the total value of such consideration, so received or accepted, or both, as the case may be.

(b)   (1)   Any licensee or permittee of a broadcast station who—

(A)   willfully or repeatedly fails to operate such station substantially as set forth in his license or permit,

(B)   willfully or repeatedly fails to observe any of the provisions of this Act or of any rule or regulation of the Commission prescribed under authority of this Act or under authority of any treaty ratified by the United States,

(C)   fails to observe any final cease and desist order issued by the Commission,

(D)   violates section 317(c) or section 509(a)(4) of this Act, or

(E)   violates section 1304, 1343, or 1464 of title 18 of the United States Code,

shall forfeit to the United States a sum not to exceed $1,000. Each day during which such violation occurs shall constitute a separate offense. Such forfeiture shall be in addition to any other penalty provided by this Act.

(2)   No forfeiture liability under paragraph (1) of this subsection (b) shall attach unless a written notice of apparent liability shall have been issued by the Commission and such notice has been received by the licensee or permittee or the Commission shall have sent such notice by registered or certified mail to the last known address of the licensee or permittee. A licensee or permittee so notified shall be granted an opportunity to show in writing, within such reasonable period as the Commission shall by regulations prescribe, why he should not be held liable. A notice issued under this paragraph shall not be valid unless it sets forth the date, facts, and nature of the act or omission with which the licensee or permittee is charged and specifically identifies the particular provision or provisions of the law, rule, or regulation or the license, permit, or cease and desist order involved.

(3)   No forfeiture liability under paragraph (1) of this subsection (b) shall attach for any violation occurring more than one year prior to the date of issuance of the notice of apparent liability and in no event shall the forfeiture imposed for the acts or omission set forth in any notice of apparent liability exceed $10,000.

Provisions relating to forfeitures

Sec. 504.   (a)   The forfeitures provided for in this Act shall be payable into the Treasury of the United States, and shall be recoverable in a civil suit in the name of the United States brought in the district where the person or carrier has its principal operating office or in any district through which the line or system of the carrier runs: *Provided*, That any suit for the recovery of a forfeiture imposed pursuant to the provisions of this Act shall be a trial de novo: *Provided further*, That in the case of forfeiture by a ship, said forfeiture may also be recoverable by way of libel in any district in which such ship shall arrive or depart. Such forfeitures shall be in addition to any other general or specific penalties herein provided. It shall be the duty of the various district attorneys, under the direction of the Attorney General of the United States, to prosecute for the recovery of forfeitures under this Act. The costs and expenses of such prosecutions shall be paid from the appropriation for the expenses of the courts of the United States.

(b)   The forfeitures imposed by parts II and III of title III and sections 503(b) and 507 of this Act shall be subject to remission or mitigation by the Commission, upon application therefor, under such regulations and methods of ascertaining the facts as may seem to it advisable, and, if suit has been instituted, the Attorney General, upon request of the Commission, shall direct the discontinuance of any prosecution to recover such forfeitures : *Provided, however*, That no forfeiture shall be remitted or mitigated after determination by a court of competent jurisdiction.

(c)   In any case where the Commission issues a notice of apparent liability looking toward the imposition of a forfeiture under this Act, that fact shall not be used, in any other proceeding before the Commission, to the prejudice of the person to whom such notice was issued, unless (i) the forfeiture has been paid, or (ii) a court of competent jurisdiction has ordered payment of such forfeiture, and such order has become final.

Venue of offenses

Sec. 505.   The trial of any offense under this Act shall be in the district in which it is committed; or if the offense is committed upon the high seas, or out of the jurisdiction of any particular State or district, the trial shall be in the district where the offender may be found or into which he shall be first brought. Whenever the offense is begun in one jurisdiction and completed in another it may be dealt with, inquired of, tried, determined, and punished in either jurisdiction in the same manner as if the offense had been actually and wholly committed therein.

Coercive practices affecting broadcasting

Sec. 506. (a) It shall be unlawful, by the use or express or implied threat of the use of force, violence, intimidation, or duress, or by the use or express or implied threat of the use of other means, to coerce, compel or constrain or attempt to coerce, compel, or constrain a licensee—

(1) to employ or agree to employ, in connection with the conduct of the broadcasting business of such licensee, any person or persons in excess of the number of employees needed by such licensee to perform actual services; or

(2) to pay or give or agree to pay or give any money or other thing of value in lieu of giving, or on account of failure to give, employment to any person or persons, in connection with the conduct of the broadcasting business of such licensee, in excess of the number of employees needed by such licensee to perform actual services; or

(3) to pay or agree to pay more than once for services performed in connection with the conduct of the broadcasting business of such licensee; or

(4) to pay or give or agree to pay or give any money or other thing of value for services, in connection with the conduct of the broadcasting business of such licensee, which are not to be performed; or

(5) to refrain, or agree to refrain, from broadcasting or from permitting the broadcasting of a noncommercial educational or cultural program in connection with which the participants receive no money or other thing of value for their services, other than their actual expenses, and such licensee neither pays nor gives any money or other thing of value for the privilege of broadcasting such program nor receives any money or other thing of value on account of the broadcasting of such program; or

(6) to refrain, or agree to refrain, from broadcasting or permitting the broadcasting of any radio communication originating outside the United States.

(b) It shall be unlawful, by the use or express or implied threat of the use of force, violence, intimidation or duress, or by the use or express or implied threat of the use of other means, to coerce, compel or constrain or attempt to coerce, compel or constrain a licensee or any other person—

(1) to pay or agree to pay any exaction for the privilege of, or on account of, producing, preparing, manufacturing, selling, buying, renting, operating, using, or maintaining recordings, transcriptions, or mechanical, chemical, or electrical reproductions, or any other articles, equipment, machines, or materials, used or intended to be used in broadcasting or in the production, preparation, performance, or presentation of a program or programs for broadcasting; or

(2) to accede to or impose any restriction upon such production, preparation, manufacture, sale, purchase, rental, operation, use, or maintenance, if such restriction is for the purpose of preventing or limiting the use of such

articles, equipment, machines, or materials in broadcasting or in the production, preparation, performance, or presentation of a program or programs for broadcasting; or

(3)   to pay or agree to pay any exaction on account of the broadcasting, by means of recordings or transcriptions, of a program previously broadcast, payment having been made, or agreed to be made, for the services actually rendered in the performance of such program.

(c)   The provisions of subsection (a) or (b) of this section shall not be held to make unlawful the enforcement or attempted enforcement, by means lawfully employed, of any contract right heretofore or hereafter existing or of any legal obligation heretofore or hereafter incurred or assumed.

(d)   Whoever willfully violates any provision of subsection (a) or (b) of this section shall, upon conviction thereof, be punished by imprisonment for not more than one year or by a fine of not more than $1,000, or both.

(e)   As used in this section the term "licensee" includes the owner or owners, and the person or persons having control or management, of the radio station in respect of which a station license was granted.

Which on political duress.
thus to curtail polit. influence   *W. Post.*   *govt - lic . power*
purse strings

Disclosure of certain payments
Which for some . — bribery

Sec. 508.   (a)   Subject to subsection (d), any employee of a radio station who accepts or agrees to accept from any person (other than such station), or any person (other than such station) who pays or agrees to pay such employee, any money, service or other valuable consideration for the broadcast of any matter over such station shall, in advance of such broadcast, disclose the fact of such acceptance or agreement to such station.

(b)   Subject to subsection (d), any person who, in connection with the *those in* production or preparation of any program or program matter which is intended *prod.* for broadcasting over any radio station, accepts or agrees to accept, or pays or *rec. #* agrees to pay, any money, service or other valuable consideration for the *shall* inclusion of any matter as a part of such program or program matter, shall, in *disclose* advance of such broadcast, disclose the fact of such acceptance or payment or *this.* agreement to the payee's employer, or to the person for whom such program or program matter is being produced, or to the licensee of such station over which such program is broadcast.

(c)   Subject to subsection (d), any person who supplies to any other *supplier* person any program or program matter which is intended for broadcasting over *of* any radio station shall, in advance of such broadcast, disclose to such other *prog.* person any information of which he has knowledge, or which has been disclosed *must* to him, as to any money, service or other valuable consideration which any *disclose* person has paid or accepted, or has agreed to pay or accept, for the inclusion of any matter as a part of such program or program matter.

(d)   The provisions of this section requiring the disclosure of information shall not apply in any case where, because of a waiver made by the Commission under section 317(d), an announcement is not required to be made under section 317.

(e)   The inclusion in the program of the announcement required by section 317 shall constitute the disclosure required by this section.

waive

(f)   The term "service or other valuable consideration" as used in this section shall not include any service or property furnished without charge or at a nominal charge for use on, or in connection with, a broadcast, or for use on a program which is intended for broadcasting over any radio station, unless it is so furnished in consideration for an identification in such broadcast or in such program of any person, product, service, trademark, or brand name beyond an identification which is reasonably related to the use of such service or property in such broadcast or such program.

payola

(g)   Any person who violates any provision of this section shall, for each such violation, be fined not more than $10,000 or imprisoned not more than one year, or both.

Prohibited practices in case of contests of intellectual knowledge, intellectual skill, or chance

Sec. 509.   (a)   It shall be unlawful for any person, with intent to deceive the listening or viewing public—

(1)   To supply to any contestant in a purportedly bona fide contest of intellectual knowledge or intellectual skill any special and secret assistance whereby the outcome of such contest will be in whole or in part prearranged or predetermined.

(2)   By means of persuasion, bribery, intimidation, or otherwise, to induce or cause any contestant in a purportedly bona fide contest of intellectual knowledge or intellectual skill to refrain in any manner from using or displaying his knowledge or skill in such contest, whereby the outcome thereof will be in whole or in part prearranged or predetermined.

(3)   To engage in any artifice or scheme for the purpose of prearranging or predetermining in whole or in part the outcome of a purportedly bona fide contest of intellectual knowledge, intellectual skill, or chance.

(4)   To produce or participate in the production for broadcasting of, to broadcast or participate in the broadcasting of, to offer to a licensee for broadcasting, or to sponsor, any radio program, knowing or having reasonable ground for believing that, in connection with a purportedly bona fide contest of intellectual knowledge, intellectual skill, or chance constituting any part of such program, any person has done or is going to do any act or thing referred to in paragraph (1), (2), or (3) of this subsection.

(5)   To conspire with any other person or persons to do any act or thing prohibited by paragraph (1), (2), (3), or (4) of this subsection, if one or more of such persons do any act to effect the object of such conspiracy.

(b)   For the purposes of this section—

(1)   The term "contest" means any contest broadcast by a radio station in connection with which any money or any other thing of value is offered as a prize or prizes to be paid or presented by the program sponsor or by any other person or persons, as announced in the course of the broadcast.

(2)   The term "the listening or viewing public" means those members of the public who, with the aid of radio receiving sets, listen to or view programs broadcast by radio stations.

(c)   Whoever violates subsection (a) shall be fined not more than $10,000 or imprisoned not more than one year, or both.

TITLE VI
MISCELLANEOUS PROVISIONS

War emergency — Powers of President

Sec. 606.   (a)   During the continuance of a war in which the United States is engaged, the President is authorized, if he finds it necessary for the national defense and security, to direct that such communications as in his judgment may be essential to the national defense and security shall have preference or priority with any carrier subject to this Act. He may give these directions at and for such times as he may determine, and may modify, change, suspend, or annul them and for any such purpose he is hereby authorized to issue orders directly, or through such person or persons as he designates for the purpose, or through the Commission. Any carrier complying with any such order or direction for preference or priority herein authorized shall be exempt from any and all provisions in existing law imposing civil or criminal penalties, obligations, or liabilities upon carriers by reason of giving preference or priority in compliance with such order or direction.

(b)   It shall be unlawful for any person during any war in which the United States is engaged to knowingly or willfully, by physical force or intimidation by threats of physical force, obstruct or retard or aid in obstructing or retarding interstate or foreign communication by radio or wire. The President is hereby authorized, whenever in his judgment the public interest requires, to employ the armed forces of the United States to prevent any such obstruction or retardation of communication: *Provided*, That nothing in this section shall be construed to repeal, modify, or affect either section 6 or section 20 of the Act entitled "An Act to supplement existing laws against unlawful restraints and monopolies, and for other purposes," approved October 15, 1914.

(c)   Upon proclamation by the President that there exists war or a threat of war, or a state of public peril or disaster or other national emergency, or in order to preserve the neutrality of the United States, the President, if he deems it necessary in the interest of national security, or defense, may suspend or amend, for such time as he may see fit, the rules and regulations applicable to any or all stations or devices capable of emitting electromagnetic radiations within the jurisdiction of the United States as prescribed by the Commission, and may cause the closing of any station for radio communication, or any device capable of emitting electromagnetic radiations between 10 kilocycles and 100,000 megacycles, which is suitable for use as a navigational aid beyond five miles, and the removal therefrom of its apparatus and equipment, or he may authorize the use or control of any such station or device and/or its apparatus and equipment, by any department of the Government under such regulations as he may prescribe upon just compensation to the owners. The authority granted to the President, under this subsection, to cause the closing of any station or device and the removal therefrom of its apparatus and equipment, or to authorize the use or control of any station or device and/or its apparatus and equipment, may be exercised in the Canal Zone.

(d)   Upon proclamation by the President that there exists a state or threat of war involving the United States, the President, if he deems it necessary in the interest of the national security and defense, may, during a period ending not later than six months after the termination of such state or threat of war and not later than such earlier date as the Congress by concurrent resolution may designate, (1) suspend or amend the rules and regulations applicable to any or all facilities or stations for wire communication within the jurisdiction of the United States as prescribed by the Commission, (2) cause the closing of any facility or station for wire communication and the removal therefrom of its apparatus and equipment, or (3) authorize the use or control of any such facility or station and its apparatus and equipment by any department of the Government under such regulations as he may prescribe, upon just compensation to the owners.

(e)   The President shall ascertain the just compensation for such use or control and certify the amount ascertained to Congress for appropriation and payment to the person entitled thereto. If the amount so certified is unsatisfactory to the person entitled thereto, such person shall be paid only 75 per centum of the amount and shall be entitled to sue the United States to recover such further sum as added to such payment of 75 per centum will make such amount as will be just compensation for the use and control. Such suit shall be brought in the manner provided by paragraph 20 of section 24, or by section 145, of the Judicial Code, as amended.

(f)   Nothing in subsection (c) or (d) shall be construed to amend, repeal, impair, or affect existing laws or powers of the States in relation to taxation or the lawful police regulations of the several States, except wherein such laws, powers, or regulations may affect the transmission of Government communications, or the issue of stocks and bonds by any communication system or systems.

(g)   Nothing in subsection (c) or (d) shall be construed to authorize the President to make any amendment to the rules and regulations of the Commission which the Commission would not be authorized by law to make; and nothing in subsection (d) shall be construed to authorize the President to take any action the force and effect of which shall continue beyond the date after which taking of such action would not have been authorized.

(h)   Any person who willfully does or causes or suffers to be done any act prohibited pursuant to the exercise of the President's authority under this section, or who willfully fails to do any act which he is required to do pursuant to the exercise of the President's authority under this section, or who willfully causes or suffers such failure, shall, upon conviction thereof, be punished for such offense by a fine of not more than $1,000 or by imprisonment for not more than one year, or both, and, if a firm, partnership, association, or corporation, by fine of not more than $5,000, except that any person who commits such an offense with intent to injure the United States, or with intent to secure an advantage to any foreign nation, shall, upon conviction thereof, be punished by a fine of not more than $20,000 or by imprisonment for not more than 20 years, or both.

10
THE CRIMINAL CODE

Title 18, U.S.C.
(1964 Edition)

These selected sections of the Criminal Code pertaining to broadcasting supplement the provisions of the Communications Act of 1934, as amended. Sections 1304 and 1464 of the Code, below, originally appeared in modified form in the Act as Sections 316 and 326, respectively.

§ 1304.   Broadcasting lottery information

Whoever broadcasts by means of any radio station for which a license is required by any law of the United States, or whoever, operating any such station, knowingly permits the broadcasting of, any advertisement of or information concerning any lottery, gift enterprise, or similar scheme, offering prizes dependent in whole or in part upon lot or chance, or any list of the prizes drawn or awarded by means of any such lottery, gift enterprise, or scheme, whether said list contains any part or all of such prizes, shall be fined not more than $1,000 or imprisoned not more than one year, or both.

Each day's broadcasting shall constitute a separate offense.
(Codified June 25, 1948, Ch. 645, 62 Stat. 763.)

§ 1343.   Fraud by wire, radio, or television

Whoever, having devised or intending to devise any scheme or artifice to defraud, or for obtaining money or property by means of false or fraudulent pretenses, representations, or promises, transmits or causes to be transmitted by means of wire, radio, or television communication in interstate or foreign commerce, any writings, signs, signals, pictures, or sounds for the purpose of executing such scheme or artifice, shall be fined not more than $1,000 or imprisoned not more than five years, or both.

(Codified July 16, 1952, Ch. 879, sec. 18(a), 66 Stat. 722; amended July 11, 1956, Ch. 561, 70 Stat. 523.)

§ 1464.   Broadcasting obscene language

Whoever utters any obscene, indecent, or profane language by means of radio communication shall be fined not more than $10,000 or imprisoned not more than two years, or both.

(Codified June 25, 1948, Ch. 645, 62 Stat. 769.)

11

PRESIDENT JOHNSON'S

MESSAGE TO CONGRESS

**H.R. Doc. 68, 90th Congress, 1st Session
February 28, 1967**

Although educational institutions were numerous among early radio station licensees, noncommercial broadcasting became a nearly forgotten cause in America as commercial broadcasting grew and television emerged as a potent mass medium. The turning point for noncommercial broadcasting was signalled by the passage of the ETV Facilities Act of 1962 (Public Law 87-447) and the Public Broadcasting Act of 1967 (Public Law 90-129), which are incorporated into Part IV of Title III of the Communications Act of 1934 (see pp. 86—98).

The 1967 Act stems from the recommendations of the Carnegie Commission on Educational Television as endorsed and modified by President Lyndon B. Johnson in the following portion of his comprehensive message on education and health in America.

The number of noncommercial TV stations on the air had almost doubled within five years of the Act's approval on November 7, 1967, but no permanent means of financing Public Broadcasting had been adopted.

Building for tomorrow

Public television

In 1951, the Federal Communications Commission set aside the first 242 television channels for noncommercial broadcasting, declaring: "The public interest will be clearly served if these stations contribute significantly to the educational process of the Nation."

The first educational television station went on the air in May 1953.

Today, there are 178 noncommercial television stations on the air or under construction. Since 1963 the Federal Government has provided $32 million under the Educational Television Facilities Act to help build towers, transmitters and other facilities. These funds have helped stations with an estimated potential audience of close to 150 million citizens.

Yet we have only begun to grasp the great promise of this medium, which, in the words of one critic, has the power to "arouse our dreams, satisfy our hunger for beauty, take us on journeys, enable us to participate in events, present great drama and music, explore the sea and the sky and the winds and the hills."

Noncommercial television can bring its audience the excitement of excellence in every field. I am convinced that a vital and self-sufficient noncommercial television system will not only instruct, but inspire and uplift our people.

Practically all noncommercial stations have serious shortages of the facilities, equipment, money and staff which they need to present programs of high quality. There are not enough stations. Interconnections between stations are inadequate and seldom permit the timely scheduling of current programs.

Noncommercial television today is reaching only a fraction of its potential audience — and achieving only a fraction of its potential worth.

Clearly, the time has come to build on the experience of the past 14 years, the important studies that have been made, and the beginnings we have made.

I recommend that Congress enact the Public Television Act of 1967 to:

—Increase federal funds for television and radio facility construction to $10.5 million in fiscal 1968, more than three times this year's appropriations.

—Create a Corporation for Public Television authorized to provide support to noncommercial television and radio.

—Provide $9 million in fiscal 1968 as initial funding for the Corporation.

Next year, after careful review, I will make further proposals for the Corporation's long-term financing.

Noncommercial television and radio in America, even though supported by Federal funds, must be absolutely free from any Federal Government interference over programming. As I said in the state of the Union message, "We should insist that the public interest be fully served through the public's airwaves."

The Board of Directors of the Corporation for Public Television should include American leaders in education, communications and the creative arts. I recommend that the Board be comprised of 15 members, appointed by the President and confirmed by the Senate.

The Corporation would provide support to establish production centers and to help local stations improve their proficiency. It would be authorized to accept funds from other sources, public and private.

The strength of public television should lie in its diversity. Every region and community should be challenged to contribute its best.

Other opportunities for the Corporation exist to support vocational training for young people who desire careers in public television, to foster research and development, and to explore new ways to serve the viewing public.

One of the Corporation's first tasks should be to study the practicality and the economic advantages of using communication satellites to establish an educational television and radio network. To assist the Corporation, I am directing the Administrator of the National Aeronautics and Space Administration and the Secretary of Health, Education, and Welfare to conduct experiments on the requirements for such a system, and for instructional television, in cooperation with other interested agencies of the Government and the private sector.

Formulation of long-range policies concerning the future of satellite communications requires the most detailed and comprehensive study by the executive branch and the Congress. I anticipate that the appropriate committees of Congress will hold hearings to consider these complex issues of public policy. The executive branch will carefully study these hearings as we shape our recommendations.

Instructional television

I recommend legislation to authorize the Secretary of Health, Education, and Welfare to launch a major study of the value and the promise of instructional television which is being used more and more widely in our classrooms, but whose potential has not been fully developed.

12

PRESIDENT NIXON'S
MESSAGE TO CONGRESS

**H.R. Doc. 222, 91st Congress, 2d Session
February 9, 1970**

The growing complexity of electronic communication has resulted in increased federal involvement in this sphere. The creation of the centralized, executive branch Office of Telecommunications Policy, following the request of President Richard M. Nixon, adds a powerful new voice to the already impressive chorus that determines public policy in broadcasting and related media. Dr. Clay T. Whitehead, President Nixon's former telecommunications aide, was appointed as the first Director of the Office of Telecommunications Policy in mid-1970.

The White House, February 9, 1970.

To the Congress of the United States:

We live in a time when the technology of telecommunications is undergoing rapid change which will dramatically affect the whole of our society. It has long been recognized that the executive branch of the Federal government should be better equipped to deal with the issues which arise from telecommunications growth. As the largest single user of the nation's telecommunications facilities, the Federal government must also manage its internal communications operations in the most effective manner possible.

Accordingly, I am today transmitting to the Congress Reorganization Plan No. 1 of 1970, prepared in accordance with chapter 9 of title 5 of the United States Code.

That plan would establish a new Office of Telecommunications Policy in the Executive Office of the President. The new unit would be headed by a Director and a Deputy Director who would be appointed by the President with the advice and consent of the Senate. The existing office held by the Director of Telecommunications Management in the Office of Emergency Preparedness would be abolished.

In addition to the functions which are transferred to it by the reorganization plan, the new Office would perform certain other duties which I intend to assign to it by Executive order as soon as the reorganization plan takes effect. That order would delegate to the new Office essentially those functions which are now assigned to the Director of Telecommunications Management. The Office of Telecommunications Policy would be assisted in its research and analysis responsibilities by the agencies and departments of the Executive Branch including another new office, located in the Department of Commerce.

The new Office of Telecommunications Policy would play three essential roles:

1.   It would serve as the President's principal adviser on tele-communications policy, helping to formulate government policies concerning a wide range of domestic and international telecommunications issues and helping to develop plans and programs which take full advantage of the nation's technological capabilities. The speed of economic and technological advance in our time means that new questions concerning communications are constantly arising, questions on which the government must be well informed and well advised. The new Office will enable the President and all government officials to share more fully in the experience, the insights, and the forecasts of government and non-government experts.

2.   The Office of Telecommunications Policy would help formulate policies and coordinate operations for the Federal government's own vast communications systems. It would, for example, set guidelines for the various departments and agencies concerning their communications equipment and services. It would regularly review the ability of government communications systems to meet the security needs of the nation and to perform effectively in time of emergency. The Office would direct the assignment of those portions of the radio spectrum which are reserved for government use, carry out responsibilities conferred on the President by the Communications Satellite Act, advise State and local governments, and provide policy direction for the National Communications System.

3.   Finally, the new Office would enable the executive branch to speak with a clearer voice and to act as a more effective partner in discussions of communications policy with both the Congress and the Federal Communications Commission. This action would take away none of the prerogatives or functions assigned to the Federal Communications Commission by the Congress. It is my hope, however, that the new Office and the Federal Communications Commission would cooperate in achieving certain reforms in telecom-munications policy, especially in their procedures for allocating portions of the radio spectrum for government and civilian use. Our current procedures must be more flexible if they are to deal adequately with problems such as the worsening spectrum shortage.

Each reorganization included in the plan which accompanies this message is necessary to accomplish one or more of the purposes set forth in section

901(a) of title 5 of the United States Code. In particular, the plan is responsive to section 901(a)(1), "to promote the better execution of the laws, the more effective management of the executive branch and of its agencies and functions, and the expeditious administration of the public business;" and section 901(a)(3), "to increase the efficiency of the operations of the government to the fullest extent practicable."

The reorganizations provided for in this plan make necessary the appointment and compensation of new officers, as specified in sections 3(a) and 3(b) of the plan. The rates of compensation fixed for these officers are comparable to those fixed for other officers in the executive branch who have similar responsibilities.

This plan should result in the more efficient operation of the government. It is not practical, however, to itemize or aggregate the exact expenditure reductions which will result from this action.

The public interest requires that government policies concerning telecommunications be formulated with as much sophistication and vision as possible. This reorganization plan — and the executive order which would follow it — are necessary instruments if the government is to respond adequately to the challenges and opportunities presented by the rapid pace of change in communications. I urge that the Congress allow this plan to become effective so that these necessary reforms can be accomplished.

Richard Nixon.

RELATED READING

Archer, Gleason L. *History of Radio to 1926.* New York: American Historical Society, 1938 (reprinted New York: Arno Press, 1971).

Bensman, Marvin R. "The Zenith-WJAZ Case and the Chaos of 1926-27." *Journal of Broadcasting* 14 (Fall 1970), 423-440.

"A Bibliography of Articles about Telecommunications in Law Periodicals, 1920-1968." *Journal of Broadcasting* 14: Part II (Winter 1969-70), 83-156. (Identical to *Federal Communications Bar Journal* 23: Part II (1969).)

Blakely, Robert J. *The People's Instrument: A Philosophy for Public Television.* Washington: Public Affairs Press, 1971.

Burke, John E. "The Public Broadcasting Act of 1967 — Parts I-III." *Educational Broadcasting Review* 6 (1972), 105-119, 178-192, 251-266.

Carlson, Robert A. "1951: A Pivotal Year for ETV." *Educational Broadcasting Review* 1:2 (December 1967), 47-54.

Carnegie Commission on Educational Television. *Public Television: A Program for Action.* New York: Harper & Row, 1967.

Cater, Douglass. "The Politics of Public TV." *Columbia Journalism Review* 11 (July-August 1972), 8-15.

Chafee, Zechariah, Jr. *Government and Mass Communications.* 2 vols. Chicago: University of Chicago Press, 1947.

Coase, Ronald H., and Edward W. Barrett. "Educational Television: Who Should Pay?" *Educational Broadcasting Review* 2:2 (April 1968), 5-17.

Codel, Martin, ed. *Radio and Its Future.* New York: Harper, 1930 (reprinted New York: Arno Press 1971).

Code of Federal Regulations, Title 47. Washington: Government Printing Office, 1972. (Published annually.)

Davis, Stephen. *The Law of Radio Communication.* New York: McGraw-Hill, 1927.

Davis, Stephen B. "The Law of the Air." In *The Radio Industry.* New York: A. W. Shaw, 1928.

Federal Communications Commission. *The Communications Act of 1934 with Amendments and Index Thereto.* Washington: Government Printing Office, 1972.

Ford, Frederick W. "The Meaning of the 'Public Interest, Convenience or Necessity.'" *Journal of Broadcasting* 5 (Summer 1961), 205-218.

Frost, S. E., Jr. *Education's Own Stations.* Chicago: University of Chicago Press, 1937 (reprinted New York: Arno Press, 1971).

Gumpert, Gary, and Dan F. Hahn. "An Historical and Organizational Perspective of the Office of Telecommunications Policy." *Educational Broadcasting Review* 6 (1972), 309-314.

Herring, James M., and Gerald C. Gross. *Telecommunications: Economics and Regulation*. New York: McGraw-Hill, 1936.

Holt, Darrel. "The Origin of 'Public Interest' in Broadcasting." *Educational Broadcasting Review* 1:1 (October 1967), 15-19.

Interpreting FCC Broadcast Rules and Regulations. 3 vols. Blue Ridge Summit, Pa.: Tab Books, 1966, 1968, and 1972.

Jansky, C. M., Jr. "The Contribution of Herbert Hoover to Broadcasting." *Journal of Broadcasting* 1 (Summer 1957), 241-249.

Koenig, Allen E., and Ruane B. Hill, eds. *The Farther Vision: Educational Television Today*. Madison: University of Wisconsin Press, 1967.

Kohlmeier, Louis M., Jr. *The Regulators: Watchdog Agencies and the Public Interest*. New York: Harper & Row, 1969.

Krasnow, Erwin G., and Lawrence D. Longley. *The Politics of Broadcast Regulation*. New York: St. Martin's Press, 1973.

Le Duc, Don R., and Thomas A. McCain. "The Federal Radio Commission in Federal Court: Origins of Broadcast Regulatory Doctrines." *Journal of Broadcasting* 14 (Fall 1970), 393-410.

Lichty, Lawrence W. "The Impact of FRC and FCC Commissioners' Backgrounds on the Regulation of Broadcasting." *Journal of Broadcasting* 6 (Spring 1962), 97-110.

Millard, Steve. "The Story of Public Broadcasting." *Broadcasting* (November 8, 1971), 30-36.

Pierson, W. Theodore. "What Is the American System of Broadcasting?" *Journal of Broadcasting* 10 (Summer 1966), 191-198.

President's Advisory Council on Executive Organization. *A New Regulatory Framework: Report on Selected Independent Regulatory Agencies*. Washington: Government Printing Office, 1971.

President's Communications Policy Board. *Telecommunications: A Program for Progress*. Washington: Government Printing Office, 1951.

President's Task Force on Communications Policy. *Final Report*. Washington: Government Printing Office, 1969.

Radio: Selected A.A.P.S.S. Surveys, 1929-1941. New York: Arno Press, 1971. (Reprints of three issues of *The Annals of the American Academy of Political and Social Science*.)

Rosenbloom, Joel. "Authority of the Federal Communications Commission." In *Freedom and Responsibility in Broadcasting*. Edited by John E. Coons. Evanston, Ill.: Northwestern University Press, 1961.

Sarno, Edward F., Jr. "The National Radio Conferences." *Journal of Broadcasting* 13 (Spring 1969), 189-202.

Schmeckebier, Laurence F. *The Federal Radio Commission: Its History, Activities and Organization*. Washington: Brookings Institution, 1932.

Sorauf, Frank J. "The Public Interest Reconsidered." *Journal of Politics* 19 (1957), 616-639.

"Special Report [on 50 years of broadcasting]." *Broadcasting* (November 2, 1970), 65-160.

Sperry, Robert. "A Selected Bibliography of Works on the Federal Communications Commission." *Journal of Broadcasting* 12 (Winter 1967-68),

83-93. (A 1967-69 supplement is found in *Journal of Broadcasting* 14 (Summer 1970), 377-389.)

Spievack, Edwin B. "Presidential Assault on Telecommunications." *Federal Communications Bar Journal* 23: Part I (1969), 155-181.

Udell, Gilman G., comp. *Radio Laws of the United States.* Washington: Government Printing Office, 1968.

United States Congress, House, Committee on Interstate and Foreign Commerce. *Regulation of Broadcasting: Half a Century of Government Regulation of Broadcasting and the Need for Further Legislative Action.* Study for the Committee [by Robert S. McMahon], 85th Congress, 2d Session, on H. Res. 99. Washington: Government Printing Office, 1958.

United States Congress, Senate, Committee on Commerce. *Federal Election Campaign Act of 1971.* Hearings before Subcommittee on Communications, 92nd Congress, 1st Session, on S. 1, S. 382, and S. 956, March 2-April 1, 1971. Washington: Government Printing Office, 1971.

————. *The Public Television Act of 1967.* Hearings before Subcommittee on Communications, 90th Congress, 1st Session, on S. 1160, April 11-14, 25-28, 1967. Washington: Government Printing Office, 1967.

PART TWO

FREEDOM OF EXPRESSION:
REGULATION OF PROGRAMMING

The determinants of broadcast programming include audience preferences, sponsor needs, the availability of creative talent, relationships between stations and program sources, and the temper of the times. Federal regulation of radio and television content is among the most feared and least influential of the myriad forces that bear on what the public perceives on the picture tube and loudspeaker.

Governmental censorship of broadcast content is expressly forbidden by Section 326 of the Communications Act, which reinforces the First Amendment to the Constitution. Yet, the Federal Communications Commission is charged with the task of regulating broadcasting in the "public interest, convenience, and necessity." Accordingly, the Commission has found it necessary to exercise some control over programming, however obliquely.

The FCC's stance in the area of program regulation is that of an acrobat trying to balance himself on a slack rope suspended between the public interest at one end and Section 326 at the other. To impose prior restraints on programming is contrary to the legal and philosophical underpinnings of freedom of speech. To exercise absolutely no influence over what is broadcast seems inimical to the concept of the public interest.

With the exception of blatantly offensive programming,

125

e.g., defamation and obscenity, the FCC has generally allowed licensees complete freedom in deciding what to include in their program schedules, on the condition that this freedom be exercised with conjoint responsibility. The broadcaster, then, is given the responsibility to determine what programs will serve the public interest. The Commission accepts the licensee's well-considered judgment in this area, unless there is evidence to indicate that the programs broadcast by the licensee are clearly contrary to the public interest.

Federal regulation of programming is not confined to such tangibles as court cases and policy statements. On occasion a commissioner's speech or a proposed (but not enacted) FCC rule will stimulate program decisions in the industry. This phenomenon is known as "regulation by raised eyebrow," and is often as imprecise in effect as it is subtle in method.

Governmental codifications are hardly the only institutionalized guidelines that affect the output of radio and television stations. The codes of the National Association of Broadcasters, together with the program policy statements and continuity acceptance standards of stations and networks, are self-regulatory devices which are more palatable to the industry as instruments of content control than government decrees. Self-regulation, frequently pointed to by broadcasters as a sign of professionalism, is more often a meagerly enforced attempt to allay threats of increased external regulation. Without federal saber rattling, genuine professional concern, or meaningful enforcement, the codes are swords rusting in their scabbards.

Federal regulation of programming has been criticized for being ineffectual by some, an abridgment of free speech by others. Self-regulation has been similarly attacked on two contradictory fronts — for encouraging only "bland" programming, and for being overly permissive by not clearly prohibiting that which is "daring" or "risqué." Both forms of regulation evolve only so long as such healthy debate continues.

1

FRC PROGRAMMING
POLICY

The following statements by the Federal Radio Commission, the FCC's predecessor agency, describe and clarify the earliest official views of the relationship between broadcast programming and the "public interest, convenience, or necessity" standard contained in the Radio Act of 1927. Although some of the narrower programming guidelines seem hopelessly archaic today, the Federal Communications Commission's "Fairness Doctrine" and its *1960 Programming Policy Statement* are but two of the numerous contemporary applications of these basic principles of regulatory philosophy.

A

STATEMENT OF

AUGUST 23, 1928

**Statement Made by the Commission on August 23, 1928,
Relative to Public Interest, Convenience, or Necessity
2 FRC Ann. Rep. 166 (1928)**

Federal Radio Commission, *Washington, D.C.*

The Federal Radio Commission announced on August 23, 1928, the basic principles and its interpretation of the public interest, convenience, or necessity

127

clause of the radio act, which were invoked in reaching decisions in cases recently heard of radio broadcasting stations whose public service was challenged. The commission's statement follows:

Public interest, convenience, or necessity

The only standard (other than the Davis amendment) which Congress furnished to the commission for its guidance in the determination of the complicated questions which arise in connection with the granting of licenses and the renewal or modification of existing licenses is the rather broad one of "public interest, convenience, or necessity." . . .

. . . No attempt is made anywhere in the act to define the term "public interest, convenience, or necessity," nor is any illustration given of its proper application.

The commission is of the opinion that Congress, in enacting the Davis amendment, did not intend to repeal or do away with this standard. While the primary purpose of the Davis amendment is to bring about equality as between the zones, it does not require the commission to grant any application which does not serve public interest, convenience, or necessity simply because the application happens to proceed from a zone or State that is under its quota. The equality is not to be brought about by sacrificing the standard. On the other hand, where a particular zone or State is over its quota, it is true that the commission may on occasions be forced to deny an application the granting of which might, in its opinion, serve public interest, convenience, or necessity. The Davis amendment may, therefore, be viewed as a partial limitation upon the power of the commission in applying the standard.

The cases which the commission has considered as a result of General Order No. 32 are all cases in which it has had before it applications for renewals of station licenses. Under section 2 of the act the commission is given full power and authority to follow the procedure adhered to in these cases, when it has been unable to reach a decision that granting a particular application would serve public interest, convenience, or necessity. In fact, the entire radio act of 1927 makes it clear that no renewal of a license is to be granted, unless the commission shall find that public interest, convenience, or necessity will be served. The fact that all of these stations have been licensed by the commission from time to time in the past, and the further fact that most of them were licensed prior to the enactment of the radio act of 1927 by the Secretary of Commerce, do not, in the opinion of the commission, demonstrate that the continued existence of such stations will serve public interest, convenience, or necessity. The issuance of a previous license by the commission is not in any event to be regarded as a finding further than for the duration of the limited period covered by the license (usually 90 days). There have been a variety of considerations to which the commission was entitled to give weight. For example, when the commission first entered upon its duties it found in existence a large number of stations, much larger than could satisfactorily operate simultaneously and permit good radio reception. Nevertheless, in order to avoid injustice and in order to give the commission an opportunity to determine which stations ·were best serving the public, it was perfectly consistent for the commission to relicense all of these stations for limited periods. It was in the public interest that a fair test should be conducted to determine which stations were rendering the best service. Furthermore, even if the relicensing of a station in the past would be some indication that it met the test, there is no reason why the United States Government, the commission, or the radio-listening public should be bound by a mistake which has been made in the past. There were no hearings preliminary to granting these licenses in the past, and it can hardly be said that the issue has been adjudicated in any of the cases.

The commission has been urged to give a precise definition of the phrase "public interest, convenience, or necessity," and in the course of the hearings has been frequently criticized for not having done so. It has also been urged that the statute itself is unconstitutional because of the alleged uncertainty and indefiniteness of the phrase. So far as the generality of the phrase is concerned, it is no less certain or definite than other phrases which have found their way into Federal statutes and which have been upheld by the Supreme Court of the United States. An example is "unfair methods of competition." To be able to arrive at a precise definition of such a phrase which will foresee all eventualities is manifestly impossible. The phrase will have to be defined by the United States Supreme Court, and this will probably be done by a gradual process of decisions on particular combinations of fact.

It must be remembered that the standard provided by the act applies not only to broadcasting stations but to each type of radio station which must be licensed, including point-to-point communication, experimental, amateur, ship, airplane, and other kinds of stations. Any definition must be broad enough to include all of these and yet must be elastic enough to permit of definite application to each.

It is, however, possible to state a few general principles which have demonstrated themselves in the course of the experience of the commission and which are applicable to the broadcasting band.

In the first place, the commission has no hesitation in stating that it is in the public interest, convenience, and necessity that a substantial band of frequencies be set aside for the exclusive use of broadcasting stations and the radio listening public, and under the present circumstances believes that the band of 550 to 1,500 kilocycles meets that test.

In the second place, the commission is convinced that public interest, convenience, or necessity will be served by such action on the part of the commission as will bring about the best possible broadcasting reception conditions throughout the United States. By good conditions the commission means freedom from interference of various types as well as good quality in the operation of the broadcasting station. So far as possible, the various types of interference, such as heterodyning, cross talk, and blanketing must be avoided. The commission is convinced that the interest of the broadcast listener is of superior importance to that of the broadcaster and that it is better that there should be a few less broadcasters than that the listening public should suffer from undue interference. It is unfortunate that in the past the most vociferous public expression has been made by broadcasters or by persons speaking in their behalf and the real voice of the listening public has not sufficiently been heard.

The commission is furthermore convinced that within the band of frequencies devoted to broadcasting, public interest, convenience, or necessity will be best served by a fair distribution of different types of service. Without attempting to determine how many channels should be devoted to the various types of service, the commission feels that a certain number should be devoted to stations so equipped and financed as to permit the giving of a high order of service over as large a territory as possible. This is the only manner in which the distant listener in the rural and sparsely settled portions of the country will be reached. A certain number of other channels should be given over to stations which desire to reach a more limited region and as to which there will be large intermediate areas in which there will be objectionable interference. Finally, there should be a provision for stations which are distinctly local in character and which aim to serve only the smaller towns in the United States without any attempt to reach listeners beyond the immediate vicinity of such towns.

The commission also believes that public interest, convenience, or necessity will be best served by avoiding too much duplication of programs and types of programs. Where one community is underserved and another community is receiving duplication of the same order of programs, the second community should be restricted in order to benefit the first. Where one type of service is being rendered by several stations in the same region, consideration should be given to a station which renders a type of service which is not such a duplication.

In view of the paucity of channels, the commission is of the opinion that the limited facilities for broadcasting should not be shared with stations which give the sort of service which is readily available to the public in another form. For example, the public in large cities can easily purchase and use phonograph records of the ordinary commercial type. A station which devotes the main portion of its hours of operation to broadcasting such phonograph records is not giving the public anything which it can not readily have without such a station. If, in addition to this, the station is located in a city where there are large resources in program material, the continued operation of the station means that some other station is being kept out of existence which might put to use such original program material. The commission realizes that the situation is not the same in some of the smaller towns and farming communities, where such program resources are not available. Without placing the stamp of approval on the use of phonograph records under such circumstances, the commission will not go so far at present as to state that the practice is at all times and under all conditions a violation of the test provided by the statute. It may be also that the development of special phonograph records will take such a form that the result can be made available by broadcasting only and not available to the public commercially, and if such proves to be the case the commission will take the fact into consideration. The commission can not close its eyes to the fact that the real purpose of the use of phonograph records in most communities is to provide a cheaper method of advertising for advertisers who are thereby saved the expense of providing an original program.

While it is true that broadcasting stations in this country are for the most part supported or partially supported by advertisers, broadcasting stations are not given these great privileges by the United States Government for the primary benefit of advertisers. Such benefit as is derived by advertisers must be incidental and entirely secondary to the interest of the public.

The same question arises in another connection. Where the station is used for the broadcasting of a considerable amount of what is called "direct advertising," including the quoting of merchandise prices, the advertising is usually offensive to the listening public. Advertising should be only incidental to some real service rendered to the public, and not the main object of a program. The commission realizes that in some communities, particularly in the State of Iowa, there seems to exist a strong sentiment in favor of such advertising on the part of the listening public. At least the broadcasters in that community have succeeded in making an impressive demonstration before the commission on each occasion when the matter has come up for discussion. The commission is not fully convinced that it has heard both sides of the matter, but is willing to concede that in some localities the quoting of direct merchandise prices may serve as a sort of local market, and in that community a service may thus be rendered. That such is not the case generally, however, the commission knows from thousands and thousands of letters which it has had from all over the country complaining of such practices.

Another question which must be taken seriously is the location of the transmitter of the station. This is properly a question of interference. Generally speaking, it is not in the public interest, convenience, or necessity for a station of substantial power (500 watts or more) to be located in the midst of a thickly inhabited community. The question of the proper location of a station with respect to its power is a complicated one and can not here be discussed in detail. Obviously it is desirable that a station serving a particular community or region should cover that community or region with a signal strong enough to constitute adequate service.

It is also desirable that the signal be not so strong as to blanket reception from other stations operating on other frequencies. There is a certain amount of blanketing in the vicinity of every transmitter, even one of 5, 10, or 50 watts.

The frequencies used by stations in the same geographical region can be widely enough separated, however, so that the blanketing will not be serious from a transmitter of less than 500 watts, even when located in a thickly inhabited community. With stations of that amount of power, or greater, the problem becomes a serious one. In order to serve the whole of a large metropolitan area a 500-watt station has barely sufficient power even when it is located in the center of the area. If its transmitter is located away from the thickly inhabited portions and out in the country it will not give satisfactory service. Such an area can only be adequately served, without blanketing, by stations of greater power located in sparsely settled portions of the near-by country.

Theoretically, therefore, it may be said that it will not serve public interest, convenience, or necessity to permit the location of a low-powered station in a large city. It can not hope to serve the entire city, and yet it renders the frequency useless for the listeners of the city outside of the small area immediately surrounding the station. On the other hand, such a station might give very good service to a small town or city.

The commission is furthermore convinced that in applying the test of public interest, convenience, or necessity, it may consider the character of the licensee or applicant, his financial responsibility, and his past record, in order to determine whether he is more or less likely to fulfill the trust imposed by the license than others who are seeking the same privilege from the same community, State, or zone.

A word of warning must be given to those broadcasting (of which there have been all too many) who consume much of the valuable time allotted to them under their licenses in matters of a distinctly private nature, which are not only uninteresting but also distasteful to the listening public. Such is the case where two rival broadcasters in the same community spend their time in abusing each other over the air.

A station which does not operate on a regular schedule made known to the public through announcements in the press or otherwise is not rendering a service which meets the test of the law. If the radio listener does not know whether or not a particular station is broadcasting, or what its program will be, but must rely on the whim of the broadcaster and on chance in tuning his dial at the proper time, the service is not such as to justify the commission in licensing such a broadcaster as against one who will give a regular service of which the public is properly advised. A fortiori, where a licensee does not use his transmitter at all and broadcasts his programs, if at all, over some other transmitter separately licensed, he is not rendering any service. It is also improper that the zone and State in which his station is located should be charged with a license under such conditions in connection with the quota of that zone and that State under the Davis amendment.

A broadcaster who is not sufficiently concerned with the public's interest in good radio reception to provide his transmitter with an adequate control or check on its frequency is not entitled to a license. The commission in allowing a latitude of 500 cycles has been very lenient and will necessarily have to reduce this margin in the future. Instability in frequency means that the radio-listening public is subjected to increased interference by heterodyne (and, in some cases, cross-talk) on adjacent channels as well as on the assigned channels.

In conclusion, the commission desires to point out that the test — "public interest, convenience, or necessity" — becomes a matter of a comparative and not an absolute standard when applied to broadcasting stations. Since the number of channels is limited and the number of persons desiring to broadcast is far greater than can be accommodated, the commission must determine from among the applicants before it which of them will, if licensed, best serve the public. In a measure, perhaps, all of them give more or less service. Those who give the least, however, must be sacrificed for those who give the most. The emphasis must be first and foremost on the interest, the convenience, and the necessity of the listening public, and not on the interest, convenience, or necessity of the individual broadcaster or the advertiser.

B

THE GREAT LAKES

STATEMENT

In the Matter of the Application of Great Lakes Broadcasting Co.
   FRC Docket No. 4900
   3 FRC Ann. Rep. 32 (1929)

. . . Broadcasting stations are licensed to serve the public and not for the purpose of furthering the private or selfish interests of individuals or groups of individuals. The standard of public interest, convenience, or necessity means nothing if it does not mean this. The only exception that can be made to this rule has to do with advertising; the exception, however, is only apparent because advertising furnishes the economic support for the service and thus makes it possible. As will be pointed out below, the amount and character of advertising must be rigidly confined within the limits consistent with the public service expected of the station.

The service to be rendered by a station may be viewed from two angles, (1) as an instrument for the communication of intelligence of various kinds to the general public by persons wishing to transmit such intelligence, or (2) as an instrument for the purveying of intangible commodities consisting of entertainment, instruction, education, and information to a listening public. As an instrument for the communication of intelligence, a broadcasting station has frequently been compared to other forms of communication, such as wire telegraphy or telephony, or point-to-point wireless telephony or telegraphy, with the obvious distinction that the messages from a broadcasting station are addressed to and received by the general public, whereas toll messages in point-to-point service are addressed to single persons and attended by safeguards to preserve their confidential nature. If the analogy were pursued with the usual legal incidents, a broadcasting station would have to accept and transmit for all persons on an equal basis without discrimination in charge, and according to rates fixed by a governmental body; this obligation would extend to anything and everything any member of the public might desire to communicate to the listening public, whether it consist of music, propaganda, reading, advertising, or what-not. The public would be deprived of the advantage of the self-imposed censorship exercised by the program directors of broadcasting stations who, for the sake of the popularity and standing of their stations, will select entertainment and educational features according to the needs and desires of their invisible audiences. In the present state of the art there is no way of increasing the number of stations without great injury to the listening public, and yet thousands of stations might be necessary to accommodate all the individuals who insist on airing their views through the microphone. If there are many such persons, as there undoubtedly are, the results would be, first, to crowd most or all of the better programs off the air, and second, to create an almost insoluble problem, i.e., how to choose from among an excess of applicants who shall be given time to address the public and who shall exercise the power to make such a choice.

To pursue the analogy of telephone and telegraph public utilities is, therefore, to emphasize the right of the sender of messages to the detriment of the listening public. The commission believes that such an analogy is a mistaken one when applied to broadcasting stations; the emphasis should be on the receiving of service and the standard of public interest, convenience or necessity should be construed accordingly. This point of view does not take broadcasting stations out of the category of public utilities or relieve them of corresponding obligations; it simply assimilates them to a different group of public utilities, i.e., those engaged in purveying commodities to the general public, such, for example, as heat, water, light, and power companies, whose duties are to consumers, just as the duties of broadcasting stations are to listeners. The commodity may be intangible but so is electric light; the broadcast program has become a vital part of daily life. Just as heat, water, light, and power companies use franchises obtained from city or State to bring their commodities through pipes, conduits, or wires over public highways to the home, so a broadcasting station uses a franchise from the Federal Government to bring its commodity over a channel through the ether to the home. The Government does not try to tell a public utility such as an electric-light company that it must obtain its materials such as coal or wire, from all comers on equal terms; it is not interested so long as the service rendered in the form of light is good. Similarly, the commission believes that the Government is interested mainly in seeing to it that the program service of broadcasting stations is good, i.e., in accordance with the standard of public interest, convenience, or necessity.

It may be said that the law has already written an exception into the foregoing viewpoint in that, by section 18 of the radio act of 1927, a broadcasting station is required to afford equal opportunities for use of the station to all candidates for a public office if it permits any of the candidates to use the station. It will be noticed, however, that in the same section it is provided that "no obligation is hereby imposed upon any licensee to allow the use of its station by any such candidate." This is not only not inconsistent with, but on the contrary it supports, the commission's viewpoint. Again the emphasis is on the listening public, not on the sender of the message. It would not be fair, indeed it would not be good service to the public to allow a one-sided presentation of the political issues of a campaign. In so far as a program consists of discussion of public questions, public interest requires ample play for the free and fair competition of opposing views, and the commission believes that the principle applies not only to addresses by political candidates but to all discussions of issues of importance to the public. The great majority of broadcasting stations are, the commission is glad to say, already tacitly recognizing a broader duty than the law imposes upon them. . . .

An indispensable condition to good service by any station is, of course, modern efficient apparatus, equipped with all devices necessary to insure fidelity in the transmission of voice and music and to avoid frequency instability or other causes of interference. . . .

There are a few negative guides to the evaluation of broadcasting stations. First of these in importance are the injunctions of the statute itself, such, for example, as the requirement for nondiscrimination between political candidates and the prohibition against the utterance of "any obscene, indecent, or profane language" (sec. 29). In the same connection may be mentioned rules and regulations of the commission, including the requirements as to the announcing of call letters and as to the accurate description of mechanical reproductions (such as phonograph records) in announcements. . . .

For more positive guides the commission again finds itself persuaded of the applicability of doctrines analogous to those governing the group of public utilities to which reference has already been made. If the viewpoint is found that the service to the listening public is what must be kept in contemplation in construing the legal standard with reference to broadcasting stations, the service must first of all be continuous during hours when the public usually listens, and must be on a schedule upon which the public may rely. . . .

Furthermore, the service rendered by broadcasting stations must be without discrimination as between its listeners. Obviously, in a strictly physical sense, a station can not discriminate so as to furnish its programs to one listener and not to another; in this respect it is a public utility by virtue of the laws of nature. Even were it technically possible, as it may easily be as the art progresses, so to design both transmitters and receiving sets that the signals emitted by a particular transmitter can be received only by a particular kind of receiving set not available to the general public, the commission would not allow channels in the broadcast band to be used in such fashion. By the same token, it is proceeding very cautiously in permitting television in the broadcast band because, during the hours of such transmission, the great majority of the public audience in the service area of the station, not being equipped to receive television signals, are deprived of the use of the channel.

There is, however, a deeper significance to the principle of nondiscrimination which the commission believes may well furnish the basic formula for the evaluation of broadcasting stations. The entire listening public within the service area of a station, or of a group of stations in one community, is entitled to service from that station or stations. If, therefore, all the programs transmitted are intended for, and interesting or valuable to, only a small portion of that public, the rest of the listeners are being discriminated against. This does not mean that every individual is entitled to his exact preference in program items. It does mean, in the opinion of the commission, that the tastes, needs, and desires of all substantial groups among the listening public should be met, in some fair proportion, by a well-rounded program, in which entertainment, consisting of music of both classical and lighter grades, religion, education and instruction, important public events, discussions of public questions, weather, market reports, and news, and matters of interest to all members of the family find a place. With so few channels in the spectrum and so few hours in the day, there are obvious limitations on the emphasis which can appropriately be placed on any portion of the program. There are parts of the day and of the evening when one type of service is more appropriate than another. There are differences between communities as to the need for one type as against another. The commission does not propose to erect a rigid schedule specifying the hours or minutes that may be devoted to one kind of program or another. What it wishes to emphasize is the general character which it believes must be conformed to by a station in order to best serve the public. . . .

In such a scheme there is no room for the operation of broadcasting stations exclusively by or in the private interests of individuals or groups so far as the nature of the programs is concerned. There is not room in the broadcast band for every school of thought, religious, political, social, and economic, each to have its separate broadcasting station, its mouthpiece in the ether. If franchises are extended to some it gives them an unfair advantage over others, and results in a corresponding cutting down of general public-service stations. It favors the interests and desires of a portion of the listening public at the expense of the rest. Propaganda stations (a term which is here used for the sake of convenience and not in a derogatory sense) are not consistent with the most beneficial sort of discussion of public questions. As a general rule, postulated on the laws of nature as well as on the standard of public interest, convenience, or necessity, particular doctrines, creeds, and beliefs must find their way into the market of ideas by the existing public-service stations, and if they are of sufficient importance to the listening public the microphone will undoubtedly be available. If it is not, a well-founded complaint will receive the careful consideration of the commission in its future action with reference to the station complained of.

The contention may be made that propaganda stations are as well able as other stations to accompany their messages with entertainment and other program features of interest to the public. Even if this were true, the fact remains that the station is used for what is essentially a private purpose for a substantial portion of the time and in addition, is constantly subject to the very human temptation not to be fair to opposing schools of thought and their representatives. By and large, furthermore, propaganda stations do not have the financial resources nor do they have the standing and popularity with the public necessary to obtain the best results in programs of general interest. The contention may also be made that to follow out the commission's viewpoint is to make unjustifiable concessions to what is popular at the expense of what is important and serious. This bears on a consideration which the commission realizes must always be kept carefully in mind and in so far as it has power under the law it will do so in its reviews of the records of particular stations. A defect, if there is any, however, would not be remedied by a one-sided presentation of a controversial subject, no matter how serious. The commission has great confidence in the sound judgment of the listening public, however, as to what types of programs are in its own best interest.

If the question were now raised for the first time, after the commission has given careful study to it, the commission would not license any propaganda station, at least, to an exclusive position on a cleared channel. Unfortunately, under the law in force prior to the radio act of 1927 (see particularly Hoover v. Intercity Radio Co., 286 Fed. 1003), the Secretary of Commerce had no power to distinguish between kinds of applicants and it was not possible to foresee the present situation and its problems. Consequently there are and have been for a long time in existence a number of stations operated by religious or similar organizations. Certain enterprising organizations, quick to see the possibilities of radio and anxious to present their creeds to the public, availed themselves of license privileges from the earlier days of broadcasting, and now have good records and a certain degree of popularity among listeners. The commission feels that the situation must be dealt with on a common-sense basis. It does not seem just to deprive such stations of all right to operation and the question must be solved on a comparative basis. While the commission is of the opinion that a broadcasting station engaged in general public service has, ordinarily, a claim to preference over a propaganda station, it will apply this principle as to existing stations by giving preferential facilities to the former and assigning less desirable positions to the latter to the extent that engineering principles permit. In rare cases it is possible to combine a general public-service station and a high-class religious station in a division of time which will approximate a well-rounded program. In other cases religious stations must accept part time on inferior channels or on daylight assignments where they are still able to transmit during the hours when religious services are usually expected by the listening public.

It may be urged that the same reasoning applies to advertising. In a sense this is true. The commission must, however, recognize that, without advertising, broadcasting would not exist, and must confine itself to limiting this advertising in amount and in character so as to preserve the largest possible amount of service for the public. The advertising must, of course, be presented as such and not under the guise of other forms on the same principle that the newspaper must not present advertising as news. It will be recognized and accepted for what it is on such a basis, whereas propaganda is difficult to recognize. If a rule against advertising were enforced, the public would be deprived of millions of dollars worth of programs which are being given out entirely by concerns simply for the resultant good will which is believed to accrue to the broadcaster or the advertiser by the announcement of his name and business in connection with programs. Advertising must be accepted for the present as the sole means of support for broadcasting, and regulation must be relied upon to prevent the abuse and overuse of the privilege.

It may be urged that if what has heretofore been said is law, the listening public is left at the mercy of the broadcaster. Even if this were so, the commission doubts that any improvement would be effected by placing the public at the mercy of each individual in turn who desired to communicate his hobby, his theory, or his grievance over the microphone, or at the mercy of every advertiser without regard to the standing either of himself or his product. That it is not so, however, is demonstrable from two considerations. In the first place, the listener has a complete power of censorship by turning his dial away from a program which he does not like; this results in a keen appreciation by the broadcaster of the necessity of pleasing a large portion of his listeners if he is to hold his audience, and of not displeasing, annoying, or offending the sensibilities of any substantial portion of the public. His failure or success is immediately reflected on the telephone and in the mail, and he knows that the same reaction to his programs will reach the licensing authority. In the second place, the licensing authority will have occasion, both in connection with renewals of his license and in connection with applications of others for his privileges, to review his past performances and to determine whether he has met with the standard. A safeguard which some of the leading stations employ, and which appeals to the commission as a wise precaution, is the association with the station of an advisory board made up of men and women whose character, standing, and occupations will insure a well-rounded program best calculated to serve the greatest portion of the population in the region to be served.

2

THE BRINKLEY CASE

KFKB Broadcasting Association, Inc., v.
Federal Radio Commission*
47 F.2d 670 (D.C. Cir.)
February 2, 1931

Dr. John R. Brinkley was hardly the only malpractitioner, medical or other, who gained access to the airwaves during radio's formative era. His station, KFKB, was among the most popular in the country for several years, much to the dismay of the American Medical Association.

This Court of Appeals decision affirmed the Federal Radio Commission's denial of Brinkley's application for license renewal. The famed purveyor of the "goat gland" operation subsequently broadcast to his American audience from a Mexican station. The *Brinkley* case stands, nevertheless, as the first judicial affirmation of the Commission's right to consider a station's past programming with relation to the "public interest, convenience, and necessity" when license renewal is sought.

Robb, Associate Justice.

Appeal from a decision of the Federal Radio Commission denying appellant's application for the renewal of its station license.

The station is located at Milford, Kan., is operating on a frequency of 1,050 kilocycles with 5,000 watts power and is known by the call letters KFKB. The station was first licensed by the Secretary of Commerce on September 20, 1923, in the name of the Brinkley-Jones Hospital Association, and intermittently operated until June 3, 1925. On October 23, 1926, it was relicensed to

*Reprinted with the permission of West Publishing Company © 1931.

Dr. J. R. Brinkley with the same call letters and continued to be so licensed until November 26, 1929, when an assignment was made to appellant corporation.

On March 20, 1930, appellant filed its application for renewal of license (Radio Act of 1927, c. 169, 44 Stat. 1162, U. S. C. Supp. 3, tit. 47, § 81, et seq. [47 USCA § 81 et seq.]). The commission, failing to find that public interest, convenience, or necessity would be served thereby, accorded appellant opportunity to be heard. Hearings were had on May 21, 22, and 23, 1930, at which appellant appeared by counsel and introduced evidence on the question whether the granting of the application would be in the public interest, convenience, or necessity. Evidence also was introduced in behalf of the commission. Upon consideration of the evidence and arguments, the commission found that public interest, convenience, or necessity would not be served by granting the application and, therefore, ordered that it be denied, effective June 13, 1930. A stay order was allowed by this court, and appellant has since been operating thereunder.

The evidence tends to show that Dr. J. R. Brinkley established Station KFKB, the Brinkley Hospital, and the Brinkley Pharmaceutical Association, and that these institutions are operated in a common interest. While the record shows that only 3 of the 1,000 shares of the capital stock of appellant are in Dr. Brinkley's name and that his wife owns 381 shares, it is quite apparent that the doctor actually dictates and controls the policy of the station. The Brinkley Hospital, located at Milford, is advertised over Station KFKB. For this advertising the hospital pays the station from $5,000 to $7,000 per month.

The Brinkley Pharmaceutical Association, formed by Dr. Brinkey, is composed of druggists who dispense to the public medical preparations prepared according to formulas of Dr. Brinkley and known to the public only by numerical designations. Members of the association pay a fee upon each sale of certain of those preparations. The amounts thus received are paid the station, presumably for advertising the preparations. It appears that the income of the station for the period February, March, and April, 1930, was as follows :

Brinkley Pharmaceutical Association	$27,856.40
Brinkley Hospital	6,500.00
All other sources	3,544.93
Total	$37,901.33

Dr. Brinkley personally broadcasts during three one-half hour periods daily over the station, the broadcast being referred to as the "medical question box," and is devoted to diagnosing and prescribing treatment of cases from symptoms given in letters addressed either to Dr. Brinkley or to the station. Patients are not known to the doctor except by means of their letters, each letter containing a code signature, which is used in making answer through the broadcasting station. The doctor usually advises that the writer of the letter is suffering from a certain ailment, and recommends the procurement from one of the members of the Brinkley Pharmaceutical Association, of one or more of Dr. Brinkley's prescriptions, designated by numbers. In Dr. Brinkley's broadcast for April 1, 1930, presumably representative of all, he prescribed for forty-four different patients and in all, save ten, he advised the procurement of from one to four of his own prescriptions. We reproduce two as typical:

Here's one from Tillie. She says she had an operation, had some trouble 10 years ago. I think the operation was unnecessary, and it isn't very good sense to have an ovary removed with the expectation of motherhood resulting therefrom. My advice to you is to use Women's Tonic No. 50, 67, and 61. This combination will do for you what you desire if any combination will, after three months' persistent use.

Sunflower State, from Dresden Kans. Probably he has gall stones. No, I don't mean that, I mean kidney stones. My advice to you is to put him on Prescription No. 80 and 50 for men, also 64. I think that he will be a whole lot better. Also drink a lot of water.

In its "Facts and Grounds for Decision," the commission held "that the practice of a physician prescribing treatment for a patient whom he has never seen, and bases his diagnosis upon what symptoms may be recited by the patient in a letter addressed to him, is inimical to the public health and safety, and for that reason is not in the public interest"; that "the testimony in this case shows conclusively that the operation of Station KFKB is conducted only in the personal interest of Dr. John R. Brinkley. While it is to be expected that a licensee of a radio broadcasting station will receive some remuneration for serving the public with radio programs, at the same time the interest of the listening public is paramount, and may not be subordinated to the interests of the station licensee."

This being an application for the renewal of a license, the burden is upon the applicant to establish that such renewal would be in the public interest, convenience, or necessity (Technical Radio Lab. v. Fed. Radio Comm., 59 App. D.C. 125, 36 F.(2d) 111, 114, 66 A.L.R. 1355; Campbell v. Galeno Chem. Co., 281 U.S. 599, 609, 50 S.Ct. 412, 74 L. Ed. 1063), and the court will sustain the findings of fact of the commission unless "manifestly against the evidence." Ansley v. Fed. Radio Comm., 60 App. D.C. 19, 46 F.(2d) 600.

We have held that the business of broadcasting, being a species of interstate commerce, is subject to the reasonable regulation of Congress. Technical Radio Lab. v. Fed. Radio Comm., 59 App. D.C. 125, 36 F.(2d) 111, 66 A.L.R. 1355; City of New York v. Fed. Radio Comm., 59 App. D.C. 129, 36 F.(2d) 115; Chicago Federation of Labor v. Fed. Radio Comm., 59 App. D.C. 333, 41 F.(2d) 422. It is apparent, we think, that the business is impressed with a public interest and that, because the number of available broadcasting frequencies is limited, the commission is necessarily called upon to consider the character and quality of the service to be rendered. In considering an application for a renewal of the license, an important consideration is the past conduct of the applicant, for "by their fruits ye shall know them." Matt. VII:20. Especially is this true in a case like the present, where the evidence clearly justifies the conclusion that the future conduct of the station will not differ from the past.

In its Second Annual Report (1928), p. 169, the commission cautioned broadcasters "who consume much of the valuable time allotted to them under their licenses in matters of a distinctly private nature which are not only uninteresting, but also distasteful to the listening public." When Congress provided that the question whether a license should be issued or renewed should be dependent upon a finding of public interest, convenience, or necessity, it very evidently had in mind that broadcasting should not be a mere adjunct of a particular business but should be of a public character. Obviously, there is no room in the broadcast band for every business or school of thought.

In the present case, while the evidence shows that much of appellant's programs is entertaining and unobjectionable in character, the finding of the commission that the station "is conducted only in the personal interest of Dr. John R. Brinkley" is not "manifestly against the evidence." We are further of the view that there is substantial evidence in support of the finding of the Commission that the "medical question box" as conducted by Dr. Brinkley "is inimical to the public health and safety, and for that reason is not in the public interest."

Appellant contends that the attitude of the commission amounts to a censorship of the station contrary to the provisions of section 29 of the Radio Act of 1927 (47 USCA § 109). This contention is without merit. There has been no attempt on the part of the commission to subject any part of appellant's broadcasting matter to scrutiny prior to its release. In considering the question whether the public interest, convenience, or necessity will be served by a renewal of appellant's license, the commission has merely exercised its undoubted right to take note of appellant's past conduct, which is not censorship.

As already indicated, Congress has imposed upon the commission the administrative function of determining whether or not a station license should be renewed, and the commission in the present case has in the exercise of judgment and discretion ruled against the applicant. We are asked upon the record and evidence before the commission to substitute our judgment and discretion for that of the commission. While section 16 of the Radio Act of 1927 (44 Stat. 1162, 1169, U. S. C., Supp. 3, tit. 47, § 96) authorized an appeal to this court, we do not think it was the intent of Congress that we should disturb the action of the commission in a case like the present. Support is found for this view in the Act of July 1, 1930 (46 Stat. 844 [47 USCA § 96]), amending section 16 of the 1927 Act. The amendment specifically provides "that the review by the court shall be limited to questions of law and that findings of fact by the commission, if supported by substantial evidence, shall be conclusive unless it shall clearly appear that the findings of the commission are arbitrary or capricious." As to the interpretation that should be placed upon such provision, see Ma-King v. Blair, 271 U.S. 479, 483, 46 S. Ct. 544, 70 L.Ed. 1046.

We are therefore constrained, upon a careful review of the record, to affirm the decision.

Affirmed.

3

THE SHULER CASE

Trinity Methodist Church, South, v.
Federal Radio Commission*
>   62 F.2d 850 (D.C. Cir.)
>   November 28, 1932

> This Court of Appeals decision, building on the prior *Brinkley* case, held that the Federal Radio Commission's refusal to renew the license of Reverend Shuler's radio station, KGEF, because of his defamatory and otherwise objectionable utterances over the station, violated neither the First nor the Fifth Amendments to the Constitution. The Supreme Court declined to review this decision (288 U.S. 599 (1933)).

Groner, Associate Justice.

Appellant, Trinity Methodist Church, South, was the lessee and operator of a radio-broadcasting station at Los Angeles, Cal., known by the call letters KGEF. The station had been in operation for several years. The Commission, in its findings, shows that, though in the name of the church, the station was in fact owned by the Reverend Doctor Shuler and its operation dominated by him. Dr. Shuler is the minister in charge of Trinity Church. The station was operated for a total of 23¼ hours each week.

In September, 1930, appellant filed an application for renewal of station license. Numerous citizens of Los Angeles protested, and the Commission, being unable to determine that public interest, convenience, and necessity would be served, set the application down for hearing before an examiner. In January, 1931, the matter was heard, and the testimony of ninety witnesses taken. The examiner recommended renewal of the license. Exceptions were filed by one of the objectors, and oral argument requested. This was had before the

*Reprinted with the permission of West Publishing Company ©1933.

Commission, sitting in banc, and, upon consideration of the evidence, the examiner's report, the exceptions, etc., the Commission denied the application for renewal upon the ground that the public interest, convenience, and/or necessity would not be served by the granting of the application. Some of the things urging it to this conclusion were that the station had been used to attack a religious organization, meaning the Roman Catholic Church; that the broadcasts by Dr. Shuler were sensational rather than instructive; and that in two instances Shuler had been convicted of attempting in his radio talks to obstruct the orderly administration of public justice.

This court denied a motion for a stay order, and this appeal was taken. The basis of the appeal is that the Commission's decision is unconstitutional, in that it violates the guaranty of free speech, and also that it deprives appellant of his property without due process of law. It is further insisted that the decision violates the Radio Act because not supported by substantial evidence, and therefore is arbitrary and capricious.

We have been at great pains to examine carefully the record of a thousand pages, and have reached the conclusion that none of these assignments is well taken.

We need not stop to review the cases construing the depth and breadth of the first amendment. The subject in its more general outlook has been the source of much writing since Milton's *Areopagitica*, the emancipation of the English press by the withdrawal of the licensing act in the reign of William the Third, and the *Letters* of Junius. It is enough now to say that the universal trend of decisions has recognized the guaranty of the amendment to prevent previous restraints upon publications, as well as immunity of censorship, leaving to correction by subsequent punishment those utterances or publications contrary to the public welfare. In this aspect it is generally regarded that freedom of speech and press cannot be infringed by legislative, executive, or judicial action, and that the constitutional guaranty should be given liberal and comprehensive construction. It may therefore be set down as a fundamental principle that under these constitutional guaranties the citizen has in the first instance the right to utter or publish his sentiments, though, of course, upon condition that he is responsible for any abuse of that right. Near v. Minnesota ex rel. Olson, 283 U.S. 697, 51 S. Ct. 625, 75 L.Ed. 1357. "Every freeman has an undoubted right to lay what sentiments he pleases before the public; to forbid this is to destroy the freedom of the press; but if he publishes what is improper, mischievous, or illegal, he must take the consequences of his own temerity." 4th Bl. Com. 151, 152. But this does not mean that the government, through agencies established by Congress, may not refuse a renewal of license to one who has abused it to broadcast defamatory and untrue matter. In that case there is not a denial of the freedom of speech, but merely the application of the regulatory power of Congress in a field within the scope of its legislative authority. See KFKB Broadcasting Ass'n v. Federal Radio Commission, 60 App. D.C. 79, 47 F.(2d) 670.

Section 1 of the Radio Act of 1927 (44 Stat. 1162, title 47, USCA, § 81) specifically declares the purpose of the act to be to regulate all forms of interstate and foreign radio transmissions and communications within the United States, its territories and possessions; to maintain the control of the United States over all the channels of interstate and foreign radio transmissions; and to provide for the use of such channels for limited periods of time, under licenses granted by federal authority. The federal authority set up by the act to carry out its terms is the Federal Radio Commission, and the Commission is given power, and required, upon examination of an application for a station license, or for a renewal or modification, to determine whether "public interest, convenience, or necessity" will be served by the granting thereof, and any applicant for a renewal of license whose application is refused may of right appeal from such decision to this court.

We have already held that radio communication, in the sense contemplated by the act, constituted interstate commerce, KFKB Broadcasting Ass'n v. Federal Radio Commission, supra; General Elec. Co. v. Federal Radio Commission, 58 App. D.C. 386, 31 F.(2d) 630, and in this respect we are supported by many decisions of the Supreme Court, Pensacola Telegraph Co. v. Western Union Tel. Co., 96 U.S. 1, 9, 24 L.Ed. 708; International Text-Book Co. v. Pigg, 217 U.S. 91, 106, 107, 30 S. Ct. 481, 54 L.Ed. 678, 27 L.R.A. (N.S.) 493, 18 Ann. Cas. 1103; Western Union Teleg. Co. v. Pendelton, 122 U.S. 347, 356, 7 S. Ct. 1126, 30 L. Ed. 1187. And we do not understand it is contended that where, as in the case before us, there is no physical substance between the transmitting and the receiving apparatus, the broadcasting of programs across state lines is not interstate commerce, and, if this be true, it is equally true that the power of Congress to regulate interstate commerce, complete in itself, may be exercised to its utmost extent, and acknowledges no limitation, other than such as prescribed in the Constitution (Gibbons v. Ogden, 9 Wheat. 1, 6 L. Ed. 23), and these powers, as was said by the Supreme Court in Pensacola Tel. Co. v. Western Union Tel. Co., supra, "keep pace with the progress of the country, and adapt themselves to the new developments of time and circumstances."

In recent years the power under the commerce clause has been extended to legislation against interstate commerce in stolen automobiles, Brooks v. United States, 267 U.S. 432, 45 S. Ct. 345, 69 L. Ed. 699, 37 A.L.R. 1407; to transportation of adulterated foods, Hipolite Egg Co. v. United States, 220 U.S. 45, 31 S. Ct. 364, 55 L. Ed. 364; in the suppression of interstate commerce for immoral purposes, Hoke v. United States, 227 U.S. 308, 33 S. Ct. 281, 57 L. Ed. 523, 43 L.R.A. (N.S.) 906, Ann. Cas. 1913E, 905; and in a variety of other subjects never contemplated by the framers of the Constitution. It is too late now to contend that Congress may not regulate, and, in some instances, deny, the facilities of interstate commerce to a business or occupation which it deems inimical to the public welfare or contrary to the public interest. Lottery Cases, 188 U.S. 321, 352, 23 S. Ct. 321, 47 L. Ed. 492. Everyone interested in radio legislation approved the principle of limiting the number of broadcasting stations, or, perhaps, it would be more nearly correct to say, recognized the inevitable necessity. In these circumstances Congress intervened and asserted its paramount authority, and, if it be admitted, as we think it must be, that, in the present condition of the science with its limited facilities, the regulatory provisions of the Radio Act are a reasonable exercise by Congress of its powers, the exercise of these powers is no more restricted by the First Amendment than are the police powers of the States under the Fourteenth Amendment. See In re Kemmler, 136 U.S. 436, 448, 449, 10 S. Ct. 930, 34 L. Ed. 519; Hamilton v. Kentucky, etc., Co., 251 U.S. 146, at page 156, 40 S. Ct. 106, 64 L. Ed. 194. In either case the answer depends upon whether the statute is a reasonable exercise of governmental control for the public good.

In the case under consideration, the evidence abundantly sustains the conclusion of the Commission that the continuance of the broadcasting programs of appellant is not in the public interest. In a proceeding for contempt against Dr. Shuler, on appeal to the Supreme Court of California, that court said (In re Shuler, 210 Cal. 377, 292 P. 481, 492) that the broadcast utterances of Dr. Shuler disclosed throughout the determination on his part to impose on the trial courts his own will and views with respect to certain causes then pending or on trial, and amounted to contempt of court. Appellant, not satisfied with attacking the judges of the courts in cases then pending before them, attacked the bar association for its activities in recommending judges, charging it with ulterior and sinister purposes. With no more justification, he charged particular judges with sundry immoral acts. He made defamatory statements against the board of health. He charged that the labor temple in Los Angeles was a bootlegging and gambling joint. In none of these matters, when called on to explain or justify his statements, was he able to do more than declare that the statements expressed his own sentiments. On one occasion he announced over the radio that he had certain damaging information against a prominent unnamed man which, unless a contribution (presumably to the church) of a hundred dollars was forthcoming, he would disclose. As a result, he received contributions from several persons. He freely spoke of "pimps" and prostitutes. He alluded slightingly to the Jews as a race, and made frequent and bitter attacks on the Roman Catholic religion and its relations to government. However inspired Dr. Shuler may have been by what he regarded as patriotic zeal, however sincere in denouncing conditions he did not approve, it is manifest, we think, that it is not narrowing the ordinary conception of "public interest" in declaring his broadcasts — without facts to sustain or to justify them — not within that term, and, since that is the test the Commission is required to apply, we think it was its duty in considering the application for renewal to take notice of appellant's conduct in his previous use of the permit, and, in the circumstances, the refusal, we think, was neither arbitrary nor capricious.

If it be considered that one in possession of a permit to broadcast in interstate commerce may, without let or hindrance from any source, use these facilities, reaching out, as they do, from one corner of the country to the other, to obstruct the administration of justice, offend the religious susceptibilities of thousands, inspire political distrust and civic discord, or offend youth and innocence by the free use of words suggestive of sexual immorality, and be answerable for slander only at the instance of the one offended, then this great science, instead of a boon, will become a scourge, and the nation a theater for the display of individual passions and the collision of personal interests. This is neither censorship nor previous restraint, nor is it a whittling away of the rights guaranteed by the First Amendment, or an impairment of their free exercise. Appellant may continue to indulge his strictures upon the characters of men in public office. He may just as freely as ever criticize religious practices of which he does not approve. He may even indulge private malice or personal slander — subject, of course, to be required to answer for the abuse thereof — but he may not, as we think, demand, of right, the continued use of an instrumentality of commerce for such purposes, or any other, except in subordination to all reasonable rules and regulations Congress, acting through the Commission, may prescribe.

Nor are we any more impressed with the argument that the refusal to renew a license is a taking of property within the Fifth Amendment. There is a marked difference between the destruction of physical property, as in Pennsylvania Coal Co. v. Mahon, 260 U.S. 393, 43 S. Ct. 158, 67 L. Ed. 322, 28 A.L.R. 1321, and the denial of a permit to use the limited channels of the air. As was pointed out in American Bond & Mtg. Co. v. United States (C.C.A.) 52 F.(2nd) 318, 320, the former is vested, the latter permissive, and, as was said by the Supreme Court in Chicago, B. & Q. R. Co. v. Illinois, 200 U.S. 561, 593, 26 S. Ct. 341, 350, 50 L.Ed. 596, 4 Ann. Cas. 1175: "If the injury complained of is only incidental to the legitimate exercise of governmental powers for the public good, then there is no taking of property for the public use, and a right to compensation, on account of such injury, does not attach under the Constitution." When Congress imposes restrictions in a field falling within the scope of its legislative authority and a taking of property without compensation is alleged, the test is whether the restrictive measures are reasonably adapted to secure the purposes and objects of regulation. If this test is satisfied, then "the enforcement of uncompensated obedience" to such regulation "is not an unconstitutional taking of property without compensation or without due process of law." Atlantic Coast Line R. Co. v. Goldsboro, 232 U.S. 548, 558, 34 S. Ct. 364, 368, 58 L. Ed. 721.

A case which illustrates this principle is Greenleaf-Johnson Lumber Co. v. Garrison, 237 U.S. 251, 35 S. Ct. 551, 59 L. Ed. 939. In that case the state of Virginia had established lines of navigability in the harbor of Norfolk. The lumber company applied for and obtained permission from the state to build a wharf from its upland into the river to the line of navigability. Some twenty years later the government, in the exercise of its control of the navigable waters and in the interest of commerce and navigation, adopted the lines of navigability formerly established by the state of Virginia, but a few years prior to the commencement of the suit the Secretary of War, by authority conferred on him by the Congress, re-established the lines, as a result of which the riparian proprietor's wharf extended some two hundred feet within the new lines of navigability. The Secretary of War asserted the right to require the demolition of the wharf as an obstruction to navigation. The owner insisted that, having received a grant of privilege from the state of Virginia prior to the exercise by the government of its power over the river, and subsequently acquiesced in by its adoption of the state lines, the property right thus acquired became as stable as any other property, and the privilege so granted irrevocable, and that it could be taken for public use only upon the payment of just compensation. The contention was rejected on the principle that the control of Congress over the navigable streams of the country is conclusive, and its judgment and determination the exercise of a legislative power in respect of a subject wholly within its control. To the same effect is Gibson v. United States, 166 U.S. 269, 17 S. Ct. 578, 41 L. Ed. 996, in which a work of public improvement in the Ohio river diminished greatly the value of the riparian owner's property by destroying his access to navigable water; and Union Bridge Co. v. United States, 204 U.S. 364, 27 S. Ct. 367, 51 L. Ed. 523, where the owner of a bridge was required to remodel the same as an obstruction to navigation, though erected under authority of the state when it was not an obstruction to navigation; and Louisville Bridge Co. v. United States, 242 U.S. 409, 37 S. Ct. 158, 61 L. Ed. 395, in which the same rule was applied in the case of a bridge erected expressly pursuant to an act of Congress. So also in United States v. Chandler-Dunbar Water Power Co., 229 U.S. 53; 33 S. Ct. 667, 57 L. Ed. 1063, the right of the government to destroy the water power of a riparian owner was upheld; and in Lewis Blue Point Oyster Cultivation Co. v. Briggs, 229 U.S. 82, 33 St. Ct. 679, 57 L. Ed. 1083, the right of compensation for the destruction of privately owned oyster beds was denied. All of these cases indubitably show adherence to the principle that one who applies for and obtains a grant or permit from a state, or the United States, to make use of a medium of interstate commerce, under the control and subject to the dominant power of the government, takes such grant or right subject to the exercise of the power of government, in the public interest, to withdraw it without compensation.

Appellant was duly notified by the Commission of the hearing which it ordered to be held to determine if the public interest, convenience, or necessity would be served by granting a renewal of its license. Due notice of this hearing was given and opportunity extended to furnish proof to establish the right under the provisions of the act for a renewal of the grant. There was, therefore, no lack of due process, and, considered from every point of view, the action of the Commission in refusing to renew was in all respects right, and should be, and is, affirmed.

Affirmed.

Van Orsdel, Associate Justice, concurs in the result.

4

THE BLUE BOOK

Public Service Responsibility of Broadcast Licensees
March 7, 1946

The "Blue Book," so called because of the color of its cover, is the most thoroughly substantiated and reasoned expression of FCC programming policy yet issued. Largely the work of Charles A. Siepmann, then a consultant to the Commission, this document elicited cries of protest from the broadcasting industry on the ground that freedom of speech was being abridged. Neither vigorously enforced nor officially repudiated by the Commission, the "Blue Book" remains a more forceful potential instrument of program regulation in the public interest than has hitherto been promulgated.

PART I.   THE COMMISSION'S CONCERN
WITH PROGRAM SERVICE

On April 10, 1945, the Federal Communications Commission announced "a policy of a more detailed review of broadcast station performance when passing upon applications for license renewals."[1]

The need for such a policy had earlier been set forth by Chairman Paul A. Porter in an address to the National Association of Broadcasters March 12, 1945. The Chairman stated:

... Briefly the facts are these: an applicant seeks a construction permit for a new station and in his application makes the usual representations as to the type of service he proposes. These representations include specific pledges that time will be made available for civic, educational, agricultural and other public service programs. The station is constructed and begins operations. Subsequently the

---

[1] FCC Mimeograph No. 81575, April 10, 1945.

licensee asks for a three-year renewal and the record clearly shows that he has not fulfilled the promises made to the Commission when he received the original grant. The Commission in the past has, for a variety of reasons, including limitations of staff, automatically renewed these licenses even in cases where there is a vast disparity between promises and performance.

We have under consideration at the present time, however, a procedure whereby promises will be compared with performance. I think the industry is entitled to know of our concern in this matter and should be informed that there is pending before the Commission staff proposals which are designed to strengthen renewal procedures and give the Commission a more definite picture of the station's overall operation when licenses come up for renewal.

A procedure involving more detailed review of renewal applications was instituted experimentally in April 1945; and this report is based in part upon experience since then with renewal applications.

The need for detailed review on renewal can best be illustrated by a series of specific instances. The cases which follow are *not* presented for any substantive light they may throw on policy with respect to program service. Part III of this report will deal with substantive program service matters. The following cases are set forth to show various occasions for detailed review on renewal rather than the principles in terms of which such review should proceed.

A.   Comparison of promise and performance: Station KIEV

The KIEV case (8 F.C.C. 207) illustrates primarily the need for sound procedures to compare promises with performance when acting on renewal of licenses.

Under date of January 27, 1932, the Cannon System, Ltd., applied for a construction permit for a new standard broadcast station at Glendale, California. Because the quota[2] for the zone in which California was located had been filled, the Cannon System, Ltd., further requested that the facilities assigned to Station KGIX, Las Vegas, Nevada, be withdrawn, in order to make possible a grant of its application.

In prosecuting its application (Docket No. 1595), Cannon System, Ltd., represented that it proposed to operate the station as a civic project; that the

---

[2] Under Section 9 of the Radio Act of 1927, as amended March 28, 1928, each zone and each state in the United States was assigned a quota, and new applications could not be granted, with certain exceptions, in a zone or state whose quota was already filled. Since the Fifth Zone quota was filled, KIEV was of the opinion that its application would be granted only at the expense of some other station, and hence requested the withdrawal of the facilities assigned to KGIX. A subsequent change in California quota facilities rendered this question moot. (*In re Cannon System, Ltd.*, F.R.C. Docket 1595, decided Sept. 23, 1932.)

central location of its proposed studios would be convenient for the program talent to be broadcast; that the applicant proposed to cooperate with the Glendale Chamber of Commerce and all the local civic, educational, fraternal and religious institutions in donating to them, without charge, periods of time for broadcasting programs of special interest to Glendale listeners; that one-third of the broadcasting time would be devoted to educational and semi-educational matters; that agricultural features would be presented and that programs would include local, state and national news items; that special features would be presented for the large Spanish population in the Glendale area; that 20 percent of all its broadcast hours would be devoted to sustaining programs of an agricultural nature; etc. It further represented that the lack of a broadcast station in Glendale discriminated against "the use of Glendale's excellent talent."

On the basis of such representations, the renewal application of Station KGIX was designated for hearing jointly with the application of the Cannon System, Ltd., for a new station. Following this hearing, the Federal Radio Commission found that "although the Glendale area now receives service from a number of stations situated elsewhere, there appears to be a need in that city for the purely local service, largely civic and educational in character, proposed to be rendered therein by applicant, Cannon System, Ltd."

With respect to Station KGIX, the Commission found that cutting its hours from unlimited to limited would permit the station "to render any substantial service theretofore rendered or proposed to be rendered." Accordingly, the application of the Cannon System, Ltd., was granted, and the authorized time of Station KGIX was cut in half in its renewed license.

On May 22, 1939, Station KIEV filed an application for renewal of its license and the Commission was unable to determine from an examination of the application that a renewal would be in the public interest. Accordingly, the application was designated for hearing[3] and was heard beginning December 7, 1939.

Commission inspectors had made recordings of the programs broadcast by the applicant on December 15, 21, and 27, 1938. On the basis of these recordings, the Commission found:

. . . On the first of these days the programs consisted of 143 popular records and 9 semi-classical records. There were 264 commercial announcements and 3 minutes of announcements concerning lost and found pets. On December 21,

---

[3] The issues in the hearing included the following:

"1. To determine the nature and character of the program service rendered by the applicant;

"2. To determine whether the station's program service has been and is now in conformity with the representations made to the Commission in support of the original application for construction permit or license, and all subsequent applications by the licensee. . . ."

1938, the programs were made up of 156 popular and 10 semi-classical records and were accompanied by 258 commercial announcements. Ten minutes were devoted to the lost and found pet column. On December 27, 1938, 165 popular, 12 semi-classical records, 10 minutes of the lost and found pet column and 199 commercial announcements made up the day's schedule. During these 3 days, which represented a total of 36 hours of broadcast time, only 23 minutes were devoted to programs other than records and commercial announcements. [4] The alleged policy of the station had been to limit commercial announcements to 160 announcements for each 10-hour day but it appears that the manager, employed on a commission basis, permitted a greater number to be broadcast. Even if the station's definition of a "commercial," which excludes time signals and introductions in the name of the sponsor, is accepted, the number of commercial programs on the dates recorded would be far in excess of those originally proposed.

Further examples of the divergence between promise and performance are found in the following record facts. For a period of over a year no regular news was broadcast over the station. Little effort was made to promote any programs other than those characterized by purely commercial continuity. The musical portions were composed almost entirely of popular records. Each 5-minute program contains at least one commercial announcement and some recorded music. While the licensee made its station available free of charge to civic, charitable, fraternal, and educational organizations, it expended no substantial effort actively to assist and aid such organizations in the preparation and production of programs. As a result, programs of this character became in most instances mere announcements for such organizations. (8 F.C.C. 207, 208-209.)

The Commission's decision, dated September 25, 1940, set forth at some length its views with respect to "the disparity between the proposed service and the programs actually broadcast." It stated:

In the Commission's view the licensee of Station KIEV did not make a reasonable effort to make its programs conform to its representations. The disparity between the proposed service and the programs actually broadcast indicates such a disregard of the representations made as to cast doubt on their sincerity in the first instance, and, therefore, on the qualifications of the licensee. Furthermore, false statements of talent expenditures were made in successive renewal applications. The Commission, in the allocation of frequencies to the various communities, must rely upon the testimony of applicants and upon the representations made in original and renewal

---

[4] In originally urging that its own application be granted and that the renewal application of Station KGIX be denied, Cannon Systems, Ltd., had called attention to the fact that the KGIX programs were 75 percent transcribed or recorded, and had characterized this as "reprehensible and inexcusable." It appears, however, that the Cannon System programs on the three days monitored were more than 98 percent recorded.

applications, to determine whether the public interest will be served by a grant of such applications. Faced here by such a disregard for representations so made, particularly upon the question of service to the public, the Commission is satisfied that a denial of the renewal application might well be justified. It should be noted that the emphasis is here placed upon the question of the truth of representations made to the Commission as a basis for the grant and renewal of a broadcast license. No adverse criticism is directed at the use of a proper proportion of high quality records or electrical transcriptions.

Upon all the facts, however, it has been concluded not to deny the pending application. The record shows that attempts to improve programs have been made. An additional member has been placed on the staff with the duty of arranging programs of a civic, educational and charitable nature. The percentage of time devoted to recorded music and to commercialization has been much reduced, and the remainder of the program schedule dedicated to diversified nonrecorded program material. News programs have been added and a 5-year contract entered into with the United Press. Religious programs are being prepared by the Ministerial Association. Local civic and fraternal organizations are being more actively assisted in the preparation of programs. To a substantial extent the public has come to utilize the transmitting facilities and the broadcast service.

There is, therefore, ground for urging that we may expect the present trend of improvement in program service to be carried forward. With some reluctance the Commission concludes that this application may be granted. The facts developed in this proceeding will, however, be given cumulative weight in dealing with any future questions involving the conduct of this station. (8 F.C.C. 207, 209-210.)

Despite the additional representations made in connection with its 1940 renewal, the KIEV logs for the week beginning April 23, 1944, show that more than 88 percent of its program time was still being devoted to mechanically reproduced music. Less than 3.7 percent of its program time — or 30 minutes a day — was devoted to the "talent" which the applicant assured the Commission was available in the community. This consisted of one singer who sang for 15 minutes 6 times a week, one pianist for 15 minutes on Saturday, one 15-minute school program, and a devotional program daily except Sunday from 6:30 to 6:45 a.m., when audiences, of course, are small. U.P. news was broadcast. The station's programs were still being interspersed with spot announcements on an average of one every 5.5 minutes. A total of 1042 spot announcements were broadcast during the week, of which 1034 were commercial and 8 were broadcast as a public service. A search of the week's logs fails to disclose any "duets, quartets, excerpts from operas, cuttings from great poems," or other special features originally promised when the Cannon System, Ltd., was seeking a license at the expense of Station KGIX. Nor does it reveal an adherence to the representations made in connection with its renewal granted in January 1940.

B.   Competing applications: Station WSNY

In the *Cannon System* case (KIEV), there was an element of competition between applicants, since the Cannon System proposed that the license of an existing station not be renewed. In the *Western Gateway* case (9 F.C.C. 92), the issue of two competing applications for a single available assignment was squarely raised.[1]

On December 8, 1939, the Van Curler Broadcasting Corporation filed an application for a new station to operate in Schenectady, New York, on a frequency of 1210 kilocycles, with power of 250 watts. A month later the Western Gateway Broadcasting Corporation filed a competing application for a new station in the same city, utilizing the same power on the same frequency. The two mutually exclusive applications were jointly heard.

Since both applicants specified similar or identical equipment and both appeared initially to be qualified financially and legally, the hearings were primarily concerned with the program representations of the two applicants. The Van Curler Broadcasting Corporation, for example, represented that it would regularly broadcast programs of the American Legion, the Schenectady Municipal Housing Authority, the Schenectady Council of Churches, etc.; that school programs for the city school system would be broadcast from 1:30 to 2 p.m. daily; that a local town-meeting program, patterned after the "American Town Meeting of the Air," would be broadcast Tuesday evenings from 8 to 9 p.m.; that a special line and studios would be installed at Union College for the broadcasting of its educational programs; etc.[2]

---

[1] This need to decide between competing applicants is a commonplace in the standard broadcast band. It may be somewhat less frequent in the new FM band because of the possibility of a larger number of stations in most communities; but competing applications for FM along the Eastern seaboard and in other metropolitan areas are already on file with the Commission. Television will also in all probability give rise to competing applications for identical facilities.

[2] "The Schenectady Municipal Housing Authority would broadcast a weekly one-quarter hour program, publicizing its activities. The Council of Churches of Schenectady would cooperate with the applicant in presenting religious programs. The proposed religious programs consist of: A one-quarter hour morning devotional program, presented 5 days a week by local ministers; a one-quarter hour Jewish program on Saturday afternoons; morning church services, presented from local churches for 1 hour on Sundays; and Vesper services for one-half hour on Sunday afternoons. Definite arrangements have been made with the city superintendent of schools for the broadcasting of school programs from 1:30 to 2 p.m. daily. Arrangements have been made with the State Forum Counselor, assigned by the United States Office of Education, to the New York Council of School Superintendents to broadcast programs in connection with this group's work in promoting adult civic education. The broadcasts to be presented would consist of: A local town meeting program (patterned after the well-known program, 'American Town Meeting of the Air'), which would be carried on Tuesday evenings from 8 to 9 p.m.; and three one-quarter hour programs each week. The Federation of Women's Clubs of Schenectady,

The other applicant, Western Gateway, also made detailed program representations — for example, that it would broadcast book reviews; a music appreciation series; a local "Radio Workshop" patterned after the CBS program of the same title; round table religious discussions embracing all religious faiths; programs of various local civic organizations, etc. The percentage of time to be devoted to each type of program was explicitly set forth.[3]

On the basis in part of these program service representations, the Commission on February 24, 1942, granted the application of Western Gateway and denied the application of Van Curler. With respect to the successful applicant, the Commission concluded:

Western Gateway Broadcasting Corporation is qualified in every respect to construct and operate the station proposed; it proposes to render a balanced program service comparable to that normally provided by local broadcast stations; and its proposed station would provide a satisfactory technical service throughout the City of Schenectady and the rural areas contiguous thereto. (9 F.C.C. 92, 101.)

---

representing some 38 clubs, would broadcast a one-half hour program each week during the seasons of the year when the clubs are most active. Definite arrangements have already been made for the presentation of some 43 programs by affiliates of the Federation. A one-quarter hour book review would be presented each week in cooperation with the city public library; and the applicant has also agreed to broadcast special announcements concerning the library. The City of Scotia would broadcast a weekly program devoted to matters of local interest to the listeners living in that community. The applicant has agreed to contribute to these groups the use of the facilities of the projected station, as well as professional production assistance, and to reserve specific periods of time on an immovable-sustaining basis for their regular programs." (9 F.C.C. 92, 100-101.)

[3] "The proposed station would be operated on the average of about 17 hours daily. According to the applicant's proposed program plans, time would be devoted as follows: Entertainment (51.41 percent), includes various types of music (presented by local and professional talent, records and transcriptions), drama, quiz programs, and programs designed especially for the women (such as shopping and household hints, fashion comments, and advice on the care of children); educational (16.53 percent), includes safety programs, book reviews, a music appreciation series, a program entitled "Radio Workshop" (a local version of CBS program of the same title), patriotic broadcasts, dramatized historical events, local round table discussions, and others; religious (6 percent), includes a morning program of religious hymns (presented by talent furnished by local churches and schools), a daily devotional program conducted by local clergymen, round table discussions embracing all religious faiths, and Sunday services from local churches; agricultural (1.27 percent), includes market and other reports, Farm Bureau topics, Grange notices, and others; news (16.95 percent), includes during each day, 5-minute newscasts every hour, a 10-minute sports review, a one-quarter hour news commentary presented by James T. Healey, two five-minute local newscasts, and two one-quarter hour news digests; civic (7.84 percent), includes programs concerning the activities of various local organizations and institutions, discussions of governmental and civic problems, and programs designed to promote interest in the community, state and nation. Programs presented by means of mechanical reproduction would be broadcast for about 20 percent of the time. Material for newscasts would be obtained from a well-known news service and local newspapers," etc. (9 F.C.C. 92, 96.)

With respect to the unsuccessful applicant, Van Curler Broadcasting Corporation, the Commission found that, "while this applicant has made a showing of the public-service programs, newscasts, transcribed features, musical clock programs, and time and other reports, it expects to broadcast, it has not adduced evidence as to its other program plans." Moreover, the Commission raised the question of credibility with respect to the representations made by the unsuccessful applicant. It noted that one of the directors had first testified that $5,000 which he had invested in the company was his own, and subsequently testified instead that it had been borrowed from a brother-in-law. Said the Commission:

In the performance of our duties we must, among other things, determine whether the operation of proposed stations, or the continued operation of existing stations, would serve public interest, and in so doing we are, of necessity, required to rely to a large extent upon statements made by station licensees, or those connected therewith. Caution must, therefore, be exercised to grant station licenses only to those persons whose statements are trustworthy. (9 F.C.C. 92, 102.)

Examinations of the logs of Station WSNY, the Western Gateway station, for the week beginning January 18, 1945, and a consideration of the statement concerning the public service rendered by Station WSNY filed by the licensee under date of May 24, 1945, in connection with its license renewal, warrant the conclusion that while a very genuine effort is being made by the licensee to serve the Schnectady area,[4] nevertheless, the station's present operations clearly fall short of the extreme representations made when Western Gateway was competitively seeking approval of a new station as against Van Curler. For example, Station WSNY represented that approximately 20 percent of its time would be devoted to programs presented by means of mechanical reproduction. An examination of the WSNY logs for the week beginning January 18, 1945, shows in contrast, that 78 percent of the program time of the station is devoted to mechanically reproduced programs. At least some of the types of programs specifically set forth in the original representations do not appear on the program schedules less than 3 years after the station went on the air.

C.   Applications for increased facilities: Station WTOL

The relation between the Commission's renewal procedures and its actions in connection with applications for increased facilities for existing broadcast stations is illustrated in the case of Station WTOL, Toledo. (7 F.C.C. 194.)

---

[4]With respect to its statements filed May 24, 1945, Station WSNY declares: "WE BELIEVE THAT NO OTHER STATION IN AMERICA CAN MATCH THE RECORD OF COMMUNITY INTEREST AND PUBLIC SERVICE BROADCASTING INDICATED IN THESE VARIOUS STATEMENTS."

Station WTOL was originally licensed to operate daytime only; but in 1938 it applied for authority to broadcast unlimited time. In the hearing on its application, the station relied heavily on the need for added evening hours in order to serve local organizations in Toledo, and to make use of the live talent in Toledo after 6 p.m. The applicant represented, for example, that after 6 p.m., 84 percent of its time would be devoted to live-talent broadcasts; that the Toledo Council of Churches, the American Legion, the YMCA and "other worthwhile organizations" desired time over the station *at night*, and that the only other station in Toledo was unable to clear sufficient time for such programs because it was affiliated with a national network.[1]

The president of the licensee corporation testified as follows on direct examination:

Q.   What is the purpose of this application for night-time hours?

A.   It is to give the people of Toledo an opportunity to have a station which can broadcast a great many events which can not at the present time be broadcast, because the only other station there is a regional station with a chain hook-up. For instance, we had during the summer civic opera which, by special permission of the Federal Communications Commission was broadcast. We have had a great many other musical occasions which could not be broadcast, although request was made by the managers of musical organizations for broadcasts. We have many important and interesting speakers who come to Toledo for dinner meetings, and other occasions, where there is a demand made for broadcasting, and these and other educational features can be carried if we have full time operation. (F.C.C. Docket 5320, Tr. 81-82.)

In granting the WTOL application for unlimited time, the Commission concluded:

Station WTOL is rendering a satisfactory local program service to the Toledo, Ohio, audience during daytime hours and a similar program service is

---

[1] "The applicant's proposed weekly program schedule was admitted in evidence, and shows, among other things, that approximately 35.5 percent of the station's time will be devoted to news, drama, education, religious, civic, and sports broadcasts, and the remaining 64.5 percent will be devoted to musical entertainment, approximately one-half of which will be commercial broadcasts. The program service proposed appears somewhat similar in character to its existing service, except that a greater percentage of the total time will be devoted to the use of live talent broadcasts. Approximately 62 percent of the station's time will be devoted to broadcasts using live talent and after 6 p.m. live talent will be used approximately 84 percent of the time. . . .

"The policy of the station has been, and will continue to be, to give free time to the Toledo Council of Churches for religious broadcasts. This organization desires time at night over Station WTOL. The station has also cooperated with the municipal and county governments and the various agencies of both the State and Federal Governments in giving free time to the Toledo Post of the American Legion, the Y.M.C.A., Boy Scouts of America, and other worthwhile organizations. These organizations desire time over the station at night and will cooperate in furnishing program material for broadcasts. Station WSPD is at the present time affiliated with the National Broadcasting Company and has been unable to give sufficient time to these organizations at night." (7 F.C.C. 194, 196-7.)

proposed for the evening hours which is not now available from any radio broadcast station serving this area. The other existing station (WSPD) in Toledo is of a regional classification and does not adequately meet the local needs of the Toledo area during the evening hours. There is a need in the Toledo, Ohio, area for the service proposed by the applicant. (7 F.C.C. 194, 198.)

The WTOL application was granted on April 17, 1939, and eight months later Station WTOL, like the only other station in Toledo, became affiliated with a national network. By 1944 the "local" programs upon which WTOL had relied were conspicuous by their absence. During the week beginning November 13, 1944, for example, approximately 15 percent of the station's time was devoted to "live" broadcasts rather than the 62 percent originally represented. After 6 p.m., instead of devoting 84 percent of the time to local live broadcasts, as represented, Station WTOL devoted only 13.7 percent of its time to such programs. Nearly half of the "live" programs, moreover, were wire news involving no live talent other than the voice of a news announcer.[2]

In contrast to its allegations that time after 6 p.m. was sought for local public service, the station broadcast only 20 minutes of local live sustaining programs after 6 p.m. during the entire week — 10 minutes of bowling scores and 10 minutes of sports news.

Throughout the week, 91.8 percent of the broadcast time was commercial. No evening time whatever during the week was given to the Toledo American Legion, YMCA, Boy Scouts, or any other local organizations which, according to the representations, desired time over the station at night.

Nor was the time after 6 p.m. filled with commercial programs of such outstanding merit as to leave no room for local service. From 6:15 to 6:30 p.m. on Tuesday, for example, a 15-minute program of transcribed music was interrupted by seven spot announcements — at 6:18, 6:19, 6:22, 6:24½, 6:25½, 6:26½, and 6:29 p.m. From 10:10 to 10:30 the same evening, a transcribed musical program entitled "Music Hall" was interrupted by 10 spot announcements in 20 minutes — at 10:15, 10:16, 10:20, 10:21, 10:22, 10:23, 10:25, 10:26, 10:27, and 10:29½ p.m.

D.   Transfer of Control: Station WBAL

In recent years, the purchase of an existing standard broadcast station has become a more common means of entering broadcasting than the erection of a

---

[2] For discussion of "wire programs" as distinguished from "local live" programs, see "Uniform Definitions and Program Logs."

new station.[1] The case of Station WBAL, Baltimore, illustrates the extent to which the service rendered by a station may be affected by a transfer or assignment of license to a purchaser, and the need for integrating Commission transfer and renewal procedures.

Station WBAL was originally licensed to the Consolidated Gas, Electric Light and Power Company of Baltimore, by the Department of Commerce. It began operations November 2, 1925.[2]

When the Federal Radio Commission was established in 1927, Station WBAL was one of many stations which sought to procure a "cleared channel," 25 of which were then being proposed. In support of its claim to a cleared channel, the station submitted "A Description of WBAL, Baltimore," prepared for the information of the Federal Radio Commission, August 1927. The "Description" stated: "Although WBAL is owned by a private corporation, its operation closely approximates that of a public enterprise." The Station's program policy was described as follows:

WBAL has endeavored to be a distinctive personality among broadcasting stations. To attain this end its programs have maintained high musical and artistic standards. The Station's "No Jazz" policy is indicative.

The Station Director is also head of the Baltimore Municipal Department of Music. The direct connections which the Director and various members of the musical staff have with the private and public musical activities of the City make possible a selection of the best artistic personnel, and provides a means of coordination which is seldom found possible. The Station has maintained its own features to a unique degree, until quite recently, over ninety percent of its programs being rendered by its own studio organizations.

In addition to the regular features of the Studio, the programs of the Station have included as a regular feature during the winter months, semi-weekly organ recitals from the Peabody Conservatory of Music, at which institution is located the largest single pipe organ south of New York. The Station has also

---

[1] During the four years 1941 through 1944, inclusive, 98 new standard broadcast stations were licensed, while 110 were assigned or transferred in toto, excluding merely formal transfers or assignments involving no actual change of control.

[2] The station began broadcasting with the following statement by the president of the then licensee corporation:

"It is my privilege on this, our opening night, to dedicate this new radio station to Baltimore and Maryland, and to the service of their people in such ways as may be found most useful to them. This station is to be known as 'Baltimore,' and it will be so designated and referred to in the future announcing and operation. The company which has financed its construction and will operate it now dedicates it to the public service of this city and Commonwealth. It will be satisfied to participate along with all others in this great community in such progress and advantage as its operation may bring forth. After tonight the name of this company may not be heard in the announcements of this station, nor is it proposed to commercialize its operation."

broadcast each season, a number of the most important musical services from various churches throughout the city. During the summer these features were supplanted by outdoor programs from a permanent pick-up point in one of the public parks of the city, featuring two programs each week, one by the Baltimore Municipal Band, the other by the Baltimore City Park Orchestra. Programs of the Baltimore Symphony Orchestra and other orchestral and choral programs of city-wide interest have also been included in the station's broadcasting each season.

The station also employed regular musical organizations:

The following staff organizations which, in line with the policy of not referring to the Gas and Electric Company, are designated simply by the call letters of the Station, have been retained as regular features to insure a uniformly high standard of program. Some appear daily, others semi-weekly, or weekly.

WBAL Concert Orchestra	WBAL String Quartet
WBAL Opera Company	WBAL Dance Orchestra
WBAL Salon Orchestra	WBAL Male Quartet
WBAL Ensemble	WBAL Mixed Quartet
WBAL Dinner Orchestra	WBAL Trio

From the personnel of the various organizations is also drawn talent for special presentations, such as continuity programs, musical scenarios and programs for special events.

The competition among the several hundred stations then on the air for the 25 proposed clear channels was very strenuous, and the Commission made it clear that "superior programs" would be one test, or perhaps the principal test, of eligibility.[3]

On November 20, 1934, application was made for transfer of control of the WBAL Broadcasting Company from the Consolidated Gas, Electric Light and Power Company to American Radio News Corporation, an absentee holding company. An amended application was filed December 1, 1934, and the transfer was approved, without a hearing, on January 8, 1935. At that time, no representations concerning program service were required of transferees, so that the purchasers were able to enter broadcasting without the representations

---

[3]Thus on December 5, 1927, Commissioner O. H. Caldwell wrote to the Mayor of Baltimore:

"The members of the Commission have asked me to acknowledge yours of December 1st., and to assure you that *the Commission desires to facilitate in every way the presentation of good programs* to the people of Baltimore through the local stations.

"If there are any channels now in use by other stations to which any Baltimore station feels better entitled, *by reason of superior programs*, the Baltimore station has but to make application, and after a hearing has been held, at which both sides will be given an opportunity to present full testimony, the members of the Commission will endeavor to assign the channel in the best public interest." (Emphasis supplied.)

which would have been required had they applied for a new station. Currently, transferees are required to state whether the transfer will affect the service, and if so, in what respects.

An examination of the program logs of Station WBAL for the week beginning Sunday, April 23, 1944, shows that its present mode of operation is in marked contrast to its operation described above under the previous licensee.

Thus, during the week beginning Sunday, April 23, 1944, only 12.5 percent of the program time between 8 a.m. and 11 p.m. was sustaining, and no sustaining programs whatever were broadcast on those days between 2 p.m. and 11 p.m. — a total of 45 hours.[4]

Between 8 a.m. and 11 p.m. of the week beginning April 23, 1944, Station WBAL broadcast 507 spot announcements, of which 6 were sustaining public service announcements. An example — not unique — of the piling up of spot announcements is found in the 45-minute period from 8:15 a.m. to 9:00 a.m. on Monday, April 24, 1944, during which 16 spot announcements were broadcast or one every 2.8 minutes.

Less than 2.5 percent of the station's time between 8 a.m. and 11 p.m. during the week was devoted to sustaining programs of local live origin. The only live sustaining programs carried during the entire week, 8 a.m. to 11 p.m., were as follows:

News at various time	95 minutes
"Gif-Ted Children," by remote control, Saturday, 9:45 – 10:00 a.m.	15 minutes
"The Family Hour," Saturday, 10:15 – 10:30 a.m.	15 minutes
"Musical Maneuvers," Saturday, 2:00 – 2:30 p.m.	30 minutes
Total live sustaining for the week	155 minutes

Station WBAL devoted 9 hours and 50 minutes to religious programs during the week — only 30 minutes of which was on a sustaining basis. The remaining 9 hours and 20 minutes were paid for by the religious organizations involved.

Station WBAL carried one forum or round table discussion-type program, either local or of network origin, during the week. The University of Chicago Round Table was made available to WBAL by NBC; but WBAL carried instead

---

[4] As used in this paragraph a "commercial" program is any program which is either paid for by a sponsor, or interrupted more than once per 15 minutes by commercial spot announcements. A 15-minute program preceded, followed, and interrupted once by commercial spot announcements is nevertheless classified as sustaining. For the Commission's proposed future definitions of "commercial" and "sustaining" programs, see "Uniform Definitions and Program Logs." For a discussion of the importance of and need for sustaining programs, see below, pp.173-198.

two transcribed commercial music programs and two 5-minute commercial talk programs.

The extent to which Baltimore has long been a world-renowned music center is noted above. During the entire week in question, the only local live music broadcast by Station WBAL between 8 a.m. and 11 p.m. was as follows:

A 10-minute "Music Award" commercial program.

"Musical Maneuvers," Saturday, 2:00–2:30 p.m.

"Songs of Romance," commercial, at various times, totalling 50 minutes for the week.

The National Broadcasting Company designates certain of its outstanding sustaining programs as "Public Service Programs": These programs were until 1945 marked with an American shield on its program schedules. During the week beginning April 23, 1944, NBC designated 19 programs as "Public Service Programs." Of these, Station WBAL carried five[5] and failed to carry 14. The 14 NBC "Public Service Programs" not carried and the programs carried by WBAL in lieu thereof are shown below [pp. 166-167].

E.   Representations made in court: Station KHMO

The *KHMO* case (4 F.C.C. 505; 70 App. D.C. 80) is of interest because it involves an element of judicial review, and a comparison of representations made in court with present performance.

The Courier Post Publishing Company of Hannibal, Missouri, now the licensee of Station KHMO, originally applied for a new station at Hannibal in 1936, as did a competing applicant. The Commission, after a hearing, was unable to find that a need existed for a local station in Hannibal and accordingly both applications were denied.

On appeal to the U.S. Court of Appeals for the District of Columbia (70 App. D.C. 80, 104 F. (2d) 213), the Court found that the Commission was in error, and that a need did exist for a local broadcast station to serve the particular local interests of the Hannibal community. Speaking through Judge Vinson, the Court noted (pp. 82-83) that service was available from other stations, but that "none of these stations provide for the local needs of Hannibal." The Court cited a Commission definition of a local station as one which would serve "to present programs of local interest to the residents of that community; to utilize and develop local entertainment talent which the record indicates is available; to serve local, religious, educational, civic, patriotic, and

---

[5] "Here's to Youth," "Doctors at War," "American Story," "Army Hour," and "Catholic Hour," all half-hour programs.

other organizations; to broadcast local news; and to generally provide a means of local public expression and a local broadcast service to listeners in that area."[1]

The Court cited in detail the programs which the applicant proposed to broadcast[2] and relied in particular on the applicant's representations that it "planned to use local talent — an abundance of which was shown to be available — and in this manner serve public interest of that area. Thus, it appears that the petition for a construction permit is supported by overwhelming evidence showing *the local need for a local station to serve in the manner set out.*" (Emphasis supplied.)

Pursuant to this decision of the Court of Appeals, the Commission granted a license. It appears, however, that the program service rendered is markedly different from the representations upon which the Court relied. For example, only 14.2 percent of the station's time for the week beginning April 22, 1945, was devoted to the "local talent"[3] said to be so abundant in the area. More than 85.8 percent of its time, in contrast, was devoted to network programs and transcriptions. Instead of giving its time "without charge" to local religious organizations, as represented, Station KHMO sold 4¾ hours of time during the week to such organizations on a commercial basis, and provided no time for local religious programs without charge.

PART II.   COMMISSION JURISDICTION WITH RESPECT TO PROGRAM SERVICE

The contention has at times been made that Section 326 of the Communications Act, which prohibits censorship or interference with free speech by the

---

[1] *Okmulgee Broadcasting Corporation*, 4 FCC 302.
[2] Thus the Court noted that the applicant "proposed to give portions of its time, without charge, to the various local civic, educational, athletic, farming, fraternal, religious, and charitable organizations. Its proposed program consists of: Entertainment 42%, educational 20%, news 9%, religious 9%, agriculture 10%, fraternal 5%, and civic activities 5%. The tentative program contemplated, particularly, the use of the facilities of the station to aid education in supplementing classroom work, and in broadcasting from a secondary studio located at Hannibal La Grange College subjects of scholastic interest and athletic events; the use by the Hannibal Chamber of Commerce to further business relations; the use by the County Agriculture Agent to bring before farmers and farm clubs the subject matter that is offered through the United States Department of Agriculture and Missouri College of Agriculture on farm problems; the use by the County Health Department to give information concerning maternity and child health, public health problems, particularly prevention of disease, food and milk control, and general sanitation; the use of the station by business in advertising; the promotion of literary and philanthropic activities; the promotion of better civic spirit; the furtherance of physical culture, and social activities of the Y.M.C.A. and Boy Scouts; and the broadcasting of daily religious services of the several Hannibal churches." (70 App. D.C. 80, 82-3.)
[3] Including news programs read off the ticker by a local announcer.

Time	NBC Public Service Program	WBAL Program
SUNDAY		
9:15–9:30 a.m.	"Commando Mary." – War Work for Women.	"Good Tidings Hour." Reverend Peters, commercial program.
10–10:30 a.m.	"National Radio Pulpit"–Reverend John Milton Phillips of the Grand Avenue Baptist Church in Omaha, Guest Speaker; Radio Choristers. Direction George Shackley. (From WOW, Omaha, and New York.)	10–10:05, News; 10:05–10:30, "Sunday Morning Round-up," transcribed music with four spot announcements for Anderson Motors, Fava Fruit Co., Four Besske Brothers, and Cactus Pills.
		"Willis Jones," commercial program sponsored by the Willis Jones committee.
1:15–1:30 p.m.	"Labor for Victory"–Congress of Industrial Organizations; guest speakers.	1:30–1:45, transcribed commercial music; 1:45–1:50, commercial talk, "Listen, Motorist"; 1:50–1:55, transcribed commercial music; 1:55–2:00, "Stay Out of Court," commercial talk.
1:30–2:00 p.m.	"University of Chicago Round Table Discussion"–guest speakers.	
		"Women of the Week," local commercial, drama, sponsored by the Schleisner Company.
4:30–4:55 p.m.	"Land of the Free"–"Indians of the North." Drama: Inter-American University of the Air; guest speaker (from Canada).	"The Open Bible," commercial program sponsored by the Hamilton Baptist Church.
11:30–12:00 mid.	"The Pacific Story–Hirohito: Eclipse of the Son of Heaven." Dramatization. (From Hollywood.)	
MONDAY		
12:30–1:00 p.m.	"U.S. Navy Band" (from Washington).	12:30–12:45, "Masters of Rhythm," transcribed music with six spot announcements; 12:45–1, "Treasury Salute," transcribed music.

TUESDAY

12:30–1:00 p.m.   "U.S. Coast Guard on Parade" (from WTIC, Hartford).

12:30–12:45, "Masters of Rhythm," transcribed music with six spot announcements; 12:45–1, "Treasury Salute," transcribed music.

11:30–12:00 mid.   "Words at War"–dramatized stories.

11:30–11:45, "Open Bible," commercial transcribed program sponsored by Hamilton Baptist Church; 11:45–12, "Treasury Salute," transcribed music.

WEDNESDAY

12:30–1:00 p.m.   "U.S. Air Force Band"–Capt. George S. Howard, Conductor (from Washington).

12:30–12:45, "Masters of Rhythm," transcribed music with six spot announcements; 12:45–1, "Treasury Salute," transcribed music.

FRIDAY

12:30–1:00 p.m.   "U.S. Marine Band" (from Washington).

12:30–12:45, "Masters of Rhythm," transcribed music with six spot announcements; 12:45–1, "Treasury Salute," transcribed music.

SATURDAY

1:30–1:45 p.m.   "The Baxters Invest in Health," drama; National Congress of Parent and Teachers Associations.

1:45–2:00 p.m.   "War Telescope"–John MacVane from London via shortwave.

6:00–6:30 p.m.   "I Sustain the Wings"–Army Air Force Band, Capt. Glenn Miller conducting.

1:30–1:35, "Latest News"; spot announcement for Arrid deodorant; 1:35–1:45, "Behind the News."

"Front-Page Drama," electrical transcription, commercial program sponsored by Sunday *American.*

6–6:05, "Esso News," sponsored by Standard Oil Co.; 6:05–6:15, "National Sports," sponsored by National Beer Co.; transcribed spot announcement for "Whiz Candy"; 6:15–6:30, "Paul Robertson Talk," political speech.

Commission, precludes any concern on the part of the Commission with the program service of licensees. This contention overlooks the legislative history of the Radio Act of 1927, the consistent administrative practice of the Federal Radio Commission, the re-enactment of identical provisions in the Communications Act of 1934 with full knowledge by the Congress that the language covered a Commission concern with program service, the relevant court decisions, and this Commission's concern with program service since 1934.

The Communications Act, like the Radio Act of 1927, directs the Commission to grant licenses and renewals of licenses only if public interest, convenience and necessity will be served thereby. The first duty of the Federal Radio Commission, created by the Act of 1927, was to give concrete meaning to the phrase "public interest" by formulating standards to be applied in granting licenses for the use of practically all the then available radio frequencies. From the beginning it assumed that program service was a prime factor to be taken into consideration. The renewal forms prepared by it in 1927 included the following questions:

(11)   Attach printed program for the last week.

(12)   *Why will the operation of the station be in the public convenience, interest and necessity?*

      (a)   Average amount of time weekly devoted to the following services (1) entertainment (2) religious (3) commercial (4) educational (5) agricultural (6) fraternal.

      (b)   Is direct advertising conducted in the interest of the applicant or others?

Copies of this form were submitted for Congressional consideration.[1]

In its Annual Report to Congress for 1928, the Commission stated (p. 161):

The Commission believes it is entitled to consider the program service rendered by the various applicants, to compare them, and to favor those which render the best service.

The Federal Radio Commission was first created for a term of one year only. In 1928 a bill was introduced to extend this term and extensive hearings were held before the House Committee on Merchant Marine and Fisheries. The Commissioners appeared before the Committee and were questioned at length as to their administration of the Act. At that time Commissioner Caldwell reported that the Commission had taken the position that

. . . each station occupying a desirable channel should be kept on its toes to produce and present the best programs possible and, if any station slips from that high standard, another station which is putting on programs of a better

---

[1] *Hearings on Jurisdiction of Radio Commission,* House Committee on Merchant Marine and Fisheries, 1928, p. 26.

standard should have the right to contest the first station's position and after hearing the full testimony, to replace it. (Hearings on Jurisdiction, p. 188.)

The Commissioner also reported that he had concluded, after 18 months' experience, that station selections should not be made on the basis of priority in use and stated that he had found that a policy —

. . . of hearings, by which there is presented full testimony on the demonstrated capacity of the station to render service, is a much better test of who is entitled to those channels. (Ibid.)

By 1929 the Commission had formulated its standard of the program service which would meet, in fair proportion, "the tastes, needs and desires of all substantial groups among the listening public." A well-rounded program service, it said, should consist of

entertainment, consisting of music of both classical and lighter grades, religion, education, and instruction, important public events, discussion of public questions, weather, market reports, and news and matters of interest to all members of the family. (Great Lakes Broadcasting Co., reported in F.R.C., 3d Annual Report, pp. 33-35.)

By the time Congress had under consideration replacing the Radio Act of 1927 with a new regulatory statute, there no longer existed any doubt that the Commission did possess the power to take over-all program service into account. The broadcasting industry itself recognized the "manifest duty" of the Commission to consider program service. In 1934, at hearings before the House Committee on Interstate Commerce on one of the bills which finally culminated in the Communications Act of 1934, the National Association of Broadcasters submitted a statement which contained the following (*Hearings on H.R. 8301,* 73rd Cong., p. 117):

It is the manifest duty of the licensing authority, in passing upon applications for licenses or the renewal thereof, to determine whether or not the applicant is rendering or can render an adequate public service. *Such service necessarily includes* broadcasting of a considerable proportion of programs devoted to education, religion, labor, agricultural and similar activities concerned with human betterment. In actual practice over a period of 7 years, as the records of the Federal Radio Commission amply prove, this has been *the principal test* which the Commission has applied in dealing with broadcasting applications. (Emphasis supplied.)

In hearings before the same committee on the same bill (*H.R. 8301,* 73rd Cong.) Chairman Sykes of the Federal Radio Commission testified (pp. 350-352):

That act puts upon the individual licensee of a broadcast station the private initiative to see that those programs that he broadcasts are in the public interest.

. . . Then that act makes those individual licensees responsible to the licensing authority to see that their operations are in the public interest.

Our licenses to broadcasting stations last for 6 months. *The law says that they must operate in the public interest, convenience, and necessity.* When the time for a renewal of those station licenses comes up, *it is the duty of the Commission in passing on whether or not that station should be relicensed for another licensing period, to say whether or not their past performance during the last license period has been in the public interest.* (Emphasis supplied.)

Under the law, of course, we cannot refuse a renewal until there is a hearing before the Commission. We would have to have a hearing before the Commission, to go thoroughly into the nature of all of the broadcasts of those stations, consider all of those broadcasts, and then say whether or not it was operating in the public interest.

In the full knowledge of this established procedure of the Federal Radio Commission, the Congress thereupon re-enacted the relevant provisions in the Communications Act of 1934.

In the course of the discussion of the 1934 Act, an amendment to the Senate bill was introduced which required the Commission to allocate 25 percent of all broadcasting facilities for the use of educational, religious, agricultural, labor, cooperative and similar non-profit-making organizations. Senator Dill, who was the sponsor in the Senate of both the 1927 and 1934 Acts, spoke against the amendment, stating that the Commission already had the power to reach the desired ends (78 *Cong. Rec.* 8843):

The difficulty probably is in the failure of the present Commission to take the steps that it ought to take to see to it that a larger use is made of radio facilities for education and religious purposes.

I may say, however, that the owners of large radio stations now operating have suggested to me that it might be well to provide in the license that a certain percentage of the time of a radio station shall be allotted to religious, educational, or non-profit users.

Senator Hatfield, a sponsor of the amendment, had also taken the position that the Commission's power was adequate, saying (78 *Cong. Rec.* 8835):

I have no criticism to make of the personnel of the Radio Commission, except that *their refusal literally to carry out the law of the land warrants the Congress of the United States writing into legislation the desire of Congress that educational institutions be given a specified portion of the radio facilities of our country.* (Emphasis supplied.)

The amendment was defeated and Section 307(c) of the Act was substituted which required the Commission to study the question and to report to Congress its recommendations.

The Commission made such a study and in 1935 issued a report advising against the enactment of legislation. The report stated:

Commercial stations are now responsible under the law, to render a public service, and the tendency of the proposal would be to lessen this responsibility.

The Commission feels that present legislation has the flexibility essential to attain the desired ends without necessitating at this time any changes in the law.

There is no need for a change in the existing law to accomplish the helpful purposes of the proposal.

In order for non-profit organizations to obtain the maximum service possible, cooperation in good faith by the broadcasters is required. *Such cooperation should, therefore, be under the direction and supervision of the Commission.* (Report of the Federal Communications Commission to Congress Pursuant to Sec. 307(c) of the Communications Act of 1934, Jan. 22, 1935.) (Emphasis supplied.)

On the basis of the foregoing legislative history there can be no doubt that Congress intended the Commission to consider overall program service in passing on applications. The Federal Communications Commission from the beginning accepted the doctrine that its public interest determinations, like those of its predecessor, must be based in part at least on grounds of program service. Thus early in 1935 it designated for joint hearing the renewal applications of Stations KGFJ, KFWB, KMPC, KRKD, and KIEV, in part "to determine the nature and character of the program service rendered . . ." *In re McGlasham et al.,* 2 F.C.C. 145, 149. In its decision, the Commission set forth the basis of its authority as follows:

Section 309(a) of the Communications Act of 1934 is an exact restatement of Section 11 of the Radio Act of 1927. This section provides that subject to the limitations of the Act the Commission may grant licenses if the public interest, convenience, and necessity will be served thereby. The United States Court of Appeals for the District of Columbia in the case of *KFKB Broadcasting Association, Inc.* v. *Federal Radio Commission,* 60 App. D.C. 79, held that under Section 11 of the Radio Act of 1927 the Radio Commission was necessarily called upon to consider the character and quality of the service to be rendered and that in considering an application for renewal an important consideration is the past conduct of the applicant. (2 F.C.C. 145, 149.)

The courts have agreed that the Commission may consider program service of a licensee in passing on its renewal application. In the first case in which an applicant appealed from a Commission decision denying the renewal of a station license in part because of its program service, the court simply assumed that program service should be considered in determining the question of public interest and summarized and adopted the Commission's findings concerning program service as a factor in its own decision.[2] In 1931, however, the question was squarely presented to the Court of Appeals when the KFKB Broadcasting

---

[2] *Technical Radio Laboratory* v. *Federal Radio Commission,* 59 App. D.C. 125, 36 F. (2d) 111.

Association contended that the action of the Commission in denying a renewal of its license because of the type of program material and advertising which it had broadcast, constituted censorship by the Commission. The Court sustained the Commission, saying:

It is apparent, we think, that the business is impressed with a public interest and that, because the number of available broadcasting frequencies is limited, *the Commission is necessarily called upon to consider the character and quality of the service to be rendered.* In considering an application for a renewal of a license, an important consideration is the past conduct of the applicant, for "by their fruits shall ye know them." Matt. VII:20. Especially is this true in a case like the present, where the evidence clearly justifies the conclusion that the future conduct of the station will not differ from the past. (*KFKB Broadcasting Association* v. *Federal Radio Commission*, 47 F. 2d 670.) (Emphasis supplied.)

In 1932, the Court affirmed this position in *Trinity Methodist Church* v. *Federal Radio Commission*, 62 F. (2d) 850, and went on to say that it is the "duty" of the Commission "to take notice of the appellant's conduct in his previous use of the permit."

The question of the nature of the Commission's power was presented to the Supreme Court in the *network* case. The contention was then made that the Commission's power was limited to technological matters only. The Court rejected this, saying (*National Broadcasting Company* v. *United States*, 319 U.S. 190, 216-217):

The Commission's licensing function cannot be discharged, therefore, merely by finding that there are no technological objections to the granting of a license. If the criterion of "public interest" were limited to such matters, how could the Commission choose between two applicants for the same facilities, each of whom is financially and technically qualified to operate a station? Since the very inception of federal regulation by radio, comparative considerations as to the service to be rendered have governed the application of the standard of "public interest, convenience, or necessity."

The foregoing discussion should make it clear not only that the Commission has the authority to concern itself with program service, but that it is under an affirmative duty, in its public interest determinations, to give full consideration to program service. Part III of this Report will consider some particular aspects of program service as they bear upon the public interest.

PART III.   SOME ASPECTS OF "PUBLIC INTEREST" IN PROGRAM SERVICE

As has been noted, the Commission must determine, with respect to each application granted or denied or renewed, whether or not the program service proposed is "in the public interest, convenience, and necessity."

The Federal Radio Commission was faced with this problem from the very beginning, and in 1928 it laid down a broad definition which may still be cited in part:

Broadcasting stations are licensed to serve the public and not for the purpose of furthering the private or selfish interests of individuals or groups of individuals. The standard of public interest, convenience, or necessity means nothing if it does not mean this. . . . The emphasis should be on the *receiving* of service and the standard of public interest, convenience, or necessity should be construed accordingly. . . . The *entire* listening public within the service area of a station, or of a group of stations in one community, is entitled to service from that station or stations. . . . In a sense a broadcasting station may be regarded as a sort of mouthpiece on the air for the community it serves, over which its public events of general interest, its political campaigns, its election results, its athletic contests, its orchestras and artists, and discussion of its public issues may be broadcast. *If . . . the station performs its duty in furnishing a well rounded program, the rights of the community* have been achieved. (In re Great Lakes Broadcasting Co., F.R.C. Docket No. 4900; cf. 3rd Annual Report of the F.R.C., pp. 32-36.) (Emphasis supplied.)

Commission policy with respect to public interest determinations is for the most part set by opinions in particular cases. (See, for example, cases indexed under "Program Service" in Volumes 1 through 9 of the Commission's Decisions.) A useful purpose is served, however, by occasional overall reviews of Commission policy. This Part will discuss four major issues currently involved in the application of the "public interest" standard to program service policy; namely, (A) the carrying of sustaining programs, (B) the carrying of local live programs, (C) the carrying of programs devoted to public discussion, and (D) the elimination of commercial advertising excesses.

A.   The carrying of sustaining programs

The commercial program, paid for and in many instances also selected, written, casted, and produced by advertisers and advertising agencies, is the staple fare of

American listening. More than half of all broadcast time is devoted to commercial programs; the most popular programs on the air are commercial. The evidence is overwhelming that the popularity of American broadcasting as we know it is based in no small part upon its commercial programs.

Nevertheless, since the early days of broadcasting, broadcasters and the Commission alike have recognized that sustaining programs also play an integral and irreplaceable part in the American system of broadcasting. The sustaining program has five distinctive and outstanding functions.

1. To secure for the station or network a means by which in the overall structure of its program service, it can achieve a *balanced* interpretation of public needs.
2. To provide programs which by their very nature may not be sponsored with propriety.
3. To provide programs for significant minority tastes and interests.
4. To provide programs devoted to the needs and purposes of nonprofit organizations.
5. To provide a field for experiment in new types of programs, secure from the restrictions that obtain with reference to programs in which the advertiser's interest in selling goods predominates.

(1)   Balance-wheel function of the sustaining program

The sustaining program is the balance-wheel by means of which the imbalance of a station's or network's program structure, which might otherwise result from commercial decisions concerning program structure, can be redressed.

Dr. Frank N. Stanton, then Director of Research and now vice-president of the Columbia Broadcasting System, explained this function to the House Committee on Interstate and Foreign Commerce (*Hearings on H.R. 4597,* 77th Cong., 2nd Sess., May 7, 1942, page 289):

One use Columbia makes of sustaining programs is to supplement commercial offerings in such ways as to achieve, so far as possible, a full and balanced network service. For example, if the commercial programs should be preponderantly musical, Columbia endeavors to restore program balance with drama or the like in its sustaining service.

The Commission, as well as broadcasters themselves, has always insisted that a "well-balanced program structure" is an essential part of broadcasting in the public interest. At least since 1928, and continuing to the present, stations have been asked, on renewal, to set forth the average amount of time, or percentage of time, devoted to entertainment programs, religious programs, educational programs, agricultural programs, fraternal programs, etc.; and the Commission has from time to time relied upon the data thus set forth in determining whether a station has maintained a well-balanced program structure.[1]

In metropolitan areas where the listener has his choice of several stations, balanced service to listeners can be achieved either by means of a balanced program structure for each station or by means of a number of comparatively specialized stations which, considered together, offer a balanced service to the community. In New York City, a considerable degree of specialization on the part of particular stations has already arisen — one station featuring a preponderance of classical music, another a preponderance of dance music, etc. With the larger number of stations which FM will make possible, such specialization may arise in other cities. To make possible this development on a sound community basis, the Commission proposes in its application forms hereafter to afford applicants an opportunity to state whether they propose a balanced program structure or special emphasis on program service of a particular type or types.

Experience has shown that in general advertisers prefer to sponsor programs of news and entertainment. There are exceptions; but they do not alter the fact that if decisions today were left solely or predominantly to advertisers, news and entertainment would occupy substantially all of the time. The concept of a well-rounded structure can obviously not be maintained if the decision is left wholly or preponderantly in the hands of advertisers in search of a market, each concerned with his particular half hour, rather than in the hands of stations and networks responsible under the statute for overall program balance in the public interest.

A device by which some networks and stations are seeking to prevent program imbalance is the "package" program, selected, written, casted and

---

[1] The question asked on renewal in recent years is as follows:

"State the average percentage of time per month (combined total should equal 100%) devoted to—

"Commercial Programs	*"Sustaining Programs*
"1. Entertainment	[The categories specified under
2. Educational	this column are the same as
3. Religious	those in the adjacent column.—
4. Agricultural	Ed.]
5. Civic (include in this item fraternal, Chamber of Commerce, charitable, and other civic but non-governmental programs)	
6. Governmental (include in this item all municipal, state, and federal programs, including political or controversial broadcasts by public officials, or candidates for public office, and regardless of whether or not the programs included under this item are entertainment, educational, agricultural, etc., in character)	
7. News	
8. —	
9. Total"	

produced by the network or station itself, and sold to the advertiser as a ready-built package, with the time specified by the station or network. In order to get a particular period of time, the advertiser must take the package program which occupies that period. This practice, still far from general, appears to be a step in the direction of returning control of programs to those licensed to operate in the public interest. The commercial "package" program is not a substitute for the sustaining program, however, for reasons set forth in subsections (2) through (5) of this section.

What happens when the balance-wheel function of the sustaining program is neglected can be illustrated by the case of the "soap opera," defined as "a continuing serial in dramatic form, in which an understanding of today's episode is dependent upon previous listening."

In January 1940, the four networks provided listeners with 59½ daytime hours of sponsored programs weekly. Of these, 55 hours were devoted to soap operas. *Only 4½ sponsored daytime hours a week on the four networks were devoted to any other type of program.* Advertisers, in short, were permitted to destroy overall program balance by concentration on one type of program. The number of soap operas subsequently increased, reaching in April 1941 a total of some 50 commercially sponsored network soap operas a day.[2] Since then, there has been some decline, and the introduction of some sustaining programs in daytime hours has begun to modify the picture.

The extent of program imbalance still prevalent is indicated by the fact that in September 1945 the National Broadcasting Company was still devoting 4¾ hours per day, Monday through Friday, to 19 soap operas, and the Columbia Broadcasting System was similarly devoting 4¼ hours daily, Monday through Friday, to 17 such programs.

The following table presents data concerning soap operas during the period December 1944–April 1945.[2a] Column 1 shows the "rating" of the 19 soap operas broadcast by NBC and the 17 broadcast by CBS — that is, the percentage of telephone homes in 32 large cities where a respondent stated that the radio was tuned to the program in question or the station carrying the program. Column 2 shows the size of the available audience as determined by the same telephone calls — that is, the percentage of telephone homes in which someone was at home and awake to answer the telephone. Column 3, which is the "resultant" of columns 1 and 2, thus shows the recruiting power of the program — that is, the percentage of the available audience actually tuned to each soap opera. It will be noted that the most popular soap opera on the air during the period in question recruited 12.5 percent of the available audience. The average NBC soap opera recruited 8.4 percent of the available audience, and the average CBS soap opera recruited 6.7 percent of the available audience. In contrast, approximately 76.8 percent of the available audience answering the telephone during the soap opera hours reported that they had their radios turned off altogether.

[2] C. E. Hooper, Inc., "Year End Review of 1943 Daytime Radio Listening."
[2a] See *Fortune*, March 1946, p. 119, "Soap Opera."

NBC SOAP OPERAS

		Program Rating	Available Audience	Recruiting Efficiency
Mon.—Fri.	10:15 a.m. Lora Lawton	3.3	75.3	4.4
	10:30 a.m. Road of Life	3.0	75.4	4.0
	10:45 a.m. Joyce Jordan	3.0	73.6	4.1
	11:45 a.m. David Harum	2.9	72.2	4.0
	2:00 p.m. Guiding Light	5.5	68.2	8.1
	2:15 p.m. Today's Children	6.0	67.1	8.9
	2:30 p.m. Woman in White	5.6	66.0	8.5
	3:00 p.m. A Woman of America	4.6	66.1	7.0
	3:15 p.m. Oxydol's Own Ma Perkins	6.1	66.2	9.2
	3:30 p.m. Pepper Young's Family	7.1	65.9	10.7
	3:45 p.m. Right to Happiness	7.0	66.4	10.5
	4:00 p.m. Backstage Wife	6.7	67.6	9.9
	4:15 p.m. Stella Dallas	6.9	67.4	10.2
	4:30 p.m. Lorenzo Jones	6.7	68.7	9.8
	4:45 p.m. Young Widder Brown	7.5	69.6	10.7
	5:00 p.m. When a Girl Marries	8.9	71.1	12.5
	5:15 p.m. Portia Faces Life	7.9	71.6	11.0
	5:30 p.m. Just Plain Bill	6.5	73.4	8.9
	5:45 p.m. Front Page Farrell	5.6	74.7	7.5

CBS SOAP OPERAS

		Program Rating	Available Audience	Recruiting Efficiency
Mon.—Fri.	10:00 a.m. Valiant Lady	2.9	76.1	3.8
	10:15 a.m. Light of the World	3.7	75.3	4.9
	10:30 a.m. The Strange Romance of Evelyn Winters	3.4	75.4	4.5
	10:45 a.m. Bachelor's Children	4.3	73.6	5.8
	11:00 a.m. Amanda of Honeymoon Hill	2.8	74.5	3.8
	11:15 a.m. Second Husband	3.3	73.3	4.5
	11:30 a.m. Bright Horizon	4.5	73.1	6.2
	12:15 p.m. Big Sister	6.7	72.1	9.3
	12:30 p.m. The Romance of Helen Trent	7.0	72.1	9.7
	12:45 p.m. Our Gal Sunday	6.8	70.8	9.6
	1:00 p.m. Life Can Be Beautiful	7.2	70.4	10.2
	1:15 p.m. Ma Perkins	7.7	69.7	11.0
	1:45 p.m. Young Dr. Malone	5.1	68.2	7.5
	2:00 p.m. Two On a Clue	4.3	68.2	6.3
	2:15 p.m. Rosemary	4.1	67.1	6.1
	2:30 p.m. Perry Mason	3.8	66.0	5.8
	2:45 p.m. Tena & Tim	3.8	66.1	5.7

Source: "Sectional" Hooperatings, Dec. 1944—April 1945, Winter—Spring.

The "ratings" of the NBC and CBS soap operas must be considered in the light of the dominant position in the spectrum occupied by the stations concerned. Thus in the 32 cities in which the surveys in question were made, the power of the stations affiliated with each network was as follows:

	Total power	*Average power per station*
32 CBS stations	925,000 w	28,906 w
32 NBC stations	835,000 w	26,093 w
32 ABC stations	222,250 w	6,945 w
32 Mutual stations	200,000 w	6,250 w

Several reasons may be suggested for the popularity of soap operas among advertisers.[3] First, the soap opera is among the cheapest of all network shows to produce. The weekly production costs of the ordinary soap opera are reported to be less, for five 15-minute periods, than some advertisers spend on a one-minute transcribed spot announcement. Second, advertisers are not interested merely or primarily in the size of the audience which they achieve. They are interested also, and perhaps primarily, in two other indices of program effectiveness. One is the "sponsor identification index" which is defined as "the percent of listeners to a specific program which knows the name of the program's advertiser, or of any of his products." The other is the "product use index," defined as "the use of a sponsor's brand of product and that of his competitors among listeners to his program compared with non-listeners." An advertiser relying on the sponsor identification index, for example, may prefer a soap opera which appeals to only one million listeners and indelibly impresses the name of his product on two-thirds of them, rather than a non-soap opera program which appeals to two million listeners but impresses the sponsor's name on less than one-third. Similarly, an advertiser may prefer a soap opera which, as in an actual instance, results in the use of his product by 46.5 percent of those who listen (as compared with 25.1 percent of use among non-listeners), even though the program in question appeals to comparatively few listeners.

Mr. Duane Jones, head of an advertising agency reputed to be one of the

---

[3] According to the Cooperative Analysis of Broadcasting (CAB), network commercial time during the day from October 1943 to April 1944 was divided as follows:

Serial drama	57.4%
News and talks	10.7%
Variety	8.7%
Drama	6.8%
Children's Programs	4.7%
Classical and Semi-Classical	4.5%
Audience Participation	2.8%
Popular Music	2.2%
Familiar Music	1.3%
Hymns	0.9%
	100 %

five largest in New York, clearly was considering the special interests of advertisers rather than the public interest, when he declared:

> The best radio program is the one that sells the most goods, not necessarily the one that holds the highest Hooper or Crossley rating. [4]

Whether or not the reasons cited for the popularity of soap operas among advertisers are the decisive ones, it is clear that the result on many stations has been a marked imbalance of program structure during the daytime hours; and it is significant that the first steps recently taken to redress this imbalance have been the addition of sustaining programs. It is by means of the sustaining program that program imbalance, consequent upon sponsor domination of excessive blocks of time, can be redressed by those responsible for program structure − balance − the licensees, including the networks.

(2)   Programs inappropriate for commercial sponsorship

A second role of the sustaining program is to provide time for broadcasts which by their very nature may not be appropriate for sponsorship. As early as 1930, Mr. Merlin H. Aylesworth, then president of the National Broadcasting Company, recognized this role of the sustaining program in testimony before the Senate Committee on Interstate Commerce, even proposing that college football games were by their nature inappropriate for commercial sponsorship. [5] More recently, in 1941, Mr. Niles Trammell, president of the National Broadcasting Co., has stated:

> Another reason for the use of sustaining programs was the voluntary recognition on the part of broadcasters that programs of certain types, such as religious programs, informative programs furnished by various governmental agencies and certain programs involving discussions of political principles and other controversial issues, were not suited to advertising sponsorship. The use of high types of sustaining programs also creates goodwill for the station and

---

[4]The advertiser view cited may be contrasted with one of the "basic principles" in the interpretation of the phrase "public interest, convenience or necessity" laid down by the Federal Radio Commission in 1928:

"While it is true that broadcasting stations in this country are for the most part supported or partially supported by advertisers, broadcasters are not given these great privileges by the United States Government for the primary benefit of advertisers. *Such benefit as is derived by advertisers must be incidental and entirely secondary to the interest of the public.*" (Emphasis in original.)

[5]"*Mr. Aylesworth.* . . . We have refused to permit from our system the sponsoring of football games by commercial institutions. That may be a wrong policy; I do not know; but I have assumed that with all these youngsters in their management boards and with all of the commercialism that is talked about, and so forth, that I just did not quite like to see the Yale-Harvard game announced 'through the courtesy of so and so.' " (*Hearings on S. 6, 1930, p. 1711.*)

induces people to become accustomed to listening to certain stations in preference to others.[6]

The *Code of the National Association of Broadcasters* similarly recognized, until 1945, that the presentation of controversial issues (except forums) should be exclusively in sustaining programs. While the Commission has recently held that an absolute ban on the sale of time for the discussion of public issues may under certain circumstances not serve the public interest,[7] it is nevertheless clear that such broadcasts should be primarily of a sustaining nature.

The Commission has never set forth and does not now propose to set forth the particular types of program which, for one reason or another, must remain free from commercial sponsorship. It does, however, recognize along with the stations and networks themselves that there are such programs.[8] Self-regulation consonant with public sentiment, and a responsible concern for the public interest, can best insure a suitable interpretation of the basic principle which the industry itself has always recognized, that some programs are by their nature unsuitable for commercial sponsorship. Public interest requires that sustaining time be kept available for such broadcasts.

(3) Significant minority tastes and interests

It has long been an established policy of broadcasters themselves and of the Commission that the American system of broadcasting must serve significant minorities among our population, and the less dominant needs and tastes which most listeners have from time to time. Dr. Frank Stanton, in his testimony before the House Committee on Interstate and Foreign Commerce in 1942, previously cited, set forth this function of the sustaining program as follows:

There is another feature of sustaining service which differentiates it from commercial programs. While the CBS sustaining service recognizes the broad popular tastes, it also gives attention to smaller groups. It is known that the New York Philharmonic Symphony Orchestra, the Columbia Work Shop, Invitation

---

[6] Affidavit of Niles Trammel, in *National Broadcasting Co.* v. *United States* in the Supreme Court of the U.S., October Term, 1941, No. 1025, Transcript of Record, p. 228.

[7] *In the Matter of United Broadcasting Co. (WHKC)*, decided June 26, 1945.

[8] For example, one station has recently stated its refusal to exploit the problems of returning veterans on commercial programs, preferring programs devoted to veteran problems on a sustaining basis. *Variety*, for March 14, 1945, reports:

"WMCA FEELS VETS WOULD RESENT COM'L EXPLOITATION OF REHABILITATION SHOW.

"Plans for the production of a new program helping returning GIs rehabilitate themselves, and to aid their families in the readjustment period, are being planned by WMCA, N.Y. Move further reflects the industry-wide consciousness of the vital issue. . . .

"Show will not be for sale, station feeling vets would resent having solution of their problems made the subject of commercial exploitation. As result it's going on as a public service show."

to Learning, Columbia Broadcasting Symphony, and many other ambitious classical programs never reach the largest audience, but Columbia, nonetheless, puts them on year after year for minorities which are growing steadily.

Many sustaining programs, originally designed for comparatively small audiences, have proved so popular that they have subsequently acquired commercial sponsorship. "Of Men and Books," for example, was a sustaining feature of a literary nature for more than seven years, from May 26, 1938 to September 8, 1945, before a sponsor was obtained. When such a program becomes sponsored, the way is open for devoting sustaining time to still other types of programs having less than maximum audience appeal.

But even if they may not be able to compete, initially or ever, with Fibber McGee and Molly in size of audience, "sponsor identification index," and "product use index," such programs are essential to a well-balanced program structure. It is no doubt partly due to recognition of this fact that time has always been reserved from sponsorship for the carrying of such programs on a sustaining basis.

(4)   Service to non-profit organizations

A well-balanced program structure has always been deemed to include programs devoted to the needs and purposes of non-profit organizations.

Section 307(c) of the Communications Act of 1934 specifically directed the Commission to "study the proposal that Congress by statute allocate fixed percentages of radio broadcasting facilities to particular types or kinds of non-profit activities," and to report to Congress its recommendations. The Commission undertook prolonged hearings on the question, at which witnesses for non-profit organizations, networks and stations were heard at length. Such organizations as the National Committee on Education by Radio, individual educational institutions, representatives of many religious organizations, the American Federation of Labor, the Women's National Radio Committee, the Farmers' Union, and many others testified concerning the importance of broadcasting to their organizations and the services which their organizations could render to the public through broadcasting. Networks and stations, in turn, testified without hesitation to their willingness to assist and to supply time for the non-profit organizations.[9]

---

[9] Merlin A. Aylesworth, then president of the National Broadcasting Company, testified in particular: "We know if we do not render a public service, the Commission will give the license to others who will render better public service." (*Hearings* pursuant to Sec. 307(c), p. A23.)

William S. Paley, until recently president of the Columbia Broadcasting System, similarly testified: "We hold our license by serving the public interest, convenience, and necessity. And only by adequate cooperation with all public spirited groups can we be deemed to perform the conditions of our contract." (*Ibid.*, p. 11151.)

The Commission, in its report to Congress pursuant to Section 307(c) of the Communications Act, recommended that specific percentages of facilities *not* be reserved by statute for non-profit organizations, specifically on the ground that existing commercial stations were ready and willing to carry programs of non-profit organizations and that non-profit organizations would benefit thereby. Said the Commission:

It would appear that the interests of the non-profit organizations may be better served by the use of the existing facilities, thus giving them access to costly and efficient equipment and to established audiences, than by the establishment of new stations for their peculiar needs. In order for non-profit organizations to obtain the maximum service possible, cooperation in good faith by the broadcasters is required. *Such cooperation should, therefore, be under the direction and supervision of the Commission. . . . It is our firm intention to assist the non-profit organizations to obtain the fullest* opportunities for expression. (Pp. 6, 9-10; emphasis supplied.)

Cooperation between networks, stations, and non-profit organizations has always been present in greater or less degree, and it may be noted that many outstanding programs, both network and local, have resulted from such cooperation. Among the programs honored at the 9th Annual Exhibition of Educational Radio Programs, 1945 (the Ohio State University Awards), for example, were the following:

Group I — Regional web, regional or clear-channel station

RELIGIOUS BROADCASTS: First Award, "Salute to Valor" series, planned and produced by National Council of Catholic Men, WEAF, New York, and NBC. Honorable Mention: "Victorious Living" series, planned and produced by International Council of Religious Education, widely used over regional and clear-channel stations.

CULTURAL PROGRAMS: Honorable Mention: "Words at War" series, planned by Council on Books in Wartime, WEAF, New York, and NBC.

PUBLIC DISCUSSION PROGRAMS: First Award, "University of Chicago Round Table" series, planned and produced by U. of Chicago, WMAQ, Chicago, and NBC.

PERSONAL AND FAMILY LIFE PROGRAMS: Honorable Mention: "The Baxters" series, planned by National Congress of Parents-Teachers, WMAQ, Chicago, and NBC. Special Mention: "Alcoholics Anonymous" series, WWJ, Detroit.

PROGRAMS FURTHERING WAR, PEACE: First Award: "The March of Minnesota" series, planned and produced by Minnesota Resources Committee, WCCO, Minneapolis, and special state network. First Award, "Russian War Relief Presents" series, planned and produced by Russian War Relief,

Inc.; produced by members of Radio Directors Guild of New York City; released to many stations.

CHILDREN'S PROGRAM, OUT-OF-SCHOOL: First Award, "Books Bring Adventure" series, planned and produced by Association of Junior Leagues of America.

IN SCHOOL PROGRAMS, PRIMARY CHILDREN: First Award, "Your Story Parade" series, planned and produced by Texas State Department of Education, WBAP, Fort Worth, and Texas Quality web.

Group II — Local station or organization

CULTURAL PROGRAMS: Special Mention: "New World A-Coming" series, planned and produced by station WMCA in cooperation with Citywide Citizens Committee on Harlem; WMCA, New York.

PUBLIC DISCUSSION PROGRAMS: First Award, "Free Speech Forum" series, planned and produced by WMCA and New York Newspaper Guild; WMCA, New York.

NEWS INTERPRETATION: First Award, "History in the Making" series, planned and produced by University of Colorado and Rocky Mountain Radio Council; KVOD, Denver.

CHILDREN'S PROGRAMS, OUT-OF-SCHOOL: First Award, "Story Time" series, planned and produced by Colorado State College of Education and Rocky Mountain Radio Council; KLZ, Denver.

IN SCHOOL PROGRAMS, ELEMENTARY CHILDREN: Honorable Mention: "News Today — History Tomorrow" series, planned and produced by Rochester Public Schools, WHAM, Rochester, N.Y.

IN SCHOOL PROGRAMS, JUNIOR-SENIOR HIGHS: First Award, "Our America" series, planned and produced by Radio Council of Chicago Public Schools; WBEZ, Chicago Public Schools.

The *Peabody* and *Variety* awards similarly feature such programs as the WTIC temperance series prepared in cooperation with Alcoholics Anonymous, "Worcester and the World," broadcast by station WTAG in cooperation with the United Nations Information Office; programs of the American Jewish Committee; "Assignment Home," produced by CBS in cooperation with Army Service Forces, etc.

Such programs as these have done much to enrich American broadcasting. It may well be that they have kept in the radio audience many whose tastes and interests would otherwise cause them to turn to other media. Radio might easily deteriorate into a means of amusing only one cultural stratum of the American public if commercially sponsored entertainment were not leavened by programs having a different cultural appeal. Just as the programs of non-profit organizations benefit from being aired along with the mass-appeal programs of advertisers, so, it may be, the programs of the advertisers reach a larger and more varied audience by reason of the serious sustaining programs produced in cooperation with non-profit organizations. The furnishing of time and assistance to non-profit organizations is thus not merely a responsibility of networks and stations, but also an opportunity.

Special problems are involved in connection with program service designed especially for farmers — market reports, crop reports, weather reports, talks on farming, and other broadcasts specifically intended for rural listeners. The question of programs particularly adapted to the needs of rural listeners has been made an issue in the Commission's forthcoming Clear Channel Hearings (Docket No. 6741) and surveys of rural listeners have been made for the Commission by the Division of Program Surveys, Bureau of Agricultural Economics, Department of Agriculture, and by the Bureau of the Census.[10]

(5)   Program experimentation

Dr. Stanton, in his testimony previously cited, has described still another role of the sustaining program in the American system of broadcasting:

. . . It is through the sustaining or noncommercial program service that Columbia has developed its greatest contributions to network radio broadcasting. On its own time and at its own expense, Columbia has pioneered in such experimental fields as that of original radio drama through the Columbia Workshop Series. Further, it was the first to originate news broadcasts involving on-the-spot reports from correspondents located over all the world. The Columbia School of the Air, now in its thirteenth year, is another example of the use to which Columbia puts its sustaining time by providing a balanced curriculum of broadcasts, 5 days a week throughout the school year, suitable for use in the classrooms. Columbia has also taken the leadership in the matter of new program content in adult education, music and public debate.

Various advertisers and advertising agencies have frankly stated the extent to which their commercial requirements make necessary a special tailoring of commercial programs. The president of the American Tobacco Company, a sponsor of many network commercial programs, has been quoted to this effect:

We have some funny things here about radio, and we have been criticized for it. Taking 100% as the total radio value, we give 90% to commercials, to what's said about the product, and we give 10% to the show.

We are commercial and we cannot afford to be anything else. I don't have the right to spend the stockholder's money just to entertain the public. In particular, sponsors are naturally loath to sponsor any program which may

---

[10] *Attitudes of Rural People Toward Radio Service*, Bureau of Agricultural Economics, U.S. Department of Agriculture, January 1946.

offend even a minority of listeners. . . . The last thing I could afford to do is to offend the public.

Similarly Procter & Gamble, probably the largest sponsor in American broadcasting, has been described as having "a policy never to offend a single listener."

In 1935, to take an extreme example, Alexander Woollcott's "Town Crier" broadcasts were discontinued when the sponsor complained Mr. Woollcott had criticized Hitler and Mussolini, and might thus offend some listeners.

In the field of creative and dramatic writing for radio, the sponsor's understandable desire to please, to avoid offense to anyone, and to integrate the tone and content of his program with his sales appeal, may exert an especially restrictive influence on artistic self-expression, and on the development of the radio art. Not a few distinguished writers are known to be unwilling to accept sponsorship because of restraints and stereotypes imposed which reflect the commercial as against the artistic preoccupations of the sponsor. *Variety* comments on this situation in its issue of June 20, 1945:

Radio script writers are turning in increasing numbers to the legit field. . . . What is particularly significant, however, is the motive behind the wholesale transfer of allegiance of the scripters from radio to Broadway. For some time the feeling has been mounting among many of the serious writers for radio that they've been retarded by a lack of freedom of expression . . . and that as long as radio remains more or less of a "duplicating machine" without encouraging creative expression and without establishing an identity of its own, it's inevitable that the guy who has something to say will seek other outlets.

Norman Rosten, himself a writer of commercial programs and winner of a grant from the American Academy of Arts and Letters for his radio writing, has stated the point of view of some radio writers in part as follows:

The sponsor and the advertising agency have taken over radio quietly in this matter of writing. Except for sustaining shows (often worthy, such as "Assignment Home") or special public service programs magnanimously aired after 11:30 p.m., the broadcasting company sells Time. It owns the air. It will sell you a piece. Period.

By "non-commercial radio" I do not mean simply any sustaining series. I mean a non-format show, an experimental show, one which does not have limitations of content or form. Something like the old Columbia Workshop. I mean a half hour each week on each network for a program of original radio plays. With or without love in a cottage. In poetry or prose. Any way we please. No commercial and no strings. All we want is a piece of wavelength and your good auspices. Not a seasonal replacement, but an all-year-round proposition. The present hit-or-miss, one-shot system is a phony. Nor does a new "Thirteen by Corwin" mean the millennium. Mr. Corwin's triumph has not saved his fellow-writers. How about a "Thirteen by Thirteen?" or "Twenty-six by Twenty-six?" The writers are here and some good ones. How about setting the Saga of Lux or the creaking door aside one half hour per week per network? It might well usher in a renaissance in radio drama. How about it NBC, CBS, American and Mutual? Put up or, as the saying quaintly goes, shut up. Prove it, or forever hold your pronouncements about radio coming of age. We are nearing the middle of the 20th century. Shall the singing commercial and the Lone Ranger inherit the earth?

There is no reason to believe that the present boundaries of program service are the ultimate boundaries. If broadcasting is to explore new fields, to devise new types of programs for the American listener, it is clear that the sustaining program must continue as a means by which experimentation and innovation may have the fullest scope, undeterred by the need for immediate financial success or the imposition on writers of restraints deriving from the natural, but limiting, preoccupations of the advertiser.

It is especially important that some sustaining programs be reserved from commercial restraints in view of the degree of concentration of control currently existing among advertisers and advertising agencies. In 1944, for example:

20% of CBS business came from 4 advertisers.
38% of CBS business was handled by 4 advertising agencies.
25% of ABC (Blue Network) business came from 4 advertisers.
37% of ABC (Blue Network) business was handled by 4 advertising agencies.
23% of MBS business came from 4 advertisers.
31% of MBS business was handled by 4 advertising agencies.[11]

One advertiser, Procter & Gamble, is reputed to have spent $22,000,000 on radio advertising in 1944. It purchased approximately 2,000 hours a week of station time — equivalent to the entire weekly time, from sign-on to sign-off, of more than 18 broadcast stations. Procter & Gamble, of course, produces many of its own shows through its own advertising agencies and has control over all its shows. This control is exercised, naturally enough, for the purpose of selling soap. It may incidentally have profound effects on the manners, mores, and opinions of the millions who listen. That is an inevitable feature of the American system of broadcasting; but it is not inevitable that only programs so produced and so controlled shall reach the ear of American listeners. The sustaining program is the necessary makeweight.

(6)   Statistics of sustaining programs

But while networks and stations alike have traditionally recognized the importance of the sustaining program as an integral part of the American system

---

[11] *Broadcasting Yearbook*, 1945, pp. 30, 32. Comparable data for NBC not available.

of broadcasting, there is evidence to suggest that such programs are disappearing from the program service of some stations, especially during the best listening hours.

No accurate statistical series has yet been established to determine the proportion of time devoted to sustaining programs, or the trends from year to year. In the most recent annual reports of stations and networks to the Commission, however, station licensees have analyzed their program structure for the month of January 1945. Since no definition of "sustaining" has heretofore been promulgated, these figures must be approached with caution. Some stations, for example, classify a 15-minute "participating" program as sustaining, even though it is interrupted by three, four, or five spot announcements. Some "bonus" stations which carry network programs without direct remuneration from the network classify all their network commercial programs as "sustaining." The returns to the Commission are in some cases carelessly prepared; some stations, for example, report more than 5 hours of programs daily between 6 and 11 p.m. Some of the returns are wholly unusable. Nevertheless, the returns of 703 stations for the month of January 1945 appeared sufficiently complete to warrant tabulation.

These 703 stations were on the air an average of 16 hours and 5 minutes daily. Of this time, they reported 8 hours and 40 minutes, or 53.9 percent, as commercial, and the remaining 7 hours and 25 minutes, or 46.1 percent, as sustaining.

These overall figures suggest that the sustaining program remains a major part of broadcasting today. On closer analysis, however, certain questions arise.

First, it should be noted that in general, the larger stations carried a considerably smaller percentage of sustaining programs than the smaller stations, as shown on the following table:

AVERAGE HOURS PER DAY AND PERCENTAGE OF TIME ON
THE AIR DEVOTED TO COMMERCIAL AND SUSTAINING
PROGRAMS BY CLASS OF STATION
FOR MONTH OF JANUARY, 1945

	Commercial		Sustaining	
	Hours per day	% of time on air	Hours per day	% of time on air
50 kw stations (41)	12:50	67.3	6:14	32.7
500 w–50 kw stations (214)	10:41	61.3	6:45	38.7
250 w or less stations (376)	7:37	47.6	8:23	52.4
Part time stations (72)	5:46	53.3	5:30	46.7
All stations (703)	8:40	53.9	7:25	46.1

Source: Annual Financial Reports, 1944.

Second, the proportion of time devoted to sustaining programs during the best listening hours from 6 to 11 p.m. was lower than during other hours:

AVERAGE HOURS AND PERCENTAGE OF TIME ON THE AIR, 6 TO 11 P.M., DEVOTED TO COMMERCIAL AND SUSTAINING PROGRAMS BY CLASS OF STATION FOR MONTH OF JANUARY, 1945

	Commercial		Sustaining	
	Hours per day	% of time on air	Hours per day	% of time on air
6 P.M. to 11 P.M. only				
50 kw stations (41)	4:16	84.7	:46	15.3
500 w—50 kw stations (214)	3:38	72.9	1:21	27.1
250 w or less stations (376)	2:38	53.9	2:16	46.1
Part time stations (72)	:46	60.5	:31	39.5
All stations (703)	2:51	62.4	1:43	37.6

Source: Annual Financial Reports, 1944.

The above statistics are, of course, averages, and hence do not illustrate the paucity of sustaining programs on particular stations. The four following charts* show in black the commercial programs, and in white the sustaining programs, of Stations WLW, WBAL, WCAU, and WSIX for a random week. Especially noteworthy is the tendency to crowd sustaining programs into the Saturday afternoon and Sunday morning segments, and to crowd them out of the best listening hours from 6 to 11 p.m.

The following eight charts† similarly illustrate the paucity of sustaining programs during the best listening hours on the stations designated as "basic affiliates" by the four major networks. . . . It will be noted that on Sunday, April 23, 1944, the following stations carried no sustaining programs whatever between the hours of 6 and 11 p.m.:

WHO	WIRE	WCED	WXYZ
WSYR	WTMJ	KOIL	WING
WSPD	WDEL	KMBC	WMAL
WAVE	WHT	WCKY	WEMP

Similarly on Monday, April 24, 1944, the following stations carried no sustaining programs whatever between the hours of 6 and 11 p.m.:

WAGE	WSAI	WFBL	WSPD
WAKR	WNBH	WTOP	WBAL
WXYZ	WEMP	WTAG	WAVE
WING	WTOL	WBBM	WIRE
WENR—WLS	WABC	WADC	WTMJ
WISH	WJR	WMT	WOW
		WHAS	WMAQ

*The four charts are omitted. [Ed.]
†The eight charts are omitted. [Ed.]

(7)   Statistics of network sustaining programs

More striking even than the dearth on some stations and during some hours of sustaining programs generally, is the dearth of *network* sustaining programs.

The five-fold function of sustaining programs, earlier outlined, has particular significance as it applies to network sustaining programs. These are unique in character. They command resources of talent, of writers, actors, producers, beyond the capacity of all or at least most local stations to offer. They cover many issues and subjects, treatment of which can best be given in the great metropolitan centers where network headquarters are situated. Even more important, the network sustaining program is the primary channel through which a nation-wide audience can be reached for treatment of the subjects earlier referred to as the peculiar province of sustaining programs. It is the very essence of network service that it should reach a nation-wide audience. Any factor intervening to prevent this militates against the principle of network operations.

The failure of American broadcasters to provide nation-wide distribution for even outstanding network sustaining programs can be illustrated by a few examples.

The Columbia Broadcasting System describes "Invitation to Learning" in these terms:

Distinguished scholars, authors, and critics meet informally on this series to discuss the outstanding classics of literature. The summer and fall schedules include a series of 31 great books to bring the total number discussed on the program to 285.

On Sunday, April 2, 1944, the most recent date for which data are available, 39 CBS stations carried this program, while 97 rejected it.

"Transatlantic Call: People to People" is described by CBS as follows:

On alternate Sundays the British Broadcasting Corporation and the Columbia Broadcasting System shake hands across the ocean. In this half-hour program, British and American audiences are presented with a picture of the national characteristics and attitudes of the two countries. The audiences of the two nations learn the reasons for the apparent differences between them, at the same time realizing the basic similarity of their attitudes and behavior.

This program was carried on Sunday, April 2, 1944, by 50 CBS stations and rejected by 86.

"Columbia's Country Journal" is described by CBS as follows:

The farmer's role in war time, his "food for victory" campaign, and his daily problems form the weekly theme of Charles ("Chuck") Worcester's "radio farm magazine." Originating in Washington for national farm news, it frequently switches to various farm regions of the country highlighting local problems. Occasional reports from abroad and native folk music are regular features.

On April 8, 1944, this program was carried by 53 and rejected by 83 CBS affiliates.

"Words at War" is described by NBC as follows:

WORDS AT WAR, a weekly series of dramatizations of current books relating to the war, is presented by NBC in cooperation with the Council on Books in Wartime. This series served as the summer replacement for "Fibber McGee and Molly," and four times in eight months was cited by the Writers' War Board for its programs. Among the outstanding books dramatized on "Words at War" were "Der Fuehrer," by Konrad Heiden; "The Veteran Comes Back," by Dr. William Waller; "Assignment U.S.A.," by Seldon Menefee; "War Crimes and Punishment," by George Creel; . . .

This program was carried on Tuesday, May 2, 1944, the last date for which data are available, by 52 NBC stations and rejected by 61. It was broadcast over the network at 11:30 p.m., E.W.T., when listeners are comparatively few, and has since been discontinued altogether.

"The NBC Inter-American University of the Air" is described by NBC as:

presenting an integrated schedule of programs of high educational and cultural value . . . Its 1943 schedule included Lands of the Free, Music of the New World, For This We Fight, The Editors Speak, and Music at War — each a series of stimulating programs that proved the worth of radio as an educational medium. Programs of the NBC University of the Air are now "assigned listening" in more than 100 colleges and universities throughout the United States. School teachers taking the "in-service" training courses of the Board of Education of the City of New York receive credits and promotion based upon their study of Lands of the Free and Music of the New World.

The only two programs of the Inter-American University of the Air noted during the week beginning Sunday, April 30, 1944, were "Lands of the Free," broadcast from 4:30 to 4:55 p.m. on Sunday, April 30, and "Music of the New World," broadcast from 11:30 to midnight on Thursday, May 4. *"Lands of the Free" was carried by 24 NBC stations and refused by 114; "Music of the New World" was carried by 66 and refused by 60.*[12]

The NBC labor program was described by the network as follows:

[12] One station broadcast only the second half of "Music of the New World." For the first half it substituted a participating program of spot announcements interspersed with transcribed music.

Labor for Victory brought authoritative speakers to discuss labor's role in the war effort, in programs produced by the American Federation of Labor alternating with the Congress of Industrial Organizations.

This program was carried on Sunday, April 30, 1944 by 35 NBC stations and rejected by 104.

"The Reviewing Stand" is an MBS program described by the network as follows:

Roundtable discussion of current problems under auspices of Northwestern University.

It was made available by MBS on Sunday, April 23, 1944 to its full network of 216 stations. Of these, only 40 MBS affiliates carried it.

"Halls of Montezuma," a Marine Corps series from the U.S. Marine Corps base at San Diego, featured the "Sea Soldiers' Chorus" and the "Marine Symphony Orchestra." *It was carried by 50 of the 215 MBS affiliates to which it was made available on Wednesday, April 26, 1944.*

"Mutual's Radio Chapel," a sustaining religious program, was made available to all MBS affiliates. *On Sunday, April 23, 1944, thirteen MBS stations carried it.*

No comparable figures were available from the Blue Network (now the American Broadcasting Company). The extent to which network sustaining programs have been neglected is well illustrated by this failure of the Blue Network even to determine whether or not its sustaining programs were being carried. It is difficult to see how a network can maintain a well-balanced program structure or can determine which of its network sustaining programs to continue and which to replace, if it has not even determined the extent to which such programs are being carried by its affiliates.

The eight charts . . . show the rarity of network sustaining programs from 6 to 11 p.m. on the "basic affiliate" stations of the four major networks. Network sustaining programs are shown by a white "S" superimposed on a black square. It will be noted that the following "basic affiliates" carried no network sustaining programs whatever from 6 to 11 p.m. on Sunday, April 23, 1944:

WXYZ	WTOL	WPRO	WLW
WING	WMT	WJR	WAVE
WHDH	WGAR	WBBM	WCSH
WMAL	WCED	WKRC	WHAM
WISH	KOIL	WIBC	WIRE
WTCN	KMBC	WHO	WTMJ
WCOL	WKBW	WSYR	WDEL
WEMP	WCKY	WSPD	WTIC

Similarly, the following "basic affiliates" carried no network sustaining programs whatever on Monday, April 24, 1944 from 6 to 11 p.m.:

WELI	WISH	WCED	WCKY	WBZA
WAGE	WFIL	WDRC	KMOX	WTIC
WWVA	WEBR	WCAU	WGAR	WDEL
WAKR	WOWO	WPRO	WMT	WRC
WJW	WSAI	WFBL	WHAS	WWJ
WXYZ	WNBH	WTOP	WFBM	WLW
WING	WEMP	WTAG	KDKA	WAVE
WENR–WLS	WTOL	WJAS	KYW	WIRE
KCMO	WABC	KRNT	WSPD	WTMJ
WHDH	WEEI	WBBM	WBAL	KSTP
WMAL	WJR	KMBC	WHAM	WOW
		WADC	WBZ	WMAQ

The paucity of network sustaining programs . . . results from two factors: first, the failure of the networks to supply sustaining programs in quantity during the best listening hours and second, the failure of some stations to carry even those network sustaining programs which are offered.

The mere fact that a station does not carry an outstanding network sustaining program does not mean, of course, that it has sacrificed public interest for private gain. In any particular case, the decision to cancel a network sustaining program may be a wise one, reached on the basis of the availability of a local program of still greater public interest. To determine whether this is the case, it is necessary to compare the network sustaining program rejected with the program scheduled in its stead, and to view the network sustaining program as part of a particular station's schedule.

An example of this technique may be supplied with respect to Station WCAU. This is a 50,000-watt station, occupying an entire clear channel by itself. Station WCAU is affiliated with the Columbia Broadcasting System and is owned by the group which also controls CBS. Hence WCAU might be expected to make available to its listeners at least the outstanding CBS sustaining programs. Indeed, one of the grounds relied on by the Federal Radio Commission when awarding a clear channel to Station WCAU as against competing applicants for such assignments was that WCAU would carry the programs of the Columbia Broadcasting System. (F.R.C. Docket No. 880, decided November 17, 1931.)

Of the 3,165 minutes of network sustaining programs made available to Station WCAU by CBS during the week beginning February 8, 1945, Station WCAU broadcast 1,285 minutes, or 40.6%. From 6 p.m. to 11 p.m. throughout the week, however, Station WCAU broadcast only 55 minutes of network sustaining programs, or 20.8% of the network sustaining programs available to it during this time. On Mondays, Wednesdays, and Thursdays, WCAU broadcast no network sustaining programs whatever from 9:45 a.m. to 11 p.m. The full schedule of network sustaining programs carried by Station WCAU was as follows:

	8 a.m.– 1 p.m.	1 p.m.– 6 p.m.	6 p.m.– 11 p.m.	11 p.m.– 1:02 a.m.	Total
Sunday	180	30	none	95	305
Monday	45	none	none	65	110
Tuesday	45	none	30	65	140
Wednesday	45	none	none	65	110
Thursday	45	none	none	100	145
Friday	45	none	15	65	125
Saturday	45	200	10	95	350
Total	450	230	55	550	1,285

More than 63% of all network sustaining programs carried by WCAU between the hours of 8 a.m. and 11 p.m. were on Saturday and Sunday. Network sustaining programs from 8 a.m. to 11 p.m., by days, were broadcast as follows:

Sunday	210 minutes
Monday	45 minutes
Tuesday	75 minutes
Wednesday	45 minutes
Thursday	45 minutes
Friday	60 minutes
Saturday	255 minutes
Total	735 minutes

Among the CBS sustaining programs not carried by WCAU, and the WCAU programs substituted therefor, were the following:

SOME NETWORK SUSTAINING PROGRAMS AVAILABLE TO BUT REFUSED BY STATION WCAU

Name of CBS Sustaining Program	Description[13]	WCAU Program Substituted
FEATURE STORY 4:30–4:45 p.m. Monday through Friday	"Members of CBS' world-wide staff of news correspondents bring to the microphone the many human interest stories that lie under the surface of the latest military and political events and usually miss being told."	"Rhona Lloyd," local talk sponsored by Aristocrat.

[13] Quoted from "CBS Program Book – Winter, 1945."

Name of CBS Sustaining Program	Description	WCAU Program Substituted
TRANS-ATLANTIC CALL: PEOPLE TO PEOPLE 12:30–1 p.m. Sunday	"On alternate Sundays, the British Broadcasting Corporation and the Columbia Broadcasting System shake hands across the ocean. In this half hour program, British and American audiences are presented with a picture of the national characteristics and attitudes of the two countries. The audiences of the two nations learn the reasons for the apparent differences between them, at the same time realizing the basic similarity in their attitudes and behavior."	"Ranger Joe," transcribed music sponsored by Ranger Joe, Inc.; "Perry Coll," music sponsored by Western Savings Fund.
CALLING PAN-AMERICA 6:15–6:45 p.m. Thursday	"CBS draws the Americas closer together with this weekly program shortwaved from Latin-American capitals. The series 'calls' a different nation to the microphone each Saturday, and presents a vivid radio picture of its life, culture and music."	"Ask Washington," commercial talk sponsored by Hollingshead, 15 minutes; transcribed commercial spot announcement for movie, "National Velvet," sponsored by Metro-Goldwyn-Mayer; phonograph records, "Songs of the Stars" sponsored by Breitenbach, 15 minutes.
SERVICE TIME 5:00–5:30 p.m. Monday through Friday	"Presented in cooperation with the fighting forces, this program devotes itself to the branches of the armed service, spotlighting the activities of a different branch each day. Various service bands and glee clubs are featured, and high ranking officials make	"Monday – Phonograph records interspersed with spot announcements for Household Finance Company (5:03:30–5:04: 30); Panther Panco Bilt Rite (5:07:30–5:08:30); National Biscuit Premium Crackers (5:11:40–5:12: 40); Cuticura-Potter Chemical Company (5:16:00–

Name of CBS Sustaining Program	Description	WCAU Program Substituted
	personal appearances. There are also interviews with personnel returned from combat zones." Monday — Waves on Parade. Tuesday — It's Maritime. Wednesday — Wacs on Parade. Thursday — Marines in the Making. Friday — First in The Air.	5:17:00); Glenwood Range (5:19:50–5:20:50); Civil Service (Sustaining) (5:24: 15–5:24:35); and weather report (5:29:00–5:29:35). *Tuesday through Friday* — similar phonograph records interspersed with similar spot announcements.
SALT LAKE TABER-NACLE CHOIR AND ORGAN 12 noon–12:30 p.m. Sunday	"This is the oldest consecutively presented public-service series in radio, having celebrated its 785th network broadcast on July 30, 1944. The Tabernacle Choir is conducted by J. Spencer Cornwall and Richard P. Condie, assistant. Organists are Alexander Schreiner, Dr. Frank Asper and Wade M. Stephens."	"Children's Hour," sponsored by Horn & Hardart, 11:30–12:20; news comment by Carroll Alcott, sponsored by Horn & Hardart, 12:20–12:30.
SALLY MOORE AND THE COLUMBIA CONCERT ORCHESTRA 6:30–6:45 p.m. Monday and Friday	"The young American contralto, CBS' most recent discovery, presents distinctive song recitals of semi-classical music accompanied by the Columbia Concert Orchestra."	Phonograph records sponsored by Groves Laxative Bromo Quinine.
ENCORE APPEAR-ANCE 6:30–6:45 p.m. Wednesday	"The program offers further opportunity to the new singers who have given outstanding performance on CBS' 'New Voices in Song.' They are accompanied by the Columbia Concert Orchestra."	Phonograph records sponsored by Groves Laxative Bromo Quinine.
WILDERNESS ROAD 5:45–6:00 p.m. Monday through Friday	"A dramatic serial of a pioneering American family that went through the hazardous Cumberland	*Monday* — Music by Eliot Lawrence interspersed with commercial spot announcements for

Name of CBS Sustaining Program	Description	WCAU Program Substituted
	Gap in 1783 with Daniel Boone as their guide. The story recreates that adventure-filled period in American history when every frontier presented a challenge to the New World settlers."	Rinso (5:48:20—5:49:20); Bell Telephone (5:51:15—5:52:15); and Household Finance Company (5:55:40—5:56:40). *Tuesday through Friday —* similar music interspersed with spot announcements.
INVITATION TO LEARNING 11:30—12 noon Sunday	"Distinguished scholars, authors, and critics meet informally on this series to discuss the outstanding classics of literature. The winter schedule includes a new series of 30 great books to bring the total number discussed on the program to 254."	"Children's Hour," local commercial program sponsored by Horn & Hardart.
THE PEOPLE'S PLATFORM 6:15—6:45 p.m. Saturday	"The vital issues of today and the postwar world are analyzed weekly on this program, one of radio's most interesting forums. Four eminent guests and Lyman Bryson, CBS Director of Education, who acts as moderator gather informally for these sessions."	"Listen to Lawrence," local commercial music program sponsored by Sun Ship Company.

A special case of failure to carry a network sustaining program is to be noted on Sunday from 2:55 to 3:00 p.m. Beginning at 3 p.m., Station WCAU carries the New York Philharmonic program sponsored by U.S. Rubber. This program is preceded over CBS by a 5-minute introductory talk by Olin Downes, the well-known music critic, on a sustaining basis. WCAU carried the symphony for which it is paid, but rejected the sustaining introduction to the symphony in favor of a five-minute commercial program, "Norman Jay Postscript," sponsored by the Yellow Cab Company.

For a similar analysis of network sustaining programs not carried by Station WBAL, an NBC affiliate, see pp. 166-167.

It has been urged that the network sustaining program is doomed by reason of the fact that a network affiliate can carry local programs only during network sustaining periods, and that station owners quite properly reject network sustaining programs in order to leave some time available for local programs of great public interest. Station owners, on this view, should be praised for eliminating network sustaining programs from their schedules, since in this way they make possible local service to their own communities.

Prior to the enactment of Regulation 3.104, when many stations had all or substantially all of their time under option to the networks, this viewpoint had some cogency. Chain broadcasting Regulation 3.104, however, allows each station freedom to reject network *commercial* programs for two hours out of each five. Thus the individual station licensee's choice is not between broadcasting local live programs during network sustaining hours and not broadcasting them at all. On the contrary, a licensee is free to present during each segment of the broadcast day a well-balanced schedule of network and local, commercial and sustaining programs alike (except to the extent that the network fails to deliver a reasonable proportion of network sustaining programs). The choice is not between network sustaining programs and local programs; rather it is between a balanced program structure and one which lacks such balance.

In recent months, the Commission before renewing the license of a broadcast station has compared the percentage of commercial programs actually broadcast during a sample week with the percentage which the station stated that it would broadcast in its original application. Where a serious discrepancy was noted, and where the proportion of sustaining programs appeared to be so low as to raise a question concerning the station's operation in the public interest, the station's comments were requested. The replies received indicate several widespread misconceptions concerning the basis of Commission policy respecting commercial and sustaining programs.

First, many station licensees stated that they saw no differences between a commercial and a sustaining program, and a few even stated their belief that a station could operate in the public interest with no sustaining programs. (The need for sustaining programs as a balance-wheel to make possible a well-balanced program structure, as a means of broadcasting programs inappropriate for commercial sponsorship, as a service for significant minority tastes and interests, as a service to non-profit organizations, and as a vehicle for program experimentation has been set forth on pp. 174-186.)

Second, a number of stations pointed out that many of their commercial programs were clearly in the public interest. The Commission is in full accord with this view. The fact that some advertisers are broadcasting programs which serve an important public interest, however, does not relieve a station of its responsibility in the public interest. Broadcast licensees properly consider their status to be very different from the status of a common carrier, merely providing physical facilities for the carrying of matter paid for and produced by others. Broadcasters rightly insist that their function in the community and the nation is of a higher order. The maintenance of this independent status and significance, however, is inconsistent with the abnegation of independent responsibility, whether to a network or to advertisers. The conceded merit of many or most programs broadcast during periods which a broadcaster has sold to others does not relieve him of the responsibility for broadcasting his own programs during periods which he has reserved from sponsorship for public service.

Third, a few licensees have alleged that they are unable to estimate the amount of time which they will devote to sustaining programs hereafter because they cannot predict how much demand for time there will be from commercial advertisers. Such licensees have obviously abdicated to advertisers the control over their stations. The requirement of a well-balanced program structure, firmly founded in the public interest provisions of the Communications Act, is a responsibility of the station licensee. To permit advertisers to dictate either the proportion of time which the station shall devote to sustaining programs or any other major policy decision is inconsistent with the basic principles of licensee responsibility on which American broadcasting has always rested.

In their replies, many licensees have pointed out that a comparison of promise and performance with respect to sustaining programs and other categories is difficult or impossible without uniform definitions of what constitutes a commercial program, a sustaining program, etc. To meet this difficulty, the Commission is promulgating herewith uniform definitions of various program categories. (See "Uniform Definitions and Program Logs.")

B.   The carrying of local live programs

All or substantially all programs currently broadcast are of four kinds: (1) network programs, including programs furnished to a station by telephone circuit from another station; (2) recorded (including transcribed) programs; (3) wire programs (chiefly wire news, syndicated to many stations by telegraph or teletype and read off the wire by a local announcer); and (4) local live programs, including remote broadcasts. For definitions of these four main classes, see "Uniform Definitions and Program Logs."

Network programs.   The merit of network programs is universally recognized; indeed, the Commission's Chain Broadcasting Regulations 3.101 and 3.102 were designed in considerable part to insure a freer flow of network programs to the listener. In January 1945, approximately 47.9% of all the time of standard broadcast stations was devoted to network programs.

Transcriptions.   The transcribed or recorded program has not had similar recognition. As early as 1922, the Department of Commerce by regulation prohibited the playing of phonograph records by stations having the better (Class B) channel assignments except in emergencies or to fill in between program periods; and later in the year it amended the regulation to prohibit even such use of records by Class B stations. Through the years the phonograph record, and to a lesser extent the transcription, have been considered inferior program sources.

No good reason appears, however, for not recognizing today the significant role which the transcription and the record, like the network, can play in radio programming. Five particular advantages may be cited:

(a)   Transcriptions are a means of disposing of radio's most ironic anomaly — the dissipation during a single broadcast, in most cases for all time, of all the skill and labor of writer, director, producer, and cast. Transcriptions make possible the compilation of a permanent archive of the best in radio, comparable in other types of programs to the recorded symphony or chamber music. Good programs with timeless interest can thus be repeated not once but many times.

(b)   Transcriptions make possible the placing of programs at convenient hours. For example, a network broadcast may either be inconvenient in time for listeners in a given time zone or may conflict with a station's commitment to its locality. By transcribing the program at the station as it comes in on the network line, the program can be made available at another and still convenient hour.[1]

(c)   Transcriptions make possible the sharing of programs among stations not directly connected by wire lines. Several New York stations, for example, are currently making their outstanding programs available via transcription to stations throughout the country. Similarly, non-radio organizations can produce and distribute programs via transcription, as in the case of the award-winning children's transcription series of the Junior League.

(d)   Transcriptions offer to the writer, director, and producer of programs the same technical advantages that the moving picture industry achieves through cutting-room techniques. Imperfections can be smoothed out; material recorded at different times and places can be blended into a single program, etc. While the basic advantages of this more plastic technique may not yet be fully utilized, recent developments in the transcription field, including those pioneered by the armed forces and the introduction of wire recorders, suggest a significant role for such programs in the future.

(e)   Portable recorders make it possible to present to the listener the event as it occurs rather than a subsequent re-creation of it. The recording of actual press conferences, for example, and the actual battlefront recordings by the Marine Corps and Army Signal Corps point the way to an expansion of recording techniques as a means of radio reporting.

In January, 1945, approximately 32.3% of all the time of standard broadcast stations was devoted to transcriptions and recordings.

Wire Programs.   The wire service, by which spot news and sometimes also other program texts are telegraphically distributed to stations, has in recent

---

[1] Conversely, however, some stations appear to use the transcription technique for shifting an outstanding network public service program from a good hour to an off hour when listeners are few and commercial programs not available.

years assumed a role of increasing importance.[2] By means of wire service for news and other texts of a timely nature, plus transcriptions for programs of less urgent timeliness, the unaffiliated station can very nearly achieve the breadth of service attained through network affiliation No statistics are currently available concerning the proportion of time devoted to wire service programs.

Local Live Programs.   There remains for discussion the local live program, for which also, no precise statistics are available. It is known, however, that in January, 1945, approximately 19.7% of all the time of standard broadcast stations was devoted to local live *and* wire service programs; and that during the best listening hours from 6 to 11 p.m., approximately 15.7% of all the time was devoted to these two classes of programs combined.

In granting and renewing licenses, the Commission has given repeated and explicit recognition to the need for adequate reflection in programs of local interests, activities and talent. Assurances by the applicant that "local talent will be available"; that there will be "a reasonable portion of time for programs which include religious, educational, and civic matters"; that "time will be devoted to local news at frequent intervals, to market reports, agricultural topics and to various civic and political activities that occur in the city" have contributed to favorable decision on many applications. As the Commission noted in its *Supplemental Report on Chain Broadcasting* (1941):

It has been the consistent intention of the Commission to assure that an adequate amount of time *during the good listening hours* shall be made available to meet the needs of the community in terms of public expression and of local interest. If these regulations do not accomplish this objective, the subject will be given further consideration. (Emphasis supplied.)

The networks themselves have recognized the importance of local live programs. Under date of October 9, 1944, the National Broadcasting Company, when requesting the Commission to amend Chain Broadcasting Regulation 3.104, stated:

Over the years our affiliated stations have been producing highly important local programs in these three open hours of the morning segment. From 8 a.m. to 10 a.m. N.Y.T., most of the stations have developed variety or "morning clock" programs which have met popular acceptance. These periods are not only profitable to the individual station but are sought for use by civic, patriotic and religious groups for special appeals because of their local listening audience appeal. Likewise, from 12 noon to 1 p.m. they have developed highly important farm news programs or other local interest shows. *To interfere with local program schedules of many years' standing would deprive our stations of their full opportunity to render a desirable local public service.* (Emphasis supplied.)

[2] For a proposed definition of "wire" programs, see "Uniform Definitions and Program Logs."

The Commission's reply, released December 20, 1944, as Mimeograph No. 79574, stated in part:

One purpose of Regulation 3.104 was to leave 14 of the 35 evening hours in each week free of network option, *in order to foster the development of local programs.*[3] . . . The Commission . . . concurs fully in your statement that interference with local programs which have met with public acceptance and which are sought for use by local civic, patriotic and religious groups, local church services, and other highly important local program schedules of years' standing is to be avoided. (Emphasis supplied.)

The courts have also supported the position taken by the Commission that the interests of the whole listening public require that provision be made for local program service. Where the record showed that of the two stations already functioning in an area, one carried 50 percent network programs and the other 85 percent, the court stated: "In view of this situation it is not difficult to see why the Commission decided that public interest would be served by the construction of a local non-network station."[4]

But the soundness of a local program policy does not rest solely on the consistent Commission policy of encouraging a reasonable proportion of local programs as part of a well-balanced program service. Three examples will serve to suggest that local programming may also be good business policy and may contribute to the popularity of the station. These examples were noted by Professor C. H. Sandage of the Harvard School of Business Administration, during a survey of radio advertising possibilities for retailers financed by the Columbia Broadcasting System.

(a)   One 250-watt station located in the Middle West had struggled along for 4 years and lost money each year until a reorganization was forced in 1942.

The former management had attempted to compete directly with outside stations whose signals were strong in the local community. Good entertainment was provided, but no attempt was made to establish the station as a local institution interested in the life of the community. Neither local listeners nor local businessmen supported the station.

The new management reversed this policy completely. All attempts at copying outside stations were eliminated. Management not only studied the

---

[3] The failure of Regulation 3.104 to achieve this purpose is illustrated by the eight charts. . . . showing many stations which carried no non-network programs whatever during the evening hours on the two days analyzed.

[4] *Great Western Broadcasting Association* v. *F.C.C.* 94 F. 2d 244, 248. In the KHMO case, the court ordered the Commission to issue a license to an applicant for a local station in an area where three stations were already operating, none of which gave genuine local service. The court expressed approval of the Commission's findings in similar cases, that "under the direct provisions of the statute the *rights of the citizens to enjoy local broadcasting privileges were being denied."* (*Courier Post Broadcasting Co.* v. *F.C.C.*, 104 F. 2d 213, 218) (Emphasis supplied.)

activities peculiar to that community but also took a personal interest in them. Station facilities were made available on a free basis to civic institutions such as the Chamber of Commerce, women's clubs, parent-teacher association, public schools, and Community Chest. School sports contests were broadcast, and other programs of distinctly local interest were developed. In a relatively short time an audience of more than 50 percent of all local radio listeners had been attracted to the station ... At the time the new management came in, gross monthly income was $2,400 and at the end of 12 months this amount has been increased to $6,000. *The new manager attributed all improvement to the policy of making the station a real local institution and a true voice of the community.* [5]

(b)   Amateur shows have been used effectively in developing local talent.

An Illinois retailer has used this type of show for a number of years and has built an audience which in 1942 surpassed in size the audience for any other radio program broadcast at the same time ... It was competing with John Charles Thomas, New York Philharmonic, and the Army Hour. Only the John Charles Thomas program approached the rating for the local program. As in all programs which make use of local talent of fair quality, a considerable audience was attracted because of an interest in local people. [6]

(c)   A feed mill in Missouri developed a quartet called the "Happy Millers" which sang hillbilly and western music.

Public acceptance has been phenomenal, partly *because of the interest of rural people in the type of entertainment afforded but also because the entertainers are all local people and well known in the community.* [7]

These few examples can no doubt be supplemented from their own experience by many alert station managers throughout the country.

While parallels between broadcast stations and newspapers must be approached with caution, their common elements with respect to local interest may be significant. The local newspaper achieves world-wide news coverage through the great press associations, taps the country's foremost writers and cartoonists through the feature syndicates, and from the picture services procures photographs from everywhere in abundant quantity. But the local newspaper editor, faced with such abundant incoming material, does not therefore discharge his local reporters and photographers, nor does he seek to reproduce locally the New York *Times* or *Daily News.* He appreciates the keen interest in local material and makes the most of that material — especially on the front page. The hours from 6 to 11 p.m. are the "front page" of the broadcast station. The statistics of local programming during these hours, or generally, are not impressive.

[5] Sandage, *Radio Advertising for Retailers*, p. 210. (Emphasis supplied.)
[6] *Ibid.*, pp. 166–167.
[7] *Ibid.*, p. 161. (Emphasis supplied.)

Extent of local live program service

No reliable statistics are currently available concerning the time devoted to local live programs, partly because there has heretofore been no accepted definition of "local live," partly because "wire" programs of news syndicated to many stations have been included in the local live classification, and partly because programs of phonograph records have been classified as "local live" by some stations if a live announcer intersperses advertising comments among the records. The paucity of local live, and especially local live sustaining programs, is indicated, however, by the following table which shows the time reported by 703 stations as having been devoted to local live programs in January, 1945. The table can perhaps be best interpreted as showing the time devoted to non-network, non-transcribed programs:

AVERAGE HOURS PER DAY AND PERCENTAGE OF TIME ON
THE AIR DEVOTED TO LOCAL LIVE PROGRAMS BY CLASS OF
STATION FOR MONTH OF JANUARY, 1945

	Commercial		Sustaining	
	Hours per day	% of time on air	Hours per day	% of time on air
50 kw stations (41)	3:02	15.9	1:52	9.8
500 w − 50 kw stations (214)	2:23	13.6	1:11	6.8
250 w or less stations (376)	1:43	10.7	1:00	6.3
Part time stations (72)	2:11	20.3	1:09	10.7
All stations (703)	2:02	12.7	1:07	7.0

Source: Annual Financial Reports, 1944.

From 6 to 11 p.m., moreover, non-network, non-transcribed programs are considerably rarer, amounting on the average to only 42 minutes in five hours for all stations. *Sustaining* programs of this type average only 13 minutes in five hours.

AVERAGE HOURS AND PERCENTAGE OF TIME ON THE AIR,
6–11 P.M., DEVOTED TO LOCAL LIVE PROGRAMS BY CLASS
OF STATION FOR MONTH OF JANUARY, 1945

	Commercial		Sustaining	
	Hours per day	% of time on air	Hours per day	% of time on air
6 p.m. to 11 p.m. only				
50 kw stations (41)	:36	12.0	:12	3.9
500 w − 50 kw stations (214)	:34	11.4	:14	4.7
250 w or less stations (376)	:29	9.8	:15	4.9
Part time stations (72)	:11	15.0	:07	8.7
All stations (703)	:29	10.6	:13	4.9

Source: Annual Financial Reports, 1944.

On particular stations, of course, the picture is even more extreme. The eight charts . . . for example, show in white the time devoted to non-network programs by the "basic affiliates" of the four major networks. It will be noted that on Sunday, April 23, 1944, the following stations carried no non-network programs whatever — and hence no local live programs — during the best listening hours from 6 to 11 p.m.:

WORC	WAGE	WMT	WCAU	KDB	WGY
WFCI	KQV	WDRC	WJAS	WBZ	WTAM
WNBC	WADC	WFBM	WTOP	WBZA	WMAQ
WCBM	WCAO	KFAB	WHBF	WJAR	WOW
WTRY	WEEI	WHAS	KWK	WRC	

In the face of this progressive blackout of non-network programs during the best listening hours on many stations, it has been proposed that some stations be licensed exclusively for non-network broadcasting, and that the Commission regulations prohibit the carrying of network programs by stations so licensed. This proposal appears impracticable. In communities where the number of stations does not exceed the number of networks, the result would be to deprive listeners of regular network service from one or more of the networks. In communities where the number of stations exceeds the number of networks, moreover, the regulation would be of little practical value since in such communities one or more of the stations will remain without a network affiliation in any event. The solution to network monopolization of a station's time, accordingly, must be found in terms of a balance of network and non-network programs, rather than in a distinction between network and non-network stations.

The most immediately profitable way to run a station, may be to procure a network affiliation, plug into the network line in the morning, and broadcast network programs throughout the day — interrupting the network output only to insert commercial spot announcements, and to substitute spot announcements and phonograph records for outstanding network sustaining programs. The record on renewal since April, 1945, of standard broadcast stations shows that some stations are approaching perilously close to this extreme. Indeed, it is difficult to see how some stations can do otherwise with the minimal staffs currently employed in programming.

For every three writers employed by 834 broadcast stations in October, 1944, there were four salesmen employed. For every dollar paid to the average writer, the average salesman was paid $2.39. And in terms of total compensation paid to writers and salesmen, the stations paid $3.30 for salesmen for every $1.00 paid for writers. The comparable relationship for 415 local stations is even more unbalanced.[8]

[8] In the week of October 15, 1944, 834 stations employed 863 writers at an average compensation of $40.14, totalling $34,641; and 1195 salesmen at an average compensation of $95.92, totalling $114,624. The 415 local stations employed 259 writers full time at an average salary of $31.87 but employed 409 salesmen at an average of $68.85.

The average local station employed less than $\frac{1}{3}$ of a full time musician and less than $\frac{1}{6}$ of a full time actor.[9]

Such figures suggest, particularly at the local station level, that few stations are staffed adequately to meet their responsibilities in serving the community. A positive responsibility rests upon local stations to make articulate the voice of the community. Unless time is earmarked for such a purpose, unless talent is positively sought and given at least some degree of expert assistance, radio stations have abdicated their local responsibilities and have become mere common carriers of program material piped in from outside the community.

C. Discussion of public issues

American broadcasters have always recognized that broadcasting is not merely a means of entertainment, but also an unequaled medium for the dissemination of news, information, and opinion, and for the discussion of public issues. Radio's role in broadcasting the election returns of November 1920 is one of which broadcasters are justly proud; and during the quarter of a century which has since elapsed, broadcasting has continued to include news, information, opinion and public discussion in its regular budget of program material.

Especially in recent years, such information programs as news and news commentaries have achieved a popularity exceeding the popularity of any other single type of program. The war, of course, tremendously increased listener interest in such programs; but if broadcasters face the crucial problems of the post-war era with skill, fairness, and courage, there is no reason why broadcasting cannot play as important a role in our democracy hereafter as it has achieved during the war years.

The use of broadcasting as an instrument for the dissemination of news, ideas, and opinions raises a multitude of problems of a complex and sometimes delicate nature, which do not arise in connection with purely entertainment programs. A few such problems may be briefly noted, without any attempt to present an exhaustive list:

(1) Shall time for the presentation of one point of view on a public issue be sold, or shall all such presentations of points of view be on sustaining time only?

(2) If presentations of points of view are to be limited only to sustaining time, what measures can be taken to insure that adequate sustaining time during good listening hours is made available for such presentations, and that such time is equitably distributed?

(3) If time is also on occasion to be sold for presentation of a point of

[9]Many or most stations are financially able to employ far larger program staffs than at present. . . .

view, what precautions are necessary to insure that the most time shall not gravitate to the side prepared to spend the most money?

(4) Are forums, town meetings, and round-table type broadcasts, in which two or more points of view are aired together, intrinsically superior to the separate presentation of points of view at various times?

(5) Should such programs be sponsored?

(6) What measures will insure that such programs be indeed fair and well-balanced among opposing points of view?

(7) Should locally originated discussion programs, in which residents of a community can themselves discuss issues of local, national, or international importance be encouraged, and if so, how?

(8) How can an unbiased presentation of the news be achieved?

(9) Should news be sponsored, and if so, to what extent should the advertiser influence or control the presentation of the news?

(10) How and by whom should commentators be selected?

(11) Should commentators be forbidden, permitted, or encouraged to express their own personal opinions?

(12) Is a denial of free speech involved when a commentator is discharged or his program discontinued because something which he has said has offended (a) the advertiser, (b) the station, (c) a minority of his listeners, or (d) a majority of his listeners?

(13) What provisions, over and above Section 315 of the Communications Act of 1934,[10] are necessary or desirable in connection with the operation of broadcast stations during a political campaign?

(14) Does a station operate in the public interest which charges a higher rate for political broadcasts than for commercial programs?

(15) The Federal Communications Commission is forbidden by law to censor broadcasts. Should station licensees have the absolute right of censorship, or should their review of broadcasts be limited to protection against libel, dissemination of criminal matter, etc.?

(16) Should broadcasters be relieved of responsibility for libel with respect to broadcasts over which they exercise no control?

(17) Should the "right to reply" to broadcasts be afforded; and if so, to whom should the right be afforded, and under what circumstances?

(18) When a station refuses time on the air requested for the discussion of public issues, should it be required to state in writing its reasons for refusal?

---

[10] "Sec. 315. If any licensee shall permit any person who is a legally qualified candidate for any public office to use a broadcasting station, he shall afford equal opportunities to all other such candidates for that office in the use of such broadcasting station, and the Commission shall make rules and regulations to carry this provision into effect: *Provided*, That such licensee shall have no power of censorship over the material broadcast under the provisions of this section. No obligation is hereby imposed upon any licensee to allow the use of its station by any such candidate."

Should it be required to maintain a record of all such requests for time, and of the disposal made of them?

(19)   What measures can be taken to open broadcasting to types of informational programs which contravene the interests of large advertisers — for example, news of the reports and decisions of the Federal Trade Commission concerning unfair advertising; reports of the American Medical Association concerning the effects of cigarette-smoking; temperance broadcasts; etc?

These are only a few of the many questions which are raised in complaints to the Commission from day to day. The future of American broadcasting as an instrument of democracy depends in no small part upon the establishment of sound solutions to such problems, and on the fair and impartial application of general solutions to particular cases.

Under the Communications Act, primary responsibility for solving these and similar issues rests upon the licensees of broadcast stations themselves. Probably no other type of problem in the entire broadcasting industry is as important, or requires of the broadcaster a greater sense of objectivity, responsibility, and fair play.

While primary responsibility in such matters rests with the individual broadcaster, the Commission is required by the statute to review periodically the station's operation, in order to determine whether the station has in fact been operated in the public interest. Certainly, the establishment of sound station policy with respect to news, information, and the discussion of public issues is a major factor in operation in the public interest.

The Commission has never laid down, and does not now propose to lay down, any categorical answers to such questions as those raised above. Rather than enunciating general policies, the Commission reaches decisions on such matters in the crucible of particular cases.[11]

One matter of primary concern, however, can be met by an over-all statement of policy, and must be met as part of the general problem of overall program balance. This is the question of the *quantity* of time which should be made available for the discussion of public issues.

The problems involved in making time available for the discussion of public issues are admittedly complex. Any vigorous presentation of a point of view will of necessity annoy or offend at least some listeners. There may be a temptation, accordingly, for broadcasters to avoid as much as possible any discussion over their stations, and to limit their broadcasts to entertainment programs which offend no one.

To operate in this manner, obviously, is to thwart the effectiveness of broadcasting in a democracy.

---

[11] See, for example, the *Mayflower* case, 8 F.C.C. 333, and *United Broadcasting Company (WHKC)* case, decided June 26, 1945.

A test case may illustrate the problem here raised. At the request of the Senate Committee on Interstate Commerce, the Commission undertook a study of all network and local programs broadcast from January 1, 1941 through May 31, 1941, relative to the foreign policy issue then before the country, that of isolationism versus intervention in the world conflict. The period reviewed was one of great crisis. The issue at stake would affect the history and even the survival of our country and its institutions. Five major questions of foreign policy were involved — lend-lease, the convoying of ships to Britain, the acquisition of foreign bases, the acquisition of foreign ships, and the maintenance of the British blockade. From this study the following facts emerged.

The four major networks submitted 532 programs. Upon analysis only 203 scripts were deemed relevant; 14 scripts were unobtainable.

Assuming all 14 of these scripts to have been relevant, this means that 217 scripts during a 5-month period dealt with the 5 major issues of foreign policy listed above. Put another way, each network broadcast a program devoted to one or more of these issues every third day.

But while the networks made these programs available, not all affiliated stations carried them. Of 120 CBS affiliates, 59.3% carried the average lend-lease program. Of 165 MBS affiliates, 45.5% carried it. Of the approximately 200 NBC stations on both Red and Blue networks of NBC, 69 stations carried the average NBC program on lend-lease.

Even more significant are the figures relating to non-network programs. Of 742 stations reporting, only 288 claimed to have originated even one program on any subject relevant to this study. The remaining 454 denied having broadcast a single non-network program on foreign policy during the entire 5-month period. While subject to possible sampling error, the study indicates that station time devoted to discussion programs distributed by the four networks exceeded station time devoted to discussion programs originated by the stations in the ratio of 30 to 1.

The carrying of any particular public discussion, of course, is a problem for the individual broadcaster. But the public interest clearly requires that an adequate amount of time be made available for the discussion of public issues; and the Commission, in determining whether a station has served the public interest, will take into consideration the amount of time which has been or will be devoted to the discussion of public issues.

D.   Advertising excesses

(1)   Value of advertising

Advertising represents the only source of revenue for most American broadcasting stations, and is therefore an indispensable part of our system of broadcasting. In return for spending some 397 million dollars per year[1] on American broadcasting, the advertiser can expect that his name and wares will be effectively made known to the public.

Advertising in general, moreover, and radio advertising in particular, plays an essential role in the distribution of goods and services within our economy. During the postwar era if manufacturers are to dispose of the tremendous output of which our postwar industry will be capable, they must keep their products before the public.

Finally, informative advertising which gives reliable factual data concerning available goods and services is itself of direct benefit to the listener in his role as consumer. Consumer knowledge of the new and improved products which contribute to a higher standard of living is one of the steps toward achieving that higher standard of living.

However, the fact that advertisers have a legitimate interest and place in the American system of broadcasting does not mean that broadcasting should be run solely in the interest of the advertisers rather than that of the listeners. Throughout the history of broadcasting, a limitation on the amount and character of advertising has been one element of "public interest." A brief review will illustrate this point.

(2)   Historic background

Commercial broadcasting began in 1920 or 1921, and by 1922 the dangers of excessive advertising had already been noted. Thus at the First Annual Radio Conference in 1922, Secretary of Commerce Herbert Hoover declared:

It is inconceivable that we should allow so great a possibility for service, for news, for entertainment, for education and for vital commercial purposes to be drowned in advertising chatter. . . .

The Conference itself took heed of Secretary Hoover's warning and recommended:

. . . that direct advertising in radio broadcasting service be absolutely prohibited and that indirect advertising be limited to the announcements of the call letters of the station and of the name of the concern responsible for the matter broadcasted, subject to such regulations as the Secretary of Commerce may impose.

In 1927, following the passage of the Radio Act, advertising abuses were among the first topics to engage the attention of the newly established Federal

---

[1] See p. . . . [This footnote refers to a table, omitted here, comparing annual expenditures for broadcast advertising and listeners' costs for receiver acquisition, operation, and maintenance. – Ed.]

Radio Commission. Thus, in its first formal statement of the "broad underlying principles which . . . must control its decisions on controversies arising between stations in their competition for favorable assignments," one of the "broad underlying principles" set forth was that "the amount and character of advertising must be rigidly confined within the limits consistent with the public service expected of the station." To quote further:

. . . The Commission must . . . recognize that without advertising, broadcasting would not exist, and *must confine itself to limiting this advertisement in amount and in character* so as to preserve the largest possible amount of service to the public. Advertising must be accepted for the present as the sole means of support of broadcasting, and *regulation must be relied upon to prevent the abuse and over use of the privilege.*[2] (Emphasis supplied.)

This general principle was applied in particular cases, especially in connection with actions on renewal of station licenses. Thus in announcing, on August 23, 1928, its decision not to renew the license of Station WCRW, the Commission stated:

It is clear that a large part of the program is distinctly commercial in character, consisting of advertisers' announcements and of direct advertising, including the quoting of prices. An attempt was made to show a very limited amount of educational and community civic service, but the amount of time thus employed is negligible and evidence of its value to the community is not convincing. Manifestly this station is one which exists chiefly for the purpose of deriving an income from the sale of advertising of a character which must be objectionable to the listening public and without making much, if any, endeavor to render any real service to the public.

The station's license was not renewed.

It was urged in some quarters, then as now, that the Commission need not concern itself with program service because whenever the public found a broadcast irksome, listeners would shift to other stations and the situation would thus automatically correct itself. The Federal Radio Commission, in announcing on August 29, 1928 its decision to place Stations WRAK, WABF, WBRE, and WMBS "on probation" by renewing their license for 30 days only, rather than for the customary 90 days, gave short shrift to this argument. It stated:

Listeners are given no protection unless it is given to them by this Commission, for they are powerless to prevent the ether waves carrying the unwelcome messages from entering the walls of their homes. Their only alternative, which is not to tune in on the station, is not satisfactory, particularly when in a city such as Erie only the local stations can be received during a large

[2] *In re Great Lakes Broadcasting Co.*, F.R.C. Docket No. 4900.

part of the year. When a station is misused for such a private purpose the entire listening public is deprived of the use of a station for a service in the public interest.

Despite the Federal Radio Commission's concern with excessive advertising, there is reason to believe that substantial Congressional sentiment considered the Commission too lax in the exercise of its functions with respect to advertising. Thus on January 12, 1932, the Senate passed Senate Resolution 129, introduced by Senator Couzens, then chairman of the Senate Committee on Interstate Commerce, which provided in part as follows:

Whereas there is growing dissatisfaction with the present use of radio facilities for purposes of commercial advertising: Be it

Resolved, That the Federal Radio Commission is hereby authorized and instructed to make a survey and to report to the Senate on the following questions:

1. What information there is available on the feasibility of Government ownership and operation of broadcasting facilities.
2. To what extent the facilities of a representative group of broadcasting stations are used for commercial advertising purposes.
3. To what extent the use of radio facilities for purposes of commercial advertising varies as between stations having power of one hundred watts, five hundred watts, one thousand watts, five thousand watts, and all in excess of five thousand watts.
4. What plans might be adopted to reduce, to limit, to control, and perhaps, to eliminate the use of radio facilities for commercial advertising purposes.
5. What rules or regulations have been adopted by other countries to control or to eliminate the use of radio facilities for commercial advertising purposes.
6. Whether it would be practicable and satisfactory to permit only the announcement of sponsorship of programs by persons or corporations.[3]

(3)   Evolution of industry standards

(a)   *Commercials in sponsored programs.*   Broadcasters and advertisers themselves have always recognized the basic doctrine that advertising must be limited and abuses avoided. Thus, Mr. Herbert Wilson Smith, of the National Carbon Company, sponsors of the Ever-Ready Hour, testified before the House Merchant Marine and Fisheries Committee concerning radio legislation on January 7, 1926:

[3] The Commission's study made pursuant to this Resolution was published as Senate Document 137, 72nd Cong. 1st sess.

. . . When these musical and semi-dramatic programs are given, we precede the program by some such announcement as this one, for example, on December 15, 1925.

"Tuesday evening means the Ever-Ready Hour, for it is on this day and at this time each week that the National Carbon Company, makers of Ever-Ready flashlights and radio batteries, engages the facilities of these 14 radio stations to present its artists in original radio creations. Tonight the sponsors of the hour have included in the program, etc."

Now, that is the extent of the advertising, direct or indirect, of any character which we do in connection with our program. . . . The statement of the name of your company or the sponsorship of the program must be delicately handled so that the listener will not feel that he is having advertising pushed over on him; then throughout the rest of the entertainment, there is given a very high-class program, a musical program, entirely for the pleasure of the listeners. (*Hearings on H.R. 5589*, 69th Cong., 1st sess., pp. 81-82.)

On March 25, 1929 the National Association of Broadcasters, composed at that time of 147 broadcast stations throughout the country, adopted "Standards of Commercial Practice" which specifically provided:

Commercial announcements, as the term is generally understood, shall not be broadcast between 7 and 11 p.m.

In 1930 Mr. William S. Hedges of Station WMAQ, then president of the National Association of Broadcasters and now vice-president of the National Broadcasting Company, testified before the Senate Committee on Interstate Commerce concerning the quantitative limits on advertising which he then enforced.[4]

The Chairman (Senator Couzens).　What portion of a 30-minute program would you say should be devoted to advertising?
Mr. Hedges.　It all depends on the way you do it. Our rule, however, in our station is that no more than one minute out of the 30 minutes is devoted to advertising sponsorship. In other words, the radio listener gets 29 minutes of corking good entertainment, and all he has to do is to learn the name of the organization that has brought to him this fine program.
The Chairman.　Do all of the advertisers on your station confine themselves to 1 minute of advertising out of thirty minutes?
Mr. Hedges.　Some of them do not use as much as that.
The Chairman.　And some use more?
Mr. Hedges.　Very few. (pp. 1752-3)

Mr. William S. Paley, until recently president of the Columbia Broadcasting System, testified in the same hearings that only 22 percent of the time of

---

[4] Senate Committee on Interstate Commerce, *Hearings on S. 6*, 71st. Cong., 2d sess.

CBS, or 23 hours per week out of 109½ hours of operation, was devoted to commercial programs; the remaining 78 percent of the time was sustaining (pp. 1796-9). He cited the "CBS Credo" on advertising:

No overloading of a program with advertising matter, either through announcements that are too long or by too frequent mention of a trade name or product. (p. 1801)

Mr. Paley testified further:

Senator Dill.   How much of the hour do you allow for advertising in a program of an hour, or how much in a program of half an hour?

Mr. Paley.   Well, that varies, Senator Dill. I do not know how many seconds or how many minutes during an hour we actually give for the advertising time, but a few weeks ago our research department told me that of all the time used on the air during a particular week, that the actual time taken for advertising mention was seven-tenths of 1 percent of all our time. (p. 1802)

Since 1930, there has been a progressive relaxation of industry standards, so that the NAB standards at present permit as much as one and three-quarter minutes of advertising in a five-minute period, and do not even require this limit on participating programs, "musical clocks," etc. The *NAB Code* provisions in effect from 1937 to 1945 were as follows:

Member stations shall hold the length of commercial copy, including that devoted to contests and offers, to the following number of minutes and seconds:

Daytime

Five-minute programs	2:00
Five-minute news programs*	1:45
Ten-minute programs	2:30
Fifteen-minute programs	3:15
Twenty-five minute programs	4:15
Thirty-minute programs	4:30
Sixty-minute programs	9:00

Nighttime

Five-minute programs	1:45
Five-minute news programs*	1:30
Ten-minute programs	2:00
Fifteen-minute programs	2:30
Twenty-five minute programs	2:45
Thirty-minute programs	3:00
Sixty-minute programs	6:00

*Further restriction by individual stations is recommended.

Exceptions:

The above limitations do not apply to participation programs, announcement programs, "musical clocks," shoppers' guide and local programs falling within these general classifications.

Because of the varying economic and social conditions throughout the United States, members of the NAB shall have the right to present to the NAB for special ruling local situations which in the opinion of the member may justify exceptions to the above prescribed limitations.

In August 1945 these standards were further amended to eliminate the day-night differential, and to apply the former nighttime maxima to all hours.

(b) *Spot Announcements.*   In addition to the commercials within sponsored programs, there are, of course, commercial spot announcements within or between programs. No standard appears to be generally accepted for limiting spot announcements — though one network has recently announced with respect to its owned stations that commercial spot announcements must be limited to 1 minute or 125 words, that not more than three may be broadcast in any quarter-hour, that "station-break" spot announcements must be limited to 12 seconds or 25 words, and that these must not be more frequent than one each quarter-hour. The result is to permit 12 minutes and 48 seconds of spot announcements per hour. The NAB standards place no limitations whatever on spot announcements.

(4) Present practices: time devoted to commercials

In addition to the general relaxation of advertising standards in recent years, there is abundant evidence that even the present NAB standards are being flouted by some stations and networks.

As a rough index to contemporary advertising practices, the Commission recorded the programs of the six Washington, D.C., stations for Friday, July 6, 1945, and analyzed the recordings and station logs for that day. The Washington stations comprise:

WRC — a 5,000-watt regional station, owned by the National Broadcasting Company.

WTOP — a 50,000-watt clear-channel station, owned and operated by the Columbia Broadcasting System.

WMAL — a 5,000-watt regional station, owned by the Washington *Evening Star*, affiliated with the American Broadcasting Company (Blue Network).

WOL — a 1,000-watt regional station licensed to the Cowles Broadcasting Company and affiliated with the Mutual Broadcasting System.

WINX — a 250-watt local station licensed to the Washington *Post.*

WWDC — a 250-watt local station licensed to the Capital Broadcasting Company.

It seems reasonable to suppose that these six stations, operating in a major metropolitan area and the capital of the country, including two stations owned by major networks and two others affiliated with major networks would represent practices superior to the practices of stations generally.

Frequent examples of commercial advertising in excess of NAB standards were noted on all four networks and all six stations. The results of the study suggest that on networks and stations alike, the NAB standards are as honored in the breach as in the observance.

(5)   Other advertising problems

The proportion of overall time devoted to advertising commercials, discussed above, is only one of a series of problems raised by present network and station policies. No thorough study has been made of these other advertising problems, and accordingly, the following paragraphs should be considered as suggestive only, and designed to stimulate further research in this field. More light is needed both on the nature of existing practices and on their effect. A partial list of advertising problems other than the proportion of time devoted to advertising includes:

(a)   *Length of individual commercials.*   One commercial recorded by the Commission ran for just five minutes, without program interruption of any kind.

That many advertisers are content with spot announcements of reasonable length is indicated by the following table showing the scheduled length of 70 commercial spot announcements broadcast over Station WCAU on Monday, February 12, 1945, between 8 a.m. and 11 p.m.:

No. of 15-second commercial spot announcements	2
No. of 20-second '' '' ''	2
No. of 25-second '' '' ''	36
No. of 30-second '' '' ''	2
No. of 45-second '' '' ''	1
No. of 60-second '' '' ''	26
No. of 95-second '' '' ''	1
	70

On the other hand, some advertisers are frankly of the opinion that the longer the commercial plug, the more effective the program. Mr. Duane Jones, president of an advertising agency said to be one of the five largest in New York, placing more than 2,000 commercials a week for 26 clients, has given forceful expression to this view:

In dealing with advertising on the air, we in the Duane Jones Co. have found that, when we increase the length and number of commercials on the air to test our programs, invariably their Crossley ratings go up. . . . When making these tests, we load the programs to the limit under NAB rulings with commercials that precede, interrupt, and follow these broadcasts. And we know from the results that any arbitrary curtailment of commercials would seriously impair the audience value of these shows.

This view does not appear to be universally held; and evidence is available that lengthy commercials result in listeners tuning out a program. Thus *Variety* for May 2, 1945, reported:

TOO MANY PLUGS COOL "ROMANCE"

Colgate's "Theatre of Romance" is going way overboard on commercial spiels each week, CBS execs pointed out to Sherman, Marquette agency chiefs on Friday (27) — and it must stop immediately for the good of the program and the web's rating, they added.

A chart-check over a two-month period shows that the commercials on "Romance" run anywhere from three minutes and 15 seconds to four and one-half minutes. CBS' ruling on the commercial's time-limit for 30-minute sponsored shows, proved over the years, is three minutes. Over that, according to researchers at the network, listeners become restless, continuity is uneven and the stanza suffers in rating....

Charts show that the drama picks up rating shortly after going on the air, and that every time a commercial is spieled, the rating sags. On "Romance," too, for a full two minutes before it goes off each week during which the surveys were taken, ratings drop as much as three points. And on many shows, besides the Colgate blurbs, the announcer pitches in with a government-agency plug as well.

Sherman, Marquette will have to hold the commercials within the three-minute limit, or less, from here on in, CBS has informed them.[5]

A study of the six Washington stations for Friday, July 6, 1945, from 8 a.m. to 11 p.m. suggests that commercials one minute or more in length are quite common. More than 150 such announcements were noted on the six Washington stations during that period.

(b) *Number of commercials.*   The extreme case of an excessive *number* of spots noted to date is Station KMAC, which broadcast 2215 commercial announcements in 133 hours on the air during the week beginning January 21, 1945. This was an average of 16.7 spots per hour. Spot

---

[5] Television may bring still longer commercials. *Variety* for March 14, 1945, reports:

"A new venture in video experimentation, as far as a Chicago station is concerned, will be tried Tuesday (20) when a 3½-minute commercial is aired over WBKB, Balaban & Katz station here. Designed to fill in the air time between studio programs, the package is completely canned and is composed of slide film, synchronized to a recorded musical background and narration with the video part entirely cartooned.

"Set up as a Red Heart dog food commercial, it was produced by David W. Doyle, associate radio director of the Henri, Hurst & McDonald, Inc., agency; written by Betty Babcock and narrated by Ray Suber. Following tests here it may later be used on WNBT (NBC) and WABD (DuMont), New York."

announcements in excess of 1,000 per week have been noted on a number of stations.

(c) *Piling up of commercials.*   The listener who has heard one program and wants to hear another has come to expect a commercial plug to intervene. Conversely, the listener who has heard one or more commercial announcements may reasonably expect a program to intervene. Listed below is a series of commercial spot announcements broadcast by Station WTOL in Toledo, on November 14, 1944, during the dinner hour, without program interruption:

6:39:30 p.m.	Transcribed spot announcement.
6:40:00	Live spot announcement.
6:41:00	Transcribed spot announcement.
6:42:00	” ” ”
6:43:00	” ” ”
6:44:00	” ” ”

This programless period occurred each weekday dinner hour during the week of November 13, 1945, except on Thursday, when Station WTOL interrupted its spots to broadcast one minute of transcribed music.[6]

Such series are not unique. The "hitch-hiker" and "cowcatcher" on network programs, now rarer but not yet exterminated, have at times meant that a listener desiring to hear two consecutive network programs must survive five intervening commercial plugs — the closing plug of the first program, a "hitch-hiker" plug for another product of the same sponsor, a local plug in the station break between programs, a "cowcatcher" for a minor product of the sponsor of the second network program, and finally the opening commercial of the second program.

Professor C. H. Sandage, in his survey of radio advertising by retailers, has pointed out that excessive spot announcements may even destroy advertiser confidence in broadcasting:

There is real danger that excessive use of spots will drive not only listeners away from a station but also a number of advertisers whom some refer to as the more respectable. A Midwest jeweler who operated a first-class, noninstallment credit store reported that he had cancelled his use of radio because he felt that radio management in his city had allowed the air to become too crowded with spot announcements. He also believed that many announcements were purchased by firms selling cheap and shoddy merchandise. Another advertiser reported: "Radio announcements are O.K. for loan sharks but not for me." Similar comments were sufficiently frequent to indicate that this factor had kept a number of retailers from using the facilities of radio.[6]

[6] Sandage, *Radio Advertising for Retailers*, p. 186.

(d) *Time between commercials.*   Listener satisfaction may depend in part upon the length of the intervals between commercials. The National Association of Broadcasters may have been recognizing this feature of the commercial when in 1929 it banned commercial announcements between 7 and 11 p.m., thus affording four hours of listening uninterrupted by commercial advertising — as distinguished from announcement of the name of the advertiser and of his product.

Some stations and some advertisers are becoming aware of the value of uninterrupted listening. Thus the WOL program on July 9, 1945 from 7:30 to 7:58 p.m. made a point of announcing that the four movements of a symphony would be played "without interruption."

(e) *The middle commercial.*   The Radio Council of Greater Cleveland, composed of representatives of 112 organizations having a total membership of 155,000, conducted a questionnaire survey in 1945 with respect to the "middle commercial" and related problems. The study, while perhaps subject to considerable sampling error, nevertheless indicates roughly the extent of listener dissatisfaction. More than 95 percent of those responding stated that they preferred commercials only at the beginning and end.

Canadian regulations prohibit the middle commercial on newscasts altogether. Canadian Regulation 13(2), adopted November 17, 1941, provides in part:

> The only announcement of sponsorship for news . . . shall be two in number, one at the beginning and one at the end, and shall be as follows:
> "Through the courtesy of (name and business of sponsor) Station ___ presents (presented) the news of the day furnished by (name of news service)."

The Association of Radio News Analysts, a group whose own livelihood depends upon commercial newscasts, has been among those who believe the middle commercial to be an unhealthy growth. Article IV of the *ARNA Code* of Ethics states:

> The association deplores the interruption of a news analysis by commercial announcements.

Many members of the ARNA, which includes outstanding news analysts and commentators throughout the country, refuse to appear on a program which is interrupted by a middle commercial. Raymond Swing, in a telegram to the St. Louis *Post-Dispatch* published February 5, 1945, described his own experience with the middle commercial:

> I made my own rebellion against them on May 10, 1940, when writing my broadcast reporting German violation of French, Belgian, Dutch and Luxembourg neutrality in launching the Western offensive. It seemed hideous to have this account interrupted by a sales talk, and I balked.
>   To the credit of Mutual officials, for whom I was then broadcasting, and the advertising agency handling the program, they supported my stand. Since

then my contracts for broadcasts on the Blue network have specified that my program not be interrupted by middle commercials.

Listeners are entitled to hear the news without jarring interruptions, and I feel confident it is sound advertising policy to recognize the right.

Despite the successful revolt of Mr. Swing and some others, it should be noted that as late as Friday, July 6, 1945, recording of broadcasts on the six Washington stations showed some news and analysis programs being interrupted by commercials on all four networks and all six stations.

The St. Louis *Post-Dispatch* has carried on for some months a concerted campaign against the middle commercial in newscasts, and has been followed by newspapers throughout the country. Leaders in the campaign have been other newspapers which, like the *Post-Dispatch*, are themselves the licensees of standard broadcast stations.

Judge Justin Miller, then of the United States Circuit Court of Appeals and now president of the National Association of Broadcasters, commented on the middle commercial and the *Post-Dispatch* campaign in a letter to the editor published April 20, 1945:

I have just read in *Broadcasting* a reprint of your editorial of April 10, "In the Interest of Radio." Let me add my voice to that of others who have commended you for the position which you have taken.

There is no more reason why a newscast should be interrupted for a plug-ugly than that such ads should be inserted in the middle of news stories or editorials in a newspaper; especially when the interruption — deliberately or unconsciously, whichever it may be — is in nauseating contrast to the subject under discussion by the commentator.

It is particularly encouraging that this insistence upon higher professional standards should come from a newspaper — a representative of the profession which has most intelligently through the years defended the guarantees of the first amendment. Only by intelligent anticipation of public reaction and by equally intelligent self-discipline can we prevent legislative intemperance.

While many stations and some sponsors deleted the middle commercial on newscasts following the *Post-Dispatch* campaign, others adopted measures which fall short of elimination. One network, for example, divides 15 minutes of news and comment into a 10-minute program for one sponsor and a 5-minute program for another — with a station-break announcement between. The result is to move the middle commercial from the precise mid-point to the two-thirds point of the quarter-hour — and to subject the listener to two or even three interrupting impacts. Another network claims to have eliminated the middle commercial, but actually it requires that commercials be limited to the first two and the last three minutes of the 15-minute period — as a result of which the news is interrupted twice instead of once. It is clear that such devices, while they eliminate the commercial at the exact middle, fail to meet the chief listener complaint — which is that the news is *interrupted.* Some sponsors, in contrast, have made a sound asset of actual elimination of the middle commercial; their opening announcement ends with some such phrase as: "We bring you now the news — *uninterrupted.*" It may well be that such emphasis upon the essentials of good programming, made explicit to listeners by appropriate announcement over the air, will do much to eliminate inferior procedures indulged in by other networks, stations, or sponsors.

(f)   *The patriotic appeal.*   Patriotism, especially in time of war, is an emotion near the forefront of the minds of most listeners. To misuse the listener's deepest patriotic feelings for the sale of commercial products over the air is a violation of a public trust. It is well established that the American flag shall not be used in visual advertising;[7] and the aural symbols of our national life should be similarly immune from commercialization. An example of the patriotic appeal to buy headache remedies is the following announcement over Station WBT, Charlotte, on September 4, 1944:

As every one of you well knows, the United States is face to face with a great challenge. People everywhere are seriously concerned about the Nation's all-out effort. Regardless of how or where you serve, your first duty is to keep well. Get adequate rest. Follow a reasonable diet. Exercise properly. Avoid unnecessary exposures or excesses. When a simple headache develops, or the pain of neuralgia strikes, try a BC Headache Powder. The quick-acting, prescription-type ingredients in the BC formula usually work fast and relieve in a hurry. Remember this. Get one of the 25-cent packages of BC today. You'll like the way BC eases tantalizing headaches and soothes nerves ruffled or upset by pain. USE ONLY ACCORDING TO DIRECTIONS, and consult a physician when pains persist or recur frequently.

Another announcement over the same station said in part:

All of us have a big job on our hands if we want to keep America the land of the free and the home of the brave. The all-out effort means hard work, and lots of it. Production must move forward — fast! . . . Get one of the 10 or 25-cent packages of BC today. . . .

(g)   *The physiological commercial.*   Appeals to listeners to "take an internal bath," inquiring of the listener whether he has the common ailment known as "American stomach," discussions of body odors, sluggish bile, etc., are a distinguishing characteristic of American broadcasting.

Various networks and stations impose various restrictions on such physiological advertising. Mr. Lewis Gannett, well-known book critic, sums up listener reaction thus in the New York *Herald Tribune* for February 28, 1945:

The aspect of home-front life which most disgusted me on return was the radio. BBC programs may be dull and army radio programs may be shallow, but

---

[7]Public Law 623, approved June 22, 1942, provides: "The flag should never be used for advertising purposes in any manner whatsoever."

if the soldier in Europe has had a chance to hear the radio at all, he has heard it straight, without the neurotic advertising twaddle which punctuates virtually every American program. . . . The first evening that I sat by a radio at home, I heard one long parade of headaches, coughs, aching muscles, stained teeth, "unpleasant full feeling," and gastric hyperacidity. . . . Our radio evenings are a sick parade of sicknesses and if they haven't yet made us a sick nation, I wonder why.

According to data compiled by the Publisher's Information Bureau, more money is spent for network advertising of drugs and toilet goods than for any other products; 27.9% of all network gross billings is for such products. Drug and cosmetic advertising is said to have trebled between 1939 and 1944. The increasing identification of radio as a purveyor of patent medicines and proprietary remedies raises serious problems which warrant careful consideration by the broadcasting industry.

Professor Sandage's survey, cited above, asked various advertisers who did not use radio advertising the reason for their refraining. His study states:

A common reason for nonuse in a few communities was the character of advertising carried by local stations. Leading merchants commented that radio messages carried on these stations were too much like the patent medicine advertisements of pre-Federal Trade Commission days. These merchants did not wish to be associated on the air with such advertisers.[8]

(h) *Propaganda in commercials.* The commercial announcement is sometimes used to propagandize for a point of view or one side of a debated issue rather than to sell goods and services. An example is the following announcement over Station KWBU, Corpus Christi, Texas, on August 1, 1944:

When you see a C[entral] P[ower and] L[ight Company] lineman hanging on a pole with one foot in heaven so to speak and hear him holler "headache," you better start running. He is not telling you how he feels but giving warning that he dropped a wrench or hammer and everyone had better look out below. The C[entral] P[ower and] L[ight Company] lineman has a tough job of keeping the electricity flowing to your home. They work night and day to keep headaches from you — to keep your lamps lit and your radio running despite lightning, floods, and storms. Only carefully trained and experienced men could do this job, but there are some in this country who think that the Government should own and operate the light and power industry. Then a lineman might hold his job for political reasons rather than for his ability to render good service to you. Business management under public regulation has brought you good reliable electric service at low prewar prices. That is the American way — let's keep it.

A second example is the following, broadcast over 12 Michigan stations in 1944:

[8] Sandage, *Radio Advertising for Retailers*, p. 73.

American Medicine, the private practice of which represents the cumulative knowledge of decades, the heritage of centuries, the sacrifices and discoveries of countless individuals, has made the United States the healthiest country in the world. Spinal meningitis, diphtheria, smallpox, typhoid fever and other fatal diseases, scourges of yesteryear, are today either preventable or curable, a credit to the tireless efforts of the American medical profession. Thirty-seven states now have voluntary prepayment medical or hospital plans developed by the medical profession and the hospitals. *No theoretical plan, government controlled and operated, and paid for by you, should replace the tried and proved system of the private practice of medicine now in use.*[9]

On January 10, 1944, four days after the U.S. Department of Justice filed suit against the DuPont Company in connection with an alleged cartel agreement, DuPont used its commercial advertising period on the well-known "Cavalcade of America" program over NBC to explain one side of a controversial issue. To quote:

I want to talk to you tonight about an agreement current in the news and of wide public interest. This is the agreement which the DuPont Company has had for years with a British chemical company, Imperial Chemical Industries, Ltd. It provides for a mutual opportunity to acquire patent licenses and technical and scientific information relating to important chemical developments. It has been a matter of public record and known to our government for ten years.

Literally hundreds of transfers of technical and scientific information have occurred for the advancement of chemical science and the benefit of the American people in peace and war. Agreements of a similar character, but limited to specific chemical fields have been made from time to time with continental European companies for the use of scientific data obtained from abroad. Many valuable products have resulted for the use of the American public and necessary to our armed forces. In this war, DuPont chemists have materially improved and have further developed the scientific data flowing from these contractual arrangements.

The scientific and technical information gained has contributed substantially to American progress and to the success of American arms. Many important products have resulted from these agreements to which reference may be made without disclosing military secrets. Developments were made incident to synthetic ammonia manufactured from nitrogen extracted from the air. Without this we could not have smokeless powder and TNT in anything like the quantities needed. The development of Methyl Methacrylate plastic used for the transparent enclosures to be found on every combat airplane stems from these agreements. A new process vital to quantity production of aircraft engines and a

---

[9] *Journal of the American Medical Association,* Vol. 127, No. 5, p. 283 (February 3, 1945). (Emphasis supplied.)

new plastic polythene, which has gone into the production of new electrical items urgently needed by the Army and Navy. Also high in this last are rayon, dyes, celophane, zelan, — water repellent for military apparel, as well as many other chemical products. All have been improved and perfected here but they came originally from abroad.

These agreements have been of the greatest benefit in giving to the American public products and processes which in the past have materially raised the standard of living, products and processes which are a part of the promise for the future of "Better Things for Better Living Through Chemistry."

(i)   *Intermixture of program and advertising.*   A listener is entitled to know when the program ends and the advertisement begins. The *New York Times* comment on this and related topics is here in point:

The virtual subordination of radio's standards to the philosophy of advertising inevitably has led the networks into an unhealthy and untenable position. It has permitted Gabriel Heatter to shift without emphasis from a discussion of the war to the merits of hair tonic. It has forced the nation's best entertainers to act as candy butchers and debase their integrity as artists. It has permitted screeching voices to yell at our children to eat this or that if they want to be as efficient as some fictional character. . . . The broadcaster often has argued that it is not his function to "reform" the public taste, but, be that as it may, it certainly is the broadcaster's responsibility not to lower it.

The Association of Radio News Analysts has particularly inveighed against the practice of having the announcements read by the same voice as the news analysis. Article IV of the ARNA Code of Ethics provides:

The association believes the reading of commercial announcements by radio news analysts is against the best interests of broadcasting.

According to the president of the ARNA, John W. Vandercook:

ARNA has . . . consistently arrayed itself in opposition to the reading of such commercial announcements by news analysts. It is our belief that the major networks and all of the more reputable American advertising agencies are in substantial agreement with us and support our stand.

We, however, recognize and applaud the necessity for perpetual vigilance and unremitting efforts to extirpate the all-too-common breaches of these principles. (St. Louis *Post-Dispatch*, Feb. 5, 1945.)

The above is not to be taken as an exhaustive list of advertising excesses. Since it is not the intention of the Commission to concern itself with advertising excesses other than an excessive ratio of advertising time to program time, no exhaustive study has been undertaken. There is need, however, for a thorough review by the industry itself of current advertising practices, with a view towards the establishment and enforcement of sound standards by the industry itself.

PART IV.   ECONOMIC ASPECTS

The problem of program service is intimately related to economic factors. A prosperous broadcasting industry is obviously in a position to render a better program service to the public than an industry which must pinch and scrape to make ends meet. Since the revenues of American broadcasting come primarily from advertisers, the terms and conditions of program service must not be such as to block the flow of advertising revenues into broadcasting. Finally, the public benefits when the economic foundations of broadcasting are sufficiently firm to insure a flow of new capital into the industry, especially at present when the development of FM and television is imminent.

A review of the economic aspects of broadcasting during recent years indicates that there are no economic considerations to prevent the rendering of a considerably broader program service than the public is currently afforded.*

PART V.   SUMMARY AND CONCLUSIONS –
PROPOSALS FOR FUTURE COMMISSION POLICY

A.   Role of the public

Primary responsibility for the American system of broadcasting rests with the licensee of broadcast stations, including the network organizations. It is to the stations and networks rather than to federal regulation that listeners must primarily turn for improved standards of program service. The Commission, as the licensing agency established by Congress, has a responsibility to consider overall program service in its public interest determinations, but affirmative improvement of program service must be the result primarily of other forces.

One such force is self-regulation by the industry itself, through its trade associations.

Licensees acting individually can also do much to raise program service standards, and some progress has indeed been made. Here and there across the country, some stations have evidenced an increased awareness of the importance of sustaining programs, live programs, and discussion programs. Other stations have eliminated from their own program service the middle commercial, the transcribed commercial, the piling up of commercials, etc. This trend toward self-improvement, if continued, may further buttress the industry against the rising tide of informed and responsible criticism.

Forces outside the broadcasting industry similarly have a role to play in

---

*Sixteen tables of economic data supporting this view are omitted. [Ed.]

improved program service. There is need, for example, for professional radio critics, who will play in this field the role which literary and dramatic critics have long assumed in the older forms of artistic expression. It is, indeed, a curious instance of the time lag in our adjustment to changed circumstances that while plays and concerts performed to comparatively small audiences in the "legitimate" theater or concert hall are regularly reviewed in the press, radio's best productions performed before an audience of millions receive only occasional and limited critical consideration. *Publicity* for radio programs is useful, but limited in the function it performs. Responsible criticism can do much more than mere promotion; it can raise the standards of public appreciation and stimulate the free and unfettered development of radio as a new medium of artistic expression. The independent radio critic, assuming the same role long occupied by the dramatic critic and the literary critic, can bring to bear an objective judgment on questions of good taste and of artistic merit which lie outside the purview of this Commission. The reviews and critiques published weekly in *Variety* afford an illustration of the role that independent criticism can play; newspapers and periodicals might well consider the institution of similar independent critiques for the general public.

Radio listener councils can also do much to improve the quality of program service. Such councils, notably in Cleveland, Ohio, and Madison, Wisconsin, have already shown the possibilities of independent listener organization. First, they can provide a much needed channel through which listeners can convey to broadcasters the wishes of the vast but not generally articulate radio audience. Second, listener councils can engage in much needed research concerning public tastes and attitudes. Third, listener councils can check on the failure of network affiliates to carry outstanding network sustaining programs, and on the local programs substituted for outstanding network sustaining programs. Fourth, they can serve to publicize and to promote outstanding programs — especially sustaining programs which at present suffer a serious handicap for lack of the vast promotional enterprise which goes to publicize many commercial programs. Other useful functions would also no doubt result from an increase in the number and an extension of the range of activities of listener councils, cooperating with the broadcasting industry but speaking solely for the interest of listeners themselves.

Colleges and universities, some of them already active in the field, have a like distinctive role to play. Together with the public schools, they have it in their power to raise a new generation of listeners with higher standards and expectations of what radio can offer.

In radio workshops, knowledge may be acquired of the techniques of radio production. There are already many examples of students graduating from such work who have found their way into the industry, carrying with them standards and conceptions of radio's role, as well as talents, by which radio service cannot fail to be enriched.

Even more important, however, is the role of colleges and universities in the field of radio research. There is room for a vast expansion of studies of the commercial, artistic and social aspects of radio. The cultural aspects of radio's influence provide in themselves a vast and fascinating field of research.

It is hoped that the facts emerging from this report and the recommendations which follow will be of interest to the groups mentioned. With them rather than with the Commission rests much of the hope for improved broadcasting quality.

B.   Role of the Commission

While much of the responsibility for improved program service lies with the broadcasting industry and with the public, the Commission has a statutory responsibility for the public interest, of which it cannot divest itself. The Commission's experience with the detailed review of broadcast renewal applications since April 1945, together with the facts set forth in this report, indicate some current trends in broadcasting which, with reference to licensing procedure, require its particular attention.

In issuing and in renewing the licenses of broadcast stations the Commission proposes to give particular consideration to four program service factors relevant to the public interest. These are: (1) the carrying of sustaining programs, including network sustaining programs, with particular reference to the retention by licensees of a proper discretion and responsibility for maintaining a well-balanced program structure; (2) the carrying of local live programs; (3) the carrying of programs devoted to the discussion of public issues, and (4) the elimination of advertising excesses.

(1)   *Sustaining programs.*   The carrying of sustaining programs has always been deemed one aspect of broadcast operation in the public interest. Sustaining programs, as noted above (pp. 174-186), perform a five-fold function in (a) maintaining an overall program balance, (b) providing time for programs inappropriate for sponsorship, (c) providing time for programs serving particular minority tastes and interests, (d) providing time for non-profit organizations — religious, civic, agricultural, labor, educational, etc., and (e) providing time for experiment and for unfettered artistic self-expression.

Accordingly, the Commission concludes that one standard of operation in the public interest is a reasonable proportion of time devoted to sustaining programs.

Moreover, if sustaining programs are to perform their traditional functions in the American system of broadcasting, they must be broadcast at hours when the public is awake and listening. The time devoted to sustaining programs, accordingly, should be reasonably distributed among the various segments of the broadcast day.

For the reasons set forth on pages 189-198, the Commission, in considering overall program balance, will also take note of network sustaining programs available to but not carried by a station, and of the programs which the station substitutes therefor.

(2)   *Local live programs.*   The Commission has always placed a marked emphasis, and in some cases perhaps an undue emphasis, on the carrying of local live programs as a standard of public interest. The development of network, transcription, and wire news services is such that no sound public interest appears to be served by continuing to stress local live programs exclusively at the expense of these other categories. Nevertheless, reasonable provision for local self-expression still remains an essential function of a station's operation (pp. 198-205), and will continue to be so regarded by the Commission. In particular, public interest requires that such programs should not be crowded out of the best listening hours.

(3)   *Programs devoted to the discussion of public issues.*   The crucial need for discussion programs, at the local, national, and international levels alike is universally realized, as set forth on pp. 205-208. Accordingly, the carrying of such programs in reasonable sufficiency, and during good listening hours, is a factor to be considered in any finding of public interest.

(4)   *Advertising   excesses.*   The   evidence   set   forth   above (pp. 208-223), warrants the conclusion that some stations during some or many portions of the broadcast day have engaged in advertising excesses which are incompatible with their public responsibilities, and which threaten the good name of broadcasting itself.

As the broadcasting industry itself has insisted, the public interest clearly requires that the amount of time devoted to advertising matter shall bear a reasonable relationship to the amount of time devoted to programs. Accordingly, in its application forms the Commission will request the applicant to state how much time he proposes to devote to advertising matter in any one hour.

This by itself will not, of course, result in the elimination of some of the particular excesses described on pp. 215-223. This is a matter in which self-regulation by the industry may properly be sought and indeed expected. The Commission has no desire to concern itself with the particular length, content, or irritating qualities of particular commercial plugs.

C.   Procedural proposals

In carrying out the above objectives, the Commission proposes to continue substantially unchanged its present basic licensing procedures — namely, the requiring of a written application setting forth the proposed program service of the station, the consideration of that application on its merits, and subsequently the comparison of promise and performance when an application is received for a renewal of the station license. The ends sought can best be achieved, so far as presently appears, by appropriate modification of the particular forms and procedures currently in use and by a generally more careful consideration of renewal applications.

The particular procedural changes proposed are set forth below. They will not be introduced immediately or simultaneously, but rather from time to time as circumstances warrant. Meanwhile, the Commission invites comment from licensees and from the public.

(1)   Uniform definitions and program logs

The Commission has always recognized certain basic categories of programs — e.g., commercial and sustaining, network, transcribed, recorded, local, live, etc. Such classifications must, under Regulation 3.404, be shown upon the face of the program log required to be kept by each standard broadcast station; and the Commission, like its predecessor, has always required data concerning such program classifications in its application forms.

Examination of logs shows, however, that there is no uniformity or agreement concerning what constitutes a "commercial" program, a "sustaining" program, a "network" program, etc. Accordingly, the Commission will adopt uniform definitions of basic program terms and classes, which are to be used in all presentations to the Commission. The proposed definitions are set forth below.

A *commercial program* (C) is any program the time for which is paid for by a sponsor *or* any program which is interrupted by a spot announcement (as defined below), at intervals of less than 15 minutes. A network program shall be classified as "commercial" if it is commercially sponsored on the network, even though the particular station is not paid for carrying it — unless all commercial announcements have been deleted from the program by the station.

(It will be noted that any program which is *interrupted* by a commercial announcement is classified as a commercial program, even though the purchaser of the interrupting announcement has not also purchased the time preceding and following. The result is to classify so-called "participating" programs as commercial. Without such a rule, a 15-minute program may contain 5 or even more minutes of advertising and still be classified as "sustaining." Under the proposed definition, a program may be classified as "sustaining" although preceded and followed by spot announcements, but if a spot announcement *interrupts* a program, the program must be classified as "commercial.")

A *sustaining* program (S) is any program which is *neither* paid for by a sponsor *nor* interrupted by a spot announcement (as defined below).

A *network* program (N) is any program furnished to the station by a network or another station. Transcribed delayed broadcasts of network programs are classified as "network," not "recorded." Programs are classified as network whether furnished by a nationwide, regional, or special network or by another station.

A *recorded* program (R) is any program which uses phonograph records, electrical transcriptions, or other means of mechanical reproduction in whole or in part − except where the recording is wholly incidental to the program and is limited to background sounds, sound effects, identifying themes, musical "bridges," etc. A program part transcribed or recorded and part live is classified as "recorded" unless the recordings are wholly incidental, as above. A transcribed delayed broadcast of a network program, however, is not classified as "recorded" but as "network."

A *wire* program (W) is any program the text of which is distributed to a number of stations by telegraph, teletype, or similar means, and read in whole or in part by a local announcer. Programs distributed by the wire news services are "wire" programs. A news program which is part wire and in part of local non-syndicated origin is classified as "wire" if more than half of the program is usually devoted to the reading verbatim of the syndicated wire text, but is classified as "live" if more than half is usually devoted to local news or comment.

(The above is a new program category. Programs in this category resemble network and transcribed programs in the respect that they are syndicated to scores or hundreds of stations. They resemble local live programs only in the respect that the words are vocalized by a local voice; the text is not local but syndicated. Such programs have an important role in broadcasting, especially in the dissemination of news. With respect to stations not affiliated with a network, the wire program for timely matter, plus the transcription for less urgent broadcasts affords a close approach to the services of a regular network. The only difficulty is that with respect to program classifications heretofore, the wire program has been merged with the local live program, which it resembles only superficially, preventing a statistical analysis of either. By establishing definitions for "wire commercial" and "wire sustaining," the Commission expects to make possible statistical studies with respect to such programs, and also to make more significant the statistical studies with respect to the "local live commercial" and "local live sustaining" categories.)

A *local live* program (L) is any local program which uses live talent exclusively, whether originating in the station's studios or by remote control. Programs furnished to a station by a network or another station, however, are not classified as "live" but as "network." A program which uses recordings in whole or in part, except in a wholly incidental manner, should not be classified as "live" but as "recorded." Wire programs, as defined above, should likewise not be classified as "live."

A *sustaining public service announcement* (PSA) is an annoucement which is not paid for by a sponsor and which is devoted to a non-profit cause − e.g., war bonds, Red Cross, public health, civic announcements, etc. Promotional, "courtesy," participating announcements, etc. should not be classified as "sustaining public service announcements" but as "spot announcements." War Bond, Red Cross, civic and similar announcements for which the station receives remuneration should not be classified as "sustaining public service announcements" but as "spot announcements."

A *spot announcement* (SA) is any announcement which is neither a sustaining public service announcement (as above defined) nor a station identification announcement (call letters and location). An announcement should be classified as a "spot announcement," whether or not the station receives remuneration, unless it is devoted to a nonprofit cause. Sponsored time signals, sponsored weather announcements, etc. are spot announcements. Unsponsored time signals, weather announcements, etc., are program matter and not classified as announcements. Station identification announcements should *not* be classified as either sustaining public service or spot announcements, if limited to call letters, location, and identification of the licensee and network.

The Commission further proposes to amend Regulation 3.404 to provide in part that the program log shall contain:

An entry classifying each program as "network commercial" (NC); "network sustaining" (NS); "recorded commercial" (RC); "recorded sustaining" (RS); "wire commercial" (WC); "wire sustaining" (WS); "local live commercial" (LC); or "local live sustaining" (LS); and classifying each announcement as "spot announcement" (SA) or "sustaining public service announcement" (PSA).

The adoption of uniform definitions will make possible a fairer comparison of program representations and performance, and better statistical analyses.

(2)   Segments of the broadcast day

The Commission has always recognized, as has the industry, that different segments of the broadcast day have different characteristics and that different types of programming are therefore permissible. For example, the *NAB Code*, until recently, and many stations permit a greater proportion of advertising during the day than at night. The Commission's Chain Broadcasting Regulations recognize four segments: 8 a.m.–1 p.m., 1 p.m.–6 p.m., 6 p.m.–11 p.m., and all other hours. Most stations make distinctions of hours in their rate cards.

In general, sustaining and live programs have tended to be crowded out of the best listening hours from 6 to 11 p.m., and also in a degree out of the period from 8 a.m. to 6 p.m. At least some stations have improved the ratios shown in reports to the Commission, but not the service rendered the public, by crowding sustaining programs into the hours after 11 p.m. and before dawn when listeners are few and sponsors fewer still. Clearly the responsibility for public service cannot be met by broadcasting public service programs only during such hours. A well-balanced program structure requires balance during the best listening hours.

	8 a.m. 6 p.m.	6 p.m. 11 p.m.	All other hours	Total
Network commercial (NC)				
Network sustaining (NS)				
Recorded commercial (RC)				
Recorded sustaining (RS)				
Wire commercial (WC)				
Wire sustaining (WS)				
Live commercial (LC)				
Live sustaining (LS)				
Total[1]				
No. of Spot Announcements (SA)				
No. of Sustaining Public Service Announcements (PSA)				

[1]Totals should equal full operating time during each segment.

Statistical convenience requires that categories be kept to a minimum. In general, the segments of the broadcast day established in the Chain Broadcasting Regulations appear satisfactory, except that no good purpose appears to be served in connection with program analysis by calculating separately the segments from 8 a.m. to 1 p.m. and from 1 p.m. to 6 p.m. Accordingly, for present purposes it is proposed to merge these segments, so that the broadcast day will be composed of three segments only: 8 a.m.–6 p.m., 6 p.m.–11 p.m., and all other hours.

The categories set forth above, plus the segments herein defined, make possible a standard program log analysis as in the form shown on page 231.

The above schedule will be uniformly utilized in Commission application forms and annual report forms in lieu of the various types of schedules now prevailing. In using it, stations may calculate the length of programs to the nearest five minutes.

(3)   Annual reports and statistics

For some years, the Commission has called for a statement of the number of hours devoted to various classes of programs each year, in connection with the Annual Financial Reports of broadcast stations and networks. Requiring such figures for an entire year may constitute a considerable accounting burden on the stations, and may therefore impair the quality of the reports. Accordingly, the Commission proposes hereafter to require these data in the Annual Financial Reports only for one week.

To make the proposed week as representative as possible of the year as a whole, the Commission will utilize a procedure heretofore sometimes used by stations in presentations to the Commission. At the end of each year, it will select at random a Monday in January or February, a Tuesday in March, a Wednesday in April, a Thursday in May or June, a Friday in July or August, a Saturday in September or October, and a Sunday in November or December, and will ask for detailed program analyses for these seven days. The particular days chosen will vary from year to year, and will be drawn so as to avoid holidays and other atypical occasions.

The information requested will be in terms of the definitions and time periods set forth above. Statistical summaries and trends will be published annually.

The Commission will also call upon the networks for quarterly statements of the stations carrying and failing to carry network sustaining programs during a sample week in each quarter.

(4)   Revision of application forms

Since the establishment of the Federal Radio Commission, applicants for new stations have been required to set forth their program plans, and applications have been granted in part on the basis of representations concerning program plans. Applications for renewal of license, assignment of license, transfer of control of licensee corporation, and modification of license have similarly included, in various forms, representations concerning program service rendered or to be rendered. The program service questions now asked on the Commission's application forms are not uniform, and not closely integrated with current Commission policy respecting program service. It is proposed, accordingly, to revise the program service questions on all Commission forms to bring them into line with the policies set forth in this report.

Specifically, applicants for new stations will be required to fill out, as part of Form 301 or Form 319, a showing of their proposed program structure, utilizing the uniform schedule set forth on page 231. Applicants for renewal of license, consent to transfer of assignment, and modification of license will be required to fill out the same uniform schedule, both for a sample week under their previous licenses, and as an indication of their proposed operation if the application in question is granted.

The Commission, of course, recognizes that there is need for flexibility in broadcast operation. An application to the Commission should not be a straitjacket preventing a licensee from rendering an even better service than originally proposed. To provide the necessary flexibility, the information supplied in the uniform schedule will be treated as a responsible estimate rather than a binding pledge. However, attention should be called to the fact that the need for trustworthiness is at least as important with respect to representations concerning program service as with respect to statements concerning financial matters.

Stations will also be asked whether they propose to render a well-balanced program service, or to specialize in programs of a particular type or addressed to a particular audience. If their proposal is for a specialized rather than a balanced program service, a showing will be requested concerning the relative need for such service in the community as compared with the need for an additional station affording a balanced program service. On renewal, stations which have proposed a specialized service will be expected to show the extent to which they have in fact fulfilled their proposals during the period of their license.

Stations affiliated with a network will further be required to list network sustaining programs not carried during a representative week, and the programs carried in place of such programs.

If the Commission is able to determine from an examination of the application that a grant will serve the public interest, it will grant forthwith, as heretofore. If the Commission is unable to make such a determination on the basis of the application it will, as heretofore, designate the application for hearing.

(5)   Action on renewals

With the above changes in Commission forms and procedures, the Commission will have available in connection with renewal applications, specific data relevant to the finding of public interest required by the statute.

First, it will have available all the data concerning engineering, legal, accounting and other matters, as heretofore.

Second, it will have available a responsible estimate of the overall program structure appropriate for the station in question, as estimated by the licensee himself when making his previous application.

Third, it will have available affirmative representations of the licensee concerning the time to be devoted to sustaining programs, live programs, discussion programs, and advertising matter.

Fourth, it will have available from the annual reports to the Commission data concerning the actual program structure of the station during a sample week in each year under the existing license.

Fifth, it will have available a statement of the overall program structure of the station during a week immediately preceding the filing of the application being considered, and information concerning the carrying of network sustaining programs.

Sixth, it will have available the station's representations concerning program service under the license applied for.

If the Commission is able to determine on the basis of the data thus available that a grant will serve the public interest, it will continue as heretofore, to grant forthwith; otherwise, as heretofore, it will designate the renewal application for hearing.

5

THE 1960 PROGRAMMING
POLICY STATEMENT

Report and Statement of Policy re:
Commission en banc Programming Inquiry
       25 Fed. Reg. 7291
       July 29, 1960

> Issued fourteen years after the "Blue Book," this programming policy statement was both milder in tone and more effectively enforced than its predecessor. This document is the one to which the Federal Communications Commission currently adheres.

On October 3, 1957, the Commission's Network Study Staff submitted its report on network broadcasting. While the scope and breadth of the network study as set forth in Order Number 1 issued November 21, 1955 encompassed a comprehensive study of programming, it soon became apparent that due to factors not within the control of the staff or the committee consideration of programming would be subject to substantial delay making it impracticable that the target dates for the overall report could be met in the program area. The principal reasons were: (a) the refusal of certain program distributors and producers to provide the committee's staff with certain information which necessitated protracted negotiations and ultimately legal action (FCC v. Ralph Cohn, et al., 154 F. Supp. 899); and (b) the fact that a coincidental and collateral investigation into certain practices was instituted by the Department of Justice. Accordingly the network study staff report recommended that the study of programming be continued and completed. The Director of the Network Study in his memorandum of transmittal of the Network Study Report stated:

The staff regrets that it was unable to include in the report its findings and conclusions in its study of programming. It is estimated that more than one-fourth of the time of the staff was expended in this area. However, the extended negotiations and litigation with some non-network program producers relative to supplying financial data necessary to this aspect of the study made it impossible to obtain this information from a sufficient number of these program producers to draw definitive conclusions on all the programming issues. Now that the Commission's right to obtain this information has been sustained, it is the hope of the staff that this aspect of the study will be completed and the results included in a supplement to the report. Unless the study of programming is completed, the benefit of much labor on this subject will have been substantially lost.

As a result on February 26, 1959, the Commission issued its "Order for Investigatory Proceeding," Docket No. 12782. That Order stated that during the course of the Network Study and otherwise, the Commission had obtained information and data regarding the acquisition, production, ownership, distribution, sale, licensing, and exhibition of programs for television broadcasting. Also, that that information and data had been augmented from other sources including hearings before Committees of Congress and from the Department of Justice, and that the Commission had determined that an overall inquiry should be made to determine the facts with respect to the television network program selection process. On November 9, 1959, the proceeding instituted by the Commission's Order of February 26, 1959 was amended and enlarged to include a general inquiry with respect to programming to determine, among other things, whether the general standards heretofore laid down by the Commission for the guidance of broadcast licensees in the selection of programs and other material intended for broadcast are currently adequate; whether the Commission should, by the exercise of its rule-making power, set out more detailed and precise standards for such broadcasters; whether the Commission's present review and consideration in the field of programming and advertising are adequate, under present conditions in the broadcast industry; and whether the Commission's authority under the Communications Act of 1934, as amended, is adequate, or whether legislation should be recommended to Congress.

This inquiry was heard by the Commission *en banc* between December 7, 1959, and February 1, 1960, and consumed 19 days in actual hearings. Over 90 witnesses testified relative to the problems involved, made suggestions and otherwise contributed from their background and experience to the solution of these problems. Several additional statements were submitted. The record in the *en banc* portion of the inquiry consisted of 3,775 pages of transcript plus 1,000 pages of exhibits. The Interim Report of the staff of the Office of Network Study was submitted to the Commission for consideration on June 15, 1960.

The Commission will make every effort to expedite its consideration of the entire docket proceeding and will take such definitive action as the Commission determines to be warranted. However, the Commission feels that a general statement of policy responsive to the issues in the *en banc* inquiry is warranted at this time.

Prior to the *en banc* hearing, the Commission had made its position clear that, in fulfilling its obligation to operate in the public interest, a broadcast station is expected to exercise reasonable care and prudence with respect to its broadcast material in order to assure that no matter is broadcast which will deceive or mislead the public. In view of the extent of the problem existing with respect to a number of licensees involving such practices as deceptive quiz shows and payola which had become apparent, the Commission concluded that certain proposed amendments to our Rules as well as proposed legislation would provide a basis for substantial improvements. Accordingly, on February 5, 1960, we adopted a Notice of Proposed Rule Making to deal with fixed quiz and other non-bona fide contest programs involving intellectual skill. These rules would prohibit the broadcasting of such programming unless accompanied by an announcement which would in all cases describe the nature of the program in a manner to sufficiently apprise the audience that the events in question are not in fact spontaneous or actual measures of knowledge or intellectual skill. Announcements would be made at the beginning and end of each program. Moreover, the proposed rules would require a station if it obtained such a program from networks, to be assured similarly that the network program has an accompanying announcement of this nature. This, we believe, would go a long way toward preventing any recurrence of problems such as those encountered in the recent quiz show programs.

We have also felt that this sort of conduct should be prohibited by statute. Accordingly, we suggested legislation designed to make it a crime for anyone to wilfully and knowingly participate or cause another to participate in or cause to be broadcast a program of intellectual skill or knowledge where the outcome thereof is prearranged or predetermined. Without the above-described amendment, the Commission's regulatory authority is limited to its licensing function. The Commission cannot reach networks directly or advertisers, producers, sponsors, and others who, in one capacity or another, are associated with the presentation of radio and television programs which may deceive the listening or viewing public. It is our view that this proposed legislation will help to assure that every contest of intellectual skill or knowledge that is broadcast will be in fact a bona fide contest. Under this proposal, all those persons responsible in any way for the broadcast of a deceptive program of this type would be penalized. Because of the far reaching effects of radio and television, we believe such sanctions to be desirable.

The Commission proposed on February 5, 1960 that a new section be added to the Commission's rules which would require the licensee of radio broadcast stations to adopt appropriate procedures to prevent the practice of payola amongst his employees. Here again the standard of due diligence would have to be met by the licensee. We have also approved on February 11 the language of proposed legislation which would impose criminal penalties for failure to announce sponsored programs, such as payola and others, involving hidden payments or other considerations. This proposal looks toward amending the United States Code to provide fines up to $5,000 or imprisonment up to one year, or both, for violators. It would prohibit the payment to any person or the receipt of payment by any person for the purpose of having as a part of the broadcast program any material on either a radio or television show unless an announcement is made as a part of the program that such material has been paid for or furnished. The Commission now has no direct jurisdiction over the employees of a broadcast station with respect to this type of activity. The imposition of a criminal penalty appears to us to be an effective manner for dealing with this practice. In addition, the Commission has made related legislative proposals with respect to fines, temporary suspension of licenses, and temporary restraining orders.

In view of our mutual interest with the Federal Trade Commission and in order to avoid duplication of effort, we have arrived at an arrangement whereby any information obtained by the FCC which might be of interest to FTC will be called to that Commission's attention by our staff. Similarly, FTC will advise our Commission of any information or data which it acquires in the course of its investigations which might be pertinent to matters under jurisdiction of the FCC. This is an understanding supplemental to earlier liaison arrangements between FCC and FTC.

Certain legislative proposals recently made by the Commission as related to the instant inquiry have been mentioned. It is appropriate now to consider whether the statutory authority of the Commission with respect to programming and program practices is, in other respects, adequate.

In considering the extent of the Commission's authority in the area of programming it is essential first to examine the limitations imposed upon it by the First Amendment to the Constitution and Section 326 of the Communications Act.

The First Amendment to the United States Constitution reads as follows:

Congress shall make no law respecting an establishment of religion or prohibiting the free exercise thereof; or abridging the freedom of speech, or of the press; or the right of the people peaceably to assemble, and to petition the Government for a redress of grievances.

Section 326 of the Communications Act of 1934, as amended, provides that:

Nothing in this chapter shall be understood or construed to give the Commission the power of censorship over the radio communications or signals transmitted by any radio station, and no regulation or condition shall be promulgated or fixed by the Commission which shall interfere with the right of free speech by means of radio communication.

The communication of ideas by means of radio and television is a form of expression entitled to protection against abridgement by the First Amendment to the Constitution. In *United States* v. *Paramount Pictures*, 334 U.S. 131, 166 (1948) the Supreme Court stated:

We have no doubt that moving pictures, like newspapers and radio are included in the press, whose freedom is guaranteed by the First Amendment.

As recently as 1954 in *Superior Films* v. *Department of Education*, 346 U.S. 587, Justice Douglas in a concurring opinion stated:

Motion pictures are, of course, a different medium of expression than the radio, the stage, the novel or the magazine. But the First Amendment draws no distinction between the various methods of communicating ideas.

Moreover, the free speech protection of the First Amendment is not confined solely to the exposition of ideas nor is it required that the subject matter of the communication be possessed of some value to society. In *Winters* v. *New York*, 333 U.S. 507, 510 (1948) the Supreme Court reversed a conviction based upon a violation of an ordinance of the City of New York which made it punishable to distribute printed matter devoted to the publication of accounts of criminal deeds and pictures of bloodshed, lust or crime. In this connection the Court said:

We do not accede to appellee's suggestion that the constitutional protection for a free press applies only to the exposition of ideas. The line between the informing and the entertaining is too elusive for the protection of that basic right. . . . Though we can see nothing of any possible value to society in these magazines, they are as much entitled to the protection of free speech as the best of literature.

Notwithstanding the foregoing authorities, the right to the use of the airwaves is conditioned upon the issuance of a license under a statutory scheme established by Congress in the Communications Act in the proper exercise of its power over commerce.[1] The question therefore arises as to whether because of the characteristics peculiar to broadcasting which justifies the government in regulating its operation through a licensing system, there exists the basis for a distinction as regards other media of mass communication with respect to application of the free speech provisions of the First Amendment? In other words, does it follow that because one may not engage in broadcasting without first obtaining a license, the terms thereof may be so framed as to unreasonably abridge the free speech protection of the First Amendment?

We recognize that the broadcasting medium presents problems peculiar to itself which are not necessarily subject to the same rules governing other media of communication. As we stated in our Petition in *Grove Press, Inc.* and *Readers Subscription, Inc.* v. *Robert K. Christenberry* (Case No. 25,861) filed in the U.S. Court of Appeals for the Second Circuit,

radio and TV programs enter the home and are readily available not only to the average normal adult but also to children and to the emotionally immature. . . . Thus, for example, while a nudist magazine may be within the protection of the First Amendment . . . the televising of nudes might well raise a serious question

---

[1] *NBC* v. *United States*, 319 U.S. 190 (1943).

of programming contrary to 18 U.S.C. 1464. . . . Similarly, regardless of whether the "four-letter words" and sexual description, set forth in "Lady Chatterley's Lover," (when considered in the context of the whole book) make the book obscene for mailability purposes, the utterance of such words or the depiction of such sexual activity on radio or TV would raise similar public interest and Section 1464 questions.

Nevertheless it is essential to keep in mind that "the basic principles of freedom of speech and the press like the First Amendment's command do not vary."[2]

Although the Commission must determine whether the total program service of broadcasters is reasonably responsive to the interests and needs of the public they serve, it may not condition the grant, denial or revocation of a broadcast license upon its own subjective determination of what is or is not a good program. To do so would "lay a forbidden burden upon the exercise of liberty protected by the Constitution."[3] The Chairman of the Commission during the course of his testimony recently given before the Senate Independent Offices Subcommittee of the Committee on Appropriations expressed the point as follows:

Mr. Ford. When it comes to questions of taste, unless it is downright profanity or obscenity, I do not think that the Commission has any part in it.

I don't see how we could possibly go out and say this program is good and that program is bad. That would be a direct violation of the law.[4]

In a similar vein Mr. Whitney North Seymour, President-elect of the American Bar Association, stated during the course of this proceeding that while the Commission may inquire of licensees what they have done to determine the needs of the community they propose to serve, the Commission may not impose upon them its private notions of what the public ought to hear.[5]

Nevertheless, several witnesses in this proceeding have advanced persuasive arguments urging us to require licensees to present specific types of programs on the theory that such action would enhance freedom of expression rather than tend to abridge it. With respect to this proposition we are constrained to point out that the First Amendment forbids governmental interference asserted in aid of free speech, as well as governmental action repressive of it. The protection against abridgement of freedom of speech and press flatly forbids governmental interference, benign or otherwise. The First Amendment "while regarding freedom in religion, in speech and printing and in assembling and petitioning the government for redress of grievances as fundamental and precious to all, seeks

---

[2] *Burstyn* v. *Wilson*, 343 U.S. 495, 503 (1952).
[3] *Cantwell* v. *Connecticut*, 310 U.S. 926, 307 [*sic*].
[4] Hearings before the Subcommittee of the Committee on Appropriations, United States Senate, 86th Congress, 2nd Session on H.R. 11776 at page 775.
[5] Memorandum of Mr. Whitney North Seymour, Special Counsel to the National Association of Broadcasters at page 7.

only to forbid that Congress should meddle therein." (*Powe* v. *United States*, 109 F. 2nd 147)

As recently as 1959 in *Farmers Educational and Cooperative Union of America* v. *WDAY, Inc.* 360 U.S. 525, the Supreme Court succinctly stated:

. . . expressly applying this country's tradition of free expression to the field of radio broadcasting, Congress has from the first emphatically forbidden the Commission to exercise any power of censorship over radio communication.

An examination of the foregoing authorities serves to explain why the day-to-day operation of a broadcast station is primarily the responsibility of the individual station licensee. Indeed, Congress provided in Section 3(h) of the Communications Act that a person engaged in radio broadcasting shall not be deemed a common carrier. Hence, the Commission in administering the Act and the courts in interpreting it have consistently maintained that responsibility for the selection and presentation of broadcast material ultimately devolves upon the individual station licensee, and that the fulfillment of the public interest requires the free exercise of his independent judgment. Accordingly, the Communications Act "does not essay to regulate the business of the licensee. The Commission is given no supervisory control over programs, of business management or of policy . . . The Congress intended to leave competition in the business of broadcasting where it found it . . ."[6] The regulatory responsibility of the Commission in the broadcast field essentially involves the maintenance of a balance between the preservation of a free competitive broadcast system, on the one hand, and the reasonable restriction of that freedom inherent in the public interest standard provided in the Communications Act, on the other.

In addition, there appears a second problem quite unrelated to the question of censorship that would enter into the Commission's assumption of supervision over program content. The Commission's role as a practical matter, let alone a legal matter, cannot be one of program dictation or program supervision. In this connection we think the words of Justice Douglas are particularly appropriate.

The music selected by one bureaucrat may be as offensive to some as it is soothing to others. The news commentator chosen to report on the events of the day may give overtones to the news that pleases the bureaucrat but which rile the . . . audience. The political philosophy which one radio sponsor exudes may be thought by the official who makes up the programs as the best for the welfare of the people. But the man who listens to it . . . may think it marks the destruction of the Republic. . . . Today it is a business enterprise working out a radio program under the auspices of government. Tomorrow it may be a dominant, political or religious group. . . . Once a man is forced to submit to one type of program, he can be forced to submit to another. It may be but a

---

[6] *FCC* v. *Sanders Brothers*, 309 U.S. 470 (1940).

short step from a cultural program to a political program. . . . The strength of our system is in the dignity, resourcefulness and the intelligence of our people. Our confidence is in their ability to make the wisest choice. That system cannot flourish if regimentation takes hold.[7]

Having discussed the limitations upon the Commission in the consideration of programming, there remains for discussion the exceptions to those limitations and the area of affirmative responsibility which the Commission may appropriately exercise under its statutory obligation to find that the public interest, convenience and necessity will be served by the granting of a license to broadcast.

In view of the fact that a broadcaster is required to program his station in the public interest, convenience and necessity, it follows despite the limitations of the First Amendment and Section 326 of the Act, that his freedom to program is not absolute. The Commission does not conceive that it is barred by the Constitution or by statute from exercising any responsibility with respect to programming. It does conceive that the manner or extent of the exercise of such responsibility can introduce constitutional or statutory questions. It readily concedes that it is precluded from examining a program for taste or content, unless the recognized exceptions to censorship apply: for example, obscenity, profanity, indecency, programs inciting to riots, programs designed or inducing toward the commission of crime, lotteries, etc. These exceptions, in part, are written into the United States Code and, in part, are recognized in judicial decision. See Sections 1304, 1343, and 1464 of Title 18 of the United States Code (lotteries; fraud by radio; utterance of obscene, indecent or profane language by radio). It must be added that such traditional or legislative exceptions to a strict application of the freedom of speech requirements of the United States Constitution may very well also convey wider scope in judicial interpretation as applied to licensed radio than they have had or would have as applied to other communications media. The Commission's petition in the *Grove* case, *supra*, urged the court not unnecessarily to refer to broadcasting, in its opinion, as had the District Court. Such reference subsequently was not made though it must be pointed out there is no evidence that the motion made by the FCC was a contributing factor. It must nonetheless be observed that this Commission conscientiously believes that it should make no policy or take any action which would violate the letter or the spirit of the censorship prohibitions of Section 326 of the Communications Act.

As stated by the Supreme Court of the United States in *Joseph Burstyn, Inc.* v. *Wilson, supra*:

. . . Nor does it follow that motion pictures are necessarily subject to the precise rule governing any other particular method of expression. Each method tends to present its own peculiar problem. But the basic principles of freedom of speech

---

[7]*Public Utilities Commission v. Pollak*, 343 U.S. 451, 468, Dissenting Opinion.

and the press, like the First Amendment's command, do not vary. Those principles, as they have frequently been enunciated by this Court, make freedom of expression the rule.

A review of the Communications Act as a whole clearly reveals that the foundation of the Commission's authority rests upon the public interest, convenience and necessity.[8] The Commission may not grant, modify or renew a broadcast station license without finding that the operation of such station is in the public interest. Thus, faithful discharge of its statutory responsibilities is absolutely necessary in connection with the implacable requirement that the Commission approve no such application for license unless it finds that "public interest, convenience, and necessity would be served." While the public interest standard does not provide a blueprint of all of the situations to which it may apply, it does contain a sufficiently precise definition of authority so as to enable the Commission to properly deal with the many and varied occasions which may give rise to its application. A significant element of the public interest is the broadcaster's service to the community. In the case of *NBC* v. *United States*, 319 U.S. 190, the Supreme Court described this aspect of the public interest as follows:

An important element of public interest and convenience affecting the issue of a license is the ability of the licensee to render the best practicable service to the community reached by broadcasts. . . . The Commission's licensing function cannot be discharged, therefore, merely by finding that there are no technological objections to the granting of a license. If the criterion of "public interest" were limited to such matters, how could the Commission choose between two applicants for the same facilities, each of whom is financially and technically qualified to operate a station? Since the very inception of federal regulation of radio, comparative considerations as to the services to be rendered have governed the application of the standard of "public interest, convenience, or necessity."

Moreover, apart from this broad standard which we will further discuss in a moment, there are certain other statutory indications.

It is generally recognized that programming is of the essence of radio service. Section 307(b) of the Communications Act requires the Commission to "make such distribution of licenses . . . among the several States and communities as to provide a fair, efficient, and equitable distribution of radio service to each of the same." Under this section the Commission has consistently licensed stations with the end objective of either providing new or additional programming service *to* a community, area or state, or of providing a new or additional "outlet" for broadcasting *from* a community, area, or state. Implicit in the former alternative is increased radio reception; implicit in the latter

---

[8] §307(d), 308, 309, *inter alia.*

alternative is increased radio transmission and, in this connection, appropriate attention to local live programming is required.

Formerly by reason of administrative policy, and since September 14, 1959, by necessary implication from the amended language of Section 315 of the Communications Act, the Commission has had the responsibility for determining whether licensees "afford reasonable opportunity for the discussion of conflicting views on issues of public importance." This responsibility usually is of the generic kind and thus, in the absence of unusual circumstances, is not exercised with regard to particular situations but rather in terms of operating policies of stations as viewed over a reasonable period of time. This, in the past, has meant a review, usually in terms of filed complaints, in connection with the applications made each three year period for renewal of station licenses. However, that has been a practice largely traceable to workload necessities, and therefore not so limited by law. Indeed the Commission recently has expressed its views to the Congress that it would be desirable to exercise a greater discretion with respect to the length of licensing periods within the maximum three year license period provided by Section 307(d). It has also initiated rulemaking to this end.

The foundation of the American system of broadcasting was laid in the Radio Act of 1927 when Congress placed the basic responsibility for all matter broadcast to the public at the grass roots level in the hands of the station licensee. That obligation was carried forward into the Communications Act of 1934 and remains unaltered and undivided. The licensee, is, in effect, a "trustee" in the sense that his license to operate his station imposes upon him a non-delegable duty to serve the public interest in the community he had chosen to represent as a broadcaster.

Great confidence and trust are placed in the citizens who have qualified as broadcasters. The primary duty and privilege to select the material to be broadcast to his audience and the operation of his component of this powerful medium of communication is left in his hands. As was stated by the Chairman in behalf of this Commission in recent testimony before a Congressional Committee:[9]

Thus far Congress has not imposed by law an affirmative programming requirement on broadcast licenses. Rather, it has heretofore given licensees a broad discretion in the selection of programs. In recognition of this principle, Congress provided in section 3(h) of the Communications Act that a person engaged in radio broadcasting shall not be deemed a common carrier. To this end the Commission in administering the Act and the courts in interpreting it have consistently maintained that responsibility for the selection and presentation of

---

[9] Testimony of Frederick W. Ford, May 16, 1960, before the Subcommittee on Communications of the Committee on Interstate & Foreign Commerce, United States Senate.

broadcast material ultimately devolves upon the individual station licensee, and that the fulfillment of such responsibility requires the free exercise of his independent judgment.

As indicated by former President Hoover, then Secretary of Commerce, in the Radio Conference of 1922-25:

The dominant element for consideration in the radio field is, and always will be, the great body of the listening public, millions in number, country wide in distribution. There is no proper line of conflict between the broadcaster and the listener, nor would I attempt to array one against the other. Their interests are mutual, for without the one the other could not exist.

There have been few developments in industrial history to equal the speed and efficiency with which genius and capital have joined to meet radio needs. The great majority of station owners today recognize the burden of service and gladly assume it. Whatever other motive may exist for broadcasting, the pleasing of the listener is always the primary purpose . . .

The greatest public interest must be the deciding factor. I presume that few will dissent as to the correctness of this principle, for all will agree that public good must ever balance private desire; but its acceptance leads to important and far-reaching practical effects, as to which there may not be the same unanimity, but from which, nevertheless, there is no logical escape.

The confines of the licensee's duty are set by the general standard "the public interest, convenience or necessity."[10] The initial and principal execution of that standard, in terms of the area he is licensed to serve, is the obligation of the licensee. The principal ingredient of such obligation consists of a diligent, positive and continuing effort by the licensee to discover and fulfill the tastes, needs and desires of his service area. If he has accomplished this, he has met his public responsibility. It is the duty of the Commission, in the first instance, to select persons as licensees who meet the qualifications laid down in the Act, and on a continuing basis to review the operations of such licensees from time to time to provide reasonable assurance to the public that the broadcast service it receives is such as its direct and justifiable interest requires.

Historically it is interesting to note that in its review of station performance the Federal Radio Commission sought to extract the general principles of broadcast service which should (1) guide the licensee in his determination of the public interest and (2) be employed by the Commission as an "index" or general frame of reference in evaluating the licensee's discharge of his public duty. The Commission attempted no precise definition of the components of the public interest but left the discernment of its limit to the practical operation of broadcast regulation. It required existing stations to report

---

[10] *Cf.* Communications Act of 1934, as amended, *inter alia*, Secs. 307, 309.

the types of service which had been provided and called on the public to express its views and preferences as to programs and other broadcast services. It sought information from as many sources as were available in its quest of a fair and equitable basis for the selection of those who might wish to become licensees and the supervision of those who already engaged in broadcasting.

The spirit in which the Radio Commission approached its unprecedented task was to seek to chart a course between the need of arriving at a workable concept of the public interest in station operation, on the one hand, and the prohibition laid on it by the First Amendment to the Constitution of the United States and by Congress in Section 29 of the Federal Radio Act against censorship and interference with free speech, on the other. The Standards or guidelines which evolved from that process, in their essentials, were adopted by the Federal Communications Commission and have remained as the basis for evaluation of broadcast service. They have in the main, been incorporated into various codes and manuals of network and station operation.

It is emphasized, that these standards or guidelines should in no sense constitute a rigid mold for station performance, nor should they be considered as a Commission formula for broadcast service in the public interest. Rather, they should be considered as indicia of the types and areas of service which, on the basis of experience, have usually been accepted by the broadcasters as more or less included in the practical definition of community needs and interests.

Broadcasting licensees must assume responsibility for all material which is broadcast through their facilities. This includes all programs and advertising material which they present to the public. With respect to advertising material the licensee has the additional responsibility to take all reasonable measures to eliminate any false, misleading, or deceptive matter and to avoid abuses with respect to the total amount of time devoted to advertising continuity as well as the frequency with which regular programs are interrupted for advertising messages. This duty is personal to the licensee and may not be delegated. He is obligated to bring his positive responsibility affirmatively to bear upon all who have a hand in providing broadcast matter for transmission through his facilities so as to assure the discharge of his duty to provide acceptable program schedule consonant with operating in the public interest in his community. The broadcaster is obligated to make a positive, diligent and continuing effort, in good faith, to determine the tastes, needs and desires of the public in his community and to provide programming to meet those needs and interests. This again, is a duty personal to the licensee and may not be avoided by delegation of the responsibility to others.

Although the individual station licensee continues to bear legal responsibility for all matter broadcast over his facilities, the structure of broadcasting, as developed in practical operation, is such — especially in television — that, in reality, the station licensee has little part in the creation, production, selection, and control of network program offerings. Licensees place "practical reliance" on networks for the selection and supervision of network programs which, of course, are the principal broadcast fare of the vast majority of television stations throughout the country.[11]

In the fulfillment of his obligation the broadcaster should consider the tastes, needs and desires of the public he is licensed to serve in developing his programming and should exercise conscientious efforts not only to ascertain them but also to carry them out as well as he reasonably can. He should reasonably attempt to meet all such needs and interests on an equitable basis. Particular areas of interest and types of appropriate service may, of course, differ from community to community, and from time to time. However, the Commission does expect its broadcast licensees to take the necessary steps to inform themselves of the real needs and interests of the areas they serve and to provide programming which in fact constitutes a diligent effort, in good faith, to provide for those needs and interests.

The major elements usually necessary to meet the public interest, needs and desires of the community in which the station is located as developed by the industry, and recognized by the Commission, have included: (1) Opportunity for Local Self-Expression, (2) The Development and Use of Local Talent, (3) Programs for Children, (4) Religious Programs, (5) Educational Programs, (6) Public Affairs Programs, (7) Editorialization by Licensees, (8) Political Broadcasts, (9) Agricultural Programs, (10) News Programs, (11) Weather and Market Reports, (12) Sports Programs, (13) Service to Minority Groups, (14) Entertainment Programming.

The elements set out above are neither all-embracing nor constant. We re-emphasize that they do not serve and have never been intended as a rigid mold or fixed formula for station operations. The ascertainment of the needed elements of the broadcast matter to be provided by a particular licensee for the audience he is obligated to serve remains primarily the function of the licensee. His honest and prudent judgments will be accorded great weight by the Commission. Indeed, any other course would tend to substitute the judgment of the Commission for that of the licensee.

The programs provided first by "chains" of stations and then by networks have always been recognized by this Commission as of great value to the station licensee in providing a well-rounded community service. The importance of network programs need not be re-emphasized as they have constituted an integral part of the well-rounded program service provided by the broadcast business in most communities.

Our own observations and the testimony in this inquiry have persuaded us that there is no public interest basis for distinguishing between sustaining and commercially sponsored programs in evaluating station performance. However, this does not relieve the station from responsibility for retaining the flexibility to accommodate public needs.

---

[11] The Commission, in recognition of this problem as it affects the licensees, has recently recommended to the Congress enactment of legislation providing for direct regulation of networks in certain respects.

Sponsorship of public affairs, and other similar programs may very well encourage broadcasters to greater efforts in these vital areas. This is borne out by statements made in this proceeding in which it was pointed out that under modern conditions sponsorship fosters rather than diminishes the availability of important public affairs and "cultural" broadcast programming. There is some convincing evidence, for instance, that at the network level there is a direct relation between commercial sponsorship and "clearance" of public affairs and other "cultural" programs. Agency executives have testified that there is unused advertising support for public affairs type programming. The networks and some stations have scheduled these types of programs during "prime time."

The Communications Act[12] provides that the Commission may grant construction permits and station licenses, or modifications or renewals thereof, "only upon written application" setting forth the information required by the Act and the Commission's Rules and Regulations. If, upon examination of any such application, the Commission shall find the public interest, convenience, and necessity would be served by the granting thereof, it shall grant said application. If it does not so find, it shall so advise the applicant and other known parties in interest of all objections to the application and the applicant shall then be given an opportunity to supply additional information. If the Commission cannot then make the necessary finding, the application is designated for hearing and the applicant bears the burden of providing proof of the public interest.

During our hearings there seemed to be some misunderstanding as to the nature and use of the "statistical" data regarding programming and advertising required by our application forms. We wish to stress that no one may be summarily judged as to the service he has performed on the basis of the information contained in his application. As we said long ago:

It should be emphasized that the statistical data before the Commission constitute an index only of the manner of operation of the stations and are not considered by the Commission as conclusive of the over-all operation of the stations in question.

Licensees will have an opportunity to show the nature of their program service and to introduce other relevant evidence which would demonstrate that in actual operation the program service of the station is, in fact, a well rounded program service and is in conformity with the promises and representations previously made in prior applications to the Commission.[13]

As we have said above, the principal ingredient of the licensee's obligation to operate his station in the public interest is the diligent, positive, and continuing effort by the licensee to discover and fulfill the tastes, needs, and desires of his community or service area, for broadcast service.

To enable the Commission in its licensing functions to make the necessary public interest finding, we intend to revise Part IV of our application forms to

---

[12] Section 308(a).

[13] Public Notice (98501), Sept. 20, 1946, "Status of Standard Broadcast Applications."

require a statement by the applicant, whether for new facilities, renewal or modification, as to: (1) the measures he has taken and the effort he has made to determine the tastes, needs and desires of his community or service area, and (2) the manner in which he proposes to meet those needs and desires.

Thus we do not intend to guide the licensee along the path of programming; on the contrary the licensee must find his own path with the guidance of those whom his signal is to serve. We will thus steer clear of the bans of censorship without disregarding the public's vital interest. What we propose will not be served by pre-planned program format submissions accompanied by complimentary references from local citizens. What we propose is documented program submissions prepared as the result of assiduous planning and consultation covering two main areas: first, a canvass of the listening public who will receive the signal and who constitute a definite public interest figure; second, consultation with leaders in community life — public officials, educators, religious, the entertainment media, agriculture, business, labor — professional and eleemosynary organizations, and others who bespeak the interests which make up the community.

By the care spent in obtaining and reflecting the views thus obtained, which clearly cannot be accepted without attention to the business judgment of the licensee if his station is to be an operating success, will the standard of programming in the public interest be best fulfilled. This would not ordinarily be the case if program formats have been decided upon by the licensee before he undertakes his planning and consultation, for the result would show little stimulation on the part of the two local groups above referenced. And it is the composite of their contributive planning, led and sifted by the expert judgment of the licensee, which will assure to the station the appropriate attention to the public interest which will permit the Commission to find that a license may issue. By his narrative development, in his application, of the planning, consulting, shaping, revising, creating, discarding and evaluation of programming thus conceived or discussed, the licensee discharges the public interest facet of his business calling without Government dictation or supervision and permits the Commission to discharge its responsibility to the public without invasion of spheres of freedom properly denied to it. By the practicality and specificity of his narrative the licensee facilitates the application of expert judgment by the Commission. Thus, if a particular kind of educational program could not be feasibly assisted (by funds or service) by educators for more than a few time periods, it would be idle for program composition to place it in weekly focus. Private ingenuity and educational interest should look further, toward implemental suggestions of practical yet constructive value. The broadcaster's license is not intended to convert his business into "an instrumentality of the federal government"; [14] neither, on the other hand, may he ignore the public interest

---

[14] "The defendant is not an instrumentality of the federal government but a privately owned corporation." *McIntire* v. *Wm. Penn Broadcasting Co.*, 151 F. 2d 597, 600.

which his application for a license should thus define and his operations thereafter reasonably observe.

Numbers of suggestions were made during the *en banc* hearings concerning possible uses by the Commission of codes of broadcast practices adopted by segments of the industry as part of a process of self-regulation. While the Commission has not endorsed any specific code of broadcast practices, we consider the efforts of the industry to maintain high standards of conduct to be highly commendable and urge that the industry persevere in these efforts.

The Commission recognizes that submissions, by applicants, concerning their past and future programming policies and performance provide one important basis for deciding whether — insofar as broadcast services are concerned — we may properly make the public interest finding requisite to the grant of an application for a standard FM or television broadcast station. The particular manner in which applicants are required to depict their proposed or past broadcast policies and services (including the broadcasting of commercial announcements) may therefore, have significant bearing upon the Commission's ability to discharge its statutory duties in the matter. Conscious of the importance of reporting requirements, the Commission on November 24, 1958 initiated proceedings (Docket No. 12673) to consider revisions to the rules prescribing the form and content of reports on broadcast programming.

Aided by numerous helpful suggestions offered by witnesses in the recent *en banc* hearings on broadcast programming, the Commission is at present engaged in a thorough study of this subject. Upon completion of that study we will announce, for comment by all interested parties, such further revisions to the present reporting requirements as we think will best conduce to an awareness, by broadcasters, of their responsibilities to the public and to effective, efficient processing, by the Commission, of applications for broadcast licenses and renewals.

To this end, we will initiate further rule making on the subject at the earliest practicable date.

Separate statement of Commissioner Hyde

I believe that the Commission's "Interim Report and Statement of Policy" in Docket No. 12782 misses the central point of the hearing conducted by the Commission en banc, December 7, 1959, to February 1, 1960.

It reiterates the legal position which was taken by the Federal Radio Commission in 1927, and which has been adhered to by the Federal Communications Commission since it was organized in 1934. This viewpoint was accepted by the executives of the leading networks and by most other units of the broadcasting industry as well as the National Association of Broadcasters. The main concern requiring a fresh approach is what to do in the light of the law and the matters presented by many witnesses in the hearings. This, I understand, is to be the subject of a rule-making proceeding still to be initiated. I urged the preparation of an appropriate rule-making notice prior to the preparation of the instant statement.

I also disagree with the decision of the Commission to release the document captioned "Interim Report by the Office of Network Study, Responsibility for Broadcast Matter, Docket No. 12782." Since it deals in part with a hearing in which the Commission itself sat en banc, I feel that it does not have the character of a separate staff-study type of document, and that its release with the Commission policy statement will create confusion. Moreover, a substantial portion of the document is concerned with matter still under investigation process in Docket 12782. I think issuance of comment on these matters under the circumstances is premature and inappropriate.

6

THE SUBURBAN CASE

Patrick Henry et al., d/b as Suburban Broadcasters v.
Federal Communications Commission*
302 F.2d 191 (D.C. Cir.)
March 29, 1962

This Court of Appeals decision affirmed the FCC's right to apply the standards contained in its *1960 Programming Policy Statement* when considering applications for permits to construct new stations. The Supreme Court declined review of the case (371 U.S. 821 (1962)). The appellate court's ruling relies heavily on the Supreme Court's 1943 *Network* decision, contained in Part IV.

Bazelon, Circuit Judge.

Appellants, doing business as Suburban Broadcasters, filed the sole application for a permit to construct the first commercial F.M. station in Elizabeth, New Jersey.[1] Although the Federal Communications Commission found Suburban legally, technically and financially qualified, it designated the application for hearing on the issues raised by the claim of Metropolitan Broadcasting Company, the licensee of WNEW in New York, that a grant would result in objectionable interference. At Metropolitan's request, the Commission subsequently added another issue for hearing:

To determine whether the program proposals of Suburban Broadcasters are designed to and would be expected to serve the needs of the proposed service area.

---

[1] The Communications Act of 1934 § 319, 48 Stat. 1089, 47 U.S.C.A. § 319 (1958), forbids the Commission to license a station unless its construction has previously been authorized by a permit issued pursuant to §§ 308 and 309, 48 Stat. 1084-1085 (1934), 47 U.S.C.A. §§ 308, 309 (1958).

Upon hearing, the trial examiner found for Suburban on both issues. The Commission affirmed on the issue of objectionable interference but reversed on the issue relating to the program proposals and denied the application. Suburban appeals.

These are the pertinent facts disclosed by the record. None of Suburban's principals were residents of Elizabeth. They made no inquiry into the characteristics or programming needs of that community and offered no evidence thereon. Suburban's program proposals were identical with those submitted in its application for an F.M. facility in Berwyn, Illinois, and in the application of two of its principals for an F.M. facility in Alameda, California.[2]

Although the trial examiner resolved the program planning issue in favor of Suburban, he noted that its approach might be characterized as "cavalier" or little more than a "quick shrug." He also referred to the "Program Policy Statement," released by the Commission July 29, 1960, to the effect that the broadcaster's programming responsibility is measured by the statutory standard of "public interest, convenience or necessity," and that in meeting such standard the broadcaster is "obligated to make a positive, diligent and continuing effort, in good faith, to determine the tastes, needs and desires of the public in his community and to provide programming to meet those needs and interests." But the examiner stated that these standards were intended for existing licensees, rather than applicants for new stations, and were therefore inapplicable here.

In reversing the examiner, the Commission (with one Commissioner absent and two dissenting) stated:

We agree [with the examiner] that Elizabeth has a presumptive need for a first local FM transmission service. We have generally presumed that an applicant for such a community would satisfy its programming needs, assuming that the applicant had at least a rudimentary knowledge of such needs. However, we cannot indulge in that presumption where the validity of the underlying assumption is questioned, a specific issue is added, and it is demonstrated that the applicant has taken no steps to familiarize himself with the community or its needs. It is not sufficient that the applicant will bring a first transmission service to the community — it must in fact provide a first local outlet for community self-expression. Communities may differ, and so may their needs; an applicant has the responsibility of ascertaining his community's needs and of programming to meet those needs. As found by the Examiner, Suburban's principals made no inquiry into the characteristics of Elizabeth or its particular programming needs. The instant program proposals were drawn up on the basis of the principals' apparent belief — unsubstantiated by inquiry, insofar as the record shows — that Elizabeth's needs duplicated those of Alameda, California, and Berwyn, Illinois, or, in the words of the Examiner, could "be served in the same manner that such 'needs' are served by FM broadcasters generally."

[2]The application for the Berwyn facility was dismissed; the one for Alameda was granted.

The Commission found that the "program proposals were not 'designed' to serve the needs of Elizabeth"; and that it could not determine whether the proposals "would be expected" to serve these needs, since no evidence of these needs was offered. "In essence," said the Commission, "we are asked to grant an application prepared by individuals totally without knowledge of the area they seek to serve. We feel the public deserves something more in the way of preparation for the responsibilities sought by applicant than was demonstrated on this record." Accordingly, the Commission held that "it cannot be concluded that a grant . . . would serve the public interest, convenience and necessity."

Appellants contend that the statutory licensing scheme requires a grant where, as here, it is established that the sole applicants for a frequency are legally, financially and technically qualified. This view reflects an arbitrarily narrow understanding of the statutory words "public convenience, interest, or necessity."[3] It leaves no room for Commission consideration of matters relating to programming. Moreover, appellants urge that consideration of such matters is precluded by the statute's proscription of censorship[4] and the constitutional guarantee of free speech.

We think these broad contentions are beside the narrow point at issue upon this record. It may be that a licensee must have freedom to broadcast light opera even if the community likes rock and roll music, although that question is not uncomplicated. Even more complicated is the question whether he may feed a diet of rock and roll music to a community which hungers for opera. These are questions, however, that we need not here decide. As we see it, the question presented on the instant record is simply whether the Commission may require that an applicant demonstrate an earnest interest in serving a local community by evidencing a familiarity with its particular needs and an effort to meet them.

We think National Broadcasting Co. v. United States, 319 U.S. 190, 63 S.Ct. 997, 87 L.Ed. 1344 (1943), settles the narrow question before us in the affirmative. There, the Commission promulgated regulations which provided, *inter alia*, that no license would be granted to stations whose network contracts would prevent them from developing programs "to serve the needs of the local community." 319 U.S. at 203, 63 S.Ct. at 1003. National Broadcasting Company challenged the regulations on precisely the grounds appellants advance here: that since the regulations were calculated to affect program content, they exceeded statutory and constitutional limitations. In sustaining the regulations, the Supreme Court held that the Commission may impose reasonable restrictions

---

[3] Communications Act of 1934 § 307(a), 48 Stat. 1083, 47 U.S.C.A. § 307(a) (1958). The statute directs the Commission to grant a station license to any applicant "if public convenience, interest, or necessity will be served thereby."

[4] "Nothing in this Act shall be understood or construed to give the Commission the power of censorship over the radio communications or signals transmitted by any radio station, and no regulation or condition shall be promulgated or fixed by the Commission which shall interfere with the right of free speech by means of radio communication." Communications Act of 1934 § 326, 48 Stat. 1091, 47 U.S.C.A. § 326 (1958).

upon the grant of licenses to assure programming designed to meet the needs of the local community. We think it clear that the Commission's action in the instant case reflects no greater interference with a broadcaster's alleged right to choose its programs free from Commission control than the interference involved in National Broadcasting Co.[5]

Affirmed.

---

[5] Appellants also complain that they were surprised by the Commission's insistence that they be familiar with the needs of the community they sought to serve. But that requirement is not new. See Kentucky Broadcasting Corp. v. Federal Communications Comm., 84 U.S. App. D.C. 383, 174 F. 2d 38 (1949); Sanders, 2 F.C.C. 365, 372 (1936); Egeland, 6 F.C.C. 278 (1938); Brownsville Broadcasting Co., 2 F.C.C. 336, 340 (1936) (alternative ground); Martin, 3 F.C.C. 461 (1936) (alternative ground); Goldwasser, 4 F.C.C. 223 (1937) (alternative ground); Kraft, 4 F.C.C. 354 (1937) (alternative ground). And the question whether appellants had demonstrated such familiarity was within the scope of the issues designated for hearing.

7

THE PACIFICA CASE

In re Pacifica Foundation
    36 FCC 147
    January 22, 1964

> This decision resulted in grants to the Pacifica Foundation for an
> initial license for KPFK, Los Angeles, renewals of the licenses of
> KPFA-FM and KPFB, Berkeley, and WBAI-FM, New York, and
> permission to transfer control of the stations. The authorizations
> were made by the Commission despite the fact that complaints
> had been received regarding the stations' programming, which
> some persons found offensive. The *Pacifica* decision can be
> considered the FCC's affirmation of principles of free speech as
> applied to broadcasting.

BY THE COMMISSION: COMMISSIONER LEE CONCURRING AND
ISSUING A STATEMENT.

1. The Commission has before it for consideration the above-pending
applications of the listed broadcast stations licensed to Pacifica Foundation.
There are three aspects to our consideration: (*a*) Certain programming issues
raised by complaints;   (*b*) issues of possible Communist Party affiliation of
principals of Pacifica;   and (*c*) a question of possible unauthorized transfer of
control. We shall consider each in turn.
    2.   *The programming issues.* — The principal complaints are concerned
with five programs: (i) a December 12, 1959, broadcast over KPFA, at 10 p.m.,
of certain poems by Lawrence Ferlinghetti (read by the poet himself); (ii) "The
Zoo Story," a recording of the Edward Albee play broadcast over KPFK at 11
p.m., January 13, 1963; (iii) "Live and Let Live," a program broadcast over
KPFK at 10:15 p.m. on January 15, 1963, in which eight homosexuals discussed
their attitudes and problems; (iv) a program broadcast over KPFA at 7:15 p.m.

on January 28, 1963, in which the poem, "Ballad of the Despairing Husband," was read by the author Robert Creeley; and (v) "The Kid," a program broadcast at 11 p.m. on January 8, 1963, over KPFA, which consisted of readings by Edward Pomerantz from his unfinished novel of the same name. The complaints charge that these programs were offensive or "filthy" in nature, thus raising the type of issue we recently considered in *Palmetto Bctg. Co.*, 33 FCC 483; 34 FCC 101. We shall consider the above five matters in determining whether, on an overall basis, the licensee's programing met the public-interest standard laid down in the Communications Act.[1] *Report and Statement of Policy re: Commission En Banc Programing Inquiry,* 20 Pike & Fischer R.R. 1901.

3.   When the Commission receives complaints of the general nature here involved, its usual practice is to refer them to the licensee so as to afford the latter an opportunity to comment. When the Commission reviews, on an overall basis, the station's operation at the time of renewal, it thus has before it a complete file, containing all the sides of any matter which may have arisen during the license period. Specifically, with respect to the programing issue in this case, the Commission, barring the exceptions noted in the *Programing Statement (supra,* at p. 1909), is not concerned with individual programs — nor is it at any time concerned with matters essentially of licensee taste or judgment. Cf. *Palmetto Bctg. Co., supra,* paragraph 22. As shown by the cited case, its very limited concern in this type of case is whether, upon the overall examination, some substantial pattern of operation inconsistent with the public-interest standard clearly and patently emerges. Unlike *Palmetto* where there was such a substantial pattern (id. at par. 23; see par. 7, infra), here we are dealing with a few isolated programs, presented over a 4-year period. It would thus appear that there is no substantial problem, on an overall basis, warranting further inquiry.[2] While this would normally conclude the matter, we have determined to treat the issues raised by Pacifica's response to the complaints, because we think it would serve a useful purpose, both to the industry and the public. We shall therefore turn to a more detailed consideration of the issues raised by the complaints as to these five programs. Because of Pacifica's different response to the complaints as to (i) and (iv), paragraph 2 above, we shall treat these two broadcasts separately. (See pars. 6-7, infra.)

4.   There is, we think, no question but that the broadcasts of the programs, "The Zoo Story," "Live and Let Live," and "The Kid," lay well

---

[1] The Commission may also enforce the standard of sec. 1464 of title 18 (dealing with "obscene, indecent, or profane language"). See secs. 312(a), (b); sec. 503(b)(1)(E). In our view, enforcement proceedings under sec. 1464 are not warranted, and therefore, no further consideration need be given this section.

[2] While, for reasons developed in this opinion, it is unnecessary to detail the showings here, we have examined the licensee's overall showings as to its stations' operations and find that those operations did serve the needs and interests of the licensee's areas. *Programing Statement, supra,* at pp. 1913-1916. In this connection, we have also taken into account the showing made in the letter of Apr. 16, 1963.

within the licensee's judgment under the public-interest standard. The situation here stands on an entirely different footing than *Palmetto, supra*, where the licensee had devoted a substantial period of his broadcast day to material which we found to be patently offensive – however much we weighed that standard in the licensee's favor – and as to which programming the licensee himself never asserted that it was not offensive or vulgar, *or that it served the needs of his area or had any redeeming features.* In this case, Pacifica has stated its judgment that the three above-cited programs served the public interests and specifically, the needs and interests of its listening public. Thus, it has pointed out that in its judgment, "The Zoo Story" is a "serious work of drama" by an eminent and "provocative playwright" – that it is "an honest and courageous play" which Americans "who do not live near Broadway ought to have the opportunity to hear and experience. . . ." Similarly, as to "The Kid," Pacifica states, with supporting authority, that Mr. Pomerantz is an author who has obtained notable recognition for his writings and whose readings from his unfinished novel were fully in the public interest as a serious work meriting the attention of its listeners; Pacifica further states that prior to broadcast, the tape was auditioned by one of its employees who edited out two phrases because they did not meet Pacifica's broadcast standards of good taste; and that while "certain minor swear words are used, . . . these fit well within the context of the material being read and conform to the standards of acceptability of reasonably intelligent listeners." Finally, as to the program, "Live and Let Live," Pacifica states that "so long as the program is handled in good taste, there is no reason why subjects like homosexuality should not be discussed on the air"; and that it "conscientiously believes that the American people will be better off as a result of hearing a constructive discussion of the problem rather than leaving the subject to ignorance and silence."

5. We recognize that as shown by the complaints here, such provocative programing as here involved may offend some listeners. But this does not mean that those offended have the right, through the Commission's licensing power, to rule such programing off the airwaves. Were this the case, only the wholly inoffensive, the bland, could gain access to the radio microphone or TV camera. No such drastic curtailment can be countenanced under the Constitution, the Communications Act, or the Commission's policy, which has consistently sought to insure "the maintenance of radio and television as a medium of freedom of speech and freedom of expression for the people of the Nation as a whole" (*Editorializing Report,* 13 FCC 1246, 1248). In saying this, we do not mean to indicate that those who have complained about the foregoing programs are in the wrong as to the worth of these programs and should listen to them. This is a matter solely for determination by the individual listeners. Our function, we stress, is not to pass on the merits of the program – to commend or to frown. Rather, as we stated (par. 3), it is the very limited one of assaying, at the time of renewal, whether the licensee's programming, on an overall basis, has been in the public interest and, in the context of this issue, whether he has made programing

judgments reasonably related to the public interest. This does not pose a close question in the case: Pacifica's judgments as to the above programs clearly fall within the very great discretion which the act wisely vests in the licensee. In this connection, we also note that Pacifica took into account the nature of the broadcast medium when it scheduled such programing for the late evening hours (after 10 p.m., when the number of children in the listening audience is at a minimum).[3]

6.   As to the Ferlinghetti and Creeley programs, the licensee asserts that in both instances, some passages did not measure up to "Pacifica's own standards of good taste." Thus, it states that it did not carefully screen the Ferlinghetti tape to see if it met its standards, "because it relied upon Mr. Ferlinghetti's national reputation and also upon the fact that the tape came to it from a reputable FM station." It acknowledges that this was a mistake in its procedures and states that "in the future, Pacifica will make its own review of all broadcasts. . . ." With respect to the Creeley passage (i.e., the poem, "Ballad of a Despairing Husband"),[4] Pacifica again states that in its judgment it should not have been broadcast. It "does not excuse the broadcast of the poem in question," but it does explain how the poem "slipped by" KPFA's drama and literature editor who auditioned the tape. It points out that prior to the offending poem, Mr. Creeley, who "has a rather flat, monotonous voice," read 18 other perfectly acceptable poems — and that the station's editor was so lulled thereby that he did not catch the few offensive words on the 19th poem. It also points out that each of the nine poems which followed was again perfectly acceptable, and that before rebroadcasting the poem on its Los Angeles station, it deleted the objectionable verse.

7.   In view of the foregoing, we find no impediment to renewal on this score. We are dealing with two isolated errors in the licensee's application of its own standards — one in 1959 and the other in 1963. The explanations given for these two errors are credible. Therefore, even assuming, arguendo, that the broadcasts were inconsistent with the public-interest standard, it is clear that no unfavorable action upon the renewal applications is called for. The standard of public interest is not so rigid that an honest mistake or error on the part of a licensee results in drastic action against him where his overall record demonstrates a reasonable effort to serve the needs and interests of his community. (See note 2, supra.) Here again, this case contrasts sharply with *Palmetto*, where instead of two isolated instances, years apart, we found that the patently offensive material was broadcast for a substantial period of the station's broadcast day for many years. (See par. 3, supra.)

---

[3]Pacifica states that it "is sensitive to its responsibilities to its listening audience and carefully schedules for late night broadcasts those programs which may be misunderstood by children although thoroughly acceptable to an adult audience."

[4]The program containing this passage was a taped recording of Mr. Creeley's readings of selections from his poetry to students at the University of California. KPFA broadcasts many such poetry readings at the university, which are recorded by a university employee for the school's archives (and made available to the station).

8.   We find, therefore, that the programing matters raised with respect to the Pacifica renewals pose no bar to a grant of renewal.[5] Our holding, as is true of all such holdings in this sensitive area, is necessarily based on, and limited to, the facts of the particular case. But we have tried to stress here, as in *Palmetto*, an underlying policy — that the licensee's judgment in this freedom-of-speech area is entitled to very great weight and that the Commission, under the public-interest standard, will take action against the licensee at the time of renewal only where the facts of the particular case, established in a hearing record, flagrantly call for such action. We have done so because we are charged under the act with "promoting the larger and more effective use of radio in the public interest" (sec. 303(g)), and obviously, in the discharge of that responsibility, must take every precaution to avoid inhibiting broadcast licensees' efforts at experimenting or diversifying their programing. Such diversity of programing has been the goal of many Commission policies (e.g., multiple ownership, development of UHF, the fairness doctrine). Clearly, the Commission must remain faithful to that goal in discharging its functions in the actual area of programing itself. . . .

Conclusion

14.   In view of the foregoing, *It is ordered*, This 22d day of January 1964, that the above-entitled applications of Pacifica Foundation *Are granted* as serving the public interest, convenience, and necessity.

Concurring statement of Commissioner Robert E. Lee

I concur in the action of the Commission in granting the several applications of Pacifica Foundation. However, I feel constrained to comment on at least one program coming to our attention insofar as it may or may not reflect these stations' program policies.

Having listened carefully and painfully to a 1½-hour tape recording of a program involving self-professed homosexuals, I am convinced that the program was designed to be, and succeeded in being, contributory to nothing but sensationalism. The airing of a program dealing with sexual aberrations is not to

[5]One other programing aspect deserves emphasis. Complaint has also been made concerning Pacifica's presentation of "far-left" programing. Pacifica has stated that it follows a policy of presenting programs covering the widest range of the political or controversial issue spectrum — from the members of the Communist Party on the left to members of the John Birch Society on the right. Again, we point out that such a policy (which must, of course, be carried out consistently with the requirements of the fairness doctrine) is within the licensee's area of programing judgment.

my mind, per se, a violation of good taste nor contrary to the public interest. When these subjects are discussed by physicians and sociologists, it is conceivable that the public could benefit. But a panel of eight homosexuals discussing their experiences and past history does not approach the treatment of a delicate subject one could expect by a responsible broadcaster. A microphone in a bordello, during slack hours, could give us similar information on a related subject. Such programs, obviously designed to be lurid and to stir the public curiosity, have little place on the air.

I do not hold myself to be either a moralist or a judge of taste. Least of all do I have a clear understanding of what may constitute obscenity in broadcasting.

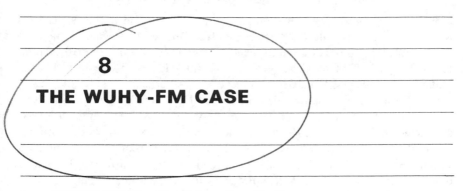

8

THE WUHY-FM CASE

In re WUHY-FM, Eastern Education Radio
24 FCC 2d 408
April 3, 1970

Obscenity, profanity, and indecency on the air are not protected by the provisions of the First Amendment to the Constitution or Section 326 of the Communications Act. Such forms of expression are punishable under Section 1464 of the Criminal Code.

This test case fails to resolve the legal issues involved, since WUHY-FM declined to accept the FCC's invitation to appeal the Commission's decision. The separate opinions of Commissioners Cox and Johnson, however, pinpoint the legal and social conflicts inherent in any such governmental foray into regulation of program content.

While the material stakes were low in this case, they could well have been higher (e.g., loss of license as in *Palmetto*, 33 FCC 250 (1962), or short-term renewal as in *Jack Straw Memorial Foundation*, 21 FCC 2d 833 (1970), *reversed following hearing*, 29 FCC 2d 334 (1971)), though never as lofty as the philosophical principles at issue.

NOTICE OF APPARENT LIABILITY

BY THE COMMISSION: CHAIRMAN BURCH CONCURRING IN THE RESULT; COMMISSIONER COX CONCURRING IN PART AND DISSENTING IN PART AND ISSUING A STATEMENT; COMMISSIONER JOHNSON DISSENTING AND ISSUING A STATEMENT; COMMISSIONER H. REX LEE ABSENT.

1.   This constitutes Notice of Apparent Liability for forfeiture pursuant to Section 503(b)(2) of the Communications Act of 1934, as amended.

    2. *The facts.*   Noncommercial educational radio station WUHY-FM is licensed to Eastern Education Radio, Philadelphia, Pennsylvania. On January 4, 1970, WUHY-FM broadcasted its weekly program "Cycle II" from 10:00 p.m. to 11:00 p.m.[1] This broadcast featured an interview with one Jerry Garcia, leader and member of "The Grateful Dead", a California rock and roll musical group. The interview was recorded on tape in Mr. Garcia's hotel room in New York City on Saturday afternoon, January 3, 1970. The interview was conducted by Messrs. Steve Hill and David Stupplebeen, who are both architects in the Philadelphia area, and who have been engaged from time to time on a volunteer basis by WUHY-FM to assist in programming. Mr. Robert J. Bielecki, a full-time staff engineer for WUHY-FM, was in charge of the production as a volunteer producer; Mr. Bielecki had been allowed supervision of "Cycle II" since its inception in November of 1969. Hill and Stupplebeen returned to Philadelphia Sunday afternoon about 4:00 p.m. (January 4, 1970) with the tape of the recorded interview. Hill spent the next three or four hours editing the tape; i.e., allowing for musical selections. Mr. Bielecki, who was engaged in routine engineering duties at the time, listened to portions of the tape from time to time. Neither Hill, Bielecki, nor Stupplebeen discussed the tape with Mr. Nathan Shaw, the station manager, nor did they seek his clearance in any way; Mr. Shaw, though not at the station, could have been reached at home.

    3.   During the interview, about 50 minutes in length, broadcast on January 4, 1970, Mr. Garcia expressed his views on ecology, music, philosophy, and interpersonal relations. See Appendix A for the example comments on these subjects, as set forth in the licensee's letter of February 12, 1970. His comments were frequently interspersed with the words "f--k" and "s--t", used as adjectives, or simply as an introductory expletive or substitute for the phrase, et cetera. Examples are:

> S - - t man.
> I must answer the phone 900 f - - - - n' times a day, man.
> Right, and it sucks it right f - - - - - g out of ya, man.
> That kind of s - - t.
> It's f - - - - n' rotten man. Every f - - - - n' year.
> . . . this s - - t.
> . . . and all that s - - t — all that s - - t.
> . . . and s - - t like that.
> . . . so f - - - - - g long.

---

[1] The licensee states that this is a one-hour, weekly broadcast which is "underground" in its orientation and "is concerned with the avant-garde movement in music, publications, art, film, personalities, and other forms of social and artistic experimentation." It is designed to reach youthful persons (e.g., the large college population in Philadelphia and "so-called 'alienated' segments of the new generation" — p. 1. WUHY Letter of February 12, 1970). "Cycle II" is the successor program to a similar program entitled "Feed."

Everybody knows everybody so f - - - - - g well that . . .

S - - t

S - - t. I gotta get down there, man.

All that s - - t.

Readily available every f - - - - - g where.

Any of that s - - t either.

Political change is so f - - - - - g slow.

4.   At the conclusion of the Garcia interview, Mr. Hill presented a person known as "Crazy Max", whose real name is not known to the licensee. "Crazy Max" had been a visitor to the station, and he told Hill, while listening to the Garcia interview, that if there were time left in the program he wanted to make some remarks about computers and society. There was a short period left, and "Crazy Max" delivered his message, which also used the word "f--k." The licensee states that Mr. Hill did not know what "Crazy Max" was going to say in detail, or how he was going to say it. It adds that "Crazy Max" will not be allowed access to the microphone again.

5.   In its letter of February 12, 1970, written in response to the Commission's request for comments on the January 4th broadcast,[2] the licensee further states:

The licensee has a standing policy, known to all personnel including Mr. Bielecki, that all taped program material which contains controversial subject matter or language must be reviewed by Mr. Nathan Shaw, the station manager of WUHY-FM. Mr. Bielecki, the producer of this program, did not bring the program to Mr. Shaw's attention. Neither Mr. Shaw nor any other person in the station management heard or reviewed the program before it was aired. Mr. Bielecki has been removed as a producer because of this infraction of station policy. "Cycle II" has been suspended as a program pending licensee review of this entire matter. Internal procedures to insure against a similar incident are being strengthened.

6.   *Discussion – policy.*   The issue in this case is not whether WUHY-FM may present the views of Mr. Garcia or "Crazy Max" on ecology, society, computers, and so on. Clearly that decision is a matter solely within the judgment of the licensee. See Section 326 of the Communications Act of 1934, as amended. Further, we stress, as we have before, the licensee's right to present provocative or unpopular programming which may offend some listeners. *In re Renewal of Pacifica*, 36 FCC 147, 149 (1964). It would markedly disserve the

---

[2]While the licensee states that it received no complaints concerning this January 4th broadcast (nor, we note, did the Commission), the Commission had received several complaints concerning this 10:00 P.M. slot on WUHY-FM (directed to the similar "Feed" program, which "Cycle II" succeeded in November, 1969); it therefore did monitor the broadcast, and specifically that of January 4th.

public interest, were the airwaves restricted only to inoffensive, bland material. Cf. *Red Lion Broadcasting Co., Inc.* v. *F.C.C.*, 395 U.S. 367 (1969). Further, the issue here does not involve presentation of a work of art or on-the-spot coverage of a bona fide news event.[3] Rather the narrow issue is whether the licensee may present previously taped interview or talk shows where the persons intersperse or begin their speech with expressions like, "S--t, man . . .", ". . . and s--t like that", or ". . . 900 f----n' times", ". . . right f----g out of ya", etc.

7.   We believe that if we have the authority, we have a duty to act to prevent the widespread use on broadcast outlets of such expressions in the above circumstances. For, the speech involved has no redeeming social value, and is patently offensive by contemporary community standards, with very serious consequences to the "public interest in the larger and more effective use of radio" (Section 303(g)). As to the first point, it conveys no thought to begin some speech with "S--t, man . . .", or to use "f----g" as an adjective throughout the speech. We recognize that such speech is frequently used in some settings, but it is not employed in public ones. Persons who might use it without thought in a home, job or barracks setting generally avoid its usage when on a public conveyance, elevator, when testifying in court, etc. Similarly, its use can be avoided on radio without stifling in the slightest any thought which the person wishes to convey. In this connection, we note that stations have presented thousands of persons from all walks of life in talk or interview shows, without broadcasting language of the nature here involved. However much a person may like to talk this way, he has no right to do so in public arenas, and broadcasters can clearly insist that in talk shows, persons observe the requirement of eschewing such language.

8.   This brings us to the second part of the analysis — the consequence to the public interest. First, if WUHY can broadcast an interview with Mr. Garcia where he begins sentences with "S--t, man . . .", or uses "f----g" before word after word, just because he likes to talk that way, so also can any other person on radio. Newscasters or disc jockeys could use the same expressions, as could persons, whether moderators or participants, on talk shows, on the ground that

[3] In this connection, we note the licensee's apt statement of policy (pp. 5-6, Letter of February 12, 1970): "The question whether to air a program which contains controversial subject matter or language is among the most difficult a licensee is called upon to resolve. In determining whether to air any program which contains material or language which is potentially offensive or disagreeable to some listeners, licensee balances a number of considerations: The subject matter of the program; its value or relevance to the segment of listeners to which it is directed; whether the program is a work of art; whether it is a recognized classic; and whether the potentially offensive language or material is essential to the integrity of the presentation. Licensee also takes into account such factors as the time of the broadcast, the likelihood that children may be in the audience, and the necessity for appropriate cautionary announcements to listeners in advance of potentially disagreeable programming."

this is the way they talk and it adds flavor or emphasis to their speech.[4] But the consequences of any such widespread practice would be to undermine the usefulness of radio to millions of others. For, these expressions are patently offensive to millions of listeners. *And here it is crucial to bear in mind the difference between radio and other media.* Unlike a book which requires the deliberate act of purchasing and reading (or a motion picture where admission to public exhibition must be actively sought), broadcasting is disseminated generally to the public (Section 3(o) of the Communications Act, 47 U.S.C. 153(o)) under circumstances where reception requires no activity of this nature. Thus, it comes directly into the home and frequently without any advance warning of its content. Millions daily turn the dial from station to station. While particular stations or programs are oriented to specific audiences, the fact is that by its very nature, thousands of others not within the "intended" audience may also see or hear portions of the broadcast.[5] Further, in that audience are very large numbers of children.[6] Were this type of programming (e.g., the WUHY interview with the above described language) to become widespread, it would drastically affect the use of radio by millions of people. No one could ever know, in home or car listening, when he or his children would encounter what he would regard as the most vile expressions serving no purpose but to shock, to pander to sensationalism. Very substantial numbers would either curtail using radio or would restrict their use to but a few channels or frequencies, abandoning the present practice of turning the dial to find some appealing program. In light of the foregoing considerations we note also that it is not a

[4]"To give but one further example, suppose a disc jockey or a moderator on a talk show for sensational or shock purposes aimed at particular audiences, began using expressions such as "Listen to this mother f-----g record [or person]." There is no question but that such use of this vulgar term for an incestuous son is utterly without redeeming social value and, on radio, taking into account its nature (see above paragraph), patently offensive. See discussion, par. 10, *infra.*

[5]In a very real sense, the situation here is the very opposite of *Stanley* v. *Georgia*, 394 U.S. 557 (1969), which involved the private possession or use of obscene material.

[6]For example, the following tables point up the children's audience in the evening hours for radio and television:

Average quarter-hour radio audience of teenagers (12 to 17 years) as a percentage of all teenagers in metro area, 1969

Time	Los Angeles	New York City	Washington, D.C.
8 to 9 p.m.	16.5	16.6	14.1
9 to 10 p.m.	14.8	16.9	14.5
10 to 11 p.m.	10.5	13.8	14.1
11 to 12 midnight	4.8	6.5	10.9

question of what a majority of licensees might do but whether such material is broadcast to a significant extent by any significant number of broadcasters. In short, in our judgment, increased use along the lines of this WUHY broadcast might well correspondingly diminish the use for millions of people. It is one thing to say, as we properly did in *Pacifica*, that no segment, however large its size, may rule out the presentation of unpopular views or of language in a work of art which offends some people; and it is quite another thing to say that WUHY has the right to broadcast an interview in which Mr. Garcia begins many sentences with, "S--t, man . . .", an expression which conveys no thought, has no redeeming social value, and in the context of broadcasting,[7] drastically curtails the usefulness of the medium for millions of people.

9.   For the foregoing reasons, and specifically to prevent any emerging trend in the broadcast field which would be inconsistent with the "larger and more effective use of radio", we conclude that we have a duty to act, if we have the authority to act. We turn now to the issue of our authority.

10.   *Discussion – Law (Authority)*. There are two aspects of this issue. First, there is the question of the applicability of 18 U.S.C. 1464, which makes it a criminal offense to "utter any obscene, indecent, or profane language by means of radio communication." This standard, we note, is incorporated in the Communications Act. See Sections 312(a)(6) and 503(b)(1)(E), 47 U.S.C. 312(a)(6); 503(b)(1)(E). The licensee urges that the broadcast was not obscene "because it did not have a dominant appeal to prurience or sexual matters" (Letter, p. 5). We agree, and thus find that the broadcast would not necessarily come within the standard laid down in *Memoirs* v. *Massachusetts*, 383 U.S. 413, 418 (1965); see also *Jacobelli* v. *Ohio*, 378 U.S. 184, 191 (1963); *Roth* v. *United*

Children (2 to 17 years) viewing TV as a percentage of total persons viewing based on New York and Los Angeles survey, February-March

Time period	Children as percent of total			Child total (percent)
	2 to 6 years	6 to 11 years	11 to 17 years	
Sunday to Saturday, 7:30 to 9 p.m.	5	13	12	30
Sunday to Saturday, 9 to 11 p.m.	1	5	13	19
Average prime time:				
Sunday to Saturday, 7:30 to 11 p.m.	3	10	13	26
Monday to Friday, 11:30 p.m. to 1 a.m.	½	½	5	6

---

[7]We stress that our analysis is limited to broadcasting because of its unique nature of dissemination into millions of homes. The difference is pointed up by this very document. It is perfectly proper, in the analysis here, to use the pertinent expressions of Mr. Garcia. There is no other way to deal intelligently with the subject. But in any event it takes a conscious act by someone interested in the subject to obtain this document and study its contents.

States, 354 U.S. 476 (1956). However, we believe that the statutory term, "indecent", should be applicable, and that, in the broadcast field, the standard for its applicability should be that the material broadcast is (a) patently offensive by contemporary community standards; and (b) is utterly without redeeming social value. The Court has made clear that different rules are appropriate for different media of expression in view of their varying natures. "Each method tends to present its own peculiar problems." *Burstyn* v. *Wilson*, 343 U.S. 495, 502-503 (1951). We have set forth in par. 8, *supra*, the reasons for applicability of the above standard in defining what is indecent in the broadcast field. We think that the factors set out in par. 8 are cogent, powerful considerations for the different standard in this markedly different field.

    11.   There is no precedent, judicial or administrative, for this case. There have been few opinions construing 18 U.S.C. 1464 (e.g., *Duncan* v. *U.S.*, 48 F. 2d 128 (C.C.A. Or. 1931), certiorari denied 283 U.S. 863; *Gagliardo* v. U.S., 366 F. 2d 720 (1966)), and none in the broadcast field here involved. The issue whether the term, "indecent", has a meaning different from "obscene" in Section 1464 was raised in *Gagliardo* (366 F. 2d at pp. 725-26) but not resolved. Support for giving it a different meaning is indicated by *U.S.* v. *Limehouse*, 285 U.S. 424 (1932) which held that the word "filthy" which was added to the postal obscenity law by amendment, now 18 U.S.C. § 1461, meant something other than "obscene, lewd, or lascivious", and permitted a prosecution of the sender of a letter which "plainly related to sexual matters" and was "coarse, vulgar, disgusting, indecent; and unquestionably filthy within the popular meaning of that term." However, in line with the principle set out above in *Burstyn*, the matter is one of first impression, and can only be definitively settled by the courts. We hold as we do, since otherwise there is nothing to prevent the development of the trend which we described in par. 8, from becoming a reality.

    12.   The licensee argues that the program was not indecent, because its basic subject matters "... are obviously decent"; "the challenged language though not essential to the meaning of the program as a whole, reflected the personality and life style of Mr. Garcia"; and "the realistic portrayal of such an interview cannot be deemed 'indecent' because the subject incidentally used strong or salty language." (Letter, p. 5). We disagree with this approach in the broadcast field. Were it followed, any newscaster or talk moderator could intersperse his broadcast with these expressions, or indeed a disc jockey could speak of his records and related views with phrases like, "S--t, man . . ., listen to this mother f----r", on the ground that his overall broadcast was clearly decent, and that this manner of presentation reflected the "personality and life style" of the speaker, who was only "telling it like it is." The licensee itself notes that the language in question "was not essential to the presentation of the subject matter . . ." but rather was ". . . essentially gratuitous." We think that is the precise point here — namely, that the language *is* "gratuitous" — i.e., "unwarranted or [having] no reason for its existence" (Webster's Collegiate Dictionary, Fifth Ed., p. 435). There is no valid basis in these circumstances for permitting its

widespread use in the broadcast field, with the detrimental consequences described in par. 8, *supra*.

13.   The matter could also be approached under the public interest standard of the Communications Act. Broadcast licensees must operate in the public interest (Section 315(a)), and the Commission does have authority to act to insure such operation. *Red Lion Broadcasting Co., Inc.* v. *F.C.C.* 395 U.S. 367, 380 (1969). This does not mean, of course, that the Commission could properly assess program after program, stating that one was consistent with the public interest and another was not. That would be flagrant censorship. See Section 326 of the Communications Act, 47 U.S.C. 326; *Banzhaf* v. *F.C.C.*, 132 U.S. App. D.C. 14, 27; 405 F. 2d 1082, 1095 (1968), certiorari denied, 395 U.S. 973 (1969). However, we believe that we can act under the public interest criterion in this narrow area against those who present programming such as is involved in this case. The standard for such action under the public interest criterion is the same as previously discussed — namely, that the material is patently offensive by contemporary community standards and utterly without redeeming social value. These were the standards employed in *Palmetto Broadcasting Co.*, 33 FCC 483; 34 FCC 101 (1963), affirmed on other grounds, *E. G. Robinson, Jr.* v. *F.C.C.*, 108 U.S. App. D.C. 144, 344 F. 2d 534 (1964), certiorari denied, 379 U.S. 843, where the Commission denied the application for renewal of a licensee which, inter alia, had presented smut during a substantial period of the broadcasting day.[8]

14.   In sum, we hold that we have the authority to act here under Section 1464 (i.e. 503(b)(1)(E)) or under the public interest standard (Section 503(b)(1)(A)(B) — for failure to operate in the public interest as set forth in the license or to observe the requirement of Section 315(a) to operate in the public interest). Cf. *Red Lion Broadcasting Co., Inc.* v. *F.C.C.*, 395 U.S. 367, 376, n. 5. However, whether under Section 1464 or the public interest standard, the criteria for Commission action thus remains the same, in our view — namely, that the material be patently offensive and utterly without redeeming value. Finally, as we stressed before in sensitive areas like this (Report and Order on Personal Attack Rules, 8 FCC 2d 721, 725 (1968)), the Commission can appropriately act only in clear-cut, flagrant cases; doubtful or close cases are clearly to be resolved in the licensee's favor.

15.   *Discussion — Application of the above principles to this case.* In view of the foregoing, little further discussion is needed on this aspect. We believe that the presentation of the Garcia material quoted in par. 3 falls clearly within the two above criteria,[9] and hence may be the subject of a forfeiture

---

[8] The Commission there found the programming patently offensive by contemporary community standards and no evidence that it ". . . in some way served the needs and interests of the area."

[9] There does not appear to be any factual dispute. However, the licensee has the opportunity to advance any pertinent factual considerations in response to this Notice and may of course obtain a trial de novo of the matter in the district court. See Section 504(a).

under Section 503(b)(1)(A)(B) and (E). We further find that the presentation was "willful" (503(b)(1)(A)(B)). We note that the material was taped. Further the station employees could have cautioned Mr. Garcia either at the outset or after the first few expressions to avoid using these "gratuitous" expressions; they did not do so.[10] That the material was presented without obtaining the station manager's approval — contrary to station policy — does not absolve the licensee of responsibility. See *KWK, Inc.*, 34 FCC 1039, affirmed 119 U.S. App. D.C. 144, 337 F. 2d 540 (1964). Indeed, in light of the facts here, there would appear to have been gross negligence on the part of the licensee with respect to its supervisory duties.

16.   We turn now to the question of the appropriate sanction. The licensee points out that this is one isolated occurrence, and that therefore the *Palmetto* decision is inapposite. We agree that there is no question of revocation or denial of license on the basis of the matter before us, even without taking into account the overall record of the station, as described in the licensee's letter, pp. 6-8. See also *In re Renewal of Pacifica*, 36 FCC 147 (1964). Rather, the issue in this case is whether to impose a forfeiture (since one of the reasons for the forfeiture provision is that it can be imposed for the isolated occurrence, such as an isolated lottery, etc.). On this issue, we note that, in view of the fact that this is largely a case of first impression, particularly as to the Section 1464 aspect, we could appropriately forego the forfeiture and simply act prospectively in this field. See, *Taft Broadcasting Co.*, 18 FCC 2d 186; *Bob Jones University*, 18 FCC 2d 8; *WBRE-TV, Inc.*, 18 FCC 2d 96. However, were we to do so, we would prevent any review of our action and in this sensitive field we have always sought to insure such reviewability. See *Red Lion Broadcasting Co., Inc.* v. *F.C.C.*, 395 U.S. 367, 376, n. 5. We believe that a most crucial peg underlying all Commission action in the programming field is the vital consideration that the courts are there to review and reverse any action which runs afoul of the First Amendment. Thus, while we think that our action is fully consistent with the law, there should clearly be the avenue of court review in a case of this nature (see Section 504 (a)). Indeed, we would welcome such review, since only in that way can the pertinent standards be definitively determined. Accordingly, in light of that consideration, the new ground which we break with this decision, and the overall record of this noncommercial educational licensee, we propose to assess a forfeiture of only $100.00.

Conclusion

17.   We conclude this discussion as we began it. We propose no change from our commitment to promoting robust, wide-open debate. *Red Lion Broadcasting*

---

[10] Indeed, one of the station participants stated at the outset of the interview, "We are going to do a lot of illegal things before this is over."

Co. v. *F.C.C., supra; Pacifica Foundation, supra.* Simply stated, our position— limited to the facts of this case — is that such debate does not require that persons being interviewed or station employees on talk programs have the right to begin their speech with, "S--t, man . . .", or use "f-----g," or "mother f-----g" as gratuitous adjectives throughout their speech. This fosters no debate, serves no social purpose, and would drastically curtail the usefulness of radio for millions of people. Indeed, significantly, in this case, under the licensee's policy (which was by-passed by its volunteer employees), Mr. Garcia's views would have been presented *without* the gratuitous expressions, but with them, the public would never have heard his views.

18.   In view of the foregoing, we determine that, pursuant to Section 503(b)(1)(A), (B), (E) of the Communications Act of 1934, as amended, Eastern Education Radio has incurred an apparent liability of one hundred dollars ($100).

19.   Eastern Education Radio is hereby notified that it has the opportunity to file with the Commission, within thirty (30) days of the date of the receipt of this Notice, a statement in writing as to why it should not be held liable, or, if liable, why the amount of liability should be reduced or remitted. Any such statement should be filed in duplicate and should contain complete details concerning the allegations heretofore made by the Commission, any justification for the violations involved, and any other information which Eastern Education Radio may desire to bring to the attention of the Commission. Statements of circumstances should be supported by copies of relevant documents where available. Upon receipt of any such reply, the Commission will determine whether the facts set forth therein are sufficient to relieve Eastern Education Radio of liability, or to justify either reduction or remission of the amount of liability. If it is unable to find that Eastern Education Radio should be relieved of liability, the Commission will issue an Order of Forfeiture and the forfeiture will be payable to the Treasurer of the United States.

20.   If Eastern Education Radio does not file, within thirty (30) days of the date of receipt of this Notice, either a statement of nonliability or a statement setting forth facts and reasons why the forfeiture should be of a lesser amount, the Commission will enter an Order of Forfeiture in the amount of one hundred dollars ($100).

21.   In accordance with our established procedures, we also state that if Eastern Education Radio does not wish to file a statement which denies liability and, in addition, it does not wish to await the issuance of an Order, it may, within thirty (30) days of the date of the receipt of this Notice, make payment of the forfeiture by mailing to the Commission a check, or similar instrument, in the amount of one hundred dollars ($100) drawn payable to the Treasurer of the United States.

By Direction of the Commission,
Ben F. Waple, *Secretary.*

Appendix A

Excerpts from licensee's letter of February 12, 1970:

"... During the interview, Mr. Garcia expressed his views on ecology, music, philosophy, and interpersonal relations. [footnote omitted] Some of Mr. Garcia's comments on these subjects are set forth below:

The problem essentially ... the basic problem is how can you live on the planet earth without wreckin' it, right?

... like you know a couple of weeks ago the thing was in the paper that the headline was in the paper that there was no more clean air in the United States, period. Yeah, and it's like uh that kind of stuff is all of a sudden comin' up real fast. You know, and it's like it looks like that's the most important thing going on and that nothing else is as important as that as far as I know, that is *the* most important thing.

For example, like uh I have friends who I've known since like they started college, you know, and like now it's eight years later and you know, and they're all Ph.Ds — stuff like that. It's just coming out in those terms, uh, I know quite a few of these people who have switched their major in the last year to Ecology and that kind of s--t, because it's like really important right. It's a big emergency going on. Okay, so — and their approach to it is generally to get together on the level of bodies of influence — that is to say, governmental s--t, you know, things like that business and so forth, and stuff like that.

But the big thing is that it's really super, you know — it's ... it's ... it definitely looks bad outside man. When you fly over New York, it looks f----n' rotten, man, but it's like that way every f----n' where, man, you know, and like I'm from San Francisco, man, and there wasn't like five or six years ago when it was like the sky was blue, crystal clear, you know; you know and that whole thing that you hardly ever see any more, man — you know you just hardly ever see it any more.

What I'd really love to do would be live on a perfect, peaceful earth and devote all my time to music. But I can't do it man, because you just can't do that. You know, I mean it's a ... there's a more important thing going on, that's all.

Politics is a form and music is a form and they're both ways of dealing with people, man. When you play music with people, though, you're not attacking them, you know. It isn't, it's not a competition between the two of you or the four of you or the seven of you, or however many of you. There are — it's like a cooperative effort which gets everybody high, so like that's and that's of course the thing that's really a great trip about music. It's really a great thing. It's really a good trip, right, and uh so like the things that that I've wanted to see happen and lots of other people you know it's like some way of getting people together to do things but having it be like music and not like business and not like politics, you know, uh just because that's a uh high watermark in a way. I mean it seems like people should be able to do that.

If you get together with four or five people and produce something that's greater than yourself you know, and that also doesn't only reflect your attitude, but it's like a little closer to the center because it has to do with more perceptions than your own and like for a plan to work. I think, it has to be approached on those kinds of levels and those kind of terms because uh it won't work if uh this is a planet full of people, each of whom is in a universe of his own. Everybody has to agree to give a little, and so forth, and so on."

STATEMENT OF COMMISSIONER KENNETH A. COX, CONCURRING IN PART AND DISSENTING IN PART

I agree with a good deal that is said in the Notice of Apparent Liability, but do not agree with the result reached.

I agree that broadcasting differs in significant respects from books, magazines, motion pictures and other means of communications. I agree that this may lead the courts to apply different standards in determining the degree of control which government may exercise over the content of broadcast programming. And I agree that it would be well to get this matter resolved by the courts in the near future. But I do not agree that the problem is as great as the majority say it is, or that it is likely to become endemic. I do not agree that the licensee of WUHY-FM was grossly negligent in this case or merits any more than a warning because of this incident. And I am afraid that this precedent may cause licensees not to carry programming they would otherwise have broadcast, out of fear that someone will be offended, will complain to the Commission, and the latter will find the broadcast improper. It should be noted that Cycle II has been suspended, so that whatever of value it had to offer will no longer be available to WUHY's audience.

At least the majority are now listing the words, and the usage of those words, which they regard as contrary to the public interest. I think that is desirable, although I am sure that broadcasters are going to worry about other words which they feel may be added to the list later on. And I applaud the majority for indicating that licensees will not be punished for presenting works of art or on-the-spot coverage of bona fide news events which may contain these words or others like them. I am glad they restrict their action to gratuitous use of words in circumstances where the offensive language has no redeeming social value.

However, I do not think the broadcast here involved posed a problem so serious as to justify the imposition of a sanction for the mere utterance of words. This weekly series was intended as an "underground" program dealing "with the avant-garde movement in music, publications, art, film, personalities, and other forms of social and artistic experimentation." It was presented between 10 and 11 p.m. on Sunday night, and was designed to appeal to the large college population in Philadelphia and to alienated segments of the new generation. It seems clear that a program with such a purpose — a perfectly valid one, I'm sure everyone would agree — would be different in approach and content from programs aimed at children, or women 30 to 40 years of age, or professional men, or adults generally. And it seems likely, in view of the widespread ferment among young people and their rejection of many of the standards of their parents' generation, that not only the ideas discussed but the language used to express them will sometimes be offensive to the older generation. But people who do not like the ideas or the language do not need to listen to programs of this kind. WUHY received no complaints about the broadcast here in question, nor did the Commission. However, we had received earlier complaints about the 10 to 11 p.m. time period and were monitoring the station on the night of January 4, 1970. So far as I can tell, my colleagues are the only people who have encountered this program who are greatly disturbed by it.

I agree that the language complained of is offensive to many and that it was gratuitous — that Mr. Garcia could have expressed the same ideas without using this language. However, I think it magnifies the impact of the words to set them out starkly, as the majority do in Paragraph 3 of the Notice, alone and out of context. I have not read the full transcript of the broadcast, and doubt if my colleagues have, but certainly a reading of the seven paragraphs quoted in the licensee's response gives a different perspective of the matter. While one might wish that Mr. Garcia had been able to express himself without using words which many people find offensive, it would appear that he was not trying to shock or titillate the audience. Apparently this is the way he talks — and I guess a lot of others in his generation do so, too. I find such poverty of expression depressing, and am afraid it may impair clarity of thought. My concern is not limited to the words which trouble the majority. In the seven paragraphs quoted by the licensee, Mr. Garcia uses only four words cited by the majority. But he uses the word "like" in an improper and redundant way sixteen times, and uses "man" as a word of emphasis seven times. These patterns of speech seem common among today's young. But I expect our language will survive — as it has withstood the slang and fads of generation after generation.

WUHY decided that it wanted to let Mr. Garcia communicate his views in a number of important areas to the station's audience — a decision which no one questions. At least the station was trying to do something more than play records and read wire news. Assuming the propriety of the station's program judgment, how could it have achieved its desired result without getting into trouble with the Commission? The majority suggest, in Paragraph 7, that while Mr. Garcia may talk this way in many other places, he should have been told that he cannot do so on radio. However, while I have had very limited contact with people of his age and background, I am of the impression that such an approach might not have been productive. I think one of the reasons for their use of such language is that it is *intended* to show disrespect for the standards of their elders, which they regard as outmoded, without real basis, and "irrelevant." It might have been difficult for Mr. Garcia to change his habits of speech without interfering with the flow of his ideas — or he might simply have refused to give the interview at all on those terms. Admittedly this is speculative, but there is no way to explore these possibilities without making some assumptions — and I think mine are not unreasonable.

The only other alternative would have been to delete the offending language. The licensee, in its response to the Commission's letter of inquiry, argued persuasively that the Garcia interview was neither obscene nor profane. I am glad that the majority agree that it was not obscene, and while they do not address themselves to the issue of profanity, they certainly make no claim that the language was profane. Instead, they hold that the language was indecent, within the meaning of 18 U.S.C. 1464, which makes it a crime to "utter any obscene, indecent, or profane language by means of radio communication." The licensee argued to the contrary in its letter:

. . . Nor was the program indecent simply because certain language not normally heard in polite circles, was uttered. The basic subject matters of the program — ecology, philosophy, music — are obviously decent. The challenged language though not essential to the meaning of the program as a whole, reflected the personality and life style of Mr. Garcia. In this sense, the interview was in the nature of a documentary. The realistic portrayal of such an interview cannot be deemed "indecent" because the subject incidentally used strong or salty language. . . .

I think this position has a good deal of merit. In addition, I think that the word "indecent" in the statute may not have a clear enough meaning to satisfy the constitutional requirement that criminal statutes must put the public on notice of just precisely what conduct will constitute a violation.

Having made this contention, the licensee nonetheless said that it would not have aired the program had it been submitted for review by the station manager, as required by established station procedures. It went on to say:

Licensee would not have aired the Jerry Garcia interview because the questioned language was not essential to the presentation of the subject matter and its potential for offense was not outweighed by considerations of subject matter or artistic integrity. While the program had value in terms of subject matter and in depicting the total personality of Jerry Garcia, licensee does not believe that these values were sufficient to warrant airing the program, at least without deletion of the offending and essentially gratuitous passages.[3]

[3] Licensee does not believe that editing and deletion are an automatically acceptable solution to this kind of problem. Such deletions often damage the entire program. Moreover, they do not protect the sensibilities of the listener. Indeed such censorship may be more distracting than the deleted language itself.

A licensee is responsible for everything broadcast over its station. WUHY therefore very properly has adopted a policy that all taped program material containing "controversial subject matter or language" must be reviewed by the station manager. If those who produced and broadcast the Garcia interview had followed that procedure and the licensee had decided not to use the interview, or to do so only after deleting the language here in issue, that would have represented a licensee's efforts to discharge its responsibilities in the exercise of its own judgment. What we have here is quite a different thing. The majority are exercising government power in the area of speech. They have imposed a sanction — though admittedly a nominal one — for a single broadcast[11] containing what they, but not the licensee, regard as indecent matter. This action, binding on all licensees, is obviously far different from letting licensees make their own judgments — even if many of them would conclude, with the majority, that language of this kind should not be broadcast.

I'm afraid it has taken me a long time to get around to discussing an idea mentioned in the first sentence of the third paragraph back — the possible deletion of the offensive words. I think the licensee has pointed out some problems with this procedure in the footnote to the last quotation above. It says that bleeping out words may disrupt the program, and that it may not be too

[11] It is important to keep in mind that we are dealing with a single incident, within the doctrine of *In re Renewal of Pacifica*, 36 FCC 147, rather than with a substantial pattern of coarse, vulgar, or suggestive material such as was involved in *Palmetto Broadcasting Corporation*, 34 FCC 101. In the last sentence of Paragraph 15, the majority find the licensee guilty of gross negligence with respect to its supervisory duties. I think this is an unfair effort to bolster the action here, and that this conclusion is without basis in the record before us. The licensee adopted appropriate procedures for review of programming, and there is no suggestion in the majority's opinion — nor was any offered during our discussion of this matter — that it has knowingly permitted disregard of its policies. So far as we know, this is the first time an employee of WUHY has failed to present a questionable program for review. So far as we know, the licensee has taken steps regularly to remind its staff of this requirement. There is no pattern of laxity or open disregard for paper policies such as we have found in other cases where we have ruled that licensees had been guilty of failure to enforce policies essential to the discharge of their responsibilities. The majority are saying that a licensee whose sound policies to detect objectionable matter are disregarded in a single case, resulting in the broadcast of language which the majority regard as indecent, can be subjected to a forfeiture. The reference to "gross negligence" is sheer window dressing.

difficult for those who dislike such language to tell what was said despite the deletion — indeed, that this may actually emphasize the fact that language which the licensee apparently regards as improper had been used. It seems to me that WUHY — when put on notice that the Commission on its own motion is challenging the broadcast — is saying that it would not have broadcast the Garcia interview at all. I think that most licensees who may consider presenting similar programming in the future — that is taped material involving statements by blacks, students, or those who have dropped out of our society — will decide that if the use of words which may offend the Commission is interspersed too regularly throughout the tape to make deletion feasible, the safe course will be just not to broadcast the program. While I hold no brief for flooding the air with the views of members of these groups, I think it may be dangerous if we do not understand what they are trying to say — even if it sometimes involves the monotonous use of four letter words. Some of their complaints are probably well founded, and even if they are not, I think we need to know what troubles them and what they are talking about doing about these matters. It may be that using radio and television to help bridge the generation gap would be an example of "the larger and more effective use of radio" which the majority are so eager to preserve. If, instead, we narrow our concept of the use of radio in order to protect the sensibilities of those who seem more concerned with suppressing words and pictures they find offensive than with solving the problems that are tearing our society apart, I think we may find that the majority are wrong in stating — in Paragraph 7 — that we can exorcise these words from radio "without stifling in the slightest any thought which the person wishes to convey." One safe course for the timid will be simply to avoid interviewing people who can be expected to use troublesome language, or inviting them to participate in panels, or asking them to comment on current developments. This may be "safe" for the licensee but I'm not sure it will be safe for our society.

This brings me, at last, to my principal problem with the majority's decision, which is that I think they are exaggerating this problem out of all proportion. It is true that in recent months we have been receiving more complaints about the broadcast of allegedly obscene, indecent, or profane matter, but most of these involve matters outside the ambit of this ruling. That is, they deal with claims that certain records contain cryptic references to the use of drugs, that others are sexually suggestive, that the skits and blackouts on the Rowan and Martin Laugh-In are similarly suggestive, that the costumes on many variety programs are indecent, that the dances are too sensuous, that the performers are too free with each other, etc. But I think I could count on the fingers of both hands the complaints that have come to my notice which involve the gratuitous use of four letter words in situations comparable to the one in this case. This has simply not been a problem.

Nor do I agree that if we do not punish WUHY for this broadcast, there is going to be such "widespread use" of the offending words as to "drastically affect the use of radio by millions of people," because "very substantial numbers would either curtail using radio or would restrict their use to but a few channels." I just do not believe there are many broadcasters waiting eagerly to flood the country with such language on an around the clock basis in the event we were to impose no sanction here. Indeed, if the Commission had not decided to make a test case of this incident, I doubt if many people would ever have heard of it. Actually, if the majority's theory is right, they are running a rather serious risk. If the courts do not sustain their action, that would be a signal to the industry that it could freely engage in the "widespread use" of four letter words which the majority fear they are anxious to embark upon. But I don't think many of our licensees have any desire to follow such a course, nor do I believe that there is any great audience to be won by such tactics. I think most broadcasters have too high a regard for their profession and its responsibilities to fall into the patterns the majority envisage in Paragraphs 7 through 9.

Similarly, I think there is a great and clear difference between presenting an occasional late night program featuring people not on the staff of the station who use offensive language and employing newscasters and disc jockeys and allowing them to use similar expressions all day long. It is one thing to permit certain elements in society to use such language on the air so that interested members of the public can find out how they think about various problems. It is quite different to turn the operation of a station over to people who talk that way. I think this, like the more generalized claim that we are about to be inundated with indecent language, is a figment of the majority's imagination designed to justify the intrusion of governmental power into this sensitive area.

I have studied broadcasting for some time, and while I think we may expect to hear strong language on the air somewhat more often in the future as a reflection of our troubled times, I simply do not believe there is any likelihood that licensees will broadcast indecent language to such an extent that they will drive millions of listeners away from radio entirely. Broadcasters make money by attracting audiences. They have developed a number of ways to win the attention of differing segments of the total audience. I do not think that four letter words are likely to become the format of the future, since I doubt if even people who use such language themselves would regard it as enhancing a station's service.

Finally, I think it should be noted that the majority have held that someone involved in this broadcast violated a criminal statute. This means that such person or persons can be prosecuted and subjected to rather severe penalties. However, I do not think this is likely to happen because I suspect that the United States Attorney in Philadelphia has more important matters to occupy his time and that of his staff. (See my dissent in the Commission's letter addressed to Jack Straw Memorial Foundation, dated January 21, 1970, FCC 70-93.) I submit that the same thing should be true of the Federal Communications Commission.

PRELIMINARY DISSENTING OPINION OF COMMISSIONER NICHOLAS JOHNSON

"Oaths are but words, and words but wind."
—Samuel Butler, *Hudibras* (1664).

What this Commission condemns today are not words, but a culture — a lifestyle it fears because it does not understand. Most of the people in this country are under 28 years of age; over 56 million students are in our colleges and schools. Many of them will "smile" when they learn that the Federal Communications Commission, an agency of their government, has punished a radio station for broadcasting the words of Jerry Garcia, the leader of what the FCC calls a "rock and roll musical group." To call The Grateful Dead a "rock and roll musical group" is like calling the Los Angeles Philharmonic a "jug band." And that about shows "where this Commission's at."

Today the Commission simply ignores decades of First Amendment law, carefully fashioned by the Supreme Court into the recognized concepts of "vagueness" and "overbreadth," see, *e.g.*, *Swickler v. Koota*, 389 U.S. 241, 249-50 (1967), and punishes a broadcaster for speech it describes as "indecent" — without so much as *attempting* a definition of that uncertain term. What the Commission tells the broadcaster he cannot say is anyone's guess — and therein lies the constitutional deficiency.

Today the Commission turns its back on Supreme Court precedent, see, *e.g., Interstate Circuit, Inc. v. Dallas.* 390 U.S. 676 (1968), citing *Holmby Productions, Inc. v. Vaughn,* 350 U.S. 870 (1954), as well as recent federal court precedent, see, *e.g., Williams v. District of Columbia*, No. 20,927 (D.C. Cir., June 20, 1969) (en banc), which invalidated statutes with similarly vague descriptions of allegedly "indecent" speech.

Today the Commission decides that certain forms of speech and expression are "patently offensive by contemporary community standards" — although neither the station nor the FCC received *a single complaint* about the broadcast in question, and the FCC conducted not a single survey among the relevant population groups in Philadelphia, nor compiled a single word of testimony on contemporary community standards, nor attempted even to define the relevant "community" in question.

I am aware that there *are* members of the public who are offended by some of what they hear or see on radio or television. I too am offended by much of what I hear or see on radio or television — though more often for what it fails to do than what it does. I am sympathetic to the outrage of any minority group — Black or Puritan — that feels its values are not honored by the society of which it is a part. (What the Commission decides, after all, is that the swear words of the lily-white middle class may be broadcast, but that those of the young, the poor, or the blacks may not.) There are scenes, subjects and words used on television which I would not use personally as a guest on camera. The words used here fall in that category. But I do not believe I sit here as an FCC Commissioner to enforce my moral standards upon the nation. Yet four other Commissioners do precisely that.

Furthermore, when we do go after broadcasters, I find it pathetic that we always seem to pick upon the small, community service stations like a KPFK, WBAI, KRAB, and now WUHY-FM. See, *e.g., Pacifica Foundation (KPFK-FM)*, 36 F.C.C. 147 (1964); *United Federation of Teachers (WBAI-FM)*, 17 F.C.C. 2d 204 (1969); *Jack Straw Memorial Foundation (KRAB-FM)*, FCC 70-93 (released Jan. 21, 1970). It is ironic to me that of the public complaints about broadcasters' "taste" received in my office, there are probably a hundred or more about network television for every one about stations of this kind. Surely if anyone were genuinely concerned about the impact of broadcasting upon the moral values of this nation — and that impact has been considerable — he ought to consider the ABC, CBS and NBC television networks before picking on little educational FM radio stations that can scarcely afford the postage to answer our letters, let alone hire lawyers. We have plenty of complaints around this Commission involving the networks. Why are they being ignored? I shan't engage in speculation.

Today this Commission acts against a station that broadcasts 77 hours a week of locally-originated fine music, public and cultural affairs, and community-oriented programming. Ironically, the Commission censures language broadcast by the station that received one of the Corporation for Public Broadcasting's first program grants for its experimental program in participatory democracy, "Free Speech." In 1969 alone, WUHY-FM received two "major" Armstrong Awards, one of the highest achievements in radio, two awards from Sigma Delta Chi, a professional journalism group, and the Corporation for Public Broadcasting's "Public Criteria" award — the only such award given to a Philadelphia station. I do not believe it a coincidence that this Commission has often moved against the programming of innovative and experimental stations (such as KPFK, WBAI and KRAB). I do not see how licensees (particularly ones that rely on the help of talented volunteers) can develop new and creative programming concepts without approaching the line that separates the orthodox from the unconventional and controversial. I believe today's decision will deter the few innovative stations that do exist from approaching that line.

Today the Commission rules that the speech in question has "no redeeming social value," although Professor Ashley Montagu, a leading authority on the subject, believes that such speech "serves clearly definable social as well as personal purposes." A. Montagu, *The Anatomy of Swearing* 1 (1967).

Today the Commission declares that a four-letter word "conveys no thought" — and proceeds to punish a broadcaster for speech which apparently conveys so much thought that it must be banned.

Today the Commission punishes a licensee for speech in order to encourage the courts to do our work for us — forgetting that the First

Amendment binds *this* agency as well as the courts. I do not believe any governmental body can stifle free speech merely to produce a "test case." We cannot, constitutionally, abdicate our responsibilities to the courts. Yet today this is what we have done.

I believe it is our responsibility to adopt precise and clear guidelines for the broadcasting industry to follow in this murky area, if we are to wade into it at all — the wisdom of which I seriously question. I believe no governmental agency can punish for the content of speech by invoking statutory prohibitions which are so broad, sweeping, vague, and potentially all-encompassing that no man can foretell when, why, or with what force the Commission will strike.

In *Joseph Burstyn, Inc. v. Wilson*, 343 U.S. 495 (1952), the Supreme Court held that the First Amendment protected motion pictures as well as normal speech. There, the Court invalidated a New York statute banning "sacrilegious" films. The Court said:

> This is far from the kind of narrow exception to freedom of expression which a state may carve out to satisfy the adverse demands of other interests of society. In seeking to apply the broad and all-inclusive definition of "sacrilegious" given by the New York courts, the censor is set adrift upon a boundless sea amid a myriad of conflicting currents of religious views, with no charts but those provided by the most vocal and powerful orthodoxies ... [I]t is enough to point out that the state has no legitimate interest in protecting any or all religions from views distasteful to them ...

If the term, "sacrilegious," is subject to the dangers of sweeping all-inclusive interpretations, what then of "indecent"? The FCC has not attempted even a "broad and all-inclusive definition" of "indecent," as the New York courts did of "sacrilegious." Rather, the FCC has cast itself adrift upon the "boundless sea" of a search for "indecency" without compass or polestar for guidance. We have only the obscure charts of the orthodox (presumably represented by a majority of Commissioners) to guide us on our way.

Groups in this country interested in civil liberties and speech freedoms should understand that the Commission today enters a new and untested area of federal censorship — censorship over the words, thoughts and ideas that can be conveyed over the most powerful medium of communication known to man: the *broadcasting* medium. To my knowledge, there are no judicial precedents, no law review articles, no FCC decisions, and no scholarly thinking that even attempt to define the standards of permissible free speech for the broadcasting medium. Should this case be appealed, therefore, these questions may be posed. All those who hold speech freedoms dear should participate. It will be regrettable if the Federal Communications Bar Association, like the big broadcasting industry generally, once again proves itself to be more interested in profitable speech than free speech. We will be waiting to see if they vigorously enter an *amicus* appearance in this case.

An anonymous poet has written:

Oh perish the use of the four-letter words
    Whose meanings are never obscure;
The Angles and Saxons, those bawdy old birds,
    Were vulgar, obscene and impure.
But cherish the use of the weaseling phrase
    That never says quite what you mean.
You had better be known for your hypocrite ways
    Than vulgar, impure and obscene.
Let your morals be loose as an alderman's vest
    If your language is always obscure.
Today, not the act, but the word is the test
    Of vulgar, obscene and impure.

Whatever else may be said about the words we censor today, their meanings are not "obscure." I cannot say as much for the majority's standards for "indecency."

In 1601, William Shakespeare wrote in *Twelfth Night* (III, iv), "Nay, let me alone for swearing." Most of the fresh and vital cultures in our country, not the least of which are the young, have learned this lesson. This Commission has not.

I regret the double standard that causes many significant matters to languish in FCC files for years, while rushing other more questionable matters to decision within days. It is extraordinary that the majority would choose to act on an issue of this consequence without even taking the time to *read*, let alone carefully consider, the full dissenting and concurring opinions of all Commissioners in this case. I may, nevertheless, take the time to prepare such a fuller opinion in the future for the record. Meanwhile, I feel it useful to put forward at least these views today, as the majority announces its decision. I dissent.

9

BROUHAHA OVER DRUG LYRICS

In re Licensee Responsibility to Review Records Before Their Broadcast

The delicate balance between the requirement that broadcast programming serve the public interest and the prohibition of government interference with broadcast free expression is exemplified in the following FCC Public Notice, Commissioner Johnson's forceful dissent, and the subsequently promulgated Commission explanation of its previously misunderstood Notice. In early 1973 the Court of Appeals upheld the FCC's position.*

The public health and free speech aspects of the FCC decision are further complicated by the tension stemming from a federal bureaucracy appearing to influence content in a medium that many young people regard as their very own.

---

*The Supreme Court refused to review the case on October 15, 1973. [Ed.]

A

THE PUBLIC NOTICE

28 FCC 2d 409

March 5, 1971

LICENSEE RESPONSIBILITY TO REVIEW RECORDS BEFORE THEIR BROADCAST

A number of complaints received by the Commission concerning the lyrics of records played on broadcasting stations relate to a subject of current and pressing concern: the use of language tending to promote or glorify the use of illegal drugs as marijuana, LSD, "speed", etc. This Notice points up the licensee's long-established responsibilities in this area.

Whether a particular record depicts the dangers of drug abuse, or, to the contrary, promotes such illegal drug usage is a question for the judgment of the licensee. The thrust of this Notice is simply that the licensee must make that judgment and cannot properly follow a policy of playing such records without someone in a responsible position (i.e., a management level executive at the station) knowing the content of the lyrics. Such a pattern of operation is clearly a violation of the basic principle of the licensee's responsibility for, and duty to exercise adequate control over, the broadcast material presented over his station. It raises serious questions as to whether continued operation of the station is in the public interest, just as in the case of a failure to exercise adequate control over foreign-language programs.[1]

In short, we expect broadcast licensees to ascertain, before broadcast, the words or lyrics of recorded musical or spoken selections played on their stations. Just as in the case of the foreign-language broadcasts, this may also entail reasonable efforts to ascertain the meaning of words or phrases used in the lyrics. While this duty may be delegated by licensees to responsible employees, the licensee remains fully responsible for its fulfillment.

Thus, here as in so many other areas, it is a question of responsible, good

[1] See Public Notice concerning Foreign Language Programs adopted March 22, 1967, FCC 67-368, 9 R.R. 2d 1901.

283

faith action by the public trustee to whom the frequency has been licensed. No more, but certainly no less, is called for.

Action by the Commission February 24, 1971. Commissioners Burch (Chairman), Wells and Robert E. Lee with Commissioner Lee issuing a statement, Commissioners H. Rex Lee and Houser concurring and issuing statements, Commissioner Johnson dissenting and issuing a statement, and Commissioner Bartley abstaining from voting.

B

COMMISSIONER JOHNSON'S DISSENT

28 FCC 2d 412
March 5, 1971

DISSENTING OPINION OF COMMISSIONER NICHOLAS JOHNSON

This public notice is an unsuccessfully-disguised effort by the Federal Communications Commission to censor song lyrics that the majority disapproves of; it is an attempt by a group of establishmentarians to determine what youth can say and hear; it is an unconstitutional action by a Federal agency aimed clearly at controlling the content of speech.

Under the guise of assuring that licensees know what lyrics are being aired on their stations, the FCC today gives a loud and clear message: get those "drug lyrics" off the air (and no telling what other subject matter the Commission majority may find offensive), or you may have trouble at license renewal time. The majority today approves a public notice which (1) singles out as "a subject of current and pressing concern: the use of language tending to promote or glorify the illegal use of drugs such as marijuana, LSD, 'speed,' etc.;" (2) emphasizes the importance of "someone in a responsible position . . . knowing the content of the lyrics;" and (3) raises the specter of loss of license unless the "pattern of operation" is such that a "responsible" employee knows the content of song lyrics played on broadcasting stations.

The contrived nature of this offensive against modern music is demonstrated by the fact that, as the majority itself concedes, "the licensee's responsibility for, and duty to exercise adequate control over, the material presented over his station," is "a basic principle" of FCC regulation; it is so basic that today's action is completely unnecessary. Licensees (that is, owners of stations) simply *can't* listen to *everything* broadcast over their stations; they have to delegate responsibility for knowledge of content to their employees; and we can assume under existing regulations that those employees *do* know what is being played. We can also assume that licensees are well aware of the Commission's power to prohibit material that falls within statutory prohibitions and beyond constitutional protection. Why, then, this focus on "language strongly suggestive of, or tending to glorify, the illegal use of drugs ..." — whatever that means — unless the intention is in fact to censor by threat what cannot be constitutionally prohibited?

Moreover, there is a serious question as to whether the majority is in fact really as concerned about drug abuse as it is in striking out blindly at a form of music which is symbolic of a culture which the majority apparently fears — in part because it totally fails to comprehend it. If the majority were in fact concerned about drug abuse, they surely would not choose to ignore song lyrics "strongly suggestive of, and tending to glorify" the use of alcohol, which is the number one drug abuse problem in this country.

It is common knowledge that drunken drivers kill *each year* nearly as many Americans as have been killed during the entire history of the war in Southeast Asia. There are more alcoholics in San Francisco alone than there are narcotics addicts in the entire country. Kenneth Eaton, Deputy Director of the Division of Alcohol Abuse and Alcoholism at the National Institute of Mental Health, recently declared: "In relative terms, the physical consequences of heavy drinking are far larger and more serious than those of heroin use"; he added that the likelihood of death in withdrawal from chronic alcoholism is much greater than in withdrawal from heroin addiction.[1] Dr. Robert L. Dupont, Director of the Washington, D.C. Narcotics Treatment Agency, agrees "absolutely" with Eaton:

It's non-controversial.

Heroin as a drug is really quite benign compared to alcohol, which is a poison.

*   *   *

We have two really serious drug problems in Washington, heroin and alcohol.[2]

I do not think it's the business of the FCC to be discouraging or banning *any* song lyrics. But if the Commission majority is *really* interested in doing

---

[1] *The Washington Post*, Feb. 7, 1971, p. A7, col. 1.
[2] *Id.*

something about the drug problems in this country, and is not just striking out at the youth culture, why does it ignore songs like "Day Drinking" . . .[3] or "California Grapevine" . . .[4] or countless other similar lyrics?[5]

And why has the Commission chosen to focus on record lyrics and yet ignore commercials which use language "tending to glorify the use of drugs generally"? In asking Congress for a study of the effects on the nation's youth of nearly $300 million worth of annual drug advertising on television, Senator Frank Moss of Utah has said:

The drug culture finds its fullest flowering in the portrait of American society which can be pieced together out of hundreds of thousands of advertisements and commercials. It is advertising which mounts so graphically the message that pills turn rain to sunshine, gloom to joy, depression to euphoria, solve problems, dispel doubt.

Not just pills; cigarette and cigar ads; soft drink, coffee, tea and beer ads — all portray the key to happiness as things to swallow, inhale, chew, drink and eat.[6]

Commissioners Rex Lee and Thomas Houser have expressed similar concerns in this very proceeding. How can anyone possibly justify the FCC's failure to examine the impact of commercials such as the following on television:

(Music) ANNOUNCER: Leave your feeling of tension behind and step into a quiet world. You'll feel calmer, more relaxed with Quiet World. The new modern calmative. Each tablet contains a special calming ingredient plus a tension reliever to let you feel relaxed. More peaceful. So leave your feeling of tension behind with Quiet World. The new modern calmative.[7]

This commercial was broadcast over WCBS-TV in New York at 3:25 p.m. to an audience made up primarily of mothers and children. Why do the majority choose to ignore these gray flannel pushers?[8]

---

[3] T. T. Hall, "Day Drinking" (© 1970, Newkeys Music, Inc.), *Song Hits*, March 1971, p. 43.

[4] H. J. Joy, "California Grapevine" (© 1970, Blue Book Music), *Song Hits*, February 1971, p. 43.

[5] . . . T. T. Hall, "This Night (Ain't Fit for Nothing But Drinking)" (© 1970, Newkeys Music, Inc.), *Song Hits*, November 1970, p. 41. . . .

H. X. Lewis G. Sutton, "Blues Sells a Lot of Booze" (© 1970, Al Gallico Music Corp.), *Song Hits*, March 1971. p. 45. . . .

J. Owen, "Here Come the Elephants" (© 1970, Bluebook Music Co.), *Song Hits*, May 1971, p. 40.

[6] *Year of Challenge, Year of Crisis*, The du Pont-Columbia University Survey of Broadcast Journalism 1969-1970, at 88.

[7] Shown on "To Tell the Truth," WCBS-TV, New York, Sept. 9, 1968, 3:25 p.m.

[8] It cannot be argued that the illegality of the drugs is the reason behind the majority's action, since the majority says nothing at all about lyrics extolling other illegal activities, such as cohabitation.

The answer to these questions is simple: the exclusive concern with song lyrics is in reality an effort to harass the youth culture, a crude attempt to suppress the anti-establishment music of the counter-culture and the "movement."

It is a thinly veiled political move. This Administration has, for reasons best known to the President, chosen to divert the American people's attention to "the drug menace," and away from problems like: the growing Southeast Asian war, racial prejudice, inflation, unemployment, hunger, poverty, education, growing urban blight, and so forth. When the broadcasters support this effort they are taking a political stance. Especially is this so when they, simultaneously, keep *off* the air contrary political views.[9] When we encourage this trend, we are taking equally political action.

The majority's interest in the whole song lyrics issue was substantially increased by the Defense Department's Drug Briefing, which was originally prepared for a briefing of radio and record executives under the President's auspices at the White House. It is not surprising that the Nixon Administration and the Defense Department, two primary targets of the youth culture, should try to strike back. But it is revealing and somewhat frightening that many of the song lyrics singled out as objectionably pro-drug-use by the White House and Defense Department turn out, in fact, to have nothing whatsoever to do with drugs. They relate instead to social commentary. Thus, the Defense Department spokesmen singled out a song by the Doors which says: "War is out — peace is the new thing." The White House finds alarming another which says:

> Itemize the things you covet
> As you squander through your life
> Bigger cars, bigger houses,
> Term insurance for your wife. . . .[10]

Is anything that attacks the values of corporate America or the military-industrial-complex now to be interpreted by the FCC and broadcasters as an incitement to drugs?

Beyond the hypocrisy of this blind attack on the youth culture, this action is legally objectionable because it ignores the Supreme Court's ruling that the First Amendment protects speech which has any socially redeeming importance. People differ as to how they feel about the reasonableness of the drug life as a way out of the often absurd qualities of life in a corporate state. I happen to

---

[9] See *Fairness Doctrine Ruling*, 25 F.C.C. 2d 242, 249 (1970); N. Johnson, "Public Channels and Private Censors," *The Nation* (March 23, 1970), p. 329; N. Johnson, "The Wasteland Revisited," *Playboy* (Dec. 1970), p. 229; N. Johnson, *How to Talk Back to Your Television Set* 71 (1970).

[10] Transcript of White House Radio Producers Briefing, Aug. 31, 1970, presented in the same form to the FCC, Dec. 9, 1970, p. 4 and lyrics of appendix, p. 1.

believe in getting high on life — the perpetual high without drugs.[11] But no one can argue that the use of drugs — by rich and poor, middle-aged and young — is not a controversial issue of public importance today. How can the FCC possibly outlaw the subject as suitable for artistic comment? How can it possibly repeal the applicability of the fairness doctrine to this subject?

The courts have frequently invalidated licensing schemes which give the licensing agency such unbridled discretion, or which are so broad, that a licensee is deterred from engaging in activity protected by the First Amendment. Thus, in *Weiman v. Updegraff*, 344 U.S. 183, 195 (1952), a case involving loyalty oaths demanded of prospective teachers, the Supreme Court condemned the provision, saying: "It has an unmistakable tendency to chill that free play of spirit which all teachers ought especially to cultivate and practice; it makes for caution and timidity in their associations by potential teachers."

As Mr. Justice Black has written:

[A] statute broad enough to support infringement of speech ... necessarily leaves all persons to guess just what the law really means to cover, and fear of a wrong guess inevitably leads people to forego the very rights the Constitution sought to protect above all others.

Barenblatt v. United States, 360 U.S. 109, 137 (1959) (dissenting opinion). This danger, inherent in the overbroad and necessarily vague action which the Commission takes today, is compounded when it involves the natural sensitivity of those whose very existence depends on the licensing power of the censoring agency.

Simply by announcing its concern with the content of song lyrics as they relate to drugs, the Commission is effectively censoring protected speech. The breadth of the regulation is aggravated by the vagueness of the standard used — "tending to glorify." What does that mean? It could include "Up, Up and Away" sung by the Mormon Tabernacle Choir. Some so-called "drug lyrics" are clearly *dis*couraging the use of drugs. Others, while less clear, can most reasonably be read to be opposing drug usage. Many informed people argue that even the programs and public service spots designed to *discourage* drug usage are often as likely to have the opposite effect. How is the poor licensee to know which lyrics are "tending to glorify"? Will he risk his license over such an interpretation?

In *Burstyn v. Wilson*, 343 U.S. 495 (1952), a statute which authorized denial of a license if the licensor concluded that the film reviewed was "sacrilegious" was held by the Supreme Court to be an unconstitutionally

---

[11] See, N. Johnson, "Life Before Death in the Corporate State," Barbara Weinstock Lecture, University of California, Berkeley, California, Nov. 5, 1970 (FCC 57177); N. Johnson, "The Careening of America or How to Talk Back to Your Corporate State," Poynter Fellow Lecture, Yale University, New Haven, Connecticut, March 8, 1971 (FCC 64807).

overbroad delegation of discretion. The Commission's action today is bound to be interpreted as a threat that the playing of certain song lyrics could threaten license renewals.

Justice Brennan summarized the Supreme Court's concern with actions which have a "chilling effect" on the exercising of rights protected by the First Amendment:

> To give these freedoms the necessary "breathing space to survive," . . . [w]e have molded both substantive rights and procedural remedies in the face of varied conflicting interests to conform to *our overriding duty to insulate all individuals from the "chilling effect" upon exercise of First Amendment freedoms* generated by vagueness, overbreadth and unbridled discretion to limit their exercise.

Walker v. City of Birmingham, 388 U.S. 307, 344-45 (1967) (dissenting opinion) (emphasis added). This is a classic case of Federal agency action which is bound to have a "chilling effect" on the exercise of First Amendment rights.

The Commission's action today will have a chilling effect on the free spirit of our songwriters, because of the caution and timidity which today's action will produce among licensees. It will have a similar effect on the record industry, because of the relationship between the radio play of a record and its economic success. And where, after all, do we get authority to regulate *that* industry by putting pressure on the move to require the printing of lyrics on dust jackets?

We are more dependent upon the creative people in our society than we have ever fully comprehended. "Legalize Freedom" says the latest bumper sticker. Full human flowering requires the opportunity to know, and express creativity, one's most honest-as-possible self. Governments are instituted among men — according to our Declaration of Independence — to promote "life, liberty, and the pursuit of happiness." We seem to have drifted quite a way from that goal. Not only do we need creative freedom to promote individual growth, we also need creative artists to divert social disaster. The artists are our country's outriders. They are out ahead of our caravan, finding the mountain passes and the rivers. They pick up the new vibrations a decade or more before the rest of us, and try to tell us what's about to happen to us as a people — in the form of painting, theater, novels, and in music. In order to function at all, they have to function free. When we start the process of Kafkaesque institutional interference with that freedom — whether by Big Business or Big Government — we are encouraging, rather than preventing, the decline and fall of the American Empire: its view of the future, and the fulfillment of its people.

I hope the recording and broadcasting industries will have the courage and commitment to respond to this brazen attack upon them with all the enthusiasm it calls for. Given the power of this Commission, I am afraid they may not.

For all these reasons, I dissent.

C

EXPLANATORY MEMORANDUM

OPINION AND ORDER

31 FCC 2d 377
April 16, 1971

BY THE COMMISSION: COMMISSIONERS BARTLEY, H. REX LEE
AND WELLS CONCURRING AND ISSUING STATEMENTS: COM-
MISSIONER JOHNSON DISSENTING AND ISSUING A STATEMENT

1. The Commission has before it petitions for reconsideration of its Public
Notice of March 5, 1971, FCC 71-205, entitled "Licensee Responsibility to
Review Records Before Their Broadcast", filed by the Federal Communications
Bar Association; Pierson, Ball & Dowd on behalf of Dick Broadcasting, Inc., Lee
Enterprises, Inc., RKO General, Inc., and Time-Life Broadcast, Inc.; the
Recording Industry Association of America (RIAA),[1] and Pacifica Foundation.[2]
The latter also submitted a petition for stay. In view of this latter request and
the considerations in the next paragraph, we agree that there is a need for
expedited action, and therefore go directly to the merits, without summarizing
the petition.

2. The Commission's public notice of March 5 stated, in most pertinent
part:

Whether a particular record depicts the dangers of drug abuse, or, to the
contrary, promotes such illegal drug usage is a question for the judgment of the
licensee. The thrust of this Notice is simply that the licensee must make that
judgment and cannot properly follow a policy of playing such records without
someone in a responsible position (i.e., a management level executive at the
station) knowing the content of the lyrics.

The Notice thus simply reflected the well established concept of licensee
responsibility. However, as the petitions point up, it was widely reported in the
press as a directive by the Commission not to play certain kinds of records.

---

[1] RIAA's Motion for Acceptance of Pleading in Excess of Page Limitations IS GRANTED.
[2] We also take note that a Petition for Reconsideration was filed late by the Stern
Community Law Firm and also a Memorandum of the Authors League of America, Inc. in
support of RIAA's Petition for Reconsideration. These materials were received during our
determination on this Memorandum Opinion and Order.

(E.G., "Stations Told to Halt Drug-Oriented Music", Associated Press, The Washington Evening Star, March 6, 1971; "FCC Bars Broadcasting of Drug-Linked Lyrics", United Press International, The Washington Post, March 7, 1971.) Since the purpose of a public notice is to inform the industry and public of a Commission policy, it follows that where a notice is so erroneously depicted, we should appropriately call attention to the error. We do so in this Memorandum Opinion and Order. While it adheres fully to the above noted established policy of licensee responsibility, this opinion treats the matter in greater detail and thus constitutes the Commission's definitive statement in this respect.

3.   As the Notice stated at the outset, the Commission has received a number of complaints concerning the broadcast of records with lyrics tending to promote or glorify the use of illegal drugs. The Commission's own experience indicated that there was some tendency by broadcasters to be indifferent to the matter of licensee responsibility in this area because all that is involved is the playing of a record. The Commission therefore believed it appropriate to point up that the licensee's responsibility for the material broadcast over his facilities extends to records. Clearly, in a time when there is an epidemic of illegal drug use — when thousands of young lives are being destroyed by use of drugs like heroin, methedrine ("speed"), cocaine — the licensee should not be indifferent to the question of whether his facilities are being used to promote the illegal use of harmful drugs.

4.   But nothing in the prior Notice stated, directly or indirectly, that a licensee is barred from presenting a particular type of record. On the contrary, the Notice made clear that selection of records was a matter for the licensee's judgment. Some records point up drug dangers, some may glorify drugs, some may simply reflect the drug scene as it is today. Here, as in so many programming areas, it is often a most difficult judgment whether a record promotes drug usage. Licensees could reasonably and understandably reach differing judgments as to a particular record. We stress that such an evaluation process is one solely for the licensee. The Commission cannot properly make or review such individual licensee judgments. Indeed, at renewal time our function is solely limited to a review of whether a licensee's programming efforts, on an overall basis, have been in the public interest. *Report and Statement of Policy Re: Commission En Banc Programming Inquiry*, 20 Pike & Fischer, Radio Regulation 1901 (1960); *In re Pacifica Foundation*, 36 FCC 147, 149 (1964).

5.   Any attempt to review or condemn a licensee's judgment to play a particular record is, as indicated, beyond the scope of federal regulatory authority with perhaps the exception of the so-called "clear and present danger" test. In this connection, in *Anti-Defamation League of B'Nai B'rith against Radio Station KTYM*, 4 FCC 2d 190, 191, 6 FCC 2d 385 (1967),[3] the Commission stated:

---

[3] *Aff'd*, Anti-Defamation League v. FCC, 403 F. 2d 169 (C.A.D.C. 1968), *cert. denied*, 394 U.S. 930 (1969).

It is the judgment of the Commission, as it has been the judgment of those who drafted our Constitution and of the overwhelming majority of our legislators and judges over the years, that the public interest is best served by permitting the expression of any views that do not involve "a clear and present danger of serious substantive evil that rises far above public convenience, annoyance or unrest."[4] *Terminiello* v. *Chicago*, 337 U.S. 1, 4 (1949).

6.   The question of formulating a definitive concrete standard is not presented in this matter. For, we hold, based on our experience and the complaints received, that whether to play a particular record in this area does not raise an issue as to which the Government may intervene. That is the reason why the Commission has not referred a single complaint concerning the playing of records with drug lyrics to licensees for their comments;[5] instead, we have informed the complainants of the provisions of Section 326. There could be extraordinary, unforeseen circumstances where the stringent requirements of the "clear and present danger" test might be met in this field. No one can today write a constitutional blueprint for every possible future happenstance and changed circumstance. It is sufficient to hold that we do not now perceive such a problem, based upon our present experience, and that our prior Notice and this Opinion are not premised upon it.

7.   The Commission did make clear in the Notice that the broadcaster could jeopardize his license by failing to exercise licensee responsibility in this area. Except as to broadcasts by political candidates, the licensee is responsible for the material broadcast over his facilities. That obviously calls for a reasonable degree and exercise of responsibility. It is nonsense to assert that the licensee can be indifferent to this responsibility. If a person approaches a station to buy time to attack his neighbor, or simply to let loose a torrent of vile language, he will not be presented. While these are egregious examples of the need for licensee responsibility, the plain fact is that the licensee is not a common carrier — that the Act makes him a public trustee who is called upon to make thousands of

---

[4]Similarly, in Brandenburg v. Ohio, 395 U.S. 444 (1969), the Supreme Court struck down the conviction of a Ku Klux Klan leader for advocating violence at a KKK rally, stating (at p. 447):

These later [Supreme Court] decisions have fashioned the principle that the constitutional guarantees of free speech and free press do not permit a State to forbid or proscribe advocacy of the use of force or of law violation except where such advocacy is directed to inciting or producing imminent lawless action and is likely to incite or produce such action.

[5]It has come to our attention that pursuant to a request by a broadcasting station's news department, a Commission employee furnished it with the titles of some songs which had been among those included in a presentation to the Commission some months ago by the Department of the Army. The song titles, furnished in response to the station's inquiry, comprised, as was made clear to the station at the time, "A partial list of song titles brought to the attention of the FCC in connection with the subject of so-called drug-oriented song lyrics." We wish to make it clear that such list does not represent any official or even unofficial pronouncement by the Commission, and will not be circulated, utilized or applied by us in any manner whatsoever. The Commission has made no judgment on any song and most emphatically has not compiled or issued any list of songs which it believes should not be broadcast. Nor does it intend to do so in the future.

programming judgments over his license term. The thrust of the Notice is simply that this concept of licensee responsibility extends to the question of records which may promote or glorify the use of illegal drugs.[6] A licensee should know whether his facilities are being used to present again and again a record which urges youth to take heroin or cocaine — that it is a wonderful, joyous experience. This example is egregious, but it serves to point up the obvious bedrock policy of the *responsible* public trustee. The point is that such records are not withdrawn from the area of licensee responsibility.

8.   Nor are the mechanics of licensee responsibility difficult or onerous. Again, it may be desirable to proceed by analogy. Licensees instruct their employees that before presenting taped material containing questionable language (i.e., of an indecent or obscene nature), the matter should be brought to the attention of a responsible management official (see *Eastern Educational Radio*, 24 FCC 2d 408, 414 (1970)). We note that this is the policy of petitioner Pacifica. See *In re Pacifica Foundation*, 36 FCC 147, 150 (1964). Further, while such material might be presented once in a series part of which has been screened and approved, its presentation is then picked up, either by complaint or station personnel, and a judgment made as to further presentation. So also here, disc jockeys could be instructed that where there is a question as to whether a record promotes the illegal drug usage, a responsible management official should be notified so he can exercise his judgment. It may be that a record which raises an issue in this respect is played once, but then the station personnel who have heard it will be in a position to bring it to the attention of the appropriate management official for his judgment. Finally, we are not calling for an extensive investigation of each such record. We recognized in the *ADL* case, *supra*, that imposition of any undue verification process "could significantly inhibit the presentation of controversial issue programming" (6 FCC 2d at p. 386); cf. *The Washington Post* v. *Keogh*, 365 F. 2d 965 (C.A.D.C., 1966). That is equally so here. Therefore, what is required is simply reasonable and good faith attention to the problem. We would conclude this aspect as we did in the prior Notice.

Thus, here as in so many other areas, it is a question of responsible, good faith action by the public trustee to whom the frequency has been licensed. No more, but certainly no less is called for.

9.   We think that the foregoing is dispositive of the major arguments presented. The licensee is not a book store, but a public trustee of an inherently limited resource who is fully responsible for its operation in the public interest. We have made clear that we are not seeking through a euphemism, licensee responsibility, to effect the wholly improper result of barring certain kinds of speech. We have imposed no onerous requirements in this respect, and have further stressed that the judgment whether to play a particular record is to be

---

[6]We thus fully agree with the FCBA position that the Commission should make clear ". . . it was announcing a policy dealing solely with licensee responsibility to be familiar with what the licensee is broadcasting and that it did not intend to pass judgment on the desirability of broadcasting any song . . ." (p. 8, FCBA petition).

made by the licensee alone. We have noted the arguments that some licensees have dropped all records referring to drugs — in erroneous reaction to our Notice. If that is the case, we trust that with the issuance of this opinion such licensees will cease such grossly inappropriate policy and rather will make a judgment based on the particular record. Finally, to the argument that suggests impropriety in our issuance of a Notice concerning the need for licensee responsibility in the area of records promoting drugs, the short answer is set forth in par. 3, *supra* — that this is an area of great concern in view of the epidemic proportions of the problem, that we had numerous complaints, and that we had some indication of licensee indifference because all that is involved is the playing of records. We have in the past issued similar Notices when there was indifference to the policy of licensee responsibility in other areas. See, e.g., Public Notice concerning Foreign Language Programs adopted March 22, 1967, FCC 67-368, 9 R.R. 2d 1901. Of course, the policy of licensee responsibility is applicable generally, but that does not mean that we cannot issue appropriate Notices when there is an indicated need therefor.

10.   An argument is also advanced as to the necessity for rule making notice under the Administrative Procedure Act. But our Notice establishes no new rule or indeed even a new policy. It reiterates an established bedrock policy — licensee responsibility. If this opinion were withdrawn, licensees would still be required to observe that policy based on scores of prior decisions. We therefore do not perceive how the rule making notice requirements of the APA are at all applicable here.

11.   As a final point, we wish to stress that the issue of drug lyrics is but one facet of the overall drug problem, and it would be unfortunate if it were to be blown out of proportion. For, consideration of this aspect is, of course, not the be-all and end-all of what a broadcaster can do to serve the public interest in this important area. The public generally is now aware of the existence of the drug abuse problem. The alert has been sounded, and broadcasters have played an important role in informing the public. The present challenge and opportunity, for those broadcasters who wish to help, is to inform our citizens as to what can be done to find solutions to the problem of drug abuse. Indeed, because the drug problem is complex, and fraught with emotion, there is the possibility of a good deal of misinformation being circulated. Broadcasters who develop their own materials and programs relating to drug abuse could, if they wish, consult with experts in the field, both in the public and private sectors to insure the accuracy and reliability of their programming. In short, we believe that licensees can play a constructive role in helping the nation seek solutions to the drug problem, just as many of them have done, through public service time, in alerting the nation to the existence of the problem.

12.   Accordingly, the request of Pacifica for stay IS DENIED, in view of the above discussion. The requests of the petitioners IS GRANTED to the extent reflected above (see, e.g., footnote 6, *supra*; pp. 9-10, Pierson, Ball & Dowd petition), and in all other respects IS DENIED.

Federal Communications Commission,
Ben F. Waple, *Secretary.*

10

FCC PROGRAM PROPOSAL

QUESTIONNAIRE

FCC Form 301, Section IV-A
January, 1971

FCC Form 301 must be filled out by any applicant wishing to construct a new commercial broadcast station or make changes in an existing station. Section IV-A of the form pertains to the programming plans of radio station applicants; it is similar to Section IV-B, which must be completed by applicants for television stations. Other sections of the application form deal with the legal, financial, and technical qualifications of the prospective broadcaster.

Section IV becomes particularly crucial when there are competing applications for the same broadcast facilities. If the several applicants are equal in all other respects, then the Federal Communications Commission will award a grant to the applicant whose programming proposal best serves the public interest.

Although licensees are not expected to "adhere inflexibly in day-to-day operation to the representations" made in Section IV, the proposal is again taken into account when it is compared with the station's performance at license renewal time. Renewal applicants must list information regarding their past programming during a "composite week" and must also indicate the nature of the program service they intend to render in the future on the application for renewal, FCC Form 303.

FCC Form 301	FEDERAL COMMUNICATIONS COMMISSION	Section IV-A

STATEMENT OF AM OR FM PROGRAM SERVICE (See instructions, Sec. IV-A, pages 7 and 8.)	Name of Applicant
	City and state which station is licensed to serve

Call letters of station	

PART I

Ascertainment of Community Needs

1. A. State in Exhibit No._____ the methods used by the applicant to ascertain the needs and interests of the public served by the station. Such information shall include (1) identification of representative groups, interests and organizations which were consulted and (2) the major communities or areas which applicant principally undertakes to serve.

   B. Describe in Exhibit No._____ the significant needs and interests of the public which the applicant believes his station will serve during the coming license period, including those with respect to national and international matters.

   C. List in Exhibit No._____ typical and illustrative programs or program series (excluding Entertainment and News) that applicant plans to broadcast during the coming license period to meet those needs and interests.

NOTE: Sufficient records shall be kept on file at the station, open for inspection by the Commission, for a period of 3 years from the date of filing of this statement (unless requested to be kept longer by the Commission) to support the representations required in answer to Question 1. These records should *not* be submitted with this application and need not be available for public inspection.

PART II

Past Programming

2. A. State the total hours of operation during the composite week: _____

   B. Attach as Exhibit No._____ one exact copy of the program logs for the composite week used as a basis for responding to questions herein. Applicants utilizing automatic program logging devices must comply with the provisions of Sections 73.112(c) and 73.282(c). Automatic recordings will be returned to the applicant. Exact copies will not be returned.

   If applicant has not operated during all of the days of the composite week which would be applicable to the use of this form, applicant should so notify the Commission and request the designation of substitute day or days as required.

3. A. State the amount of time (rounded to the nearest minute) the applicant devoted in the composite week to the program types (see Definitions) listed below. Commercial matter within a program segment shall be excluded in computing time

(1) News .... %

(2) Public Affairs .... %

(3) All other programs, exclusive
of Entertainment and Sports .... %

B. If in the applicant's judgment the composite week does not adequately represent the station's past programming, applicant may in addition provide in Exhibit No. _____ the same information as required in 3-A above (using the same format) for a calendar month or longer during the year preceding the filing of this application. Applicant shall identify the time period used. Applicant need not file the program logs used in responding to this question unless requested by the Commission.

4. List in Exhibit No. _____ typical and illustrative programs or program series (excluding Entertainment and News) broadcast during the year preceding the filing of this application which have served public needs and interests in applicant's judgment. Denote, by underlining the Title, those programs, if any, designed to inform the public on local, national or international problems of greatest public importance in the community served by the applicant. Use the format below.

Title	Source*	Type*	Brief Description	Time Broadcast & Duration	How Often Broadcast

5. Submit in Exhibit No. _____ the following information concerning the applicant's news programs:

A. The staff, news gathering facilities, news services and other sources utilized; and

B. An estimate of the percentage of news program time devoted to local and regional news during the composite week.

6. In connection with the applicant's public affairs programming, describe its policy during the past renewal period with respect to making time available for the discussion of public issues and the method of selecting subjects and participants.

*See Definitions Section IV-A, Page 7

297

7. Describe briefly the applicant's program format(s) during the past 12 months (e.g., country and western music, talk, folk music, classical music, foreign language, jazz, standard pops, etc.) and the approximate percentage of time per week devoted to such format(s).

8. State how and to what extent (if any) applicant's station contributed during the past license period to the over-all diversity of program services available in the area or communities served.

9. Was the applicant affiliated with one or more national, regional or special radio networks during the past license period? Yes _____ No _____ . If "yes," give name(s) of network(s): _____

10. State the number of public service announcements broadcast by the applicant during the composite week: _____

11. A. If this application is for an FM station, did the programming duplicate that of any AM station?

Yes _____ No _____ .("Duplicate" means simultaneous broadcasting of a particular program over both the AM and FM stations or the broadcast of a particular FM program within 24 hours before or after the identical program is broadcast over the AM station—Section 73.242(a) of the Rules and Regulations.)

B. If the answer is "yes," identify the AM station by call letters; describe its relation to the FM station; and state the number of hours each day in the composite week that were duplicated.

12. A. In applicant's judgment, does the information supplied in this Part II adequately reflect its past programming?
Yes _____ No _____ .

B. If "no," applicant may attach as Exhibit No. _____ such additional information as may be necessary to describe accurately and present fairly its program service.

C. If applicant's programming practices for the period covered by this statement varied substantially from the programming representations made in applicant's last renewal application, the applicant shall submit as Exhibit No. _____ a statement explaining the variations and the reasons therefor.

PART III

Proposed Programming

13. State the proposed total hours of operation during a typical week: _____

14. State the minimum amount of time the applicant proposes to devote normally each week to the program types (see Definitions) listed below. Commercial matter within a program segment shall be excluded in computing time devoted to that particular program segment. (e.g., a fifteen-minute news program containing 3 minutes' commercial matter shall be computed as a 12-minute news program.)

	Hours	Minutes	% of Total Time on Air
(1) News....................	....	....	.... %
(2) Public Affairs	....	....	.... %
(3) All other programs, exclusive of Entertainment and Sports............	....	....	.... % .... %

15. Submit in Exhibit No. _____ the following information concerning the applicant's proposed news programs:

A. . The staff, news gathering facilities, news services and other sources to be utilized; and

B. An estimate of the percentage of news program time to be devoted to local and regional news during a typical week.

16. In connection with the applicant's proposed public affairs programming describe its policy with respect to making time available for the discussion of public issues and the method of selecting subjects and participants.

17. Describe the applicant's proposed programming format(s), e.g., country and western music, talk, folk music, classical music, foreign language, jazz, standard pops, etc., and the approximate percentage of time per week to be devoted to such format(s).

18. State how and to what extent (if any) applicant proposes to contribute to the over-all diversity of program services available in the area or communities to be served.

19. State the minimum number of public service announcements applicant proposes to present during a typical week: _____

20. Will the applicant be affiliated with one or more national, regional, or special radio networks? Yes _____ No _____.
If "yes," give name(s) of networks(s): _____

21. A. If this application is for an FM station will the programming duplicate that of any AM station? Yes _____ No _____.
("Duplicate" means simultaneous broadcasting of a particular program over both AM and FM stations or the broadcast of a particular FM program within 24 hours before or after the identical program is broadcast over the AM station—Section 73.242(a) of the Rules and Regulations.)

B. If the answer is "yes," identify the AM station by call letters; describe its relation to the FM station; and state the number of hours each day proposed to be duplicated.

PART IV

Past Commercial Practices

22. Give the following information with respect to the composite week:

	All Hours	6 A.M. - 6 P.M.
A. Total broadcast time	....	....
B. Time devoted to commercial matter:		
(1) Amount in hours and minutes	....	....
(2) Percentage	.... %	.... %

301

23. State the number of 60-minute segments of the composite week (beginning with the first full clock hour and ending with the last clock hour of each broadcast day) containing the following amounts of commercial matter:

   A. Up to and including 10 minutes ....

   B. Over 10 and up to and including 14 minutes ....

   C. Over 14 and up to and including 18 minutes ....

   D. Over 18 minutes ....

List each segment in category (D) above, specifying the amount of commercial time in the segment, and the day and time broadcast.

24. A. In the applicant's judgment, does the information supplied in this Part IV for the composite week adequately reflect its commercial practices?   Yes_____ No_____ .

     B. If "no," applicant may attach as Exhibit No._____ such additional material as may be necessary to describe adequately and present fairly its commercial practices.

     C. If applicant's commercial practices for the period covered by this statement varied substantially from the commercial representations made in applicant's last renewal application, the applicant shall submit as Exhibit No._____ a statement explaining the variations and the reasons therefor.

25. State the maximum percentage of commercial matter which the applicant proposes normally to allow during the following segments of a typical week:

    6 a.m. - 6 p.m. .... _____ %

    All hours .... _____ %

If applicant proposes to permit this level to be exceeded at times, state under what circumstances and how often this is expected to occur, and the limits that would then apply.

26. What is the maximum amount of commercial matter in any 60-minute segment which the applicant proposes normally to allow?

If applicant proposes to permit this amount to be exceeded at times, state under what circumstances and how often this is expected to occur, and the limits that would then apply.

PART VI

General Station Policies and Procedures

27. State the name(s) and position of the person(s) who determines the day-to-day programming, makes decisions, and directs the operation of the station covered by this application and whether he is employed full-time in the operation of the station.

28. A. Does the applicant have established policies with respect to programming and advertising standards (whether developed by the station or contained in a code of broadcasting standards and practices) to guide the operation of the station?

    Yes _____ No _____ .

    B. If "yes," attach as Exhibit No. _____ a brief summary of such policies. (If the station relies exclusively upon the published code of any national organization or trade association, a statement to that effect will suffice)

29. State the methods by which applicant undertakes to keep informed of the requirements of the Communications Act and the Commission's Rules and Regulations, and a description of the procedures established to acquaint applicant's employees and agents with such requirements and to ensure their compliance.

30. If, as an integral part of its station identification announcements, applicant makes or proposes to make reference to any business, profession or activity other than broadcasting in which applicant or any affiliate or stockholder is engaged or financially interested, directly or indirectly, set forth typical examples and approximate frequency of their use.

31. State the number of station employees: _____ . If the station has or proposes to have ten or more employees, state in Exhibit No._____ the number of full-time and part-time employees in the programming, sales, technical, and general and administrative departments. Do not list the same employee in more than one category. However, if an employee performs multiple services, this may be so shown by identifying him with his various duties e.g., if two employees are combination announcers and salesmen, the list would include an entry of "two programming-sales".

PART VII

Other Matters and Certification

32. Applicant may submit as Exhibit No. _____ any additional information which, in its judgment, is necessary adequately to describe or to present fairly its services and operations in relation to the public interest.

33. The undersigned has familiarized himself with paragraph 7 of the Instructions on page 7 of Section IV-A concerning signature requirements and in light of its provisions does hereby:

  A. Acknowledge that all the statements made in this Section IV-A and the attached exhibits are considered material representations and that all the exhibits are a material part hereof and are incorporated herein as if set out in full in the application form; and

  B. Certify that the statements herein are true, complete, and correct to the best of his knowledge and belief and are made in good faith.

SIGNED AND DATED this .... day of .... , 19 ....

....
(NAME OF APPLICANT)

By: ....
(SIGNATURE)

....
(PLEASE PRINT NAME OF PERSON SIGNING)

(TITLE)

WILLFUL FALSE STATEMENTS MADE IN THIS FORM ARE PUNISHABLE BY FINE AND IMPRISONMENT. U. S. CODE, TITLE 18, SECTION 1001.

307

Instructions, General Information and Definitions
for AM-FM Broadcast Application

1. **Applicants for new AM or FM stations, and major changes when required** *(see paragraph 2)* shall file this Section IV-A with respect to Ascertainment of Community Needs (Part I), Proposed Programming (Part III), Proposed Commercial Practices (Part V), General Station Policies and Practices (Part VI) and Other Matters and Certification (Part VII).

2. **Applicants for major changes in facilities** (as defined in Sections 1.571(a)(1) and 1.573(a)(1) of the Commission's Rules) need not file this Section IV-A unless there is proposed a substantial change in programming, increased facilities serving a substantial amount of new area or population, or unless the information is requested by the Commission.

3. A. The replies to the following questions constitute representations on which the Commission will rely in considering this application. Thus time and care should be devoted to the replies so that they will reflect accurately applicant's responsible consideration of the questions asked. It is not, however, expected that the licensee will or can adhere inflexibly in day-to-day operation to the representations made herein.

   B. Replies relating to future operation constitute representations against which the subsequent operation of the station will be measured. Accordingly, if during the license period the station substantially alters its programming format or commercial practices, the licensee should notify the Commission of such changes; otherwise it is presumed the station is being operated substantially as last proposed.

4. The applicant's attention is called to the Commission's "Report and Statement of Policy re: Commission En Banc Programming Inquiry," (FCC 60-970; 25 Federal Register 7291; 20 Pike and Fischer Radio Regulation 1902), copies of which are available upon request to the Commission; and also to the material contained in Attachment A and Attachment B to this Section.

5. A legible copy of this Section IV-A and the exhibits submitted therewith shall be kept on file available for public inspection at any time during regular business hours. It shall be maintained at the main studio of the station or any other accessible place (such as a public registry for documents or an attorney's office) in the community to which the station is or is proposed to be licensed.

6. **Network Programs.** Where information for the composite week is called for herein with respect to commercial matter or program type classification in connection with national network programs, the applicant may rely on information furnished by the network.

7. **Signature.**

   This Section IV-A shall be signed in the space provided at the end hereof. It shall be personally signed by the applicant, if the applicant is an individual; by one of the partners, if the applicant is a partnership; by an officer of applicant, if a corporation or association. *SIGNING OF THIS SECTION IS A REPRESENTATION _____ THE _____ WHO SIGNS IS FAMILIAR WITH THE CONTENTS OF THIS SECTION AND ASSOCIATED*

Definitions

The definitions set out below are to be followed in furnishing the information called for by the questions of this Section IV-A. The inclusion of various types and sources of programs in the paragraphs which follow is not intended to establish a formula for station operation, but is a method for analyzing and reporting station operation.

8. **Sources** of programs are defined as follows:

(a) **A local program** (L) is any program originated or produced by the station, or for the production of which the station is primarily responsible, and employing live talent more than 50% of the time. Such a program, taped or recorded for later broadcast, shall be classified as local. A local program fed to a network shall be classified by the originating station as local. All non-network news programs may be classified as local. Programs primarily featuring records or transcriptions shall be classified as recorded even though a station announcer appears in connection with such material. However, identifiable units of such programs which are live and separately logged as such may be classified as local (e.g., if during the course of a program featuring records or transcriptions a non-network 2-minute news report is given and logged as a news program, the report may be classified as local).

(b) **A network program** (NET) is any program furnished to the station by a network (national, regional or special) Delayed broadcasts of programs originated by networks are classified as network.

(c) **A recorded program** (REC) is any program not defined above, including, without limitation, those using recordings, transcriptions, or tapes.

9. **Types** of programs are defined as follows:

If a program contains two or more identifiable units of program material which constitute different program types as herein defined, each such unit may be separately logged and classified.

The definitions of the first eight types of programs, (a) through (h) are not intended to overlap each other, and these types will normally include all the programs broadcast. The programs classified under (i) through (k) will have been classified under the first eight and there may be further duplication among types (i) through (k).

(a) **Agricultural programs** (A) include market reports, farming or other information specifically addressed, or primarily of interest, to the agricultural population.

Definitions - Cont.

(b) *Entertainment programs* (E) include all programs intended primarily as entertainment, such as music, drama, variety, comedy, quiz, etc.

(c) *News programs* (N) include reports dealing with current local, national, and international events, including weather and stock market reports; and when an integral part of a news program, commentary, analysis and sports news.

(d) *Public Affairs programs* (PA) include talks, commentaries, discussions, speeches, editorials, political programs, documentaries, forums, panels, round tables, and similar programs primarily concerning local, national, and international public affairs.

(e) *Religious programs* (R) include sermons or devotionals; religious news; and music, drama, and other types of programs designed primarily for religious purposes.

(f) *Instructional programs* (I) include programs, other than those classified under Agricultural, News, Public Affairs, Religious or Sports, involving the discussion of, or primarily designed to further an appreciation or understanding of, literature, music, fine arts, history, geography, and the natural and social sciences; and programs devoted to occupational and vocational instruction, instruction with respect to hobbies, and similar programs intended primarily to instruct.

(g) *Sports programs* (S) include play-by-play and pre- or post-game related activities and separate programs of sports instruction, news, or information (e.g., fishing opportunities, golfing instruction, etc.).

(h) *Other programs* (O) include all programs not falling within definitions (a) through (g).

★   ★   ★   ★   ★

(i) *Editorials* (EDIT) include programs presented for the purpose of stating opinions of the licensee.

(j) *Political programs* (POL) include those which present candidates for public office or which give expression (other than in station editorials) to views on such candidates or on issues subject to public ballot.

(k) *Educational Institution programs* (ED) include any program prepared by, in behalf of, or in cooperation with, educational institutions, educational organizations, libraries, museums, PTA's or similar organizations. Sports programs shall not be included.

10. *Commercial matter* (CM) includes commercial continuity (network and non-network) and commercial announcements (network and non-network) as follows:

(a) *Commercial continuity* (CC) is the advertising message of a program sponsor.

(b) *A commercial announcement* (CA) is any other advertising message for which a charge is made, or other consideration is received.

of the future program beyond mention of the sponsor's name as an integral part of the title of the program (e.g., where the agreement for the sale of time provides that the sponsor will receive promotional announcements, or when the promotional announcement contains a statement such as "LISTEN TOMORROW FOR THE [NAME OF PROGRAM] BROUGHT TO YOU BY [SPONSOR'S NAME]").

(2) Other announcements including but not limited to the following are *not* commercial announcements:

(i) Promotional announcements, except as defined above;

(ii) Station identification announcements;

(iii) Mechanical reproduction announcements;

(iv) Public service announcements;

(v) Announcements made pursuant to Sections 73.119(d) or 73.289(d) of the Rules that materials or services have been furnished as an inducement to broadcast a political program or a program involving the discussion of controversial public issues;

(vi) Announcements made pursuant to the local notice requirements of Sections 1.580 (pre-grant) and 1.594 (designation for hearing) of the Rules.

11. **A *public service announcement* (PSA)** is any announcement (including network) for which no charge is made and which promotes programs, activities, or services of federal, state or local governments (e.g., recruiting, sales of bonds, etc.) or the programs, activities or services of non-profit organizations (e.g., UGF, Red Cross blood donations, etc.), and other announcements regarded as serving community interests, excluding time signals, routine weather announcements and promotional announcements.

12. **A *program*** is an identifiable unit of program material, logged as such, which is not an announcement as defined above (e.g., if, within a 30-minute entertainment program, a station broadcasts a one-minute news and weather report, this news and weather report may be separately logged and classified as a one-minute news program and the entertainment portion as a 29-minute program).

13. ***Composite Week*** - Seven days designated annually by the Commission in a Public Notice and consisting of seven different days of the week.

14. ***Typical Week*** - A week which an applicant projects as typical of his proposed weekly operation.

ATTACHMENT A

Attention is invited to the Commission's "Report and Statement of Policy Re: Commission En Banc Programming Inquiry" released July 29, 1960 - FCC 60-970 (25 Federal Register 7291; 20 Pike and Fischer Radio Regulation 1902).

Pursuant to the Communications Act of 1934, as amended, the Commission cannot grant, renew or modify a broadcast authorization unless it makes an affirmative finding that the operation of the station, as proposed, will serve the public interest, convenience and necessity. Programming is of the essence of broadcasting.

A broadcast station's use of a channel for the period authorized is premised on its serving the public. Thus, the public has a legitimate and continuing interest in the program service offered by the station, and it is the duty of all broadcast permittees and licensees to serve as trustees for the public in the operation of their stations. Broadcast permittees and licensees must make positive, diligent and continuing efforts to provide a program schedule designed to serve the needs and interests of the public in the areas to which they transmit an acceptable signal.

In its above-referenced "Policy Statement," the Commission has indicated the general nature of the inquiry which should be made in the planning and devising of a program schedule:

"Thus we do not intend to guide the licensee along the path of programming; on the contrary, the licensee must find his own path with the guidance of those whom his signal is to serve. We will thus steer clear of the bans of censorship without disregarding the public's vital interest. What we propose will not be served by pre-planned program format submissions accompanied by complimentary references from local citizens. What we propose is documented program submissions prepared as the result of assiduous planning and consultation covering two main areas: first, a canvass of the listening public who will receive the signal and who constitute a definite public interest figure; second, consultation with leaders in community life -- public officials, educators, religious (groups), the entertainment media - agriculture, business, labor, professional and eleemosynary organizations, and others who bespeak the interests which make up the community."

of broadcast service have frequently been found necessary or desirable to serve the broadcast needs and interests of many communities. In the Policy Statement, referred to above, the Commission set out fourteen such elements. The Commission stated:

"The major elements usually necessary to meet the public interest, needs and desires of the community in which the station is located as developed by the industry, and recognized by the Commission, have included: (1) Opportunity for Local Self-Expression, (2) The Development and Use of Local Talent (3) Programs for Children, (4) Religious Programs, (5) Educational Programs, (6) Public Affairs Programs, (7) Editorialization by licensees, (8) Political Broadcasts, (9) Agricultural Programs, (10) News Programs, (11) Weather and Market Reports, (12) Sports Programs, (13) Service to Minority Groups, (14) Entertainment Programming."

It is emphasized that broadcasters, mindful of the public interest, must assume and discharge responsibility for planning, selecting and supervising all matter broadcast by their stations, whether such matter is produced by them or provided by networks or others. This duty was made clear in the Commission's Policy Statement, page 14, paragraph 3:

" Broadcasting licensees must assume responsibility for all material which is broadcast through their facilities. This includes all programs and advertising material which they present to the public. With respect to advertising material the licensee has the additional responsibility to take all reasonable measures to eliminate any false, misleading, or deceptive matter and to avoid abuses with respect to the total amount of time devoted to advertising continuity as well as the frequency with which regular programs are interrupted for advertising messages. This duty is personal to the licensee and may not be delegated. He is obligated to bring his positive responsibility affirmatively to bear upon all who have a hand in providing broadcast matter for transmission through his facilities so as to assure the discharge of his duty to provide (an) acceptable program schedule consonant with operating in the public interest in his community. The broadcaster is obligated to make a positive, diligent and continuing effort, in good faith, to determine the tastes, needs and desires of the public in his community and to provide programming to meet those needs and interests. This, again, is a duty personal to the licensee and may not be avoided by delegation of the responsibility to others."

ATTACHMENT B

Attention is invited to the Commission's Public Notice entitled "Ascertainment of Community Needs By Broadcast Applicants." released August 22, 1968 - FCC 68-847, (33 Federal Register 12113).

The Commission issues this Public Notice to provide broadcast applicants with a better understanding of the showing called for in response to Part 1, Sections IV-A and IV-B, the programming sections of application forms. Deficient showings delay definitive action on applications and impose a costly workload burden on the Commission.

In a recent case, Minshall Broadcasting Company, Inc. (petition to enlarge issues) 11 FCC 2d 796 (1968), the Commission reiterated the four elements of the showing to be made in response to Part 1:

(a) Full information on the steps the applicant has taken to become informed of the real community needs and interests of the area to be served.

(b) Suggestions which the applicant has received as to how the station could help meet the area's needs.

(c) The applicant's evaluation of those suggestions.

(d) The programming service which the applicant proposes in order to meet those needs as they have been evaluated

In another recent case, Andy Valley Broadcasting System, Inc. (petition to deny) FCC 68-290 (1968), the Commission held that a survey of community needs is mandatory and that "applicants, despite long residence in the area, may no longer be considered, ipso facto, familiar with the programming needs and interests of the community."

Before detailing the information needed in the four elements set forth above, it is appropriate to state our belief that if the processes of Part 1 are carried out in good faith, the programming service will be rooted in the people whom the station is obligated to serve and who will be in a much better position to see that the obligation to them is fulfilled, thus lessening the enforcement burden of the Commission.

Part 1, Question 1.A., requires consultation with leaders in community life—public officials, educators, religious, the entertainment media, agriculture, business, labor, professional and eleemosynary organizations, and others who bespeak the interests which make up the community. Report and Statement of Policy Re: Commission En Banc Program Inquiry, 20 RR 1902.

point of the group represented by the leader being consulted; should include a representative range of groups and leaders to give the applicant a better basis for determining the total needs of the community; and should identify them by name, position and organization. The purpose of such consultations should be to elicit constructive information concerning community needs, and not mere approval of existing or pre-planned programming.

Suggestions received: The second of the above four elements is largely self-explanatory, but, importantly, the listing should include the significant suggestions as to community needs received through the consultations with community leaders, whether or not the applicant proposes to treat them through its programing service.

Applicant's evaluation: What is expected of the applicant is that he will evaluate the relative importance of those suggestions and consider them in formulating the station's over-all program service.

Programming service proposed to meet the needs as evaluated: The fourth element set out in Minshall should be set out in response to Question 1.C., and calls for relating the program service to the needs of the community as evaluated, i.e., what programming service is proposed to meet what needs.

The foregoing information is also expected of all applicants for increased facilities serving a substantial amount of new area or population. KTBS, Inc., 1 RR 2d 1054 (1964).

Section 1.526 of the Commission Rules requires licensees of broadcast stations to keep on file locally for public inspection a copy of its applications (which include Sections IV-A and IV-B) as well as exhibits, letters, other documents, and correspondence with the Commission pertaining to the application.

11

FCC ASCERTAINMENT PRIMER

Federal Communications Commission Primer on Part I, Section IV-A and IV-B of Application Forms Concerning Ascertainment of Community Problems and Broadcast Matter To Deal With Those Problems

> 27 FCC 2d 650, 682
>
> February 23, 1971
>
> (as amended by 33 FCC 2d 394,
>
> January 12, 1972)

> Ever since the FCC issued its *1960 Programming Policy Statement*, the element of broadcaster ascertainment of community problems, needs, and interests has grown in importance. The 1962 *Suburban* case is an early indication of this continuing trend, as is the major modification of Section IV of the FCC application forms carried out in the 1960s.
>
> The *Ascertainment Primer*, a product of a proceeding initiated by the Federal Communications Bar Association, is designed to clarify FCC standards pertaining to Part I of its program proposal questionnaires, and thereby to "aid broadcasters in being more responsive to the problems of their communities, add more certainty to their efforts in meeting Commission standards, make available to other interested parties standards by which they can judge applications for stations licensed to their community, and aid [the FCC] staff in applying ... standards uniformly" (27 FCC 2d 650, 651 (1971)).

A.   GENERAL

1.   *Question*:   With what applications does this Primer apply in answering Part I, Section IV (A or B) of the application forms?

Answer: With applications for:

a.   construction permit for new broadcast stations;
b.   construction permit for a change in authorized facilities when the station's proposed field intensity contour (Grade B for television, 1 mV/m for FM, or 0.5 mV/m for AM) encompasses a new area that is equal to or greater than 50% of the area within the authorized field intensity contours;
c.   construction permit or modification of license to change station location;
d.   construction permit for satellite television station, including a 100% satellite;
e.   the assignee's or transferee's portion of applications for assignment of broadcast license or transfer of control, except in *pro forma* cases where Form 316 is appropriate.

Educational organizations filing applications for educational noncommercial stations are exempt from the provisions of this Primer.

2.   *Question*:   If Section IV (A or B) has been recently submitted, must an applicant conduct a new ascertainment of community problems and submit a new Section IV?

Answer: Needless duplication of effort will not be required. Prior filings within the year previous to the tender of the present application will generally be acceptable, where they were filed by the same applicant, for the same station or for another station in the same community and there are no significant coverage differences involved. Parties relying on previous filings must specifically refer to the application relied on and state that in their judgment there has been no change since the earlier filing. Proposed assignors and transferors of control are not required to file Part I even where they must file other parts of Section IV.

3.   *Question*:   What is the general purpose of Part I, Section IV-A or IV-B?

Answer: To show what the applicant has done to ascertain the problems, needs and interests of the residents of his community of license and other areas he undertakes to serve (See Question 6, below), and what broadcast matter he proposes to meet those problems, needs and interests, as evaluated. The word "problems" will be used subsequently in this Primer as a short form of the phrase "problems, needs and interests." The phrase "to meet community problems" will be used to include the obligation to meet, aid in meeting, be responsive to, or stimulate the solution for community problems.

4.   *Question*:   How should ascertainment of community problems be made?

Answer: By consultations with leaders of the significant groups in the community to be served and surrounding areas the applicant has undertaken to serve, and by consultations with members of the general public. In order to know what significant groups are found in a particular community, its composition must be determined, see Question and Answer 9. The word "group" as used here is broad enough to include population segments, such as racial and ethnic groups, and informal groups, as well as groups with formal organization.

5. *Question*:   Can an applicant rely upon long-time residency in or familiarity with, the area to be served instead of making a showing that he has ascertained community problems?
Answer: No. Such an ascertainment is mandatory.

6. *Question*:   Is an applicant expected to ascertain community problems outside the community of license?
Answer: Yes. Of course, an applicant's principal obligation is to ascertain the problems of his community of license. But he should also ascertain the problems of the other communities that he undertakes to serve, as set forth in his response to Question 1(A) (2) of Section IV-A or IV-B. Applicants for stations licensed to more than one city, or for channels assigned to two or more cities, or proposed transferees or assignees of stations which have obtained waiver of the station identification rules to permit secondary identification with additional cities, are expected to ascertain problems in each of the cities. If an applicant chooses not to serve a major community that falls within his service contours a showing must be submitted explaining why. However, no major city more than 75 miles from the transmitter site need be included in the applicant's ascertainment, even if the station's contours exceed that distance.

7. *Question*:   Must the ascertainment of community problems for the other areas the applicant undertakes to serve be as extensive as for the city of license?
Answer: No. Normally, consultations with community leaders who can be expected to have a broad overview of community problems would be sufficient to ascertain community problems.

8. *Question*:   Should an applicant for a major change in facilities (see Answer 1(b), above) make a new ascertainment of community problems for the entire service area or just the additional area to be served?
Answer: Only the additional area to be served need be subjected to a new ascertainment of community problems. Only communities or areas covered by Question and Answer 6 need be ascertained, to the extent indicated in Answer 7.

9. *Question*:   How does an applicant determine the composition of his city of license?
Answer: The applicant may use any method he chooses, but guesswork or estimates based upon alleged area familiarity are inadequate. Current data from the U.S. Census Bureau, Chamber of Commerce and other reliable studies or reports are acceptable. The applicant must submit such data as is necessary to indicate the minority, racial, or ethnic breakdown of the community, its economic activities, governmental activities, public service organizations, and any other factors or activities that make the particular community distinctive.

10.   *Question*:   If the applicant shows consultations with leaders of groups and organizations that represent various economic, social, political, cultural and other elements of the community, such as government, education, religion, agriculture, business, labor, the professions, racial and/or ethnic groups, and eleemosynary organizations, is the applicant still required to submit a showing in support of its determination of the composition of the community?

Answer: Yes. The purpose of requiring a determination of the community is to inform the applicant and the Commission what groups comprise the community. The applicant must use that information to select those who are to be consulted as representatives of those groups. That determination may be challenged on a showing, including supporting data, that a significant group has been omitted. The "significance" of a group may rest on several criteria, including its size, its influence, or its lack of influence in the community.

B.   CONSULTATIONS WITH COMMUNITY LEADERS AND MEMBERS OF THE GENERAL PUBLIC

11(a).   *Question*: Who should conduct consultations with community leaders?

Answer: Principals or management-level employees. In the case of newly formed applicants who have not hired a full staff and are applying for new stations, or for transfer or assignment of an authorization, principals, management-level employees, or prospective management-level employees, must be used to consult with community leaders.

11(b).   *Question*:   Who should consult with members of the general public?

Answer: Principals or employees. In the case of newly formed applicants who have not hired a full staff and are applying for new stations, or for transfer or assignment of an authorization, principals, employees or prospective employees may conduct consultations. If consultations are conducted by employees who are below the management level, the consultation process must be supervised by principals, management-level employees, or prospective management-level employees. In addition, the applicant may choose to use a professional research or survey service to conduct consultations with members of the general public.

12.   *Question*:   To what extent may a professional research or survey service be used in the ascertainment process?

Answer: A professional service would not establish a dialogue between decision-making personnel in the applicant and community leaders. Therefore, such a service may not be used to consult community leaders. However, a professional service, as indicated in Answer 11(b), may be used to conduct consultations with the general public. A professional service may also be used to provide the applicant with background data, including information as to the composition of the city of license. The use of a professional research or survey service is not required to meet Commission standards as to ascertaining community problems. The applicant will be responsible for the reliability of such a service.

13(a). *Question*: With what community leaders should consultations be held?
Answer: The applicant has already determined the composition of the community, and should select for consultations those community leaders that reflect that composition. Groups with the greatest problems may be the least organized and have the fewest recognized spokesmen. Therefore, additional efforts may be necessary to identify their leaders so as to better establish a dialogue with such groups and better ascertain their problems.

13(b). *Question*: With what members of the general public should consultations be held?
Answer: A random sample of members of the general public should be consulted. The consultations should be designed to further ascertain community problems which may not have been revealed by consultations with community leaders. In addition to a random sample, if the applicant has reason to believe that further consultations with a particular group may reveal further problems or may elicit viewpoints that will give him further insight into its problems, he is encouraged to consult with additional members of that group.

14. *Question*: How many should be consulted?
Answer: No set number or formula has been adopted. Community leaders from each significant group must be consulted. A sufficient number of members of the general public to assure a generally random sample must also be consulted. The number of consultations will vary, of course, with the size of the city in question and the number of distinct groups or organizations. No formula has been adopted as to the number of consultations in the city of license compared to other communities falling within the station's coverage contours. Applicants for stations in relatively small communities that are near larger communities are reminded that an ascertainment of community problems primarily in the larger community raises a question as to whether the station will realistically serve the small city, or intends to abandon its obligation to the smaller city.

15. *Question*: When should consultations be held?
Answer: In preparing applications for major changes in the facilities of operating stations, a complete new ascertainment must be made within six (6) months prior to filing the application. Applicants for a new facility, or the party filing the assignee or transferee portion of an application for assignment or transfer, are also required to hold consultations within six (6) months prior to filing an appropriate application.

16.   *Question*:   Is a showing on the ascertainment of community problems defective if leaders of one of the groups that comprise the community, as disclosed by the applicant's study, are not consulted?
Answer: The omission of consultations with leaders of a significant group would make the applicant's showing defective, since those consulted would not reflect the composition of the community.

17.   *Question*:   In consultations to ascertain community problems, may a preprinted form or questionnaire be used?
Answer: Yes. A questionnaire may serve as a useful guide for consultations with community leaders, but cannot be used in lieu of personal consultations. Members of the general public may be asked to fill out a questionnaire to be collected by the applicant. The applicant may also permit members of the general public to return the questionnaires by mail, but only if the applicant submits an appropriate showing that this method has resulted in responses from members of the general public who are generally distributed throughout the community to be served. If the applicant uses a form or questionnaire, a copy should be submitted with the application.

18.   *Question*:   In consulting with community leaders to ascertain community problems, should an applicant also elicit their opinion on what programs the applicant should broadcast?
Answer: It is not the purpose of the consultations to elicit program suggestions. (See Question and Answer 3.) Rather, it is to ascertain what the person consulted believes to be the problems of the community from the standpoint of a leader of the particular group or organization. Thus, a leader in the educational field would be a useful source of information on educational matters; a labor leader, on labor matters; and a business leader on business matters. However, it is also recognized that individual leaders may have significant comments outside their respective fields, and the applicant should consider their comments with respect to all community problems. The applicant has the responsibility for determining what broadcast matter should be presented to meet the ascertained community problems as he has evaluated them.

19.   *Question*:   If, in consulting with community leaders and members of the general public, an applicant receives little information as to the existence of community problems, can he safely assume that only a few problems actually exist?
Answer: No. The assumption is not safe. The applicant should re-examine his efforts to determine whether his consultations have been designed to elicit sufficient information. Obviously, a brief or chance encounter will not provide adequate results. The person interviewed should be specifically advised of the purpose of the consultation. The applicant should note that many individuals, when consulting with a broadcast applicant, either jump to the conclusion that

the applicant is seeking programming preferences, or express community problems in terms of exposure or publicity for the particular group or groups with which they are affiliated. The applicant may properly note these comments, but should ask further questions designed to elicit more extensive responses as to community problems.

20.   *Question*:   In responding to Part I of Section IV-A or IV-B how should the applicant identify the community leaders consulted?
Answer: By name, position, and/or organization of each. If further information is required to clearly identify a specific leader, it should be submitted.

21.   *Question*:   Should the information elicited from a community leader, from the standpoint of the group he represents, be set forth after his name?
Answer: It is not required, but the applicant may find it desirable. The information can be set forth in a general list of community problems.

C.   INFORMATION RECEIVED

22.   *Question*:   Must all community problems which were revealed by the consultations be included in the applicant's showing?
Answer: All ascertained community problems should be listed, whether or not he proposes to treat them through his broadcast matter. An applicant need not, however, list comments as to community problems that are clearly frivolous.

D.   APPLICANT'S EVALUATION

23.   *Question*:   What is meant by an "applicant's evaluation" of information received as to community problems?
Answer: The applicant's evaluation is the process by which he determines the relative importance of the community problems he has ascertained, the timeliness of the various comments, and the extent to which he can present broadcast matter to meet the problems.

24.   *Question*:   Is the applicant's evaluation to be included in his application?
Answer: It is not required. Where the applicant's broadcast matter does not appear to be sufficiently responsive to the community problems disclosed by his consultations, the applicant may be asked for an explanation by letter of inquiry from the Commission. See Questions and Answers 25 and 26.

25. *Question*: Must an applicant plan broadcast matter to meet all community problems disclosed by his consultations?

Answer: Not necessarily. However, he is expected to determine in good faith which of such problems merit treatment by the station. In determining what kind of broadcast matter should be presented to meet those problems, the applicant may consider his program format and the composition of his audience, but bearing in mind that many problems affect and are pertinent to diverse groups of people.

26. *Question*: If an applicant lists a number of community problems but in his evaluation determines that he will present broadcast matter to meet only one or two of them, would the proposal be defective?

Answer: A *prima facie* question would arise as to how the proposal would serve the public interest, and the applicant would have the burden of establishing the validity of his proposal.

27. *Question*: As a result of the evaluation process, is an applicant expected to propose broadcast matter to meet community problems in proportion to the number of people involved in the problem?

Answer: No. For example, the applicant, in his evaluation (see Question and Answer 23) might determine that a problem concerning a beautification program affecting all the people would not have the relative importance and immediacy of a problem relating to inadequate hospital facilities affecting only a small percentage of the community, but in a life-or-death way.

E. BROADCAST MATTER TO MEET THE PROBLEMS AS EVALUATED

28. *Question*: What is meant by "broadcast matter"?

Answer: Programs and announcements.

29. *Question*: In the application, must there be a showing as to *what* broadcast matter the applicant is proposing to *what* problem?

Answer: Yes. See Public Notice of August 22, 1968, FCC 68-847, 13 RR 2d 1303. The applicant should give the description, and anticipated time segment, duration and frequency of broadcast of the program or program series, and the community problem or problems which are to be treated by it. One appropriate way would be to list the broadcast matter and, after it, the particular problem or problems the broadcast matter is designed to meet. Statements such as "programs will be broadcast from time to time to meet community problems," or "news, talk and discussion programs will be used to meet community problems," are clearly insufficient. Applicants should note that they are expected to make a positive, diligent and continuing effort to meet community problems. Therefore, they are expected to modify their broadcast matter if warranted in light of changed community problems. If announcements are proposed, they should be identified with the community problem or problems they are designed to meet.

30.   *Question*:   Can an applicant specify only announcements and no programs to meet community problems?
Answer: A proposal to present announcements only would raise a question as to the adequacy of the proposal. The applicant would have the burden of establishing that announcements would be the most effective method for meeting the community problems he proposes to meet. If the burden is not met by the showing in the application, it will be subject to further inquiry.

31.   *Question*:   What is meant by devoting a "significant proportion" of a station's programming to meeting community problems? [*City of Camden*, 18 FCC 2d 412, 421, 16 RR 2d 555, 568 (1969).]
Answer: There is no single answer for all stations. The time required to deal with community problems can vary from community to community and from time to time within a community. Initially, this is a matter that falls within the discretion of the applicant. However, where the amount of broadcast matter proposed to meet community problems appears patently insufficient to meet significantly the community problems disclosed by the applicant's consultations, he will be asked for an explanation by letter of inquiry from the Commission.

32.   *Question*:   Can station editorials be used as a part of a licensee's efforts to meet community problems?
Answer: Yes.

33.   *Question*:   Can news programming be considered as programming to meet community problems?
Answer: Yes. However, they can not be relied upon exclusively. Most broadcast stations, of course, carry news programs regardless of community problems. News programs are usually considered by the people to be a factual report of events and matters — to keep the public informed — and, therefore, are not designed primarily to meet community problems.

34.   *Question*:   If an applicant proposes a specialized format (all news, rock and roll, religious, etc.), must it present broadcast matter to meet community problems?
Answer: Yes. The broadcast matter can be fitted into the format of the station.

35. *Question*: May an applicant rely upon activities other than programming to meet community problems?

Answer: No. Many broadcasters do participate personally in civic activities, but the Commission's concern must be with the licensee's stewardship of his broadcast time in serving the public interest.

36. *Question*: Are there any requirements as to when broadcast matter meeting community problems should be presented?

Answer: The applicant is expected to schedule the time of presentation on a good faith judgment as to when it could reasonably be expected to be effective.

12

SELF-REGULATION

Broadcasters first voluntarily imposed regulation on themselves through their trade association, the National Association of Broadcasters (NAB), in 1929. The remarkable growth and increased complexity of self-regulation are made evident by comparing the original codes with their contemporary counterparts.

About half of all commercial radio and television stations subscribe to the current codes. Additionally, all networks and many stations have their own formulations of programming standards to which they adhere, although the NAB codes have gained wider acceptance than any others.

A

NAB CODE OF ETHICS*

March 25, 1929

First.   Recognizing that the Radio audience includes persons of all ages and all types of political, social and religious belief, every broadcaster will endeavor to

*Reprinted by permission of The Code Authority, National Association of Broadcasters.

prevent the broadcasting of any matter which would commonly be regarded as offensive.

Second.   When the facilities of a broadcaster are used by others than the owner, the broadcaster shall ascertain the financial responsibility and character of such client, that no dishonest fraudulent or dangerous person, firm or organization may gain access to the Radio audience.

Third.   Matter which is barred from the mails as fraudulent, deceptive or obscene shall not be broadcast.

Fourth.   Every broadcaster shall exercise great caution in accepting any advertising matter regarding products or services which may be injurious to health.

Fifth.   No broadcaster shall permit the broadcasting of advertising statements or claims which he knows or believes to be false, deceptive or grossly exaggerated.

Sixth.   Every broadcaster shall strictly follow the provisions of the Radio Act of 1927 regarding the clear identification of sponsored or paid-for material.

Seventh.   Care shall be taken to prevent the broadcasting of statements derogatory to other stations, to individuals, or to competing products or services, except where the law specifically provides that the station has no right of censorship.

Eighth.   Where charges of violation of any article of the Code of Ethics of The National Association of Broadcasters are filed in writing with the Managing Director, the Board of Directors shall investigate such charges and notify the station of its findings.

B

NAB STANDARDS OF COMMERCIAL PRACTICE *

March 25, 1929

I.   *Program Content and Presentation*

   (A)   There is a decided difference between what may be broadcast before and after 6:00 p.m. Time before 6:00 p.m. is included in the

*Reprinted by permission of The Code Authority, National Association of Broadcasters.

business day and, therefore, may be devoted in part, at least, to broadcasting programs of a business nature; while time after 6:00 p.m. is for recreation and relaxation, and commercial programs should be of the good-will type.

(B)   Commercial announcements, as the term is generally understood, should not be broadcast between 7:00 and 11:00 p.m.

(C)   A client's business and his product should be mentioned sufficiently to insure him an adequate return on his investment — but never to the extent that it loses listeners to the station.

(D)   The use of records should be governed by the following:

1.   The order of the Commission with reference to identifying "Phonograph Records" and other means of mechanical reproduction should be completely carried out.

2.   Phonograph records (those for sale to the public) should not be broadcast between 6:00 and 11:00 p.m. except in the case of pre-release records used in programs sponsored either by the manufacturer or the local distributor.

3.   When mechanical reproductions prepared for radio use only are not for public sale, and are of such quality to recommend their being broadcast, no limitation should be placed on their use, except as individual station policy may determine.

II.   *Salesmen and Representatives*

(A)   Salesmen on commission or salary should have:

1.   Definite responsibility to the station for which they solicit;

2.   Some means of identification.

Furthermore, contracts should state specifically that they will not be considered as acceptable until signed by an officer of the station; that no agreements, verbal or understood, can be considered as part of the contract. The salesman's conference with the client should always be confirmed by an officer of the station.

(B)   The standard commission allowed by all advertising media to recognized agencies should be allowed by broadcasting stations. If selling representatives are maintained by stations in cities where they otherwise have no representation, the station itself should make its own arrangements as to payment for such representation.

(C)   Blanket time should not be sold to clients to be resold by them as they see fit.

III.   *Agencies*

(A)   Agencies have three functions in broadcasting:

1.   Credit responsibility.

2.   Account service and contact.

3.   Program supervision in the interest of the client.

    (B)   Commission should be allowed only to agencies of recognized standing.

IV.   *Sales Data.* — The best sales data is result data.

V.   *Rate Cards*

    (A)   There should be no deviation whatsoever from rates quoted on a rate card or cards.

    (B)   Wherever practicable, the standard rate card form recommended by this Association should be used.

VI.   *Clients*

    (A)   Client standards of credit should be maintained similar to those established in other fields of advertising.

    (B)   In deciding what accounts or classes of business are acceptable for broadcast advertising, member stations should be governed by the Code of Ethics adopted by this Association.

C

NAB RADIO CODE*

17th Edition, April, 1972

THE RADIO BROADCASTER'S CREED

We Believe:

That Radio Broadcasting in the United States of America is a living symbol of democracy; a significant and necessary instrument for maintaining freedom of expression, as established by the First Amendment to the Constitution of the United States;

That its influence in the arts, in science, in education, in commerce, and upon the public welfare is of such magnitude that the only proper measure of its responsibility is the common good of the whole people;

That it is our obligation to serve the people in such manner as to reflect credit upon our profession and to encourage aspiration toward a better estate for all mankind; by making available to every person in America such programs as will perpetuate the traditional leadership of the United States in all phases of the broadcasting art;

That we should make full and ingenious use of man's store of knowledge, his talents, and his skills and exercise critical and discerning judgment concerning all broadcasting operations to the end that we may, intelligently and sympathetically:

Observe the proprieties and customs of civilized society;

Respect the rights and sensitivities of all people;

Honor the sanctity of marriage and the home;

Protect and uphold the dignity and brotherhood of all mankind;

Enrich the daily life of the people through the factual reporting and analysis of news, and through programs of education, entertainment, and information;

Provide for the fair discussion of matters of general public concern; engage in works directed toward the common good; and volunteer our aid and comfort in times of stress and emergency;

Contribute to the economic welfare of all by expanding the channels of trade, by encouraging the development and conservation of natural resources, and by bringing together the buyer and seller through the broadcasting of information pertaining to goods and services.

Toward the achievement of these purposes we agree to observe the following:

I.   PROGRAM STANDARDS

A.   News

Radio is unique in its capacity to reach the largest number of people first with reports on current events. This competitive advantage bespeaks caution — being first is not as important as being right. The following Standards are predicated upon that viewpoint.

    1. *News sources.*   Those responsible for news on radio should exercise constant professional care in the selection of sources — for the integrity

of the news and the consequent good reputation of radio as a dominant news medium depend largely upon the reliability of such sources.

2. *News reporting.* News reporting shall be factual and objective. Good taste shall prevail in the selection and handling of news. Morbid, sensational, or alarming details not essential to factual reporting should be avoided. News should be broadcast in such a manner as to avoid creation of panic and unnecessary alarm. Broadcasters shall be diligent in their supervision of content, format, and presentation of news broadcasts. Equal diligence should be exercised in selection of editors and reporters who direct news gathering and dissemination, since the station's performance in this vital informational field depends largely upon them.

3. *Commentaries and analyses.* Special obligations devolve upon those who analyze and/or comment upon news developments, and management should be satisfied completely that the task is to be performed in the best interest of the listening public. Programs of news analysis and commentary shall be clearly identified as such, distinguishing them from straight news reporting.

4. *Editorializing.* Broadcasts in which stations express their own opinions about issues of general public interest should be clearly identified as editorials and should be clearly distinguished from news and other program material.

5. *Coverage of news and public events.* In the coverage of news and public events the broadcaster has the right to exercise his judgment consonant with the accepted standards of ethical journalism and especially the requirements for decency and decorum in the broadcast of public and court proceedings.

6. *Placement of advertising.* A broadcaster should exercise particular discrimination in the acceptance, placement and presentation of advertising in news programs so that such advertising should be clearly distinguishable from the news content.

B.   Controversial public issues

1.   Radio provides a valuable forum for the expression of responsible views on public issues of a controversial nature. The broadcaster should develop programs relating to controversial public issues of importance to his fellow citizens; and give fair representation to opposing sides of issues which materially affect the life or welfare of a substantial segment of the public.

2.   Requests by individuals, groups or organizations for time to discuss their views on controversial public issues should be considered on the basis of their individual merits, and in the light of the contributions which the use requested would make to the public interest.

3.   Programs devoted to the discussion of controversial public issues should be identified as such. They should not be presented in a manner which would create the impression that the program is other than one dealing with a public issue.

C.   Community responsibility

1.   A broadcaster and his staff occupy a position of responsibility in the community and should conscientiously endeavor to be acquainted with its needs and characteristics in order to serve the welfare of its citizens.

2.   Requests for time for the placement of public service announcements or programs should be carefully reviewed with respect to the character and reputation of the group, campaign or organization involved, the public interest content of the message, and the manner of its presentation.

D.   Political broadcasts

1.   Political broadcasts, or the dramatization of political issues designed to influence an election, shall be properly identified as such.

2.   They should be presented in a manner which would properly identify the nature and character of the broadcast.

3.   Because of the unique character of political broadcasts and the necessity to retain broad freedoms of policy void of restrictive interference, it is incumbent upon all political candidates and all political parties to observe the canons of good taste and political ethics, keeping in mind the intimacy of broadcasting in the American home.

E.   Advancement of education and culture

1.   Because radio is an integral part of American life, there is inherent in radio broadcasting a continuing opportunity to enrich the experience of living through the advancement of education and culture.

2.   The radio broadcaster, in augmenting the educational and cultural influences of the home, the church, schools, institutions of higher learning, and other entities devoted to education and culture:

(a)   Should be thoroughly conversant with the educational and cultural needs and aspirations of the community served;

(b)   Should cooperate with the responsible and accountable educational and cultural entities of the community to provide enlightenment of listeners;

(c)   Should engage in experimental efforts designed to advance the community's cultural and educational interests.

F.   Religion and religious programs

1.   Religious programs shall be presented by responsible individuals, groups or organizations.

2.   Radio broadcasting, which reaches men of all creeds simultaneously, shall avoid attacks upon religious faiths.

3.   Religious programs shall be presented respectfully and without prejudice or ridicule.

4.   Religious programs shall place emphasis on religious doctrines of faith and worship.

G.   Dramatic programs

1.   In determining the acceptability of any dramatic program containing any element of crime, mystery, or horror, proper consideration should be given to the possible effect on all members of the family.

2.   Radio should reflect realistically the experience of living, in both its pleasant and tragic aspects, if it is to serve the listener honestly. Nevertheless, it holds a concurrent obligation to provide programs which will encourage better adjustments to life.

3.   This obligation is apparent in the area of dramatic programs particularly. Without sacrificing integrity of presentation, dramatic programs on radio shall avoid:

(a)   Techniques and methods of crime presented in such manner as to encourage imitation, or to make the commission of crime attractive, or to suggest that criminals can escape punishment;

(b)   Detailed presentation of brutal killings, torture, or physical agony, horror, the use of supernatural or climactic incidents likely to terrify or excite unduly;

(c)   Sound effects calculated to mislead, shock, or unduly alarm the listener;

(d)   Disrespectful portrayal of law enforcement;

(e)   The portrayal of suicide as a satisfactory solution to any problem.

H.   Responsibility toward children

The education of children involves giving them a sense of the world at large. It is not enough that programs broadcast for children shall be suitable for the young and immature. In addition, programs which might reasonably be expected to hold the attention of children and which are broadcast during times when children may be normally expected to constitute a substantial part of the audience should be presented with due regard for their effect on children.

1.   Programs specifically designed for listening by children shall be based upon sound social concepts and shall reflect respect for parents, law and order, clean living, high morals, fair play, and honorable behavior.

2.   They shall convey the commonly accepted moral, social and ethical ideals characteristic of American life.

3.   They should contribute to the healthy development of personality and character.

4.   They should afford opportunities for cultural growth as well as for wholesome entertainment.

5.   They should be consistent with integrity of realistic production, but they should avoid material of extreme nature which might create undesirable emotional reaction in children.

6.   They shall avoid appeals urging children to purchase the product specifically for the purpose of keeping the program on the air or which, for any reason, encourage the children to enter inappropriate places.

7.   They should present such subjects as violence and sex without undue emphasis and only as required by plot development or character delineation. Crime should not be presented as attractive or as a solution to human problems, and the inevitable retribution should be made clear.

8.   They should avoid reference to kidnapping or threats of kidnapping of children.

I.   General

1.   The intimacy and confidence placed in Radio demand of the broadcaster, the networks and other program sources that they be vigilant in protecting the audience from deceptive program practices.

2.   Sound effects and expressions characteristically associated with news broadcasts (such as "bulletin," "flash," "we interrupt this program to bring you," etc.) shall be reserved for announcement of news, and the use of any deceptive techniques in connection with fictional events and non-news programs shall not be employed.

3.   The acceptance of cash payments or other considerations for including identification of commercial products or services, trade names or advertising slogans, including the identification of prizes, etc., must be disclosed in accordance with provisions of the Communications Act.

4.   When plot development requires the use of material which depends upon physical or mental handicaps, care should be taken to spare the sensibilities of sufferers from similar defects.

5.   Stations should avoid broadcasting program material which would tend to encourage illegal gambling or other violations of federal, state and local laws, ordinances, and regulations.

6.   Simulation of court atmosphere or use of the term "court" in a program title should be done only in such manner as to eliminate the possibility of creating the false impression that the proceedings broadcast are vested with judicial or official authority.

7.   Quiz and similar programs that are presented as contests of knowledge, information, skill or luck must in fact, be genuine contests and the results must not be controlled by collusion with or between contestants, or any other action which will favor one contestant against any other.

8.   No program shall be presented in a manner which through artifice or simulation would mislead the audience as to any material fact. Each broadcaster must exercise reasonable judgment to determine whether a particular method of presentation would constitute a material deception, or would be accepted by the audience as normal theatrical illusion.

9.   Legal, medical and other professional advice will be permitted only in conformity with law and recognized ethical and professional standards.

10.   Narcotic addiction shall not be presented except as a vicious habit. The misuse of hallucinogenic drugs shall not be presented or encouraged as desirable or socially acceptable.

11.   Program material pertaining to fortune-telling, occultism, astrology, phrenology, palm-reading, numerology, mind-reading, character-reading, or subjects of a like nature, is unacceptable when presented for the purpose of fostering belief in these subjects.

12.   The use of cigarettes shall not be presented in a manner to impress the youth of our country that it is a desirable habit worthy of imitation in that it contributes to health, individual achievement or social acceptance.

13.   Profanity, obscenity, smut and vulgarity are forbidden. From time to time, words which have been acceptable, acquire undesirable meanings, and broadcasters should be alert to eliminate such words.

14.   Words (especially slang) derisive of any race, color, creed, nationality or national derivation, except wherein such usage would be for the specific purpose of effective dramatization, such as combating prejudice, are forbidden.

15.   Respect is maintained for the sanctity of marriage and the value of the home. Divorce is not treated casually as a solution for marital problems.

16.   Broadcasts of actual sporting events at which on-the-scene betting is permitted should concentrate on the subject as a public sporting event and not on the aspects of gambling.

II.   ADVERTISING STANDARDS

Advertising is the principal source of revenue of the free, competitive American system of radio broadcasting. It makes possible the presentation to all American people of the finest programs of entertainment, education, and information.

Since the great strength of American radio broadcasting derives from the public respect for and the public approval of its programs, it must be the purpose of each broadcaster to establish and maintain high standards of performance, not only in the selection and production of all programs, but also in the presentation of advertising.

This Code establishes basic standards for all radio broadcasting. The principles of acceptability and good taste within the Program Standards section govern the presentation of advertising where applicable. In addition, the Code establishes in this section special standards which apply to radio advertising.

A.   General advertising standards

1.   A commercial radio broadcaster makes his facilities available for the advertising of products and services and accepts commercial presentations for such advertising. However, he shall, in recognition of his responsibility to the public, refuse the facilities of his station to an advertiser where he has good reason to doubt the integrity of the advertiser, the truth of the advertising representations, or the compliance of the advertiser with the spirit and purpose of all applicable legal requirements.

2.   In consideration of the customs and attitudes of the communities served, each radio broadcaster should refuse his facilities to the advertisement of products and services, or the use of advertising scripts, which the station has good reason to believe would be objectionable to a substantial and responsible segment of the community. These standards should be applied with judgment and flexibility, taking into consideration the characteristics of the medium, its home and family audience, and the form and content of the particular presentation.

B.   Presentation of advertising

1.   The advancing techniques of the broadcast art have shown that the quality and proper integration of advertising copy are just as important as measurement in time. The measure of a station's service to its audience is determined by its overall performance.

2.   The final measurement of any commercial broadcast service is quality. To this, every broadcaster shall dedicate his best effort.

3.   Great care shall be exercised by the broadcaster to prevent the presentation of false, misleading or deceptive advertising. While it is entirely appropriate to present a product in a favorable light and atmosphere, the presentation must not, by copy or demonstration, involve a material deception as to the characteristics or performance of a product.

4.   The broadcaster and the advertiser should exercise special caution with the content and presentation of commercials placed in or near programs designed for children. Exploitation of children should be avoided. Commercials directed to children should in no way mislead as to the product's performance and usefulness. Appeals involving matters of health which should be determined by physicians should be avoided.

5.   Reference to the results of research, surveys or tests relating to the product to be advertised shall not be presented in a manner so as to create an impression of fact beyond that established by the study. Surveys, tests or other research results upon which claims are based must be conducted under recognized research techniques and standards.

C.   Acceptability of advertisers and products

In general, because radio broadcasting is designed for the home and the entire family, the following principles shall govern the business classifications:

1.   The advertising of hard liquor shall not be accepted.

2.   The advertising of beer and wines is acceptable when presented in the best of good taste and discretion.

3.   The advertising of fortune-telling, occultism, astrology, phrenology, palm-reading, numerology, mind-reading, character-reading, or subjects of a like nature, is not acceptable.

4.   Because the advertising of all products and services of a personal nature raises special problems, such advertising, when accepted, should be treated with emphasis on ethics and the canons of good taste, and presented in a restrained and inoffensive manner.

5. The advertising of lotteries is unacceptable. The advertising of tip sheets and other publications seeking to advertise for the purpose of giving odds or promoting betting is unacceptable.

The advertising of organizations, private or governmental, which conduct legalized betting on sporting contests is acceptable, provided it is limited to institutional type advertising which does not exhort the public to bet.

6. An advertiser who markets more than one product shall not be permitted to use advertising copy devoted to an acceptable product for purposes of publicizing the brand name or other identification of a product which is not acceptable.

7. Care should be taken to avoid presentation of "bait-switch" advertising whereby goods or services which the advertiser has no intention of selling are offered merely to lure the customer into purchasing higher-priced substitutes.

8. Advertising should offer a product or service on its positive merits and refrain from discrediting, disparaging or unfairly attacking competitors, competing products, other industries, professions or institutions.

Any identification or comparison of a competitive product or service, by name, or other means, should be confined to specific facts rather than generalized statements or conclusions, unless such statements or conclusions are not derogatory in nature.

9. Advertising testimonials should be genuine and reflect an honest appraisal of personal experience.

10. Advertising by institutions or enterprises offering instruction with exaggerated claims for opportunities awaiting those who enroll, is unacceptable.

11. The advertising of firearms/ammunition is acceptable provided it promotes the product only as sporting equipment and conforms to recognized standards of safety as well as all applicable laws and regulations. Advertisements of firearms/ammunition by mail order are unacceptable.

D.   Advertising of medical products

Because advertising for over-the-counter products involving health considerations are of intimate and far-reaching importance to the consumer, the following principles should apply to such advertising:

1. When dramatized advertising material involves statements by doctors, dentists, nurses or other professional people, the material should be presented by members of such profession reciting actual experience, or it should be made apparent from the presentation itself that the portrayal is dramatized.

2.   Because of the personal nature of the advertising of medical products, the indiscriminate use of such words as "Safe," "Without Risk," "Harmless," or other terms of similar meaning, either direct or implied, should not be expressed in the advertising of medical products.

3.   Advertising material which offensively describes or dramatizes distress or morbid situations involving ailments is not acceptable.

E.   Time standards for advertising copy

1.   The amount of time to be used for advertising should not exceed 18 minutes within any clock hour. The Code Authority, however, for good cause may approve advertising exceeding the above standard for special circumstances.

2.   Any reference to another's products or services under any trade name, or language sufficiently descriptive to identify it, shall, except for normal guest identification, be considered as advertising copy.

3.   For the purpose of determining advertising limitations, such program types as "classified," "swap shop," "shopping guides," and "farm auction" programs, etc., shall be regarded as containing one and one-half minutes of advertising for each five-minute segment.

F.   Contests

1.   Contests shall be conducted with fairness to all entrants and shall comply with all pertinent laws and regulations.

2.   All contest details, including rules, eligibility requirements, opening and termination dates, should be clearly and completely announced or easily accessible to the listening public; and the winners' names should be released as soon as possible after the close of the contest.

3.   When advertising is accepted which requests contestants to submit items of product identification or other evidence of purchase of products, reasonable facsimiles thereof should be made acceptable. However, when the award is based upon skill and not upon chance, evidence of purchase may be required.

4.   All copy pertaining to any contest (except that which is required by law) associated with the exploitation or sale of the sponsor's product or service, and all references to prizes or gifts offered in such connection should be considered a part of and included in the total time limitations heretofore provided. (See Time Standards for Advertising Copy.)

G.   Premiums and offers

1.   The broadcaster should require that full details of proposed offers be submitted for investigation and approval before the first announcement of the offer is made to the public.

2.   A final date for the termination of an offer should be announced as far in advance as possible.

3.   If a consideration is required, the advertiser should agree to honor complaints indicating dissatisfaction with the premium by returning the consideration.

4.   There should be no misleading descriptions or comparisons of any premiums or gifts which will distort or enlarge their value in the minds of the listeners.

D

NAB TELEVISION CODE*

16th Edition, April, 1972
(Amended to January 10, 1973)

PREAMBLE

Television is seen and heard in nearly every American home. These homes include children and adults of all ages, embrace all races and all varieties of philosophic or religious conviction and reach those of every educational background. Television broadcasters must take this pluralistic audience into account in programming their stations. They are obligated to bring their positive responsibility for professionalism and reasoned judgment to bear upon all those involved in the development, production and selection of programs.

*Copyright 1972, National Association of Broadcasters.

The free, competitive American system of broadcasting which offers programs of entertainment, news, general information, education and culture is supported and made possible by revenues from advertising. While television broadcasters are responsible for the programming and advertising on their stations, the advertisers who use television to convey their commercial messages also have a responsibility to the viewing audience. Their advertising messages should be presented in an honest, responsible and tasteful manner. Advertisers should also support the endeavors of broadcasters to offer a diversity of programs that meet the needs and expectations of the total viewing audience.

The viewer also has a responsibility to help broadcasters serve the public. All viewers should make their criticisms and positive suggestions about programming and advertising known to the broadcast licensee. Parents particularly should oversee the viewing habits of their children, encouraging them to watch programs that will enrich their experience and broaden their intellectual horizons.

PROGRAM STANDARDS

I. Principles governing program content

It is in the interest of television as a vital medium to encourage programs that are innovative, reflect a high degree of creative skill, deal with significant moral and social issues and present challenging concepts and other subject matter that relate to the world in which the viewer lives.

Television programs should not only reflect the influence of the established institutions that shape our values and culture, but also expose the dynamics of social change which bear upon our lives.

To achieve these goals, television broadcasters should be conversant with the general and specific needs, interests and aspirations of all the segments of the communities they serve. They should affirmatively seek out responsible representatives of all parts of their communities so that they may structure a broad range of programs that will inform, enlighten and entertain the total audience.

Broadcasters should also develop programs directed toward advancing the cultural and educational aspects of their communities.

To assure that broadcasters have the freedom to program fully and responsibly, none of the provisions of this Code should be construed as preventing or impeding broadcast of the broad range of material necessary to help broadcasters fulfill their obligations to operate in the public interest.

The challenge to the broadcaster is to determine how suitably to present the complexities of human behavior. For television, this requires exceptional awareness of considerations peculiar to the medium.

Accordingly, in selecting program subjects and themes, great care must be exercised to be sure that treatment and presentation are made in good faith and not for the purpose of sensationalism or to shock or exploit the audience or appeal to prurient interests or morbid curiosity.

II.   Responsibility toward children

Broadcasters have a special responsibility to children. Programs designed primarily for children should take into account the range of interests and needs of children, and should contribute to the sound, balanced development of children.

In the course of a child's development, numerous social factors and forces, including television, affect the ability of the child to make the transition to adult society.

The child's training and experience during the formative years should include positive sets of values which will allow the child to become a responsible adult, capable of coping with the challenges of maturity.

Children should also be exposed, at the appropriate times, to a reasonable range of the realities which exist in the world sufficient to help them make the transition to adulthood.

Because children are allowed to watch programs designed primarily for adults, broadcasters should take this practice into account in the presentation of material in such programs when children may constitute a substantial segment of the audience.

All the standards set forth in this section apply to both program and commercial material designed and intended for viewing by children.

III.   Community responsibility

1.   Television broadcasters and their staffs occupy positions of unique responsibility in their communities and should conscientiously endeavor to be acquainted fully with the community's needs and characteristics in order better to serve the welfare of its citizens.

2.   Requests for time for the placement of public service announcements or programs should be carefully reviewed with respect to the character and reputation of the group, campaign or organization involved, the public interest content of the message, and the manner of its presentation.

IV.   Special program standards

1.   Violence, physical or psychological, may only be projected in

responsibly handled contexts, not used exploitatively. Programs involving violence should present the consequences of it to its victims and perpetrators.

Presentation of the details of violence should avoid the excessive, the gratuitous and the instructional.

The use of violence for its own sake and the detailed dwelling upon brutality or physical agony, by sight or by sound, are not permissible.

2.   The treatment of criminal activities should always convey their social and human effects.

The presentation of techniques of crime in such detail as to be instructional or invite imitation shall be avoided.

3.   Narcotic addiction shall not be presented except as a destructive habit. The use of illegal drugs or the abuse of legal drugs shall not be encouraged or shown as socially acceptable.

4.   The use of gambling devices or scenes necessary to the development of plot or as appropriate background is acceptable only when presented with discretion and in moderation, and in a manner which would not excite interest in, or foster, betting nor be instructional in nature.

5.   Telecasts of actual sports programs at which on-the-scene betting is permitted by law shall be presented in a manner in keeping with Federal, state and local laws, and should concentrate on the subject as a public sporting event.

6.   Special precautions must be taken to avoid demeaning or ridiculing members of the audience who suffer from physical or mental afflictions or deformities.

7.   Special sensitivity is necessary in the use of material relating to sex, race, color, creed, religious functionaries or rites, or national or ethnic derivation.

8.   Obscene, indecent or profane matter, as proscribed by law, is unacceptable.

9.   The presentation of marriage, the family and similarly important human relationships, and material with sexual connotations, shall not be treated exploitatively or irresponsibly, but with sensitivity. Costuming and movements of all performers shall be handled in a similar fashion.

10.   The use of liquor and the depiction of smoking in program content shall be de-emphasized. When shown, they should be consistent with plot and character development.

11.   The creation of a state of hypnosis by act or detailed demonstration on camera is prohibited and hypnosis as a form of "parlor game" antics to create humorous situations within a comedy setting is forbidden.

12.   Program material pertaining to fortune-telling, occultism, astrology, phrenology, palm-reading, numerology, mind-reading, character-reading, and the like is unacceptable if it encourages people to regard such fields as providing commonly accepted appraisals of life.

13.   Professional advice, diagnosis and treatment will be presented in conformity with law and recognized professional standards.

14.   Any technique whereby an attempt is made to convey information

to the viewer by transmitting messages below the threshold of normal awareness is not permitted.

15.   The use of animals, consistent with plot and character delineation, shall be in conformity with accepted standards of humane treatment.

16.   Quiz and similar programs that are presented as contests of knowledge, information, skill or luck must, in fact, be genuine contests and the results must not be controlled by collusion with or between contestants, or by any other action which will favor one contestant against any other.

17.   The broadcaster shall be constantly alert to prevent inclusion of elements within a program dictated by factors other than the requirements of the program itself. The acceptance of cash payments or other considerations in return for including scenic properties, the choice and identification of prizes, the selection of music and other creative program elements and inclusion of any identification of commercial products or services, their trade names or advertising slogan within the program are prohibited except in accordance with Sections 317 and 508 of the Communications Act.

18.   Contests may not constitute a lottery.

19.   No program shall be presented in a manner which through artifice or simulation would mislead the audience as to any material fact. Each broadcaster must exercise reasonable judgment to determine whether a particular method of presentation would constitute a material deception, or would be accepted by the audience as normal theatrical illusion.

20.   A television broadcaster should not present fictional events or other non-news material as authentic news telecasts or announcements, nor should he permit dramatizations in any program which would give the false impression that the dramatized material constitutes news.

21.   The standards of this Code covering program content are also understood to include, wherever applicable, the standards contained in the advertising section of the Code.

V.   Treatment of news and public events

General

Television Code standards relating to the treatment of news and public events are, because of constitutional considerations, intended to be exhortatory. The standards set forth hereunder encourage high standards of professionalism in broadcast journalism. They are not to be interpreted as turning over to others the broadcaster's responsibility as to judgments necessary in news and public events programming.

News

1.   A television station's news schedule should be adequate and well-balanced.

2.   News reporting should be factual, fair and without bias.

3.   A television broadcaster should exercise particular discrimination in the acceptance, placement and presentation of advertising in news programs so that such advertising should be clearly distinguishable from the news content.

4.   At all times, pictorial and verbal material for both news and comment should conform to other sections of these standards, wherever such sections are reasonably applicable.

5.   Good taste should prevail in the selection and handling of news:

Morbid, sensational or alarming details not essential to the factual report, especially in connection with stories of crime or sex, should be avoided. News should be telecast in such a manner as to avoid panic and unnecessary alarm.

6.   Commentary and analysis should be clearly identified as such.

7.   Pictorial material should be chosen with care and not presented in a misleading manner.

8.   All news interview programs should be governed by accepted standards of ethical journalism, under which the interviewer selects the questions to be asked. Where there is advance agreement materially restricting an important or newsworthy area of questioning, the interviewer will state on the program that such limitation has been agreed upon. Such disclosure should be made if the person being interviewed requires that questions be submitted in advance or if he participates in editing a recording of the interview prior to its use on the air.

9.   A television broadcaster should exercise due care in his supervision of content, format, and presentation of newscasts originated by his station, and in his selection of newscasters, commentators, and analysts.

Public events

1.   A television broadcaster has an affirmative responsibility at all times to be informed of public events, and to provide coverage consonant with the ends of an informed and enlightened citizenry.

2.   The treatment of such events by a television broadcaster should provide adequate and informed coverage.

VI.   Controversial public issues

1.   Television provides a valuable forum for the expression of responsible views on public issues of a controversial nature. The television broadcaster should seek out and develop with accountable individuals, groups and organizations, programs relating to controversial public issues of import to his fellow citizens; and to give fair representation to opposing sides of issues which materially affect the life or welfare of a substantial segment of the public.

2.   Requests by individuals, groups or organizations for time to discuss their views on controversial public issues, should be considered on the basis of their individual merits, and in the light of the contribution which the use requested would make to the public interest, and to a well-balanced program structure.

3.   Programs devoted to the discussion of controversial public issues should be identified as such. They should not be presented in a manner which would mislead listeners or viewers to believe that the program is purely of an entertainment, news, or other character.

4.   Broadcasts in which stations express their own opinions about issues of general public interest should be clearly identified as editorials. They should be unmistakably identified as statements of station opinion and should be appropriately distinguished from news and other program material.

VII.   Political telecasts

1.   Political telecasts should be clearly identified as such. They should not be presented by a television broadcaster in a manner which would mislead listeners or viewers to believe that the program is of any other character.

(Ref.: Communications Act of 1934, as amended, Secs. 315 and 317, and FCC Rules and Regulations, Secs. 3.654, 3.657, 3.663, as discussed in NAB's "Political Broadcast Catechism & The Fairness Doctrine.")

VIII.   Religious programs

1.   It is the responsibility of a television broadcaster to make available to the community appropriate opportunity for religious presentations.

2.   Programs reach audiences of all creeds simultaneously. Therefore, both the advocates of broad or ecumenical religious precepts, and the exponents of specific doctrines, are urged to present their positions in a manner conducive to viewer enlightenment on the role of religion in society.

3.   In the allocation of time for telecasts of religious programs the television station should use its best efforts to apportion such time fairly among responsible individuals, groups and organizations.

ADVERTISING STANDARDS

IX.   General advertising standards

1.   This Code establishes basic standards for all television broadcasting.

The principles of acceptability and good taste within the Program Standards section govern the presentation of advertising where applicable. In addition, the Code establishes in this section special standards which apply to television advertising.

2. A commercial television broadcaster makes his facilities available for the advertising of products and services and accepts commercial presentations for such advertising. However, a television broadcaster should, in recognition of his responsibility to the public, refuse the facilities of his station to an advertiser where he has good reason to doubt the integrity of the advertiser, the truth of the advertising representations, or the compliance of the advertiser with the spirit and purpose of all applicable legal requirements.

3. Identification of sponsorship must be made in all sponsored programs in accordance with the requirements of the Communications Act of 1934, as amended, and the Rules and Regulations of the Federal Communications Commission.

4. Representations which disregard normal safety precautions shall be avoided.

Children shall not be represented, except under adult supervision, as being in contact with, or demonstrating a product recognized as potentially dangerous to them.

5. In consideration of the customs and attitudes of the communities served, each television broadcaster should refuse his facilities to the advertisement of products and services, or the use of advertising scripts, which the station has good reason to believe would be objectionable to a substantial and responsible segment of the community. These standards should be applied with judgment and flexibility, taking into consideration the characteristics of the medium, its home and family audience, and the form and content of the particular presentation.

6. The advertising of hard liquor (distilled spirits) is not acceptable.

7. The advertising of beer and wines is acceptable only when presented in the best of good taste and discretion, and is acceptable only subject to Federal and local laws.

8. Advertising by institutions or enterprises which in their offers of instruction imply promises of employment or make exaggerated claims for the opportunities awaiting those who enroll for courses is generally unacceptable.

9. The advertising of firearms/ammunition is acceptable provided it promotes the product only as sporting equipment and conforms to recognized standards of safety as well as all applicable laws and regulations. Advertisements of firearms/ammunition by mail order are unacceptable. The advertising of fireworks is acceptable subject to all applicable laws.

10. The advertising of fortune-telling, occultism, astrology, phrenology, palm-reading, numerology, mind-reading, character reading or subjects of a like nature is not permitted.

11. Because all products of a personal nature create special problems, acceptability of such products should be determined with especial emphasis on

ethics and the canons of good taste. Such advertising of personal products as is accepted must be presented in a restrained and obviously inoffensive manner.

 12. The advertising of tip sheets, race track publications, or organizations seeking to advertise for the purpose of giving odds or promoting betting or lotteries is unacceptable.

 13. An advertiser who markets more than one product should not be permitted to use advertising copy devoted to an acceptable product for purposes of publicizing the brand name or other identification of a product which is not acceptable.

 14. "Bait-switch" advertising, whereby goods or services which the advertiser has no intention of selling are offered merely to lure the customer into purchasing higher-priced substitutes, is not acceptable.

 15. Personal endorsements (testimonials) shall be genuine and reflect personal experience. They shall contain no statement that cannot be supported if presented in the advertiser's own words.

X. Presentation of advertising

 1. Advertising messages should be presented with courtesy and good taste; disturbing or annoying material should be avoided; every effort should be made to keep the advertising message in harmony with the content and general tone of the program in which it appears.

 2. The role and capability of television to market sponsors' products are well recognized. In turn, this fact dictates that great care be exercised by the broadcaster to prevent the presentation of false, misleading or deceptive advertising. While it is entirely appropriate to present a product in a favorable light and atmosphere, the presentation must not, by copy or demonstration, involve a material deception as to the characteristics, performance or appearance of the product. Broadcast advertisers are responsible for making available, at the request of the Code Authority, documentation adequate to support the validity and truthfulness of claims, demonstrations and testimonials contained in their commercial messages.

 3. The broadcaster and the advertiser should exercise special caution with the content and presentation of television commercials placed in or near programs designed for children. Exploitation of children should be avoided. Commercials directed to children should in no way mislead as to the product's performance and usefulness.

 Appeals involving matters of health which should be determined by physicians should not be directed primarily to children.

 4. Children's program hosts or primary cartoon characters shall not be utilized to deliver commercial messages within or adjacent to the programs which feature such hosts or cartoon characters. This provision shall also apply to

lead-ins to commercials when such lead-ins contain sell copy or imply endorsement of the product by program host or primary cartoon character.

5.   Appeals to help fictitious characters in television programs by purchasing the advertiser's product or service or sending for a premium should not be permitted, and such fictitious characters should not be introduced into the advertising message for such purposes.

6.   Commercials for services or over-the-counter products involving health considerations are of intimate and far-reaching importance to the consumer. The following principles should apply to such advertising:

a.   Physicians, dentists or nurses, or actors representing physicians, dentists or nurses shall not be employed directly or by implication. These restrictions also apply to persons professionally engaged in medical services (e.g., physical therapists, pharmacists, dental assistants, nurses' aides).

b.   Visual representations of laboratory settings may be employed, provided they bear a direct relationship to bona fide research which has been conducted for the product or service. (*See Television Code, X, 11*) In such cases, laboratory technicians shall be identified as such and shall not be employed as spokesmen or in any other way speak on behalf of the product.

c.   Institutional announcements not intended to sell a specific product or service to the consumer and public service announcements by non-profit organizations may be presented by accredited physicians, dentists or nurses, subject to approval by the broadcaster. An accredited professional is one who has met required qualifications and has been licensed in his resident state.

7.   Advertising should offer a product or service on its positive merits and refrain from discrediting, disparaging or unfairly attacking competitors, competing products, other industries, professions or institutions.

8.   A sponsor's advertising messages should be confined within the framework of the sponsor's program structure. A television broadcaster should avoid the use of commercial announcements which are divorced from the program either by preceding the introduction of the program (as in the case of so-called "cow-catcher" announcements) or by following the apparent sign-off of the program (as in the case of so-called trailer or "hitch-hike" announcements). To this end, the program itself should be announced and clearly identified, both audio and video, before the sponsor's advertising material is first used, and should be signed off, both audio and video, after the sponsor's advertising material is last used.

9.   Since advertising by television is a dynamic technique, a television broadcaster should keep under surveillance new advertising devices so that the spirit and purpose of these standards are fulfilled.

10.   A charge for television time to churches and religious bodies is not recommended.

11.   Reference to the results of bona fide research, surveys or tests relating to the product to be advertised shall not be presented in a manner so as to create an impression of fact beyond that established by the work that has been conducted.

XI.   Advertising of medical products

1.   The advertising of medical products presents considerations of intimate and far-reaching importance to the consumer because of the direct bearing on his health.

2.   Because of the personal nature of the advertising of medical products, claims that a product will effect a cure and the indiscriminate use of such words as "safe," "without risk," "harmless," or terms of similar meaning should not be accepted in the advertising of medical products on television stations.

3.   A television broadcaster should not accept advertising material which in his opinion offensively describes or dramatizes distress or morbid situations involving ailments, by spoken word, sound or visual effects.

XII.   Contests

1.   Contests shall be conducted with fairness to all entrants, and shall comply with all pertinent laws and regulations. Care should be taken to avoid the concurrent use of the three elements which together constitute a lottery — prize, chance and consideration.

2.   All contest details, including rules, eligibility requirements, opening and termination dates should be clearly and completely announced and/or shown, or easily accessible to the viewing public, and the winners' names should be released and prizes awarded as soon as possible after the close of the contest.

3.   When advertising is accepted which requests contestants to submit items of product identification or other evidence of purchase of products, reasonable facsimiles thereof should be made acceptable unless the award is based upon skill and not upon chance.

4.   All copy pertaining to any contest (except that which is required by law) associated with the exploitation or sale of the sponsor's product or service, and all references to prizes or gifts offered in such connection should be considered a part of and included in the total time allowances as herein provided. (*See Television Code, XIV*)

XIII.   Premiums and offers

1.   Full details of proposed offers should be required by the television broadcaster for investigation and approved before the first announcement of the offer is made to the public.

2.   A final date for the termination of an offer should be announced as far in advance as possible.

3.   Before accepting for telecast offers involving a monetary consideration, a television broadcaster should satisfy himself as to the integrity of the advertiser and the advertiser's willingness to honor complaints indicating dissatisfaction with the premium by returning the monetary consideration.

4.   There should be no misleading descriptions or visual representations of any premiums or gifts which would distort or enlarge their value in the minds of the viewers.

5.   Assurances should be obtained from the advertiser that premiums offered are not harmful to person or property.

6.   Premiums should not be approved which appeal to superstition on the basis of "luck-bearing" powers or otherwise.

XIV.   Time standards for non-program material

In order that the time for non-program material and its placement shall best serve the viewer, the following standards are set forth in accordance with sound television practice:

1.   Non-Program Material Definition:

Non-program material, in both prime time and all other time, includes billboards, commercials, promotional announcements and all credits in excess of 30 seconds per program, except in feature films. In no event should credits exceed 40 seconds per program. The 40-second limitation on credits shall not apply, however, in any situation governed by a contract entered into before October 1, 1971. Public service announcements and promotional announcements for the same program are excluded from this definition.

2.   Allowable Time for Non-Program Material.

a.   In prime time on network affiliated stations, non-program material shall not exceed nine minutes 30 seconds in any 60-minute period.

In prime time on independent stations, non-program material shall not exceed 12 minutes in any 60-minute period.

In the event that news programming is included within the three and one-half hour prime time period, not more than one 30-minute segment of news programming may be governed by time standards applicable to all other time.

Prime time is a continuous period of not less than three and one-half consecutive hours per broadcast day as designated by the station between the hours of 6:00 p.m. and Midnight.

b.   In all other time, non-program material shall not exceed 16 minutes in any 60-minute period.

c.   Children's Weekend Programming Time — Defined as that

contiguous period of time between the hours of 7:00 a.m. and 2:00 p.m. on Saturday and Sunday. In programming designed primarily for children within this time period, non-program material shall not exceed 12 minutes in any 60-minute period.

3.   Program Interruptions.

a.   Definition: A program interruption is any occurrence of non-program material within the main body of the program.

b.   In prime time, the number of program interruptions shall not exceed two within any 30-minute program, or four within any 60-minute program.

Programs longer than 60 minutes shall be pro-rated at two interruptions per half-hour.

The number of interruptions in 60-minute variety shows shall not exceed five.

c.   In all other time, the number of interruptions shall not exceed four within any 30-minute program period.

d.   In children's weekend time, as above defined in 2c, the number of program interruptions shall not exceed two within any 30-minute program or four within any 60-minute program.

e.   In both prime time and all other time, the following interruption standard shall apply within programs of 15 minutes or less in length:

5-minute program – 1 interruption;
10-minute program – 2 interruptions;
15-minute program – 2 interruptions.

f.   News, weather, sports and special events programs are exempt from the interruption standard because of the nature of such programs.

4.   No more than four non-program material announcements shall be scheduled consecutively within programs, and no more than three non-program material announcements shall be scheduled consecutively during station breaks. The consecutive non-program material limitation shall not apply to a single sponsor who wishes to further reduce the number of interruptions in the program.

5.   A multiple product announcement is one in which two or more products or services are presented within the framework of a single announcement. A multiple product announcement shall not be scheduled in a unit of time less than 60 seconds, except where integrated so as to appear to the viewer as a single message. A multiple product announcement shall be considered integrated and counted as a single message if:

a.   the products or services are related and interwoven within the framework of the announcement (related products or services shall be defined as those having a common character, purpose and use); and

b.   the voice(s), setting, background and continuity are used consistently throughout so as to appear to the viewer as a single message. Multiple product announcements of 60 seconds in length or longer not meeting this definition of integration shall be counted as two or more announcements under this section of the Code. This provision shall not apply to retail or service establishments. (Effective September 1, 1973.)

6.   The use of billboards, in prime time and all other time, shall be confined to programs sponsored by a single or alternate week advertiser and shall be limited to the products advertised in the program.

7.   Reasonable and limited identification of prizes and donors' names where the presentation of contest awards or prizes is a necessary part of program content shall not be included as non-program material as defined above.

8.   Programs presenting women's service features, shopping guides, fashion shows, demonstrations and similar material provide a special service to the public in which certain material normally classified as non-program is an informative and necessary part of the program content. Because of this, the time standards may be waived by the Code Authority to a reasonable extent on a case-by-case basis.

9.   Gratuitous references in a program to a non-sponsor's product or service should be avoided except for normal guest identification.

10.   Stationary backdrops or properties in television presentations showing the sponsor's name or product, the name of his product, his trade-mark or slogan should be used only incidentally and should not obtrude on program interest or entertainment.

RELATED READING

Baird, Frank L. "Program Regulation on the New Frontier." *Journal of Broadcasting* 11 (Summer 1967), 231-243.

Baldwin, Thomas F., and Stuart H. Surlin. "A Study of Broadcast Station License Application Exhibits on Ascertainment of Community Needs." *Journal of Broadcasting* 14 (Spring 1970), 157-170.

Bennett, Sandra W. "Ascertainment of Community Needs: Where is Public Broadcasting?" *Educational Broadcasting Review* 6 (February 1972), 20-25.

Bogart, Leo. *The Age of Television*. 3d ed. New York: Frederick Ungar, 1972.

Broadcasting and the Bill of Rights. Washington: National Association of Broadcasters, 1947.

Brown, Les. *Television: The Business Behind the Box*. New York: Harcourt, Brace, Jovanovich, 1971.

Carson, Gerald. *The Roguish World of Doctor Brinkley*. New York: Holt, Rinehart and Winston, 1960.

Cogley, John. *Report on Blacklisting: Radio-Television*. Vol. II. New York: Fund for the Republic, 1956 (reprinted New York: Arno Press, 1971).

Cole, Barry G., ed. *Television: A Selection of Readings from* TV Guide *Magazine*. New York: Free Press, 1970.

Coons, John E., ed. *Freedom and Responsibility in Broadcasting*. Evanston, Ill.: Northwestern University Press, 1961.

Emery, Walter B. "Government's Role in the American System of Broadcasting." *Television Quarterly* 1:1 (February 1962), 7-13.

Foley, Joseph M. "Ascertaining Ascertainment: Impact of the FCC Primer on TV Renewal Applications." *Journal of Broadcasting* 16 (Fall 1972), 387-406.

Helffrich, Stockton. "The Radio and Television Codes and the Public Interest." *Journal of Broadcasting* 14 (Summer 1970), 267-274.

Kelly, Frank. *Who Owns the Air?* Santa Barbara, Cal.: Center for the Study of Democratic Institutions, 1960.

Kroeger, Albert R. "A Long, Hard Look at the Genealogy of Network TV." *Television*, April 1966, 33-39.

Lacy, Dan. *Freedom and Communications*. 2d ed. Urbana: University of Illinois Press, 1965.

Lee, Robert E. "Self-Regulation or Censorship." *Educational Broadcasting Review* 3:5 (October 1969), 17-20.

Linton, Bruce A. *Self-Regulation in Broadcasting: A Three-Part College-Level Study Guide*. Washington: National Association of Broadcasters, 1967.

Loevinger, Lee. "The Role of Law in Broadcasting." *Journal of Broadcasting* 8 (Spring 1964), 113-126.

Longley, Lawrence D. "The FCC's Attempt to Regulate Commercial Time."
    Journal of Broadcasting 11 (Winter 1966-67), 83-89.
"A Lurch Toward Tighter Program Control." *Broadcasting,* February 22, 1971,
    28-30.
Meyer, Richard J. "Reaction to the 'Blue Book.'" *Journal of Broadcasting* 6
    (Fall 1962), 295-312.
————. "'The Blue Book.'" *Journal of Broadcasting* 6 (Summer 1962),
    197-207.
Miller, Merle, and Evan Rhodes. *Only You, Dick Daring!* New York: William
    Sloane Associates, 1964.
Minow, Newton N. *Equal Time: The Private Broadcaster and the Public Interest.*
    Edited by Lawrence Laurent. New York: Atheneum, 1964.
"Note: Offensive Speech and the FCC." *Yale Law Journal* 79 (June 1970),
    1343-1368.
Pennybacker, John H., and Waldo W. Braden, eds. *Broadcasting and the Public
    Interest.* New York: Random House, 1969.
Pierson, W. Theodore. "The Active Eyebrow — A Changing Style for Censorship."
    Television Quarterly 1:1 (February 1962), 14-21.
The Report of the Commission on Obscenity and Pornography. New York:
    Bantam, 1970.
Rintels, David W. "Censorship on Television: How Much Truth Does 'The FBI'
    Tell About the FBI?" *New York Times,* March 5, 1972, sec. 2, 1, 17.
————. "Will Marcus Welby Always Make You Well?" *New York Times,*
    March 12, 1972, sec. 2, 1, 17-18.
Schwartz, Bernard. *The Professor and the Commissions.* New York: Knopf, 1959.
Seldes, Gilbert. *The Public Arts.* New York: Simon and Schuster, 1956.
Serling, Rod. "About Writing for Television." *Patterns.* New York: Bantam,
    1958.
Siepmann, Charles A. *Radio's Second Chance.* Boston: Little, Brown, 1946.
————. *Radio, Television, and Society.* New York: Oxford University Press,
    1950.
————. "What is Wrong with TV — and With Us." *New York Times Magazine,*
    April 19, 1964, 13, 112-114.
Skornia, Harry J. *Television and Society.* New York: McGraw-Hill, 1965.
Smead, Elmer E. *Freedom of Expression by Radio and Television.* Washington:
    Public Affairs Press, 1959.
Spalding, John W. "1928: Radio Becomes a Mass Advertising Medium." *Journal
    of Broadcasting* 8 (Winter 1963-64), 31-44.
Stebbins, Gene R. "Pacifica's Battle for Free Expression." *Educational Broad-
    casting Review* 4:3 (June 1970), 19-28.
Steiner, Gary A. *The People Look at Television: A Study of Audience Attitudes.*
    New York: Knopf, 1963.
Summers, Harrison B., comp. *Radio Censorship.* New York: H. W. Wilson, 1939
    (reprinted New York: Arno Press, 1971).
Summers, Robert E., and Harrison B. Summers. *Broadcasting and the Public.*
    Belmont, Cal.: Wadsworth, 1966.

United States Congress, House, Committee on Interstate and Foreign Commerce. *Regulation of Radio and Television Cigarette Advertisements.* Hearing before the Committee, 91st Congress, 1st Session, on Self-Regulation by the Broadcasting Industry of Radio and Television Cigarette Advertisements, June 10, 1969. Washington: Government Printing Office, 1969.

Weinberg, Meyer. *TV in America: The Morality of Hard Cash.* New York: Ballantine, 1962.

Wesolowski, James Walter. "Obscene, Indecent, or Profane Broadcast Language as Construed by the Federal Courts." *Journal of Broadcasting* 13 (Spring 1969), 203-219.

Winick, Charles. *Taste and the Censor in Television.* New York: Fund for the Republic, 1959.

Wolfe, G. Joseph. "Norman Baker and KTNT." *Journal of Broadcasting* 12 (Fall 1968), 389-399.

2·|2   2·|2
2·|2   2·|8
2·|8   2·|2
————
7·|2
359
45/
40 7

FREEDOM OF EXPRESSION: BROADCAST JOURNALISM

492
.365

12 7.

492
360
132

> *"Tonight I want to discuss the importance of the television news medium to the American people. No nation depends more on the intelligent judgment of its citizens. No medium has a more profound influence over public opinion. . . ."* (Spiro T. Agnew, November 13, 1969)

News has been a staple of broadcasting ever since KDKA's 1920 report of election returns. Radio gained its greatest journalistic impetus during World War II. Its ability to be "on the spot" surpassed the best efforts of competing newspapers which could only put out "extra" editions hours after the public heard vivid eyewitness accounts of events broadcast directly from the scene.

While newspapers still occupy a prominent position, broadcasting, especially television, appears to be the primary and most credible source of news for most people.[1] The spread of "all-news" radio formats, the popularity of regularly scheduled TV newscasts, and broadcasting's extensive coverage of public events, coupled with the decline of the daily newspaper, signify the journalistic shift from print to electronic media.

Radio and television are largely responsible for the pictures in our minds that we come to accept as reality. These media allow everyone to accompany astronauts to the moon, eavesdrop on a

---

[1]Burns W. Roper. *An Extended View of Public Attitudes toward Television and Other Mass Media, 1959-1971* (New York: Television Information Office, 1971).

132

national political convention, mourn the violent death of a president, and then watch the assassination of his alleged assassin. When the events of the world don't involve us personally, then our very awareness of them depends on the coverage given by the news media. Whether the public's understanding is deep or shallow, sophisticated or naive, is a reflection of the media's reciprocal relationship to the public. Just as an important TV news special will inform no one if it isn't watched, the public will fail to develop an interest in the issues of the day unless broadcasting exposes those issues in a manner appropriate to the appetites of its audience.

That broadcasting is supported in the main by advertising revenues has positive and negative implications for the health of American public opinion. While commercial support insulates news from partisan political influences to a degree, it also subjects professional journalism to economic pressures, often to the detriment of the former.

Broadcasting has changed the conduct of American politics. Presidents since Franklin D. Roosevelt have used radio and television to bypass reporters and editors and speak directly to the citizenry. Presidential news conferences, veto messages, and ceremonial activities have been adapted with TV's requirements and potential in mind. Following the "Great Debates" of 1960, broadcast political campaign costs rose from 34.6 million dollars in 1964 to almost 60 million dollars in 1968, exclusive of production expenses. Most of this money was spent to broadcast political "spots," carefully contrived messages of one minute or less, whose potential to illuminate campaign issues is surpassed by their ability to create "brand awareness" and convey an "image" of a candidate. Though Congress set limits on campaign spending in a 1972 law, it provided no means of enriching the quality of candidates' political dialogue as carried by broadcasting.

Broadcasters fulfill their journalistic responsibilities under greater restraints than their newspaper colleagues, who have no equivalent of Section 315 or the "Fairness Doctrine." Canon 35 permits the pencil-and-pad reporter to ply his trade in the courtroom, but denies broadcasters the use of their tools — microphones and cameras. Whether such restrictions might properly be applied to the print media, or whether the removal of such restrictions on electronic media would better serve the information needs of the public, dependent as it is on broadcast news, are questions every person must decide for himself. In doing so, it may help to recall the paradox in two of Thomas Jefferson's remarks.

> Ignorance is preferable to error; and he is less remote from the truth who believes nothing, than he who believes what is wrong. (From *Notes on the State of Virginia*.)

> The basis of our government being the opinion of the people, the very first object should be to keep that right; and were it left to me to decide whether we should have a government without newspapers, or newspapers without a government, I should not hesitate a moment to prefer the latter. But I should mean that every man should receive those papers, and be capable of reading them. (From a letter to Colonel Edward Carrington.)

C. in classroom.
1st, 6th,
5th.

1

A BENCHMARK

The Requirements for A Free and Responsible Press* (1947)

A Free and Responsible Press was a report by the Commission on Freedom of the Press, a group whose independent inquiry was supported by grants from Time, Inc., and Encyclopaedia Britannica, Inc. Among the notable individuals who served on this distinguished Commission were Harold Lasswell, Archibald MacLeish, Reinhold Niebuhr, Beardsley Ruml, and Arthur M. Schlesinger. The Commission was chaired by Robert M. Hutchins, then Chancellor of The University of Chicago.

The selection that follows comprises the chapter entitled "The Requirements" in the Commission's report. It is as clear and concise a description of what the press (including broadcasting) should be as has yet been issued.

If the freedom of the press is freighted with the responsibility of providing the current intelligence needed by a free society, we have to discover what a free society requires. Its requirements in America today are greater in variety, quantity, and quality than those of any previous society in any age. They are the requirements of a self-governing republic of continental size, whose doings have become, within a generation, matters of common concern in new and important ways. Its internal arrangements, from being thought of mainly as matters of private interest and automatic market adjustments, have become affairs of conflict and conscious compromise among organized groups, whose powers appear not to be bounded by "natural law," economic or other. Externally, it has suddenly assumed a leading role in the attempt to establish peaceful relationships among all the states on the globe.

Today our society needs, first, a truthful, comprehensive, and intelligent account of the day's events in a context which gives them meaning; second, a

assess for needs

full account of events

*Reprinted from the April 1947 issue of *Fortune Magazine* by special permission; © 1947 Time Inc.

forum for the exchange of comment and criticism; third, a means of projecting the opinions and attitudes of the groups in the society to one another; fourth, a method of presenting and clarifying the goals and values of the society; and, fifth, a way of reaching every member of the society by the currents of information, thought, and feeling which the press supplies.

The Commission has no idea that these five ideal demands can ever be completely met. All of them cannot be met by any one medium; some do not apply at all to a particular unit; nor do all apply with equal relevance to all parts of the communications industry. The Commission does not suppose that these standards will be new to the managers of the press; they are drawn largely from their professions and practices.

> **A truthful, comprehensive, and intelligent account of the day's events in a context which gives them meaning**

The first requirement is that the media should be accurate. They should not lie.

Here the first link in the chain of responsibility is the reporter at the source of the news. He must be careful and competent. He must estimate correctly which sources are most authoritative. He must prefer firsthand observation to hearsay. He must know what questions to ask, what things to observe, and which items to report. His employer has the duty of training him to do his work as it ought to be done.

Of equal importance with reportorial accuracy are the identification of fact as fact and opinion as opinion, and their separation, so far as possible. This is necessary all the way from the reporter's file, up through the copy and makeup desks and editorial offices, to the final, published product. The distinction cannot, of course, be made absolute. There is no fact without a context and no factual report which is uncolored by the opinions of the reporter. But modern conditions require greater effort than ever to make the distinction between fact and opinion. In a simpler order of society published accounts of events within the experience of the community could be compared with other sources of information. Today this is usually impossible. The account of an isolated fact, however accurate in itself, may be misleading and, in effect, untrue.

The greatest danger here is in the communication of information internationally. The press now bears a responsibility in all countries, and particularly in democratic countries, where foreign policies are responsive to popular majorities, to report international events in such a way that they can be understood. It is no longer enough to report *the fact* truthfully. It is now necessary to report *the truth about the fact.*

In this country a similar obligation rests upon the press in reporting domestic news. The country has many groups which are partially insulated from *media – an on-going process.*

on-going peep how flow of info going

one another and which need to be interpreted to one another. Factually correct but substantially untrue accounts of the behavior of members of one of these social islands can intensify the antagonisms of others toward them. A single incident will be accepted as a sample of group action unless the press has given a flow of information and interpretation concerning the relations between two racial groups such as to enable the reader to set a single event in its proper perspective. If it is allowed to pass as a sample of such action, the requirement that the press present an accurate account of the day's events in a context which gives them meaning has not been met.

A forum for the exchange of comment and criticism

repres. all viewpoint

The second requirement means that the great agencies of mass communication should regard themselves as common carriers of public discussion.[1] The units of the press have in varying degrees assumed this function and should assume the responsibilities which go with it, more generally and more explicitly.

It is vital to a free society that an idea should not be stifled by the circumstances of its birth. The press cannot and should not be expected to print everybody's ideas. But the giant units can and should assume the duty of publishing significant ideas contrary to their own, as a matter of objective reporting, distinct from their proper function of advocacy. Their control over the various ways of reaching the ear of America is such that, if they do not publish ideas which differ from their own, those ideas will never reach the ear of America. If that happens, one of the chief reasons for the freedom which these giants claim disappears.

Access to a unit of the press acting as a common carrier is possible in a number of ways, all of which, however, involve selection on the part of the managers of the unit. The individual whose views are not represented on an editorial page may reach an audience through a public statement reported as news, through a letter to the editor, through a statement printed in advertising space, or through a magazine article. But some seekers for space are bound to be disappointed and must resort to pamphlets or such duplicating devices as will spread their ideas to such public as will attend to them.

But all the important viewpoints and interests in the society should be represented in its agencies of mass communication. Those who have these viewpoints and interests cannot count on explaining them to their fellow-citizens through newspapers or radio stations of their own. Even if they could make the necessary investment, they could have no assurance that their publications

---

[1] By the use of this analogy the Commission does not intend to suggest that the agencies of communication should be subject to the legal obligations of common carriers, such as compulsory reception of all applicants for space, the regulation of rates, etc.

would be read or their programs heard by the public outside their own adherents. An ideal combination would include general media, inevitably solicitous to present their own views, but setting forth other views fairly. As checks on their fairness, and partial safeguards against ignoring important matters, more specialized media of advocacy have a vital place. In the absence of such a combination the partially insulated groups in society will continue to be insulated. The unchallenged assumptions of each group will continue to harden into prejudice. The mass medium reaches across all groups; through the mass medium they can come to understand one another.

Whether a unit of the press is an advocate or a common carrier, it ought to identify the sources of its facts, opinions, and arguments so that the reader or listener can judge them. Persons who are presented with facts, opinions, and arguments are properly influenced by the general reliability of those who offer them. If the veracity of statements is to be appraised, those who offer them must be known.

Identification of source is necessary to a free society. Democracy, in time of peace, at least, has a justifiable confidence that full and free discussion will strengthen rather than weaken it. But, if the discussion is to have the effect for which democracy hopes, if it is to be really full and free, the names and the characters of the participants must not be hidden from view.

The projection of a representative picture of the constituent groups in the society

This requirement is closely related to the two preceding. People make decisions in large part in terms of favorable or unfavorable images. They relate fact and opinion to stereotypes. Today the motion picture, the radio, the book, the magazine, the newspaper, and the comic strip are principal agents in creating and perpetuating these conventional conceptions. When the images they portray fail to present the social group truly, they tend to pervert judgment.

Such failure may occur indirectly and incidentally. Even if nothing is said about the Chinese in the dialogue of a film, yet if the Chinese appear in a succession of pictures as sinister drug addicts and militarists, an image of China is built which needs to be balanced by another. If the Negro appears in the stories published in magazines of national circulation only as a servant, if children figure constantly in radio dramas as impertinent and ungovernable brats — the image of the Negro and the American child is distorted. The plugging of special color and "hate" words in radio and press dispatches, in advertising copy, in news stories — such words as "ruthless," "confused," "bureaucratic" — performs inevitably the same image-making function.

Responsible performance here simply means that the images repeated and emphasized be such as are in total representative of the social group as it is. The truth about any social group, though it should not exclude its weaknesses and vices, includes also recognition of its values, its aspirations, and its common humanity. The Commission holds to the faith that if people are exposed to the inner truth of the life of a particular group, they will gradually build up respect for and understanding of it.

The presentation and clarification of the goals and values of the society

The press has a similar responsibility with regard to the values and goals of our society as a whole. The mass media, whether or not they wish to do so, blur or clarify these ideals as they report the failings and achievements of every day.[2] The Commission does not call upon the press to sentimentalize, to manipulate the facts for the purpose of painting a rosy picture. The Commission believes in realistic reporting of the events and forces that militate against the attainment of social goals as well as those which work for them. We must recognize, however, that the agencies of mass communication are an educational instrument, perhaps the most powerful there is; and they must assume a responsibility like that of educators in stating and clarifying the ideals toward which the community should strive.

Full access to the day's intelligence

It is obvious that the amount of current information required by the citizens in a modern industrial society is far greater than that required in any earlier day. We do not assume that all citizens at all times will actually use all the material they receive. By necessity or choice large numbers of people voluntarily delegate analysis and decision to leaders whom they trust. Such leadership in our society is freely chosen and constantly changing; it is informal, unofficial, and flexible. Any citizen may at any time assume the power of decision. In this way government is carried on by consent.

---

[2] A striking indication of the continuous need to renew the basic values of our society is given in the recent poll of public opinion by the National Opinion Research Center at Denver, in which one out of every three persons polled did not think the newspapers should be allowed to criticize the American form of government, even in peacetime. Only 57 per cent thought that the Socialist party should be allowed, in peacetime, to publish newspapers in the United States. Another poll revealed that less than a fourth of those questioned had a "reasonably accurate idea" of what the Bill of Rights is. Here is widespread ignorance with regard to the value most cherished by the press — its own freedom — which seems only dimly understood by many of its consumers.

But such leadership does not alter the need for the wide distribution of news and opinion. The leaders are not identified; we can inform them only by making information available to everybody.

The five requirements listed in this chapter suggest what our society is entitled to demand of its press. We can now proceed to examine the tools, the structure, and the performance of the press to see how it is meeting these demands.

Let us summarize these demands in another way.

The character of the service required of the American press by the American people differs from the service previously demanded, first, in this — that it is essential to the operation of the economy and to the government of the Republic. Second, it is a service of greatly increased responsibilities both as to the quantity and as to the quality of the information required. In terms of quantity, the information about themselves and about their world made available to the American people must be as extensive as the range of their interests and concerns as citizens of a self-governing, industrialized community in the closely integrated modern world. In terms of quality, the information provided must be provided in such a form, and with so scrupulous a regard for the wholeness of the truth and the fairness of its presentation, that the American people may make for themselves, by the exercise of reason and of conscience, the fundamental decisions necessary to the direction of their government and of their lives.

2

THE MAYFLOWER DECISION

C. P.

In the Matter of The Mayflower Broadcasting Corporation
and The Yankee Network, Inc. (WAAB)
    8 FCC 333, 338
    January 16, 1941

> This case began when the Mayflower Broadcasting Corporation
> filed an application for a construction permit, requesting the
> facilities of station WAAB in Boston, whose license was being
> considered for renewal by the FCC. Although Mayflower's
> application was denied because of misrepresentations made to the
> Commission and lack of financial qualifications, the proceedings
> revealed that WAAB had editorialized for some period of time.
> The Commission's ruling on this matter effectively discouraged
> broadcast editorials until the FCC issued its "Fairness Doctrine"
> in 1949.

*WAAB use. did not deal w/ editorial.
issues
FCC*

DECISION AND ORDER

These proceedings were instituted upon the filing by The Mayflower Broadcasting Corporation of an application for a construction permit to authorize a new radiobroadcast station at Boston, Mass., to operate on the frequency 1410 kilocycles with power of 500 watts night and 1 kilowatt day, unlimited time. These are the facilities now assigned to Station WAAB, Boston, Mass. The Commission designated this application for hearing along with the applications of The Yankee Network, Inc. (licensee of Station WAAB) for renewal of licenses for this station's main and auxiliary transmitters. The hearing was held in Boston, Mass., during November 1939. On May 31, 1940, the Commission issued proposed findings of fact and conclusions proposing to deny the application of The Mayflower Broadcasting Corporation and to grant the applications of The Yankee Network, Inc., for renewal of licenses. Exceptions to the proposed findings and conclusions were filed by Mayflower Broadcasting Corporation and at its request oral argument was held on July 25, 1940, with The Yankee Network, Inc., participating. Due to the absence of a quorum of the Commission at that time, the case was reargued before the full Commission by counsel for both parties on September 26, 1940.

In its proposed findings the Commission concluded that The Mayflower Broadcasting Corporation was not shown to be financially qualified to construct and operate the proposed station and, moreover, that misrepresentations of fact were made to the Commission in the application. After careful consideration of the applicant's exceptions and of the oral arguments presented, the Commission is unable to change these conclusions. The proposed findings and conclusions as to the application of The Mayflower Broadcasting Corporation will therefore, be adopted and made final.

More difficult and less easily resolvable questions are, however, presented by the applications for renewal of The Yankee Network, Inc. The record shows without contradiction that beginning early in 1937 and continuing through September 1938, it was the policy of Station WAAB to broadcast so-called editorials from time to time urging the election of various candidates for political office or supporting one side or another of various questions in public controversy. In these editorials, which were delivered by the editor-in-chief of the station's news service, no pretense was made at objective, impartial reporting. It is clear — indeed the station seems to have taken pride in the fact — that the purpose of these editorials was to win public support for some person or view favored by those in control of the station.

No attempt will be made here to analyze in detail the large number of broadcasts devoted to editorials. The material in the record has been carefully considered and compels the conclusion that this licensee during the period in question, has revealed a serious misconception of its duties and functions under the law. Under the American system of broadcasting it is clear that responsibility for the conduct of a broadcast station must rest initially with the broadcaster. It is equally clear that with the limitations in frequencies inherent in the nature of radio, the public interest can never be served by a dedication of any broadcast facility to the support of his own partisan ends. Radio can serve as an instrument of democracy only when devoted to the communication of information and the exchange of ideas fairly and objectively presented. A truly free radio cannot be used to advocate the causes of the licensee. It cannot be used to support the candidacies of his friends. It cannot be devoted to the support of principles he happens to regard most favorably. In brief, the broadcaster cannot be an advocate.

Freedom of speech on the radio must be broad enough to provide full and equal opportunity for the presentation to the public of all sides of public issues. Indeed, as one licensed to operate in a public domain the licensee has assumed the obligation of presenting all sides of important public questions, fairly, objectively and without bias. The public interest — not the private — is paramount. These requirements are inherent in the conception of public interest set up by the Communications Act as the criterion of regulation. And while the day to day decisions applying these requirements are the licensee's responsibility, the ultimate duty to review generally the course of conduct of the station over a period of time and to take appropriate action thereon is vested in the Commission.

Upon such a review here, there can be no question that The Yankee Network, Inc., in 1937 and 1938 continued to operate in contravention of these principles. The record does show, however, that, in response to a request of the Commission for details as to the conduct of the station since September 1938, two affidavits were filed with the Commission by John Shepard 3d, president of The Yankee Network, Inc. Apparently conceding the departures from the requirements of public interest by the earlier conduct of the station, these affidavits state, and they are uncontradicted, that no editorials have been broadcast over Station WAAB since September 1938 and that it is not intended to depart from this uninterrupted policy. The station has no editorial policies. In the affidavits there is further a description of the station's procedure for handling news items and the statement is made that since September 1938 "no attempt has ever been or will ever be made to color or editorialize the news received" through usual sources. In response to a question from the bench inquiring whether the Commission should rely on these affidavits in determining whether to renew the licenses, counsel for The Yankee Network, Inc., stated at the second argument, "There are absolutely no reservations whatsoever, or mental reservations of any sort, character, or kind with reference to those affidavits. They mean exactly what they say in the fullest possible amplification that the Commission wants to give to them."

Relying upon these comprehensive and unequivocal representations as to the future conduct of the station and in view of the loss of service to the public involved in the deletion of this station, it has been concluded to grant the applications for renewal. Should any future occasion arise to examine into the conduct of this licensee, however, the Commission will consider the facts developed in this record in its review of the activities as a whole. . . .

3

GLIMMERINGS OF "FAIRNESS"

The *WHKC* and *Scott* decisions both deal with the programming of controversial issues and with requests for license non-renewal or revocation by those who alleged that their right of free speech was denied by the stations in question. The FCC's disposition of the two cases can be regarded as a portent of the "Fairness Doctrine" which was issued a few years later.

WHKC presages the current inclination of renewal applicants and their opponents to arrive at written understandings by mutual agreement so as to avoid lengthy and expensive renewal hearings. When the FCC, in 1970, permitted licensees to reject editorial advertising as a matter of station policy (thereby repudiating paragraph 6 of *WHKC*), it was reversed by the Court of Appeals (*Business Executives' Move for Peace* and *Democratic National Committee* v. *FCC*, 450 F.2d 642 (D.C. Cir. 1971)). The Commission's appeal of this reversal to the Supreme Court was pending during the preparation of this volume (*cert. granted* February 28, 1972).*

Scott is of special interest because of the Commission's treatment of religious liberty as related to freedom of expression in broadcasting. Mr. Scott fared no better with the FCC even after promulgation of the "Fairness Doctrine" (see 19 FCC 2d 920 (1969) and 25 FCC 2d 239 (1970)).

---

*On May 29, 1973, the Supreme Court reversed the Court of Appeals and upheld the FCC in *Columbia Broadcasting System, Inc.*, v. *Democratic National Committee*, 412 U.S. 94. [Ed.]

A

THE WHKC CASE

[handwritten: lic. issued to them. chall., revised when aqq. to present controv. issues.]

In re United Broadcasting Co. (WHKC)
10 FCC 515
June 26, 1945

DECISION AND ORDER

By the Commission:

   1.   The Commission has before it a joint motion filed by the International Union, United Automobile, Aircraft, and Agricultural Implement Workers of America, affiliated with the Congress of Industrial Organizations and Local 927, UAW-CIO, Columbus, Ohio (herein called the "UAW-CIO" or the petitioner), and the United Broadcasting Co., licensee of Station WHKC (herein called the licensee), requesting the Commission to adopt a statement of policy which has been agreed upon by the parties, and to enter an order dismissing the proceedings.

   2.   The background of this matter may be set forth as follows: On June 2, 1944, the UAW-CIO filed a petition directed against the Commission's action granting the application of the licensee for renewal of license for operation of Station WHKC. The petition alleged that the licensee was throttling free speech and was therefore not operating in the public interest for the following reasons. *[handwritten: w.t. granted lic.= bcg move did not dscr. controv. subj.]*

   (a)   The station had a policy not to permit the sale of time for programs which solicit memberships, discuss controversial subjects, race, religion, and politics.

   (b)   The station did not apply this practice uniformly, but on the contrary applied that policy "strictly to those with whom the management of Station WHKC disagrees, including petitioners, and loosely or not at all with respect to others."

   (c)   The station unfairly censored scripts submitted by petitioners. *[handwritten: censored scripts]*

   ·   Upon consideration of this petition and an opposition thereto filed by the licensee, the Commission designated the petition for hearing, and pursuant to the provisions of section 308(b) and 312(a) of the Communications Act of

371

1934, as amended, directed the station licensee to file with the Commission on or before the 5th day of August 1944, a statement of fact concerning the operation of WHKC with particular reference to the allegations of the petition and as to whether the station had been operated in the public interest. The Commission further directed the licensee to be prepared at said hearing to offer evidence in support of its statement of fact. Pursuant to the Commission's action, the licensee filed its statement of fact and a hearing was held before a member of the Commission from August 16 through August 24, 1944.

3.   The evidence adduced at the hearing showed that the station's policy upon which the petition was predicated was governed by the provisions of the Code of the National Association of Broadcasters. The code is a voluntary one without legal effect upon the members of the National Association of Broadcasters. The purpose of the Code as stated in its foreword is "to formulate basic standards" for the guidance of broadcasters. At pages 3 and 4 it provides that no time shall be sold for the presentation of public controversial issues, with the exception of political broadcasts and the public forum type of programs; and that solicitation of memberships in organizations, whether on paid or free time, should not be permitted except for charitable organizations, such as the American Red Cross and "except where such memberships are incidental to the rendering of commercial services, such as an insurance plan either in respect to casualty, to life, or to property."

4.   On October 20, 1944, the petitioner and the licensee filed the instant joint motion which contained the following agreed statement:

The record of the hearing discloses that Station WHKC in the past had pursued a policy which it believed to be in the best interests of the public and at no time did the station believe that the application of this policy was contrary to the interests of labor. The record testimony further discloses that at the time of the hearing the station enunciated a revised policy which it had adopted prior to the hearing and which it intends to follow in the future. This policy is as follows:

(a)   It will be the future policy of Station WHKC to consider each request for time solely on its individual merits without discriminations and without prejudice because of the identity of the personality of the individual, corporation, or organization desiring such time.

(b)   With respect to public issues of a controversial nature, the station's policy will be one of open-mindedness and impartiality. Requests of all individuals, groups, or organizations will of necessity have to be considered in the light of the contribution which their use of time would make toward a well-balanced program schedule, which the station will try at all times to maintain in the interest of the people it serves.

(c)   Station WHKC will make time available, primarily on a sustaining basis, but also on a commercial basis, for the full and free discussion of issues of public importance, including controversial issues, and dramatizations thereof, in order that broadcasting may achieve its full possibilities as a significant medium for the dissemination of news, ideas, and opinions. And, in doing so, there will be no discrimination between business concerns and nonprofit organizations either in making time available or restricting the use of such time. Nonprofit organizations will have the right to purchase time for solicitation of memberships.

(d) Station WHKC will, if it refuses time for public discussion, do so in writing showing reasons for such denial to the extent that requests for time are made in writing.

[margin: the refusal will write why]

(e) The censorship of scripts is an evil repugnant to the American tradition of free speech and a free press, whether enforced by a Government agency or by a private radio station licensee. Broadcasts by candidates for public office may not be censored under the law. But as to all other broadcasts, Station WHKC will not censor scripts, or delete any matter contained in them, except for reasons which it believes to be in accordance with the law and existing regulations as set forth in its statement of policy and as explained and interpreted in the record testimony. In the light of future experience this policy may be changed through action by the courts, the legislature, or by rules of Government bodies having jurisdiction over particular subject matter. It will be the policy of the station to adjust its practices to such changes, reflecting at all times the tolerance which the interest of the public renders essential.

[margin: will no longer censor scripts except in accordance w/ the law.]

(f) The station will see that its broadcasts on controversial issues, considered on an over-all basis, maintain a fair balance among the various points of view, i.e., over the weeks and months it will maintain such a balance with respect to local and network programs, both sustaining and commercial alike.

[margin: will be fair to all points of view.]

The parties believe that the above statement of policy properly sets forth the duties of a licensee under the Communications Act of 1934 with respect to the availability of time for discussion of issues of public importance, the censoring of scripts by licensees, and the maintenance of an over-all program balance.

5. As indicated in paragraph 2 hereof, the present proceeding puts in issue the duties of a licensee, under the statutory mandate, to operate in the public interest, convenience, and necessity, to maintain an over-all program balance by providing time on a nondiscriminatory basis for discussion of public controversial issues and for the solicitation of memberships for nonprofit organizations. It is recognized, of course, that the physical limitations on the amount of spectrum space available for radio broadcasting and the large demands upon radio stations for use of time make it impossible for every person desiring to use the facilities of a station to be granted this privilege. Under section 3(h) of the act, broadcast stations are expressly declared not to be common carriers. These facts, however, in no way impinge upon the duty of each station licensee to be sensitive to the problems of public concern in the community and to make sufficient time available, on a nondiscriminatory basis, for full discussion thereof, without any type of censorship which would undertake to impose the views of the licensee upon the material to be broadcast. The spirit of

[margin: PIC N]

the Communications Act of 1934 requires radio to be an instrument of free speech, subject only to the general statutory provisions imposing upon the licensee the responsibility of operating its station in the public interest.

6.   No single or exact rule of thumb for providing time, on a non-discriminatory basis, can be stated for application to all situations which may arise in the operation of all stations. The Commission, however, is of the opinion that the operation of any station under the extreme principles that no time shall be sold for the discussion of controversial public issues and that only charitable organizations and certain commercial interests may solicit memberships is inconsistent with the concept of public interest established by the Communications Act as the criterion of radio regulations (cf. in re the Mayflower Broadcasting Co., 8 FCC 338). The Commission recognizes that good program balance may not permit the sale or donation of time to all who may seek it for such purposes and that difficult problems calling for careful judgment on the part of station management may be involved in deciding among applicants for time when all cannot be accommodated. However, competent management should be able to meet such problems in the public interest and with fairness to all concerned. The fact that it places an arduous task on management should not be made a reason for evading the issue by a strict rule against the sale of time for any programs of the type mentioned.

7.   The agreed statement of policy submitted by the parties herein appears to set forth generally a fair and nondiscriminatory policy which WHKC, the licensee, has undertaken to apply to the presentation of controversial public issues and to the solicitation of memberships by nonprofit organizations in the maintenance of over-all program balance. On the basis of this undertaking, we are of the opinion that the joint motion should be granted and the proceeding dismissed, and it is so ordered this 26th day of June 1945.

B

THE SCOTT CASE

In re Petition of Robert Harold Scott for Revocation of
Licenses of Radio Stations KQW, KPO and KFRC
11 FCC 372
July 19, 1946

MEMORANDUM OPINION AND ORDER

On March 27, 1945, Robert Harold Scott, of Palo Alto, Calif., filed a petition requesting that the Commission revoke the licenses of radio stations KQW, San Jose, Calif., and KPO and KFRC, both of San Francisco, Calif. The ground on which the petitioner seeks to have the Commission take this action is that these stations have refused to make any time available to him, by sale or otherwise, for the broadcasting of talks on the subject of atheism, while they have permitted the use of their facilities for direct statements and arguments against atheism as well as for indirect arguments, such as church services, prayers, Bible readings, and other kinds of religious programs. It is petitioner's contention that the question of the existence or nonexistence of a Divine Being is, in itself a controversial issue, and that in refusing to make time available for arguments in support of the atheistic point of view, the stations complained of are not presenting all sides of the issue and, therefore, are not operating in the public interest.

After having secured further information from the petitioner, the Commission notified the stations of the petition and invited their comments on the matter. Don Lee Broadcasting System, licensee of Station KFRC, expressed its "firm belief that it would not be in the public interest to lend our facilities to Mr. Scott for the dissemination and propagation of atheism." National Broadcasting Co., Inc., licensee of KPO, asserted that "it is difficult to imagine that a controversial public issue exists in the usual sense of that phrase, on the subject of the existence of a God merely because of the nonbelief of a relatively few." Station KQW, in its reply, stated that it refused time to petitioner for the "broadcasting of atheistic talks," and contended that such talks would not be in the public interest. The answer stated that the management of KQW did not

Scott Hg. lic. denial — stat. refused to make x avail. for atheism, bud others can todise relig. ag. hum

Is God a controv. subject.

Not in public interest

375

consider the "proposed atheistic broadcasts" as presenting a "controversial" public question and that, in any event, "if a public controversial question was tendered, it was not of sufficient public moment and did not present a question so uppermost or important in the minds of the public to justify its broadcast in the public interest with consequent displacement of an existing program service." The answer alleged further that "KQW acted within its legal rights and the Commission is not by statute authorized to substitute its judgment for that of the licensee under the circumstances here presented."

In his petition, Mr. Scott says: "I do not throw stones at church windows. I do not mock a people kneeling in prayer. I respect every man's right to have and to express any religious belief whatsoever. But I abhor and denounce those who, while asserting this right, seek, in one way or another, to prevent others from expressing contrary views."

It therefore appears, both from licensees' responses to Mr. Scott's requests for time and from his statement of his own position, that the question here presented does not involve blasphemous attacks upon the Deity, or abusive or intemperate attacks upon any religious belief or organization, but only such criticisms as would necessarily be implied in the logical development of arguments supporting atheism. The licensees of the stations involved appear to have treated atheism as a special type of controversy and to have interpreted their obligation to operate in the public interest as requiring or permitting them to bar access to their facilities for the presentation of the atheistic point of view, not because of the manner in which the point of view is to be presented, but because they believe its substance to be distasteful or objectionable to a large majority of the listening audience.

As in the case of the petition of the Reverend Sam Morris for a denial of the application of renewal of license of Station KRLD, Dallas, Tex. (file No. B3-R-397), the issue here involved is one of broad scope and it is not restricted to the three stations which are the subject of Mr. Scott's complaint. We therefore do not feel that we would be warranted on the basis of this single complaint in selecting these three stations as the subject of a hearing looking toward terminations of their licenses, when there is no urgent ground for selecting them rather than many other stations. But, lest our dismissal of Mr. Scott's petition be misconstrued, we feel that we should make our position entirely clear, as we did in dismissing the petition of the Reverend Sam Morris.

The first amendment to our Constitution guarantees both religious freedom[1] and freedom of speech. While these guarantees are expressed in terms of limitation on governmental action, they are far more than narrow legalistic

[1] No principle is more firmly inbedded in our Constitution than that of religious freedom. In addition to the first amendment, art. VI repudiates any religious tests as to qualification to any office of political trust under the United States. The same section, in the interests of freedom of conscience, permits affirmation rather than oath in the pledge to support the Constitution required of State and Federal officials. Likewise, sec. 1 of art. II permits the substitution of an affirmation for the oath of office required of the President of the United States.

concepts. They are essential parts of the fundamental philosophy underlying the form of government and the way of life which we call "American."

Freedom of religious belief necessarily carries with it freedom to disbelieve, and freedom of speech means freedom to express disbeliefs as well as beliefs. If freedom of speech is to have meaning, it cannot be predicated on the mere popularity or public acceptance of the ideas sought to be advanced. It must be extended as readily to ideas which we disapprove or abhor as to ideas which we approve. Moreover, freedom of speech can be as effectively denied by denying access to the public means of making expression effective — whether public streets, parks, meeting halls, or the radio — as by legal restraints or punishment of the speaker.

It is true that in this country an overwhelming majority of the people profess a belief in the existence of a Divine Being. But the conception of the nature of the Divine Being is as varied as religious denominations and sects and even differs with the individuals belonging to the same denominations or sects.

God is variously thought of as a "Spirit, infinite, eternal, and unchangeable," and as having a tangible form resembling man who, in turn, was created in His image; as consisting of a Trinity and a single Godhead; as a Divine Lawgiver, laying down infallible natural and moral laws by which man is governed, and as a God who concerns himself with the personal affairs of individuals, however petty; as a God to whom each person is individually accountable and as a God to be approached only through ordained intermediaries; a God of the powerful who divinely appoints kings and other rulers of men, and as a God of the meek and lowly; as a God of stern justice and a God of mercy; as a God to be worshipped or appeased primarily through ritual and as a God to be served primarily through service to one's fellow man; as a God whose rewards and punishments are mainly reserved for a future life and as a God who also rewards or punishes through spiritual enrichment or impoverishment of man's present existence. These are only a few of the many differing conceptions which might be cited by way of illustration.

So diverse are these conceptions that it may be fairly said, even as to professed believers, that the God of one man does not exist for another. And so strongly may one believe in his own particular conception of God that he may easily be led to say, "Only my God exists, and therefore he who denies my God is an atheist, irrespective of his professed belief in a God." For example, the early Christians were to the Romans atheists because they denied the existence of the pagan gods in which the Romans believed.[2]

[2] "Atheism is a term of varying application and significance. . . . Its meaning is dependent upon the particular type of 'theism' with which at the moment it is being contrasted. . . . The atheist is conceived as the man who denies or despises what he ought not only to fear but to respect. It is intelligible, then, that the early Christians should be called 'atheists' by their persecutors. The Christians denied, after all, many more gods than they acknowledged. The pagan was morally offended at this wholesale rejection of familiar loyalties." [Encyclopedia Britannica, 14th Ed., vol. 2 (article on "Atheism" by the Reverend Charles John Shebbeare, M.A., rector of Stanhope, County Durham, and chaplain to His Majesty the King).]

A rule which denies freedom of expression to the professed atheist should certainly be applied with equal, if not greater, strictness to one whose views are, in fact, atheistic, but who seeks to deny or conceal his atheism. Thus, the necessity arises of making determinations on the basis of personal judgment as to whether views sought to be expressed are, in fact, atheistic. The power then is vested in those making such determination to attach the label of atheism to the believer whose particular belief they may happen to disapprove, and thus of effectively denying the believer the right to express his views. Under such a course, Jefferson, Jackson, Lincoln, and others whose names we revere could, today, be barred from access to the air to express their own particular religious philosophies. The first two were denounced with particular vigor from the pulpits of some of the wealthier and better established churches, and the label of "atheist" was freely attached to Jefferson by those who had come to feel that their favored positions, which were threatened by his social, economic, and political philosophies, were rewards which the Deity had bestowed upon them because of their special virtues and accomplishments.

Underlying the conception of freedom of speech is not only the recognition of the importance of the free flow of ideas and information to the effective functioning of democratic forms of government and ways of life, but also belief that immunity from criticism is dangerous — dangerous to the institution or belief to which the immunity is granted as well as to the freedom of the people generally. Sound and vital ideas and institutions become strong and develop with criticism so long as they themselves have full opportunity for expression; it is dangerous that the unsound be permitted to flourish for want of criticism.

Moreover, however strongly we may feel about the sacredness of religious beliefs, we should be mindful of the fact that immunity from criticism cannot be granted to religion without, at the same time, granting it to those who use the guise of religion to further their ends of personal profit or power, to promote their own particular political or economic philosophies, or to give vent to their personal frustrations and hatreds. "False prophets" are not phenomena peculiar to Biblical days. Their danger now, as then, lies essentially in the difficulty of recognizing them as such. This difficulty is increased to the extent that their doctrines and motives are shielded from critical examination.

We recognize that in passing upon requests for time, a station licensee is constantly confronted with most difficult problems. Since the demands for time may far exceed the amount available for broadcasting a licensee must inevitably make a selection among those seeking it for the expression of their views. He may not even be able to grant time to all religious groups who might desire the use of his facilities, much less to all who might want to oppose religion. Admittedly, a very real opportunity exists for him to be arbitrary and unreasonable, to indulge his own preferences, prejudices, or whims; to pursue his own private interest or to favor those who espouse his views, and discriminate against those of opposing views. The indulgence of that opportunity could not conceivably be characterized as an exercise of the broadcaster's right of freedom of speech. Nor could it fairly be said to afford the listening audience that opportunity to hear a diversity and balance of views, which is an inseparable corollary of freedom of expression. In making a selection with fairness, the licensee must, of course, consider the extent of the interest of the people in his service area in a particular subject to be discussed, as well as the qualifications of the person selected to discuss it. Every idea does not rise to the dignity of a "public controversy," and every organization, regardless of membership or the seriousness of its purposes, is not per se entitled to time on the air. But an organization or idea may be projected into the realm of controversy by virtue of being attacked. The holders of a belief should not be denied the right to answer attacks upon them or their belief solely because they are few in number.

The fact that a licensee's duty to make time available for the presentation of opposing views on current controversial issues of public importance may not extend to all possible differences of opinion within the ambit of human contemplation cannot serve as the basis for any rigid policy that time shall be denied for the presentation of views which may have a high degree of unpopularity. The criterion of the public interest in the field of broadcasting clearly precludes a policy of making radio wholly unavailable as a medium for the expression of any view which falls within the scope of the constitutional guarantee of freedom of speech.

Because, as we have stated above, the problem here presented is far broader in scope than the complaint against the particular stations here involved, we feel that the petition should be denied, notwithstanding the views which we have expressed.

It is therefore ordered, this 19th day of July 1946, that the petition be and it is hereby denied.

4

THE FAIRNESS DOCTRINE

In the Matter of Editorializing by Broadcast Licensees
13 FCC 1246
June 1, 1949

> This document served to reverse the Commission's previous policy regarding broadcast editorials enunciated in the *Mayflower* decision. FCC adherence to the "Fairness Doctrine" from 1949 to date has encouraged increasing numbers of stations to express their editorial views on the air. The edited version below omits the additional views of Commissioner Webster and the separate opinion of Commissioner Jones.

REPORT OF THE COMMISSION

1. This report is issued by the Commission in connection with its hearings on the above entitled matter held at Washington, D.C., on March 1, 2, 3, 4, and 5, and April 19, 20, and 21, 1948. The hearing had been ordered on the Commission's own motion on September 5, 1947, because of our belief that further clarification of the Commission's position with respect to the obligations of broadcast licensees in the field of broadcasts of news, commentary and opinion was advisable. It was believed that in view of the apparent confusion concerning certain of the Commission's previous statements on these vital matters by broadcast licensees and members of the general public, as well as the professed disagreement on the part of some of these persons with earlier Commission pronouncements, a reexamination and restatement of its views by the Commission would be desirable. And in order to provide an opportunity to interested persons and organizations to acquaint the Commission with their views, prior to any Commission determination, as to the proper resolution of the difficult and complex problems involved in the presentation of radio news and

380

comment in a democracy, it was designated for public hearing before the Commission *en banc* on the following issues:

1. To determine whether the expression of editorial opinions by broadcast station licensees on matters of public interest and controversy is consistent with their obligations to operate their stations in the public interest.

2. To determine the relationship between any such editorial expression and the affirmative obligation of the licensees to insure that a fair and equal presentation of all sides of controversial issues is made over their facilities.

2.   At the hearings testimony was received from some 49 witnesses representing the broadcasting industry and various interested organizations and members of the public. In addition, written statements of their position on the matter were placed into the record by 21 persons and organizations who were unable to appear and testify in person. The various witnesses and statements brought forth for the Commission's consideration, arguments on every side of both of the questions involved in the hearing. Because of the importance of the issues considered in the hearing, and because of the possible confusion which may have existed in the past concerning the policies applicable to the matters which were the subject of the hearing, we have deemed it advisable to set forth in detail and at some length our conclusions as to the basic considerations relevant to the expression of editorial opinion by broadcast licensees and the relationship of any such expression to the general obligations of broadcast licensees with respect to the presentation of programs involving controversial issues.

3.   In approaching the issues upon which this proceeding has been held, we believe that the paramount and controlling consideration is the relationship between the American system of broadcasting carried on through a large number of private licensees upon whom devolves the responsibility for the selection and presentation of program material, and the congressional mandate that this licensee responsibility is to be exercised in the interests of, and as a trustee for the public at large which retains ultimate control over the channels of radio and television communications. One important aspect of this relationship, we believe, results from the fact that the needs and interests of the general public with respect to programs devoted to news commentary and opinion can only be satisfied by making available to them for their consideration and acceptance or rejection, of varying and conflicting views held by responsible elements of the community. And it is in the light of these basic concepts that the problems of insuring fairness in the presentation of news and opinion and the place in such a picture of any expression of the views of the station licensee as such must be considered.

4.   It is apparent that our system of broadcasting, under which private persons and organizations are licensed to provide broadcasting service to the

various communities and regions, imposes responsibility in the selection and presentation of radio program material upon such licensees. Congress has recognized that the requests for radio time may far exceed the amount of time reasonably available for distribution by broadcasters. It provided, therefore, in Section 3(h) of the Communications Act that a person engaged in radio broadcasting shall not be deemed a common carrier. It is the licensee, therefore, who must determine what percentage of the limited broadcast day should appropriately be devoted to news and discussion or consideration of public issues, rather than to the other legitimate services of radio broadcasting, and who must select or be responsible for the selection of the particular news items to be reported or the particular local, State, national or international issues or questions of public interest to be considered, as well as the person or persons to comment or analyze the news or to discuss or debate the issues chosen as topics for radio consideration: "The life of each community involves a multitude of interests some dominant and all pervasive such as interest in public affairs, education and similar matters and some highly specialized and limited to few. The practical day-to-day problem with which every licensee is faced is one of striking a balance between these various interests to reflect them in a program service which is useful to the community, and which will in some way fulfill the needs and interests of the many." *Capital Broadcasting Company*, 4 Pike & Fischer, R.R. 21; *The Northern Corporation (WMEX)*, 4 Pike & Fischer, R.R. 333, 338. And both the Commission and the courts have stressed that this responsibility devolves upon the individual licensees, and can neither be delegated by the licensee to any network or other person or group, or be unduly fettered by contractual arrangements restricting the licensee in his free exercise of his independent judgments. *National Broadcasting Company* v. *United States*, 319 U.S. 190 (upholding the Commission's chain broadcasting regulations, Section 3.101-3.108, 3.231-3.238, 3.631-3.638), *Churchhill Tabernacle* v. *Federal Communications Commission*, 160 F. 2d 244 (See, rules and regulations, Sections 3.109, 3.239, 3.639); *Allen T. Simmons* v. *Federal Communications Commission*, 169 F. 2d 670, *certiorari denied* 335 U.S. 846.

5. But the inevitability that there must be some choosing between various claimants for access to a licensee's microphone, does not mean that the licensee is free to utilize his facilities as he sees fit or in his own particular interests as contrasted with the interests of the general public. The Communications Act of 1934, as amended, makes clear that licenses are to be issued only where the public interest, convenience or necessity would be served thereby. And we think it is equally clear that one of the basic elements of any such operation is the maintenance of radio and television as a medium of freedom of speech and freedom of expression for the people of the Nation as a whole. Section 301 of the Communications Act provides that it is the purpose of the act to maintain the control of the United States over all channels of interstate and foreign commerce. Section 326 of the act provides that this control of the United States shall not result in any impairment of the right of

free speech by means of such radio communications. It would be inconsistent with these express provisions of the act to assert that, while it is the purpose of the act to maintain the control of the United States over radio channels, but free from any regulation or condition which interferes with the right of free speech, nevertheless persons who are granted limited rights to be licensees of radio stations, upon a finding under Sections 307(a) and 309 of the act that the public interest, convenience, or necessity would be served thereby, may themselves make radio unavailable as a medium of free speech. The legislative history of the Communications Act and its predecessor, the Radio Act of 1927 shows, on the contrary, that Congress intended that radio stations should not be used for the private interest, whims, or caprices of the particular persons who have been granted licenses, but in manner which will serve the community generally and the various groups which make up the community.[1] And the courts have consistently upheld Commission action giving recognition to and fulfilling that intent of Congress. *KFKB Broadcasting Association* v. *Federal Radio Commission*, 47 F. 2d 670; *Trinity Methodist Church, South* v. *Federal Radio Commission*, 62 F. 2d 850, *certiorari denied*, 288 U.S. 599.

6.   It is axiomatic that one of the most vital questions of mass communication in a democracy is the development of an informed public opinion through the public dissemination of news and ideas concerning the vital public issues of the day. Basically, it is in recognition of the great contribution which radio can make in the advancement of this purpose that portions of the radio spectrum are allocated to that form of radio communications known as radiobroadcasting. Unquestionably, then, the standard of public interest, convenience and necessity as applied to radiobroadcasting must be interpreted in the light of this basic purpose. The Commission has consequently recognized the

---

[1] Thus in the Congressional debates leading to the enactment of the Radio Act of 1927 Congressman (later Senator) White stated (67 Cong. Rec. 5479, March 12, 1926):

"We have reached the definite conclusion that the right of all our people to enjoy this means of communication can be preserved only by the repudiation of the idea underlying the 1912 law that anyone who will, may transmit and by the assertion in its stead of the doctrine that the right of the public to service is superior to the right of any individual to use the ether ... the recent radio conference met this issue squarely. It recognized that in the present state of scientific development there must be a limitation upon the number of broadcasting stations and it recommended that licenses should be issued only to those stations whose operation would render a benefit to the public, are necessary in the public interest or would contribute to the development of the art. This principle was approved by every witness before your committee. We have written it into the bill. *If enacted into law, the broadcasting privilege will not be a right of selfishness. It will rest upon an assurance of public interest to be served."* (Italics added.)

And this view that the interest of the listening public rather than the private interests of particular licensees was reemphasized as recently as June 9, 1948, in a unanimous report of the Senate Committee on Interstate and Foreign Commerce on S. 1333 (80th Cong.) which would have amended the present Communications Act in certain respects. See S. Rept. No. 1567, 80th Cong. 2nd Sess., pp. 14-15.

necessity for licensees to devote a reasonable percentage of their broadcast time to the presentation of news and programs devoted to the consideration and discussion of public issues of interest in the community served by the particular station. And we have recognized, with respect to such programs, the paramount right of the public in a free society to be informed and to have presented to it for acceptance or rejection the different attitudes and viewpoints concerning these vital and often controversial issues which are held by the various groups which make up the community.[2] It is this right of the public to be informed, rather than any right on the part of the Government, any broadcast licensee or any individual member of the public to broadcast his own particular views on any matter, which is the foundation stone of the American system of broadcasting.

7.   This affirmative responsibility on the part of broadcast licensees to provide a reasonable amount of time for the presentation over their facilities of programs devoted to the discussion and consideration of public issues has been reaffirmed by the Commission in a long series of decisions. The *United Broadcasting Co. (WHKC)* case, 10 FCC 675, emphasized that this duty includes the making of reasonable provision for the discussion of controversial issues of public importance in the community served, and to make sufficient time available for full discussion thereof. The *Scott* case, 3 Pike & Fischer, Radio Regulation 259, stated our conclusions that this duty extends to all subjects of substantial importance to the community coming within the scope of free discussion under the first amendment without regard to personal views and opinions of the licensees on the matter, or any determination by the licensee as to the possible unpopularity of the views to be expressed on the subject matter to be discussed among particular elements of the station's listening audience. Cf., *National Broadcasting Company* v. *United States*, 319 U.S. 190; *Allen T. Simmons*, 3 Pike & Fischer, R.R. 1029, *affirmed; Simmons* v. *Federal Communications Commission*, 169 F. 2d 670, *certiorari denied*, 335 U.S. 846; *Bay State Beacon*, 3 Pike & Fischer, R.R. 1455, *affirmed; Bay State Beacon* v. *Federal Communications Commission*, U.S. App. D.C., decided December 20, 1948; *Petition of Sam Morris*, 3 Pike & Fischer, R.R. 154; *Thomas N. Beach*, 3 Pike & Fischer R.R. 1784. And the Commission has made clear that in such presentation of news and comment the public interest requires that the licensee must operate on a basis of overall fairness, making his facilities available for the expression of the contrasting views of all responsible elements in the community on the various issues which arise. *Mayflower Broadcasting Co.*, 8 F.C.C. 333; *United Broadcasting Co. (WHKC)* 10 F.C.C. 515; Cf. *WBNX Broadcasting Co., Inc.*, 4 Pike & Fischer, R.R. 244 (memorandum opinion). Only where the licensee's discretion in the choice of the particular programs to be broadcast over his facilities is exercised so as to afford a reasonable opportunity for the

---

[2] Cf., *Thornhill* v. *Alabama*, 310 U.S. 88, 95, 102; *Associated Press* v. *United States*, 326 U.S. 1, 20.

presentation of all responsible positions on matters of sufficient importance to be afforded radio time can radio be maintained as a medium of freedom of speech for the people as a whole. These concepts, of course, do restrict the licensee's freedom to utilize his station in whatever manner he chooses but they do so in order to make possible the maintenance of radio as a medium of freedom of speech for the general public.

8. It has been suggested in the course of the hearings that licensees have an affirmative obligation to insure fair presentation of all sides of any controversial issue before any time may be allocated to the discussion or consideration of the matter. On the other hand, arguments have been advanced in support of the proposition that the licensee's sole obligation to the public is to refrain from suppressing or excluding any responsible point of view from access to the radio. We are of the opinion, however, that any rigid requirement that licensees adhere to either of these extreme prescriptions for proper station programing techniques would seriously limit the ability of licensees to serve the public interest. Forums and roundtable discussions, while often excellent techniques of presenting a fair cross section of differing viewpoints on a given issue, are not the only appropriate devices for radio discussion, and in some circumstances may not be particularly appropriate or advantageous. Moreover, in many instances the primary "controversy" will be whether or not the particular problem should be discussed at all; in such circumstances, where the licensee has determined that the subject is of sufficient import to receive broadcast attention, it would obviously not be in the public interest for spokesmen for one of the opposing points of view to be able to exercise a veto power over the entire presentation by refusing to broadcast its position. Fairness in such circumstances might require no more than that the licensee make a reasonable effort to secure responsible representation of the particular position and, if it fails in this effort, to continue to make available its facilities to the spokesmen for such position in the event that, after the original programs are broadcast, they then decide to avail themselves of a right to reply to present their contrary opinion. It should be remembered, moreover, that discussion of public issues will not necessarily be confined to questions which are obviously controversial in nature, and, in many cases, programs initiated with no thought on the part of the licensee of their possibly controversial nature will subsequently arouse controversy and opposition of a substantial nature which will merit presentation of opposing views. In such cases, however, fairness can be preserved without undue difficulty since the facilities of the station can be made available to the spokesmen for the groups wishing to state views in opposition to those expressed in the original presentation when such opposition becomes manifest.

9. We do not believe, however, that the licensee's obligations to serve the public interest can be met merely through the adoption of a general policy of not refusing to broadcast opposing views where a demand is made of the station for broadcast time. If, as we believe to be the case, the public interest is best served in a democracy through the ability of the people to hear expositions

of the various positions taken by responsible groups and individuals on particular topics and to choose between them, it is evident that broadcast licensees have an affirmative duty generally to encourage and implement the broadcast of all sides of controversial public issues over their facilities, over and beyond their obligation to make available on demand opportunities for the expression of opposing views. It is clear that any approximation of fairness in the presentation of any controversy will be difficult if not impossible of achievement unless the licensee plays a conscious and positive role in bringing about balanced presentation of the opposing viewpoints.

10.   It should be recognized that there can be no one all embracing formula which licensees can hope to apply to insure the fair and balanced presentation of all public issues. Different issues will inevitably require different techniques of presentation and production. The licensee will in each instance be called upon to exercise his best judgment and good sense in determining what subjects should be considered, the particular format of the programs to be devoted to each subject, the different shades of opinion to be presented, and the spokesmen for each point of view. In determining whether to honor specific requests for time, the station will inevitably be confronted with such questions as whether the subject is worth considering, whether the viewpoint of the requesting party has already received a sufficient amount of broadcast time, or whether there may not be other available groups or individuals who might be more appropriate spokesmen for the particular point of view than the person making the request. The latter's personal involvement in the controversy may also be a factor which must be considered, for elementary considerations of fairness may dictate that time be allocated to a person or group which has been specifically attacked over the station, where otherwise no such obligation would exist. Undoubtedly, over a period of time some licensees may make honest errors of judgment. But there can be no doubt that any licensee honestly desiring to live up to its obligation to serve the public interest and making a reasonable effort to do so, will be able to achieve a fair and satisfactory resolution of these problems in the light of the specific facts.

11.   It is against this background that we must approach the question of "editorialization" — the use of radio facilities by the licensees thereof for the expression of the opinions and ideas of the licensee on the various controversial and significant issues of interest to the members of the general public afforded radio (or television) service by the particular station. In considering this problem it must be kept in mind that such editorial expression may take many forms ranging from the overt statement of position by the licensee in person or by his acknowledged spokesmen to the selection and presentation of news editors and commentators sharing the licensee's general opinions or the making available of the licensee's facilities, either free of charge or for a fee to persons or organizations reflecting the licensee's viewpoint either generally or with respect to specific issues. It should also be clearly indicated that the question of the relationship of broadcast editorialization, as defined above, to operation in the

public interest, is not identical with the broader problem of assuring "fairness" in the presentation of news, comment or opinion, but is rather one specific facet of this larger problem.

12.   It is clear that the licensee's authority to determine the specific programs to be broadcast over his station gives him an opportunity, not available to other persons, to insure that his personal viewpoint on any particular issue is presented in his station's broadcasts, whether or not these views are expressly identified with the licensee. And, in the absence of governmental restraint, he would, if he so choose, be able to utilize his position as a broadcast licensee to weight the scales in line with his personal views, or even directly or indirectly to propagandize in behalf of his particular philosophy or views on the various public issues to the exclusion of any contrary opinions. Such action can be effective and persuasive whether or not it is accompanied by any editorialization in the narrow sense of overt statement of particular opinions and views identified as those of licensee.

13.   The narrower question of whether any overt editorialization or advocacy by broadcast licensees, identified as such is consonant with the operation of their stations in the public interest, resolves itself, primarily into the issue of whether such identification of comment or opinion broadcast over a radio or television station with the licensee, as such, would inevitably or even probably result in such overemphasis on the side of any particular controversy which the licensee chooses to espouse as to make impossible any reasonably balanced presentation of all sides of such issues or to render ineffective the available safeguards of that overall fairness which is the essential element of operation in the public interest. We do not believe that any such consequence is either inevitable or probable, and we have therefore come to the conclusion that overt licensee editorialization, within reasonable limits and subject to the general requirements of fairness detailed above, is not contrary to the public interest.

14.   The Commission has given careful consideration to contentions of those witnesses at the hearing who stated their belief that any overt editorialization or advocacy by broadcast licensee is *per se* contrary to the public interest. The main arguments advanced by these witnesses were that overt editorialization by broadcast licensees would not be consistent with the attainment of balanced presentations since there was a danger that the institutional good will and the production resources at the disposal of broadcast licensees would inevitably influence public opinion in favor of the positions advocated in the name of the licensee and that, having taken an open stand on behalf of one position in a given controversy, a license is not likely to give a fair break to the opposition. We believe, however, that these fears are largely misdirected, and that they stem from a confusion of the question of overt advocacy in the name of the licensee, with the broader issue of insuring that the station's broadcasts devoted to the consideration of public issues will provide the listening public with a fair and balanced presentation of differing viewpoints on such issues, without regard to the particular views which may be held or

expressed by the licensee. Considered, as we believe they must be, as just one of several types of presentation of public issues, to be afforded their appropriate and nonexclusive place in the station's total schedule of programs devoted to balanced discussion and consideration of public issues, we do not believe that programs in which the licensee's personal opinions are expressed are intrinsically more or less subject to abuse than any other program devoted to public issues. If it be true that station good will and licensee prestige, where it exists, may give added weight to opinion expressed by the licensee, it does not follow that such opinion should be excluded from the air any more than it should in the case of any individual or institution which over a period of time has built up a reservoir of good will or prestige in the community. In any competition for public acceptance of ideas, the skills and resources of the proponents and opponents will always have some measure of effect in producing the results sought. But it would not be suggested that they should be denied expression of their opinions over the air by reason of their particular assets. What is against the public interest is for the licensee "to stack the cards" by a deliberate selection of spokesmen for opposing points of view to favor one viewpoint at the expense of the other, whether or not the views of those spokesmen are identified as the views of the licensee or of others. Assurance of fairness must in the final analysis be achieved, not by the exclusion of particular views because of the source of the views, or the forcefulness with which the view is expressed, but by making the microphone available for the presentation of contrary views without deliberate restrictions designed to impede equally forceful presentation.

15. Similarly, while licensees will in most instances have at their disposal production resources making possible graphic and persuasive techniques for forceful presentation of ideas, their utilization for the promulgation of the licensee's personal viewpoints will not necessarily or automatically lead to unfairness or lack of balance. While uncontrolled utilization of such resources for the partisan ends of the licensee might conceivably lead to serious abuses, such abuses could as well exist where the station's resources are used for the sole use of his personal spokesmen. The prejudicial or unfair use of broadcast production resources would, in either case, be contrary to the public interest.

16. The Commission is not persuaded that a station's willingness to stand up and be counted on these particular issues upon which the licensee has a definite position may not be actually helpful in providing and maintaining a climate of fairness and equal opportunity for the expression of contrary views. Certainly the public has less to fear from the open partisan than from the covert propagandist. On many issues, of sufficient importance to be allocated broadcast time, the station licensee may have no fixed opinion or viewpoint which he wishes to state or advocate. But where the licensee, himself, believes strongly that one side of a controversial issue is correct and should prevail, prohibition of his expression of such position will not of itself insure fair presentation of that issue over his station's facilities, nor would open advocacy necessarily prevent an overall fair presentation of the subject. It is not a sufficient answer to state that

a licensee *should* occupy the position of an impartial umpire, where the licensee is *in fact* partial. In the absence of a duty to present all sides of controversial issues, overt editorialization by station licensees could conceivably result in serious abuse. But where, as we believe to be the case under the Communications Act, such a responsibility for a fair and balanced presentation of controversial public issues exists, we cannot see how the open espousal of one point of view by the licensee should necessarily prevent him from affording a fair opportunity for the presentation of contrary positions or make more difficult the enforcement of the statutory standard of fairness upon any licensee.

17. It must be recognized, however, that the licensee's opportunity to express his own views as part of a general presentation of varying opinions on particular controversial issues, does not justify or empower any licensee to exercise his authority over the selection of program material to distort or suppress the basic factual information upon which any truly fair and free discussion of public issues must necessarily depend. The basis for any fair consideration of public issues, and particularly those of a controversial nature, is the presentation of news and information concerning the basic facts of the controversy in as complete and impartial a manner as possible. A licensee would be abusing his position as public trustee of these important means of mass communication were he to withhold from expression over his facilities relevant news or facts concerning a controversy or to slant or distort the presentation of such news. No discussion of the issues involved in any controversy can be fair or in the public interest where such discussion must take place in a climate of false or misleading information concerning the basic facts of the controversy.

18. During the course of the hearing, fears have been expressed that any effort on the part of the Commission to enforce a reasonable standard of fairness and impartiality would inevitably require the Commission to take a stand on the merits of the particular issues considered in the programs broadcast by the several licensees, as well as exposing the licensees to the risk of loss of license because of "honest mistakes" which they may make in the exercise of their judgment with respect to the broadcasts of programs of a controversial nature. We believe that these fears are wholly without justification, and are based on either an assumption of abuse of power by the Commission or a lack of proper understanding of the role of the Commission, under the Communications Act, in considering the program service of broadcast licensees in passing upon applications for renewal of license. While this Commission and its predecessor, the Federal Radio Commission, have, from the beginning of effective radio regulation in 1927, properly considered that a licensee's overall program service is one of the primary indicia of his ability to serve the public interest, actual consideration of such service has always been limited to a determination as to whether the licensee's programming, taken as a whole, demonstrates that the licensee is aware of his listening public and is willing and able to make an honest and reasonable effort to live up to such obligations. The action of the station in

carrying or refusing to carry any particular program is of relevance only as the station's actions with respect to such programs fits into its overall pattern of broadcast service, and must be considered in the light of its other program activities. This does not mean, of course, that stations may, with impunity, engage in a partisan editorial campaign on a particular issue or series of issues provided only that the remainder of its program schedule conforms to the statutory norm of fairness; a licensee may not utilize the portion of its broadcast service which conforms to the statutory requirements as a cover or shield for other programing which fails to meet the minimum standards of operation in the public interest. But it is clear that the standard of public interest is not so rigid that an honest mistake or error in judgment on the part of a licensee will be or should be condemned where his overall record demonstrates a reasonable effort to provide a balanced presentation of comment and opinion on such issues. The question is necessarily one of the reasonableness of the station's actions, not whether any absolute standard of fairness has been achieved. It does not require any appraisal of the merits of the particular issue to determine whether reasonable efforts have been made to present both sides of the question. Thus, in appraising the record of a station in presenting programs concerning a controversial bill pending before the Congress of the United States, if the record disclosed that the licensee had permitted only advocates of the bill's enactment to utilize its facilities to the exclusion of its opponents, it is clear that no independent appraisal of the bill's merits by the Commission would be required to reach a determination that the licensee has misconstrued its duties and obligations as a person licensed to serve the public interest. The Commission has observed, in considering this general problem that "the duty to operate in the public interest is no esoteric mystery, but is essentially a duty to operate a radio station with good judgment and good faith guided by a reasonable regard for the interests of the community to be served." *Northern Corporation (WMEX)*, 4 Pike & Fischer, R.R. 333, 339. Of course, some cases will be clearer than others, and the Commission in the exercise of its functions may be called upon to weigh conflicting evidence to determine whether the licensee has or has not made reasonable efforts to present a fair and well-rounded presentation of particular public issues. But the standard of reasonableness and the reasonable approximation of a statutory norm is not an arbitrary standard incapable of administrative or judicial determination, but, on the contrary, one of the basic standards of conduct in numerous fields of Anglo-American law. Like all other flexible standards of conduct, it is subject to abuse and arbitrary interpretation and application by the duly authorized reviewing authorities. But the possibility that a legitimate standard of legal conduct might be abused or arbitrarily applied by capricious governmental authority is not and cannot be a reason for abandoning the standard itself. And broadcast licensees are protected against any conceivable abuse of power by the Commission in the exercising of its licensing authority by the procedural safeguards of the Communications Act and the Administrative Procedure Act, and by the right of appeal to the courts from final action claimed to be arbitrary or capricious.

19.   There remains for consideration the allegation made by a few of the witnesses in the hearing that any action by the Commission in this field enforcing a basic standard of fairness upon broadcast licensees necessarily constitutes an "abridgment of the right of free speech" in violation of the first amendment of the United States Constitution. We can see no sound basis for any such conclusion. The freedom of speech protected against governmental abridgment by the first amendment does not extend any privilege to government licensees of means of public communications to exclude the expression of opinions and ideas with which they are in disagreement. We believe, on the contrary, that a requirement that broadcast licensees utilize their franchises in a manner in which the listening public may be assured of hearing varying opinions on the paramount issues facing the American people is within both the spirit and letter of the first amendment. As the Supreme Court of the United States has pointed out in the Associated Press monopoly case:

It would be strange indeed, however, if the grave concern for freedom of the press which prompted adoption of the first amendment should be read as a command that the Government was without power to protect that freedom. . . . *That amendment rests on the assumption that the widest possible dissemination of information from diverse and antagonistic sources is essential to the welfare of the public, that a free press is a condition of free society. Surely a command that the Government itself shall not impede the free flow of ideas does not afford nongovernmental combinations a refuge if they impose restraints upon that constitutionally guaranteed freedom.* Freedom to publish means freedom for all and not for some. Freedom to publish is guaranteed by the Constitution but freedom to combine to keep others from publishing is not. (*Associated Press v. United States*, 326 U.S. 1 at p. 20.)

20.   We fully recognize that freedom of the radio is included among the freedoms protected against governmental abridgment by the first amendment. *United States* v. *Paramount Pictures, Inc., et al.*, 334 U.S. 131, 166. But this does not mean that the freedom of the people as a whole to enjoy the maximum possible utilization of this medium of mass communication may be subordinated to the freedom of any single person to exploit the medium for his own private interest. Indeed, it seems indisputable that full effect can only be given to the concept of freedom of speech on the radio by giving precedence to the right of the American public to be informed on all sides of public questions over any such individual exploitation for private purposes. Any regulation of radio, especially a system of limited licensees, is in a real sense an abridgment of the inherent freedom of persons to express themselves by means of radio communications. It is however, a necessary and constitutional abridgment in order to prevent chaotic interference from destroying the great potential of this medium for public enlightenment and entertainment. *National Broadcasting Company* v. *United States*, 319 U.S. 190, . . .; cf. *Federal Radio Commission* v. *Nelson Brothers Bond & Mortgage Co.*, 289 U.S. 266; *Fisher's Blend Station, Inc.* v. *State Tax Commission*, 277 U.S. 650. Nothing in the Communications

Act or its history supports any conclusion that the people of the Nation, acting through Congress, have intended to surrender or diminish their paramount rights in the air waves, including access to radio broadcasting facilities to a limited number of private licensees to be used as such licensees see fit, without regard to the paramount interests of the people. The most significant meaning of freedom of the radio is the right of the American people to listen to this great medium of communications free from any governmental dictation as to what they can or cannot hear and free alike from similar restraints by private licensees.

21. To recapitulate, the Commission believes that under the American system of broadcasting the individual licensees of radio stations have the responsibility for determining the specific program material to be broadcast over their stations. This choice, however, must be exercised in a manner consistent with the basic policy of the Congress that radio be maintained as a medium of free speech for the general public as a whole rather than as an outlet for the purely personal or private interests of the licensee. This requires that licensees devote a reasonable percentage of their broadcasting time to the discussion of public issues of interest in the community served by their stations and that such programs be designed so that the public has a reasonable opportunity to hear different opposing positions on the public issues of interest and importance in the community. The particular format best suited for the presentation of such programs in a manner consistent with the public interest must be determined by the licensee in the light of the facts of each individual situation. Such presentation may include the identified expression of the licensee's personal viewpoint as part of the more general presentation of views or comments on the various issues, but the opportunity of licensees to present such views as they may have on matters of controversy may not be utilized to achieve a partisan or one-sided presentation of issues. Licensee editorialization is but one aspect of freedom of expression by means of radio. Only insofar as it is exercised in conformity with the paramount right of the public to hear a reasonably balanced presentation of all responsible viewpoints on particular issues can such editorialization be considered to be consistent with the licensee's duty to operate in the public interest. For the licensee is a trustee impressed with the duty of preserving for the public generally radio as a medium of free expression and fair presentation.

DISSENTING VIEWS OF COMMISSIONER HENNOCK

I agree with the majority that it is imperative that a high standard of impartiality in the presentation of issues of public controversy be maintained by broadcast licensees. I do not believe that the Commission's decision, however, will bring about the desired end. The standard of fairness as delineated in the report is virtually impossible of enforcement by the Commission with our present lack of policing methods and with the sanctions given us by law. We should not underestimate the difficulties inherent in the discovery of unfair presentation in any particular situation, or the problem presented by the fact that the sole sanction the Commission possesses is total deprivation of broadcast privileges in a renewal or revocation proceeding which may occur long after the violation.

In the absence of some method of policing and enforcing the requirement that the public trust granted a licensee be exercised in an impartial manner, it seems foolhardy to permit editorialization by licensees themselves. I believe that we should have such a prohibition, unless we can substitute for it some more effective method of insuring fairness. There would be no inherent evil in the presentation of a licensee's viewpoint if fairness could be guaranteed. In the present circumstances, prohibiting it is our only instrument for insuring the proper use of radio in the public interest.

315= = oppor. + f.d.
(315 = opp. use of facil. by cand.
f.d. = = on controv. issues

5

THE FAIRNESS PRIMER

Applicability of the Fairness Doctrine in the Handling of Controversial Issues of Public Importance
29 Fed. Reg. 10415
Adopted July 1, 1964;
Printed July 25, 1964

Issued 15 years after promulgation of the "Fairness Doctrine," this primer clarifies the intent and administration of the basic policy through a question-answer format summarizing FCC case history through 1963. The Commission launched a full scale inquiry into the "Fairness Doctrine" in 1971 (30 FCC 2d 26), but continued to apply the doctrine and this primer during the inquiry's lengthy pendency.

PART I – INTRODUCTION

It is the purpose of this Public Notice to advise broadcast licensees and members of the public of the rights, obligations, and responsibilities of such licensees under the Commission's "fairness doctrine," which is applicable in any case in which broadcast facilities are used for the discussion of a controversial issue of public importance. For this purpose, we have set out a digest of the Commission's interpretative rulings on the fairness doctrine. This Notice will be revised at appropriate intervals to reflect new rulings in this area. In this way, we hope to keep the broadcaster and the public informed of pertinent Commission determinations on the fairness doctrine, and thus reduce the number of these cases required to be referred to the Commission for resolution. Before turning to the digest of the rulings, we believe some brief introductory discussion of the fairness doctrine is desirable.

The basic administrative action with respect to the fairness doctrine was taken in the Commission's 1949 Report, Editorializing by Broadcast Licensees,

13 FCC 1246; Vol. 1, Part 3, R.R. 91-201.[1] This report is attached hereto because it still constitutes the Commission's basic policy in this field.[2]

Congress recognized this policy in 1959. In amending Section 315 so as to exempt appearances by legally qualified candidates on certain news-type programs from the "equal opportunities" provision, it was stated in the statute that such action should not be construed as relieving broadcasters ". . . from the obligation imposed upon them under this Act to operate in the public interest and to afford reasonable opportunity for the discussion of conflicting views on issues of public importance" (Public Law 86-274, approved September 14, 1959, 73 Stat. 557).[3] The legislative history[4] establishes that this provision "is a restatement of the basic policy of the 'standard of fairness' which is imposed on broadcasters under the Communications Act of 1934" (H. Rept. No. 1069, 86th Cong., 1st Sess., p. 5).

While Section 315 thus embodies both the "equal opportunities" requirement and the fairness doctrine, they apply to different situations and in different ways. The "equal opportunities" requirement relates solely to use of broadcast facilities by candidates for public office. With certain exceptions involving specified news-type programs, the law provides that if a licensee permits a person who is a legally qualified candidate for public office to use a broadcast station, he shall afford equal opportunities to all other such candidates for that office in the use of the station. The Commission's Public Notice on Use of Broadcast Facilities by Candidates for Public Office, 27 Fed. Reg. 10063 (October 12, 1962), should be consulted with respect to "equal opportunities" questions involving political candidates.

The fairness doctrine deals with the broader question of affording reasonable opportunity for the presentation of contrasting viewpoints on controversial issues of public importance. Generally speaking, it does not apply with the precision of the "equal opportunities" requirement. Rather, the licensee, in applying the fairness doctrine, is called upon to make reasonable

---

[1] Citations in "R.R." refer to Pike & Fischer, Radio Regulations. The above report thus deals not only with the question of editorializing but also the requirements of the fairness doctrine.

[2] The report (par. 6) also points up the responsibility of broadcast licensees to devote a reasonable amount of their broadcast time to the presentation of programs dealing with the discussion of controversial issues of public importance. See Appendix A. [Appendix A, the Commission's 1949 Report, is omitted here; it appears, however, on pp. 380-393 of this volume. – Ed.]

[3] The full statement in Section 315(a) reads as follows: "Nothing in the foregoing sentence [i.e., exemption from equal time requirements for news-type programs] shall be construed as relieving broadcasters, in connection with the presentation of newscasts, news interviews, news documentaries, and on-the-spot coverage of news events, from the obligation imposed upon them under this chapter to operate in the public interest and to afford reasonable opportunity for the discussion of conflicting views on issues of public importance."

[4] See Appendix B. [Appendix B, "The History of the Fairness Doctrine," is omitted. – Ed.]

judgments in good faith on the facts of each situation — as to whether a controversial issue of public importance is involved, as to what viewpoints have been or should be presented, as to the format and spokesmen to present the viewpoints, and all the other facets of such programming. See par. 9, Editorializing Report. In passing on any complaint in this area, the Commission's role is not to substitute its judgment for that of the licensee as to any of the above programming decisions, but rather to determine whether the licensee can be said to have acted reasonably and in good faith. There is thus room for considerably more discretion on the part of the licensee under the fairness doctrine than under the "equal opportunities" requirement.

Interpretative rulings — Commission procedure

We set forth below a digest of the Commission's rulings on the fairness doctrine. References, with citations, to the Commission's decisions or rulings are made so that the researcher may, if he desires, review the complete text of the Commission's ruling. Copies of rulings may be found in a "Fairness Doctrine" folder kept in the Commission's Reference Room.

In an area such as the fairness doctrine, the Commission's rulings are necessarily based upon the facts of the particular case presented, and thus a variation in facts might call for a different or revised ruling. We therefore urge that interested persons, in studying the rulings for guidance, look not only to the language of the ruling but the specific factual context in which it was made.

It is our hope, as stated, that this Notice will reduce significantly the number of fairness complaints made to the Commission. Where complaint is made to the Commission, the Commission expects a complainant to submit specific information indicating (1) the particular station involved; (2) the particular issue of a controversial nature discussed over the air; (3) the date and time when the program was carried; (4) the basis for the claim that the station has presented only one side of the question; and (5) whether the station had afforded, or has plans to afford, an opportunity for the presentation of contrasting viewpoints.[5] (Lar Daly, 19 R.R. 1104, March 24, 1960; cf. Cullman Bctg. Co., FCC 63-849, Sept. 18, 1963.)

If the Commission determines that the complaint sets forth sufficient facts to warrant further consideration, it will promptly advise the licensee of the complaint and request the licensee's comments on the matter. Full opportunity is given to the licensee to set out all programs which he has presented, or plans to present, with respect to the issue in question during an appropriate time period. Unless additional information is sought from either the complainant or

---

[5]The complainant can usually obtain this information by communicating with the station.

the licensee, the matter is then usually disposed of by Commission action. (Letter of September 18, 1963 to Honorable Oren Harris, FCC 63-851.)

Finally, we repeat what we stated in our 1949 Report:

... It is this right of the public to be informed, rather than any right on the part of the Government, any broadcast licensee or any individual member of the public to broadcast his own particular views on any matter, which is the foundation stone of the American system of broadcasting.

PART II – COMMISSION RULINGS

A. Controversial issue of public importance

1. *Civil rights as controversial issue.* In response to a Commission inquiry, a station advised the Commission, in a letter dated March 6, 1950, that it had broadcast editorial programs in support of a National Fair Employment Practices Commission on January 15-17, 1950, and that it had taken no affirmative steps to encourage and implement the presentation of points of view with respect to these matters which differed from the point of view expressed by the station.

Ruling. The establishment of a National Fair Employment Practices Commission constitutes a controversial question of public importance so as to impose upon the licensee the affirmative duty to aid and encourage the broadcast of opposing views. It is a matter of common knowledge that the establishment of a National Fair Employment Practices Commission is a subject that has been actively controverted by members of the public and by members of the Congress of the United States and that in the course of that controversy numerous differing views have been espoused. The broadcast by the station of a relatively large number of programs relating to this matter over a period of three days indicates an awareness of its importance and raises the assumption that at least one of the purposes of the broadcasts was to influence public opinion. In our report In the Matter of Editorializing by Broadcast Licensees, we stated that:

. . . In appraising the record of a station in presenting programs concerning a controversial bill pending before the Congress of the United States, if the record disclosed that the licensee had permitted only advocates of the bill's enactment to utilize its facilities to the exclusion of its opponents, it is clear that no independent appraisal of the bill's merits by the Commission would be required to reach a determination that the licensee had misconstrued its duties and obligations as a person licensed to serve the public interest.

In light of the foregoing the conduct of the licensee was not in accord with the principles set forth in the report. (New Broadcasting Co. (WLIB), 6 R.R. 258, April 12, 1950.)

2. *Political spot announcements.*   In an election an attempt was made to promote campaign contributions to the candidates of the two major parties through the use of spot announcements on broadcast stations. Certain broadcast stations raised the question whether the airing of such announcements imposed an obligation under Section 315 of the Act and/or the fairness doctrine to broadcast such special announcements for all candidates running for a particular office in a given election.

Ruling.   The "equal opportunities" provision of Section 315 applies only to uses by candidates and not to those speaking in behalf of or against candidates. Since the above announcements did not contemplate the appearance of a candidate, the "equal opportunities" provision of Section 315 would not be applicable. The fairness doctrine is, however, applicable. (Letter to Lawrence M. C. Smith, FCC 63-358, 25 R.R. 291, April 17, 1963.) See Ruling No. 13.

3. *"Reports to the People."*   The complaint of the Chairman of the Democratic State Committee of New York alleged that an address by Governor Dewey over the facilities of the stations affiliated with the CBS network on May 2, 1949, entitled "A Report to the People of New York State," was political in nature and contained statements of a controversial nature. The CBS reply stated, in substance, that it was necessary to distinguish between the reports made by holders of office to the people whom they represented and the partisan political activities of the individuals holding office.

Ruling.   The Commission recognizes that public officials may be permitted to utilize radio facilities to report on their stewardship to the people and that "the mere claim that the subject is political does not automatically require that the opposite political party be given equal facilities for a reply." On the other hand, it is apparent that so-called reports to the people may constitute attacks on the opposite political party or may be a discussion of a public controversial issue. Consistent with the views expressed by the Commission in the Editorializing Report, it is clear that the characterization of a particular program as a report to the people does not necessarily establish such a program as noncontroversial in nature so as to avoid the requirement of affording time for the expression of opposing views. In that Report, we stated ". . . that there can be no one all embracing formula which licensees can hope to apply to insure the fair and balanced presentation of all public issues . . . The licensee will in each instance be called upon to exercise his best judgment and good sense in determining what subjects should be considered, the particular format of the programs to be devoted to each subject, the different shades of opinion to be presented, and the spokesmen for each point of view." The duty of the licensee to make time available for the expression of differing views is invoked where the facts and circumstances in each case indicate an area of controversy and differences of opinion where the subject matter is of public importance. In the light of the foregoing, the Commission concludes that "it does not appear that there has been the abuse of judgment on the part of [CBS] such as to warrant holding a hearing on its applications for renewal of license." (Paul E. Fitzpatrick, 6 R.R. 543, July 21, 1949; (see also, California Democratic State Central Committee, Public Notice 95873, 20 R.R. 867, 869, October 31, 1960.))

4. *Controversial issue within service area.* A station broadcast a statement by the President of CBS opposing pay TV; two newscasts containing the views of a Senator opposed to pay TV; one newscast reporting the introduction by a Congressman of an anti-pay TV bill; a half-hour network program on pay TV in which both sides were represented, followed by a ten-minute film clip of a Senator opposing pay TV; a half-hour program in which a known opponent of pay TV was interviewed by interrogators whose questions in some instances indicated an opinion by the questioner favorable to pay TV. In a hearing upon the station's application for modification of its construction permit, an issue was raised whether the station had complied with the requirements of the fairness doctrine. The licensee stated that while nationally pay TV was "certainly" a controversial issue, it regarded pay TV as a local controversial issue only to a very limited extent in its service area, and therefore it was under no obligation to take the initiative to present the views of advocates of pay TV.

Ruling. The station's handling of the pay TV question was improper. It could be inferred that the station's sympathies with the opposition to pay TV made it less than a vigorous searcher for advocates of subscription television. The station evidently thought the subject of sufficient general interest (beyond its own concern in the matter) to devote broadcast time to it, and even to preempt part of a local program to present the views of the Senator in opposition to pay TV immediately after the balanced network discussion program, with the apparent design of neutralizing any possible public sympathy for pay TV which might have arisen from the preceding network forum. The anti-pay TV side was represented to a greater extent on the station than the other, though it cannot be said that the station choked off the expression of all views inimical to its interest. A licensee cannot excuse a one-sided presentation on the basis that the subject matter was not controversial in its service area, for it is only through a fair presentation of all facts and arguments on a particular question that public opinion can properly develop. (In re The Spartan Radiocasting Co., 33 F.C.C., 765, 771, 794-795, 802-803, November 21, 1962.)

5. *Substance of broadcast.* A number of stations broadcast a program entitled "Living Should Be Fun," featuring a nutritionist giving comment and advice on diet and health. Complaint was made that the program presented only one side of controversial issues of public importance. Several licensees contended that a program dealing with the desirability of good health and nutritious diet should not be placed in the category of discussion of controversial issues.

Ruling. The Commission cannot agree that the program consisted merely of the discussion of the desirability of good health and nutritious diet. Anyone who listened to the program regularly — and station licensees have the obligation to know what is being broadcast over their facilities — should have been aware that at times controversial issues of public importance were discussed. In discussing such subjects as the fluoridation of water, the value of krebiozen in the treatment of cancer, the nutritive qualities of white bread, and the use of high potency vitamins without medical advice, the nutritionist emphasized the fact that his views were opposed to many authorities in these fields, and on occasions on the air, he invited those with opposing viewpoints to present such viewpoints on his program. A licensee who did not recognize the applicability of the fairness doctrine failed in the performance of his obligations to the public. (Report on "Living Should be Fun" Inquiry, 33 F.C.C. 101, 107, 23 R.R. 1599, 1606, July 18, 1962.)

6. *Substance of broadcast.*   A station broadcast a program entitled "Communist Encirclement" in which the following matters, among others, were discussed: socialist forms of government were viewed as a transitory form of government leading eventually to communism; it was asserted that this country's continuing foreign policy in the Far East and Latin America, the alleged infiltration of our government by communists, and the alleged moral weakening in our homes, schools and churches have all contributed to the advance of international communism. In response to complaints alleging one-sided presentation of these issues, the licensee stated that since it did not know of the existence of any communist organizations or communists in its community, it was unable to afford opportunity to those who might wish to present opposing views.

Ruling.   In situations of this kind, it was not and is not the Commission's intention to require licensees to make time available to communists or the communist viewpoints. But the matters listed above raise controversial issues of public importance on which persons other than communists hold contrasting views. There are responsible contrasting viewpoints on the most effective methods of combatting communism and communist infiltration. Broadcast of proposals supporting only one method raises the question whether reasonable opportunity has been afforded for the expression of contrasting viewpoints. (Letter to Tri-State Broadcasting Company, Inc., April 26, 1962 (staff letter).)

7. *Substance of broadcast.*   In 1957, a station broadcast a panel discussion entitled "The Little Rock Crisis" in which several public officials appeared, and whose purpose, a complainant stated, was to stress the maintenance of segregation and to express an opinion as to what the Negro wants or does not want. A request for time to present contrasting viewpoints was refused by the licensee who stated that the program was most helpful in preventing trouble by urging people to keep calm and look to their elected representatives for leadership, that it was a report by elected officials to the people, and that therefore no reply was necessary or advisable.

Ruling.   If the matters discussed involved no more than urging people to remain calm, it can be urged that no question exists as to fair presentation. However, if the station permitted the use of its facilities for the presentation of one side of the controversial issue of racial integration, the station incurred an obligation to afford a reasonable opportunity for the expression of contrasting views. The fact that the proponents of one particular position were elected officials did not in any way alter the nature of the program or remove the applicability of the fairness doctrine. See Ruling No. 3. (Lamar Life Insurance Co., FCC 59-651, 18 R.R. 683, July 1, 1959.)

8. *National controversial issues.* Stations broadcast a daily commentary program six days a week, in three of which views were expressed critical of the proposed nuclear weapons test ban treaty. On one of the stations the program was sponsored six days a week and on the other one day a week. A national committee in favor of the proposed treaty requested that the stations afford free time to present a tape of a program containing viewpoints opposed to those in the sponsored commentary program. The stations indicated, among other things, that it was their opinion that the fairness doctrine is applicable only to local issues.

Ruling. The keystone of the fairness doctrine and of the public interest is the right of the public to be informed — to have presented to it the "conflicting views of issues of public importance." Where a licensee permits the use of its facilities for the expression of views on controversial local or national issues of public importance such as the nuclear weapons test ban treaty, he must afford reasonable opportunities for the presentation of contrasting views by spokesmen for other responsible groups. (Letter to Cullman Broadcasting Co., Inc., FCC 63-849, September 18, 1963.) See Rulings No. 16 and 17 for other aspects of the Cullman decision.

B. Licensee's obligation to afford reasonable opportunity for the presentation of contrasting viewpoints

9. *Affirmative duty to encourage.* In response to various complaints alleging that a station had been "one-sided" in its presentations on controversial issues of public importance, the licensee concerned rested upon its policy of making time available, upon request, for "the other side."

Ruling. The licensee's obligations to serve the public interest cannot be met merely through the adoption of a general policy of not refusing to broadcast opposing views where a demand is made of the station for broadcast time. As the Commission pointed out in the Editorializing Report (par. 9):

... If, as we believe to be the case, the public interest is best served in a democracy through the ability of the people to hear expositions of the various positions taken by responsible groups and individuals on particular topics and to choose between them, it is evident that broadcast licensees have an affirmative duty generally to encourage and implement the broadcast of all sides of controversial public issues over their facilities, over and beyond their obligation to make available on demand opportunities for the expression of opposing views. It is clear that any approximation of fairness in the presentation of any controversy will be difficult if not impossible of achievement unless the licensee plays a conscious and positive role in bringing about balanced presentation of the opposing viewpoints. (John J. Dempsey, 6 R.R. 615, August 16, 1950; Editorializing Report, par. 9.) (See also Metropolitan Bctg. Corp., Public Notice 82386, 19 R.R. 602, 604, December 29, 1959.)

10.   *Non-delegable duty.*   Approximately 50 radio stations broadcast a program entitled "Living Should Be Fun," featuring a nutritionist giving comment and advice on diet and health. The program was syndicated and taped for presentation, twenty-five minutes a day, five days a week. Many of the programs discussed controversial issues of public importance. In response to complaints that the stations failed to observe the requirements of the fairness doctrine, some of the licensees relied upon (i) the nutritionist's own invitation to those with opposing viewpoints to appear on his program or (ii) upon the assurances of the nutritionist or the sponsor that the program fairly represented all responsible contrasting viewpoints on the issues with which it dealt, as an adequate discharge of their obligations under the fairness doctrine.

Ruling.   Those licensees who relied solely upon the assumed built-in fairness of the program itself, or upon the nutritionist's invitation to those with opposing viewpoints, cannot be said to have properly discharged their responsibilities. Neither alternative is likely to produce the fairness which the public interest demands. There could be many valid reasons why the advocate of an opposing viewpoint would be unwilling to appear upon such a program. In short, the licensee may not delegate his responsibilities to others, and particularly to an advocate of one particular viewpoint. As the Commission said in our Report in the Matter of Editorializing by Broadcast Licensees, "It is clear that any approximation of fairness in the presentation of any controversy will be difficult if not impossible of achievement unless the licensee plays a conscious and positive role in bringing about balanced presentation of the opposing viewpoints." (Report on "Living Should Be Fun" Inquiry, 33 FCC 101, 107, 23 R.R. 1599, 1606, July 18, 1962.)

11.   *Reliance upon other media.*   In January 1958, the issue of subscription television was a matter of public controversy, and it was generally known that the matter was the subject of Congressional hearings being conducted by the House and Senate Interstate and Foreign Commerce Committees. On Monday, January 27, 1958, between 9:30 and 10:00 p.m., WSOC-TV broadcast the program "Now It Can Be Tolled" (simultaneously with the other Charlotte television station, WBTV), a program consisting of a skit followed by a discussion in which the president of WSOC-TV and the vice president and general manager of Station WBTV were interviewed by employees of the two stations. The skit and interview were clearly weighted against

subscription TV, and in the program the station made clear its preference for the present TV system. On Saturday, February 1, 1958, WSOC-TV presented for 15 minutes, beginning at 3:35 p.m., a film clip in which a United States Representative discussed subscription television and expressed his opposition thereto. From January 24 to January 30, 1958, inclusive, WSOC-TV presented a total of 43 spot announcements, all of them against subscription television, and urged viewers, if they opposed it, to write their Congressmen without delay to express their opposition. WSOC-TV did not broadcast any programs or announcements presenting a viewpoint favorable to subscription television although on February 28, 1958, the station did (together with the management of Station WBTV) send a telegram to the three chief subscription television groups, offering them joint use of the two Charlotte stations, without charge, at a time mutually agreeable to all parties concerned, for the purpose of putting on a program by the proponents of pay TV. This offer was refused by Skiatron, one of the three groups. In its reply to the Commission's inquiry, the station referred to "the large amount of publicity already given by the Pay-TV proponents in newspapers, magazines and by direct mail," and asserted that its decision in this matter was taken "in an effort to furnish the public with the opposing viewpoints on the subject . . ."

Ruling. The station's broadcast presentation of the subscription TV issue was essentially one-sided, and, taking into account the circumstances of the situation existing at the time, the station did not make any timely effort to secure the presentation of the other side of the issue by responsible representatives. It is the Commission's view that the requirement of fairness, as set forth in the Editorializing Report, applies to a broadcast licensee irrespective of the position which may be taken by other media on the issue involved; and that the licensee's own performance in this respect, in and of itself, must demonstrate compliance with the fairness doctrine. (Letter to WSOC Broadcasting Co., FCC 58-686, 17 R.R. 548, 550, July 16, 1958.)

C. Reasonable opportunity for the presentation of contrasting viewpoints

12. *"Equal time" not required.*   Licensee broadcast over its several facilities on October 28, 1960, a 30-minute documentary concerning a North Dakota hospital. The last five minutes of the program consisted of an interview of the Superintendent of the hospital and the Chairman of the Board of Administration for State Institutions who responded to charges that the complainant, a candidate for the office of Attorney General of North Dakota, had publicly leveled against the Superintendent and Chairman concerning the administration of the hospital. On November 4, 1960 and at about the same viewing time as the preceding documentary, complainant's 30-minute broadcast

was aired over the Stations in which complainant presented his allegations about the professional, administrative, and disciplinary conditions at the hospital and a state training school. The following day (November 5) licensee presented a 30-minute documentary on the state training school, the last five minutes of which consisted of a discussion of the charges made by complainant on his November 4 program by a spokesman for the opposing political party, and by the interviewees of the October 28 program. Licensee refused complainant's request for "equal time" to reply to the November 5 broadcast.

Ruling. In view of the fact that the "equal opportunities" requirement of Section 315 becomes applicable only when an opposing candidate for the same office has been afforded broadcast time, and that the complainant's political opponent did not appear on any of the programs in question (and, in fact, was never mentioned during the broadcast of these programs), the Commission reviewed the matter in light of the fairness doctrine. Unlike the "equal opportunities" requirement of Section 315, the fairness doctrine requires that where a licensee affords time over his facilities for an expression of one opinion on a controversial issue of public importance, he is under obligation to insure that proponents of opposing viewpoints are afforded a reasonable opportunity for the presentation of such views. The Commission concludes that on the facts before it, the licensee's actions were not inconsistent with the principles enunciated in the Editorializing Report. (Hon. Charles L. Murphy, FCC 62-737, 23 R.R. 953, July 13, 1962.)

13. *"Equal time" not required.* During a state-wide election an attempt was made to promote bipartisan campaign contributions, particularly for the candidates of the two major parties running for Governor and Senator, through the use of spot announcements on broadcast stations. Several stations raised the question whether the broadcast of these announcements would impose upon them the obligation, under the fairness doctrine, to broadcast such special announcements for all candidates running for a particular office in a given election.

Ruling. If there were only the two candidates of the major parties for the office in question, fairness would obviously require that these two be treated roughly the same with respect to the announcements. But it does not follow that if there were, in addition, so-called minority party candidates for the office of Senator, these candidates also would have to be afforded a roughly equivalent number of similar announcements. In such an event, the licensee would be called upon to make a good faith judgment as to whether there can reasonably be said to be a need or interest in the community calling for some provision of announcement time to these other parties or candidates and, if so, to determine the extent of that interest or need and the appropriate way to meet it. In short, the licensee's obligation under the fairness doctrine is to afford a reasonable opportunity for the presentation of opposing views in the light of circumstances — an obligation calling for the same kind of judgment as in the case where party spokesmen (rather than candidates) appear. (Letter to Mr. Lawrence M. C. Smith, FCC 63-658, April 18, 1963.)

14.   *No necessity for presentation on same program.*   In the proceedings leading to the Editorializing Report, it was urged, in effect, that contrasting viewpoints with respect to a controversial issue of public importance should be presented on the same program.

Ruling.   The Commission concluded that any rigid requirement in this respect would seriously limit the ability of the licensees to serve the public interest. "Forums and roundtable discussions, while often excellent techniques of presenting a fair cross section of differing viewpoints on a given issue, are not the only appropriate devices for radio discussion, and in some circumstances may not be particularly appropriate or advantageous." (Par. 8, Editorializing Report.)

15.   *Overall performance on the issue.*   A licensee presented a program in which views were expressed critical of the proposed nuclear weapons test ban treaty. The licensee rejected a request of an organization seeking to present views favorable to the treaty, on the ground, among others, that the contrasting viewpoint on this issue had already been presented over the station's facilities in other programming.

Ruling.   The licensee's overall performance is considered in determining whether fairness has been achieved on a specific issue. Thus, where complaint is made, the licensee is afforded the opportunity to set out all the programs, irrespective of the programming format, which he has devoted to the particular controversial issue during the appropriate time period. In this case, the Commision files contained no complaints to the contrary, and therefore, if it was the licensee's good faith judgment that the public had had the opportunity fairly to hear contrasting views on the issue involved in his other programming, it appeared that the licensee's obligation pursuant to the fairness doctrine had been met. (Letter to Cullman Bctg. Co., FCC 63-849, September 18, 1963; Letter of September 20, 1963, FCC 63-851, to Honorable Oren Harris.)

D.   Limitations which may reasonably be imposed by the licensee

16.   *Licensee discretion to choose spokesman.*   See Ruling 8 for facts.

Ruling.   Where a licensee permits the use of its facilities for the expression of views on controversial local or national issues of public importance such as the nuclear weapons test ban treaty, he must afford reasonable opportunities for the presentation of contrasting views by spokesmen for other responsible groups. There is, of course, no single method by which this obligation is to be met. As the Editorializing Report makes clear, the licensee has considerable discretion as to the techniques or formats to be employed and the spokesmen for each point of view. In the good faith exercise of his best judgment, he may, in a particular case, decide upon a local rather than regional or national spokesman — or upon a spokesman for a group which also is willing to pay for the broadcast time. Thus, with the exception of the broadcast of personal attacks (see Part E), there is no single group or person entitled as a matter of right to present a viewpoint differing from that previously expressed on the station. (Letter to Cullman Broadcasting Co., Inc., FCC .63-849, September 18, 1963.)

17. *Non-local spokesman; paid sponsorship.*   See Ruling 8 for facts. The stations contended that their obligation under the fairness doctrine extended only to a local group or its spokesman, and also inquired whether they were required to give free time to a group wishing to present viewpoints opposed to those aired on a sponsored program.

Ruling. Where the licensee has achieved a balanced presentation of contrasting views, either by affording time to a particular group or person of its own choice or through its own programming, the licensee's obligations under the fairness doctrine — to inform the public — will have been met. But, it is clear that the public's paramount right to hear opposing views on controversial issues of public importance cannot be nullified by either the inability of the licensee to obtain paid sponsorship of the broadcast time or the licensee's refusal to consider requests for time to present a conflicting viewpoint from an organization on the sole ground that the organization has no local chapter. In short, where the licensee has chosen to broadcast a sponsored program which for the first time presents one side of a controversial issue, has not presented (or does not plan to present) contrasting viewpoints in other programming, and has been unable to obtain paid sponsorship for the appropriate presentation of the opposing viewpoint or viewpoints, he cannot reject a presentation otherwise suitable to the licensee — and thus leave the public uninformed — on the ground that he cannot obtain paid sponsorship for that presentation. (Letter to Cullman Broadcasting, Co., Inc, FCC 63-849, September 18, 1963.)

18. *Unreasonable limitation; refusal to permit appeal not to vote.*   A station refused to sell broadcast time to the complainant who, as a spokesman for a community group, was seeking to present his point of view concerning a bond election to be held in the community; the station had sold time to an organization in favor of the bond issue. The complainant alleged that the station had broadcast editorials urging people to vote in the election and that his group's position was that because of the peculiarities in the bond election law (more than 50 percent of the electorate had to vote in the election for it to be valid), the best way to defeat the proposed measure was for people not to vote in the election. The complainant alleged, and the station admitted, that the station refused to sell him broadcast time because the licensee felt that to urge people not to vote was improper.

Ruling. Because of the peculiarities of the state election law, the sale of broadcast time to an organization favoring the bond issue, and the urging of listeners to vote, the question of whether to vote became an issue. Accordingly, by failing to broadcast views urging listeners not to vote, the licensee failed to discharge the obligations imposed upon him by the Commission's Report on Editorializing. (Letter to Radio Station WMOP, January 21, 1962 (staff ruling).)

19. *Unreasonable limitation; insistence upon request from both parties to dispute.* During the period of a labor strike which involved a matter of paramount importance to the community and to the nation at large, a union requested broadcast time to discuss the issues involved. The request was denied by the station solely because of its policy to refuse time for such discussion unless both the union and the management agreed, in advance, that they would jointly request and use the station, and the management of the company involved in the strike had refused to do so.

Ruling. In view of the licensee's statement that the issue was "of paramount importance to the community . . ." the licensee's actions were not in accordance with the principles enunciated in the Editorializing Report, specifically that portion of par. 8, which states that:

. . . where the licensee has determined that the subject is of sufficient import to receive broadcast attention, it would obviously not be in the public interest for spokesmen for one of the opposing points of view to be able to exercise a veto power over the entire presentation by refusing to broadcast its position. Fairness in such circumstances might require no more than that the licensee make a reasonable representation of the particular position and if it fails in this effort, to continue to make available its facilities to the spokesmen for such position in the event that, after the original programs are broadcast, they then decide to avail themselves of a right to present their contrary opinion. (Par. 8, Report on Editorializing by Broadcast Licensees; The Evening News Ass'n (WWJ), 6 R.R. 283, April 21, 1950.)

E. Personal attack principle

20. *Personal attack.* A newscaster on a station, in a series of broadcasts, attacked certain county and state officials, charging them with nefarious schemes and the use of their offices for personal gain, attaching derisive epithets to their names, and analogizing their local administration with the political methods of foreign dictators. At the time of renewal of the station's license, the persons attacked urged that the station had been used for the licensee's selfish purposes and to vent his personal spite. The licensee denied the charge, and asserted that the broadcasts had a factual basis. On several occasions, the persons attacked were invited to use the station to discuss the matters in the broadcasts.

Ruling. Where a licensee expresses an opinion concerning controversial issues of public importance, he is under obligation to see that those holding opposing viewpoints are afforded a reasonable opportunity for the presentation of their views. He is under a further obligation not to present biased or one-sided news programming (viewing such programming on an overall basis) and not to use his station for his purely personal and private interests. Investigation established that the licensee did not subordinate his public interest obligations to his private interests, and that there was "a body of opinion" in the community "that such broadcasts had a factual basis."

As to the attacks, the *Editorializing Report* states that ". . . elementary considerations of fairness may dictate that time be allocated to a person or group which has been specifically attacked over the station, where otherwise no such obligation would exist . . ." In this case, the attacks were of a highly personal nature, impugning the character and honesty of named individuals. In such circumstances, the licensee has an affirmative duty to take all appropriate steps to see to it that the persons attacked are afforded the fullest opportunity to respond. Here, the persons attacked knew of the attacks, were generally apprised of their nature, and were aware of the opportunities afforded them to respond. Accordingly, the license was renewed. (Clayton W. Mapoles, FCC 62-501, 23 R.R. 586, May 9, 1962.)

21. *Personal attack.*   For a period of five days, September 18-22, a station broadcast a series of daily editorials attacking the general manager of a national rural electric cooperative association in connection with a pending controversial issue of public importance. The manager arrived in town on September 21 for a two-day stay and, upon being informed of the editorials, on the morning of September 22d sought to obtain copies of them. About noon of the same day, the station approached the manager with an offer of an interview to respond to the statements made in the editorials. The manager stated, however, that he would not have had time to prepare adequately a reply which would require a series of broadcasts. He complained to the Commission that the station had acted unfairly.

Ruling.   Where, as here, a station's editorials contain a personal attack upon an individual by name, the fairness doctrine requires that a copy of the specific editorial or editorials shall be communicated to the person attacked either prior to or at the time of the broadcast of such editorials so that a reasonable opportunity is afforded that person to reply. This duty on the part of the station is greater where, as here, interest in the editorials was consciously built up by the station over a period of days and the time within which the person attacked would have an opportunity to reply was known to be so limited. The Commission concludes that in failing to supply copies of the editorials promptly to the manager and delaying in affording him the opportunity to reply to them, the station had not fully met the requirements of the Commission's fairness doctrine. (Billings Bctg. Co., FCC 62-736. 23 R.R. 951, July 13, 1962.)

22. *No personal attack merely because individual is named.*   A network program discussed the applicability of Section 315 to appearances by candidates for public office on TV newscasts and the Commission's decision holding that the mayoralty candidate, Lar Daly, was entitled to equal time when the Mayor of Chicago appeared on a newscast. The program contained the editorial

views of the President of CBS opposing the interpretation of the Commission and urging that Section 315 not apply to newscasts. Three other persons on the program expressed contrasting points of view. Lar Daly's request that he be afforded time to reply to the President of CBS, because he was "directly involved" in the Commission's decision which was discussed over the air and because he was the most qualified spokesman to present opposing views, was denied by the station. Did the fairness doctrine require that his request be granted?

Ruling. It was the newscast question involved in the Commission's decision, rather than Lar Daly, which was the controversial issue which was presented. Since the network presented several spokesmen, all of whom appeared qualified to state views contrasting with those expressed by the network President, the network fulfilled its obligation to provide a "fair and balanced presentation of an important public issue of a controversial nature." (Lar Daly, 19 R.R. 1103, at 1104, Mar. 24, 1960.)[6]

23. *Licensee involvement in personal attack.* It was urged that in Mapoles, Billings, and Times-Mirror (see Rulings 20, 21, 25), the station was, in effect, "personally involved"; that the personal attack principle should be applied only when the licensee is personally involved in the attack upon a person or group (i.e., through editorials or through station commentator programming), and not where the attack is made by a party unconnected with the station.

Ruling. Under fundamental communications policy, the licensee, with the exception of appearances of political candidates subject to the equal opportunity requirements of Section 315, is fully responsible for all matter which is broadcast over his station. It follows that when a program contains a personal attack, the licensee must be fully aware of the contents of the program, whatever its source or his actual involvement in the broadcast. The crucial consideration, as the Commission stated in Mapoles, is that "his broadcast facilities [have been] used to attack a person or group." (Letter of September 18, 1963 to Douglas A. Anello, FCC 63-850.)

24. *Personal attack – no tape or transcript.* In the same inquiry as above (Ruling 23), the question was also raised as to the responsibility of the licensee when his facilities are used for a personal attack in a program dealing

---

[6] As seen from the above rulings, the personal attack principle is applicable where there are statements, in connection with a controversial issue of public importance, attacking an individual's or group's integrity, character, or honesty or like personal qualities, and not when an individual or group is simply named or referred to. Thus, while a definitive Commission ruling must await a complaint involving specific facts – see introduction, p. 396, the personal attack principle has not been applied where there is simply stated disagreement with the views of an individual or group concerning a controversial issue of public importance. Nor is it necessary to send a transcript or summary of the attack, with an offer of time for response, in the case of a personal attack upon a foreign leader, even assuming such an attack occurred in connection with a controversial issue of public importance.

with a controversial issue of public importance and the licensee has no transcript or tape of the program.

Ruling. Where a personal attack is made and no script or tape is available, good sense and fairness dictate that the licensee send as accurate a summary as possible of the substance of the attack to the person or group involved. (Letter of September 18, 1963 to Douglas A. Anello, FCC 63-850.)

25. *Personal attacks on, and criticism of, candidate; partisan position on campaign issues.* In more than 20 broadcasts, two station commentators presented their views on the issues in the 1962 California gubernatorial campaign between Governor Brown and Mr. Nixon. The views expressed on the issues were critical of the Governor and favored Mr. Nixon, and at times involved personal attacks on individuals and groups in the gubernatorial campaign, and specifically on Governor Brown. The licensee responded that it had presented opposing viewpoints but upon examination there were two instances of broadcasts featuring Governor Brown (both of which were counterbalanced by appearances of Mr. Nixon) and two instances of broadcasts presenting viewpoints opposed to two of the issues raised by the above-noted broadcasts by the commentators. It did not appear that any of the other broadcasts cited by the station dealt with the issues raised as to the gubernatorial campaign.

Ruling. Since there were only two instances which involved the presentation of viewpoints concerning the gubernatorial campaign, opposed to the more than twenty programs of the commentators presenting their views on many different issues of the campaign for which no opportunity was afforded for the presentation of opposing viewpoints, there was not a fair opportunity for presentation of opposing viewpoints with respect to many of the issues discussed in the commentators' programs. The continuous, repetitive opportunity afforded for the expression of the commentators' viewpoints on the gubernatorial campaign, in contrast to the minimal opportunity afforded to opposing viewpoints, violated the right of the public to a fair presentation of views. Further, with respect to the personal attacks by the one commentator on individuals and groups involved in the gubernatorial campaign, the principle in Mapoles and Billings should have been followed. In the circumstances, the station should have sent a transcript of the pertinent continuity on the above programs to Governor Brown and should have offered a comparable opportunity for an appropriate spokesman to answer the broadcasts. (Times-Mirror, FCC 62-1130, 24 R.R. 404, Oct. 26, 1962; FCC 62-1109, 24 R.R. 407, Oct. 19, 1962.)

26. *Personal attacks on, and criticism of candidates; partisan position on campaign issues – appropriate spokesman.* See facts above. The question was raised whether the candidate has the right to insist upon his own appearance, to respond to the broadcasts in question.

Ruling. Since a response by a candidate would, in turn, require that equal opportunities under Section 315 be afforded to the other legally-qualified candidates for the same office, the fairness doctrine requires only that the licensee afford the attacked candidate an opportunity to respond through an appropriate spokesman. The candidate should, of course, be given a substantial voice in the selection of the spokesman to respond to the attack or to the statement of support. (Times-Mirror Bctg. Co., FCC 62-1130, 24 R.R. 404, 406, Oct. 19, 1962, Oct. 26, 1962.)

27. *Personal attacks on, and criticism of, candidate; partisan position on campaign issues.*   During the fall of an election year, a news commentator on a local affairs program made several critical and uncomplimentary references to the actions and public positions of various political and non-partisan candidates for public office and of the California Democratic Clubs and demanded the resignation of an employee of the staff of the County Superintendent of Schools. In response to a request for time to respond by the local Democratic Central Committee, and after negotiations between the licensee and the complaining party, the licensee offered two five-minute segments of time on November 1 and 2, 1962, and instructed its commentator to refrain from expressing any point of view on partisan issues on November 5, or November 6, election eve and election day, respectively.

Ruling.   On the facts of this case, the comments of the news commentator constituted personal attacks on candidates and others and involved the taking of a partisan position on issues involved in a race for political office. Therefore, under the ruling of the Times-Mirror case, the licensee was under an obligation to "send a transcript of the pertinent continuity in each such program to the appropriate candidates immediately and [to] offer a comparable opportunity for an appropriate spokesman to answer the broadcast." However, upon the basis of the showing, the licensee's offer of time, in response to the request, was not unreasonable under the fairness doctrine. (Letter to The McBride Industries, Inc., FCC 63-756, July 31, 1963.)

F.   **Licensee editorializing** *— need j.d. if you editize!*

28. *Freedom to editorialize.*   The Editorializing Report and the 1960 Programming Statement, while stating that the licensee is not required to editorialize, make clear that he is free to do so, but that if he does, he must meet the requirements of the fairness doctrine.

6

THE RED LION CASE

Red Lion Broadcasting Co., Inc., et al. v.
Federal Communications Commission et al.
395 U.S. 367
June 9, 1969

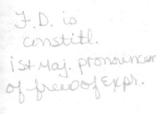

In this landmark decision the Supreme Court unanimously upheld the constitutionality of the FCC's "Fairness Doctrine" and the Commission's 1967 rules stemming from this policy. Red Lion is the High Court's first major pronouncement regarding freedom of expression in broadcasting since the "Network" case of 1943 (see pp. 503-532).

   Considerable controversy surrounds the decision. Some would limit its applicability to the immediate issues of the legality of the FCC requirement that time be provided for the airing of replies to personal attacks regardless of an aggrieved party's willingness or ability to pay. Others would interpret Red Lion as sanction for the Commission to exercise greater control over all types of broadcast programming. Finally, there are those who would extend the principle of the "Fairness Doctrine" to the nonbroadcast mass media through the establishment of a constitutionally derived "right of access."

   Broadcasting and First Amendment theory are certain to be affected by the implications of the Red Lion decision for years to come as regulators and regulated probe the contours of this attempt to reconcile the intent of a 180-year-old constitutional amendment with the realities of electronic mass communication.

Mr. Justice White delivered the opinion of the Court.

   The Federal Communications Commission has for many years imposed on radio and television broadcasters the requirement that discussion of public issues be presented on broadcast stations, and that each side of those issues must be given fair coverage. This is known as the fairness doctrine, which originated very early in the history of broadcasting and has maintained its present outlines for some time. It is an obligation whose content has been defined in a long series of FCC rulings in particular cases, and which is distinct from the statutory requirement of § 315 of the Communications Act[1] that equal time be allotted all qualified candidates for public office. Two aspects of the fairness doctrine, relating to personal attacks in the context of controversial public issues and to political editorializing, were codified more precisely in the form of FCC regulations in 1967. The two cases before us now, which were decided separately below, challenge the constitutional and statutory bases of the doctrine and component rules. *Red Lion* involves the application of the fairness doctrine to a particular broadcast, and *RTNDA* * arises as an action to review the FCC's 1967 promulgation of the personal attack and political editorializing regulations, which were laid down after the *Red Lion* litigation had begun.

---

[1]Communications Act of 1934, Tit. III, 48 Stat. 1081, as amended, 47 U.S.C. § 301 *et seq.* Section 315 now reads:

"315. Candidates for public office; facilities; rules.

"(a) If any licensee shall permit any person who is a legally qualified candidate for any public office to use a broadcasting station, he shall afford equal opportunities to all other such candidates for that office in the use of such broadcasting station: *Provided*, That such licensee shall have no power of censorship over the material broadcast under the provisions of this section. No obligation is imposed upon any licensee to allow the use of its station by any such candidate. Appearance by a legally qualified candidate on any –

"(1) bona fide newscast,

"(2) bona fide news interview,

"(3) bona fide news documentary (if the appearance of the candidate is incidental to the presentation of the subject or subjects covered by the news documentary), or

"(4) on-the-spot coverage of bona fide news events (including but not limited to political conventions and activities incidental thereto), shall not be deemed to be use of a broadcasting station within the meaning of this subsection. Nothing in the foregoing sentence shall be construed as relieving broadcasters, in connection with the presentation of newscasts, news interviews, news documentaries, and on-the-spot coverage of news events, from the obligation imposed upon them under this chapter to operate in the public interest and to afford reasonable opportunity for the discussion of conflicting views on issues of public importance.

"(b) The charges made for the use of any broadcasting station for any of the purposes set forth in this section shall not exceed the charges made for comparable use of such station for other purposes.

"(c) The Commission shall prescribe appropriate rules and regulations to carry out the provisions of this section."

*RTNDA denotes Radio Television News Directors Association. [Ed.]

I.

A.

The Red Lion Broadcasting Company is licensed to operate a Pennsylvania radio station, WGCB. On November 27, 1964, WGCB carried a 15-minute broadcast by the Reverend Billy James Hargis as part of a "Christian Crusade" series. A book by Fred J. Cook entitled "Goldwater — Extremist on the Right" was discussed by Hargis, who said that Cook had been fired by a newspaper for making false charges against city officials; that Cook had then worked for a Communist-affiliated publication; that he had defended Alger Hiss and attacked J. Edgar Hoover and the Central Intelligence Agency; and that he had now written a "book to smear and destroy Barry Goldwater."[2] When Cook heard of the broadcast he concluded that he had been personally attacked and demanded free reply time, which the station refused. After an exchange of letters among Cook, Red Lion, and the FCC, the FCC declared that the Hargis broadcast constituted a personal attack on Cook; that Red Lion had failed to meet its obligation under the fairness doctrine as expressed in *Times-Mirror Broadcasting Co.*, 24 P & F Radio Reg. 404 (1962), to send a tape, transcript, or summary of the broadcast to Cook and offer him reply time; and that the station must provide reply time whether or not Cook would pay for it. On review in the Court of Appeals for the District of Columbia Circuit,[3] the FCC's position was upheld as constitutional and otherwise proper. 127 U.S. App. D.C. 129, 381 F. 2d 908 (1967).

---

[2] According to the record, Hargis asserted that his broadcast included the following statement:

"Now, this paperback book by Fred J. Cook is entitled, 'GOLDWATER–EXTREMIST ON THE RIGHT.' Who is Cook? Cook was fired from the New York World Telegram after he made a false charge publicly on television against an un-named official of the New York City government. New York publishers and NEWSWEEK Magazine for December 7, 1959, showed that Fred Cook and his pal, Eugene Gleason, had made up the whole story and this confession was made to New York District Attorney, Frank Hogan. After losing his job, Cook went to work for the left-wing publication, THE NATION, one of the most scurrilous publications of the left which has championed many communist causes over many years. Its editor, Carry McWilliams, has been affiliated with many communist enterprises, scores of which have been cited as subversive by the Attorney General of the U.S. or by other government agencies. . . . Now, among other things Fred Cook wrote for THE NATION, was an article absolving Alger Hiss of any wrong doing . . . there was a 208 page attack on the FBI and J. Edgar Hoover; another attack by Mr. Cook was on the Central Intelligence Agency . . . now this is the man who wrote the book to smear and destroy Barry Goldwater called 'Barry Goldwater — Extremist of the Right!' "

[3] The Court of Appeals initially dismissed the petition for want of a reviewable order, later reversing itself en banc upon argument by the Government that the FCC rule used here, which permits it to issue "a declaratory ruling terminating a controversy or removing uncertainty," 47 CFR § 1.2, was in fact justified by the Administrative Procedure Act.

B.

Not long after the *Red Lion* litigation was begun, the FCC issued a Notice of Proposed Rule Making, 31 Fed. Reg. 5710, with an eye to making the personal attack aspect of the fairness doctrine more precise and more readily enforceable, and to specifying its rules relating to political editorials. After considering written comments supporting and opposing the rules, the FCC adopted them substantially as proposed, 32 Fed. Reg. 10303. Twice amended, 32 Fed. Reg. 11531, 33 Fed. Reg. 5362, the rules were held unconstitutional in the *RTNDA* litigation by the Court of Appeals for the Seventh Circuit, on review of the rule-making proceeding, as abridging the freedoms of speech and press. 400 F. 2d 1002 (1968).

As they now stand amended, the regulations read as follows:

"Personal attacks; political editorials.

"(a) When, during the presentation of views on a controversial issue of public importance, an attack is made upon the honesty, character, integrity or like personal qualities of an identified person or group, the licensee shall, within a reasonable time and in no event later than 1 week after the attack, transmit to the person or group attacked (1) notification of the date, time and identification of the broadcast; (2) a script or tape (or an accurate summary if a script or tape is not available) of the attack; and (3) an offer of a reasonable opportunity to respond over the licensee's facilities.

"(b) The provisions of paragraph (a) of this section shall not be applicable (1) to attacks on foreign groups or foreign public figures; (2) to personal attacks which are made by legally qualified candidates, their authorized spokesmen, or those associated with them in the campaign, on other such candidates, their authorized spokesmen, or persons associated with the candidates in the campaign; and (3) to bona fide newscasts, bona fide news interviews, and on-the-spot coverage of a bona fide news event (including commentary or

---

That Act permits an adjudicating agency, "in its sound discretion, with like effect as in the case of other orders, to issue a declaratory order to terminate a controversy or remove uncertainty." § 5, 60 Stat. 239, 5 U.S.C. § 1004(d). In this case, the FCC could have determined the question of Red Lion's liability to a cease-and-desist order or license revocation, 47 U.S.C. § 312, for failure to comply with the license's condition that the station be operated "in the public interest," or for failure to obey a requirement of operation in the public interest implicit in the ability of the FCC to revoke licenses for conditions justifying the denial of an initial license, 47 U.S.C. § 312(a)(2), and the statutory requirement that the public interest be served in granting and renewing licenses, 47 U.S.C. §§ 307(a), (d). Since the FCC could have adjudicated these questions it could, under the Administrative Procedure Act, have issued a declaratory order in the course of its adjudication which would have been subject to judicial review. Although the FCC did not comply with all of the formalities for an adjudicative proceeding in this case, the petitioner itself adopted as its own the Government's position that this was a reviewable order, waiving any objection it might have had to the procedure of the adjudication.

analysis contained in the foregoing programs, but the provisions of paragraph (a) of this section shall be applicable to editorials of the licensee).

"NOTE: The fairness doctrine is applicable to situations coming within [(3)], above, and, in a specific factual situation, may be applicable in the general area of political broadcasts [(2)], above. See, section 315(a) of the Act, 47 U.S.C. 315(a); Public Notice: *Applicability of the Fairness Doctrine in the Handling of Controversial Issues of Public Importance.* 29 F.R. 10415. The categories listed in [(3)] are the same as those specified in section 315(a) of the Act.

"(c) Where a licensee, in an editorial, (i) endorses or (ii) opposes a legally qualified candidate or candidates, the licensee shall, within 24 hours after the editorial, transmit to respectively (i) the other qualified candidate or candidates for the same office or (ii) the candidate opposed in the editorial (1) notification of the date and the time of the editorial; (2) a script or tape of the editorial; and (3) an offer of a reasonable opportunity for a candidate or a spokesman of the candidate to respond over the licensee's facilities: *Provided, however*, That where such editorials are broadcast within 72 hours prior to the day of the election, the licensee shall comply with the provisions of this paragraph sufficiently far in advance of the broadcast to enable the candidate or candidates to have a reasonable opportunity to prepare a response and to present it in a timely fashion." 47 CFR §§ 73.123, 73.300, 73.598, 73.679 (all identical).

C.

Believing that the specific application of the fairness doctrine in *Red Lion*, and the promulgation of the regulations in *RTNDA*, are both authorized by Congress and enhance rather than abridge the freedoms of speech and press protected by the First Amendment, we hold them valid and constitutional, reversing the judgment below in *RTNDA* and affirming the judgment below in *Red Lion*.

II.

The history of the emergence of the fairness doctrine and of the related legislation shows that the Commission's action in the *Red Lion* case did not exceed its authority, and that in adopting the new regulations the Commission was implementing congressional policy rather than embarking on a frolic of its own.

A.

Before 1927, the allocation of frequencies was left entirely to the private sector, and the result was chaos.[4] It quickly became apparent that broadcast frequencies constituted a scarce resource whose use could be regulated and rationalized only by the Government. Without government control, the medium would be of little use because of the cacophony of competing voices, none of which could be clearly and predictably heard.[5] Consequently, the Federal Radio Commission was established to allocate frequencies among competing applicants in a manner responsive to the public "convenience, interest, or necessity."[6]

Very shortly thereafter the Commission expressed its view that the "public interest requires ample play for the free and fair competition of opposing views, and the commission believes that the principle applies . . . to all discussions of issues of importance to the public." *Great Lakes Broadcasting Co.*, 3 F.R.C.

[4]Because of this chaos, a series of National Radio Conferences was held between 1922 and 1925, at which it was resolved that regulation of the radio spectrum by the Federal Government was essential and that regulatory power should be utilized to ensure that allocation of this limited resource would be made only to those who would serve the public interest. The 1923 Conference expressed the opinion that the Radio Communications Act of 1912, 37 Stat. 302, conferred upon the Secretary of Commerce the power to regulate frequencies and hours of operation, but when Secretary Hoover sought to implement this claimed power by penalizing the Zenith Radio Corporation for operating on an unauthorized frequency, the 1912 Act was held not to permit enforcement. *United States* v. *Zenith Radio Corporation*, 12 F. 2d 614 (D.C.N.D. Ill. 1926). Cf. *Hoover* v. *Intercity Radio Co.*, 52 App. D.C. 339, 286 F. 1003 (1923) (Secretary had no power to deny licenses, but was empowered to assign frequencies). An opinion issued by the Attorney General at Hoover's request confirmed the impotence of the Secretary under the 1912 Act. 35 Op. Atty. Gen. 126 (1926). Hoover thereafter appealed to the radio industry to regulate itself, but his appeal went largely unheeded. See generally L. Schmeckebier, The Federal Radio Commission 1-14 (1932).

[5]Congressman White, a sponsor of the bill enacted as the Radio Act of 1927, commented upon the need for new legislation:

"We have reached the definite conclusion that the right of all our people to enjoy this means of communication can be preserved only by the repudiation of the idea underlying the 1912 law that anyone who will may transmit and by the assertion in its stead of the doctrine that the right of the public to service is superior to the right of any individual. . . . The recent radio conference met this issue squarely. It recognized that in the present state of scientific development there must be a limitation upon the number of broadcasting stations and it recommended that licenses should be issued only to those stations whose operation would render a benefit to the public, are necessary in the public interest, or would contribute to the development of the art. This principle was approved by every witness before your committee. We have written it into the bill. If enacted into law, the broadcasting privilege will not be a right of selfishness. It will rest upon an assurance of public interest to be served." 67 Cong. Rec. 5479.

[6]Radio Act of 1927, § 4, 44 Stat. 1163. See generally Davis, The Radio Act of 1927, 13 Va. L. Rev. 611 (1927).

Ann. Rep. 32, 33 (1929), rev'd on other grounds, 59 App. D.C. 197, 37 F. 2d 993, cert. dismissed, 281 U.S. 706 (1930). This doctrine was applied through denial of license renewals or construction permits, both by the FRC, *Trinity Methodist Church, South* v. *FRC*, 61 App. D.C. 311, 62 F. 2d 850 (1932), cert. denied, 288 U.S. 599 (1933), and its successor FCC, *Young People's Association for the Propagation of the Gospel*, 6 F.C.C. 178 (1938). After an extended period during which the licensee was obliged not only to cover and to cover fairly the views of others, but also to refrain from expressing his own personal views, *Mayflower Broadcasting Corp.*, 8 F.C.C. 333 (1940), the latter limitation on the licensee was abandoned and the doctrine developed into its present form.

There is a twofold duty laid down by the FCC's decisions and described by the 1949 Report on Editorializing by Broadcast Licensees, 13 F.C.C. 1246 (1949). The broadcaster must give adequate coverage to public issues, *United Broadcasting Co.*, 10 F.C.C. 515 (1945), and coverage must be fair in that it accurately reflects the opposing views. *New Broadcasting Co.*, 6 P & F Radio Reg. 258 (1950). This must be done at the broadcaster's own expense if sponsorship is unavailable. *Cullman Broadcasting Co.*, 25 P & F Radio Reg. 895 (1963). Moreover, the duty must be met by programming obtained at the licensee's own initiative if available from no other source. *John J. Dempsey*, 6 P & F Radio Reg. 615 (1950); see *Metropolitan Broadcasting Corp.*, 19 P & F Radio Reg. 602 (1960); *The Evening News Assn.*, 6 P & F Radio Reg. 283 (1950). The Federal Radio Commission had imposed these two basic duties on broadcasters since the outset, *Great Lakes Broadcasting Co.*, 3 F.R.C. Ann. Rep. 32 (1929), rev'd on other grounds, 59 App. D.C. 197, 37 F. 2d 993, cert. dismissed, 281 U.S. 706 (1930); *Chicago Federation of Labor* v. *FRC*, 3 F.R.C. Ann. Rep. 36 (1929), aff'd, 59 App. D.C. 333, 41 F. 2d 422 (1930); *KFKB Broadcasting Assn.* v. *FRC*, 60 App. D.C. 79, 47 F. 2d 670 (1931), and in particular respects the personal attack rules and regulations at issue here have spelled them out in greater detail.

When a personal attack has been made on a figure involved in a public issue, both the doctrine of cases such as *Red Lion* and *Times-Mirror Broadcasting Co.*, 24 P & F Radio Reg. 404 (1962), and also the 1967 regulations at issue in *RTNDA* require that the individual attacked himself be offered an opportunity to respond. Likewise, where one candidate is endorsed in a political editorial, the other candidates must themselves be offered reply time to use personally or through a spokesman. These obligations differ from the general fairness requirement that issues be presented, and presented with coverage of competing views, in that the broadcaster does not have the option of presenting the attacked party's side himself or choosing a third party to represent that side. But insofar as there is an obligation of the broadcaster to see that both sides are presented, and insofar as that is an affirmative obligation, the personal attack doctrine and regulations do not differ from the preceding fairness doctrine. The simple fact that the attacked men or unendorsed candidates may respond themselves or through agents is not a critical distinction, and indeed, it is not unreasonable for the FCC to conclude that the objective of adequate presentation of all sides may best be served by allowing those most closely affected to make the response, rather than leaving the response in the hands of the station which has attacked their candidacies, endorsed their opponents, or carried a personal attack upon them.

B.

The statutory authority of the FCC to promulgate these regulations derives from the mandate to the "Commission from time to time, as public convenience, interest, or necessity requires" to promulgate "such rules and regulations and prescribe such restrictions and conditions . . . as may be necessary to carry out the provisions of this chapter . . ." 47 U.S.C. § 303 and § 303 (r).[7] The Commission is specifically directed to consider the demands of the public interest in the course of granting licenses, 47 U.S.C. §§ 307(a), 309(a); renewing them, 47 U.S.C. § 307; and modifying them. *Ibid.* Moreover, the FCC has included among the conditions of the Red Lion license itself the requirement that operation of the station be carried out in the public interest, 47 U.S.C. § 309(h). This mandate to the FCC to assure that broadcasters operate in the public interest is a broad one, a power "not niggardly but expansive," *National Broadcasting Co.* v. *United States*, 319 U.S. 190, 219 (1943), whose validity we have long upheld. *FCC* v. *Pottsville Broadcasting Co.*, 309 U.S. 134, 138 (1940); *FCC* v. *RCA Communications, Inc.*, 346 U.S. 86, 90 (1953); *FRC* v. *Nelson Bros. Bond & Mortgage Co.*, 289 U.S. 266, 285 (1933). It is broad enough to encompass these regulations.

The fairness doctrine finds specific recognition in statutory form, is in part modeled on explicit statutory provisions relating to political candidates, and is approvingly reflected in legislative history.

[7] As early as 1930, Senator Dill expressed the view that the Federal Radio Commission had the power to make regulations requiring a licensee to afford an opportunity for presentation of the other side on "public questions." Hearings before the Senate Committee on Interstate Commerce on S. 6, 71st Cong., 2d Sess., 1616 (1930):

"Senator Dill. Then you are suggesting that the provision of the statute that now requires a station to give equal opportunity to candidates for office shall be applied to all public questions?

"Commissioner Robinson. Of course, I think in the legal concept the law requires it now. I do not see that there is any need to legislate about it. It will evolve one of these days. Somebody will go into court and say, 'I am entitled to this opportunity,' and he will get it.

"Senator Dill. Has the Commission considered the question of making regulations requiring the stations to do that?

"Commissioner Robinson. Oh, no.

"Senator Dill. It would be within the power of the commission, I think, to make regulations on that subject."

In 1959 the Congress amended the statutory requirement of § 315 that equal time be accorded each political candidate to except certain appearances on news programs, but added that this constituted no exception *"from the obligation imposed upon them under this Act to operate in the public interest and to afford reasonable opportunity for the discussion of conflicting views on issues of public importance."* Act of September 14, 1959, § 1, 73 Stat. 557, amending 47 U.S.C. § 315(a) (emphasis added). This language makes it very plain that Congress, in 1959, announced that the phrase "public interest," which had been in the Act since 1927, imposed a duty on broadcasters to discuss both sides of controversial public issues. In other words, the amendment vindicated the FCC's general view that the fairness doctrine inhered in the public interest standard. Subsequent legislation declaring the intent of an earlier statute is entitled to great weight in statutory construction.[8] And here this principle is given special force by the equally venerable principle that the construction of a statute by those charged with its execution should be followed unless there are compelling indications that it is wrong,[9] especially when Congress has refused to alter the administrative construction.[10] Here, the Congress has not just kept its silence by refusing to overturn the administrative construction,[11] but has

---

[8] *Federal Housing Administration* v. *Darlington, Inc.*, 358 U.S. 84, 90 (1958); *Glidden Co.* v *Zdanok*, 370 U.S. 530, 541 (1962) (opinion of Mr. Justice Harlan, joined by Mr. Justice Brennan and Mr. Justice Stewart). This principle is a venerable one. *Alexander* v. *Alexandria*, 5 Cranch 1 (1809); *United States* v. *Freeman*, 3 How. 556 (1845); *Stockdale* v. *The Insurance Companies*, 20 Wall. 323 (1874).

[9] *Zemel* v. *Rusk*, 381 U.S. 1, 11-12 (1965); *Udall* v. *Tallman*, 380 U.S. 1, 16-18 (1965); *Commissioner* v. *Sternberger's Estate*, 348 U.S. 187, 199 (1955); *Hastings & D.R. Co.* v. *Whitney*, 132 U.S. 357, 366 (1889); *United States* v. *Burlington & Missouri River R. Co.*, 98 U.S. 334, 341 (1879); *United States* v. *Alexander*, 12 Wall. 177, 179-181 (1871); *Surgett* v. *Lapice*, 8 How. 48, 68 (1850).

[10] *Zemel* v. *Rusk*, 381 U.S. 1, 11-12 (1965); *United States* v. *Bergh*, 352 U.S. 40, 46-47 (1956); *Alstate Construction Co.* v. *Durkin*, 345 U.S. 13, 16-17 (1953); *Costanzo* v. *Tillinghast*, 287 U.S. 341, 345 (1932).

[11] An attempt to limit sharply the FCC's power to interfere with programming practices failed to emerge from Committee in 1943. S. 814, 78th Cong., 1st Sess. (1943). See Hearings on S. 814 before the Senate Committee on Interstate Commerce, 78th Cong., 1st Sess. (1943). Also, attempts specifically to enact the doctrine failed in the Radio Act of 1927, 67 Cong. Rec. 12505 (1926) (agreeing to amendment proposed by Senator Dill eliminating coverage of "question affecting the public"), and a similar proposal in the Communications Act of 1934 was accepted by the Senate, 78 Cong. Rec. 8854 (1934); see S. Rep. No. 781, 73d Cong., 2d Sess., 8 (1934), but was not included in the bill reported by the House Committee, see H. R. Rep. No. 1850, 73d Cong., 2d Sess. (1934). The attempt which came nearest success was a bill, H. R. 7716, 72d Cong., 1st Sess. (1932), passed by Congress but pocket-vetoed by the President in 1933, which would have extended "equal opportunities" whenever a public question was to be voted on at an election or by a government agency. H. R. Rep. No. 2106, 72d Cong., 2d Sess., 6 (1933). In any event, unsuccessful attempts at legislation are not the best of guides to legislative intent. *Fogarty* v. *United States*, 340 U.S. 8, 13-14 (1950); *United States* v. *United Mine*

ratified it with positive legislation. Thirty years of consistent administrative construction left undisturbed by Congress until 1959, when that construction was expressly accepted, reinforce the natural conclusion that the public interest language of the Act authorized the Commission to require licensees to use their stations for discussion of public issues, and that the FCC is free to implement this requirement by reasonable rules and regulations which fall short of abridgment of the freedom of speech and press, and of the censorship proscribed by § 326 of the Act.[12]

The objectives of § 315 themselves could readily be circumvented but for the complementary fairness doctrine ratified by § 315. The section applies only to campaign appearances by candidates, and not by family, friends, campaign managers, or other supporters. Without the fairness doctrine, then, a licensee could ban all campaign appearances by candidates themselves from the air[13] and proceed to deliver over his station entirely to the supporters of one slate of candidates, to the exclusion of all others. In this way the broadcaster could have a far greater impact on the favored candidacy than he could by simply allowing a spot appearance by the candidate himself. It is the fairness doctrine as an aspect of the obligation to operate in the public interest, rather than § 315, which prohibits the broadcaster from taking such a step.

The legislative history reinforces this view of the effect of the 1959 amendment. Even before the language relevant here was added, the Senate report on amending § 315 noted that "broadcast frequencies are limited and, therefore, they have been necessarily considered a public trust. Every licensee who is fortunate in obtaining a license is mandated to operate in the public interest and has assumed the obligation of presenting important public questions fairly and without bias." S. Rep. No. 562, 86th Cong., 1st Sess., 8-9 (1959). See also, specifically adverting to Federal Communications Commission doctrine, id., at 13.

Rather than leave this approval solely in the legislative history, Senator Proxmire suggested an amendment to make it part of the Act. 105 Cong. Rec.

Workers, 330 U.S. 258, 281-282 (1947). A review of some of the legislative history over the years, drawing a somewhat different conclusion, is found in Staff Study of the House Committee on Interstate and Foreign Commerce, Legislative History of the Fairness Doctrine, 90th Cong., 2d Sess. (Comm. Print. 1968). This inconclusive history was, of course, superseded by the specific statutory language added in 1959.

[12]" § 326. Censorship.

"Nothing in this chapter shall be understood or construed to give the Commission the power of censorship over the radio communications or signals transmitted by any radio station, and no regulation or condition shall be promulgated or fixed by the Commission which shall interfere with the right of free speech by means of radio communication."

[13]*John P. Crommelin*, 19 P & F Radio Reg. 1392 (1960).

14457. This amendment, which Senator Pastore, a manager of the bill and a ranking member of the Senate Committee, considered "rather surplusage," 105 Cong. Rec. 14462, constituted a positive statement of doctrine[14] and was altered to the present merely approving language in the conference committee. In explaining the language to the Senate after the committee changes, Senator Pastore said: "We insisted that that provision remain in the bill, to be a continuing reminder and admonition to the Federal Communications Commission and to the broadcasters alike, that we were not abandoning the philosophy that gave birth to section 315, in giving the people the right to have a full and complete disclosure of conflicting views on news of interest to the people of the country." 105 Cong. Rec. 17830. Senator Scott, another Senate manager, added that: "It is intended to encompass all legitimate areas of public importance which are controversial," not just politics. 105 Cong. Rec. 17831.

It is true that the personal attack aspect of the fairness doctrine was not actually adjudicated until after 1959, so that Congress then did not have those rules specifically before it. However, the obligation to offer time to reply to a personal attack was presaged by the FCC's 1949 Report on Editorializing, which the FCC views as the principal summary of its *ratio decidendi* in cases in this area:

"In determining whether to honor specific requests for time, the station will inevitably be confronted with such questions as . . . whether there may not be other available groups or individuals who might be more appropriate spokesmen for the particular point of view than the person making the request. The latter's personal involvement in the controversy may also be a factor which must be considered, for elementary considerations of fairness may dictate that time be allocated to a person or group which has been specifically attacked over the station, where otherwise no such obligation would exist." 13 F.C.C., at 1251-1252.

When the Congress ratified the FCC's implication of a fairness doctrine in 1959 it did not, of course, approve every past decision or pronouncement by the Commission on this subject, or give it a completely free hand for the future. The statutory authority does not go so far. But we cannot say that when a station publishes personal attacks or endorses political candidates, it is a misconstruction of the public interest standard to require the station to offer time

---

[14]The Proxmire amendment read: "[B]ut nothing in this sentence shall be construed as changing the basic intent of Congress with respect to the provisions of this act, which recognizes that television and radio frequencies are in the public domain, that the license to operate in such frequencies requires operation in the public interest, and that in newscasts, news interviews, news documentaries, on-the-spot coverage of news events, and panel discussions, all sides of public controversies shall be given as equal an opportunity to be heard as is practically possible." 105 Cong. Rec. 14457.

for a response rather than to leave the response entirely within the control of the station which has attacked either the candidacies or the men who wish to reply in their own defense. When a broadcaster grants time to a political candidate, Congress itself requires that equal time be offered to his opponents. It would exceed our competence to hold that the Commission is unauthorized by the statute to employ a similar device where personal attacks or political editorials are broadcast by a radio or television station.

In light of the fact that the "public interest" in broadcasting clearly encompasses the presentation of vigorous debate of controversial issues of importance and concern to the public; the fact that the FCC has rested upon that language from its very inception a doctrine that these issues must be discussed, and fairly; and the fact that Congress has acknowledged that the analogous provisions of § 315 are not preclusive in this area, and knowingly preserved the FCC's complementary efforts, we think the fairness doctrine and its component personal attack and political editorializing regulations are a legitimate exercise of congressionally delegated authority. The Communications Act is not notable for the precision of its substantive standards and in this respect the explicit provisions of § 315, and the doctrine and rules at issue here which are closely modeled upon that section, are far more explicit than the generalized "public interest" standard in which the Commission ordinarily finds its sole guidance, and which we have held a broad but adequate standard before. *FCC* v. *RCA Communications, Inc.*, 346 U.S. 86, 90 (1953); *National Broadcasting Co.* v. *United States*, 319 U.S. 190, 216-217 (1943); *FCC* v. *Pottsville Broadcasting Co.*, 309 U.S. 134, 138 (1940); *FRC* v. *Nelson Bros. Bond & Mortgage Co.*, 289 U.S. 266, 285 (1933). We cannot say that the FCC's declaratory ruling in *Red Lion*, or the regulations at issue in *RTNDA*, are beyond the scope of the congressionally conferred power to assure that stations are operated by those whose possession of a license serves "the public interest."

III.

The broadcasters challenge the fairness doctrine and its specific manifestations in the personal attack and political editorial rules on conventional First Amendment grounds, alleging that the rules abridge their freedom of speech and press. Their contention is that the First Amendment protects their desire to use their allotted frequencies continuously to broadcast whatever they choose, and to exclude whomever they choose from ever using that frequency. No man may be prevented from saying or publishing what he thinks, or from refusing in his speech or other utterances to give equal weight to the views of his opponents. This right, they say, applies equally to broadcasters.

A.

Although broadcasting is clearly a medium affected by a First Amendment interest, *United States* v. *Paramount Pictures, Inc.*, 334 U.S. 131, 166 (1948), differences in the characteristics of new media justify differences in the First Amendment standards applied to them.[15] *Joseph Burstyn, Inc.* v. *Wilson*, 343 U.S. 495, 503 (1952). For example, the ability of new technology to produce sounds more raucous than those of the human voice justifies restrictions on the sound level, and on the hours and places of use, of sound trucks so long as the restrictions are reasonable and applied without discrimination. *Kovacs* v. *Cooper*, 336 U.S. 77 (1949).

Just as the Government may limit the use of sound-amplifying equipment potentially so noisy that it drowns out civilized private speech, so may the Government limit the use of broadcast equipment. The right of free speech of a broadcaster, the user of a sound truck, or any other individual does not embrace a right to snuff out the free speech of others. *Associated Press* v. *United States*, 326 U.S. 1, 20 (1945).

When two people converse face to face, both should not speak at once if either is to be clearly understood. But the range of the human voice is so limited that there could be meaningful communications if half the people in the United States were talking and the other half listening. Just as clearly, half the people might publish and the other half read. But the reach of radio signals is incomparably greater than the range of the human voice and the problem of interference is a massive reality. The lack of know-how and equipment may keep many from the air, but only a tiny fraction of those with resources and intelligence can hope to communicate by radio at the same time if intelligible communication is to be had, even if the entire radio spectrum is utilized in the present state of commercially acceptable technology.

It was this fact, and the chaos which ensued from permitting anyone to use any frequency at whatever power level he wished, which made necessary the

[15] The general problems raised by a technology which supplants atomized, relatively informal communication with mass media as a prime source of national cohesion and news were discussed at considerable length by Zechariah Chafee in Government and Mass Communications (1947). Debate on the particular implications of this view for the broadcasting industry has continued unabated. A compendium of views appears in Freedom and Responsibility in Broadcasting (J. Coons ed.) (1961). See also Kalven, Broadcasting, Public Policy and the First Amendment, 10 J. Law & Econ. 15 (1967); M. Ernst, The First Freedom, 125-180 (1946); T. Robinson, Radio Networks and the Federal Government, especially at 75-87 (1943). The considerations which the newest technology brings to bear on the particular problem of this litigation are concisely explored by Louis Jaffe in The Fairness Doctrine, Equal Time, Reply to Personal Attacks, and the Local Service Obligation; Implications of Technological Change, Printed for Special Subcommittee on Investigations of the House Committee on Interstate and Foreign Commerce (1968).

enactment of the Radio Act of 1927 and the Communications Act of 1934,[16] as the Court has noted at length before. *National Broadcasting Co.* v. *United States*, 319 U.S. 190, 210-214 (1943). It was this reality which at the very least necessitated first the division of the radio spectrum into portions reserved respectively for public broadcasting and for other important radio uses such as amateur operation, aircraft, police, defense, and navigation; and then the subdivision of each portion, and assignment of specific frequencies to individual users or groups of users. Beyond this, however, because the frequencies reserved for public broadcasting were limited in number, it was essential for the Government to tell some applicants that they could not broadcast at all because there was room for only a few.

Where there are substantially more individuals who want to broadcast than there are frequencies to allocate, it is idle to posit an unabridgeable First Amendment right to broadcast comparable to the right of every individual to speak, write, or publish. If 100 persons want broadcast licenses but there are only 10 frequencies to allocate, all of them may have the same "right" to a license; but if there is to be any effective communication by radio, only a few can be licensed and the rest must be barred from the airwaves. It would be strange if the First Amendment, aimed at protecting and furthering communications, prevented the Government from making radio communication possible by requiring licenses to broadcast and by limiting the number of licenses so as not to overcrowd the spectrum.

This has been the consistent view of the Court. Congress unquestionably has the power to grant and deny licenses and to eliminate existing stations. *FRC* v. *Nelson Bros. Bond & Mortgage Co.*, 289 U.S. 266 (1933). No one has a First Amendment right to a license or to monopolize a radio frequency; to deny a station license because "the public interest" requires it "is not a denial of free speech." *National Broadcasting Co.* v. *United States*, 319 U.S. 190, 227 (1943).

By the same token, as far as the First Amendment is concerned those who are licensed stand no better than those to whom licenses are refused. A license permits broadcasting, but the licensee has no constitutional right to be the one who holds the license or to monopolize a radio frequency to the exclusion of his fellow citizens. There is nothing in the First Amendment which prevents the Government from requiring a licensee to share his frequency with others and to conduct himself as a proxy or fiduciary with obligations to present those views and voices which are representative of his community and which would otherwise, by necessity, be barred from the airwaves.

This is not to say that the First Amendment is irrelevant to public broadcasting. On the contrary, it has a major role to play as the Congress itself

---

[16]The range of controls which have in fact been imposed over the last 40 years, without giving rise to successful constitutional challenge in this Court, is discussed in W. Emery, Broadcasting and Government: Responsibilities and Regulations (1961); Note, Regulation of Program Content by the FCC, 77 Harv. L. Rev. 701 (1964).

recognized in § 326, which forbids FCC interference with "the right of free speech by means of radio communication." Because of the scarcity of radio frequencies, the Government is permitted to put restraints on licensees in favor of others whose views should be expressed on this unique medium. But the people as a whole retain their interest in free speech by radio and their collective right to have the medium function consistently with the ends and purposes of the First Amendment. It is the right of the viewers and listeners, not the right of the broadcasters, which is paramount. See *FCC* v. *Sanders Bros. Radio Station*, 309 U.S. 470, 475 (1940); *FCC* v. *Allentown Broadcasting Corp.*, 349 U.S. 358, 361-362 (1955); 2 Z. Chafee, Government and Mass Communications 546 (1947). It is the purpose of the First Amendment to preserve an uninhibited marketplace of ideas in which truth will ultimately prevail, rather than to countenance monopolization of that market, whether it be by the Government itself or a private licensee. *Associated Press* v. *United States*, 326 U.S. 1, 20 (1945); *New York Times Co.* v. *Sullivan*, 376 U.S. 254, 270 (1964); *Abrams* v. *United States*, 250 U.S. 616, 630 (1919) (Holmes, J., dissenting). "[S]peech concerning public affairs is more than self-expression; it is the essence of self-government." *Garrison* v. *Louisiana*, 379 U.S. 64, 74-75 (1964). See Brennan, The Supreme Court and the Meiklejohn Interpretation of the First Amendment, 79 Harv. L. Rev. 1 (1965). It is the right of the public to receive suitable access to social, political, esthetic, moral, and other ideas and experiences which is crucial here. That right may not constitutionally be abridged either by Congress or by the FCC.

B.

Rather than confer frequency monopolies on a relatively small number of licensees, in a Nation of 200,000,000, the Government could surely have decreed that each frequency should be shared among all or some of those who wish to use it, each being assigned a portion of the broadcast day or the broadcast week. The ruling and regulations at issue here do not go quite so far. They assert that under specified circumstances, a licensee must offer to make available a reasonable amount of broadcast time to those who have a view different from that which has already been expressed on his station. The expression of a political endorsement, or of a personal attack while dealing with a controversial public issue, simply triggers this time sharing. As we have said, the First Amendment confers no right on licensees to prevent others from broadcasting on "their" frequencies and no right to an unconditional monopoly of a scarce resource which the Government has denied others the right to use.

In terms of constitutional principle, and as enforced sharing of a scarce resource, the personal attack and political editorial rules are indistinguishable from the equal-time provision of § 315, a specific enactment of Congress

Consider'g, 315+'d. are hard to distinguish [handwritten annotation]

requiring stations to set aside reply time under specified circumstances and to which the fairness doctrine and these constituent regulations are important complements. That provision, which has been part of the law since 1927, Radio Act of 1927, § 18, 44 Stat. 1170, has been held valid by this Court as an obligation of the licensee relieving him of any power in any way to prevent or censor the broadcast, and thus insulating him from liability for defamation. The constitutionality of the statute under the First Amendment was unquestioned.[17] *Farmer Educ. & Coop. Union* v. *WDAY*, 360 U.S. 525 (1959).

Nor can we say that it is inconsistent with the First Amendment goal of producing an informed public capable of conducting its own affairs to require a broadcaster to permit answers to personal attacks occurring in the course of discussing controversial issues, or to require that the political opponents of those endorsed by the station be given a chance to communicate with the public.[18] Otherwise, station owners and a few networks would have unfettered power to make time available only to the highest bidders, to communicate only their own views on public issues, people and candidates, and to permit on the air only those with whom they agreed. There is no sanctuary in the First Amendment for unlimited private censorship operating in a medium not open to all. "Freedom of the press from governmental interference under the First Amendment does not sanction repression of that freedom by private interests." *Associated Press* v. *United States*, 326 U.S. 1, 20 (1945).

C.

It is strenuously argued, however, that if political editorials or personal attacks will trigger an obligation in broadcasters to afford the opportunity for expression to speakers who need not pay for time and whose views are unpalatable to the licensees, then broadcasters will be irresistibly forced to

[17]This has not prevented vigorous argument from developing on the constitutionality of the ancillary FCC doctrines. Compare Barrow, The Equal Opportunities and Fairness Doctrines in Broadcasting: Pillars in the Forum of Democracy, 37 U. Cin. L. Rev. 447 (1968), with Robinson, The FCC and the First Amendment: Observations on 40 Years of Radio and Television Regulation, 52 Minn. L. Rev. 67 (1967), and Sullivan, Editorials and Controversy: The Broadcaster's Dilemma, 32 Geo. Wash. L. Rev. 719 (1964).

[18]The expression of views opposing those which broadcasters permit to be aired in the first place need not be confined solely to the broadcasters themselves as proxies. "Nor is it enough that he should hear the arguments of adversaries from his own teachers, presented as they state them, and accompanied by what they offer as refutations. That is not the way to do justice to the arguments, or bring them into real contact with his own mind. He must be able to hear them from persons who actually believe them; who defend them in earnest, and do their very utmost for them." J. Mill, On Liberty 32 (R. McCallum ed. 1947).

self-censorship and their coverage of controversial public issues will be eliminated or at least rendered wholly ineffective. Such a result would indeed be a serious matter, for should licensees actually eliminate their coverage of controversial issues, the purposes of the doctrine would be stifled.

At this point, however, as the Federal Communications Commission has indicated, that possibility is at best speculative. The communications industry, and in particular the networks, have taken pains to present controversial issues in the past, and even now they do not assert that they intend to abandon their efforts in this regard.[19]   It would be better if the FCC's encouragement were never necessary to induce the broadcasters to meet their responsibility. And if experience with the administration of these doctrines indicates that they have the net effect of reducing rather than enhancing the volume and quality of coverage, there will be time enough to reconsider the constitutional implications. The fairness doctrine in the past has had no such overall effect.

That this will occur now seems unlikely, however, since if present licensees should suddenly prove timorous, the Commission is not powerless to insist that they give adequate and fair attention to public issues. It does not violate the First Amendment to treat licensees given the privilege of using scarce radio frequencies as proxies for the entire community, obligated to give suitable time and attention to matters of great public concern. To condition the granting or renewal of licenses on a willingness to present representative community views on controversial issues is consistent with the ends and purposes of those constitutional provisions forbidding the abridgment of freedom of speech and freedom of the press. Congress need not stand idly by and permit those with licenses to ignore the problems which beset the people or to exclude from the airways anything but their own views of fundamental questions. The statute, long administrative practice, and cases are to this effect.

Licenses to broadcast do not confer ownership of designated frequencies, but only the temporary privilege of using them, 47 U.S.C. § 301. Unless renewed, they expire within three years. 47 U.S.C. § 307(d). The statute mandates the issuance of licenses if the "public convenience, interest, or necessity will be served thereby." 47 U.S.C. § 307(a). In applying this standard the Commission for 40 years has been choosing licensees based in part on their program proposals. In *FRC* v. *Nelson Bros. Bond & Mortgage Co.*, 289 U.S. 266, 279 (1933), the Court noted that in "view of the limited number of available broadcasting frequencies, the Congress has authorized allocation and licenses." In determining how best to allocate frequencies, the Federal Radio Commission

---

[19]The President of the Columbia Broadcasting System has recently declared that despite the Government, "we are determined to continue covering controversial issues as a public service, and exercising our own independent news judgment and enterprise. I, for one, refuse to allow that judgment and enterprise to be affected by official intimidation." F. Stanton, Keynote Address, Sigma Delta Chi National Convention, Atlanta, Georgia, November 21, 1968. Problems of news coverage from the broadcaster's viewpoint are surveyed in W. Wood, Electronic Journalism (1967).

considered the needs of competing communities and the programs offered by competing stations to meet those needs; moreover, if needs or programs shifted, the Commission could alter its allocations to reflect those shifts. *Id.*, at 285. In the same vein, in *FCC* v. *Pottsville Broadcasting Co.*, 309 U.S. 134, 137-138 (1940), the Court noted that the statutory standard was a supple instrument to effect congressional desires "to maintain . . . a grip on the dynamic aspects of radio transmission" and to allay fears that "in the absence of governmental control the public interest might be subordinated to monopolistic domination in the broadcasting field." Three years later the Court considered the validity of the Commission's chain broadcasting regulations, which among other things forbade stations from devoting too much time to network programs in order that there be suitable opportunity for local programs serving local needs. The Court upheld the regulations, unequivocally recognizing that the Commission was more than a traffic policeman concerned with the technical aspects of broadcasting and that it neither exceeded its powers under the statute nor transgressed the First Amendment in interesting itself in general program format and the kinds of programs broadcast by licensees. *National Broadcasting Co.* v. *United States*, 319 U.S. 190 (1943).

D.

The litigants embellish their First Amendment arguments with the contention that the regulations are so vague that their duties are impossible to discern. Of this point it is enough to say that, judging the validity of the regulations on their face as they are presented here, we cannot conclude that the FCC has been left a free hand to vindicate its own idiosyncratic conception of the public interest or of the requirements of free speech. Past adjudications by the FCC give added precision to the regulations; there was nothing vague about the FCC's specific ruling in *Red Lion* that Fred Cook should be provided an opportunity to reply. The regulations at issue in *RTNDA* could be employed in precisely the same way as the fairness doctrine was in *Red Lion*. Moreover, the FCC itself has recognized that the applicability of its regulations to situations beyond the scope of past cases may be questionable, 32 Fed. Reg. 10303, 10304 and n. 6, and will not impose sanctions in such cases without warning. We need not approve every aspect of the fairness doctrine to decide these cases, and we will not now pass upon the constitutionality of these regulations by envisioning the most extreme applications conceivable, *United States* v. *Sullivan*, 332 U.S. 689, 694 (1948), but will deal with those problems if and when they arise.

We need not and do not now ratify every past and future decision by the FCC with regard to programming. There is no question here of the Commission's refusal to permit the broadcaster to carry a particular program or to publish his own views; of a discriminatory refusal to require the licensee to broadcast certain views which have been denied access to the airwaves; of government censorship of a particular program contrary to § 326; or of the official government view dominating public broadcasting. Such questions would raise more serious First Amendment issues. But we do hold that the Congress and the Commission do not violate the First Amendment when they require a radio or television station to give reply time to answer personal attacks and political editorials.

E.

It is argued that even if at one time the lack of available frequencies for all who wished to use them justified the Government's choice of those who would best serve the public interest by acting as proxy for those who would present differing views, or by giving the latter access directly to broadcast facilities, this condition no longer prevails so that continuing control is not justified. To this there are several answers.

Scarcity is not entirely a thing of the past. Advances in technology, such as microwave transmission, have led to more efficient utilization of the frequency spectrum, but uses for that spectrum have also grown apace.[20] Portions of the spectrum must be reserved for vital uses unconnected with human communication, such as radio-navigational aids used by aircraft and vessels. Conflicts have even emerged between such vital functions as defense preparedness and experimentation in methods of averting midair collisions through radio warning devices.[21] "Land mobile services" such as police, ambulance, fire department, public utility, and other communications systems have been occupying an increasingly crowded portion of the frequency spectrum[22] and there are, apart from licensed amateur radio operators' equipment, 5,000,000 transmitters operated on the "citizens' band" which is also increasingly congested.[23] Among

---

[20]Current discussions of the frequency allocation problem appear in Telecommunication Science Panel, Commerce Technical Advisory Board, U.S. Dept. of Commerce, Electromagnetic Spectrum Utilization – The Silent Crisis (1966); Joint Technical Advisory Committee, Institute of Electrical and Electronics Engineers and Electronic Industries Assn., Report on Radio Spectrum Utilization (1964); Note, The Crisis in Electromagnetic Frequency Spectrum Allocation, 53 Iowa L. Rev. 437 (1967). A recently released study is the Final Report of the President's Task Force on Communications Policy (1968).

[21]*Bendix Aviation Corp.* v. *FCC*, 106 U.S. App. D.C. 304, 272 F.2d 533 (1959), cert. denied, 361 U.S. 965 (1960).

[22]1968 FCC Annual Report 65-69.

[23]New limitations on these users, who can also lay claim to First Amendment protection, were sustained against First Amendment attack with the comment, "Here is truly a situation where if everybody could say anything, many could say nothing." *Lafayette Radio Electronics Corp.* v. *United States*, 345 F. 2d 278, 281 (1965). Accord, *California Citizens Band Assn.* v. *United States*, 375 F. 2d 43 (C.A. 9th Cir.), cert. denied, 389 U.S. 844 (1967).

the various uses for radio frequency space, including marine, aviation, amateur, military, and common carrier users, there are easily enough claimants to permit use of the whole with an even smaller allocation to broadcast radio and television uses than now exists.

Comparative hearings between competing applicants for broadcast spectrum space are by no means a thing of the past. The radio spectrum has become so congested that at times it has been necessary to suspend new applications. [24] The very high frequency television spectrum is, in the country's major markets, almost entirely occupied, although space reserved for ultra high frequency television transmission, which is a relatively recent development as a commercially viable alternative, has not yet been completely filled. [25]

The rapidity with which technological advances succeed one another to create more efficient use of spectrum space on the one hand, and to create new uses for that space by ever growing numbers of people on the other, makes it unwise to speculate on the future allocation of that space. It is enough to say that the resource is one of considerable and growing importance whose scarcity impelled its regulation by an agency authorized by Congress. Nothing in this record, or in our own researches, convinces us that the resource is no longer one for which there are more immediate and potential uses than can be accom-

---

[24] *Kessler* v. *FCC*, 117 U.S. App. D.C. 130, 326 F. 2d 673 (1963).

[25] In a table prepared by the FCC on the basis of statistics current as of August 31, 1968, VHF and UHF channels allocated to and those available in the top 100 market areas for television are set forth:

COMMERCIAL

Market Areas	Channels Allocated		Channels On the Air, Authorized, or Applied for		Available Channels	
	VHF	UHF	VHF	UHF	VHF	UHF
Top 10	40	45	40	44	0	1
Top 50	157	163	157	136	0	27
Top 100	264	297	264	213	0	84

NONCOMMERCIAL

Market Areas	Channels Reserved		Channels On the Air, Authorized, or Applied for		Available Channels	
	VHF	UHF	VHF	UHF	VHF	UHF
Top 10	7	17	7	16	0	1
Top 50	21	79	20	47	1	32
Top 100	35	138	34	69	1	69

1968 FCC Annual Report 132–135.

modated, and for which wise planning is essential.[26] This does not mean, of course, that every possible wavelength must be occupied at every hour by some vital use in order to sustain the congressional judgment. The substantial capital investment required for many uses, in addition to the potentiality for confusion and interference inherent in any scheme for continuous kaleidoscopic re-allocation of all available space may make this unfeasible. The allocation need not be made at such a breakneck pace that the objectives of the allocation are themselves imperiled.[27]

Even where there are gaps in spectrum utilization, the fact remains that existing broadcasters have often attained their present position because of their initial government selection in competition with others before new technological advances opened new opportunities for further uses. Long experience in broadcasting, confirmed habits of listeners and viewers, network affiliation, and other advantages in program procurement give existing broadcasters a substantial advantage over new entrants, even where new entry is technologically possible. These advantages are the fruit of a preferred position conferred by the Government. Some present possibility for new entry by competing stations is not enough, in itself, to render unconstitutional the Government's effort to assure that a broadcaster's programming ranges widely enough to serve the public interest.

In view of the scarcity of broadcast frequencies, the Government's role in allocating those frequencies, and the legitimate claims of those unable without governmental assistance to gain access to those frequencies for expression of

[26]RTNDA argues that these regulations should be held invalid for failure of the FCC to make specific findings in the rule-making proceeding relating to these factual questions. Presumably the fairness doctrine and the personal attack decisions themselves, such as *Red Lion*, should fall for the same reason. But this argument ignores the fact that these regulations are no more than the detailed specification of certain consequences of long-standing rules, the need for which was recognized by the Congress on the factual predicate of scarcity made plain in 1927, recognized by this Court in the 1943 *National Broadcasting Co.* case, and reaffirmed by the Congress as recently as 1959. "If the number of radio and television stations were not limited by available frequencies, the committee would have no hesitation in removing completely the present provision regarding equal time and urge the right of each broadcaster to follow his own conscience . . . However, broadcast frequencies are limited and, therefore, they have been necessarily considered a public trust." S. Rep. No. 562, 86th Cong., 1st Sess., 8-9 (1959). In light of this history; the opportunity which the broadcasters have had to address the FCC and show that somehow the situation had radically changed, undercutting the validity of the congressional judgment; and their failure to adduce any convincing evidence of that in the record here, we cannot consider the absence of more detailed findings below to be determinative.

[27]The "airwaves [need not] be filled at the earliest possible moment in all circumstances without due regard for these important factors." *Community Broadcasting Co.* v. *FCC*, 107 U.S. App. D.C. 95, 105, 274 F. 2d 753, 763 (1960). Accord, enforcing the fairness doctrine, *Office of Communication of the United Church of Christ* v. *FCC*, 123 U.S. App. D.C. 328, 343, 359 F. 2d 994, 1009 (1966).

their views, we hold the regulations and ruling at issue here are
by statute and constitutional.[28] The judgment of the Court o
Lion is affirmed and that in *RTNDA* reversed and the caus
proceedings consistent with this opinion.

Not having heard oral argument in these cases, Mr. Justice _ _ _ _ _ _ _ _ _
part in the Court's decision.

---

[28]We need not deal with the argument that even if there is no longer a technological scarcity
of frequencies limiting the number of broadcasters, there nevertheless is an economic
scarcity in the sense that the Commission could or does limit entry to the broadcasting
market on economic grounds and license no more stations than the market will support.
Hence, it is said, the fairness doctrine or its equivalent is essential to satisfy the claims of
those excluded and of the public generally. A related argument, which we also put aside,
is that quite apart from scarcity of frequencies, technological or economic, Congress does
not abridge freedom of speech or press by legislation directly or indirectly multiplying the
voices and views presented to the public through time sharing, fairness doctrines, or other
devices which limit or dissipate the power of those who sit astride the channels of
communication with the general public. Cf. *Citizen Publishing Co.* v. *United States*, 394
U.S. 131 (1969).

7

APPLICATION OF THE FAIRNESS
DOCTRINE TO ADVERTISING

During an era of growing consumer activism, the FCC, in 1967, held that health aspects of cigarette smoking constituted a controversial issue of public importance to which the "Fairness Doctrine" applied (8 FCC 2d 381). Thus, broadcasters who accepted cigarette advertising were required to "provide a significant amount of time for the other viewpoint." The FCC elaborated its position in 9 FCC 2d 921 (1967) when broadcasters and the Tobacco Institute petitioned for reconsideration.

There followed a dizzying series of events: the Court of Appeals upheld the Commission's decision on general public interest grounds (405 F.2d 1082 (1968)); the Supreme Court refused to review the case (396 U.S. 842 (1969)); the FCC proposed to bar cigarette ads entirely (16 FCC 2d 284 (1969)); the National Association of Broadcasters urged that self-regulation would effect a gradual phase-out of such ads; Congress banned all broadcast cigarette advertising effective January 2, 1971 (Public Law 91-222 (1970)); the FCC determined that in the absence of cigarette commercials, smoking was no longer a matter to which it would mandate application of the "Fairness Doctrine" (27 FCC 2d 453 (1970)). The net result seemed to be confusion about the doctrine and the loss to broadcasters of more than 200 million dollars annually in tobacco advertising. As for cigarette consumption, it was virtually unaffected.

The FCC's reluctance to apply the doctrine to other types of commercial advertising was upset in 1971 by the Court of Appeals in the *Friends of the Earth* case (449 F.2d 1164). The Commission complied with the court's remand in 1972 (33 FCC 2d 648), but the proceeding was terminated a year later (39 FCC 2d 564 (1973)) by mutual agreement of the parties.

434

A

LETTER FROM FEDERAL

COMMUNICATIONS COMMISSION TO

TELEVISION STATION WCBS-TV

8 FCC 2d 381
June 2, 1967

FEDERAL COMMUNICATIONS COMMISSION
Washington 25, D.C.
June 2, 1967

Television Station WCBS-TV
51 West 52 Street
New York, New York.

Gentlemen:

This letter constitutes the Commission's ruling upon the complaint of Mr. John F. Banzhaf, III, against Station WCBS-TV, New York, N.Y. Mr. Banzhaf, by letter dated January 5, 1967, filed a fairness doctrine complaint, asserting that WCBS-TV, after having aired numerous commercial advertisements for cigarette manufacturers, has not afforded him or some other responsible spokesman an opportunity "to present contrasting views on the issue of the benefits and advisability of smoking."

Mr. Banzhaf's letter cites as examples three particular commercials over WCBS-TV which present the point of view that smoking is "socially acceptable and desirable, manly, and a necessary part of a rich full life." Mr. Banzhaf, in his letter to you of December 1, 1966, requested free time be made available to "responsible groups" roughly approximate to that spent on the promotion of "the virtues and values of smoking."

Your responsive letter of December 30, 1966, cites programs which WCBS-TV has broadcast dealing with the effect of smoking on health, beginning in September 1962 and continuing to date. It cites six reports on this issue in its evening news programs since May 1966, five major reports by its Science Editor since September 1966 and five one minute messages, which advance the view that smoking is undesirable, broadcast without charge within the last few months for the American Cancer Society. The letter also refers to half hour and hour programs on smoking and health broadcast in 1962 and 1964. You take the position that the above programs have provided contrasting viewpoints on this issue by responsible authorities, and therefore, that it is unnecessary to consider whether the "fairness doctrine" may be applied to commercial announcements solely aimed at selling products. You state your view that it may not.

In Mr. Banzhaf's complaint to the Commission, he asserts that the programs cited by you as showing compliance with the "fairness doctrine" are insufficient to offset the effects of paid advertisements broadcast daily for a total of five to ten minutes each broadcast day. He also states that the very point of his letters is to establish the applicability of the doctrine to cigarette advertisements.

We hold that the fairness doctrine is applicable to such advertisements. We stress that our holding is limited to this product — cigarettes. Governmental and private reports (e.g., the 1964 Report of the Surgeon General's Committee) and Congressional action (e.g., the Federal Cigarette Labeling and Advertising Act of 1965) assert that normal use of this product can be a hazard to the health of millions of persons. The advertisements in question clearly promote the use of a particular cigarette as attractive and enjoyable. Indeed, they understandably have no other purpose. We believe that a station which presents such advertisements has the duty of informing its audience of the other side of this controversial issue of public importance — that however enjoyable, such smoking may be a hazard to the smoker's health.

We reject, however, Mr. Banzhaf's claim that the time to be afforded "roughly approximate" that devoted to the cigarette commercials. The fairness doctrine does not require "equal time" (see Ruling No. II C. 12, 29 F.R. 10416) and, equally important, a requirement of such "rough approximation" would, we think, be inconsistent with the Congressional direction in this field — the 1965 Cigarette Labeling and Advertising Act. The practical result of any roughly one-to-one correlation would probably be either the elimination or substantial curtailment of broadcast cigarette advertising. But in the 1965 Act Congress made clear that it did not favor such a "drastic" step, but rather wished to afford an opportunity to consider "the combined impact of voluntary limitations on advertising under the Cigarette Advertising Code, the extensive smoking education campaigns now underway, and the compulsory warning on the package . . . [on the problem of] adequately alert[ing] the public to the potential hazard from smoking" (Sen. Rept. No. 195, 89th Cong., 1st Sess., p. 5). At the conclusion of a three year period (to end July 1, 1969), and upon the basis of reports from the Federal Trade Commission and the Department of Health, Education, and Welfare (HEW) and other pertinent sources, the Congress would then decide what further remedial action, if any, is appropriate. In the meantime, Congress has promoted extensive smoking education campaigns by appropriating substantial sums for HEW in this area. See P.L. 89-156, Title II, Public Health Service, Chronic Diseases and Health of the Aged.

Our action here, therefore, must be tailored so as to carry out the above Congressional purpose. We believe that it does. It requires a station which carries cigarette commercials to provide a significant amount of time for the other viewpoint, thus implementing the "smoking education campaigns" referred to as a basis for Congressional action in the 1965 Act. See Cigarette Labeling and Advertising Act; remarks of Senator Warren Magnuson, floor manager in the Senate of the bill which became that Act, Cong. Rec. (Daily Edition) Jan. 16, 1967, p. S. 317, 319. But this requirement will not preclude or curtail presentation by stations of cigarette advertising which they choose to carry.

A station might, for example, reasonably determine that the above noted responsibility would be discharged by presenting each week, in addition to appropriate news reports or other programming dealing with the subject, a number of the public service announcements of the American Cancer Society or HEW in this field. We stress, however, that in this, as in other areas under the fairness doctrine, the type of programming and the amount and nature of time to be afforded is a matter for the good faith, reasonable judgment of the licensee, upon the particular facts of his situation. See Cullman Broadcasting Co., F.C.C. 63-849 (Sept. 18, 1963).

In this case, we note that WCBS-TV is aware of its responsibilities in this area, in light of the programming described in the third paragraph. While we have rejected Mr. Banzhaf's claim of "rough approximation of time," the question remains whether in the circumstances a sufficient amount of time is being allocated each week to cover the viewpoint of the health hazard posed by smoking. We note in this respect that, particularly in light of the recent American Cancer Society announcements, you appear to have a continuing program in this respect. The guidelines in the foregoing discussion are brought to your attention so that in connection with the above continuing program you may make the judgment whether sufficient time is being allocated each week in this area.

By Direction of the Commission
Ben F. Waple
Secretary

B

THE FRIENDS OF THE EARTH CASE

Friends of the Earth v.
Federal Communications Commission*
449 F. 2d 1164 (D.C. Cir.)
August 16, 1971

McGowan, Circuit Judge:

Petitioners in this statutory review proceeding attack the dismissal by the Federal Communications Commission, without hearing or oral argument, of their fairness doctrine complaint in respect of Station WNBC-TV in New York City. The issue raised is that of the reach of the fairness doctrine in relation to product advertising, in this instance automobile and gasoline commercials. For the reasons hereinafter appearing, we think that the Commission erred in concluding that the advertising in question did not present a point of view favorable to one side of a controversial issue of public importance; and we remand for reconsideration and further inquiry by the Commission to determine whether the licensee has been adequately discharging its public service obligations by carrying a reasonable amount of information on the other side of the question, or whether it must take further positive actions, differing in either kind or degree from what it has been doing, in order to achieve the balance contemplated by the fairness doctrine.

I

On February 6, 1970, petitioners[1] wrote a letter to WNBC-TV, complaining of the "spot advertisements for automobile and gasoline companies [which]

---

*Reprinted with the permission of West Publishing Company © 1972.

[1] The individual petitioner is a resident of New York City who serves as executive director of Friends of the Earth, the other petitioner herein. The latter is a national organization dedicated to the protection and preservation of the environment. Its headquarters are in New York City.

constantly bombard the New York area viewers with pitches for large-engine and high-test gasolines which are generally described as efficient, clean, socially responsible, and automotively necessary." Petitioners referred to the following commercials as having been selected at random in the weeks immediately preceding their letter:

(1)   January 26, 1970, 8:15 p.m., 30 sec., an advertisement for Ford Mustang, picturing the car on a lonely beach, and stressing its "performance" (large engine displacement);

(2)   Same date, 8:45 p.m., 30 sec., an advertisement for Ford Torino stressing size;

(3)   January 22, 1970, 6:51 p.m., 30 sec., an advertisement for Chevrolet Impala stressing the great value of its size ("you don't have to be a big spender to be a big rider"), including the standard 250-horsepower V-8 engine;

(4)   January 5, 1970, 8:05 p.m., 30 sec., an advertisement for Ford Mustang and Torino GT, again stressing size ("4-barrel, V-8" and "up to 429 cubic inches") and advocating "moving up to" a larger car;

(5)   December 10, 1969, 11:15 p.m., encouraging the use of high-test leaded gasoline for cold-weather starting ("the cold-weather gasoline").

Petitioners asserted, contrarily, that these products were especially heavy contributors to air pollution, which had become peculiarly oppressive and dangerous in New York City; and that they fell within the reach of the decisions of the Commission and of this court on cigarette advertising. Banzhaf v. FCC, 132 U.S. App. D.C. 14, 405 F. 2d 1082 (1968), cert. denied *sub nom.*, Tobacco Institute v. FCC, 396 U.S. 842, 90 S.Ct. 50, 24 L.Ed. 2d 93 (1969). Petitioners noted that, just as the Commission in the case of cigarette advertising relied heavily upon the report of the Surgeon General's Advisory Committee, so had the Surgeon General, in his 1962 report on "Motor Vehicles, Air Pollution and Health," concluded that automobile emissions offer significant dangers to human health and survival — a conclusion reiterated by a more recent report issued by the National Academy of Science and the National Academy of Engineering. Reference was also made to the 1969 report of Mayor Lindsay's Task Force on Air Pollution, which said that "[T]he best way to cut down on dangerous hydrocarbons in the air is to cut down on horsepower."

Thus, so it was said, the treatment by the communications media of the relationship of air pollution to automobiles occurs in the context of a public controversy in which government officials and professional and lay people concerned about health are pitted against the automobile manufacturers and the oil companies, and presents a situation to which the fairness doctrine applies.[2]

---

[2] The origins and nature of the fairness doctrine are comprehensively described in Red Lion Broadcasting Co., Inc. v. FCC, 395 U.S. 367 (1969), especially at pp. 375-386, 89 S.Ct. 1794, 23 L.Ed.2d 371.

Petitioners asked that the licensee "promptly make known the ways in which it intends to discharge its responsibility to inform the public of the other side of this critical controversy;" and, although asserting financial inability to purchase time, offered to produce and make available to the licensee spot advertisements presenting the anti-auto-pollution case. Petitioners indicated that, if a satifactory response was not forthcoming, complaint would be made to the Commission.

On February 18, the licensee replied. It took the position that the Commission's tobacco decision was limited by its terms to cigarette advertising, and that it did not, in the Commission's words in that decision, impose any fairness doctrine obligation "with respect to other product advertising." Further, said the licensee, there is no real controversy about whether transportation by automobile should continue and that, therefore, the advertising of automobiles and of the fuels which propel them is not related to any controversial issue of public importance. Finally, the licensee referred to a number of programs presented by it in which the problem of air pollution by automobiles had been discussed; and it suggested that this represented an adequate discharge of any public interest obligation it had to inform its viewers on this subject.

On March 14 petitioners wrote a letter to the Commission, attaching the foregoing exchange of correspondence with the licensee and lodging a formal complaint against WNBC-TV "for failure to fulfill its 'fairness doctrine' and 'public interest' obligations with respect to automobile and gasoline advertisements." Petitioners urged upon the Commission the applicability of its cigarette advertising decision to other health hazards, and to the increasing recognition by governmental and other experts that carbon monoxide pollution caused by automobiles had become a serious and substantial danger to health, particularly in New York City. They reasserted their contentions that the large-car and high-powered gasoline advertisements carried by the licensee were designed to promote the idea that these products presented no health hazards in fact. They also contended that the discussion programs cited by the licensee were no adequate offset to the many spot commercials which were aired repeatedly throughout the broadcast hours, including the times of maximum viewing. It was the petitioners' request of the Commission that "this complaint be investigated and that necessary and appropriate action be taken to bring WNBC-TV into compliance with the requirements of the Federal Communications Act."

This letter of complaint was supplemented on April 7 by a letter to the Commission from counsel for the petitioners in which the Commission's attention was drawn to the recently enacted National Environmental Policy Act of 1969, Public Law 91-190, 83 Stat. 852. Counsel pointed out that in this new statute Congress had emphasized the "critical importance of restoring and maintaining environmental quality," and had authorized and directed government agencies to advance these ends and to interpret and administer "the policies, regulations, and public laws of the United States . . . in accordance with the policies set forth in this Act." Counsel referred to the underlying report of the Senate Committee which indicated that this mandate was intended to extend to "the licensing functions of independent agencies as well as the ongoing activities of regular Federal agencies." S. Rep. No. 91-296, 91st Cong., 1st Sess. 14 (1969).

On June 20 the Environmental Protection Administration of the City of New York addressed a letter to the Commission in support of the petitioners' complaint. It described air pollution conditions in New York City, and asserted that they were presenting an increasingly serious danger to health. A similar supporting letter was sent to the Commission by Citizens for Clean Air, Inc., a New York membership corporation organized for the purpose of educating the citizens of the New York metropolitan area in the hazards of air pollution and the effective means of alleviating it. It pointed out that, although serious suggestions were currently being made for the prohibition of automobiles in Manhattan, the commercials in question were urging the use of cars of ever larger horsepower, thereby compounding the problem. This letter urged that the Commission conduct hearings "for the purpose of developing facts adequate to resolve the serious questions which have been raised"; and it indicated a wish to present testimony in any such hearings.

On June 13 the licensee wrote a letter to the Commission in which it reiterated its contention that the content of the commercials complained of did not constitute a discussion of the pollution issue. It also listed by title a number of programs carried by it which it characterized as a more than adequate discharge by it of any duty it may have had to inform the public of the anti-pollution viewpoint.

Counsel for the petitioners responded to this letter on June 30 in a letter which, among other things, described the ever-growing health hazard in New York City by reason of automobile-produced air pollution and challenged the claim by the licensee that its public service programs adequately countered the effect of the automobile and gasoline spot advertisements complained of. It asked the Commission to examine actual transcripts of the programs cited by the licensee as fulfilling its public interest obligations, and asserted that such an examination would demonstrate that a substantial gap remained in the licensee's presentation of the conflicting positions with respect to automotive pollution of the air.[3]

In a letter to petitioners dated August 5, 1970, the Commission reviewed the contentions made in the foregoing correspondence and reported its conclusion that "no action is warranted against WNBC." It recognized that automobiles "result in many deaths each year and because their gasoline engines constitute the main source of air pollution (S. Rep. No. 91-745, 91st Cong. 2d Sess. 3 (1970)), they raise most serious environmental problems." This was, however, said to be true of "a host of other products or services — detergents

---

[3]Petitioners professed difficulty in seeing how "The World of the Beaver" and "The Great Barrier Reef" programs, cited by the licensee, had much relevance to the problem of the pollution of the air in New York City by automobiles.

(particularly with phosphates), gasoline (especially of a leaded nature), electric power, airplanes, disposable containers, etc." Cigarettes, said the Commission, are distinguishable from products of this nature, since smoking them is a habit "which can fade away" without impact upon other aspects of life, and which official voices have urged the public to avoid or to abandon. Contrarily, the Government is not urging discontinuance of the use of automobiles, although it is beginning to recognize that far-reaching action must be taken to accommodate the impact of automobiles upon the environment. The Commission asserted that the focus should probably be on such action and "not [on] the peripheral advertising aspect."

The Commission represented itself as being without power to take the kind of action which could solve or alleviate the air pollution problems caused by the use of automobiles. That was a matter about which it was not expert, and which falls within the competence of other agencies of the Government. The Commission also stated that there was a threshold issue as to whether the commercials complained of did in fact present one side of a controversial issue. It purported not to have the information available to exercise judgment on the question of whether the differences in the amount of time respectively involved in the advertising of large and small cars is sufficiently great to call for further time to be afforded to the side taken by petitioners. "We have," said the Commission, "no such information before us, but we decline in any event to extend the cigarette advertising ruling to these other products." It stated its belief to be that "we should adhere to our previous judgment that cigarettes are a unique product permitting the simplistic approach adopted in that field."

The Commission went on to say that, even if it be assumed to be wrong in that belief, it would not extend the cigarette ruling "generally to the field of product advertising." To do so would, said the Commission, "undermine the present system which is based on product commercials, many of which have some adverse ecological effects." It justified this conclusion by pointing to the fact that a licensee had a public interest obligation to provide discussions of the environmental issues affected by some of the advertised products, although it did not address itself to the content and volume of the programs relied upon by the licensee as discharging its obligations or make any findings in this regard. It thought that the approach of regulating product advertising is one which Congress could take, but, in the absence of action by Congress, the Commission should stay its hand.

II

In this court the Commission asserted that "[T]he crucial issue in this case is whether the Commission reasonably refused to extend to gasoline and automobile commercials its ruling with respect to cigarette commercials." We have no difficulty in accepting this formulation of the issue, involving as it does a comparison of the record before us with that before the Commission and this court in *Banzhaf*.

The complainant in *Banzhaf* brought to the Commission's attention certain specific commercials which allegedly sought "to create the impression and present the point of view that smoking is socially acceptable and desirable, manly, and a necessary part of a rich full life." It was urged upon the Commission that such commercials took one side of a controversial issue of public importance, and that, under the fairness doctrine, the licensee was required affirmatively to make its facilities available for contrasting viewpoints. The licensee in *Banzhaf* represented that it had in fact broadcast a number of news and information programs about the impact of smoking upon health, and had carried some public service announcements of the American Cancer Society free of charge. Thus, said the licensee, its coverage of the health aspects of smoking had actually been in full compliance with the fairness doctrine, although it went on to insist that the fairness doctrine had no application to product advertising.

The Commission accepted the complainant's characterization of the cigarette commercials in question as presenting a distinct point of view on a controversial matter of public importance; and it regarded this as bringing the fairness doctrine into operation. The Commission did not require the licensee to provide a precisely equal amount of time for the anti-smoking position, and it left this matter of time and the type of programming to the good faith judgment of the licensee. It did, however, expressly direct licensees carrying cigarette commercials to provide "a significant amount of time for the other viewpoint." The vigorous challenge made in this court to the Commission's ruling did not prevail, and we upheld the Commission's action as against the many-faceted attack mounted against it in the tobacco case.

Petitioners' letter of complaint to the Commission in the case presently before us called attention to certain commercials of the licensee which allegedly suggested that there were special virtues in cars of greater rather than lesser horsepower, and in gasolines of the high-test, leaded character. As the petitioners said in concluding their letter to the licensee, all of these advertisements, in a manner reminiscent of the themes sounded in the cigarette advertisements, "imply that the good life is somehow inexorably connected with the use of powerful cars and high-test gasoline." For this reason, it was said, these particular commercials reflected a point of view on the merits of the use of larger cars and more powerful fuels which, in the context of the current concern about the danger of air pollution to health, invoked the fairness doctrine.

No more than in *Banzhaf* did the Commission here deny the existence or the persuasiveness of expert evidence, from both official and private quarters, of the very real dangers to health presented by air pollution, and the significant degree to which automobile emissions both create and aggravate the air pollution problem. To this point, therefore, the pattern of the problem unfolding before the Commission and its response to it are very like that in *Banzhaf*. Where the Commission departs from *Banzhaf* is in insisting that, because cigarettes are unique in the threat they present to human health, the public interest considerations which caused it to reach the result it did in *Banzhaf* have no force here.

The distinction is not apparent to us, any more than we suppose it is to the asthmatic in New York City for whom increasing air pollution is a mortal danger. Neither are we impressed by the Commission's assertion that, because no governmental agency has as yet urged the complete abandonment of the use of automobiles, the commercials in question do not touch upon a controversial issue of public importance. Matters of degree arise in environmental control, as in other areas of legal regulation. To say that all automobiles pollute the atmosphere is not to say that some do not pollute more than others. Voices have already been lifted against the fetish of unnecessary horsepower; and some gasoline refiners have begun to make a virtue of necessity by extolling their non-leaded, less dynamic, brands of gasoline. Commercials which continue to insinuate that the human personality finds greater fulfillment in the large car with the quick getaway do, it seems to us, ventilate a point of view which not only has become controversial but involves an issue of public importance. When there is undisputed evidence, as there is here, that the hazards to health implicit in air pollution are enlarged and aggravated by such products, then the parallel with cigarette advertising is exact and the relevance of *Banzhaf* inescapable.

In its *Banzhaf* ruling the Commission was at great pains to warn that it did not contemplate its extention to product advertising generally; and the Commission's action now under review reflects, more than anything else, a purpose to make good on that representation. But the Commission has since been obliged to moderate its view that commercial advertising, apart from cigarettes, is immune from the fairness doctrine. On May 12 last it issued its ruling (FCC 71-526) in the so-called *Chevron* case where complaint had been made of gasoline commercials which allegedly made deceptive and misleading claims with respect to the product's capacity to minimize air pollution.

The Commission decided to take no action in *Chevron* because (1) the commercials there in question, far from suggesting that automobile emissions do not contribute significantly to the dangers of air pollution, urged that the gasoline being advertised was designed to reduce those dangers, and (2) the commercials were the subject of a pending Federal Trade Commission proceeding on a charge of false and deceptive advertising. In this context the Commission did not think that the purposes of the fairness doctrine were served by making it the occasion for a debate with respect to the efficacy of a commercial product. Of the applicability of the doctrine generally, however, the Commission said:

This is not to say that a product commercial cannot argue a controversial issue raising fairness responsibilities. For example, if an announcement sponsored by a coal-mining company asserted that strip mining had no harmful ecological results, the sponsor would be engaging directly in debate on a controversial issue, and fairness obligations would ensue. Or, if a community were in dispute over closing a factory emitting noxious fumes and an advertisement for a product made in the factory argued that question, fairness would also come into play.

On June 30 last, the Commission in the so-called *Esso* case (FCC 71-704) sustained a fairness doctrine complaint which it thought to come within the range of these examples. Complaint had been made about commercials sponsored by Standard Oil Company of New Jersey which related to the development of oil reserves in Alaska, and which were said "to discuss one side of controversial issues of public importance, namely (1) the need of developing Alaskan oil reserves quickly and (2) the capability of the oil companies to develop and transport that oil without environmental damage." The licensee took the position that the commercials in question were institutional advertising which did not involve any controversial issue of public importance. The Commission held that this approach was unreasonable, and that the fairness doctrine was triggered by the commercials in issue.

Having decided that the fairness doctrine applied, the Commission then turned in *Esso* to the claim by the licensee that other programs carried by it were fully adequate to present the contrary side of the question. The Commission concluded that, on the basis of the information before it, it could not find that the programs cited by the licensee "afforded reasonable opportunity for the presentation of contrasting views to those presented in the commercials. . . ." The licensee was, accordingly, directed to submit within 10 days a statement indicating what additional material it had, or intended to, broadcast in order to satisfy its obligations under the fairness doctrine.

It is obvious that the Commission is faced with great difficulties in tracing a coherent pattern for the accommodation of product advertising to the fairness doctrine. It has said as much in the closing paragraphs of the *Chevron* decision, where it announced its purpose to initiate in the near future a wide ranging inquiry which "will permit a thorough re-examination and re-thinking of the broader issues suggested by this and other recent cases before us. . . ." We do not, of course, anticipate what the result of that proceeding will prove to be, nor do we minimize either the seriousness or the thorny nature of the problems to be explored therein. Pending, however, a reformulation of its position, we are unable to see how the Commission can plausibly differentiate the case presently before us from *Banzhaf* insofar as the applicability of the fairness doctrine is concerned.

It is true that fairness doctrine obligations can be met by public service programs which do give reasonable vent to points of view contrary to those reflected in the offending commercials. The Commission recognized this principle in the decision now under review, and noted that the licensee had listed programs carried by it as allegedly discharging this responsibility. The Commission, however, explicitly restricted the basis of its ruling to the inapplicability of the fairness doctrine; and it did not regard as being before it for decision the question of whether the licensee had otherwise met its fairness obligations. It indicated that this was a matter which was properly to be explored at license renewal time.

The fairness doctrine does not, of course, operate on that kind of a time schedule, as the Commission's most recent decision in the *Esso* case demonstrates. There, once the Commission found the fairness doctrine to be applicable, it directed its attention to the question of whether compliance had in effect been forthcoming by virtue of other programs aired by the licensee. Since the information before it on this point was scanty, the Commission was compelled to find the programs cited as falling short of an adequate presentation of contrasting views. It did, however, give the licensee an opportunity within 10 days to submit further information on this score.

The disposition we make here follows the *Esso* approach. Having found this case indistinguishable from *Banzhaf* in the reach of the fairness doctrine, and being without the benefit of an express finding by the Commission on the question of the possible satisfaction of that doctrine by the licensee through the medium of other programs, we remand the case to the Commission for determination by it of this second issue.[4]

It is so ordered.

Wilbur K. Miller, Senior Circuit Judge, would affirm.

[4] In Green v. FCC and G.I. Association v. FCC, – U.S. App. D.C.–, 447 F.2d 323 (decided June 18, 1971), this court left undisturbed the Commission's disallowance of a fairness doctrine complaint about military recruitment advertisements. There, however, the petitioners persisted in linking their complaints about the advertisements to the controversial issues of the Vietnam War and the draft; and the Commission found expressly that the licensees had not "failed to treat the issues of Vietnam and the draft (both concededly controversial issues of public importance) in conformance with the fairness doctrine."

8

"THE SELLING OF THE PENTAGON"

In Re Complaint Concerning the CBS Program "The Selling
of the Pentagon"
30 FCC 2d 150
April 28, 1971

Few television public affairs documentaries have caused as much
controversy as "CBS Reports: The Selling of the Pentagon."
Many lauded the program as an example of bold investigative
journalism, but others thought it to be a "calculated deception."
When the Columbia Broadcasting System refused to comply with
a congressional subpoena requiring the submission of outtakes and
other materials not actually seen on the broadcast, CBS and its
president, Frank Stanton, became the subjects of a contempt of
Congress citation which the House of Representatives ultimately
refused to pass.

Representative Harley O. Staggers, Chairman of the Special
Subcommittee on Investigations of the House Committee on
Interstate and Foreign Commerce, sent a letter of complaint to
the FCC during his subcommittee's inquiry. The Commission's
reply, below, reflects the cautious ambivalence with which a
government licensing agency must approach such delicate First
Amendment and public interest questions as alleged news slanting
by broadcast journalists.

CBS subsequently demonstrated to the FCC's satisfaction
that it had complied with the "Fairness Doctrine" with respect
to "The Selling of the Pentagon." The network also issued an
internal directive requiring that interviews and speeches forming
parts of news and public affairs documentaries be treated in such
a manner as to avoid the substance and appearance of distortion
through editorial manipulation.

April 28, 1971.

Dear Mr. Chairman:

This is in response to your letter of March 9, 1971, in which you register a complaint concerning the CBS news documentary, "The Selling of the Pentagon." You ask "what action the Commission will take" in light of allegations by Assistant Secretary of Defense Daniel Z. Henkin that his answers to questions posed by CBS newsman Roger Mudd had been so edited and rearranged as to misrepresent their content, and that a statement was attributed to a Marine colonel "when, in fact, the officer was reading a quotation of the Prime Minister of Laos." You also enclose a letter to Dr. Frank Stanton, President of CBS, asking for comment on Mr. Henkin's allegations and on techniques of editing whereby "through the editing process, answers to questions may easily be curtailed or rearranged . . . and [made] to appear to have been given in response to different questions." Similar inquiries and complaints were also received from Chairman Hébert of the House Armed Services Committee, from other members of the Congress, and from the public.

Taken together, two principal questions have thus been raised: (1) whether CBS adhered to the requirements of the fairness doctrine to afford reasonable opportunity for the presentation of contrasting viewpoints on issues of public importance covered in the program; and (2) whether CBS slanted or deliberately distorted its presentation of persons interviewed on the program. As to (1), we note that CBS presented an hour-long news special on April 18 for the stated purpose of affording an opportunity for the presentation of contrasting viewpoints on the issues of substance raised in the original program. The Commission, however, is still requesting the comments of CBS as to whether it has complied with the requirements of the fairness doctrine in this matter. A copy of the letter is attached. In this Statement, therefore, the Commission will address question (2) above.

The Factual Record

On February 23 and again on March 23, in the documentary at issue, the CBS network stated that the Department of Defense would spend $30 million this year in "public relations funds not merely to inform but to convince and persuade the public on vital issues of war and peace."

The original broadcast aroused controversy as inquiries and complaints to this Commission have attested. As a consequence, following the March 23 rebroadcast, CBS ran a series of edited film clips of critical comments derived from previous addresses and interviews by Vice President Agnew, Secretary Laird, and Chairman Hébert, plus a rebuttal by Mr. Richard Salant, President of CBS News.

The controversy has focused on two aspects of "The Selling of the

Pentagon" in particular, and the essential facts are not really in dispute. One concerns a film-clip from an address delivered by Colonel MacNeil at a symposium held in Peoria, Illinois,[1] featuring presentations by what CBS described as "the traveling colonels" (military and civilian spokesmen supplied, on request, to local civic and professional organizations). As far as the viewer could tell — and neither Colonel MacNeil nor CBS made it clear — the speaker seemed to be affirming the "domino theory" as applied to Southeast Asian nations under Communist pressure, although as the printed transcript shows he was in fact quoting the Prime Minister of Laos to this effect. Later in the course of his remarks, Col. MacNeil did return to the "domino theory" and he did affirm it in virtually the same words as the Laotian Prime Minister. As Mr. Salant observed in his March 23 rebuttal, it was "difficult to tell where Souvanna Phouma left off and the Colonel started."

The other aspect of principal controversy concerns an interview between Mr. Henkin and Mr. Mudd. In it, some portions of Mr. Henkin's answers were cut; and what appeared as answers to particular questions were in fact rearranged from answers to quite different questions. What follows is a detailed analysis of the interview as shown on the program, compared with the verbatim transcript of the original interview:

This is what the viewers of the CBS documentary were shown as a single exchange:

> *Roger Mudd.*   What about your public displays of military equipment at state fairs and shopping centers? What purpose does that serve?
>
> *Mr. Henkin.*   Well, I think it serves the purpose of informing the public about their armed forces. I believe the American public has the right to request information about the armed forces, to have speakers come before them, to ask questions, and to understand the need for our armed forces, why we ask for the funds that we do ask for, how we spend these funds, what we are doing about such problems as drugs — and we do have a drug problem in the armed forces, what we are doing about the racial problem — and we do have a racial problem. I think the public has a valid right to ask us these questions.

This, on the other hand, is how Mr. Henkin actually answered the question cited above:

> *Mr. Henkin.*   Well, I think it serves the purpose of informing the public about their armed forces. [*This is the only sentence that was retained intact in the answer as broadcast.*] It also has the ancillary benefit, I would hope, of stimulating interest in recruiting as we move or try to move to zero

---

[1] CBS, in its documentary, stated that the Defense Department's participation in the symposium "was arranged by Peoria's Caterpillar Tractor Company, which did 39 million dollars of business last year with the Defense Department." The Defense Department has stated, however, that the event was arranged and sponsored by the Peoria Association of Commerce with a Caterpillar employee serving as chairman of the symposium.

draft calls and increased reliance on volunteers for our armed forces. I think it is very important that the American youth have an opportunity to learn about the armed forces. [*Both the latter sentences were dropped entirely.*]

The answer to Mr. Henkin was shown to be giving had in fact been transposed from his answer to another and later question that dealt not only with military displays but also with the availability of military speakers. At that later point in the interview, Mr. Mudd asked Mr. Henkin whether such things as drug and racial problems constituted "the sort of information that gets passed out at state fairs by sergeants who are standing next to rockets."

Mr. Henkin replied as follows:

> *Mr. Henkin.*   No, I didn't — wouldn't limit that to sergeants standing next to any kind of exhibits. I knew — I thought we were discussing speeches and all.

But this is how the sequence was shown over the air:

> *Mr. Mudd.*   Well, is that the sort of information about the drug problem you have and the racial problem you have and the budget problems you have — is that the sort of information that gets passed out at state fairs by sergeants who are standing next to rockets?
>
> *Mr. Henkin.*   No. I wouldn't limit that to sergeants standing next to any kind of exhibits. Now, there are those who contend that this is propaganda. I do not agree with this.

The second sentence of Mr. Henkin's actual answer — the part about "speeches and all" — had been omitted. And the "new" material — about propaganda — came from an earlier point in the interview and was in fact a reference to charges that the Pentagon was using talk of an "increasing Soviet threat" as propaganda to influence the size of the military budget.[2]

Policy Considerations and Conclusions

In view of all the facts at our disposal, we conclude that further action by this Commission would be inappropriate — and not because the issues involved are insubstantial. Precisely to the contrary, they are so substantial that they reach to the bedrock principles upon which our free and democratic society is founded.

---

[2] An inquiry has been made concerning a third aspect of "The Selling of the Pentagon" in connection with edited coverage of a news briefing of Pentagon reporters by Deputy Assistant Secretary of Defense Jerry Friedheim. The facts are that CBS recorded the entire session, with answers to approximately 34 questions: only six questions and answers were shown in the documentary and, of these six, three answers were of the "no comment" type — the *only* such answers Mr. Friedheim gave during the entire briefing. Mr. Henkin asserts that answers to any of the "no comment questions" would have "revealed classified national security information." Coverage of the briefing followed comments by Mr. Mudd to the effect that Mr. Friedheim, as a "careful and respected adversary" of Pentagon reporters, does not "tell all he knows" and "wouldn't have his job long if he did."

Our basis for this conclusion is set forth in prior Commission rulings, of which two are particularly apposite: *In re Complaints Concerning CBS Program, Hunger In America,* 20 FCC 2d 143 (1969), and *Network Coverage of the Democratic National Convention,* 16 FCC 2d 650 (1969).

Lacking extrinsic evidence or documents that on their face reflect deliberate distortion, we believe that this government licensing agency cannot properly intervene. It would be unwise and probably impossible for the Commission to lay down some precise line of factual accuracy — dependent always on journalistic judgment — across which broadcasters must not stray. As we stated in the *Hunger in America* ruling, "the Commission is not the national arbiter of the truth" (20 FCC 2d at p. 151). Any presumption on our part would be inconsistent with the First Amendment and with the profound national commitment to the principle that debate on public issues should be "uninhibited, robust, [and] wide-open" (*New York Times Co.* v. *Sullivan,* 376 U.S. 254, 270). It would involve the Commission deeply and improperly in the journalistic functions of broadcasters.

This function necessarily involves selection and editorial judgment. And, in the absence of extrinsic evidence, documentary or otherwise, that a licensee has engaged in deliberate distortion, for the Commission to review this editing process would be to enter an impenetrable thicket. On every single question of judgment, and each complaint that might be registered, the Commission would have to decide whether the editing had involved deliberate distortion. Although we can conceive of situations where the documentary evidence of deliberate distortion would be sufficiently strong to require an inquiry — e.g., where a "yes" answer to one question was used to replace a "no" answer to an entirely different question — we believe that such a situation is not presented here.

We are not saying that CBS' or any other broadcaster's editorial judgment is above criticism. As we said in *Hunger in America* (20 FCC 2d at p. 151), allegations of distortion "should be referred to the licensee for its own investigation and appropriate handling." And again:

... [W]e stress that the licensee must have a policy of requiring honesty of its news staff and must take reasonable precautions to see that news is fairly handled. The licensee's investigation of substantial complaints ... must be a thorough, conscientious one, resulting in remedial action where appropriate.

Our point is that this licensing agency cannot and should not dictate the particular response to thousands of journalistic circumstances. Above all, we affirm that we must ".... eschew the censor's role, including efforts to establish news distortion in situations where government intervention would constitute a worse danger than the possible rigging itself." But to say that such intervention would be a remedy far worse than the disease is *not* to say that we can afford to shrug off the deeper questions involved.

This Commission is charged with "... promoting the public interest in the larger and more effective use of radio" (Section 303(g) of the Communications

Act). Surely there is no issue bearing more heavily on the public service role of broadcasting than the integrity of the licensee's news operation.

We have allocated so much spectrum space to broadcasting precisely because of the contribution it can make to an informed public. Thus it follows inevitably that broadcasting must discharge that function responsibly, without deliberate distortion or slanting. The nation depends on broadcasting, and increasingly on television, *fairly* to illumine the news.

We particularly urge the need for good faith, earnest self-examination. In our view, broadcast journalists should demonstrate a positive inclination to respond to serious criticism. Indeed, Mr. Chairman, the thrust of your and other congressional inquiries — reflected also in criticism in print media — was to raise questions about the editing process, particularly with respect to the Henkin interview.

It seems to us that CBS has failed to address the question raised as to splicing answers to a variety of questions as a way of creating a new "answer" to a single question. The very use of a "Question and Answer" format would seem to encourage the viewer to believe that a particular answer follows directly from the question preceding. Surely important issues are involved here, ones that every broadcast journalist should ponder most seriously.

What we urge — because we believe it will markedly serve the public interest — is an open, eager and self-critical attitude on the part of broadcast journalists. We urge them (as we did in *Hunger in America*, cited above) to examine their own processes, to subject them to the kind of hard critical analysis that is characteristic of the best traditions of the journalistic profession.

Our objective is to encourage broadcast journalism, not to hurt or hinder it. We have made clear in the past that the Commission seeks a larger role for broadcast journalism, including newscasts and documentaries. We reiterate that commitment today. For what ultimately is at stake in this entire matter is broadcasting's own reputation for probity and reliability, and thus its claim to public confidence.

In view of the foregoing discussion, we do not propose to inquire of CBS as to the second issue referred to, *supra*. A copy of this letter will be sent to CBS so that it is informed fully of the Commission's position in this important area. We shall, of course, also keep you informed of any further developments as to the application of the fairness doctrine.

This letter was adopted by the Commission on April 28, 1971.

Commissioners Burch, Chairman, and Johnson issuing separate statements.

By Direction of the Commission,
Dean Burch, *Chairman.*

9

THE GREAT DEBATES LAW

Public Law 86–677, 86th Congress

August 24, 1960

This Senate Joint Resolution, which provided the legal basis for the "Great Debates" of 1960 between John F. Kennedy and Richard M. Nixon, was passed only after the Democratic and Republican National Conventions were held and the presidential and vice presidential candidates chosen. Many broadcasters hailed the bill's passage as a step toward total elimination of the burdensome equal time requirements of Section 315 of the Communications Act. It seems unlikely, however, that future suspensions of Section 315 will occur unless neither candidate is an incumbent for the office he seeks.

The complexities inherent in the administration of Section 315 are apparent in the FCC "Political Broadcasting Primers," 24 FCC 2d 832 (1970) and 34 FCC 2d 510 (1972).

Resolved by the Senate and House of Representatives of the United States of America in Congress assembled, That that part of section 315(a) of the Communications Act of 1934, as amended, which requires any licensee of a broadcast station who permits any person who is a legally qualified candidate for any public office to use a broadcasting station to afford equal opportunities to all other such candidates for that office in the use of such broadcasting station, is suspended for the period of the 1960 presidential and vice presidential campaigns with respect to nominees for the offices of President and Vice President of the United States. Nothing in the foregoing shall be construed as relieving broadcasters from the obligation imposed upon them under this Act to operate in the public interest.

(2) The Federal Communications Commission shall make a report to the Congress, not later than March 1, 1961, with respect to the effect of the provisions of this joint resolution and any recommendations the Commission may have for amendments to the Communications Act of 1934 as a result of experience under the provisions of this joint resolution.

7 TUFP
1, 5, 6, 14
sp. red. press
asty pg
5 - due process
6 jury fair trial
14 - privileges

10

FAIR TRIAL VERSUS

FREE PRESS

Estes v. Texas
381 U.S. 532
June 7, 1965

The conflict between the First, Fifth, Sixth, and Fourteenth
Amendments illuminates the weaknesses inherent in a system that
places high value both on a free press and trial by jury. The
American Bar Association recognized this tangle when it enacted
Canon 35 after the notoriously publicized trial of Bruno
Hauptmann in 1935.

This 5-4 Supreme Court decision, in which the Justices
issued six different opinions, holds that when the First and
Fourteenth Amendments conflict the latter takes precedence over
the former. Furthermore, the Court decided such a conflict
results whenever pretrial disclosures create notorious publicity
and the proceedings of a courtroom are disrupted by television
equipment and personnel. This case constitutes an important
precedent for the Court's decision in *Sheppard* v. *Maxwell* (384
U.S. 333 (1966)).

Only the opinion of the Court and the major dissenting
opinion appear below.

Mr. Justice Clark delivered the opinion of the Court.

The question presented here is whether the petitioner, who stands
convicted in the District Court for the Seventh Judicial District of Texas at Tyler
for swindling,[1] was deprived of his right under the Fourteenth Amendment to

---

[1] The evidence indicated that petitioner, through false pretenses and fraudulent representations, induced certain farmers to purchase fertilizer tanks and accompanying
equipment, which in fact did not exist, and to sign and deliver to him chattel mortages on
the fictitious property.

454

due process by the televising and broadcasting of his trial. Both the trial court and the Texas Court of Criminal Appeals found against the petitioner. We hold to the contrary and reverse his conviction.

I

While petitioner recites his claim in the framework of Canon 35 of the Judicial Canons of the American Bar Association he does not contend that we should enshrine Canon 35 in the Fourteenth Amendment, but only that the time-honored principles of a fair trial were not followed in his case and that he was thus convicted without due process of law. Canon 35, of course, has of itself no binding effect on the courts but merely expresses the view of the Association in opposition to the broadcasting, televising and photographing of court proceedings. Likewise, Judicial Canon 28 of the Integrated State Bar of Texas, 27 Tex. B. J. 102 (1964), which leaves to the trial judge's sound discretion the telecasting and photographing of court proceedings, is of itself not law. In short, the question here is not the validity of either Canon 35 of the American Bar Association or Canon 28 of the State Bar of Texas, but only whether petitioner was tried in a manner which comports with the due process requirement of the Fourteenth Amendment.

Petitioner's case was originally called for trial on September 24, 1962, in Smith County after a change of venue from Reeves County, some 500 miles west. Massive pretrial publicity totaling 11 volumes of press clippings, which are on file with the Clerk, had given it national notoriety. All available seats in the courtroom were taken and some 30 persons stood in the aisles. However, at that time a defense motion to prevent telecasting, broadcasting by radio and news photography and a defense motion for continuance were presented, and after a two-day hearing the former was denied and the latter granted.

These initial hearings were carried live by both radio and television, and news photography was permitted throughout. The videotapes of these hearings clearly illustrate that the picture presented was not one of that judicial serenity and calm to which petitioner was entitled. Cf. *Wood* v. *Georgia*, 370 U.S. 375, 383 (1962); *Turner* v. *Louisiana*, 379 U.S. 466, 472 (1965); *Cox* v. *Louisiana*, 379 U.S. 559, 562 (1965). Indeed, at least 12 cameramen were engaged in the courtroom throughout the hearing taking motion and still pictures and televising the proceedings. Cables and wires were snaked across the courtroom floor, three microphones were on the judge's bench and others were beamed at the jury box and the counsel table. It is conceded that the activities of the television crews and news photographers led to considerable disruption of the hearings. Moreover, veniremen had been summoned and were present in the courtroom during the entire hearing but were later released after petitioner's motion for continuance had been granted. The court also had the names of the witnesses called; some answered but the absence of others led to a continuance of the case until October 22, 1962. It is contended that this two-day pretrial hearing cannot be considered in determining the question before us. We cannot agree. Pretrial can create a major problem for the defendant in a criminal case. Indeed, it may be more harmful than publicity during the trial for it may well set the community opinion as to guilt or innocence. Though the September hearings dealt with motions to prohibit television coverage and to postpone the trial, they are unquestionably relevant to the issue before us. All of this two-day affair was highly publicized and could only have impressed those present, and also the community at large, with the notorious character of the petitioner as well as the proceeding. The trial witnesses present at the hearing, as well as the original jury panel, were undoubtedly made aware of the peculiar public importance of the case by the press and television coverage being provided, and by the fact that they themselves were televised live and their pictures rebroadcast on the evening show.

When the case was called for trial on October 22 the scene had been altered. A booth had been constructed at the back of the courtroom which was painted to blend with the permanent structure of the room. It had an aperture to allow the lens of the cameras an unrestricted view of the courtroom. All television cameras and newsreel photographers were restricted to the area of the booth when shooting film or telecasting.

Because of continual objection, the rules governing live telecasting, as well as radio and still photos, were changed as the exigencies of the situation seemed to require. As a result, live telecasting was prohibited during a great portion of the actual trial. Only the opening[2] and closing arguments of the State, the return of the jury's verdict and its receipt by the trial judge were carried live with sound. Although the order allowed videotapes of the entire proceeding without sound, the cameras operated only intermittently, recording various portions of the trial for broadcast on regularly scheduled newscasts later in the day and evening. At the request of the petitioner, the trial judge prohibited coverage of any kind, still or television, of the defense counsel during their summations to the jury.

Because of the varying restrictions placed on sound and live telecasting the telecasts of the trial were confined largely to film clips shown on the stations' regularly scheduled news programs. The news commentators would use the film of a particular part of the day's trial activities as a backdrop for their reports. Their commentary included excerpts from testimony and the usual reportorial remarks. On one occasion the videotapes of the September hearings were rebroadcast in place of the "late movie."

---

[2] Due to mechanical difficulty there was no picture during the opening argument.

II

In *Rideau* v. *Louisiana*, 373 U.S. 723 (1963), this Court constructed a rule that the televising of a defendant in the act of confessing to a crime was inherently invalid under the Due Process Clause of the Fourteenth Amendment even without a showing of prejudice or a demonstration of the nexus between the televised confession and the trial. See *id.*, at 729 (dissenting opinion of Clark, J.). Here, although there was nothing so dramatic as a home-viewed confession, there had been a bombardment of the community with the sights and sounds of a two-day hearing during which the original jury panel, the petitioner, the lawyers and the judge were highly publicized. The petitioner was subjected to characterization and minute electronic scrutiny to such an extent that at one point the photographers were found attempting to picture the page of the paper from which he was reading while sitting at the counsel table. The two-day hearing and the order permitting television at the actual trial were widely known throughout the community. This emphasized the notorious character that the trial would take and, therefore, set it apart in the public mind as an extraordinary case or, as Shaw would say, something "not conventionally unconventional." When the new jury was empaneled at the trial four of the jurors selected had seen and heard all or part of the broadcasts of the earlier proceedings.

III

We start with the proposition that it is a "public trial" that the Sixth Amendment guarantees to the "accused." The purpose of the requirement of a public trial was to guarantee that the accused would be fairly dealt with and not unjustly condemned. History had proven that secret tribunals were effective instruments of oppression. As our Brother Black so well said in *In re Oliver*, 333 U.S. 257 (1948):

The traditional Anglo-American distrust for secret trials has been variously ascribed to the notorious use of this practice by the Spanish Inquisition, to the excesses of the English Court of Star Chamber, and to the French monarchy's abuse of the *lettre de cachet*. . . . Whatever other benefits the guarantee to an accused that his trial be conducted in public may confer upon our society, the guarantee has always been recognized as a safeguard against any attempt to employ our courts as instruments of persecution. At 268-270. (Footnotes omitted.)

It is said, however, that the freedoms granted in the First Amendment extend a right to the news media to televise from the courtroom, and that to refuse to honor this privilege is to discriminate between the newspapers and television. This is a misconception of the rights of the press.

The free press has been a mighty catalyst in awakening public interest in governmental affairs, exposing corruption among public officers and employees and generally informing the citizenry of public events and occurrences, including court proceedings. While maximum freedom must be allowed the press in carrying on this important function in a democratic society its exercise must necessarily be subject to the maintenance of absolute fairness in the judicial process. While the state and federal courts have differed over what spectators may be excluded from a criminal trial, 6 Wigmore, Evidence § 1834 (3d ed. 1940), the *amici curiae* brief of the National Association of Broadcasters and the Radio Television News Directors Association, says, as indeed it must, that "neither of these two amendments [First and Sixth] speaks of an unlimited right of access to the courtroom on the part of the broadcasting media. . . ." At 7. Moreover, they recognize that the "primary concern of all must be the proper administration of justice"; that "the life or liberty of any individual in this land should not be put in jeopardy because of actions of any news media"; and that "the due process requirements in both the Fifth and Fourteenth Amendments and the provisions of the Sixth Amendment require a procedure that will assure a fair trial. . . ." At 3-4.

Nor can the courts be said to discriminate where they permit the newspaper reporter access to the courtroom. The television and radio reporter has the same privilege. All are entitled to the same rights as the general public. The news reporter is not permitted to bring his typewriter or printing press. When the advances in these arts permit reporting by printing press or by television without their present hazards to a fair trial we will have another case.

IV

Court proceedings are held for the solemn purpose of endeavoring to ascertain the truth which is the *sine qua non* of a fair trial. Over the centuries Anglo-American courts have devised careful safeguards by rule and otherwise to protect and facilitate the performance of this high function. As a result, at this time those safeguards do not permit the televising and photographing of a criminal trial, save in two States and there only under restrictions. The federal courts prohibit it by specific rule. This is weighty evidence that our concepts of a fair trial do not tolerate such an indulgence. We have always held that the atmosphere essential to the preservation of a fair trial — the most fundamental of all freedoms — must be maintained at all costs. Our approach has been through rules, contempt proceedings and reversal of convictions obtained under unfair conditions. Here the remedy is clear and certain of application and it is our duty to continue to enforce the principles that from time immemorial have proven efficacious and necessary to a fair trial.

TV. maybe
too eager.

pupil. right to know.
ct. owners

V

The State contends that the televising of portions of a criminal trial does not constitute a denial of due process. Its position is that because no prejudice has been shown by the petitioner as resulting from the televising, it is permissible; that claims of "distractions" during the trial due to the physical presence of television are wholly unfounded; and that psychological considerations are for psychologists, not courts, because they are purely hypothetical. It argues further that the public has a right to know what goes on in the courts; that the court has no power to "suppress, edit, or censor events which transpire in proceedings before it," citing *Craig* v. *Harney*, 331 U.S. 367, 374 (1947); and that the televising of criminal trials would be enlightening to the public and would promote greater respect for the courts.

At the outset the notion should be dispelled that telecasting is dangerous because it is new. It is true that our empirical knowledge of its full effect on the public, the jury or the participants in a trial, including the judge, witnesses and lawyers, is limited. However, the nub of the question is not its newness but, as Mr. Justice Douglas says, "the insidious influences which it puts to work in the administration of justice." Douglas, The Public Trial and the Free Press, 33 Rocky Mt. L. Rev. 1 (1960). These influences will be detailed below, but before turning to them the State's argument that the public has a right to know what goes on in the courtroom should be dealt with.

It is true that the public has the right to be informed as to what occurs in its courts, but reporters of all media, including television, are always present if they wish to be and are plainly free to report whatever occurs in open court through their respective media. This was settled in *Bridges* v. *California*, 314 U.S. 252 (1941), and *Pennekamp* v. *Florida*, 328 U.S. 331 (1946), which we reaffirm. These reportorial privileges of the press were stated years ago:

> The law, however, favors publicity in legal proceedings, so far as that object can be attained without injustice to the persons immediately concerned. The public are permitted to attend nearly all judicial inquiries, and there appears to be no sufficient reason why they should not also be allowed to see in print the reports of trials, if they can thus have them presented as fully as they are exhibited in court, or at least all the material portion of the proceedings impartially stated, so that one shall not, by means of them, derive erroneous impressions, which he would not have been likely to receive from hearing the trial itself. 2 Cooley's Constitutional Limitations 931-932 (Carrington ed. 1927).

The State, however, says that the use of television in the instant case was "without injustice to the person immediately concerned," basing its position on the fact that the petitioner has established no isolatable prejudice and that this must be shown in order to invalidate a conviction in these circumstances. The

State paints too broadly in this contention, for this Court itself has found instances in which a showing of actual prejudice is not a prerequisite to reversal. This is such a case. It is true that in most cases involving claims of due process deprivations we require a showing of identifiable prejudice to the accused. Nevertheless, at times a procedure employed by the State involves such a probability that prejudice will result that it is deemed inherently lacking in due process. Such a case was *In re Murchison*, 349 U.S. 133 (1955), where Mr. Justice Black for the Court pointed up with his usual clarity and force:

> A fair trial in a fair tribunal is a basic requirement of due process. Fairness of course requires an absence of actual bias in the trial of cases. But our system of law has always endeavored to prevent even the *probability* of unfairness. . . . [T]o perform its high function in the best way "justice must satisfy the appearance of justice." *Offutt* v. *United States*, 348 U.S. 11, 14. At 136. (Emphasis supplied.)

And, as Chief Justice Taft said in *Tumey* v. *Ohio*, 273 U.S. 510, almost 30 years before:

> the requirement of due process of law in judicial procedure is not satisfied by the argument that men of the highest honor and the greatest self-sacrifice could carry it on without danger or injustice. Every procedure which would offer a *possible* temptation to the average man . . . to forget the burden of proof required to convict the defendant, or which might lead him not to hold the balance nice, clear and true between the State and the accused, denies the latter due process of law. At 532. (Emphasis supplied.)

This rule was followed in *Rideau, supra*, and in *Turner* v. *Louisiana*, 379 U.S. 466 (1965). In each of these cases the Court departed from the approach it charted in *Stroble* v. *California*, 343 U.S. 181 (1952), and in *Irvin* v. *Dowd*, 366 U.S. 717 (1961), where we made a careful examination of the facts in order to determine whether prejudice resulted. In *Rideau* and *Turner* the Court did not stop to consider the actual effect of the practice but struck down the conviction on the ground that prejudice was inherent in it. Likewise in *Gideon* v. *Wainwright*, 372 U.S. 335 (1963), and *White* v. *Maryland*, 373 U.S. 59 (1963), we applied the same rule, although in different contexts.

In this case it is even clearer that such a rule must be applied. In *Rideau*, *Irvin* and *Stroble*, the pretrial publicity occurred outside the courtroom and could not be effectively curtailed. The only recourse other than reversal was by contempt proceedings. In *Turner* the probability of prejudice was present through the use of deputy sheriffs, who were also witnesses in the case, as shepherds for the jury. No prejudice was shown but the circumstances were held to be inherently suspect, and, therefore, such a showing was not held to be a requisite to reversal. Likewise in this case the application of this principle is especially appropriate. Television in its present state and by its very nature, reaches into a variety of areas in which it may cause prejudice to an accused.

Still one cannot put his finger on its specific mischief and prove with particularity wherein he was prejudiced. This was found true in *Murchison, Tumey, Rideau* and *Turner*. Such untoward circumstances as were found in those cases are inherently bad and prejudice to the accused was presumed. Forty-eight of our States and the Federal Rules have deemed the use of television improper in the courtroom. This fact is most telling in buttressing our conclusion that any change in procedure which would permit its use would be inconsistent with our concepts of due process in this field.

VI

As has been said, the chief function of our judicial machinery is to ascertain the truth. The use of television, however, cannot be said to contribute materially to this objective. Rather its use amounts to the injection of an irrelevant factor into court proceedings. In addition experience teaches that there are numerous situations in which it might cause actual unfairness — some so subtle as to defy detection by the accused or control by the judge. We enumerate some in summary:

1.   The potential impact of television on the jurors is perhaps of the greatest significance. They are the nerve center of the fact-finding process. It is true that in States like Texas where they are required to be sequestered in trials of this nature the jurors will probably not see any of the proceedings as televised from the courtroom. But the inquiry cannot end there. From the moment the trial judge announces that a case will be televised it becomes a *cause célèbre*. The whole community, including prospective jurors, becomes interested in all the morbid details surrounding it. The approaching trial immediately assumes an important status in the public press and the accused is highly publicized along with the offense with which he is charged. Every juror carries with him into the jury box these solemn facts and thus increases the chance of prejudice that is present in every criminal case. And we must remember that realistically it is only the notorious trial which will be broadcast, because of the necessity for paid sponsorship. The conscious or unconscious effect that this may have on the juror's judgment cannot be evaluated, but experience indicates that it is not only possible but highly probable that it will have a direct bearing on his vote as to guilt or innocence. Where pretrial publicity of all kinds has created intense public feeling which is aggravated by the telecasting or picturing of the trial the televised jurors cannot help but feel the pressures of knowing that friends and neighbors have their eyes upon them. If the community be hostile to an accused a televised juror, realizing that he must return to neighbors who saw the trial themselves, may well be led "not to hold the balance nice, clear and true between the State and the accused. . . ."

Moreover, while it is practically impossible to assess the effect of television on jury attentiveness, those of us who know juries realize the problem of jury "distraction." The State argues this is *de minimis* since the physical disturbances have been eliminated. But we know that distractions are not caused solely by the physical presence of the camera and its telltale red lights. It is the awareness of the fact of telecasting that is felt by the juror throughout the trial. We are all self-conscious and uneasy when being televised. Human nature being what it is, not only will a juror's eyes be fixed on the camera, but also his mind will be preoccupied with the telecasting rather than with the testimony.

Furthermore, in many States, the jurors serving in the trial may see the broadcasts of the trial proceedings. Admittedly, the Texas sequestration rule would prevent this occurring there.[3] In other States following no such practice jurors would return home and turn on the TV if only to see how they appeared upon it. They would also be subjected to re-enactment and emphasis of the selected parts of the proceedings which the requirements of the broadcasters determined would be telecast and would be subconsciously influenced the more by that testimony. Moreover, they would be subjected to the broadest commentary and criticism and perhaps the well-meant advice of friends, relatives and inquiring strangers who recognized them on the streets.

Finally, new trials plainly would be jeopardized in that potential jurors will often have seen and heard the original trial when it was telecast. Yet viewers may later be called upon to sit in the jury box during the new trial. These very dangers are illustrated in this case where the court, due to the defendant's objections, permitted only the State's opening and closing arguments to be broadcast with sound to the public.

2.   The quality of the testimony in criminal trials will often be impaired. The impact upon a witness of the knowledge that he is being viewed by a vast audience is simply incalculable. Some may be demoralized and frightened, some cocky and given to overstatement; memories may falter, as with anyone speaking publicly, and accuracy of statement may be severely undermined. Embarrassment may impede the search for the truth, as may a natural tendency toward overdramatization. Furthermore, inquisitive strangers and "cranks" might approach witnesses on the street with jibes, advice or demands for explanation of testimony. There is little wonder that the defendant cannot "prove" the existence of such factors. Yet we all know from experience that they exist.

In addition the invocation of the rule against witnesses is frustrated. In most instances witnesses would be able to go to their homes and view broadcasts of the day's trial proceedings, notwithstanding the fact that they had been admonished not to do so. They could view and hear the testimony of preceding

---

3Only six States, in addition to Texas, require sequestration of the jury prior to its deliberations in a non-capital felony trial. The great majority of jurisdictions leave the matter to the trial judge's discretion, while in at least one State the jury will be kept together in such circumstances only upon a showing of cause by the defendant.

witnesses, and so shape their own testimony as to make its impact crucial. And even in the absence of sound, the influences of such viewing on the attitude of the witness toward testifying, his frame of mind upon taking the stand or his apprehension of withering cross-examination defy objective assessment. Indeed, the mere fact that the trial is to be televised might render witnesses reluctant to appear and thereby impede the trial as well as the discovery of the truth.

While some of the dangers mentioned above are present as well in newspaper coverage of any important trial, the circumstances and extraneous influences intruding upon the solemn decorum of court procedure in the televised trial are far more serious than in cases involving only newspaper coverage.

3.   A major aspect of the problem is the additional responsibilities the presence of television places on the trial judge. His job is to make certain that the accused receives a fair trial. This most difficult task requires his undivided attention. Still when television comes into the courtroom he must also supervise it. In this trial, for example, the judge on several different occasions — aside from the two days of pretrial — was obliged to have a hearing or enter an order made necessary solely because of the presence of television. Thus, where telecasting is restricted as it was here, and as even the State concedes it must be, his task is made much more difficult and exacting. And, as happened here, such rulings may unfortunately militate against the fairness of the trial. In addition, laying physical interruptions aside, there is the ever-present distraction that the mere awareness of television's presence prompts. Judges are human beings also and are subject to the same psychological reactions as laymen. Telecasting is particularly bad where the judge is elected, as is the case in all save a half dozen of our States. The telecasting of a trial becomes a political weapon, which, along with other distractions inherent in broadcasting, diverts his attention from the task at hand — the fair trial of the accused.

But this is not all. There is the initial decision that must be made as to whether the use of television will be permitted. This is perhaps an even more crucial consideration. Our judges are high-minded men and women. But it is difficult to remain oblivious to the pressures that the news media can bring to bear on them both directly and through the shaping of public opinion. Moreover, where one judge in a district or even in a State permits telecasting, the requirement that the others do the same is almost mandatory. Especially is this true where the judge is selected at the ballot box.

4.   Finally, we cannot ignore the impact of courtroom television on the defendant. Its presence is a form of mental — if not physical — harassment, resembling a police line-up or the third degree. The inevitable close-ups of his gestures and expressions during the ordeal of his trial might well transgress his personal sensibilities, his dignity, and his ability to concentrate on the proceedings before him — sometimes the difference between life and death — dispassionately, freely and without the distraction of wide public surveillance. A defendant on trial for a specific crime is entitled to his day in court, not in a

stadium, or a city or nationwide arena. The heightened public clamor resulting from radio and television coverage will inevitably result in prejudice. Trial by television is, therefore, foreign to our system. Furthermore, telecasting may also deprive an accused of effective counsel. The distractions, intrusions into confidential attorney-client relationships and the temptation offered by television to play to the public audience might often have a direct effect not only upon the lawyers, but the judge, the jury and the witnesses. See Pye, The Lessons of Dallas — Threats to Fair Trial and Free Press, National Civil Liberties Clearing House, 16th Annual Conference.

The television camera is a powerful weapon. Intentionally or inadvertently it can destroy an accused and his case in the eyes of the public. While our telecasters are honorable men, they too are human. The necessity for sponsorship weighs heavily in favor of the televising of only notorious cases, such as this one, and invariably focuses the lens upon the unpopular or infamous accused. Such a selection is necessary in order to obtain a sponsor willing to pay a sufficient fee to cover the costs and return a profit. We have already examined the ways in which public sentiment can affect the trial participants. To the extent that television shapes that sentiment, it can strip the accused of a fair trial.

The State would dispose of all these observations with the simple statement that they are for psychologists because they are purely hypothetical. But we cannot afford the luxury of saying that, because these factors are difficult of ascertainment in particular cases, they must be ignored. Nor are they "purely hypothetical." They are no more hypothetical than were the considerations deemed controlling in *Tumey, Murchison, Rideau* and *Turner.* They are real enough to have convinced the Judicial Conference of the United States, this Court and the Congress that television should be barred in federal trials by the Federal Rules of Criminal Procedure; in addition they have persuaded all but two of our States to prohibit television in the courtroom. They are effects that may, and in some combination almost certainly will, exist in any case in which television is injected into the trial process.

VII

The facts in this case demonstrate clearly the necessity for the application of the rule announced in *Rideau.* The sole issue before the court for two days of pretrial hearing was the question now before us. The hearing was televised live and repeated on tape in the same evening, reaching approximately 100,000 viewers. In addition, the courtroom was a mass of wires, television cameras, microphones and photographers. The petitioner, the panel of prospective jurors, who were sworn the second day, the witnesses and the lawyers were all exposed to this untoward situation. The judge decided that the trial proceedings would be telecast. He announced no restrictions at the time. This emphasized the notorious nature of the coming trial, increased the intensity of the publicity on the petitioner and together with the subsequent televising of the trial beginning 30 days later inherently prevented a sober search for the truth. This is underscored by the fact that the selection of the jury took an entire week. As might be expected, a substantial amount of that time was devoted to ascertaining the impact of the pretrial televising on the prospective jurors. As we have noted, four of the jurors selected had seen all or part of those broadcasts. The trial, on the other hand, lasted only three days.

Moreover, the trial judge was himself harassed. After the initial decision to permit telecasting he apparently decided that a booth should be built at the broadcasters' expense to confine its operations; he then decided to limit the parts of the trial that might be televised live; then he decided to film the testimony of the witnesses without sound in an attempt to protect those under the rule; and finally he ordered that defense counsel and their argument not be televised, in the light of their objection. Plagued by his original error — recurring each day of the trial — his day-to-day orders made the trial more confusing to the jury, the participants and to the viewers. Indeed, it resulted in a public presentation of only the State's side of the case.

As Mr. Justice Holmes said in *Patterson* v. *Colorado*, 205 U.S. 454, 462 (1907):

The theory of our system is that the conclusions to be reached in a case will be induced only by evidence and argument in open court, and not by any outside influence, whether of private talk or public print.

It is said that the ever-advancing techniques of public communication and the adjustment of the public to its presence may bring about a change in the effect of telecasting upon the fairness of criminal trials. But we are not dealing here with future developments in the field of electronics. Our judgment cannot be rested on the hypothesis of tomorrow but must take the facts as they are presented today.

The judgment is therefore reversed.

Mr. Justice Stewart, whom Mr. Justice Black, Mr. Justice Brennan, and Mr. Justice White join, dissenting.

I cannot agree with the Court's decision that the circumstances of this trial led to a denial of the petitioner's Fourteenth Amendment rights. I think that the introduction of television into a courtroom is, at least in the present state of the art, an extremely unwise policy. It invites many constitutional risks, and it detracts from the inherent dignity of a courtroom. But I am unable to escalate this personal view into a *per se* constitutional rule. And I am unable to find, on the specific record of this case, that the circumstances attending the limited televising of the petitioner's trial resulted in the denial of any right guaranteed to him by the United States Constitution.

On October 22, 1962, the petitioner went to trial in the Seventh Judicial District Court of Smith County, Texas, upon an indictment charging him with the offenses of (1) swindling, (2) theft by false pretenses, and (3) theft by a bailee. After a week spent in selecting a jury, the trial itself lasted some three and a half days. At its conclusion the jury found the petitioner guilty of the offense of swindling under the first count of the indictment. The trial judge permitted portions of the trial proceedings to be televised, under the limitations described below. He also gave news photographers permission to take still pictures in the courtroom under specified conditions.

The Texas Court of Criminal Appeals affirmed the petitioner's conviction, and we granted certiorari, limited to a single question. The question, as phrased by the petitioner, is this:

Whether the action of the trial court, over petitioner's continued objection, denied him due process of law and equal protection of the laws under the Fourteenth Amendment to the Constitution of the United States, in requiring petitioner to submit to live television of his trial, and in refusing to adopt in this all out publicity case, as a rule of trial procedure, Canon 35 of the Canons of Judicial Ethics of the American Bar Association, and instead adopting and following, over defendant's objection, Canon 28 of the Canons of Judicial Ethics, since approved by the Judicial Section of the integrated (State agency) State Bar of Texas.

The two Canons of Judicial Ethics referred to in the petitioner's statement of the question presented are set out in the margin.[1] But, as the Court rightly says, the problem before us is not one of choosing between the conflicting

---

[1]Canons of Judicial Ethics. American Bar Association: Judicial Canon 35. Improper publicizing of Court proceedings.

"Proceedings in court should be conducted with fitting dignity and decorum. The taking of photographs in the court room, during sessions of the court or recesses between sessions, and the broadcasting or televising of court proceedings detract from the essential dignity of the proceedings, distract participants and witnesses in giving testimony, and create misconceptions with respect thereto in the mind of the public and should not be permitted.

"Provided that this restriction shall not apply to the broadcasting or televising, under the supervision of the court, of such portions of naturalization proceedings (other than the interrogation of applicants) as are designed and carried out exclusively as a ceremony for the purpose of publicly demonstrating in an impressive manner the essential dignity and the serious nature of naturalization."

Canons of Judicial Ethics, Integrated State Bar of Texas: Judicial Canon 28. Improper Publicizing of Court Proceedings.

"Proceedings in court should be conducted with fitting dignity and decorum. The taking of photographs in the court room, during sessions of the court or recesses between sessions, and the broadcasting or televising of court proceedings unless properly supervised and controlled, may detract from the essential dignity of the proceedings, distract participants and witnesses in giving testimony, and create misconceptions with respect thereto in the mind of the public. The supervision and control of such trial coverage shall be left to the trial judge who has the inherent power to exclude or control coverage in the proper case in the interest of justice."

guidelines reflected in these Canons of Judicial Ethics. It is a problem rooted in the Due Process Clause of the Fourteenth Amendment. We deal here with matters subject to continuous and unforeseeable change — the techniques of public communication. In an area where all the variables may be modified tomorrow, I cannot at this time rest my determination on hypothetical possibilities not present in the record of this case. There is no claim here based upon any right guaranteed by the First Amendment. But it is important to remember that we move in an area touching the realm of free communication, and for that reason, if for no other, I would be wary of imposing any *per se* rule which, in the light of future technology, might serve to stifle or abridge true First Amendment rights.

I

The indictment was originally returned by a grand jury in Reeves County, Texas, and it engendered widespread publicity. After some preliminary proceedings there, the case was transferred for trial to Smith County, more than 500 miles away. The trial was set for September 24, 1962, but it did not commence on that date. Instead, that day and the next were spent in hearings on two motions filed by defense counsel: a motion to bar television and news cameras from the trial, and a motion to continue the trial to a later date. Those proceedings were themselves telecast "live," and news photographers were permitted to take pictures in the courtroom. The activities of the television crews and news photographers led to considerable disruption of the hearings.[2] At the conclusion

---

"In connection with the control of such coverage the following declaration of principles is adopted:

"(1) There should be no use of flash bulbs or other artificial lighting.

"(2) No witness, over his expressed objection, should be photographed, his voice broadcast or be televised.

"(3) The representatives of news media must obtain permission of the trial judge to cover by photograph, broadcasting or televising, and shall comply with the rules prescribed by the judge for the exercise of the privilege.

"(4) Any violation of the Court's Rules shall be punished as a contempt.

"(5) Where a judge has refused to allow coverage or has regulated it, any attempt, other than argument by representatives of the news media directly with the Court, to bring pressure of any kind on the judge, pending final disposition of the cause in trial, shall be punished as a contempt."

[2] A contemporary newspaper account described the scene as follows:

"A television motor van, big as an intercontinental bus, was parked outside the courthouse and the second-floor courtroom was a forest of equipment. Two television cameras had been set up inside the bar and four more marked cameras were aligned just outside the gates.

"A microphone stuck its 12-inch snout inside the jury box, now occupied by an overflow of reporters from the press table, and three microphones confronted Judge Dunagan on his bench. [C]ables and wires snaked over the floor." The New York Times, September 25, 1962, p. 46, col. 4.

of the hearings the motion for a continuance was granted, and the case reset for trial on October 22. The motion to bar television and news photographers from the trial was denied.[3]

On October 1, the trial judge issued an order delineating what coverage he would permit during the trial.[4] As a result of that order and ensuing conferences

[3]In ruling on the motion, the trial judge stated:

"In the past, it has been the policy of this Court to permit televising in the court room under the rules and supervision of the Court. Heretofore, I have not encountered any difficulty with it. I was unable to observe any detraction from the witnesses or the attorneys in those cases. We have watched television, of course, grow up from its infancy and now into its maturity; and it is a news media. So I really do not see any justified reason why it should not be permitted to take its proper seat in the family circle. However, it will be under the strict supervision of the Court. I know there has been pro and con about televising in the court room. I have heard some say that it makes a circus out of the Court. I had the privilege yesterday morning of sitting in my home and viewing a sermon by the First Baptist Church over in Dallas and certainly it wasn't any circus in that church; and I feel that if it is a proper instrument in the house of the Lord, it is not out of place in the court room, if properly supervised.

"Now, television is going to be televising whatever the scene is here. If you want to watch a ball game and that is what they televise, you are going to see a ball game. If you want to see a preacher and hear a sermon, you tune in on that and that is what you are going to get. If the Court permits a circus in this court room, it will be televised, that is true, but they will not be creating a circus.

"Now, the most important point is whether or not it would interfere with a fair and impartial trial of this Defendant. That is the most important point, and that is the purpose, or will be the primary purpose of the Court, to insure that he gets that fair trial. . . .

"There is not anything the Court can do about the interest in this case, but I can control your activities and your conduct here; and I can assure you now that this Court is not going to be turned into a circus with TV or without it. Whatever action is necessary for the Court to take to insure that, the Court will take it. . . .

"There has been one consideration that the Court has given and it is that this is a small court room and there will be hundreds of people trying to get into this court room to witness this trial. I believe we would have less confusion if they would stay at home and stay out of the court room and look in on the trial. With all of those people trying to crowd in and push into this court room, that is another consideration I have given to it."

[4]"In my statement of September 24, 1962, admitting television and other cameras in the court room during the trial of Billie Sol Estes, I said cameras would be allowed under the control and direction of the Court so long as they did not violate the legal rights of the Defendant or the State of Texas. . . .

"In line with my statement of September 24, 1962, I am at this time informing both television and radio that live broadcasting or telecasting by either news media cannot and will not be permitted during the interrogation of jurors in testing their qualifications, or of the testimony given by the witnesses, as to do so would be in violation of Art. 644 of the Code of Criminal Procedure of Texas, which provides as follows: 'At the request of either party, the witnesses on both sides may be sworn and placed in the custody of an officer and removed out of the court room to some place where they can not hear the testimony as delivered by any other witness in the case. This is termed placing witnesses under rule.'

" . . . [E]ach television network and the local television station will be allowed one

between the judge and representatives of the news media, the environment for the trial, which began on October 22, was in sharp contrast to that of the September hearings. The actual extent of television and news photography in the courtroom was described by the judge, after the trial had ended, in certifying the petitioner's bill of exceptions. This description is confirmed by my understanding of the entire record and was agreed to and accepted by defense counsel:

Prior to the trial of October 22, 1962, there was a booth constructed and placed in the rear of the courtroom painted the same or near the same color as the courtroom with a small opening across the top for the use of cameras. . . .

Live telecasting and radio broadcasting were not permitted and the only telecasting was on film without sound, and there was not any broadcasting of the trial by radio permitted. Each network, ABC, NBC, CBS and KRLD [KLTV] Television in Tyler was allowed a camera in the courtroom. . . . The telecasting on film of this case was not a continuous camera operation and only pictures being taken at intervals during the day to be used on regular news casts later in the day. There were some days during the trial that the cameras of only one or two stations were in operation, the others not being in attendance upon the Court each and every day. The Court did not permit any cameras other than those that were noiseless nor were flood lights and flash bulbs allowed to be used in the courtroom. The Court permitted one news photographer with Associated Press, United Press International and Tyler Morning Telegraph and Courier Times. However, they were not permitted inside the Bar; and the Court did not permit any telecasting or photographing in the hallways leading into the courtroom or on the second floor of the courthouse where the courtroom is situated, in order that the Defendant and his attorneys would not be hindered, molested or harassed in approaching or leaving the courtroom. The Court did permit live telecasting of the arguments of State's counsel and the returning of the verdict by the Jury and its acceptance by the Court. The opening argument of the District Attorney of Smith County was carried by sound and because of transmission difficulty, there was not any picture. The closing argument for the State by the District Attorney of Reeves County was carried live by both picture and sound. The arguments of attorneys for Defendant, John D. Cofer and Hume Cofer, were not telecast or broadcast as the Court granted their Motion that same not be permitted.

There was not any televising at any time during the trial except from the

---

film camera without sound in the court room and the film will be made available to other television stations on a pool basis. Marshall Pengra, manager of Television Station KLTV, Tyler, will be in charge of the independent pool and independent stations may contact him. The same will be true of cameras for the press, which will be limited to the local press, Associated Press and United Press. . . .

"I am making this statement at this time in order that the two news media affected may have sufficient notice before the case is called on October 22nd.

"The rules I have set forth above concerning the use of cameras are subject to change if I find that they are too restrictive or not workable, for any reason."

booth in the rear of the courtroom, and during the argument of counsel to the jury, news photography was required to operate from the booth so that they would not interfere or detract from the attention of either the jurors or the attorneys.

During the trial that began October 22nd, there was never at any time any radio broadcasting equipment in the courtroom. There was some equipment in a room off of the courtroom where there were periodic news reports given; and throughout the trial that began October 22nd, not any witness requested not to be televised or photographed while they were testifying. Neither did any juror, while being interrogated on voir dire or at any other time, make any request of the Court not to be televised.

Thus, except for the closing arguments for the prosecution and the return of the jury's verdict, there was no "live" telecasting of the trial. And, even for the purposes of delayed telecasting on later news programs, no words or other sounds were permitted to be recorded while the members of the jury were being selected or while any witness was testifying. No witnesses and no jurors were televised or photographed over their objection.[5]

Finally, the members of the jury saw no telecasts and no pictures of anything that went on during the trial. In accord with Texas law, the jurors were sequestered, day and night, from the beginning of the trial until it ended.[6] The jurors were lodged each night in quarters provided for that purpose in the courthouse itself. On the evening of November 6, by agreement of counsel and special permission of the court, the members of the jury were permitted to watch the election returns on television for a short period. For this purpose a portable television was brought into the jury's quarters by a court officer, and operated by him. Otherwise the jurors were not permitted to watch television at any time during the trial. The only newspapers permitted the jury were ones from which all coverage of the trial had been physically removed.

II

It is important to bear in mind the precise limits of the question before us in this case. The petition for a writ of certiorari asked us to review four separate constitutional claims. We declined to review three of them, among which was the claim that the members of the jury "had received through the news media damaging and prejudicial evidence. . . ."[7] We thus left undisturbed the

[5]There were nine witnesses for the prosecution and no witnesses for the defense.
[6]Arts. 668, 745, and 725, Tex. Code Crim. Proc.
[7]Petition for Writ of Certiorari, Question 3, p. 3.

determination of the Texas Court of Criminal Appeals that the members of the jury were *not* prejudiced by the widespread publicity which preceded the petitioner's trial. One ingredient of this pretrial publicity was the telecast of the September hearings. Despite the confusion in the courtroom during those hearings, all that a potential juror could have possibly learned from watching them on television was that the petitioner's case had been called for trial, and that motions had been made and acted upon for a continuance, and to exclude cameras and television. At those hearings, there was no discussion whatever of anything bearing on the petitioner's guilt or innocence. This was conceded by the petitioner's counsel at the trial.[8]

Because of our refusal to review the petitioner's claim that pretrial publicity had a prejudicial effect upon the jurors in this case, and because, insofar as the September hearings were an element of that publicity, the claim is patently without merit, that issue is simply not here. Our decision in *Rideau* v. *Louisiana*, 373 U.S. 723, therefore, has no bearing at all in this case. There the record showed that the inhabitants of the small Louisiana parish where the trial was held had repeatedly been exposed to a television film showing "Rideau, in jail, flanked by the sheriff and two state troopers, admitting in detail the commission of the robbery, kidnapping, and murder, in response to leading questions by the sheriff." 373 U.S., at 725. We found that "[a]ny subsequent court proceedings in a community so pervasively exposed to such a spectacle could be but a hollow formality." *Id.*, at 726. See also *Irvin* v. *Dowd*, 366 U.S. 717.

The *Rideau* case was no more than a contemporary application of enduring principles of procedural due process, principles reflected in such earlier cases as *Moore* v. *Dempsey*, 261 U.S. 86; *Brown* v. *Mississippi* 297 U.S. 278; and *Chambers* v. *Florida*, 309 U.S. 227, 235-241. "Under our Constitution's guarantee of due process," we said, "a person accused of committing a crime is vouchsafed basic minimal rights. Among these are the right to counsel, the right to plead not guilty, and the right to be tried in a courtroom presided over by a judge." 373 U.S., at 726-727. We had occasion to apply the same basic concepts of procedural due process earlier this Term in *Turner* v. *Louisiana*, 379 U.S. 466. "In the constitutional sense, trial by jury in a criminal case necessarily implies at the very least that the 'evidence developed' against a defendant shall come from the witness stand in a public courtroom where there is full judicial protection of the defendant's right of confrontation, of cross-examination, and of counsel." 379 U.S., at 472-473.

---

[8]"A. [Mr. Hume Cofer, counsel for petitioner] . . . The publicity that was given this trial on the last occasion and the number of cameras here, I think was sufficient to spread the news of the case throughout the county, to every available juror; and it is my opinion that on that occasion, there were so many cameras and so much paraphernalia here that it gave an opportunity for every prospective juror in Smith County to know about this case.

"Q. Not about the facts of the case?

"A. No, sir; not about the facts, nor any of the evidence."

But we do not deal here with mob domination of a courtroom, with a kangaroo trial, with a prejudiced judge or a jury inflamed with bias. Under the limited grant of certiorari in this case, the sole question before us is an entirely different one. It concerns only the regulated presence of television and still photography at the trial itself, which began on October 22, 1962. Any discussion of pretrial events can do no more than obscure the important question which is actually before us.

III

tv trial has constitutional hazards.

It is obvious that the introduction of television and news cameras into a criminal trial invites many serious constitutional hazards. The very presence of photographers and television cameramen plying their trade in a courtroom might be so completely and thoroughly disruptive and distracting as to make a fair trial impossible. Thus, if the scene at the September hearing had been repeated in the courtroom during this jury trial, it is difficult to conceive how a fair trial in the constitutional sense could have been afforded the defendant.[9] And even if, as was true here, the television cameras are so controlled and concealed as to be hardly perceptible in the courtroom itself, there are risks of constitutional dimensions that lurk in the very process of televising court proceedings at all.

Some of those risks are catalogued in the *amicus curiae* brief filed in this case by the American Bar Association: "[P]otential or actual jurors, in the absence of enforceable and effective safeguards, may arrive at certain misconceptions regarding the defendant and his trial by viewing televised pre-trial hearings and motions from which the jury is ordinarily excluded. Evidence otherwise inadmissible may leave an indelible mark. . . . Once the trial begins, exposure to nightly rebroadcasts of selected portions of the day's proceedings will be difficult to guard against, as jurors spend frequent evenings before the television set. The obvious impact of witnessing repeated trial episodes and hearing accompanying commentary, episodes admittedly chosen for their news value and not for evidentiary purposes, can serve only to distort the jurors' perspective. . . . Despite the court's injunction not to discuss the case, it seems undeniable that jurors will be subject to the pressure of television-watching family, friends and, indeed, strangers. . . . It is not too much to imagine a juror being confronted with his wife's television-oriented viewpoint. . . . Additionally, the jurors' daily television appearances may make them recognizable celebrities, likely to be stopped by passing strangers, or perhaps harried by intruding telephone calls. . . ." Constitutional problems of another kind might arise if a witness or juror were subjected to being televised over his objection.

[9]See note 2.

The plain fact of the matter, however, is that none of these things happened or could have happened in this case. The jurors themselves were prevented from seeing any telecasts of the trial, and completely insulated from association with any members of the public who did see such telecasts. This case, therefore, does not remotely resemble *Turner* v. *Louisiana,* 379 U.S. 466, where, during the trial, the jurors were subjected outside the courtroom to unmeasured and unmeasurable influences by key witnesses for the prosecution.

In the courtroom itself, there is nothing to show that the trial proceeded in any way other than it would have proceeded if cameras and television had not been present. In appearance, the courtroom was practically unaltered. There was no obtrusiveness and no distraction, no noise and no special lighting. There is no indication anywhere in the record of any disturbance whatever of the judicial proceedings. There is no claim that the conduct of the judge, or that any deed or word of counsel, or of any witness, or of any juror, was influenced in any way by the presence of photographers or by television.

Furthermore, from a reading of the record it is crystal clear that this was not a trial where the judge was harassed or confused or lacking in command of the proceedings before the jury. Not once, after the first witness was called, was there any interruption at all of the trial proper to secure a ruling concerning the presence of cameramen in the courtroom. There was no occasion, during the entire trial − until after the jury adjourned to reach its verdict − for any cautionary word to members of the press in the courtroom. The only time a motion was made, the jury was not in the courtroom. The trial itself was a most mundane affair, totally lacking in the lurid and completely emotionless. The evidence related solely to the circumstances in which various documents had been signed and negotiated. It was highly technical, if not downright dull. The petitioner called no witnesses, and counsel for petitioner made only a brief closing argument to the jury. There is nothing to indicate that the issues involved were of the kind where emotion could hold sway. The transcript of the trial belies any notion that frequent interruptions and inconsistent rulings communicated to the jury any sense that the judge was unable to concentrate on protecting the defendant and conducting the trial in a fair manner, in accordance with the State and Federal Constitutions.

IV

What ultimately emerges from this record, therefore, is one bald question − whether the Fourteenth Amendment of the United States Constitution prohibits all television cameras from a state courtroom whenever a criminal trial is in progress. In the light of this record and what we now know about the impact of television on a criminal trial, I can find no such prohibition in the Fourteenth

Amendment or in any other provision of the Constitution. If what occurred did not deprive the petitioner of his constitutional right to a fair trial, then the fact that the public could view the proceeding on television has no constitutional significance. The Constitution does not make us arbiters of the image that a televised state criminal trial projects to the public.

While no First Amendment claim is made in this case, there are intimations in the opinions filed by my Brethren in the majority which strike me as disturbingly alien to the First and Fourteenth Amendments' guarantees against federal or state interference with the free communication of information and ideas. The suggestion that there are limits upon the public's right to know what goes on in the courts causes me deep concern. The idea of imposing upon any medium of communications the burden of justifying its presence is contrary to where I had always thought the presumption must lie in the area of First Amendment freedoms. See *Speiser* v. *Randall*, 357 U.S. 513, 525. And the proposition that nonparticipants in a trial might get the "wrong impression" from unfettered reporting and commentary contains an invitation to censorship which I cannot accept. Where there is no disruption of the "essential requirement of the fair and orderly administration of justice," "[f]reedom of discussion should be given the widest range." *Pennekamp* v. *Florida*, 328 U.S. 331, 347; *Bridges* v. *California*, 314 U.S. 252. Cf. *Cox* v. *Louisiana*, 379 U.S. 559, 563.

I do not think that the Constitution denies to the State or to individual trial judges all discretion to conduct criminal trials with television cameras present, no matter how unobtrusive the cameras may be. I cannot say at this time that it is impossible to have a constitutional trial whenever any part of the proceedings is televised or recorded on television film. I cannot now hold that the Constitution absolutely bars television cameras from every criminal courtroom, even if they have no impact upon the jury, no effect upon any witness, and no influence upon the conduct of the judge.

For these reasons I would affirm the judgment.

11

DEFAMATION AND
BROADCAST NEWS

Rosenbloom v. Metromedia, Inc.
     403 U.S. 29
     June 7, 1971

> The exercise of enshrined First Amendment rights by the mass
> media occasionally trespasses upon the more nebulous rights of
> personal privacy. Defamation (i.e., libel and slander) is not
> protected by the Constitution. Legal defenses against defamation
> charges have evolved so as to favor free expression over privacy
> rights.
>   *Rosenbloom* v. *Metromedia* carries the evolution one step
> farther by extending the Supreme Court's 1964 *New York Times*
> doctrine to private individuals involved in matters of general
> concern to the public. This 5-3 decision produced five separate
> opinions, of which only the Court's judgment is reproduced
> below.

Mr. Justice Brennan announced the judgment of the Court and an opinion in
which The Chief Justice [Burger] and Mr. Justice Blackmun join.

In a series of cases beginning with *New York Times Co.* v. *Sullivan*, 376
U.S. 254 (1964), the Court has considered the limitations upon state libel laws
imposed by the constitutional guarantees of freedom of speech and of the press.
New York Times held that in a civil libel action by a public official against a
newspaper those guarantees required clear and convincing proof that a
defamatory falsehood alleged as libel was uttered with "knowledge that it was
false or with reckless disregard of whether it was false or not." *Id.*, at 280. The
same requirement was later held to apply to "public figures" who sued in libel
on the basis of alleged defamatory falsehoods. The several cases considered since
New York Times involved actions of "public officials" or "public figures,"

usually, but not always, against newspapers or magazines.[1] Common to all the cases was a defamatory falsehood in the report of an event of "public or general interest."[2] The instant case presents the question whether the *New York Times'* knowing-or-reckless-falsity standard applies in a state civil libel action brought not by a "public official" or a "public figure" but by a private individual for a defamatory falsehood uttered in a news broadcast by a radio station about the individual's involvement in an event of public or general interest.[3] The District Court for the Eastern District of Pennsylvania held that the *New York Times* standard did not apply and that Pennsylvania law determined respondent's liability in this diversity case, 289 F. Supp. 737 (1968). The Court of Appeals for the Third Circuit held that the *New York Times* standard did apply and reversed the judgment for damages awarded to petitioner by the jury. 415 F. 2d 892 (1969). We granted certiorari, 397 U.S. 904 (1970). We agree with the Court of Appeals and affirm that court's judgment.

I

In 1963, petitioner was a distributor of nudist magazines in the Philadelphia

[1] See, *e.g. Associated Press* v. *Walker*, 388 U.S. 130 (1967) (retired Army general against a wire service); *Curtis Publishing Co.* v. *Butts*, 388 U.S. 130 (1967) (former football coach against publisher of magazine); *Beckley Newspapers Corp.* v. *Hanks*, 389 U.S. 81 (1967) (court clerk against newspaper); *Greenbelt Publishing Assn.* v. *Bresler*, 398 U.S. 6 (1970) (state representative and real estate developer against publisher of newspaper); *Ocala Star-Banner Co.* v. *Damron*, 401 U.S. 295 (1971) (defeated candidate for tax assessor against publisher of newspaper); *Monitor Patriot Co.* v. *Roy*, 401 U.S. 265 (1971) (candidate for United States Senate against publisher of newspaper); *Time, Inc.* v. *Pape* 401 U.S. 279 (1971) (police official against publisher of magazine). However, *Rosenblatt* v. *Baer*, 383 U.S. 75 (1966), involved an action against a newspaper columnist by a former county recreation area supervisor; *St. Amant* v. *Thompson*, 390 U.S. 727 (1968), involved an action of a deputy sheriff against a defeated candidate for the United States Senate; and *Linn* v. *Plant Guard Workers*, 383 U.S. 53 (1966), involved an action by an official of an employer against a labor union.

　Garrison v. *Louisiana*, 379 U.S. 64 (1964), held that the *New York Times* standard measured also the constitutional restriction upon state power to impose criminal sanctions for criticism of the official conduct of public officials. The *Times* standard of proof has also been required to support the dismissal of a public school teacher based on false statements made by the teacher in discussing issues of public importance. *Pickering* v. *Board of Education*, 391 U.S. 563 (1968). The same test was applied to suits for invasion of privacy based on false statements where, again, a matter of public interest was involved. *Time, Inc.* v. *Hill*, 385 U.S. 374 (1967). The opinion in that case expressly reserved the question presented here whether the test applied in a libel action brought by a private individual. *Id.*, at 391.

[2] This term is from Warren & Brandeis, The Right to Privacy, 4 Harv. L. Rev. 193, 214 (1890). Our discussion of matters of "public or general interest" appears in Part IV, *infra*, of this opinion.

[3] Petitioner does not question that the First Amendment guarantees of freedom of speech and freedom of the press apply to respondent's newscasts.

metropolitan area. During the fall of that year, in response to citizen complaints, the Special Investigations Squad of the Philadelphia Police Department initiated a series of enforcement actions under the city's obscenity laws. The police, under the command of Captain Ferguson, purchased various magazines from more than 20 newsstands throughout the city. Based upon Captain Ferguson's determination that the magazines were obscene,[4] police on October 1, 1963, arrested most of the newsstand operators[5] on charges of selling obscene material. While the police were making an arrest at one newsstand, petitioner arrived to deliver some of his nudist magazines and was immediately arrested along with the newsboy.[6] Three days later, on October 4, the police obtained a warrant to search petitioner's home and the rented barn he used as a warehouse, and seized the inventory of magazines and books found at these locations. Upon learning of the seizures, petitioner, who had been released on bail after his first arrest, surrendered to the police and was arrested for a second time.

Following the second arrest, Captain Ferguson telephoned respondent's radio station WIP and another local radio station, a wire service, and a local newspaper to inform them of the raid on petitioner's home and of his arrest. WIP broadcast news reports every half hour to the Philadelphia metropolitan area. These news programs ran either five or ten minutes and generally contained from six to twenty different items that averaged about thirty seconds each. WIP's 6 p.m. broadcast on October 4, 1963, included the following item:

City Cracks Down on Smut Merchants

The Special Investigations Squad raided the home of George Rosenbloom in the 1800 block of Vesta Street this afternoon. Police confiscated 1,000 allegedly obscene books at Rosenbloom's home and arrested him on charges of possession of obscene literature. The Special Investigations Squad also raided a barn in the 20 Hundred block of Welsh Road near Bustleton Avenue and confiscated 3,000 obscene books. Capt. Ferguson says he believes they have hit the supply of a main distributor of obscene material in Philadelphia.

This report was rebroadcast in substantially the same form at 6:30 p.m., but at 8 p.m. when the item was broadcast for the third time, WIP corrected the third sentence to read "reportedly obscene." News of petitioner's arrest was broadcast five more times in the following twelve hours, but each report described the seized books as "allegedly" or "reportedly" obscene. From October 5 to October 21, WIP broadcast no further reports relating to petitioner.

On October 16 petitioner brought an action in Federal District Court

---

[4] At trial, Captain Ferguson testified that his definition of obscenity was "anytime the private parts is showing of the female or the private parts is shown of males."

[5] Several more newsstand operators were arrested between October 1 and October 4.

[6] The record neither confirms nor refutes petitioner's contention that his arrest was fortuitous. Nor does the record reflect whether or not petitioner's magazines were the subject either of the original citizens' complaints or of the initial police purchases.

against various city and police officials and against several local news media.[7] The suit alleged that the magazines petitioner distributed were not obscene and sought injunctive relief prohibiting further police interference with his business as well as further publicity of the earlier arrests. The second series of allegedly defamatory broadcasts related to WIP's news reports of the lawsuit. There were ten broadcasts on October 21, two on October 25, and one on November 1. None mentioned petitioner by name. The first at 6:30 a.m. on October 21 was pretty much like those that followed:

> Federal District Judge Lord, will hear arguments today from two publishers and a distributor all seeking an injunction against Philadelphia Police Commissioner Howard Leary . . . District Attorney James C. Crumlish . . . a local television station and a newspaper . . . ordering them to lay off the smut literature racket.
>
> The girlie-book peddlers say the police crackdown and continued reference to their borderline literature as smut or filth is hurting their business. Judge Lord refused to issue a temporary injunction when he was first approached. Today he'll decide the issue. It will set a precedent . . . and if the injunction is not granted . . . it could signal an even more intense effort to rid the city of pornography.

On October 27, petitioner went to WIP's studios after hearing from a friend that the station had broadcast news about his lawsuit. Using a lobby telephone to talk with a part-time newscaster, petitioner inquired what stories WIP had broadcast about him. The newscaster asked him to be more specific about dates and times. Petitioner then asked for the noon news broadcast on October 21, 1963, which the newscaster read to him over the phone; it was similar to the above 6:30 a.m. broadcast. According to petitioner, the ensuing interchange was brief. Petitioner told the newscaster that his magazines were "found to be completely legal and legitimate by the United States Supreme Court." When the newscaster replied the district attorney had said the magazines were obscene, petitioner countered that he had a public statement of the district attorney declaring the magazines legal. At that point, petitioner testified, "the telephone conversation was terminated . . . He just hung up." Petitioner apparently made no request for a retraction or correction, and none was forthcoming. WIP's final report on petitioner's lawsuit — the only one after petitioner's unsatisfactory conversation at the station — occurred on November 1 after the station had checked the story with the judge involved.[8]

---

[7] The complaint named as defendants the publishers of two newspapers, a television station, the city of Philadelphia, and the district attorney, but not respondent WIP. The plaintiffs were petitioner, the partnership of himself and his wife which carried on the business, and the publisher of the nudist magazines that he distributed.
[8] The text of the final broadcast read as follows:

> "U.S. District Judge John Lord told WIP News just before airtime that it may be

II

In May 1964 a jury acquitted petitioner in state court of the criminal obscenity charges under instructions of the trial judge that, as a matter of law, the nudist magazines distributed by petitioner were not obscene. Following his acquittal, petitioner filed this diversity action in District Court seeking damages under Pennsylvania's libel law. Petitioner alleged that WIP's unqualified characterization of the books seized as "obscene" in the 6 and 6:30 p.m. broadcasts of October 4, describing his arrest, constituted libel *per se* and was proved false by petitioner's subsequent acquittal. In addition, he alleged that the broadcasts in the second series describing his court suit for injunctive relief were also false and defamatory in that WIP characterized petitioner and his business associates as "smut distributors" and "girlie-book peddlers" and, further, falsely characterized the suit as an attempt to force the defendants "to lay off the smut literature racket."

At the trial WIP's defenses were truth and privilege. WIP's news director testified that his eight-man staff of reporters prepared their own newscasts and broadcast their material themselves, and that material for the news programs usually came either from the wire services or from telephone tips. None of the writers or broadcasters involved in preparing the broadcasts in this case testified. The news director's recollection was that the primary source of information for the first series of broadcasts about petitioner's arrest was Captain Ferguson, but that, to the director's knowledge, the station did not have any further verification. Captain Ferguson testified that he had informed WIP and other media of the police action and that WIP had accurately broadcast what he told the station. The evidence regarding WIP's investigation of petitioner's lawsuit in the second series of broadcasts was even more sparse. The news director testified that he was "sure we would check with the District Attorney's office also and with the Police Department," but "it would be difficult for me to specifically state what additional corroboration we had." In general, he testified that WIP's half-hour deadlines required it to rely on wire-service copy and oral reports from previously reliable sources subject to the general policy that "we will contact as many sources as we possibly can on any kind of a story."

---

another week before he will be able to render a decision as to whether he has jurisdiction in the case of two publishers and a distributor who wish to restrain the D.A.'s office, the police chief, a TV station and the Bulletin for either making alleged raids of their publications, considered smut and immoral literature by the defendants named, or publicizing that they are in that category. Judge Lord then will be in a position to rule on injunction proceedings asked by the publishers and distributor claiming the loss of business in their operations."

III

Pennsylvania's libel law tracks almost precisely the Restatement (First) of Torts provisions on the subject. Pennsylvania holds actionable any unprivileged "malicious"[9] publication of matter which tends to harm a person's reputation and expose him to public hatred, contempt, or ridicule. *Schnabel* v. *Meredith*, 378 Pa. 609, 107 A. 2d 860 (1954); Restatement of Torts § § 558, 559 (1938). Pennsylvania law recognizes truth as a complete defense to a libel action. *Schonek* v. *WJAC, Inc.*, 436 Pa. 78, 84, 258 A. 2d 504, 507 (1969); Restatement of Torts § 582. It recognizes an absolute immunity for defamatory statements made by high state officials, even if published with an improper motive, actual malice, or knowing falsity. *Montgomery* v. *Philadelphia*, 392 Pa. 178, 140 A. 2d 100 (1958); Restatement of Torts § 591, and it recognizes a conditional privilege for news media to report judicial, administrative, or legislative proceedings if the account is fair and accurate, and not published solely for the purpose of causing harm to the person defamed, even though the official information is false or inaccurate. *Sciandra* v. *Lynett*, 409 Pa. 595, 600-601, 187 A. 2d 586, 588-589 (1963); Restatement of Torts § 611. The conditional privilege of the news media may be defeated, however, by " 'want of reasonable care and diligence to ascertain the truth, before giving currency to an untrue communication.' The failure to employ such 'reasonable care and diligence' can destroy a privilege which otherwise would protect the utterer of the communication." *Purcell* v. *Westinghouse Broadcasting Co.*, 411 Pa. 167, 179, 191 A. 2d 662, 668 (1963). Pennsylvania has also enacted verbatim the Restatement's provisions on burden of proof, which place the burden of proof for the affirmative defenses of truth and privilege upon the defendant.[10]

At the close of the evidence, the District Court denied respondent's

---

[9]The reference here, of course, is to common-law "malice," not to the constitutional standard of *New York Times Co.* v. *Sullivan, supra*. See n. 18, *infra*.

[10]Pa. Stat. Ann., Tit. 12, § 1584a (Supp. 1971) provides:

"(1) In an action for defamation, the plaintiff has the burden of proving, when the issue is properly raised:

"(a) The defamatory character of the communication;

"(b) Its publication by the defendant;

"(c) Its application to the plaintiff;

"(d) The recipient's understanding of its defamatory meaning;

"(e) The recipient's understanding of it as intended to be applied to the plaintiff;

"(f) Special harm resulting to the plaintiff from its publication;

"(g) Abuse of a conditionally privileged occasion.

"(2) In an action for defamation, the defendant has the burden of proving, when the issue is properly raised:

"(a) The truth of the defamatory communication;

"(b) The privileged character of the occasion on which it was published;

"(c) The character of the subject matter of defamatory comment as of public concern."

See Restatement of Torts § 613.

motion for a directed verdict and charged the jury, in conformity with Pennsylvania law, that four findings were necessary to return a verdict for petitioner: (1) that one or more of the broadcasts were defamatory; (2) that a reasonable listener would conclude that the defamatory statement referred to petitioner; (3) that WIP had forfeited its privilege to report official proceedings fairly and accurately, either because it intended to injure the plaintiff personally or because it exercised the privilege unreasonably and without reasonable care; and (4) that the reporting was false. The jury was instructed that petitioner had the burden of proof on the first three issues, but that respondent had the burden of proving that the reporting was true. The jury was further instructed that "as a matter of law" petitioner was not entitled to actual damages claimed for loss of business "not because it wouldn't ordinarily be but because there has been evidence that this same subject matter was the subject" of broadcasts over other television and radio stations and of newspaper reports, "so if there was any business lost . . . we have no proof . . . that [it] resulted directly from the broadcasts by WIP . . ." App. 331a. On the question of punitive damages, the judge gave the following instruction:

[I]f you find that this publication arose from a bad motive or malice toward the plaintiff, or if you find that it was published with reckless indifference to the truth, if you find that it was not true, you would be entitled to award punitive damages, and punitive damages are awarded as a deterrent from future conduct of the same sort.

They really are awarded only for outrageous conduct, as I have said, with a bad motive or with reckless disregard of the interests of others, and before you would award punitive damages you must find that these broadcasts were published with a bad motive or with reckless disregard of the rights of others, or reckless indifference to the rights of others . . .

The jury returned a verdict for petitioner and awarded $25,000 in general damages, and $725,000 in punitive damages. The District Court reduced the punitive damages award to $250,000 on remittitur, but denied respondent's motion for judgment n. o. v. In reversing, the Court of Appeals emphasized that the broadcasts concerned matters of public interest and that they involved "hot news" prepared under deadline pressure. The Court of Appeals concluded that "the fact that plaintiff was not a public figure cannot be accorded decisive importance if the recognized important guarantees of the First Amendment are to be adequately implemented." 415 F. 2d, at 896. For that reason, the court held that the *New York Times* standard applied and, further, directed that judgment be entered for respondent, holding that, as a matter of law, petitioner's evidence did not meet that standard.

IV

Petitioner concedes that the police campaign to enforce the obscenity laws was an issue of public interest, and, therefore, that the constitutional guarantees for freedom of speech and press imposed limits upon Pennsylvania's power to apply its libel laws to compel respondent to compensate him in damages for the alleged defamatory falsehoods broadcast about his involvement. As noted, the narrow question he raises is whether, because he is not a "public official" or a "public figure" but a private individual, those limits required that he prove that the falsehoods resulted from a failure of respondent to exercise reasonable care, or required that he prove that the falsehoods were broadcast with knowledge of their falsity or with reckless disregard of whether they were false or not. That question must be answered against the background of the functions of the constitutional guarantees for freedom of expression. *Rosenblatt* v. *Baer*, 383 U.S. 75, at 84-85, n. 10 (1966).

Self-governance in the United States presupposes far more than knowledge and debate about the strictly official activities of various levels of government. The commitment of the country to the institution of private property, protected by the Due Process and Just Compensation Clauses in the Constitution, places in private hands vast areas of economic and social power that vitally affect the nature and quality of life in the Nation. Our efforts to live and work together in a free society not completely dominated by governmental regulation necessarily encompass far more than politics in a narrow sense. "The guarantees for speech and press are not the preserve of political expression or comment upon public affairs." *Time, Inc.* v. *Hill*, 385 U.S. 374, 388 (1967). "Freedom of discussion, if it would fulfill its historic function in this nation, must embrace all issues about which information is needed or appropriate to enable the members of society to cope with the exigencies of their period." *Thornhill* v. *Alabama*, 310 U.S. 88, 102 (1940).

Although the limitations upon civil libel actions, first held in *New York Times* to be required by the First Amendment, were applied in that case in the context of defamatory falsehoods about the official conduct of a public official, later decisions have disclosed the artificiality, in terms of the public's interest, of a simple distinction between "public" and "private" individuals or institutions:

Increasingly in this country, the distinctions between governmental and private sectors are blurred. . . . In many situations, policy determinations which traditionally were channeled through formal political institutions are now originated and implemented through a complex array of boards, committees, commissions, corporations, and associations, some only loosely connected with the Government. This blending of positions and power has also occurred in the case of individuals so that many who do not hold public office at the moment are nevertheless intimately involved in the resolution of important public questions . . .

. . . Our citizenry has a legitimate and substantial interest in the conduct of such persons, and freedom of the press to engage in uninhibited debate about their involvement in public issues and events is as crucial as it is in the case of "public officials." *Curtis Publishing Co.* v. *Butts*, 388 U.S. 130, 163-164 (1967) (Warren, C. J., concurring in result).

Moreover, the constitutional protection was not intended to be limited to matters bearing broadly on issues of responsible government. "[T]he Founders ... felt that a free press would advance 'truth, science, morality, and arts in general' as well as responsible government." *Id.*, at 147 (opinion of Harlan, J.). Comments in other cases reiterate this judgment that the First Amendment extends to myriad matters of public interest. In *Time, Inc.* v. *Hill, supra,* we had "no doubt that the ... opening of a new play linked to an actual incident, is a matter of public interest," 385 U.S., at 388, which was entitled to constitutional protection. *Butts* held that an alleged "fix" of a college football game was a public issue. *Associated Press* v. *Walker,* 388 U.S. 130 (1967), a companion case to *Butts,* established that the public had a similar interest in the events and personalities involved in federal efforts to enforce a court decree ordering the enrollment of a Negro student in the University of Mississippi. Thus, these cases underscore the vitality, as well as the scope, of the "profound national commitment to the principle that debate on *public issues* should be uninhibited, robust, and wide-open." *New York Times Co.* v. *Sullivan,* 376 U.S., at 270-271 (emphasis added).

If a matter is a subject of public or general interest, it cannot suddenly become less so merely because a private individual is involved, or because in some sense the individual did not "voluntarily" choose to become involved. The public's primary interest is in the event; the public focus is on the conduct of the participant and the content, effect, and significance of the conduct, not the participant's prior anonymity or notoriety.[11] The present case illustrates the point. The community has a vital interest in the proper enforcement of its criminal laws, particularly in an area such as obscenity where a number of highly important values are potentially in conflict: the public has an interest both in seeing that the criminal law is adequately enforced and in assuring that the law is not used unconstitutionally to suppress free expression. Whether the person involved is a famous large-scale magazine distributor or a "private" businessman running a corner newsstand has no relevance in ascertaining whether the public has an interest in the issue. We honor the commitment to robust debate on public issues, which is embodied in the First Amendment, by extending constitutional protection to all discussion

---

[11]For example, the public's interest in the provocative speech that was made during the tense episode on the campus of the University of Mississippi would certainly have been the same in *Associated Press* v. *Walker,* n.1, *supra,* if the speaker had been an anonymous student and not a well-known retired Army general. *Walker* also illustrates another anomaly of focusing analysis on the public "figure" or public "official" status of the individual involved. General Walker's fame stemmed from events completely unconnected with the episode in Mississippi. It seems particularly unsatisfactory to determine the extent of First Amendment protection on the basis of factors completely unrelated to the newsworthy events being reported. See also *Greenbelt Publishing Assn.* v. *Bresler,* 398 U.S. 6 (1970).

and communication involving matters of public or general concern, without regard to whether the persons involved are famous or anonymous.[12]

Our Brother White agrees that the protection afforded by the First Amendment depends upon whether the issue involved in the publication is an issue of public or general concern. He would, however, confine our holding to the situation raised by the facts in this case, that is, limit it to issues involving "official actions of public servants." In our view that might be misleading. It is clear that there has emerged from our cases decided since *New York Times* the concept that the First Amendment's impact upon state libel laws derives not so much from whether the plaintiff is a "public official," "public figure," or "private individual," as it derives from the question whether the allegedly defamatory publication concerns a matter of public or general interest. See T. Emerson, The System of Freedom of Expression 531-532, 540 (1970). In that circumstance we think the time has come forthrightly to announce that the determinant whether the First Amendment applies to state libel actions is whether the utterance involved concerns an issue of public or general concern, albeit leaving the delineation of the reach of that term to future cases. As our Brother White observes, that is not a problem in this case, since police arrest of a person for distributing allegedly obscene magazines clearly constitutes an issue of public or general interest. [13]

V

We turn then to the question to be decided. Petitioner's argument that the Constitution should be held to require that the private individual prove only that the publisher failed to exercise "reasonable care" in publishing defamatory falsehoods proceeds along two lines. First, he argues that the private individual,

---

[12]We are not to be understood as implying that no area of a person's activities falls outside the area of public or general interest. We expressly leave open the question of what constitutional standard of proof, if any, controls the enforcement of state libel laws for defamatory falsehoods published or broadcast by news media about a person's activities not within the area of public or general interest.

　　We also intimate no view on the extent of constitutional protection, if any, for purely commercial communications made in the course of business. See *Valentine* v. *Chrestensen*, 316 U.S. 52 (1942). Compare *Breard* v. *Alexandria*, 341 U.S. 622 (1951), with *Martin* v. *Struthers*, 319 U.S. 141 (1943). But see *New York Times Co.* v. *Sullivan*, 376 U.S., at 265-266; *Linn* v. *Plant Guard Workers*, 383 U.S. 53 (1966).

[13]Our Brother White states in his opinion: "[T]he First Amendment gives . . . a privilege to report . . . the official actions of public servants in full detail, with no requirement that . . . the privacy of an individual involved in . . . the official action be spared from public view." . . . This seems very broad. It implies a privilege to report, for example, such confidential records as those of juvenile court proceedings.

unlike the public figure, does not have access to the media to counter the defamatory material and that the private individual, unlike the public figure, has not assumed the risk of defamation by thrusting himself into the public arena. Second, petitioner focuses on the important values served by the law of defamation in preventing and redressing attacks upon reputation.

We have recognized the force of petitioner's arguments, *Time, Inc.* v. *Hill, supra*, at 391, and we adhere to the caution expressed in that case against "blind application" of the *New York Times* standard. *Id.*, at 390. Analysis of the particular factors involved, however, convinces us that petitioner's arguments cannot be reconciled with the purposes of the First Amendment, with our cases, and with the traditional doctrines of libel law itself. Drawing a distinction between "public" and "private" figures makes no sense in terms of the First Amendment guarantees.[14] The *New York Times* standard was applied to libel of a public official or public figure to give effect to the Amendment's function to encourage ventilation of public issues, not because the public official has any less interest in protecting his reputation than an individual in private life. While the argument that public figures need less protection because they can command media attention to counter criticism may be true for some very prominent people, even then it is the rare case where the denial overtakes the original charge. Denials, retractions, and corrections are not "hot" news, and rarely receive the prominence of the original story. When the public official or public figure is a minor functionary, or has left the position that put him in the public eye, see *Rosenblatt* v. *Baer, supra*, the argument loses all of its force. In the vast majority of libels involving public officials or public figures, the ability to respond through the media will depend on the same complex factor on which the ability of a private individual depends: the unpredictable event of the media's continuing interest in the story. Thus the unproved, and highly improbable, generalization that an as yet undefined class of "public figures" involved in matters of public concern will be better able to respond through the media than private individuals also involved in such matters seems too insubstantial a reed on which to rest a constitutional distinction. Furthermore, in First Amendment terms, the cure seems far worse than the disease. If the States fear that private citizens will not be able to respond adequately to publicity involving them, the solution lies in the direction of ensuring their

---

[14]See *United Medical Laboratories, Inc.* v. *Columbia Broadcasting System, Inc.*, 404 F. 2d 706 (CA9 1968), cert. denied, 394 U.S. 921 (1969); *Time, Inc.* v. *McLaney*, 406 F. 2d 565 (CA5), cert. denied, 395 U.S. 922 (1969); *Bon Air Hotel, Inc.* v. *Time, Inc.*, 426 F. 2d 858, 861 n. 4, and cases cited therein (CA5 1970). See generally Cohen, A New Niche for the Fault Principle: A Forthcoming Newsworthiness Privilege in Libel Cases?, 18 U.C.L.A. L. Rev. 371 (1970); Kalven, The Reasonable Man and the First Amendment: Hill, Butts, and Walker, 1967 Sup. Ct. Rev. 267; Note, Public Official and Actual Malice Standards: The Evolution of *New York Times Co.* v. *Sullivan*, 56 Iowa L. Rev. 393, 398-400 (1970); Note, The Scope of First Amendment Protection for Good-Faith Defamatory Error, 75 Yale L. J. 642 (1966).

ability to respond, rather than in stifling public discussion of matters of public concern.[15]

Further reflection over the years since *New York Times* was decided persuades us that the view of the "public official" or "public figure" as assuming the risk of defamation by voluntarily thrusting himself into the public eye bears little relationship either to the values protected by the First Amendment or to the nature of our society. We have recognized that "[e]xposure of the self to others in varying degrees is a concomitant of life in a civilized community." *Time, Inc.* v. *Hill, supra*, at 388. Voluntarily or not, we are all "public" men to some degree. Conversely, some aspects of the lives of even the most public men fall outside the area of matters of public or general concern. See n. 12, *supra*; *Griswold* v. *Connecticut*, 381 U.S. 479 (1965).[16] Thus, the idea that certain "public" figures have voluntarily exposed their entire lives to public inspection, while private individuals have kept theirs carefully shrouded from public view is, at best, a legal fiction. In any event, such a distinction could easily produce the paradoxical result of dampening discussion of issues of public or general concern because they happen to involve private citizens while extending constitutional encouragement to discussion of aspects of the lives of "public figures" that are not in the area of public or general concern.

General references to the values protected by the law of libel conceal important distinctions. Traditional arguments suggest that libel law protects two separate interests of the individual: first, his desire to preserve a certain privacy around his personality from unwarranted intrusion, and, second, a desire to preserve his public good name and reputation. See *Rosenblatt* v. *Baer*, 383 U.S., at 92 (Stewart, J., concurring). The individual's interest in privacy — in preventing unwarranted intrusion upon the private aspects of his life — is not involved in this case, or even in the class of cases under consideration, since, by

[15]Some States have adopted retraction statutes or right-of-reply statutes. See Donnelly, The Right of Reply: An Alternative to an Action for Libel, 34 Va. L. Rev. 867 (1948); Note, Vindication of the Reputation of a Public Official, 80 Harv. L. Rev. 1730 (1967). Cf. *Red Lion Broadcasting Co.* v. *FCC*, 395 U.S. 367 (1969).

One writer, in arguing that the First Amendment itself should be read to guarantee a right of access to the media not limited to a right to respond to defamatory falsehoods, has suggested several ways the law might encourage public discussion. Barron, Access to the Press — A New First Amendment Right, 80 Harv. L. Rev. 1641, 1666-1678 (1967). It is important to recognize that the private individual often desires press exposure either for himself, his ideas, or his causes. Constitutional adjudication must take into account the individual's interest in access to the press as well as the individual's interest in preserving his reputation, even though libel actions by their nature encourage a narrow view of the individual's interest since they focus only on situations where the individual has been harmed by undesired press attention. A constitutional rule that deters the press from covering the ideas or activities of the private individual thus conceives the individual's interest too narrowly.

[16]This is not the less true because the area of public concern in the cases of candidates for public office and of elected public officials is broad. See *Monitor Patriot Co.* v. *Roy*, 401 U.S. 265 (1971).

hypothesis, the individual is involved in matters of public or general concern.[17] In the present case, however, petitioner's business reputation is involved, and thus the relevant interests protected by state libel law are petitioner's public reputation and good name.

These are important interests. Consonant with the libel laws of most of the States, however, Pennsylvania's libel law subordinates these interests of the individual in a number of circumstances. Thus, high government officials are immune from liability — absolutely privileged — even if they publish defamatory material from an improper motive, with actual malice, and with knowledge of its falsity. *Montgomery* v. *Philadelphia*, 392 Pa. 178, 140 A. 2d 100 (1958). This absolute privilege attaches to judges, attorneys at law in connection with a judicial proceeding, parties and witnesses to judicial proceedings, Congressmen and state legislators, and high national and state executive officials. Restatement of Torts §§ 585-592. Moreover, a conditional privilege allows newspapers to report the false defamatory material originally published under the absolute privileges listed above, if done accurately. *Sciandra* v. *Lynett*, 409 Pa. 595, 187 A. 2d 586 (1963).

Even without the presence of a specific constitutional command, therefore, Pennsylvania libel law recognizes that society's interest in protecting individual reputation often yields to other important social goals. In this case, the vital needs of freedom of the press and freedom of speech persuade us that allowing private citizens to obtain damage judgments on the basis of a jury determination that a publisher probably failed to use reasonable care would not provide adequate "breathing space" for these great freedoms. Reasonable care is an "elusive standard" that "would place on the press the intolerable burden of guessing how a jury might assess the reasonableness of steps taken by it to verify the accuracy of every reference to a name, picture or portrait." *Time, Inc.* v. *Hill*, 385 U.S., at 389. Fear of guessing wrong must inevitably cause self-censorship and thus create the danger that the legitimate utterance will be deterred. Cf. *Speiser* v. *Randall*, 357 U.S. 513, 526 (1958).

Moreover, we ordinarily decide civil litigation by the preponderance of the evidence. Indeed, the judge instructed the jury to decide the present case by that

[17]Our Brothers Harlan and Marshall would not limit the application of the First Amendment to private libels involving issues of general or public interest. They would hold that the Amendment covers all private libels at least where state law permits the defense of truth. The Court has not yet had occasion to consider the impact of the First Amendment on the application of state libel laws to libels where no issue of general or public interest is involved. See n.1, *supra*. However, *Griswold* v. *Connecticut*, 381 U.S. 479 (1965), recognized a constitutional right to privacy and at least one commentator has discussed the relation of that right to the First Amendment. Emerson, *supra*, at 544-562. Since all agree that this case involves an issue of public or general interest, we have no occasion to discuss that relationship. See n.12, *supra*. We do not, however, share the doubts of our Brothers Harlan and Marshall that courts would be unable to identify interests in privacy and dignity. The task may be difficult but not more so than other tasks in this field.

standard. In the normal civil suit where this standard is employed, "we view it as no more serious in general for there to be an erroneous verdict in the defendant's favor than for there to be an erroneous verdict in the plaintiff's favor." *In re Winship*, 397 U.S. 358, 371 (1970) (Harlan, J., concurring). In libel cases, however, we view an erroneous verdict for the plantiff as most serious. Not only does it mulct the defendant for an innocent misstatement — the three-quarter-million-dollar jury verdict in this case could rest on such an error — but the possibility of such error, even beyond the vagueness of the negligence standard itself, would create a strong impetus toward self-censorship, which the First Amendment cannot tolerate. These dangers for freedom of speech and press led us to reject the reasonable-man standard of liability as "simply inconsistent" with our national commitment under the First Amendment when sought to be applied to the conduct of a political campaign. *Monitor Patriot Co.* v. *Roy*, 401 U.S. 265, 276 (1971). The same considerations lead us to reject that standard here.

We are aware that the press has, on occasion, grossly abused the freedom it is given by the Constitution. All must deplore such excesses. In an ideal world, the responsibility of the press would match the freedom and public trust given it. But from the earliest days of our history, this free society, dependent as it is for its survival upon a vigorous free press, has tolerated some abuse. In 1799, James Madison made the point in quoting (and adopting) John Marshall's answer to Talleyrand's complaints about American newspapers, American State Papers, 2 Foreign Relations 196 (U.S. Cong. 1832):

"Among those principles deemed sacred in America, among those sacred rights considered as forming the bulwark of their liberty, which the Government contemplates with awful reverence and would approach only with the most cautious circumspection, there is no one of which the importance is more deeply impressed on the public mind than the liberty of the press. That this *liberty* is often carried to excess; that it has sometimes degenerated into *licentiousness*, is seen and lamented, *but the remedy has not yet been discovered. Perhaps it is an evil inseparable from the good with which it is allied; perhaps it is a shoot which cannot be stripped from the stalk without wounding vitally the plant from which it is torn. However desirable those measures might be which might correct without enslaving the press, they have never yet been devised in America.*" 6 Writings of James Madison, 1790-1802, p. 336 (G. Hunt ed. 1906) (emphasis in original).

This Court has recognized this imperative: "[T]o insure the ascertainment and publication of the truth about public affairs, it is essential that the First Amendment protect some erroneous publications as well as true ones." *St. Amant* v. *Thompson*, 390 U.S. 727, 732 (1968). We thus hold that a libel action, as here, by a private individual against a licensed radio station for a defamatory falsehood in a newscast relating to his involvement in an event of public or general concern may be sustained only upon clear and convincing proof that the defamatory falsehood was published with knowledge that it was false or with reckless disregard of whether it was false or not.[18] Calculated falsehood, of course, falls outside "the fruitful exercise of the right of free speech." *Garrison v. Louisiana*, 379 U.S. 64, 75 (1964).

Our Brothers Harlan and Marshall reject the knowing-or-reckless-falsehood standard in favor of a test that would require, at least, that the person defamed establish that the publisher negligently failed to ascertain the truth of his story; they would also limit any recovery to "actual" damages. For the reasons we have stated, the negligence standard gives insufficient breathing space to First Amendment values. Limiting recovery to actual damages has the same defects. In the first instance, that standard, too, leaves the First Amendment insufficient elbow room within which to function. It is not simply the possibility of a judgment for damages that results in self-censorship. The very possibility of having to engage in litigation, an expensive and protracted process, is threat enough to cause discussion and debate to "steer far wider of the unlawful zone" thereby keeping protected discussion from public cognizance. *Speiser* v. *Randall*, 357 U.S., at 526. Cf. *Blonder-Tongue Laboratories, Inc.* v. *University of Illinois Foundation*, 402 U.S. 313, 334-339 (1971). Too, a small newspaper suffers equally from a substantial damage award, whether the label of the award be "actual" or "punitive."

The real thrust of Brothers Harlan's and Marshall's position, however, is their assertion that their proposal will not "constitutionalize" the factfinding process. But this clearly is not the way their test would work in practice. Their approach means only that factfinding will shift from an inquiry into whether the defamatory statements were knowingly or recklessly uttered to the inquiry whether they were negligently uttered, and if so, to an inquiry whether plaintiff suffered "actual" damages. This latter inquiry will involve judges even more deeply in factfinding. Would the mere announcement by a state legislature that embarrassment and pain and suffering are measurable actual losses mean that such damages may be awarded in libel actions? No matter how the problem is approached, this Court would ultimately have to fashion constitutional definitions of "negligence" and of "actual damages."

Aside from these particularized considerations, we have repeatedly

---

[18] At oral argument petitioner argued that "the little man can't show actual malice. How can George Rosenbloom show that there was actual malice in Metromedia? They never heard of him before." Yr. of Oral Arg., Dec. 8, 1970, p. 39. But ill will toward the plaintiff, or bad motives, are not elements of the *New York Times* standard. That standard requires only that the plaintiff prove knowing or reckless falsity. That burden, and no more, is the plaintiff's whether "public official," "public figure," or "little man." It may be that jury instructions that are couched only in terms of knowing or reckless falsity, and omit reference to "actual malice," would further a proper application of the *New York Times* standard to the evidence.

recognized that courts may not avoid an excursion into factfinding in this area simply because it is time consuming or difficult. We stated in *Pennekamp* v. *Florida*, 328 U.S. 331, 335 (1946), that:

> The Constitution has imposed upon this Court final authority to determine the meaning and application of those words of that instrument which require interpretation to resolve judicial issues. With that responsibility, we are compelled to examine for ourselves the statements in issue and the circumstances under which they were made to see whether or not they . . . are of a character which the principles of the First Amendment, as adopted by the Due Process Clause of the Fourteenth Amendment, protect. (Footnote omitted.)

Clearly, then, this Court has an "obligation to test challenged judgments against the guarantees of the First and Fourteenth Amendments," and in doing so "this Court cannot avoid making an independent constitutional judgment on the facts of the case." *Jacobellis* v. *Ohio*, 378 U.S. 184, 190 (1964). The simple fact is that First Amendment questions of "constitutional fact" compel this Court's *de novo* review. See *Edwards* v. *South Carolina*, 372 U.S. 229, 235 (1963); *Blackburn* v. *Alabama*, 361 U.S. 199, 205 n. 5 (1960).

VI

Petitioner argues that the instructions on punitive damages either cured or rendered harmless the instructions permitting an award of general damages based on a finding of failure of WIP to exercise reasonable care. We have doubts of the merits of the premise,[19] but even assuming that instructions were given satisfying the standard of knowing or reckless falsity, the evidence was insufficient to sustain an award for the petitioner under that standard. In these cases our "duty is not limited to the elaboration of constitutional principles; we must also in proper cases review the evidence to make certain that those principles have been constitutionally applied." *New York Times Co.* v. *Sullivan*,

---

[19]The instructions authorized an award of punitive damages upon a finding that a falsehood "arose from a bad motive or . . . that it was published with reckless indifference to the truth . . . punitive damages are awarded as a deterrent from future conduct of the same sort." App. 333a. The summation of petitioner's counsel conceded that respondent harbored no ill-will toward petitioner, but, following the suggestion of the instructions that punitive damages are " 'smart' money," App. 313a, argued that they should be assessed because "[respondent] must be careful the way they impart news information and you can punish them if they weren't because you could say that was malicious." *Ibid.* This was an obvious invitation based on the instructions to award punitive damages for carelessness. Thus the jury was allowed, and even encouraged, to find malice and award punitive damages merely on the basis of negligence and bad motive.

376 U.S., at 285. Our independent analysis of the record leads us to agree with the Court of Appeals that none of the proofs, considered either singly or cumulatively, satisfies the constitutional standard with the convincing clarity necessary to raise a jury question whether the defamatory falsehoods were broadcast with knowledge that they were false or with reckless disregard of whether they were false or not.

The evidence most strongly supporting petitioner is that concerning his visit to WIP's studio where a part-time newscaster hung up the telephone when petitioner disputed the newscaster's statement that the District Attorney had characterized petitioner's magazines as obscene. This contact occurred, however, after all but one of the second series of broadcasts had been aired. The incident has no probative value insofar as it bears on petitioner's case as to the first series of broadcasts. That portion of petitioner's case was based upon the omission from the first two broadcasts at 6 and 6:30 p.m. on October 4 of the word "alleged" preceding a characterization of the magazines distributed by petitioner. But that omission was corrected with the 8 p.m. broadcast and was not repeated in the five broadcasts that followed. And we agree with the analysis of the Court of Appeals that led that court, and leads us, to conclude that the episode failed to provide evidence satisfying the *New York Times* standard insofar as it bore on petitioner's case based upon the broadcasts on and after October 21 concerning petitioner's lawsuit:

Only one broadcast took place after this conversation. It is attacked on the ground that it contains an inaccurate statement concerning plaintiff's injunction action in that it stated that the district attorney considered plaintiff's publications to be smut and immoral literature. The transcript of the testimony shows that plaintiff's own attorney, when questioning defendant's representative concerning the allegedly defamatory portion of the last broadcast, said that he was not questioning its "accuracy". Furthermore, his examination of the same witness brought out that defendant's representative confirmed the story with the judge involved before the broadcast was made. We think that the episode described failed to provide evidence of actual malice with the requisite convincing clarity to create a jury issue under federal standards. 415 F. 2d, at 897.

Petitioner argues finally that WIP's failure to communicate with him to learn his side of the case and to obtain a copy of the magazine for examination, sufficed to support a verdict under the *New York Times* standard. But our "cases are clear that reckless conduct is not measured by whether a reasonably prudent man would have published, or would have investigated before publishing. There must be sufficient evidence to permit the conclusion that the defendant in fact entertained serious doubts as to the truth of his publication." *St. Amant* v. *Thompson*, 390 U.S., at 731. Respondent here relied on information supplied by police officials. Following petitioner's complaint about the accuracy of the broadcasts, WIP checked its last report with the judge who presided in the case. While we may assume that the District Court correctly held to be defamatory respondent's characterizations of petitioner's business as "the smut literature racket," and of those engaged in it as "girlie-book peddlers," there is no evidence in the record to support a conclusion that respondent "in fact entertained serious doubts as to the truth" of its reports.

Affirmed.

Mr. Justice Douglas took no part in the consideration or decision of this case.

12

SELF-REGULATION

RTNDA Code of Broadcast News Ethics*
January 2, 1966

The Radio Television News Directors Association is the major national organization representing the interests of broadcast journalists. The RTNDA Code, despite its brevity and its lax enforcement, should be viewed as more than "window dressing" for the profession; it embodies principles that transcend the occasional staging of a news event or the passing trend favoring "happy" news. The self-regulatory efforts of radio-TV newsmen become increasingly important as the broadcast media supplant the print media as primary sources of information in this democracy.

The members of the Radio Television News Directors Association agree that their prime responsibility as newsmen — and that of the broadcasting industry as the collective sponsor of news broadcasting — is to provide to the public they serve a news service as accurate, full and prompt as human integrity and devotion can devise, To that end, they declare their acceptance of the standards of practice here set forth, and their solemn intent to honor them to the limits of their ability.

Article One

The primary purpose of broadcast newsmen — to inform the public of events of importance and appropriate interest in a manner that is accurate and comprehensive — shall override all other purposes.

*Printed with permission of the Radio Television News Directors Association.

Article Two

Broadcast news presentations shall be designed not only to offer timely and accurate information, but also to present it in the light of relevant circumstances that give it meaning and perspective.

This standard means that news reports, when clarity demands it, will be laid against pertinent factual background; that factors such as race, creed, nationality or prior status will be reported only when they are relevant; that comment or subjective content will be properly identified; and that errors in fact will be promptly acknowledged and corrected.

Article Three

Broadcast newsmen shall seek to select material for newscast solely on their evaluation of its merits as news.

This standard means that news will be selected on the criteria of significance, community and regional relevance, appropriate human interest, service to defined audiences. It excludes sensationalism or misleading emphasis in any form; subservience to external or "interested" efforts to influence news selection and presentation, whether from within the broadcasting industry or from without. It requires that such terms as "bulletin" and "flash" be used only when the character of the news justifies them; that bombastic or misleading descriptions of newsroom facilities and personnel be rejected, along with undue use of sound and visual effects; and that promotional or publicity material be sharply scrutinized before use and identified by source or otherwise when broadcast.

Article Four

Broadcast newsmen shall at all times display humane respect for the dignity, privacy and the well-being of persons with whom the news deals.

Article Five

Broadcast newsmen shall govern their personal lives and such nonprofessional associations as may impinge on their professional activities in a manner that will protect them from conflict of interest, real or apparent.

Article Six

Broadcast newsmen shall seek actively to present all news the knowledge of which will serve the public interest, no matter what selfish, uninformed or corrupt efforts attempt to color it, withhold it or prevent its presentation. They shall make constant effort to open doors closed to the reporting of public proceedings with tools appropriate to broadcasting (including cameras and recorders), consistent with the public interest. They acknowledge the newsman's ethic of protection of confidential information and sources, and urge unswerving observation of it except in instances in which it would clearly and unmistakably defy the public interest. — *in all cases it does.* (NK8?)

Article Seven

Broadcast newsmen recognize the responsibility borne by broadcasting for informed analysis, comment and editorial opinion on public events and issues. They accept the obligation of broadcasters, for the presentation of such matters by individuals whose competence, experience and judgment qualify them for it.

Article Eight

In court, broadcast newsmen shall conduct themselves with dignity, whether the court is in or out of session. They shall keep broadcast equipment as unobtrusive and silent as possible. Where court facilities are inadequate, pool broadcasts should be arranged.

Article Nine

In reporting matters that are or may be litigated, the newsman shall avoid practices which would tend to interfere with the right of an individual to a fair trial.

Article Ten

Broadcast newsmen shall actively censure and seek to prevent violations of these standards, and shall actively encourage their observance by all newsmen, whether of the Radio Television News Directors Association or not.

RELATED READING

Agnew, Spiro T. "Television News Coverage: Network Censorship." *Vital Speeches* 36 (December 1, 1969), 98-101.

Arlen, Michael J. *Living Room War.* New York: Viking, 1969.

Ashley, Paul P. *Say It Safely: Legal Limits in Publishing, Radio, and Television.* 4th ed. Seattle: University of Washington Press, 1969.

Bagdikian, Ben H. *The Information Machines: Their Impact on Men and the Media.* New York: Harper & Row, 1970.

_____. "Right of Access: A Modest Proposal." *Columbia Journalism Review,* Spring 1969, 10-13.

Barrett, Marvin, ed. *The Alfred I. duPont—Columbia University Survey of Broadcast Journalism, 1968-1969* (and annually thereafter). New York: Grosset & Dunlap, 1969 (and annually thereafter).

Barron, Jerome A. "Access to the Press — A New First Amendment Right." *Harvard Law Review* 80 (1967), 1641-1678.

_____. "An Emerging First Amendment Right of Access to the Media?" *George Washington Law Review* 37 (1969), 487-509.

_____. "The Meaning and Future of Red Lion." *Educational Broadcasting Review* 3:6 (December 1969), 9-11.

Blake, Jonathan D. "Red Lion Broadcasting Co. v. FCC: Fairness and the Emperor's New Clothes." *Federal Communications Bar Journal* 23 (1969), 75-92.

Bluem, A. William. *Documentary in American Television.* New York: Hastings House, 1965.

Brown, William R. "Television and the Democratic National Convention of 1968." *Quarterly Journal of Speech* 55 (October 1969), 237-246.

Chester, Edward W. *Radio, Television and American Politics.* New York: Sheed and Ward, 1969.

Clark, David G. "H. V. Kaltenborn and his Sponsors: Controversial Broadcasting and the Sponsor's Role." *Journal of Broadcasting* 12 (Fall 1968), 309-321.

Commission on Campaign Costs in the Electronic Era. *Voters' Time.* New York: Twentieth Century Fund, 1969.

Commission on Freedom of the Press. *A Free and Responsible Press.* Chicago: University of Chicago Press, 1947.

"Concepts of the Broadcast Media Under the First Amendment: A Reevaluation and a Proposal." *New York University Law Review* 47 (1972), 83-109.

Dunn, Delmer D. *Financing Presidential Campaigns.* Washington: Brookings Institution, 1972.

Efron, Edith. *The News Twisters.* Los Angeles: Nash, 1971.

"Fairness Doctrine: Television as a Marketplace of Ideas." *New York University Law Review* 45 (1970), 1222-1250.

Foote, A. Edward, ed. *CBS and Congress: "The Selling of the Pentagon" Papers* (special issue of *Educational Broadcasting Review*). Washington: National Association of Educational Broadcasters, 1971.

Friendly, Alfred, and Ronald L. Goldfarb. *Crime and Publicity.* New York: Twentieth Century Fund, 1967.

Friendly, Fred W. *Due to Circumstances Beyond Our Control . . .* New York: Random House, 1967.

Gillmor, Donald M. *Free Press and Fair Trial.* Washington: Public Affairs Press, 1967.

Green, Maury. *Television News: Anatomy and Process.* Belmont, Cal.: Wadsworth, 1969.

Guback, Thomas H. "Political Broadcasting and Public Policy." *Journal of Broadcasting* 12 (Summer 1968), 191-211.

Hohenberg, John. *Free Press/Free People: The Best Cause.* New York: Columbia University Press, 1971.

Jaffe, Louis L. "The Editorial Responsibility of the Broadcaster: Reflections on Fairness and Access." *Harvard Law Review* 85 (1972), 768-792.

"Journalism and the Kerner Report." *Columbia Journalism Review*, Fall 1968, 42-65.

Kendrick, Alexander. *Prime Time: The Life of Edward R. Murrow.* Boston: Little, Brown, 1969.

Kittross, John M., and Kenneth Harwood, eds. *Free and Fair: Courtroom Access and the Fairness Doctrine.* Philadelphia: Association for Professional Broadcasting Education, 1970.

Kraus, Sidney, ed. *The Great Debates.* Bloomington: Indiana University Press, 1962.

Lawhorne, Clifton O. *Defamation and Public Officials: The Evolving Law of Libel.* Carbondale: Southern Illinois University Press, 1971.

Legal Advisory Committee on Fair Trial and Free Press. *The Rights of Fair Trial and Free Press.* Chicago: American Bar Association, 1969.

Loevinger, Lee. "Broadcasting and Religious Liberty." *Journal of Broadcasting* 9 (Winter 1964-65), 3-23.

Lynd, Robert D. "Banzhaf v. FCC: Public Interest and the Fairness Doctrine." *Federal Communications Bar Journal* 23 (1969), 39-56.

Martin, Ernest F., Jr. "The 'Hunger in America' Controversy." *Journal of Broadcasting* 16 (Spring 1972), 185-194.

Mass Communications. Santa Barbara, Cal.: Center for the Study of Democratic Institutions, 1966.

McGinniss, Joe. *The Selling of the President 1968.* New York: Trident, 1969.

McGranery, Regina C. "Exemptions from the Section 315 Equal Time Standard: A Proposal for Presidential Elections." *Federal Communications Bar Journal* 24 (1970-71), 177-205.

Meeske, Milan D. "Broadcasting and the Law of Defamation." *Journal of Broadcasting* 15 (Summer 1971), 331-346.

Mill, John Stuart. *On Liberty.* Edited by Alburey Castell. New York: Appleton-Century-Crofts, 1947.

Milton, John. *Areopagitica and Of Education.* Edited by George H. Sabine. New York: Appleton-Century-Crofts, 1951.

"The News Media and the Disorders." *Report of the National Advisory* [Kerner] *Commission on Civil Disorders.* New York: Bantam, 1968.

Pember, Don R. *Privacy and the Press: The Law, the Mass Media, and the First Amendment.* Seattle: University of Washington Press, 1972.

Powledge, Fred. *The Engineering of Restraint: The Nixon Administration and the Press.* Washington: Public Affairs Press, 1971.

Reitman, Alan, and Trudy Hayden. "Should Government Impose the First Amendment on Media?" *Educational Broadcasting Review* 2:6 (December 1968), 26-41.

Rivers, William L., and Wilbur Schramm. *Responsibility in Mass Communication.* Revised ed. New York: Harper & Row, 1969.

Rogers, Jimmie N., and Theodore Clevenger, Jr. " 'The Selling of the Pentagon': Was CBS the Fulbright Propaganda Machine?" *Quarterly Journal of Speech* 57 (October 1971), 266-273.

Russo, Frank D. "A Study of Bias in TV Coverage of the Vietnam War: 1969 and 1970." *Public Opinion Quarterly* 35 (Winter 1971-72), 539-543.

Scalia, Antonin. "Don't Go Near the Water." *Federal Communications Bar Journal* 25 (1972), 111-120.

Seldes, Gilbert. *The New Mass Media: Challenge to a Free Society.* Washington: Public Affairs Press, 1968.

Siebert, Frederick S., Theodore Peterson, and Wilbur Schramm. *Four Theories of the Press.* Urbana: University of Illinois Press, 1956.

Skornia, Harry J. *Television and the News: A Critical Appraisal.* Palo Alto, Cal.: Pacific Books, 1968.

Small, William. *To Kill a Messenger: Television News and the Real World.* New York: Hastings House, 1970.

Smith, Robert R. "The Origins of Radio Network News Commentary." *Journal of Broadcasting* 9 (Spring 1965), 113-122.

Special Committee on Radio and Television of the Association of the Bar of the City of New York. *Freedom of the Press and Fair Trial: Final Report with Recommendations.* New York: Columbia University Press, 1967.

————. *Radio, Television, and the Administration of Justice: A Documented Survey of Materials.* New York: Columbia University Press, 1965.

Stanton, Frank. "The Case for Political Debates on TV." *New York Times Magazine,* January 19, 1964, 16, 68-70.

"Televised Presidential Addresses and the FCC's Fairness Doctrine." *Columbia Journal of Law and Social Problems* 7 (Winter 1971), 75-106.

Toohey, Daniel W. "Section 399: The Constitution Giveth and Congress Taketh Away." *Educational Broadcasting Review* 6 (February 1972), 31-37.

United States Congress, House, Committee on Interstate and Foreign Commerce. *Network News Documentary Practices — CBS "Project Nassau."* Hearings before Special Subcommittee on Investigations, 91st Congress, 1st and 2d Sessions, July 17, 1969-April 16, 1970. Washington: Government Printing Office, 1970.

————. *Subpenaed Material re Certain TV News Documentary Programs.* Hearings before Special Subcommittee on Investigations, 92nd Congress, 1st Session, April 20, May 12, and June 24, 1971. Washington: Government Printing Office, 1971.

United States Congress, Senate, Committee on Commerce. *The FCC's Actions and the Broadcasters' Operations in Connection with the Commission's Fairness Doctrine.* Staff Report for the Subcommittee on Communications [by Robert Lowe], 90th Congress, 2d Session. Washington: Government Printing Office, 1968.

United States Congress, Senate, Subcommittee on Freedom of Communications of the Subcommittee on Communications of the Committee on Commerce. *Final Report Pursuant to S. Res. 305, 86th Congress,* Parts I-VI, 87th Congress, 1st and 2d Sessions. Washington: Government Printing Office, 1961-1962.

Wheeler, Harvey. "The End of the Two Party System." *Saturday Review,* November 2, 1968, 19-22.

White, Llewellyn. *The American Radio.* Chicago: University of Chicago Press, 1947 (reprinted New York: Arno Press, 1971).

Whiteside, Thomas. "Corridor of Mirrors: The Television Editorial Process, Chicago." *Columbia Journalism Review,* Winter 1968-69, 35-54.

Wiebe, Gerhart. "An Historical Setting for Broadcast Journalism." *Journal of Broadcasting* 1 (Winter 1956-57), 33-38.

Wyckoff, Gene. *The Image Candidates.* New York: Macmillan, 1968.

PART FOUR
REGULATION OF COMPETITION

Economic considerations in broadcasting are often paramount when a new station seeks to enter an existing station's market or when a new service, such as Cable Television (CATV) or Pay-TV, threatens the status quo in radio and television. Broadcasting is, after all, a business. Business enterprises attempt to keep expenses low and revenues high in order to achieve the goal of maximum profitability. Competition enlarges the public's choice of program sources, but tends to reduce profitability and can bring about the demise of a station or service.

Current technology permits the national distribution of TV programming via space satellite and regional and local program dissemination by CATV. Such a system, by coupling efficiency with a greater abundance of program choices, would reduce the economic viability of conventional broadcast stations which rely on earlier technologies. Those whose interests are rooted in the present invariably try to delay their own extinction either by retarding the advance of the future or by turning competition into partnership by acquiring stakes in the new technology that threatens them: "If you can't fight 'em, join 'em."

How much competition should there be in broadcasting? Despite the physical limits of the broadcast spectrum and the anti-monopolistic provisions of the Communications Act of 1934,

501

the answer to this question has been left largely to the discretion of the Federal Communications Commission. In exercising its power to issue broadcast authorizations if the "public interest, convenience, and necessity" will be served, the FCC is free to determine the nature and extent of competition which will best serve the public interest.

This is by no means an easy task. In a broadcasting system almost exclusively supported by advertising revenues, is the public interest best served by licensing as many stations as the spectrum can contain, or by limiting the stations to a number dictated by available advertising revenues and estimates of capital costs and operating expenses? Is the public interest better served by a large number of competitive stations and services operating on a perhaps flimsy and insecure financial footing, or by a small number of secure, economically protected stations and services? What criteria should be applied to determine which of several applications for a broadcast authorization will be granted? To what extent can the goal of providing diverse services to meet varied needs and interests be reconciled with the requisite for a viable means of financing such services through advertising? Are there acceptable ways to underwrite the cost of popular programming other than advertising?

The FCC has vacillated between the extremes of "free competition" and "economic protectionism" in facing these questions. Its procompetitive policy is evidenced by the avoidance of so-called "economic injury" protests as well as the issuance of rules and policy statements encouraging diversity of ownership and discouraging anti-competitive network practices. But in exercising its jurisdiction over CATV and Pay-TV, the Commission has viewed the public interest as requiring it to protect the interests of broadcast stations by inhibiting the development of new services. The courts have erected no substantial barrier to the exercise of FCC judgment in such matters, while Congress has been unresponsive to the calls of the courts and the Commission to provide legislative leadership when new technologies pose alternatives and competitive threats to the established pattern of broadcasting.

CATV, which presently reaches about 10 percent of American homes, is the rising star among broadcast-related media. There will be others. Should CATV ever become as well established as conventional over-the-air broadcasting, there is every reason to believe that the cable industry will oppose its eventual successor as vigorously as its predecessor opposed it. But change is as inevitable as predictions of its direction are hazardous.

The problem of regulating competition in mass telecommunications will undoubtedly grow more complex as tomorrow's entrepreneurs develop today's laboratory experiment. In a field in which financial considerations are so central, the way economic regulation is exercised becomes crucial in achieving whatever purposes one may assign to the electronic media.

1

THE NETWORK CASE

National Broadcasting Co., Inc., et al. v.
United States et al.
> 319 U.S. 190
> May 10, 1943

A network provides programs, advertising, and revenue to its affiliated stations. Without networks, broadcasting in a vast country like the United States would not be a national communications medium. Network operations began as early as 1923 in America. The National Broadcasting Company originated in 1926, followed by the Columbia Broadcasting System in 1927 and the Mutual Broadcasting System in 1934.

In the late 1930s the FCC became aware that the power of radio networks, particularly NBC and CBS, hampered the ability of station licensees to program as they saw fit and threatened the very structure of broadcasting as envisioned by Congress and the regulatory agency. One important outcome of the FCC's inquiry and subsequent rulemaking was the creation of the American Broadcasting Company in 1945, which arose from NBC's divestiture of one of its two networks in 1943.

This key Supreme Court decision upheld the Commission's authority to issue regulations pertaining to business arrangements between networks and their affiliates. Aside from the central issue of competition, Justice Frankfurter's opinion is noteworthy for its examination of the legislative history of radio regulation and its clarification of the relationship between "public interest, convenience, and necessity" and freedom of speech in broadcasting. Justice Murphy's dissent suggests inconsistency between the Court's 1940 *Sanders Brothers* decision and this one.

Mr. Justice Frankfurter delivered the opinion of the Court.

In view of our dependence upon regulated private enterprise in discharging the far-reaching rôle which radio plays in our society, a somewhat detailed exposition of the history of the present controversy and the issues which it raises is appropriate.

These suits were brought on October 30, 1941, to enjoin the enforcement of the Chain Broadcasting Regulations promulgated by the Federal Communications Commission on May 2, 1941, and amended on October 11, 1941. We held last Term in *Columbia System* v. *United States*, 316 U.S. 407, and *National Broadcasting Co.* v. *United States*, 316 U.S. 447, that the suits could be maintained under § 402(a) of the Communications Act of 1934, 48 Stat. 1093, 47 U.S.C. § 402(a) (incorporating by reference the Urgent Deficiencies Act of October 22, 1913, 38 Stat. 219, 28 U.S.C. § 47), and that the decrees of the District Court dismissing the suits for want of jurisdiction should therefore be reversed. On remand the District Court granted the Government's motions for summary judgment and dismissed the suits on the merits. 47 F. Supp. 940. The cases are now here on appeal. 28 U.S.C. § 47. Since they raise substantially the same issues and were argued together, we shall deal with both cases in a single opinion.

On March 18, 1938, the Commission undertook a comprehensive investigation to determine whether special regulations applicable to radio stations engaged in chain broadcasting[1] were required in the "public interest, convenience, or necessity." The Commission's order directed that inquiry be made, *inter alia*, in the following specific matters: the number of stations licensed to or affiliated with networks, and the amount of station time used or controlled by networks; the contractual rights and obligations of stations under their agreements with networks; the scope of network agreements containing exclusive affiliation provisions and restricting the network from affiliating with other stations in the same area; the rights and obligations of stations with respect to network advertisers; the nature of the program service rendered by stations licensed to networks; the policies of networks with respect to character of programs, diversification, and accommodation to the particular requirements of the areas served by the affiliated stations; the extent to which affiliated stations exercise control over programs, advertising contracts, and related matters; the nature and extent of network program duplication by stations serving the same area; the extent to which particular networks have exclusive coverage in some areas; the competitive practices of stations engaged in chain broadcasting; the effect of chain broadcasting upon stations not licensed to or affiliated with networks; practices or agreements in restraint of trade, or in furtherance of monopoly, in connection with chain broadcasting; and the scope of concentration of control over stations, locally, regionally, or nationally, through contracts, common ownership, or other means.

---

[1]Chain broadcasting is defined in § 3 (p) of the Communications Act of 1934 as the "simultaneous broadcasting of an identical program by two or more connected stations." In actual practice, programs are transmitted by wire, usually leased telephone lines, from their point of origin to each station in the network for simultaneous broadcast over the air.

On April 6, 1938, a committee of three Commissioners was designated to hold hearings and make recommendations to the full Commission. This committee held public hearings for 73 days over a period of six months, from November 14, 1938, to May 19, 1939. Order No. 37, announcing the investigation and specifying the particular matters which would be explored at the hearings, was published in the Federal Register, 3 Fed. Reg. 637, and copies were sent to every station licensee and network organization. Notices of the hearings were also sent to these parties. Station licensees, national and regional networks, and transcription and recording companies were invited to appear and give evidence. Other persons who sought to appear were afforded an opportunity to testify. 96 witnesses were heard by the committee, 45 of whom were called by the national networks. The evidence covers 27 volumes, including over 8,000 pages of transcript and more than 700 exhibits. The testimony of the witnesses called by the national networks fills more than 6,000 pages, the equivalent of 46 hearing days.

The committee submitted a report to the Commission on June 12, 1940, stating its findings and recommendations. Thereafter, briefs on behalf of the networks and other interested parties were filed before the full Commission, and on November 28, 1940, the Commission issued proposed regulations which the parties were requested to consider in the oral arguments held on December 2 and 3, 1940. These proposed regulations dealt with the same matters as those covered by the regulations eventually adopted by the Commission. On January 2, 1941, each of the national networks filed a supplementary brief discussing at length the questions raised by the committee report and the proposed regulations.

On May 2, 1941, the Commission issued its Report on Chain Broadcasting, setting forth its findings and conclusions upon the matters explored in the investigation, together with an order adopting the Regulations here assailed. Two of the seven members of the Commission dissented from this action. The effective date of the Regulations was deferred for 90 days with respect to existing contracts and arrangements of network-operated stations, and subsequently the effective date was thrice again postponed. On August 14, 1941, the Mutual Broadcasting Company petitioned the Commission to amend two of the Regulations. In considering this petition the Commission invited interested parties to submit their views. Briefs were filed on behalf of all of the national networks, and oral argument was had before the Commission on September 12, 1941. And on October 11, 1941, the Commission (again with two members dissenting) issued a Supplemental Report, together with an order amending three Regulations. Simultaneously, the effective date of the Regulations was postponed until November 15, 1941, and provision was made for further postponements from time to time if necessary to permit the orderly adjustment of existing arrangements. Since October 30, 1941, when the present suits were filed, the enforcement of the Regulations has been stayed either voluntarily by the Commission or by order of court.

Such is the history of the Chain Broadcasting Regulations. We turn now to the Regulations themselves, illumined by the practices in the radio industry disclosed by the Commission's investigation. The Regulations, which the Commission characterized in its Report as "the expression of the general policy we will follow in exercising our licensing power," are addressed in terms to station licensees and applicants for station licenses. They provide, in general, that no licenses shall be granted to stations or applicants having specified relationships with networks. Each Regulation is directed at a particular practice found by the Commission to be detrimental to the "public interest," and we shall consider them *seriatim*. In doing so, however, we do not overlook the admonition of the Commission that the Regulations as well as the network practices at which they are aimed are interrelated:

In considering above the network practices which necessitate the regulations we are adopting, we have taken each practice singly, and have shown that even in isolation each warrants the regulation addressed to it. But the various practices we have considered do not operate in isolation; they form a compact bundle or pattern, and the effect of their joint impact upon licensees necessitates the regulations even more urgently than the effect of each taken singly. (Report, p. 75.)

The Commission found that at the end of 1938 there were 660 commercial stations in the United States, and that 341 of these were affiliated with national networks. 135 stations were affiliated exclusively with the National Broadcasting Company, Inc., known in the industry as NBC, which operated two national networks, the "Red" and the "Blue." NBC was also the licensee of 10 stations, including 7 which operated on so-called clear channels with the maximum power available, 50 kilowatts; in addition, NBC operated 5 other stations, 4 of which had power of 50 kilowatts, under management contracts with their licensees. 102 stations were affiliated exclusively with the Columbia Broadcasting System, Inc., which was also the licensee of 8 stations, 7 of which were clear-channel stations operating with power of 50 kilowatts. 74 stations were under exclusive affiliation with the Mutual Broadcasting System, Inc. In addition, 25 stations were affiliated with both NBC and Mutual, and 5 with both CBS and Mutual. These figures, the Commission noted, did not accurately reflect the relative prominence of the three companies, since the stations affiliated with Mutual were, generally speaking, less desirable in frequency, power, and coverage. It pointed out that the stations affiliated with the national networks utilized more than 97% of the total night-time broadcasting power of all the stations in the country. NBC and CBS together controlled more than 85% of the total night-time wattage, and the broadcast business of the three national network companies amounted to almost half of the total business of all stations in the United States.

The Commission recognized that network broadcasting had played and was continuing to play an important part in the development of radio.

The growth and development of chain broadcasting [it stated], found its impetus in the desire to give widespread coverage to programs which otherwise would not be heard beyond the reception area of a single station. Chain broadcasting makes possible a wider reception for expensive entertainment and cultural programs and also for programs of national or regional significance which would otherwise have coverage only in the locality of origin. Furthermore, the access to greatly enlarged audiences made possible by chain broadcasting has been a strong incentive to advertisers to finance the production of expensive programs. . . . But the fact that the chain broadcasting method brings benefits and advantages to both the listening public and to broadcast station licensees does not mean that the prevailing practices and policies of the networks and their outlets are sound in all respects, or that they should not be altered. The Commission's duty under the Communications Act of 1934 is not only to see that the public receives the advantages and benefits of chain broadcasting, but also, so far as its powers enable it, to see that practices which adversely affect the ability of licensees to operate in the public interest are eliminated. (Report, p. 4.)

The Commission found that eight network abuses were amenable to correction within the powers granted it by Congress:

Regulation 3.101 — Exclusive affiliation of station.   The Commission found that the network affiliation agreements of NBC and CBS customarily contained a provision which prevented the station from broadcasting the programs of any other network. The effect of this provision was to hinder the growth of new networks, to deprive the listening public in many areas of service to which they were entitled, and to prevent station licensees from exercising their statutory duty of determining which programs would best serve the needs of their community. The Commission observed that in areas where all the stations were under exclusive contract to either NBC or CBS, the public was deprived of the opportunity to hear programs presented by Mutual. To take a case cited in the Report: In the fall of 1939 Mutual obtained the exclusive right to broadcast the World Series baseball games. It offered this program of outstanding national interest to stations throughout the country, including NBC and CBS affiliates in communities having no other stations. CBS and NBC immediately invoked the "exclusive affiliation" clauses of their agreements with these stations, and as a result thousands of persons in many sections of the country were unable to hear the broadcasts of the games.

Restraints having this effect [the Commission observed], are to be condemned as contrary to the public interest irrespective of whether it be assumed that Mutual programs are of equal, superior, or inferior quality. The important consideration is that station licensees are denied freedom to choose the programs which they believe best suited to their needs; in this manner the duty of a station licensee to operate in the public interest is defeated. . . . Our conclusion is that the disadvantages resulting from these exclusive arrangements far outweigh any advantages. A licensee station does not operate in the public interest when it enters into exclusive arrangements which prevent it from giving the public the best service of which it is capable, and which, by closing the door of opportunity in the network field, adversely affects the program structure of the entire industry. (Report, pp. 52, 57.)

Accordingly, the Commission adopted Regulation 3.101, providing as follows:

No license shall be granted to a standard broadcast station having any contract, arrangement, or understanding, express or implied, with a network organization under which the station is prevented or hindered from, or penalized for, broadcasting the programs of any other network organization.

Regulation 3.102 — Territorial exclusivity.   The Commission found another type of "exclusivity" provision in network affiliation agreements whereby the network bound itself not to sell programs to any other station in the same area. The effect of this provision, designed to protect the affiliate from the competition of other stations serving the same territory, was to deprive the listening public of many programs that might otherwise be available. If an affiliated station rejected a network program, the "territorial exclusivity" clause of its affiliation agreement prevented the network from offering the program to other stations in the area. For example, Mutual presented a popular program, known as "The American Forum of the Air," in which prominent persons discussed topics of general interest. None of the Mutual stations in the Buffalo area decided to carry the program, and a Buffalo station not affiliated with Mutual attempted to obtain the program for its listeners. These efforts failed, however, on account of the "territorial exclusivity" provision in Mutual's agreements with its outlets. The result was that this program was not available to the people of Buffalo.

The Commission concluded that

It is not in the public interest for the listening audience in an area to be deprived of network programs not carried by one station where other stations in that area are ready and willing to broadcast the programs. It is as much against the public interest for a network affiliate to enter into a contractual arrangement which prevents another station from carrying a network program as it would be for it to drown out that program by electrical interference. (Report, p. 59.)

Recognizing that the "territorial exclusivity" clause was unobjectionable in so far as it sought to prevent duplication of programs in the same area, the Commission limited itself to the situations in which the clause impaired the ability of the licensee to broadcast available programs. Regulation 3.102, promulgated to remedy this particular evil, provides as follows:

No license shall be granted to a standard broadcast station having any contract, arrangement, or understanding, express or implied, with a network organization which prevents or hinders another station serving substantially the same area from broadcasting the network's programs not taken by the former station, or which prevents or hinders another station serving a substantially different area from broadcasting any program of the network organization. This regulation shall not be construed to prohibit any contract, arrangement, or understanding between a station and a network organization pursuant to which the station is granted the first call in its primary service area upon the programs of the network organization.

Regulation 3.103 — Term of affiliation.   The standard NBC and CBS affiliation contracts bound the station for a period of five years, with the network having the exclusive right to terminate the contracts upon one year's notice. The Commission, relying upon § 307(d) of the Communications Act of 1934, under which no license to operate a broadcast station can be granted for a longer term than three years, found the five-year affiliation term to be contrary to the policy of the Act:

Regardless of any changes that may occur in the economic, political, or social life of the Nation or of the community in which the station is located, CBS and NBC affiliates are bound by contract to continue broadcasting the network programs of only one network for 5 years. The licensee is so bound even though the policy and caliber of programs of the network may deteriorate greatly. The future necessities of the station and of the community are not considered. The station licensee is unable to follow his conception of the public interest until the end of the 5-year contract. (Report, p. 61.)

The Commission concluded that under contracts binding the affiliates for five years, "stations become parties to arrangements which deprive the public of the improved service it might otherwise derive from competition in the network field; and that a station is not operating in the public interest when it so limits its freedom of action." (Report, p. 62.) Accordingly, the Commission adopted Regulation 3.103:

No license shall be granted to a standard broadcast station having any contract, arrangement, or understanding, express or implied, with a network organization which provides, by original term, provisions for renewal, or otherwise for the affiliation of the station with the network organization for a period longer than two years:[2] *Provided,* That a contract, arrangement, or understanding for a period up to two years, may be entered into within 120 days prior to the commencement of such period.

Regulation 3.104 — Option time.   The Commission found that network affiliation contracts usually contained so-called network optional time

---

[2]Station licenses issued by the Commission normally last two years. Section 3.34 of the Commission's Rules and Regulations governing Standard and High-Frequency Broadcast Stations, as amended October 14, 1941.

clauses. Under these provisions the network could upon 28 days' notice call upon its affiliates to carry a commercial program during any of the hours specified in the agreement as "network optional time." For CBS affiliates "network optional time" meant the entire broadcast day. For 29 outlets of NBC on the Pacific Coast, it also covered the entire broadcast day; for substantially all of the other NBC affiliates, it included 8½ hours on weekdays and 8 hours on Sundays. Mutual's contracts with about half of its affiliates contained such a provision, giving the network optional time for 3 or 4 hours on weekdays and 6 hours on Sundays.

In the Commission's judgment these optional time provisions, in addition to imposing serious obstacles in the path of new networks, hindered stations in developing a local program service. The exercise by the networks of their options over the station's time tended to prevent regular scheduling of local programs at desirable hours. The Commission found that

shifting a local commercial program may seriously interfere with the efforts of a [local] sponsor to build up a regular listening audience at a definite hour, and the long-term advertising contract becomes a highly dubious project. This hampers the efforts of the station to develop local commercial programs and affects adversely its ability to give the public good program service. . . . A station licensee must retain sufficient freedom of action to supply the program and advertising needs of the local community. Local program service is a vital part of community life. A station should be ready, able, and willing to serve the needs of the local community by broadcasting such outstanding local events as community concerts, civic meetings, local sports events, and other programs of local consumer and social interest. We conclude that national network time options have restricted the freedom of station licensees and hampered their efforts to broadcast local commercial programs, the programs of other national networks, and national spot transcriptions. We believe that these considerations far outweigh any supposed advantages from "stability" of network operations under time options. We find that the optioning of time by licensee stations has operated against the public interest. (Report, pp. 63, 65.)

The Commission undertook to preserve the advantages of option time, as a device for "stabilizing" the industry, without unduly impairing the ability of local stations to develop local program service. Regulation 3.104 called for the modification of the option-time provision in three respects: the minimum notice period for exercise of the option could not be less than 56 days; the number of hours which could be optioned was limited; and specific restrictions were placed upon exercise of the option to the disadvantage of other networks. The text of the Regulation follows:

No license shall be granted to a standard broadcast station which options for network programs any time subject to call on less than 56 days' notice, or more time than a total of three hours within each of four segments of the broadcast day, as herein described. The broadcast day is divided into 4 segments, as follows: 8:00 a.m. to 1:00 p.m.; 1:00 p.m. to 6:00 p.m.; 6:00 p.m. to 11:00 p.m.; 11:00 p.m. to 8:00 a.m. Such options may not be exclusive as against other network organizations and may not prevent or hinder the station from optioning or selling any or all of the time covered by the option, or other time, to other network organizations.

Regulation 3.105 – Right to reject programs.   The Commission found that most network affiliation contracts contained a clause defining the right of the station to reject network commercial programs. The NBC contracts provided simply that the station "may reject a network program the broadcasting of which would not be in the public interest, convenience, and necessity." NBC required a licensee who rejected a program to "be able to support his contention that what he has done has been more in the public interest than had he carried on the network program." Similarly, the CBS contracts provided that if the station had "reasonable objection to any sponsored program or the product advertised thereon as not being in the public interest, the station may, on 3 weeks' prior notice thereof to Columbia, refuse to broadcast such program, unless during such notice period such reasonable objection of the station shall be satisfied."

While seeming in the abstract to be fair, these provisions, according to the Commission's finding, did not sufficiently protect the "public interest." As a practical matter, the licensee could not determine in advance whether the broadcasting of any particular network program would or would not be in the public interest.

It is obvious that from such skeletal information [as the networks submitted to the stations prior to the broadcasts] the station cannot determine in advance whether the program is in the public interest, nor can it ascertain whether or not parts of the program are in one way or another offensive. In practice, if not in theory, stations affiliated with networks have delegated to the networks a large part of their programming functions. In many instances, moreover, the network further delegates the actual production of programs to advertising agencies. These agencies are far more than mere brokers or intermediaries between the network and the advertiser. To an ever-increasing extent, these agencies actually exercise the function of program production. Thus it is frequently neither the station nor the network, but rather the advertising agency, which determines what broadcast programs shall contain. Under such circumstances, it is especially important that individual stations, if they are to operate in the public interest, should have the practical opportunity as well as the contractual right to reject network programs. . . .

It is the station, not the network, which is licensed to serve the public interest. The licensee has the duty of determining what programs shall be broadcast over his station's facilities, and cannot lawfully delegate this duty or transfer the control of his station directly to the network or indirectly to an advertising agency. He cannot lawfully bind himself to accept programs in every case where he cannot sustain the burden of proof that he has a better program. The licensee is obliged to reserve to himself the final decision as to what programs will best serve the public interest. We conclude that a licensee is not fulfilling his obligations to operate in the public interest, and is not operating in accordance with the express requirements of the Communications Act, if he agrees to accept programs on any basis other than his own reasonable decision that the programs are satisfactory. (Report, pp. 39, 66.)

The Commission undertook in Regulation 3.105 to formulate the obligations of licensees with respect to supervision over programs:

No license shall be granted to a standard broadcast station having any contract, arrangement, or understanding, express or implied, with a network organization which (a), with respect to programs offered pursuant to an affiliation contract, prevents or hinders the station from rejecting or refusing network programs which the station reasonably believes to be unsatisfactory or unsuitable; or which (b), with respect to network programs so offered or already contracted for, prevents the station from rejecting or refusing any program which, in its opinion, is contrary to the public interest, or from substituting a program of outstanding local or national importance.

Regulation 3.106 – Network ownership of stations.   The Commission found that NBC, in addition to its network operations, was the licensee of 10 stations, 2 each in New York, Chicago, Washington, and San Francisco, 1 in Denver, and 1 in Cleveland. CBS was the licensee of 8 stations, 1 in each of these cities: New York, Chicago, Washington, Boston, Minneapolis, St. Louis, Charlotte, and Los Angeles. These 18 stations owned by NBC and CBS, the Commission observed, were among the most powerful and desirable in the country, and were permanently inaccessible to competing networks.

Competition among networks for these facilities is nonexistent, as they are completely removed from the network-station market. It gives the network complete control over its policies. This "bottling-up" of the best facilities has undoubtedly had a discouraging effect upon the creation and growth of new networks. Furthermore, common ownership of network and station places the network in a position where its interest as the owner of certain stations may conflict with its interest as a network organization serving affiliated stations. In dealings with advertisers, the network represents its own stations in a proprietary capacity and the affiliated stations in something akin to an agency capacity. The danger is present that the network organization will give preference to its own stations at the expense of its affiliates. (Report, p. 67.)

The Commission stated that if the question had arisen as an original matter, it might well have concluded that the public interest required severance of the business of station ownership from that of network operation. But since substantial business interests have been formed on the basis of the Commission's continued tolerance of the situation, it was found inadvisable to take such a drastic step. The Commission concluded, however, that "the licensing of two stations in the same area to a single network organization is basically unsound and contrary to the public interest," and that it was also against the "public interest" for network organizations to own stations in areas where the available facilities were so few or of such unequal coverage that competition would thereby be substantially restricted. Recognizing that these considerations called for flexibility in their application to particular situations, the Commission provided that "networks will be given full opportunity, on proper application for new facilities or renewal of existing licenses, to call to our attention any reasons why the principle should be modified or held inapplicable." (Report, p. 68.) Regulation 3.106 reads as follows:

No license shall be granted to a network organization, or to any person directly or indirectly controlled by or under common control with a network organization, for more than one standard broadcast station where one of the stations covers substantially the service area of the other station, or for any standard broadcast station in any locality where the existing standard broadcast stations are so few or of such unequal desirability (in terms of coverage, power, frequency, or other related matters) that competition would be substantially restrained by such licensing.

Regulation 3.107 – Dual network operation. This regulation provides that: "No license shall be issued to a standard broadcast station affiliated with a network organization which maintains more than one network: *Provided*, That this regulation shall not be applicable if such networks are not operated simultaneously, or if there is no substantial overlap in the territory served by the group of stations comprising each such network." In its Supplemental Report of October 11, 1941, the Commission announced the indefinite suspension of this regulation. There is no occasion here to consider the validity of Regulation 3.107, since there is no immediate threat of its enforcement by the Commission.

Regulation 3.108 – Control by networks of station rates. The Commission found that NBC's affiliation contracts contained a provision empowering the network to reduce the station's network rate, and thereby to reduce the compensation received by the station, if the station set a lower rate for non-network national advertising than the rate established by the contract for the network programs. Under this provision the station could not sell time to a national advertiser for less than it would cost the advertiser if he bought the time from NBC. In the words of NBC's vice-president, "This means simply that a national advertiser should pay the same price for the station whether he buys it through one source or another source. It means that we do not believe that our stations should go into competition with ourselves." (Report, p. 73.)

The Commission concluded that "it is against the public interest for a station licensee to enter into a contract with a network which has the effect of decreasing its ability to compete for national business. We believe that the public interest will best be served and listeners supplied with the best programs if stations bargain freely with national advertisers." (Report, p. 75.) Accordingly, the Commission adopted Regulation 3.108, which provides as follows:

No license shall be granted to a standard broadcast station having any contract, arrangement, or understanding, express or implied, with a network organization under which the station is prevented or hindered from, or penalized for, fixing or altering its rates for the sale of broadcast time for other than the network's programs.

The appellants attack the validity of these Regulations along many fronts. They contend that the Commission went beyond the regulatory powers conferred upon it by the Communications Act of 1934; that even if the Commission were authorized by the Act to deal with the matters comprehended by the Regulations, its action is nevertheless invalid because the Commission misconceived the scope of the Act, particularly § 313 which deals with the application of the anti-trust laws to the radio industry; that the Regulations are arbitrary and capricious; that if the Communications Act of 1934 were construed to authorize the promulgation of the Regulations, it would be an unconstitutional delegation of legislative power; and that, in any event, the Regulations abridge the appellants' right of free speech in violation of the First Amendment. We are thus called upon to determine whether Congress has authorized the Commission to exercise the power asserted by the Chain Broadcasting Regulations, and if it has, whether the Constitution forbids the exercise of such authority.

Federal regulation of radio[3] begins with the Wireless Ship Act of June 24, 1910, 36 Stat. 629, which forbade any steamer carrying or licensed to carry fifty or more persons to leave any American port unless equipped with efficient apparatus for radio communication, in charge of a skilled operator. The enforcement of this legislation was entrusted to the Secretary of Commerce and Labor, who was in charge of the administration of the marine navigation laws. But it was not until 1912, when the United States ratified the first international radio treaty, 37 Stat. 1565, that the need for general regulation of radio communication became urgent. In order to fulfill our obligations under the treaty, Congress enacted the Radio Act of August 13, 1912, 37 Stat. 302. This

---

[3]The history of federal regulation of radio communication is summarized in Herring and Gross, Telecommunications (1936) 239-86; Administrative Procedure in Government Agencies, Monograph of the Attorney General's Committee on Administrative Procedure, Sen. Doc. No. 186, 76th Cong., 3d Sess., Part 3, dealing with the Federal Communications Commission, pp. 82-84; 1 Socolow, Law of Radio Broadcasting (1939) 38-61; Donovan, Origin and Development of Radio Law (1930).

statute forbade the operation of radio apparatus without a license from the Secretary of Commerce and Labor; it also allocated certain frequencies for the use of the Government, and imposed restrictions upon the character of wave emissions, the transmission of distress signals, and the like.

The enforcement of the Radio Act of 1912 presented no serious problems prior to the World War. Questions of interference arose only rarely because there were more than enough frequencies for all the stations then in existence. The war accelerated the development of the art, however, and in 1921 the first standard broadcast stations were established. They grew rapidly in number, and by 1923 there were several hundred such stations throughout the country. The Act of 1912 had not set aside any particular frequencies for the use of private broadcast stations; consequently, the Secretary of Commerce selected two frequencies, 750 and 833 kilocycles, and licensed all stations to operate upon one or the other of these channels. The number of stations increased so rapidly, however, and the situation became so chaotic, that the Secretary, upon the recommendation of the National Radio Conferences which met in Washington in 1923 and 1924, established a policy of assigning specified frequencies to particular stations. The entire radio spectrum was divided into numerous bands, each allocated to a particular kind of service. The frequencies ranging from 550 to 1500 kilocycles (96 channels in all, since the channels were separated from each other by 10 kilocycles) were assigned to the standard broadcast stations. But the problems created by the enormously rapid development of radio were far from solved. The increase in the number of channels was not enough to take care of the constantly growing number of stations. Since there were more stations than available frequencies, the Secretary of Commerce attempted to find room for everybody by limiting the power and hours of operation of stations in order that several stations might use the same channel. The number of stations multiplied so rapidly, however, that by November, 1925, there were almost 600 stations in the country, and there were 175 applications for new stations. Every channel in the standard broadcast band was, by that time, already occupied by at least one station, and many by several. The new stations could be accommodated only by extending the standard broadcast band, at the expense of the other types of services, or by imposing still greater limitations upon time and power. The National Radio Conference which met in November, 1925, opposed both of these methods and called upon Congress to remedy the situation through legislation.

The Secretary of Commerce was powerless to deal with the situation. It had been held that he could not deny a license to an otherwise legally qualified applicant on the ground that the proposed station would interfere with existing private or Government stations. *Hoover* v. *Intercity Radio Co.*, 52 App. D.C. 339, 286 F. 1003. And on April 16, 1926, an Illinois district court held that the Secretary had no power to impose restrictions as to frequency, power, and hours of operation, and that a station's use of a frequency not assigned to it was not a violation of the Radio Act of 1912. *United States* v. *Zenith Radio Corp.*, 12 F.

2d 614. This was followed on July 8, 1926, by an opinion of Acting Attorney General Donovan that the Secretary of Commerce had no power, under the Radio Act of 1912, to regulate the power, frequency or hours of operation of stations. 35 Ops. Atty. Gen. 126. The next day the Secretary of Commerce issued a statement abandoning all his efforts to regulate radio and urging that the stations undertake self-regulation.

But the plea of the Secretary went unheeded. From July, 1926, to February 23, 1927, when Congress enacted the Radio Act of 1927, 44 Stat. 1162, almost 200 new stations went on the air. These new stations used any frequencies they desired, regardless of the interference thereby caused to others. Existing stations changed to other frequencies and increased their power and hours of operation at will. The result was confusion and chaos. With everybody on the air, nobody could be heard. The situation became so intolerable that the President in his message of December 7, 1926, appealed to Congress to enact a comprehensive radio law:

Due to the decisions of the courts, the authority of the department [of Commerce] under the law of 1912 has broken down; many more stations have been operating than can be accommodated within the limited number of wave lengths available; further stations are in course of construction; many stations have departed from the scheme of allocations set down by the department, and the whole service of this most important public function has drifted into such chaos as seems likely, if not remedied, to destroy its great value. I most urgently recommend that this legislation should be speedily enacted. (H. Doc. 483, 69th Cong., 2d Sess., p. 10.)

The plight into which radio fell prior to 1927 was attributable to certain basic facts about radio as a means of communication — its facilities are limited; they are not available to all who may wish to use them; the radio spectrum simply is not large enough to accommodate everybody. There is a fixed natural limitation upon the number of stations that can operate without interfering with one another.[4] Regulation of radio was therefore as vital to its development as traffic control was to the development of the automobile. In enacting the Radio Act of 1927, the first comprehensive scheme of control over radio communication, Congress acted upon the knowledge that if the potentialities of radio were not to be wasted, regulation was essential.

The Radio Act of 1927 created the Federal Radio Commission, composed of five members, and endowed the Commission with wide licensing and regulatory powers. We do not pause here to enumerate the scope of the Radio Act of 1927 and of the authority entrusted to the Radio Commission, for the basic provisions of that Act are incorporated in the Communications Act of 1934, 48 Stat. 1064, 47 U.S.C. § 151 et seq., the legislation immediately before

---

[4] See Morecroft, Principles of Radio Communication (3d ed. 1933) 355-402; Terman, Radio Engineering (2d ed. 1937) 593-645.

us. As we noted in *Federal Communications Comm'n* v. *Pottsville Broadcasting Co.*, 309 U.S. 134, 137,

In its essentials the Communications Act of 1934 [so far as its provisions relating to radio are concerned] derives from the Federal Radio Act of 1927. . . . By this Act Congress, in order to protect the national interest involved in the new and far-reaching science of broadcasting, formulated a unified and comprehensive regulatory system for the industry. The common factors in the administration of the various statutes by which Congress had supervised the different modes of communication led to the creation, in the Act of 1934, of the Communications Commission. But the objectives of the legislation have remained substantially unaltered since 1927.

Section 1 of the Communications Act states its "purpose of regulating interstate and foreign commerce in communication by wire and radio so as to make available, so far as possible, to all the people of the United States a rapid, efficient, Nation-wide, and world-wide wire and radio communication service with adequate facilities at reasonable charges." Section 301 particularizes this general purpose with respect to radio:

It is the purpose of this Act, among other things, to maintain the control of the United States over all the channels of interstate and foreign radio transmission; and to provide for the use of such channels, but not the ownership thereof, by persons for limited periods of time, under licenses granted by Federal authority, and no such license shall be construed to create any right, beyond the terms, conditions, and periods of the license.

To that end a Commission composed of seven members was created, with broad licensing and regulatory powers.

Section 303 provides:

Except as otherwise provided in this Act, the Commission from time to time, as public convenience, interest, or necessity requires, shall—

    (a)   Classify radio stations;

    (b)   Prescribe the nature of the service to be rendered by each class of licensed stations and each station within any class; . . .

    (f)   Make such regulations not inconsistent with law as it may deem necessary to prevent interference between stations and to carry out the provisions of this Act . . . ;

    (g)   Study new uses for radio, provide for experimental uses of frequencies, and generally encourage the larger and more effective use of radio in the public interest; . . .

    (i)   Have authority to make special regulations applicable to radio stations engaged in chain broadcasting; . . .

    (r)   Make such rules and regulations and prescribe such restrictions and conditions, not inconsistent with law, as may be necessary to carry out the provisions of this Act. . . .

The criterion governing the exercise of the Commission's licensing power is the "public interest, convenience, or necessity." §§ 307(a)(d), 309(a), 310, 312. In addition, § 307(b) directs the Commission that

In considering applications for licenses, and modifications and renewals thereof, when and insofar as there is demand for the same, the Commission shall make such distribution of licenses, frequencies, hours of operation, and of power among the several States and communities as to provide a fair, efficient, and equitable distribution of radio service to each of the same.

The Act itself establishes that the Commission's powers are not limited to the engineering and technical aspects of regulation of radio communication. Yet we are asked to regard the Commission as a kind of traffic officer, policing the wave lengths to prevent stations from interfering with each other. But the Act does not restrict the Commission merely to supervision of the traffic. It puts upon the Commission the burden of determining the composition of that traffic. The facilities of radio are not large enough to accommodate all who wish to use them. Methods must be devised for choosing from among the many who apply. And since Congress itself could not do this, it committed the task to the Commission.

The Commission was, however, not left at large in performing this duty. The touchstone provided by Congress was the "public interest, convenience, or necessity," a criterion which "is as concrete as the complicated factors for judgment in such a field of delegated authority permit." *Federal Communications Comm'n* v. *Pottsville Broadcasting Co.*, 309 U.S. 134, 138. "This criterion is not to be interpreted as setting up a standard so indefinite as to confer an unlimited power. Compare *New York Central Securities Co.* v. *United States*, 287 U.S. 12, 24. The requirement is to be interpreted by its context, by the nature of radio transmission and reception, by the scope, character and quality of services . . ." *Federal Radio Comm'n* v. *Nelson Bros. Co.*, 289 U.S. 266, 285.

The "public interest" to be served under the Communications Act is thus the interest of the listening public in "the larger and more effective use of radio." § 303(g). The facilities of radio are limited and therefore precious; they cannot be left to wasteful use without detriment to the public interest. "An important element of public interest and convenience affecting the issue of a license is the ability of the licensee to render the best practicable service to the community reached by his broadcasts." *Federal Communications Comm'n* v. *Sanders Radio Station*, 309 U.S. 470, 475. The Commission's licensing function cannot be discharged, therefore, merely by finding that there are no technological objections to the granting of a license. If the criterion of "public interest" were limited to such matters, how could the Commission choose between two applicants for the same facilities, each of whom is financially and technically qualified to operate a station? Since the very inception of federal regulation of radio, comparative considerations as to the services to be rendered have governed the application of the standard of "public interest, convenience, or necessity." See *Federal Communications Comm'n* v. *Pottsville Broadcasting Co.*, 309 U.S. 134, 138 n. 2.

The avowed aim of the Communications Act of 1934 was to secure the maximum benefits of radio to all the people of the United States. To that end Congress endowed the Communications Commission with comprehensive powers to promote and realize the vast potentialities of radio. Section 303(g) provides that the Commission shall "generally encourage the larger and more effective use of radio in the public interest"; subsection (i) gives the Commission specific "authority to make special regulations applicable to radio stations engaged in chain broadcasting"; and subsection (r) empowers it to adopt "such rules and regulations and prescribe such restrictions and conditions, not inconsistent with law, as may be necessary to carry out the provisions of this Act."

These provisions, individually and in the aggregate, preclude the notion that the Commission is empowered to deal only with technical and engineering impediments to the "larger and more effective use of radio in the public interest." We cannot find in the Act any such restriction of the Commission's authority. Suppose, for example, that a community can, because of physical limitations, be assigned only two stations. That community might be deprived of effective service in any one of several ways. More powerful stations in nearby cities might blanket out the signals of the local stations so that they could not be heard at all. The stations might interfere with each other so that neither could be clearly heard. One station might dominate the other with the power of its signal. But the community could be deprived of good radio service in ways less crude. One man, financially and technically qualified, might apply for and obtain the licenses of both stations and present a single service over the two stations, thus wasting a frequency otherwise available to the area. The language of the Act does not withdraw such a situation from the licensing and regulatory powers of the Commission, and there is no evidence that Congress did not mean its broad language to carry the authority it expresses.

In essence, the Chain Broadcasting Regulations represent a particularization of the Commission's conception of the "public interest" sought to be safeguarded by Congress in enacting the Communications Act of 1934. The basic consideration of policy underlying the Regulations is succinctly stated in its Report:

With the number of radio channels limited by natural factors, the public interest demands that those who are entrusted with the available channels shall make the fullest and most effective use of them. If a licensee enters into a contract with a network organization which limits his ability to make the best use of the radio facility assigned him, he is not serving the public interest. . . . The net effect [of the practices disclosed by the investigation] has been that broadcasting service has been maintained at a level below that possible under a system of free competition. Having so found, we would be remiss in our statutory duty of encouraging "the larger and more effective use of radio in the public interest" if we were to grant licenses to persons who persist in these practices. (Report, pp. 81, 82.)

We would be asserting our personal views regarding the effective utilization of radio were we to deny that the Commission was entitled to find that the large public aims of the Communications Act of 1934 comprehend the considerations which moved the Commission in promulgating the Chain Broadcasting Regulations. True enough, the Act does not explicitly say that the Commission shall have power to deal with network practices found inimical to the public interest. But Congress was acting in a field of regulation which was both new and dynamic. "Congress moved under the spur of a widespread fear that in the absence of governmental control the public interest might be subordinated to monopolistic domination in the broadcasting field." *Federal Communications Comm'n* v. *Pottsville Broadcasting Co.*, 309 U.S. 134, 137. In the context of the developing problems to which it was directed, the Act gave the Commission not niggardly but expansive powers. It was given a comprehensive mandate to "encourage the larger and more effective use of radio in the public interest," if need be, by making "special regulations applicable to radio stations engaged in chain broadcasting." § 303(g)(i).

Generalities unrelated to the living problems of radio communication of course cannot justify exercises of power by the Commission. Equally so, generalities empty of all concrete considerations of the actual bearing of regulations promulgated by the Commission to the subject-matter entrusted to it, cannot strike down exercises of power by the Commission. While Congress did not give the Commission unfettered discretion to regulate all phases of the radio industry, it did not frustrate the purposes for which the Communications Act of 1934 was brought into being by attempting an itemized catalogue of the specific manifestations of the general problems for the solution of which it was establishing a regulatory agency. That would have stereotyped the powers of the Commission to specific details in regulating a field of enterprise the dominant characteristic of which was the rapid pace of its unfolding. And so Congress did what experience had taught it in similar attempts at regulation, even in fields where the subject-matter of regulation was far less fluid and dynamic than radio. The essence of that experience was to define broad areas for regulation and to establish standards for judgment adequately related in their application to the problems to be solved.

For the cramping construction of the Act pressed upon us, support cannot be found in its legislative history. The principal argument is that § 303(i), empowering the Commission "to make special regulations applicable to radio stations engaged in chain broadcasting," intended to restrict the scope of the Commission's powers to the technical and engineering aspects of chain broadcasting. This provision comes from § 4(h) of the Radio Act of 1927. It was introduced into the legislation as a Senate committee amendment to the House bill. (H. R. 9971, 69th Cong., 1st Sess.) This amendment originally read as follows:

(C) The commission, from time to time, as public convenience, interest, or necessity requires, shall— . . .

(j) When stations are connected by wire for chain broadcasting, determine the power each station shall use and the wave lengths to be used during the time stations are so connected and so operated, and make all other regulations necessary in the interest of equitable radio service to the listeners in the communities or areas affected by chain broadcasting.

The report of the Senate Committee on Interstate Commerce, which submitted this amendment, stated that under the bill the Commission was given "complete authority . . . to control chain broadcasting." Sen. Rep. No. 772, 69th Cong., 1st Sess., p. 3. The bill as thus amended was passed by the Senate, and then sent to conference. The bill that emerged from the conference committee, and which became the Radio Act of 1927, phrased the amendment in the general terms now contained in § 303(i) of the 1934 Act: the Commission was authorized "to make special regulations applicable to radio stations engaged in chain broadcasting." The conference reports do not give any explanation of this particular change in phrasing, but they do state that the jurisdiction conferred upon the Commission by the conference bill was substantially identical with that conferred by the bill passed by the Senate. See Sen. Doc. No. 200, 69th Cong., 2d Sess., p.17; H. Rep. 1886, 69th Cong., 2d Sess., p. 17. We agree with the District Court that in view of this legislative history, § 303(i) cannot be construed as no broader than the first clause of the Senate amendment, which limited the Commission's authority to the technical and engineering phases of chain broadcasting. There is no basis for assuming that the conference intended to preserve the first clause, which was of limited scope, by agreeing upon a provision which was broader and more comprehensive than those it supplanted.[5]

---

[5]In the course of the Senate debates on the conference report upon the bill that became the Radio Act of 1927, Senator Dill, who was in charge of the bill, said: "While the commission would have the power under the general terms of the bill, the bill specifically sets out as one of the special powers of the commission the right to make specific regulations for governing chain broadcasting. As to creating a monopoly of radio in this country, let me say that this bill absolutely protects the public, so far as it can protect them, by giving the commission full power to refuse a license to anyone who it believes will not serve the public interest, convenience, or necessity. It specifically provides that any corporation guilty of monopoly shall not only not receive a license but that its license may be revoked; and if after a corporation has received its license for a period of three years it is then discovered and found to be guilty of monopoly, its license will be revoked. . . . In addition to that, the bill contains a provision that no license may be transferred from one owner to another without the written consent of the commission, and the commission, of course, having the power to protect against a monopoly, must give such protection. I wish to state further that the only way by which monopolies in the radio business can secure control of radio here, even for a limited period of time, will be by the commission becoming servile to them. Power must be lodged somewhere, and I myself am unwilling to assume in advance that the commission proposed to be created will be servile to the desires and demands of great corporations of this country." 68 Cong. Rec. 2881.

A totally different source of attack upon the Regulations is found in §
311 of the Act, which authorizes the Commission to withhold licenses from
persons convicted of having violated the anti-trust laws. Two contentions are
made — first, that this provision puts considerations relating to competition
outside the Commission's concern before an applicant has been convicted of
monopoly or other restraints of trade, and second, that, in any event, the
Commission misconceived the scope of its powers under § 311 in issuing the
Regulations. Both of these contentions are unfounded. Section 311 derives from
§ 13 of the Radio Act of 1927, which expressly commanded, rather than merely
authorized, the Commission to refuse a license to any person judicially found
guilty of having violated the anti-trust laws. The change in the 1934 Act was
made, in the words of Senator Dill, the manager of the legislation in the Senate,
because "it seemed fair to the committee to do that." 78 Cong. Rec. 8825. The
Commission was thus permitted to exercise its judgment as to whether violation
of the anti-trust laws disqualified an applicant from operating a station in the
"public interest." We agree with the District Court that "The necessary
implication from this [amendment in 1934] was that the Commission might
infer from the fact that the applicant had in the past tried to monopolize radio,
or had engaged in unfair methods of competition, that the disposition so
manifested would continue and that if it did it would make him an unfit
licensee." 47 F. Supp. 940, 944.

That the Commission may refuse to grant a license to persons adjudged
guilty in a court of law of conduct in violation of the anti-trust laws certainly
does not render irrelevant consideration by the Commission of the effect of such
conduct upon the "public interest, convenience, or necessity." A licensee
charged with practices in contravention of this standard cannot continue to hold
his license merely because his conduct is also in violation of the anti-trust laws
and he has not yet been proceeded against and convicted. By clarifying in § 311
the scope of the Commission's authority in dealing with persons convicted of
violating the anti-trust laws, Congress can hardly be deemed to have limited the
concept of "public interest" so as to exclude all considerations relating to
monopoly and unreasonable restraints upon commerce. Nothing in the
provisions or history of the Act lends support to the inference that the
Commission was denied the power to refuse a license to a station not operating
in the "public interest," merely because its misconduct happened to be an
unconvicted violation of the anti-trust laws.

Alternatively, it is urged that the Regulations constitute an *ultra vires*
attempt by the Commission to enforce the anti-trust laws, and that the
enforcement of the anti-trust laws is the province not of the Commission but of
the Attorney General and the courts. This contention misconceives the basis of
the Commission's action. The Commission's Report indicates plainly enough
that the Commission was not attempting to administer the anti-trust laws:

The prohibitions of the Sherman Act apply to broadcasting. This
Commission, although not charged with the duty of enforcing that law, should

administer its regulatory powers with respect to broadcasting in the light of the purposes which the Sherman Act was designed to achieve. . . . While many of the network practices raise serious questions under the antitrust laws, our jurisdiction does not depend on a showing that they do in fact constitute a violation of the antitrust laws. It is not our function to apply the antitrust laws as such. It is our duty, however, to refuse licenses or renewals to any person who engages or proposes to engage in practices which will prevent either himself or other licensees or both from making the fullest use of radio facilities. This is the standard of public interest, convenience or necessity which we must apply to all applications for licenses and renewals. . . . We do not predicate our jurisdiction to issue the regulations on the ground that the network practices violate the antitrust laws. We are issuing these regulations because we have found that the network practices prevent the maximum utilization of radio facilities in the public interest. (Report, pp. 46, 83, 83 n. 3.)

We conclude, therefore, that the Communications Act of 1934 authorized the Commission to promulgate regulations designed to correct the abuses disclosed by its investigation of chain broadcasting. There remains for consideration the claim that the Commission's exercise of such authority was unlawful.

The Regulations are assailed as "arbitrary and capricious." If this contention means that the Regulations are unwise, that they are not likely to succeed in accomplishing what the Commission intended, we can say only that the appellants have selected the wrong forum for such a plea. What was said in *Board of Trade* v. *United States*, 314 U.S. 534, 548, is relevant here: "We certainly have neither technical competence nor legal authority to pronounce upon the wisdom of the course taken by the Commission." Our duty is at an end when we find that the action of the Commission was based upon findings supported by evidence, and was made pursuant to authority granted by Congress. It is not for us to say that the "public interest" will be furthered or retarded by the Chain Broadcasting Regulations. The responsibility belongs to the Congress for the grant of valid legislative authority and to the Commission for its exercise.

It would be sheer dogmatism to say that the Commission made out no case for its allowable discretion in formulating these Regulations. Its long investigation disclosed the existences of practices which it regarded as contrary to the "public interest." The Commission knew that the wisdom of any action it took would have to be tested by experience:

We are under no illusion that the regulations we are adopting will solve all questions of public interest with respect to the network system of program distribution. . . . The problems in the network field are interdependent, and the steps now taken may perhaps operate as a partial solution of problems not directly dealt with at this time. Such problems may be examined again at some future time after the regulations here adopted have been given a fair trial. (Report, p. 88.)

The problems with which the Commission attempted to deal could not be solved at once and for all time by rigid rules-of-thumb. The Commission therefore did not bind itself inflexibly to the licensing policies expressed in the Regulations. In each case that comes before it the Commission must still exercise an ultimate judgment whether the grant of a license would serve the "public interest, convenience, or necessity." If time and changing circumstances reveal that the "public interest" is not served by application of the Regulations, it must be assumed that the Commission will act in accordance with its statutory obligations.

Since there is no basis for any claim that the Commission failed to observe procedural safeguards required by law, we reach the contention that the Regulations should be denied enforcement on constitutional grounds. Here, as in *New York Central Securities Corp.* v. *United States*, 287 U.S. 12, 24-25, the claim is made that the standard of "public interest" governing the exercise of the powers delegated to the Commission by Congress is so vague and indefinite that, if it be construed as comprehensively as the words alone permit, the delegation of legislative authority is unconstitutional. But, as we held in that case, "It is a mistaken assumption that this is a mere general reference to public welfare without any standard to guide determinations. The purpose of the Act, the requirements it imposes, and the context of the provision in question show the contrary." *Ibid.* See *Federal Radio Comm'n* v. *Nelson Bros. Co.*, 289 U.S. 266, 285; *Federal Communications Comm'n* v. *Pottsville Broadcasting Co.*, 309 U.S. 134, 137–38. Compare *Panama Refining Co.* v. *Ryan*, 293 U.S. 388, 428; *Intermountain Rate Cases*, 234 U.S. 476, 486-89; *United States* v. *Lowden*, 308 U.S. 225.

We come, finally, to an appeal to the First Amendment. The Regulations, even if valid in all other respects, must fall because they abridge, say the appellants, their right of free speech. If that be so, it would follow that every person whose application for a license to operate a station is denied by the Commission is thereby denied his constitutional right of free speech. Freedom of utterance is abridged to many who wish to use the limited facilities of radio. Unlike other modes of expression, radio inherently is not available to all. That is its unique characteristic, and that is why, unlike other modes of expression, it is subject to governmental regulation. Because it cannot be used by all, some who wish to use it must be denied. But Congress did not authorize the Commission to choose among applicants upon the basis of their political, economic or social views, or upon any other capricious basis. If it did, or if the Commission by these Regulations proposed a choice among applicants upon some such basis, the issue before us would be wholly different. The question here is simply whether the Commission, by announcing that it will refuse licenses to persons who engage in specified network practices (a basis for choice which we hold is comprehended within the statutory criterion of "public interest"), is thereby denying such persons the constitutional right of free speech. The right of free speech does not include, however, the right to use the facilities of radio without a license. The licensing system established by Congress in the Communications Act of 1934 was a proper exercise of its power over commerce. The standard it provided for the licensing of stations was the "public interest, convenience, or necessity." Denial of a station license on that ground, if valid under the Act, is not a denial of free speech.

A procedural point calls for just a word. The District Court, by granting the Government's motion for summary judgment, disposed of the case upon the pleadings and upon the record made before the Commission. The court below correctly held that its inquiry was limited to review of the evidence before the Commission. Trial *de novo* of the matters heard by the Commission and dealt with in its Report would have been improper. See *Tagg Bros.* v. *United States*, 280 U.S. 420; *Acker* v. *United States*, 298 U.S. 426.

Affirmed.

Mr. Justice Black and Mr. Justice Rutledge took no part in the consideration or decision of these cases.

Mr. Justice Murphy, dissenting:

I do not question the objectives of the proposed regulations, and it is not my desire by narrow statutory interpretation to weaken the authority of government agencies to deal efficiently with matters committed to their jurisdiction by the Congress. Statutes of this kind should be construed so that the agency concerned may be able to cope effectively with problems which the Congress intended to correct, or may otherwise perform the functions given to it. But we exceed our competence when we gratuitously bestow upon an agency power which the Congress has not granted. Since that is what the Court in substance does today, I dissent.

In the present case we are dealing with a subject of extreme importance in the life of the nation. Although radio broadcasting, like the press, is generally conducted on a commercial basis, it is not an ordinary business activity, like the selling of securities or the marketing of electrical power. In the dissemination of information and opinion, radio has assumed a position of commanding importance, rivalling the press and the pulpit. Owing to its physical characteristics radio, unlike the other methods of conveying information, must be regulated and rationed by the government. Otherwise there would be chaos, and radio's usefulness would be largely destroyed. But because of its vast potentialities as a medium of communication, discussion and propaganda, the character and extent of control that should be exercised over it by the government is a matter of deep and vital concern. Events in Europe show that radio may readily be a weapon of authority and misrepresentation, instead of a means of entertainment and enlightenment. It may even be an instrument of oppression. In pointing out these possibilities I do not mean to intimate in the slightest that they are imminent or probable in this country, but they do suggest that the construction of the instant statute should be approached with more than ordinary restraint and caution, to avoid an interpretation that is not clearly justified by the conditions that brought about its enactment, or that would give the Commission greater powers than the Congress intended to confer.

The Communications Act of 1934 does not in terms give the Commission power to regulate the contractual relations between the stations and the networks. *Columbia System* v. *United States*, 316 U.S. 407, 416. It is only as an incident of the power to grant or withhold licenses to individual stations under § § 307, 308, 309 and 310 that this authority is claimed,[1] except as it may have been provided by subdivisions (g), (i) and (r) of § 303, and by § § 311 and 313. But nowhere in these sections, taken singly or collectively, is there to be found by reasonable construction or necessary inference, authority to regulate the broadcasting industry as such, or to control the complex operations of the national networks.

In providing for regulation of the radio, the Congress was under the necessity of vesting a considerable amount of discretionary authority in the Commission. The task of choosing between various claimants for the privilege of using the air waves is essentially an administrative one. Nevertheless, in specifying with some degree of particularity the kind of information to be included in an application for a license, the Congress has indicated what general conditions and considerations are to govern the granting and withholding of station licenses. Thus an applicant is required by § 308(b) to submit information bearing upon his citizenship, character, and technical, financial and other qualifications to operate the proposed station, as well as data relating to the ownership and location of the proposed station, the power and frequencies desired, operating periods, intended use, and such other information as the Commission may require. Licenses, frequencies, hours of operation and power are to be fairly distributed among the several States and communities to provide efficient service to each. § 307(b). Explicit provision is made for dealing with applicants and licensees who are found guilty, or who are under the control of persons found guilty of violating the federal anti-trust laws. § § 311 and 313. Subject to the limitations defined in the Act, the Commission is required to grant a station license to any applicant "if public convenience, interest, or

---

[1] The regulations as first proposed were not connected with denial of applications for initial or renewal station licenses but provided instead that: "No licensee of a standard broadcast station shall enter into any contractual arrangement, express or implied, with a network organization," which contained any of the disapproved provisions. After a short time, however, the regulations were cast in their present form, making station licensing depend upon conformity with the regulations.

necessity will be served thereby." § 307(a). Nothing is said, in any of these sections, about network contracts, affiliations, or business arrangements.

The power to control network contracts and affiliations by means of the Commission's licensing powers cannot be derived from implication out of the standard of "public convenience, interest or necessity." We have held that: "the Act does not essay to regulate the business of the licensee. The Commission is given no supervisory control of the programs, of business management or of policy. In short, the broadcasting field is open to anyone, provided there be an available frequency over which he can broadcast without interference to others, if he shows his competency, the adequacy of his equipment, and financial ability to make good use of the assigned channel." *Federal Communications Comm'n* v. *Sanders Radio Station*, 309 U.S. 470, 475. The criterion of "public convenience, interest or necessity" is not an indefinite standard, but one to be "interpreted by its context, by the nature of radio transmission and reception, by the scope, character and quality of services, . . ." *Federal Radio Comm'n* v. *Nelson Bros. Co.*, 289 U.S. 266, 285. Nothing in the context of which the standard is a part refers to network contracts. It is evident from the record that the Commission is making its determination of whether the public interest would be served by renewal of an existing license or licenses, not upon an examination of written applications presented to it, as required by § § 308 and 309, but upon an investigation of the broadcasting industry as a whole, and general findings made in pursuance thereof which relate to the business methods of the network companies rather than the characteristics of the individual stations and the peculiar needs of the areas served by them. If it had been the intention of the Congress to invest the Commission with the responsibility, through its licensing authority, of exercising far-reaching control — as exemplified by the proposed regulations — over the business operations of chain broadcasting and radio networks as they were then or are now organized and established, it is not likely that the Congress would have left it to mere inference or implication from the test of "public convenience, interest or necessity," or that Congress would have neglected to include it among the considerations expressly made relevant to license applications by § 308(b). The subject is one of such scope and importance as to warrant explicit mention. To construe the licensing sections (§ § 307, 308, 309, 310) as granting authority to require fundamental and revolutionary changes in the business methods of the broadcasting networks — methods which have been in existence for several years and which have not been adjudged unlawful — would inflate and distort their true meaning and extend them beyond the limited purposes which they were intended to serve.

It is quite possible, of course, that maximum utilization of the radio as an instrument of culture, entertainment, and the diffusion of ideas is inhibited by existing network arrangements. Some of the conditions imposed by the broadcasting chains are possibly not conducive to a freer use of radio facilities, however essential they may be to the maintenance of sustaining programs and the operation of the chain broadcasting business as it is now conducted. But I am unable to agree that it is within the present authority of the Commission to prescribe the remedy for such conditions. It is evident that a correction of these conditions in the manner proposed by the regulations will involve drastic changes in the business of radio broadcasting which the Congress has not clearly and definitely empowered the Commission to undertake.

If this were a case in which a station license had been withheld from an individual applicant or licensee because of special relations or commitments that would seriously compromise or limit his ability to provide adequate service to the listening public, I should be less inclined to make any objection. As an incident of its authority to determine the eligibility of an individual applicant in an isolated case, the Commission might possibly consider such factors. In the present case, however, the Commission has reversed the order of things. Its real objective is to regulate the business practices of the major networks, thus bringing within the range of its regulatory power the chain broadcasting industry as a whole. By means of these regulations and the enforcement program, the Commission would not only extend its authority over business activities which represent interests and investments of a very substantial character, which have not been put under its jurisdiction by the Act, but would greatly enlarge its control over an institution that has now become a rival of the press and pulpit as a purveyor of news and entertainment and a medium of public discussion. To assume a function and responsibility of such wide reach and importance in the life of the nation, as a mere incident of its duty to pass on individual applications for permission to operate a radio station and use a specific wave length, is an assumption of authority to which I am not willing to lend my assent.

Again I do not question the need of regulation in this field, or the authority of the Congress to enact legislation that would vest in the Commission such power as it requires to deal with the problem, which it has defined and analyzed in its report with admirable lucidity. It is possible that the remedy indicated by the proposed regulations is the appropriate one, whatever its effect may be on the sustaining programs, advertising contracts, and other characteristics of chain broadcasting as it is now conducted in this country. I do not believe, however, that the Commission was justified in claiming the responsibility and authority it has assumed to exercise without a clear mandate from the Congress.

An examination of the history of this legislation convinces me that the Congress did not intend by anything in § 303, or any other provision of the Act, to confer on the Commission the authority it has assumed to exercise by the issuance of these regulations. Section 303 is concerned primarily with technical matters, and the subjects of regulation authorized by most of its subdivisions are exceedingly specific — so specific in fact that it is reasonable to infer that, if Congress had intended to cover the subject of network contracts and affiliations, it would not have left it to dubious implications from general clauses, lifted out of context, in subdivisions (g), (i) and (r). I am unable to agree that in authorizing the Commission in § 303(g) to study new uses for radio, provide for experimental use of frequencies, and "generally encourage the larger and more effective use of radio in the public interest," it was the intention or the purpose of the Congress to confer on the Commission the regulatory powers now being asserted. Manifestly that subdivision dealt with experimental and development work — technical and scientific matters, and the construction of its concluding clause should be accordingly limited to those considerations. Nothing in its legislative history suggests that it had any broader purpose.

It was clearly not the intention of the Congress by the enactment of § 303(i), authorizing the Commission "to make special regulations applicable to radio stations engaged in chain broadcasting," to invest the Commission with the authority now claimed over network contracts. This section is a verbatim reënactment of § 4(h) of the Radio Act of 1927, and had its origin in a Senate amendment to the bill which became that Act. In its original form it provided that the Commission, from time to time, as public convenience, interest, or necessity required, should:

When stations are connected by wire for chain broadcasting, [the Commission should] determine the power each station shall use and the wave lengths to be used during the time stations are so connected and so operated, and make all other regulations necessary in the interest of equitable radio service to the listeners in the communities or areas affected by chain broadcasting.

It was evidently the purpose of this provision to remedy a situation that was described as follows by Senator Dill (who was in charge of the bill in the Senate) in questioning a witness at the hearings of the Senate Committee on Interstate Commerce:

... During the past few months there has grown up a system of chain broadcasting, extending over the United States a great deal of the time. I say a great deal of the time — many nights a month — and the stations that are connected are of such widely varying meter lengths that the ordinary radio set that reaches out any distance is unable to get anything but that one program, and so, in effect, that one program monopolizes the air. I realize it is somewhat of a technical engineering problem, but it has seemed to many people, at least many who have written to me, that when stations are carrying on chain programs that they might be limited to the use of wave lengths adjoining or near enough to one another that they would not cover the entire dial. I do not know whether legislation ought to restrict that or whether it had better be done by regulations of the department. I want to get your opinion as to the advisability in some way protecting people who want to hear some other program than the one being broadcasted by chain broadcast. (Report on Hearings Before Senate Committee on Interstate Commerce on S. 1 and S. 1754, 69th Cong., 1st Sess. (1926) p. 123.)

In other words, when the same program was simultaneously broadcast by chain stations, the weaker independent stations were drowned out because of the high power of the chain stations. With the receiving sets then commonly in use, listeners were unable to get any program except the chain program. It was essentially an interference problem. In addition to determining power and wave length for chain stations, it would have been the duty of the Commission, under the amendment, to make other regulations necessary for "equitable radio service to the listeners in the communities or areas affected by chain broadcasting." The last clause should not be interpreted out of context and without relation to the problem at which the amendment was aimed. It is reasonably construed as simply authorizing the Commission to remedy other technical problems of interference involved in chain broadcasting in addition to power and wave length by requiring special types of equipment, controlling locations, etc. The statement in the Senate Committee Report that this provision gave the Commission "complete authority . . . to control chain broadcasting" (S. Rep. No. 772, 69th Cong., 1st Sess., p. 3) must be taken as meaning that the provision gave complete authority with respect to the specific problem which the Senate intended to meet, a problem of technical interference.

While the form of the amendment was simplified in the Conference Committee so as to authorize the Commission "to make special regulations applicable to radio stations engaged in chain broadcasting," both Houses were assured in the report of the Conference Committee that "the jurisdiction conferred in this paragraph is substantially the same as the jurisdiction conferred upon the Commission by . . . the Senate amendment." (Sen. Doc. No. 200, 69th Cong., 2d Sess., p. 17; H. Rep. No. 1886, 69th Cong., 2d Sess., p. 17). This is further borne out by a statement of Senator Dill in discussing the conference report on the Senate floor:

What is happening to-day is that the National Broadcasting Co., which is a part of the great Radio Trust, to say the least, if not a monopoly, is hooking up stations in every community on their various wave lengths with high powered stations and sending one program out, and they are forcing the little stations off the board so that the people cannot hear anything except the one program.

There is no power to-day in the hands of the Department of Commerce to stop that practice. The radio commission will have the power to regulate and prevent it and give the independents a chance. (68 Cong. Rec. 3031.)

Section 303(r) is certainly no basis for inferring that the Commission is empowered to issue the challenged regulations. This subdivision is not an independent grant of power, but only an authorization to: "Make such rules and regulations and prescribe such restrictions and conditions, not inconsistent with law, as may be necessary to carry out the provisions of this Act." There is no provision in the Act for the control of network contractual arrangements by the Commission, and consequently § 303(r) if of no consequence here.

To the extent that existing network practices may have run counter to the anti-trust laws, the Congress has expressly provided the means of dealing with the problem. The enforcement of those laws has been committed to the courts and other law enforcement agencies. In addition to the usual penalties prescribed by statute for their violation, however, the Commission has been expressly authorized by § 311 to refuse a station license to any person "finally adjudged guilty by a Federal court" of attempting unlawfully to monopolize radio communication. Anyone under the control of such a person may also be refused a license. And whenever a court has ordered the revocation of an existing license, as expressly provided in § 313, a new license may not be granted by the Commission to the guilty party or to any person under his control. In my opinion these provisions (§ § 311 and 313) clearly do not and were not intended to confer independent authority on the Commission to supervise network contracts or to enforce competition between radio networks by withholding licenses from stations, and do not justify the Commission in refusing a license to an applicant otherwise qualified, because of business arrangements that may constitute an unlawful restraint of trade, when the applicant has not been finally adjudged guilty of violating the anti-trust laws, and is not controlled by one so adjudged.

The conditions disclosed by the Commission's investigation, if they require correction, should be met, not by the invention of authority where none is available or by diverting existing powers out of their true channels and using them for purposes to which they were not addressed, but by invoking the aid of the Congress or the service of agencies that have been entrusted with the enforcement of the anti-trust laws. In other fields of regulation the Congress has made clear its intentions. It has not left to mere inference and guess-work the existence of authority to order broad changes and reforms in the national economy or the structure of business arrangements in the Public Utility Holding Company Act, 49 Stat. 803, the Securities Act of 1933, 48 Stat. 74, the Federal Power Act, 49 Stat. 838, and other measures of similar character. Indeed the Communications Act itself contains cogent internal evidence that Congress did not intend to grant power over network contractual arrangements to the Commission. In § 215(c) of Title II, dealing with common carriers by wire and radio, Congress provided:

The Commission shall examine all contracts of common carriers subject to this Act which prevent the other party thereto from dealing with another common carrier subject to this Act, and shall report its findings to Congress, together with its recommendations as to whether additional legislation on this subject is desirable.

Congress had no difficulty here in expressing the possible desirability of regulating a type of contract roughly similar to the ones with which we are now concerned, and in reserving to itself the ultimate decision upon the matters of policy involved. Insofar as the Congress deemed it necessary in this legislation to safeguard radio broadcasting against arrangements that are offensive to the anti-trust laws or monopolistic in nature, it made specific provision in § § 311 and 313. If the existing network contracts are deemed objectionable because of monopolistic or other features, and no remedy is presently available under these provisions, the proper course is to seek amendatory legislation from the Congress, not to fabricate authority by ingenious reasoning based upon provisions that have no true relation to the specific problem.

Mr. Justice Roberts agrees with these views.

2

ECONOMIC INJURY

Economic injury is one of the most perplexing problems in broadcast regulation. Allegations of economic injury, when properly made by an existing licensee, can forestall the advent of additional competition for program material as well as for audience and advertiser support.

The FCC, by seeking to avoid direct confrontation with the issues inherent in economic injury protests, has generally promoted intramedium competition through the absence of regulation. From 1940 to 1958 the Commission interpreted the Supreme Court's *Sanders Brothers* decision to mean that economic injury to a broadcaster was no basis for refusing to grant a license to a potential competitor. The Court of Appeals' *Carroll* decision rejected this interpretation, making it mandatory for the FCC to consider economic injury protests when increased competition is alleged to affect the public interest adversely. The Commission's request to appeal this decision to the Supreme Court was refused by the Department of Justice, whereupon the FCC ingeniously developed a variety of procedural methods so as to continue to preclude its grappling with this aspect of competition in broadcasting.

A

THE SANDERS BROTHERS CASE

Federal Communications Commission v.
Sanders Brothers Radio Station
309 U.S. 470
March 25, 1940

Mr. Justice Roberts delivered the opinion of the Court.

We took this case to resolve important issues of substance and procedure arising under the Communications Act of 1934, as amended.[1]

January 20, 1936, the Telegraph Herald, a newspaper published in Dubuque, Iowa, filed with the petitioner an application for a construction permit to erect a broadcasting station in that city. May 14, 1936, the respondent, who had for some years held a broadcasting license for, and had operated, Station WKBB at East Dubuque, Illinois, directly across the Mississippi River from Dubuque, Iowa, applied for a permit to move its transmitter and studios to the last named city and install its station there. August 18, 1936, respondent asked leave to intervene in the Telegraph Herald proceeding, alleging in its petition, *inter alia*, that there was an insufficiency of advertising revenue to support an additional station in Dubuque and insufficient talent to furnish programs for an additional station; that adequate service was being rendered to the community by Station WKBB and there was no need for any additional radio outlet in Dubuque and that the granting of the Telegraph Herald application would not serve the public interest, convenience, and necessity. Intervention was permitted and both applications were set for consolidated hearing.

The respondent and the Telegraph Herald offered evidence in support of their respective applications. The respondent's proof showed that its station had operated at a loss; that the area proposed to be served by the Telegraph Herald was substantially the same as that served by the respondent and that, of the advertisers relied on to support the Telegraph Herald station, more than half had used the respondent's station for advertising.

[1] Act of June 19, 1934, c. 652, 48 Stat. 1064; Act of June 5, 1936, c. 511, 49 Stat. 1475; Act of May 20, 1937, c. 229, 50 Stat. 189, 47 U.S.C. 151, *et seq.*

An examiner reported that the application of the Telegraph Herald should be denied and that of the respondent granted. On exceptions of the Telegraph Herald, and after oral argument, the broadcasting division of petitioner made an order granting both applications, reciting that "public interest, convenience, and necessity would be served" by such action. The division promulgated a statement of the facts and of the grounds of decision, reciting that both applicants were legally, technically, and financially qualified to undertake the proposed construction and operation; that there was need in Dubuque and the surrounding territory for the services of both stations, and that no question of electrical interference between the two stations was involved. A rehearing was denied and respondent appealed to the Court of Appeals for the District of Columbia. That court entertained the appeal and held that one of the issues which the Commission should have tried was that of alleged economic injury to the respondent's station by the establishment of an additional station and that the Commission had erred in failing to make findings on that issue. It decided that, in the absence of such findings, the Commission's action in granting the Telegraph Herald permit must be set aside as arbitrary and capricious.[2]

The petitioner's contentions are that under the Communications Act economic injury to a competitor is not a ground for refusing a broadcasting license and that, since this is so, the respondent was not a person aggrieved, or whose interests were adversely affected, by the Commission's action, within the meaning of § 402(b) of the Act which authorizes appeals from the Commission's orders.

The respondent asserts that the petitioner in argument below contented itself with the contention that the respondent had failed to produce evidence requiring a finding of probable economic injury to it. It is consequently insisted that the petitioner is not in a position here to defend its failure to make such findings on the ground that it is not required by the Act to consider any such issue. By its petition for rehearing in the court below, the Commission made clear its position as now advanced. The decision of the court below, and the challenge made in petition for rehearing and here by the Commission, raise a fundamental question as to the function and power of the Commission and we think that, on the record, it is open here.

First. We hold that resulting economic injury to a rival station is not, in and of itself, and apart from considerations of public convenience, interest, or necessity, an element the petitioner must weigh, and as to which it must make findings, in passing on an application for a broadcasting license.

Section 307(a) of the Communications Act directs that "the Commission, if public convenience, interest, or necessity will be served thereby, subject to the limitations of this Act, shall grant to any applicant therefor a station license provided for by this Act." This mandate is given meaning and contour by the

---

[2]*Sanders Brothers Radio Station* v. *Federal Communications Commission*, 70 App. D.C. 297; 106 F.2d 321.

other provisions of the statute and the subject matter with which it deals.[3] The Act contains no express command that in passing upon an application the Commission must consider the effect of competition with an existing station. Whether the Commission should consider the subject must depend upon the purpose of the Act and the specific provisions intended to effectuate that purpose.

The genesis of the Communications Act and the necessity for the adoption of some such regulatory measure is a matter of history. The number of available radio frequencies is limited. The attempt by a broadcaster to use a given frequency in disregard of its prior use by others, thus creating confusion and interference, deprives the public of the full benefit of radio audition. Unless Congress had exercised its power over interstate commerce to bring about allocation of available frequencies and to regulate the employment of transmission equipment the result would have been an impairment of the effective use of these facilities by anyone. The fundamental purpose of Congress in respect of broadcasting was the allocation and regulation of the use of radio frequencies by prohibiting such use except under license.

In contradistinction to communication by telephone and telegraph, which the Communications Act recognizes as a common carrier activity and regulates accordingly in analogy to the regulation of rail and other carriers by the Interstate Commerce Commission,[4] the Act recognizes that broadcasters are not common carriers and are not to be dealt with as such.[5] Thus the Act recognizes that the field of broadcasting is one of free competition. The sections dealing with broadcasting demonstrate that Congress has not, in its regulatory scheme, abandoned the principle of free competition, as it has done in the case of the railroads,[6] in respect of which regulation involves the suppression of wasteful practices due to competition, the regulation of rates and charges, and other measures which are unnecessary if free competition is to be permitted.

An important element of public interest and convenience affecting the issue of a license is the ability of the licensee to render the best practicable service to the community reached by his broadcasts. That such ability may be assured the Act contemplates inquiry by the Commission, *inter alia*, into an applicant's financial qualifications to operate the proposed station.[7]

But the Act does not essay to regulate the business of the licensee. The Commission is given no supervisory control of the programs, of business management or of policy. In short, the broadcasting field is open to anyone, provided there be an available frequency over which he can broadcast without

[3]*Radio Commission* v. *Nelson Bros. Co.*, 289 U.S. 266, 285.
[4]See Title II §§ 201-221, 47 U.S.C. §§ 201-221.
[5]See § 3(h), 47 U.S.C. § 153(h).
[6]Compare *Texas & Pacific Ry.* v. *Gulf, C. & S.F. Ry. Co.*, 270 U.S. 266, 277; *Chicago Junction Case*, 264 U.S. 258.
[7]See § 308(b), 47 U.S.C. § 308(b).

interference to others, if he shows his competency, the adequacy of his equipment, and financial ability to make good use of the assigned channel.

The policy of the Act is clear that no person is to have anything in the nature of a property right as a result of the granting of a license. Licenses are limited to a maximum of three years' duration, may be revoked, and need not be renewed. Thus the channels presently occupied remain free for a new assignment to another licensee in the interest of the listening public.

Plainly it is not the purpose of the Act to protect a licensee against competition but to protect the public. Congress intended to leave competition in the business of broadcasting where it found it, to permit a licensee who was not interfering electrically with other broadcasters to survive or succumb according to his ability to make his programs attractive to the public.

This is not to say that the question of competition between a proposed station and one operating under an existing license is to be entirely disregarded by the Commission, and, indeed, the Commission's practice shows that it does not disregard that question. It may have a vital and important bearing upon the ability of the applicant adequately to serve his public; it may indicate that both stations — the existing and the proposed — will go under, with the result that a portion of the listening public will be left without adequate service; it may indicate that, by a division of the field, both stations will be compelled to render inadequate service. These matters, however, are distinct from the consideration that, if a license be granted, competition between the licensee and any other existing station may cause economic loss to the latter. If such economic loss were a valid reason for refusing a license this would mean that the Commission's function is to grant a monopoly in the field of broadcasting, a result which the Act itself expressly negatives,[8] which Congress would not have contemplated without granting the Commission powers of control over the rates, programs, and other activities of the business of broadcasting.

We conclude that economic injury to an existing station is not a separate and independent element to be taken into consideration by the Commission in determining whether it shall grant or withhold a license.

Second.   It does not follow that, because the licensee of a station cannot resist the grant of a license to another, on the ground that the resulting competition may work economic injury to him, he has no standing to appeal from an order of the Commission granting the application.

Section 402(b) of the Act provides for an appeal to the Court of Appeals of the District of Columbia (1) by an applicant for a license or permit, or (2) "by any other person aggrieved or whose interests are adversely affected by any decision of the Commission granting or refusing any such application."

The petitioner insists that as economic injury to the respondent was not a proper issue before the Commission it is impossible that § 402(b) was intended to give the respondent standing to appeal, since absence of right implies

[8] See § 311, 47 U.S.C. § 311, relating to unfair competition and monopoly.

absence of remedy. This view would deprive subsection (2) of any substantial effect.

Congress had some purpose in enacting s 402(b) (2). It may have been of the opinion that one likely to be financially injured by the issue of a license would be the only person having a sufficient interest to bring to the attention of the appellate court errors of law in the action of the Commission in granting the license. It is within the power of Congress to confer such standing to prosecute an appeal.[9]

We hold, therefore, that the respondent had the requisite standing to appeal and to raise, in the court below, any relevant question of law in respect of the order of the Commission.

Third.   Examination of the findings and grounds of decision set forth by the Commission discloses that the findings were sufficient to comply with the requirements of the Act in respect of the public interest, convenience, or necessity involved in the issue of the permit. In any event, if the findings were not as detailed upon this subject as might be desirable, the attack upon them is not that the public interest is not sufficiently protected but only that the financial interests of the respondent have not been considered. We find no reason for abrogating the Commission's order for lack of adequate findings.

Fourth.   The respondent here renews a contention made in the Court of Appeals to the effect that the Commission used as evidence certain data and reports in its files without permitting the respondent, as intervenor before the Commission, the opportunity of inspecting them. The Commission disavows the use of such material as evidence in the cause and the Court of Appeals has found the disavowal veracious and sufficient. We are not disposed to disturb its conclusion.

The judgment of the Court of Appeals is *Reversed.*

Mr. Justice McReynolds took no part in the decision of this case.

[9]Compare *Interstate Commerce Commission* v. *Oregon-Washington R. Co.*, 288 U.S. 14, 23-25.

B

THE CARROLL CASE

Carroll Broadcasting Company v.
Federal Communications Commission*
  258 F. 2d 440 (D.C. Cir.)
  July 10, 1958

Prettyman, Circuit Judge.

This is an appeal from the Federal Communications Commission and concerns a license for a standard broadcasting station. Carroll, our appellant, is an existing licensee. It unsuccessfully protested the grant of a license to West Georgia, our intervenor.

Carrollton and Bremen are towns in Georgia, twelve miles apart, with populations, respectively, of 8,600 and 2,300. Carroll's main studios are in Carrollton. West Georgia would broadcast from Bremen.

Three issues were prescribed by the Commission for the hearing upon the protest. One of these was upon the request of Carroll and was:

To determine whether a grant of the application would result in such an economic injury to the protestant as would impair the protestant's ability to continue serving the public, and if so, the nature and extent thereof, the areas and populations affected thereby, and the availability of other broadcast service to such areas and populations.

But the Commission ordered "That said issue is not adopted by the Commission and that the burden of proceeding with the introduction of evidence and the burden of proof as to this issue shall be on the protestant." The case was remanded to the examiner for hearings on the added issue and a possible revised decision. The hearings were held, a further initial decision rendered by the examiner, exceptions taken, and oral argument had before the Commission.

*Reprinted with the permission of West Publishing Company ©1959.

On this issue the Commission held that "Congress had determined that free competition shall prevail in the broadcasting industry" and that "The Communications Act does not confer upon the Commission the power to consider the effect of legal competition except perhaps" in Section 307(b) cases. Hence, said the Commission, "it is unnecessary for us to make findings or reach conclusions on this issue." Moreover, the Commission said, pursuant to other decisions by it, as a matter of policy "the possible effects of competition will be disregarded in passing upon applications for new broadcast stations."

It was settled by the Sanders Brothers case[1] that economic injury to an existing station is not a ground for denying a new application. But the Court, it seems to us, made clear the point that economic injury to a licensee and the public interest may be different matters. The Court said, for example:[2]

First. We hold that resulting economic injury to a rival station is not, in and of itself, and apart from considerations of public convenience, interest, or necessity, an element the petitioner must weigh, and as to which it must make findings, in passing on an application for a broadcasting license.

And the Court said:[3]

This is not to say that the question of competition between a proposed station and one operating under an existing license is to be entirely disregarded by the Commission, and, indeed, the Commission's practice shows that it does not disregard that question. It may have a vital and important bearing upon the ability of the applicant adequately to serve his public; it may indicate that both stations — the existing and the proposed — will go under, with the result that a portion of the listening public will be left without adequate service; it may indicate that, by division of the field, both stations will be compelled to render inadequate service. These matters, however, are distinct from the consideration that, if a license be granted, competition between the licensee and any other existing station may cause economic loss to the latter.

Thus, it seems to us, the question whether a station makes $5,000, or $10,000, or $50,000 is a matter in which the public has no interest so long as service is not adversely affected; service may well be improved by competition. But, if the situation in a given area is such that available revenue will not support good service in more than one station, the public interest may well be in the licensing of one rather than two stations. To license two stations where there is revenue for only one may result in no good service at all. So economic injury to an existing station, while not in and of itself a matter of moment, becomes important when on the facts it spells diminution or destruction of service. At that point the element of injury ceases to be a matter of purely private concern.

[1] *Federal Communications Commission* v. *Sanders Brothers Radio Station*, 309 U.S. 470, 60 S.Ct. 693, 84 L.Ed. 869 (1940).
[2] Id., 309 U.S. at page 473, 60 S.Ct. at page 696.
[3] Id., 309 U.S. at pages 475-476, 60 S.Ct. at pages 697-698.

The basic charter of the Commission is, of course, to act in the public interest. It grants or denies licenses as the public interest, convenience and necessity dictate. Whatever factual elements make up that criterion in any given problem — and the problem may differ from case to case — must be considered. Such is not only the power but the duty of the Commission.

So in the present case the Commission had the power to determine whether the economic effect of a second license in this area would be to damage or destroy service to an extent inconsistent with the public interest. Whether the problem actually exists depends upon the facts, and we have no findings upon the point.

This opinion is not to be construed or applied as a mandate to the Commission to hear and decide the economic effects of every new license grant. It has no such meaning. We hold that, when an existing licensee offers to prove that the economic effect of another station would be detrimental to the public interest, the Commission should afford an opportunity for the presentation of such proof and, if the evidence is substantial (*i.e.*, if the protestant does not fail entirely to meet his burden), should make a finding or findings.

The Commission says that, if it has authority to consider economic injury as a factor in the public interest, the whole basic concept of a competitive broadcast industry disappears. We think it does not. Certainly the Supreme Court did not think so in the Sanders Brothers case, supra. Private economic injury is by no means always, or even usually, reflected in public detriment. Competitors may severely injure each other to the great benefit of the public. The broadcast industry is a competitive one, but competitive effects may under some sets of circumstances produce detriment to the public interest. When that happens the public interest controls.

The Commission says it lacks the "tools" — meaning specifications of authority from the Congress — with which to make the computations, valuations, schedules, etc., required in public utility regulation. We think no such elaborate equipment is necessary for the task here. As we have just said, we think it is not incumbent upon the Commission to evaluate the probable economic results of every license grant. Of course the public is not concerned whether it gets service from A or from B or from both combined. The public interest is not disturbed if A is destroyed by B, so long as B renders the required service. The public interest is affected when service is affected. We think the problem arises when a protestant offers to prove that the grant of a new license would be detrimental to the public interest. The Commission is equipped to receive and appraise such evidence. If the protestant fails to bear the burden of proving his point (and it is certainly a heavy burden), there may be an end to the matter. If his showing is substantial, or if there is a genuine issue posed, findings should be made. Perhaps Carroll did not cast its proffer of proof exactly in terms of the public interest, or at least not in terms of the whole public interest. It may be argued that it offered to prove only detriment to its own ability for service. We are inclined to give it the benefit of the most favorable interpretation. In any event, whatever proof Carroll had is already in the record. If it does not support a finding of detriment to the public interest, but merely of a detriment to Carroll, the Commission can readily so find.

The case must be remanded for findings on this point.

Carroll also makes a point about the Commission's findings in respect to West Georgia's basic financial qualifications and about a presumption that a father-in-law, a brother-in-law, and an uncle-in-law form part of the control exercised by a family unit. We find no error in these respects.

Remanded for further findings.

3

POLICY STATEMENT ON

COMPARATIVE BROADCAST HEARINGS

1 FCC 2d 393

July 28, 1965

The Federal Communications Commission has been confronted
with a choice of broad regulatory philosophies since its for-
mation. On one hand is the desire for consistency in administrative law. On the other hand is the need for flexibility in a field
of rapid technological innovation, structural change, and
managerial ingenuity.

The Commissioners' conflicting views of consistency and
flexibility are most evident in the policy statement and con
curring and dissenting statements below.

One of the Commission's primary responsibilities is to choose among qualified
new applicants for the same broadcast facilities.[1] This commonly requires
extended hearings into a number of areas of comparison. The hearing and
decision process is inherently complex, and the subject does not lend itself to
precise categorization or to the clear making of precedent. The various factors
cannot be assigned absolute values, some factors may be present in some cases
and not in others, and the differences between applicants with respect to each
factor are almost infinitely variable.

Furthermore, membership on the Commission is not static and the views
of individual Commissioners on the importance of particular factors may change.
For these and other reasons, the Commission is not bound to deal with all cases
at all times as it has dealt in the past with some that seem comparable, *Federal
Communications Commission* v. *WOKO, Inc.*, 329 U.S. 223, 228,[2] and changes

---

[1]This statement of policy does not attempt to deal with the somewhat different problems
raised where an applicant is contesting with a licensee seeking renewal of license.

[2]"[T]he doctrine of *stare decisis* is not generally applicable to the decisions of
administrative tribunals," *Kentucky Broadcasting Corp.* v. *Federal Communications
Commission*, 84 U.S. App. D.C. 383, 385, 174 F. 2d 38, 40.

of viewpoint, if reasonable, are recognized as both inescapable and proper. *Pinellas Broadcasting Co.* v. *Federal Communications Commission*, 97 U.S. App. D.C. 236, 230 F. 2d 204, *cert. den.* 350 U.S. 1007.

All this being so, it is nonetheless important to have a high degree of consistency of decision and of clarity in our basic policies. It is also obviously of great importance to prevent undue delay in the disposition of comparative hearing cases. A general review of the criteria governing the disposition of comparative broadcast hearings will, we believe, be useful to parties appearing before the Commission. It should also be of value to the examiners who initially decide the cases and to the Review Board to which the basic review of examiners' decisions in this area has been delegated. See Section 0.365 of our Rules, 47 CFR 0.365.[3]

This statement is issued to serve the purpose of clarity and consistency of decision, and the further purpose of eliminating from the hearing process time-consuming elements not substantially related to the public interest. We recognize, of course, that a general statement cannot dispose of all problems or decide cases in advance. Thus, for example, a case where a party proposes a specialized service will have to be given somewhat different consideration. Difficult cases will remain difficult. Our purpose is to promote stability of judgment without foreclosing the right of every applicant to a full hearing.

We believe that there are two primary objectives toward which the process of comparison should be directed. They are, first, the best practicable service to the public, and, second, a maximum diffusion of control of the media of mass communications. The value of these objectives is clear. Diversification of control is a public good in a free society, and is additionally desirable where a government licensing system limits access by the public to the use of radio and television facilities.[4] Equally basic is a broadcast service which meets the needs of the public in the area to be served, both in terms of those general interests which all areas have in common and those special interests which areas do not share. An important element of such a service is the flexibility to change as local needs and interests change. Since independence and individuality of approach are elements of rendering good program service, the primary goals of good

---

[3]On June 15, 1964 the rule was amended to give the Review Board authority to review initial decisions of hearing examiners in comparative television cases, a function formerly performed only by the Commission itself.

[4]As the Supreme Court has stated, the First Amendment to the Constitution of the United States "rests on the assumption that the widest possible dissemination of information from diverse and antagonistic sources is essential to the welfare of the public," *Associated Press* v. *United States*, 326 U.S. 1, 20. That radio and television broadcast stations play an important role in providing news and opinion is obvious. That it is important in a free society to prevent a concentration of control of the sources of news and opinion and, particularly, that government should not create such a concentration, is equally apparent, and well established. *United States* v. *Storer Broadcasting Co.*, 351 U.S. 192; *Scripps-Howard Radio, Inc.* v. *Federal Communications Commission*, 89 U.S. App. D.C. 13, 189 F. 2d 677, *cert. den.* 342 U.S. 830.

service and diversification of control are also fully compatible.

Several factors are significant in the two areas of comparison mentioned above, and it is important to make clear the manner in which each will be treated.

1. *Diversification of control of the media of mass communications.* Diversification is a factor of primary significance since, as set forth above, it constitutes a primary objective in the licensing scheme.

As in the past, we will consider both common control and less than controlling interests in other broadcast stations and other media of mass communications. The less the degree of interest in other stations or media, the less will be the significance of the factor. Other interests in the principal community proposed to be served will normally be of most significance, followed by other interests in the remainder of the proposed service area[5] and, finally, generally in the United States. However, control of large interests elsewhere in the same state or region may well be more significant than control of a small medium of expression (such as a weekly newspaper) in the same community. The number of other mass communication outlets of the same type in the community proposed to be served will also affect to some extent the importance of this factor in the general comparative scale.

It is not possible, of course, to spell out in advance the relationships between any significant number of the various factual situations which may be presented in actual hearings. It is possible, however, to set forth the elements which we believe significant. Without indicating any order of priority, we will consider interests in existing media of mass communications to be more significant in the degree that they:

(A)   are larger, i.e., go towards complete ownership and control;

and to the degree that the existing media:

(B)   are in, or close to, the community being applied for;
(C)   are significant in terms of numbers and size, i.e., the area covered, circulation, size of audience, etc.;
(D)   are significant in terms of regional or national coverage; and
(E)   are significant with respect to other media in their respective localities.

2. *Full-time participation in station operation by owners.* We consider this factor to be of substantial importance. It is inherently desirable

---

[5] Sections 73.35(a), 73.240(a)(1) and 73.636(a)(1) of our rules, 47 CFR 73.35(a), 73.240(a)(1), 73.636(a)(1), prohibit common control of stations in the same service (AM, FM and TV) within prescribed overlap areas. Less than controlling ownership interests and significant managerial positions in stations and other media within and without such areas will be considered when held by persons with any ownership or significant managerial interest in an applicant.

that legal responsibility and day-to-day performance be closely associated. In addition, there is a likelihood of greater sensitivity to an area's changing needs, and of programming designed to serve these needs, to the extent that the station's proprietors actively participate in the day-to-day operation of the station. This factor is thus important in securing the best practicable service.[6] It also frequently complements the objective of diversification, since concentrations of control are necessarily achieved at the expense of integrated ownership.

We are primarily interested in full-time participation. To the extent that the time spent moves away from full time, the credit given will drop sharply, and no credit will be given to the participation of any person who will not devote to the station substantial amounts of time on a daily basis. In assessing proposals, we will also look to the positions which the participating owners will occupy, in order to determine the extent of their policy functions and the likelihood of their playing important roles in management. We will accord particular weight to staff positions held by the owners, such as general manager, station manager, program director, business manager, director of news, sports or public service broadcasting, and sales manager. Thus, although positions of less responsibility will be considered, especially if there will be full-time integration by those holding those positions, they cannot be given the decisional significance attributed to the integration of stockholders exercising policy functions. Merely consultative positions will be given no weight.

Attributes of participating owners, such as their experience and local residence, will also be considered in weighing integration of ownership and management. While, for the reasons given above, integration of ownership and management is important *per se,* its value is increased if the participating owners are local residents and if they have experience in the field. Participation in station affairs on the basis described above by a local resident indicates a likelihood of continuing knowledge of changing local interests and needs.[7] Previous broadcast experience, while not so significant as local residence, also has some value when put to use through integration of ownership and management.

Past participation in civic affairs will be considered as a part of a participating owner's local residence background, as will any other local activities indicating a knowledge of and interest in the welfare of the community. Mere diversity of business interests will not be considered. Generally speaking, residence in the principal community to be served will be of primary importance, closely followed by residence outside the community, but within the proposed service area. Proposed future local residence (which is expected to accompany meaningful participation) will also be accorded less weight than present residence of several years' duration.

---

[6] As with other proposals, it is important that integration proposals be adhered to on a permanent basis. See *Tidewater Teleradio, Inc.*, 24 Pike & Fischer, R.R. 653.

[7] Of course, full-time participation is also necessarily accompanied by residence in the area.

Previous broadcasting experience includes activity which would not qualify as a past broadcast record, i.e., where there was not ownership responsibility for a station's performance. Since emphasis upon this element could discourage qualified newcomers to broadcasting, and since experience generally confers only an initial advantage,[8] it will be deemed of minor significance. It may be examined qualitatively, upon an offer of proof of particularly poor or good previous accomplishment.

The discussion above has assumed full-time, or almost full-time, participation in station operation by those with ownership interests. We recognize that station ownership by those who are local residents and, to a markedly lesser degree, by those who have broadcasting experience, may still be of some value even where there is not the substantial participation to which we will accord weight under this heading. Thus, local residence complements the statutory scheme and Commission allocation policy of licensing a large number of stations throughout the country, in order to provide for attention to local interests, and local ownership also generally accords with the goal of diversifying control of broadcast stations. Therefore, a slight credit will be given for the local residence of those persons with ownership interests who cannot be considered as actively participating in station affairs on a substantially full-time basis but who will devote some time to station affairs, and a very slight credit will similarly be given for experience not accompanied by full-time participation. Both of these factors, it should be emphasized, are of minor significance. No credit will be given either the local residence or experience of any person who will not put his knowledge of the community (or area) or experience to any use in the operation of the station.

3. *Proposed program service.* The United States Court of Appeals for the District of Columbia Circuit has stated that, "in a comparative consideration, it is well recognized that comparative service to the listening public is the vital element, and programs are the essence of that service." *Johnston Broadcasting Co.* v. *Federal Communications Commission*, 85 U.S. App. D.C. 40, 48, 175 F. 2d 351, 359. The importance of program service is obvious. The feasibility of making a comparative evaluation is not so obvious. Hearings take considerable time and precisely formulated program plans may have to be changed not only in details but in substance, to take account of new conditions obtaining at the time a successful applicant commences operation. Thus, minor differences among applicants are apt to prove to be of no significance.

The basic elements of an adequate service have been set forth in our July 29, 1960 "Report and Statement of Policy Re: Commission *en banc* Programming Inquiry," 25 F.R. 7291, 20 Pike & Fischer, R.R. 1901, and need

---

[8] Lack of experience, unlike a high concentration of control, is remediable. See *Sunbeam Television Corp.* v. *Federal Communications Commission*, 100 U.S. App. D.C. 82, 243 F. 2d 26.

not be repeated here.[9] And the applicant has the responsibility for a reasonable knowledge of the community and area, based on surveys or background, which will show that the program proposals are designed to meet the needs and interests of the public in that area. See *Henry* v. *Federal Communications Commission*, 112 U.S. App. D.C. 257, 302 F. 2d 191, *cert. den.* 371 U.S. 821. Contacts with local civic and other groups and individuals are also an important means of formulating proposals to meet an area's needs and interests. Failure to make them will be considered a serious deficiency, whether or not the applicant is familiar with the area.

Decisional significance will be accorded only to material and substantial differences between applicants' proposed program plans. See *Johnston Broadcasting Co.* v. *Federal Communications Commission*, 85 U.S. App. D.C. 40, 175 F. 2d 351. Minor differences in the proportions of time allocated to different types of programs will not be considered. Substantial differences will be considered to the extent that they go beyond ordinary differences in judgment and show a superior devotion to public service. For example, an unusual attention to local community matters for which there is a demonstrated need, may still be urged. We will not assume, however, that an unusually high percentage of time to be devoted to local or other particular types of programs is necessarily to be preferred. Staffing plans and other elements of planning will not be compared in the hearing process except where an inability to carry out proposals is indicated.[10]

In light of the considerations set forth above, and our experience with the similarity of the program plans of competing applicants, taken with the desirability of keeping hearing records free of immaterial clutter, no comparative issue will ordinarily be designated on program plans and policies, or on staffing plans or other program planning elements, and evidence on these matters will not be taken under the standard issues. The Commission will designate an issue where examination of the applications and other information before it makes such action appropriate, and applicants who believe they can demonstrate significant differences upon which the reception of evidence will be useful may petition to amend the issues.

No independent factor of likelihood of effectuation of proposals will be utilized. The Commission expects every licensee to carry out its proposals, subject to factors beyond its control, and subject to reasonable judgment that the public's needs and interests require a departure from original plans. If there

---

[9]Specialized proposals necessarily have to be considered on a case-to-case basis. We will examine the need for the specialized service as against the need for a general-service station where the question is presented by competing applicants.

[10]We will similarly not give independent consideration to proposed studios or other equipment. These are also elements of a proposed operation which are necessary to carry out the program plans, and which are expected to be adequate. They will be inquired into only upon a petition to amend the issues which indicates a serious deficiency.

is a substantial indication that any party will not be able to carry out its proposals to a significant degree, the proposals themselves will be considered deficient.[11]

4. *Past broadcast record.* This factor includes past ownership interest and significant participation in a broadcast station by one with an ownership interest in the applicant. It is a factor of substantial importance upon the terms set forth below.

A past record within the bounds of average performance will be disregarded, since average future performance is expected. Thus, we are not interested in the fact of past ownership *per se*, and will not give a preference because one applicant has owned stations in the past and another has not.

We are interested in records which, because either unusually good or unusually poor, give some indication of unusual performance in the future. Thus, we shall consider past records to determine whether the record shows (i) unusual attention to the public's needs and interests, such as special sensitivity to an area's changing needs through flexibility of local programs designed to meet those needs, or (ii) either a failure to meet the public's needs and interests or a significant failure to carry out representations made to the Commission (the fact that such representations have been carried out, however, does not lead to an affirmative preference for the applicant, since it is expected, as a matter of course, that a licensee will carry out representations made to the Commission).

If a past record warrants consideration, the particular reasons, if any, which may have accounted for that record will be examined to determine whether they will be present in the proposed operation. For example, an extraordinary record compiled while the owner fully participated in operation of the station will not be accorded full credit where the party does not propose similar participation in the operation of the new station for which he is applying.

5. *Efficient use of frequency.*[12] In comparative cases where one of two or more competing applicants proposes an operation which, for one or more engineering reasons, would be more efficient, this fact can and should be considered in determining which of the applicants should be preferred. The nature of an efficient operation may depend upon the nature of the facilities applied for, i.e., whether they are in the television or FM bands where geographical allocations have been made, or in the standard broadcast (AM) band where there are no such fixed allocations. In addition, the possible variations of situations in comparative hearings are numerous. Therefore, it is not feasible here to delineate the outlines of this element, and we merely take

---

[11] It should be noted here that the absence of an issue on program plans and policies will not preclude cross-examination of the parties with respect to their proposals for participation in station operation, i.e., to test the validity of integration proposals.

[12] This factor as discussed here is not to be confused with the determination to be made of which of two communities has the greater need for a new station. See *Federal Communications Commission* v. *Allentown Broadcasting Corp.* 349 U.S. 358.

this occasion to point out that the element will be considered where the facts warrant.

6. *Character.*   The Communications Act makes character a relevant consideration in the issuance of a license. See Section 308(b), 47 U.S.C. 308(b). Significant character deficiencies may warrant disqualification, and an issue will be designated where appropriate. Since substantial demerits may be appropriate in some cases where disqualification is not warranted, petitions to add an issue on conduct relating to character will be entertained. In the absence of a designated issue, character evidence will not be taken. Our intention here is not only to avoid unduly prolonging the hearing process, but also to avoid those situations where an applicant converts the hearing into a search for his opponents' minor blemishes, no matter how remote in the past or how insignificant.

7. *Other Factors.*   As we stated at the outset, our interest in the consistency and clarity of decision and in expedition of the hearing process is not intended to preclude the full examination of any relevant and substantial factor. We will thus favorably consider petitions to add issues when, but only when, they demonstrate that significant evidence will be adduced.[13]

We pointed out at the outset that in the normal course there may be changes in the views of individual commissioners as membership on the Commission changes or as commissioners may come to view matters differently with the passage of time. Therefore, it may be well to emphasize that by this attempt to clarify our present policy and our views with respect to the various factors which are considered in comparative hearings, we do not intend to stultify the continuing process of reviewing our judgment on these matters. Where changes in policy are deemed appropriate they will be made, either in individual cases or in further general statements, with an explanation of the reason for the change. In this way, we hope to preserve the advantages of clear policy enunciation without sacrificing necessary flexibility and open-mindedness.

Cases to be decided by either the Review Board or, where the Review Board has not been delegated that function, by the Commission itself, will be decided under the policies here set forth. So too, future designations for hearing will be made in accordance with this statement. Where cases are now in hearing, the hearing examiner will be expected to follow this statement to the extent practicable. Issues already designated will not be changed, but evidence should be adduced only in accordance with this statement. Thus, evidence on issues which we have said will no longer be designated in the absence of a petition to add an issue, should not be accepted unless the party wishing to adduce the evidence makes an offer of proof to the examiner which demonstrates that the evidence will be of substantial value under the criteria discussed herein. Since we

---

[13] Where a narrow question is raised, for example on one aspect of financial qualification, a narrowly drawn issue will be appropriate. In other circumstances, a broader inquiry may be required. This is a matter for *ad hoc* determination.

are not adopting new criteria which would call for the introduction of new evidence, but rather restricting the scope somewhat of existing factors and explaining their importance more clearly, there will be no element of surprise which might affect the fairness of a hearing. It is, of course, traditional judicial practice to decide cases in accordance with principles in effect at the time of decision. Administrative finality is also important. Therefore, cases which have already been decided, either by the Commission or, where appropriate, by the Review Board, will not be reconsidered. We believe that our purpose to improve the hearing and decisional process in the future does not require upsetting decisions already made, particularly in light of the basically clarifying nature of this document.

Dissenting statement of Commissioner Hyde

I dissent to the adoption of the "Policy Statement on Comparative Broadcast Hearings" issued July 28, 1965.

One of the expressed objectives of the Policy Statement is the simplification and the expedition of the Commission's processes with respect to decisions in comparative cases. I agree with the majority that this is a most desirable objective; however, the policy statement as now framed will not achieve expedition. Moreover, to the extent that a degree of simplification of our decisional process may result from its adoption, this result, in my opinion, would be at a price which would be prohibitive and perhaps unlawful. It would press applicants into a mold in order to meet the Commission's preconceived standards, thus deterring perhaps better-qualified applicants from applying; it would preclude significant consideration of material differences among applicants and result in automatic preference of applicants slavishly conforming to the mold, and eventually force the Commission to decide cases on trivial differences among applicants since basically they would all have come out of the same press. I consider this much too high a price to pay to achieve the majority's objective.

I think the initiative in proposing how stations should be owned and operated should remain with the applicants, thus providing opportunities for diversified approaches. Moreover, in the interest of diversity, the initiative for the presentation of program plans should be left with applicants and without undue circumscription as to what should be included or excluded. Then, as a matter of elementary fairness, as well as due process, applicants should be entitled to examination and comparison on the merit of their respective proposals – not merely comparison with previously-adopted positions. It may be that the check-off approach (as argued in the Policy Statement) will be helpful to Examiners and others in making decisions, but even this illusion of facility is certain to disappear as to cases involving competing new applicants who can plan to conform to prescribed formulas.

When competing applications for facilities are filed, the Commission must make an election which involves a comparison of characteristics. As was stated in *Johnston Broadcasting Company* v. *F.C.C.*, U.S.C.A., D.C., May 4, 1949:

The Commission cannot ignore a material difference between two applicants and make findings in respect to selected characteristics only. Neither can it base its conclusion upon a selection from among its findings of differences and ignore all other findings. It must take into account all the characteristics which indicate differences, and reach an overall relative determination upon an evaluation of all factors, conflicting in many cases. . . .

In this situation, and in order to comply with the directive of the Court, the Commission must consider among other things differences in makeup of applicants and differences in program proposals for the purpose of making the required comparison. But this requirement to consider differences in characteristics does not warrant the Commission to presume to establish — in the abstract — standardized preferences as to how applicants should be organized or as to how programs should be planned. I think that the effort to direct and standardize is incongruous with the basic policy of the Act.

I presume that one of the reasons for the adoption of the Policy Statement is to apprise potential applicants of the views of the Commission (and individual Commissioners) as to the manner in which differences among applicants will be treated. Decisions which have been made are available for this purpose. The views of the Commission and of individual Commissioners as to the effect of differences among applicants in comparative cases are set out in decisions which touch on such differences. Similarly, the specific views of dissenting or of separately-concurring Commissioners are available for analysis.

I know of no two cases where the underlying facts are identical. I know of no two cases where differences among the applicants are identical. Therefore, the significance to be given in each decision to each difference and to each criterion must of necessity vary, and must necessarily be considered in context with the other facts of the individual cases.

If the Commission has been remiss in the past in not spelling out the decisional process in each case as carefully as it should, the obvious remedy is improvement in the preparation of decisions. Moreover, through more carefully written decisions, both the Commission and the applicants can view the weight given to each difference and to each criterion in light of all the facts in a given case. To the extent the other relevant facts in the applicant's case require the same conclusion, an applicant can assume such conclusion will be reached by the Commission. To the extent the other relevant facts require or permit a different conclusion, the Commission will be free to so conclude. However, to attempt to cure what might be considered past omissions in not fully spelling out reasons for decisions by prescribing an arbitrary order and weight to be given to each of such criteria seems to me to be idealizing form over substance, and avoiding statutory and legal requirements in doing so. This is especially true when no need exists for establishing this procedure since a simpler and more adequate solution is at hand.

The proposed fiat as to the weight which will be given to the various criteria — without sound predication of accepted data and when considered only in a vacuum and in the abstract — must necessarily result in a degree of unfairness to some applicants and in the fashioning of an unnecessary straitjacket for the Commission in its decisional process. How can we decide in advance and in a vacuum that a specific broadcaster with a satisfactory record in one community will be less likely to serve the broadcasting needs of a second community than a specific long-time resident of that second community who doesn't have broadcast experience? How can we make this decision without knowing more about each applicant? The majority now says that experience can always be acquired and, therefore, that it is less important than local residence. But the knowledge acquired from such local residence can by the same token be obtained just as easily — if not more easily — than broadcast experience. It seems clear to me that the importance to be given to the element of experience in one case or to the element of local residence in another case will necessarily vary in light of the additional factors involved in each case.

Moreover, the decision by an individual without broadcast experience (or perhaps even without business experience) to take full control of a complicated broadcast venture is held by this proposed Policy to be entitled to a significantly greater preference than a decision by a more prudent applicant who intends to secure competent, experienced and professional management to operate a station under his general direction until he acquires a reasonable degree of experience. It may be reasonable for the Commission to make such a conclusion in the light of all of the facts in a particular case, taking into consideration the specific attributes of the individual concerned, but it is obvious that the same conclusion need not be valid in a second case where the same attributes may not be present. The fact that it may be difficult to explain different decisions in the two cases is taken by the majority as sufficient reason to establish arbitrary preferences. This I cannot accept.

The evaluation of local needs and how best to provide for them is a highly subjective matter. Is the Commission competent — in advance of a review of all of the pertinent factors in a particular case — to decide that non-professional opinion as to the existence of needs or as to the manner in which the needs can best be fulfilled is automatically entitled to a greater weight than professional opinion based upon prior experience in substantially identical communities? I submit that it is not, and that although the decision might be difficult to make in any one case, and perhaps even more difficult to explain where the decisions differ on this factor in two cases, there can nevertheless be sound bases for different results in cases involving these elements. We should not be foreclosed from exploring them.

The language of the Policy Statement is quite broad in certain areas while, at the same time, the statement tries to be precise and restrictive in its proposed results. For example, terms such as "unusually high percentage of time," "unusual attention to community matters," "minor differences in the proportion of time," "ordinary differences in judgment," etc., are used without definition as to the meaning of the terms. I presume that future decisions will spell out at least some guidelines as to their meaning, but it is obvious that this will be achieved only at great cost to the applicants and after much litigation and then only in connection with the facts of a particular case. Since precise definitions are really not now feasible, why should these terms be employed? And since there appear to be no presently-existing guidelines which can be established in this document, then the ensuing wrangle in comparative cases as to what is ordinary, usual, unusual, high, etc., will take up at least the same time, if not more, than the mere introduction of proof of the basic facts.

I do not believe that the Commission has given sufficient thought to the consequences of establishing the order and weight of preferences in comparative hearing cases. The document says that the policy is to apply to "new" applicants, and that it "does not attempt to deal with the somewhat different problems raised where an applicant is contesting with a licensee seeking renewal of license." I do not believe that a logical or a legal basis can be established for making a distinction between criteria to be applied to renewal applications and criteria applicable to initial applications. The statutory test is exactly the same. The intention of Congress to require the same test was affirmed in the Communications Act Amendments of 1952. Since we must assume that the Commission will find it appropriate or necessary to make uniform application of its statement of preferences, it is essential to consider the consequences of such application. The filing of a new application — organized according to formula — to challenge a renewal applicant could lead to a facile but in many instances unfair and arbitrary decisional process. Is the Commission now ready to read out established broadcasters, not locally owned, but otherwise without blemish in favor of any locally-owned applicants? Is the Commission now ready to read out established broadcasters who are without blemish, except that they utilize competent personnel who do not have an ownership interest, in favor of applicants who propose to operate the facilities personally? Is the Commission ready to accept a new applicant formed to meet this preconceived mold in preference to an existing broadcaster who does not fit into such mold regardless of other circumstances?

I must assume that in the above cases the Commission will not reach its judgments arbitrarily and without giving consideration to all of the significant elements. Upon this assumption, I can foresee the development of case after case where exceptions to the Policy will be found to be necessary in order to reach a decision which a majority will consider to be fair and in the public interest. I can foresee a decisional process which eventually will be substantially similar — if not virtually identical — to the one in existence. Under these circumstances, I cannot believe that the public interest will be served, or the processes of the

Commission expedited, by the adoption of the proposed Policy Statement.

No useful purpose would appear to be served by further belaboring these points. While the motives of the majority may be excellent, I do not believe that its objectives can thus be achieved. Moreover, I fear that the degree of uniformity which is being sought will necessarily be detrimental to broadcasting in general and to the public interest.

An overall objection which I think I should state is that the Commission is, in effect, placing legislative-like restrictions upon performance under the responsibility Congress intended it to implement with broad discretion. It would appear that we do not trust Commissioners to exercise judgment with as much discretion as Congress intended to repose in the Agency. This restrictive approach not only limits the Agency, but, as has been indicated, threatens to inhibit the development of services which do not conform to preconceived molds.

I think that the Commission should consider — instead of the adoption of this proposed "Policy Statement" — the introduction of such modern and accepted procedural methods as "discovery" — requiring its staff to make a more careful examination of each competing applicant prior to the issuance of hearing orders so as to specify issues which will encompass all material differences among the applicants rather than ordering hearings on generalized, boiler-plate issues and preconceived conclusions; and writing its decisions with such care as to eliminate frivolous and inconsequential matter and in such a manner that applicants would be readily apprised of areas which the Commission considers to be vitally important. I believe that discovery procedure alone will do more to bring light — and to minimize heat — in comparative cases than a general abjuration of trivia. If the parties and, in fact, the Commission can secure factual information about each of the applicants before the hearing, and if thereafter, the Commission will exercise care and discretion in the framing of the issues, more will have been achieved to shorten our hearing procedures than can reasonably be expected from the adoption of this Policy Statement.

Dissenting statement of Commissioner Robert T. Bartley

I believe that our comparative hearings should be expedited by eliminating what has amounted to extensive bickering in the record over minutiae.

As I see it, however, the Commission majority is attempting the impossible here when it prejudges the decisional factors in future cases. My observation is that there are no two cases exactly alike. There are so many varying circumstances in each case that a factor in one may be more important than the same factor in another. Broadcasting — a dynamic force in our society — experiences constant change. I have expressed it differently on occasions by saying, "There's nothing static in radio but the noise." If we are to encourage the larger and more effective use of radio in the public interest, we must avoid becoming static ourselves.

Concurring statement of Commissioner Robert E. Lee

Even though I recognize the Policy Statement adopted by the Commission to be the result of a sincere effort to clarify the historical process of selecting a winner in comparative broadcast hearings, I am concurring with considerable reluctance. I am disappointed that the Commission did not examine alternative methods of "picking a winner" from a group of competing applicants, each of which may be fully qualified but only one of which may be granted. For example, in a recent case involving nine applications where I unqualifiedly concurred with the result arrived at by the majority, I said:

However, I would much prefer such appropriate changes in the Communications Act and in the Commission's practices and policies as would have permitted, in a case such as this, adoption of a procedure which would, on a comparative basis, eliminate from further consideration several of the applications, and which would have permitted us to direct the remaining applicants to endeavor to work out a satisfactory merger arrangement within a stated reasonable period. In the event that such a merger were thereafter presented to the Commission, an award could have been given to the merged entity. Failing such a merger, the Commission would thereupon proceed to select a winner from among the limited eligibles. *Veterans Broadcasting Company, Inc., et al*, decided January 19, 1965.

Over the years I have participated in decisions in hundreds of "comparative proceedings" and candor compels me to say that our method of selection of the winning applicant has given me grave concern. I realize, of course, that where we have a number of qualified applicants in a consolidated proceeding for a single facility in a given community, it is necessary that we grant one and deny the others. The ultimate choice of the winner generally sustains the Commission's choice despite the recent rash of remands from the Court. Thus, it would appear that we generally grant the "right" application. However, I am not so naive as to believe that granting the "right application" could not, in some cases, be one of several applications.

The criteria that the Commission now says will be decisive — assuming all other things are substantially equal — in choosing among qualified applicants for new broadcast facilities in comparative hearings, are not new. However, the Policy Statement does tend to restrict the scope somewhat of existing factors and if undue delay in the disposition of comparative broadcast hearings is thus prevented, some good will have been accomplished.

I wish to make clear that my concurrence here does not bind me with respect to the weight I might see fit to put upon the various criteria in a given case. For example, while I recognize the problem of diversification of the mass media, I also recognize some counter balancing in the advantages of common ownership of a radio station and a newspaper. I am also persuaded that the public interest may be served by the common ownership of a radio station and a CATV system in the same market. In other words, if it should appear to me in a given proceeding that the owner of a newspaper or of a CATV system would do the better job of serving a particular community, I would not be so concerned with the composition of such an applicant that I would select another that was not "tainted" with the media of mass communication.

Historically, a prospective applicant hires a highly skilled communications attorney, well versed in the procedures of the Commission. This counsel has a long history of Commission decisions to guide him and he puts together an application that meets all of the so-called criteria. There then follows a torturous and expensive hearing wherein each applicant attempts to tear down his adversaries on every conceivable front, while individually presenting that which he thinks the Commission would like to hear. The Examiner then makes a reasoned decision which, at first blush, generally makes a lot of sense — but comes the Oral Argument and all of the losers concentrate their fire on the "potential" winner and the Commission must thereupon examine the claims and counter claims, "weigh" the criteria and pick the winner which, if my recollection serves me correctly, is a different winner in about 50 per cent of the cases.

The real blow, however, comes later when the applicant that emerged as the winner on the basis of our "decisive" criteria sells the station to a multiple owner or someone else that could not possibly have prevailed over other qualified applicants under the criteria in an adversary proceeding. It may be that there is no better selection system than the one being followed. If so, it seems like a "helleva way to run a railroad," and I hope these few comments may inspire the Commission to find that better system even if it requires changes in the Communications Act.

4

THE CARTER MOUNTAIN CASE

In re Carter Mountain Transmission Corp.
32 FCC 459
February 14, 1962

Cable Television (CATV) systems began operating in the United States in 1949 when they were known as "community antenna television systems." As they grew in number and as audiences served by expanded CATV services also grew, increasingly vocal and complaining TV station licensees made it impossible for the FCC to avoid consideration of CATV's competitive impact on open circuit television.

At first the Commission disclaimed jurisdiction over CATV and requested that Congress authorize it to regulate the new medium. When Congress failed to provide enabling legislation, the FCC found it necessary to proceed under the Communications Act as it stood.

Carter Mountain was the Commission's first successful attempt to regulate CATV. The decision established that the FCC could lawfully deny microwave relay applications to serve CATV systems if existing TV stations — and thus the public interest — would be injured by increased competition from such additional CATV facilities. The decision was affirmed by the Court of Appeals (321 F. 2d 359 (D.C. Cir. 1963)) and the Supreme Court refused to review the case (375 U.S. 951 (1963)).

By the Commission: Commissioner Bartley not participating; Commissioner Cross dissenting and issuing a statement.

1.   This is a protest proceeding under 47 U.S.C. 309(c)[1] and 405, arising out of the application of Carter Mountain Transmission Corp. ("Carter"), for a

---

[1] The protest was filed under the then provisions of sec. 309(c) of the Communications Act of 1934, 48 Stat. 1085, as amended, 47 U.S.C.A. sec. 309(c).

permit to install microwave radio relay pickup television signals to community antenna systems in Riverton, Lander, and Thermopolis, Wyo. Our grant without hearing was protested by Joseph P. and Mildred V. Ernst, d/b as Chief Washakie TV, licensee of station KWRB-TV, channel 10, Riverton, Wyo. ("KWRB-TV"), protestants alleging, inter alia, that by providing additional service to existing and operating CATV systems located in Thermopolis, Riverton, and Lander, Wyo., the microwave facilities would enhance their competitive standing to the economic detriment of KWRB-TV; and further, that Carter "is not eligible" to hold common carrier authorizations. By memorandum opinion and order of June 29, 1959 (FCC 59-617; 24 F.R. 5402), the effective date of the grant was postponed and the protest was set for oral argument before the Commission, en banc, with the licensee of KWRB-TV, Carter, and the Chief, Common Carrier Bureau, designated as parties. By memorandum opinion and order of May 20, 1960 (FCC 60-564; 25 F.R. 4606), the matter was designated for hearing. On May 25, 1961 (FCC 61D-74), Hearing Examiner Walther W. Guenther released an initial decision looking toward a denial of the protest, a setting aside of the stay of the effectiveness of the grant, and a reinstatement of the grant of the subject application. KWRB-TV filed exceptions and requested oral argument. The National Association of Broadcasters and Tri-State TV Translator Association sought and were granted leave to file memoranda of law, and the NAB was granted further leave to participate in the oral argument, which was held December 14, 1961.

2.   The initial decision sets forth the background and history of the proceeding, which need not be repeated here. Except as modified herein and in the rulings on the exceptions, the Commission is in general agreement with the examiner's findings, which are hereby adopted. Except as modified herein, and in the rulings on the exceptions, the examiner's conclusions not inconsistent with this decision are hereby adopted. For reasons hereinafter stated, the Commission disagrees with the ultimate result reached by the examiner and, as to that portion of the decision reverses the examiner.

3.   Two basic questions are presented for determination: (a) whether Carter is in fact a bona fide common carrier eligible for a common carrier microwave facility; and (b) whether, a determination having been made that Carter is a common carrier of a microwave facility to a CATV system, the public interest is inherent and the economic impact is of no legal significance. Each will be discussed in order.

4.   KWRB-TV excepts to the examiner's findings and ultimate conclusion that Carter is a bona fide common carrier and to the examiner's failure to find that Carter is the alter ego of Western (a CATV operator). The examiner amply described the situation, adequately discussed the legal proposition, and ultimately concluded correctly. The burden of adducing facts concerning the interlocking ownership between itself and CATV was placed on the applicant, who proved to the examiner's satisfaction that Carter and CATV are separate

legal entities, and that the existing degree of common or interlocking ownership would support no contrary inference. KWRB-TV failed to prove anything adverse to this conclusion. In view of the conclusion herein, we do not reach the question of the legal significance of a greater degree of, or a total identity of, ownership, and we refrain from expressing an opinion thereon. The applicant held itself out for hire, invited the public to use its facilities, and indicated its willingness and ability to carry out this hire. As a matter of fact, station KOOK-TV, with which Carter has no affinity of interest, accepted Carter's offer and the examiner rightfully took official notice thereof. Thus, in accordance with the facts gathered pursuant to issues (3) and (4), issue (5) was properly resolved in applicant's favor.

5.   After such findings, the examiner stated "[since] a grant of the subject application will serve the public interest [because it is a bona fide common carrier], . . . it is unnecessary to consider, in particular, the nature of the showing made by protestant under issue (2). . . . whatever impact the operations of the CATV systems may have upon protestant's operation of station KWRB-TV, . . . are matters of no legal significance to the ultimate determination made that a grant of the subject application of Carter, a bona fide communications common carrier, will serve the public interest." KWRB-TV urges that the examiner erred in so concluding. The National Association of Broadcasters, Tri-State TV Translator Association, and the Broadcast Bureau join.

6.   When this application was designated for hearing, the Commission recognized that the grant of the microwave facility which is to be used to carry CATV into a community could conceivably destroy the only local television service. The Commission retained the right to make a determination on the facts by specifically including issues (1) and (2), which seek respectively to determine the areas and population now being served by KWRB-TV and the nature and type of said service; and to determine the impact which a grant of the instant application would have upon the operation of KWRB-TV, and the resulting injury, if any, to the public now served. Thus, it is clear that the Commission did not consider the impact of no legal significance, but sought facts on which an ultimate conclusion could be predicated. The examiner made adequate findings with respect to these issues, but gave these facts no weight in his conclusions.

7.   Carter urges however, that even were the Commission to find an impact and were it to take cognizance of any adverse effect this impact may have on KWRB-TV, it must recognize that the CATV not the carrier (Carter in this instance) is responsible for the impact, and that the two systems are separate legal entities. This argument, appearing meritorious on its face, is set forth by the examiner (initial decision, p. 28, footnote 8). However, the Commission does not construe its responsibilities this narrowly. We find no justification for ignoring our obligations in the field of television simply because it happens to be common carrier activities that are being regulated at the moment. A grant of common carrier radio facilities requires a finding that the public interest will be

served thereby; certainly the well-being of existing television facilities is an aspect of this public interest. Thus it is not only appropriate, it is necessary that we determine whether the use of the facility applied for would directly or indirectly bring about the elimination of the only television transmission or reception service to the public. In examining the entire instant situation, we may reasonably assume that the carrier (over which we do have jurisdiction) seeks to improve its present service and add additional services so that it may utilize any customer (i.e., CATV) potential. Carter contends that because we have no jurisdiction over the customer, we cannot consider the activities of the customer in regulating the carrier. We do not agree. If making the grant enables this customer potential to destroy a basic Commission policy, then even assuming, arguendo, that the applicant is not the direct cause of the impact, the ability to create such a situation in this particular instance is sufficient to warrant an examination into the entire problem. We will not shut our eyes to the impact upon the public service which is our ultimate concern, when it appears that the grant may serve to deprive a substantially large number of the public of a service merely because the common carrier classification is used. The Commission does not operate in a vacuum. We will not permit a subsequent grant to be issued if it be demonstrated that the same would vitiate a prior grant, without weighing the public-interest considerations involved.

8.   Carter further urges that considering the use which the common carrier subscriber may make of its facility places the Commission in the position of censoring public communications. Here again we do not agree with this position. As guardian of the public interest, we are entrusted with a wide range of discretionary authority and under that authority we may not only appraise the facts and draw inferences from them, but also bring to bear upon the problem an expert judgment from our analysis of the total situation as to just where the public interest lies.[2] We are not in this instance attempting to do anything more than make a valued judgment in this direction. There is no attempt to examine, limit, or interfere with the actual material to be transmitted. We are merely considering the question of whether the use of the facility is in the public interest, a conclusion which must be reached prior to the issuance of the grant. In seeking this ultimate answer, we must look at the situation in its entirety, and we do not agree that we are acting in any fashion which would constitute "censorship."

9.   It would be helpful at this time to set down some of the pertinent facts. KWRB-TV's grade A and B contours include a total of 36,918 persons (1950 U.S. census), in an area of 13,845 square miles, encompassing approx-

---

[2]In *Television Corporation of Michigan, Inc.* v. *FCC* (294 F. 2d 730 (1961)), the Court of Appeals for the District of Columbia Circuit stated, at p. 733, that "[N]either the statutory sections nor the 'priorities' express rigid and inflexible standards: the Commission has a broad measure of discretion in dealing with the many and complicated problems of allocation and distribution of service."

imately 10,548 homes.[3] However, only 6 of the towns included in the aforementioned area have a population in excess of 1,000 persons; namely, Lander, Riverton, Thermopolis, Worland, Basin, and Greybull. We are primarily concerned here with the first four towns, having populations of 4,182, 6,845, 3,955, and 5,806 persons, respectively, totaling 20,788 persons, or 5,940 homes. The towns of Lander and Riverton had a relatively small number of subscribers to CATV operations, although from 1958 through 1960 they slowly increased the number of homes placed on the cable. The towns of Thermopolis and Worland had a large number of CATV subscribers, and these numbers had been decreasing during the years 1958 through 1960 with resultant increased sale of spots for KWRB-TV.

10.   KWRB-TV's overall programing serves the public interest. It has permission from each of the three networks with which it is affiliated to carry their entire schedules by deleting the "commercials" and substituting "public service," and it carries public service spots on behalf of the local town and community. It has a good local operating record and programs for the community it serves. If KWRB-TV were no longer to operate, no local programs of this type would be available to persons residing within the grade B contour, and they depend on this station for the airing of this local material.

11.   The largest revenue returns are received from the towns of Lander and Riverton. Despite the fact that Worland has approximately 1,600 more persons than does Lander, the revenue from Lander is approximately 6 times that of Worland. This is attributed to the fact that CATV did not make any substantial inroad in Lander, while approximately 75 percent of the homes in Worland are on the cable. A similar type of comparison may be made between the towns of Riverton and Thermopolis.

12.   Since its inception, station KWRB-TV has been operating in the "red"; that is, its operating expenses have exceeded its income. However, in each succeeding year of operation the gap between the two has become smaller, and as contended by protestant, should eventually be closed and then changed to "black." KWRB-TV points to a number of contributing factors, some of which are: the closing of the CATV station in Thermopolis (then under another operator) for approximately 6 months during 1960; a decrease in the number of homes carried on the CATV cable in the towns of Thermopolis and Worland where CATV has 44 percent and 75 percent subscriptions; KWRB-TV's being a "family enterprise" with resultant low expense and high productivity; reduction in the amount of syndicated film purchases and the substitution of network programing for which charges are no longer being exacted; but primarily, KWRB-TV's ability to show inroads on the number of cable subscribers together with an increase in its network affiliation status, enabled it to sell its spot advertising more readily, thus increasing its revenue.

13.   Duplication of network programing exists not only between the

[3]U.S. census national average of approximately 3.5 persons per "household" or "home."

imported programs entering the towns here involved over the cable system, but also with KWRB-TV signal. Network programs carried on KWRB-TV may also appear on one or more of the cable channels, without the local spot advertising. KWRB-TV states that at the present time, however, its picture is clearer and better than the one appearing on the CATV cable in the area. Thus, although a good deal of difficulty is encountered in attempting to sell spots in face of the division of audience, it manages to do so on the basis of better performance. However, it is urged that a grant of the instant application would permit the CATV to improve its facilities to match that of KWRB-TV, rendering the sale to local advertisers impossible in view of the fact that they would not be able to guarantee any viewing on its channel. Reason and logic cause us to agree with the conclusion that should the CATV system be permitted to expand its services and furnish better technical facilities, KWRB-TV will be placed in the economically disadvantageous position of finding it more difficult to sell its advertising; it would have nothing to point to which would indicate to a potential advertiser that a popular program was being viewed over KWRB-TV vis-a-vis other potential channels. Its one balancing factor of a better picture will have been removed.

14.   Licenses are granted by the Commission only if the operations proposed are found to be in the public interest, convenience, and necessity. Hence, when the impact of economic injury is such as to adversely affect the public interest, it is not only within our power, but it is our duty to determine the ultimate effect, study the facts, and act in a manner most advantageous to the public.[4] Although most of the network programs carried by KWRB-TV would continue to be available to the present CATV subscribers in the 6 towns of over 1,000 persons, via translators or CATV's, such programs would not be available to persons not residing in the immediate vicinity of the towns in which the CATV systems and VHF translators operate, nor to persons in the towns unable to pay the CATV charges. Therefore, if KWRB-TV is eventually forced off the air as a result of a grant of the instant application, the public stands to lose its only local outlet, an outlet on which a considerable part of the population in northwestern Wyoming relies.

15.   A review of KWRB-TV's revenue for the year 1959 indicates that Lander and Riverton each return $14,191.31 and $17,429.14, respectively, as against a return of $6,457.20 and $2,485.45 from Thermopolis and Worland, respectively, notwithstanding the fact that Worland has a larger population than does Lander. Thus, the four towns made up $40,563.10 of a total revenue of $66,812.03 for the year 1959. If the CATV pattern is permitted to be altered, and the substantial return from Riverton in particular is reduced, KWRB-TV,

---

[4]The courts have held that economic injury to a licensee and public interest may be different matters. However, the former "becomes important when on the facts it spells diminution or destruction of service." *Carroll Broadcasting Company* v. *FCC*, 258 F. 2d 440, 443 (1958).

despite the fact that it would strive harder, would find it more difficult to sell its advertising in face of the split audience, and this situation, together with facts of record, results in our judgment that the demise of this local operation would result.

16.   At the time KWRB-TV was granted its license, the Commission concluded that it was in the public interest to make such a grant. The Commission must now find it in the public interest to grant the instant application. Standing alone, it might appear that each does in fact serve the public interest, with KWRB-TV showing, inter alia, that it is the only local television outlet for the community, while Carter would show that an increase in its facilities would permit the rendition of better and more efficient service to the CATV serving the community. However, neither stands alone; the effect of one upon the other must be weighed, and the ultimate conclusion must be made to the best interest of the public. True, a grant of the instant application would permit the rendition of better service by the CATV, but at the expense of destroying the local station and its rural coverage. The CATV would permit the urban areas a choice of coverage, but the local station, especially in this case of a single-station market, serves a wider area. A grant of this application will not contemplate an extension of coverage for the entire area included in KWRB-TV's contours, since it is too costly for CATV to enter the rural areas. Thus, the rural people would be left with nothing at all. This is not a true competitive situation where one or the other of the applicants would render the service. In this instance, if KWRB-TV, the local outlet, should be forced to cease operation, the rural people would be left without any service. We do not agree that we are powerless to prevent the demise of the local television station, and the eventual loss of service to a substantial population; nor do we agree that the Commission's expertise may not be invoked in this instance to predict this ultimate situation. Thus, after weighing the public interest involved in Carter's improved facility against the loss of the local station, it must be concluded, beyond peradventure of a doubt, the need for the local outlet and the service which it would provide to outlying areas outweighs the need for the improved service which Carter would furnish under the terms of the instant application. To the extent that this decision departs from our views in the report and order in docket No. 12443, 26 FCC 403 (released April 14, 1959), those views are modified.

17.   In view of the foregoing and in light of the evidence adduced, we fail to find that a grant of the instant application would serve the public interest, convenience, and necessity, and therefore the application is denied, without prejudice however, to Carter's refiling when it is able to show that the CATV operation will avoid the duplication of KWRB-TV programing which now exists and that the CATV system will carry the local KWRB-TV signal. Placing of these latter conditions upon the refiling without prejudice is being done with full recognition of the separate corporate entities of Carter and the CATV. The realities of the situation, however, force a recognition of the fact that the

conditions we impose upon Carter are a sine qua non to our finding that its operation will be in the public interest. Neither the Commission nor KWRB-TV can bring them about. Carter may accomplish this by a contract relationship between itself and the corporation with which it has some interlocking ownership [Western], or by some less formal means.

Accordingly, *It is ordered*, This 14th day of February 1962, that protest of Joseph P. Ernst and Mildred V. Ernst, d/b as Chief Washakie TV (KWRB-TV), *Is granted*; and the aforementioned application of Carter Mountain Transmission Corp. *Is denied* without prejudice to refiling when a showing can be made that the duplication of programing is adequately avoided and a satisfactory arrangement is arrived at by which the cable system will carry the local KWRB-TV service.

Dissenting statement of Commissioner Cross

I dissent. Even though I sympathize with the plight of station KWRB-TV (channel 10, Riverton, Wyo.) in this instance, I nevertheless consider the relief being granted by the majority sets an undesirable precedent that is against the best overall interests of the broadcasting industry in this country.

In docket No. 12443 (released April 14, 1959), the Commission, after lengthy consideration and deliberation, properly, in my view, determined the rationale for deciding cases like this one. In paragraph 75 of the report and order in docket No. 12443, the Commission stated:

. . . it is neither proper, pertinent, nor necessary for us to consider the specific lawful use which the common carrier subscriber may make of the facilities of the carrier. To take a different view would place the Commission in the anomalous position of acting as censor over public communications, and put us under the burden of policing, not only the use of such facilities but the content of communications transmitted on the facilities. The logical extension of such a philosophy would require us to deny communications facilities of any kind (message telephone, telegraph, etc.) to CATV's and, for example, to deny access to facilities to those acting contrary to our concept of the public welfare. The adjudication of these matters is beyond our province.

Despite this previous statement by the Commission (and the other portions of the report and order in docket No. 12443 on this general subject), the protestant and others have now apparently convinced the majority that the Commission should consider the specific lawful use which the common carrier subscriber may make of the facilities of the carrier. The thrust of their argument in this regard is that the Commission should not, on the one hand, license microwave facilities to a common carrier when part or all of such facilities will be used by a CATV system to the economic detriment of the only television station in the community, which has also been licensed by the Commission with its other hand.

Admittedly, this is a hard case, but there is an old saying that hard cases make bad law and, in my opinion, that is what is being done here by the decision of the majority. Having the Commission examine into the specific lawful use which the common carrier subscriber may make of the facilities of the carrier is, in my opinion, not only contrary to common carrier communications law and practice but could open up a veritable Pandora's box which in the end may well redound to the serious detriment of the broadcasting industry itself.

The Commission was aware of these undesirable possibilities at the time it released its report and order in docket No. 12443. Indeed, these factors were significant in persuading the Commission that the best way to protect the broadcaster in situations like this was not through the common carrier licensees but through legislation that would authorize the Commission to have some degree of regulation over the users; i.e., the CATV systems. Such legislation was, in fact, proposed to the Congress by the Commission and is still before the Congress.[5] Accordingly, it is my view that we should not try to correct one isolated situation in the instant case by departing from our previously well-considered and soundly bottomed actions on the subject; i.e., the report and order in docket No. 12443 and our subsequent request to the Congress for the legislation noted above. I would therefore deny the protest and wait for the enactment of the requested legislation to deal with this matter.

[5] S. 1044 and H.R. 6840 were introduced on Feb. 16, 1961, at the Commission's request.

5

THE SOUTHWESTERN CASE

United States et al. v.
Southwestern Cable Co. et al.
    392 U.S. 157
    June 10, 1968

Using *Carter Mountain* as a precedent, the FCC adopted the first rules placing local carriage and nonduplication requirements on microwave-served CATV systems in 1965 (38 FCC 683). A year later it applied rules to all CATV systems (2 FCC 2d 725), whether or not they used microwave facilities. The 1966 rules also prohibited CATV importation of distant television station signals into the top 100 TV markets without a hearing. The effect of the Commission's rules was to slow the growth of CATV and thus protect licensed television stations from "unfair competition."

This unanimous Supreme Court decision, sometimes referred to as the "San Diego case," declared the FCC's rules legally valid under the broad authority over interstate communication vested in the Commission by the Communications Act. Justice White's concurring opinion is omitted below.

Mr. Justice Harlan delivered the opinion of the Court.

These cases stem from proceedings conducted by the Federal Communications Commission after requests by Midwest Television[1] for relief under

[1]Midwest's petition was premised upon its status as licensee of KFMB-TV, San Diego, California. It is evidently also the licensee of various other broadcasting stations. See Second Report and Order, 2 F.C.C. 2d 725, 739.

§ § 74.1107[2] and 74.1109[3] of the rules promulgated by the Commission for the regulation of community antenna television (CATV) systems. Midwest averred that respondents' CATV systems transmitted the signals of Los Angeles broadcasting stations into the San Diego area, and thereby had, inconsistently with the public interest, adversely affected Midwest's San Diego station.[4] Midwest sought an appropriate order limiting the carriage of such signals by respondents' systems. After consideration of the petition and of various responsive pleadings, the Commission restricted the expansion of respondents' service in areas in which they had not operated on February 15, 1966, pending hearings to be conducted on the merits of Midwest's complaints.[5] 4 F.C.C. 2d 612. On petitions for review, the Court of Appeals for the Ninth Circuit held that the Commission lacks authority under the Communications Act of 1934, 48

---

[2] 47 CFR § 74.1107(a) provides that "[n]o CATV system operating in a community within the predicted Grade A contour of a television broadcast station in the 100 largest television markets shall extend the signal of a television broadcast station beyond the Grade B contour of that station, except upon a showing approved by the Commission that such extension would be consistent with the public interest, and specifically the establishment and healthy maintenance of television broadcast service in the area. Commission approval of a request to extend a signal in the foregoing circumstances will be granted where the Commission, after consideration of the request and all related materials in a full evidentiary hearing, determines that the requisite showing has been made. The market size shall be determined by the rating of the American Research Bureau, on the basis of the net weekly circulation for the most recent year." San Diego is the Nation's 54th largest television market. *Midwest Television, Inc.*, 11 Pike & Fischer Radio Reg. 2d 273, 276.

[3] 47 CFR § 74.1109 creates "procedures applicable to petitions for waiver of the rules, additional or different requirements and rulings on complaints or disputes." It provides that petitions for special relief "may be submitted informally, by letter, but shall be accompanied by an affidavit of service on any CATV system, station licensee, permittee, applicant, or other interested person who may be directly affected if the relief requested in the petition should be granted." 47 CFR § 74.1109(b). Provisions are made for comments or opposition to the petition, and for rejoinders by the petitioner. 47 CFR § § 74.1109(d), (e). Finally, the Commission "may specify other procedures, such as oral argument, evidentiary hearing, or further written submissions directed to particular aspects, as it deems appropriate." 47 CFR § 74.1109(f).

[4] Midwest asserted that respondents' importation of Los Angeles signals had fragmented the San Diego audience, that this would reduce the advertising revenues of local stations, and that the ultimate consequence would be to terminate or to curtail the services provided in the San Diego area by local broadcasting stations. Respondents' CATV systems now carry the signals of San Diego stations, but Midwest alleged that the quality of the signals, as they are carried by respondents, is materially degraded, and that this serves only to accentuate the fragmentation of the local audience.

[5] February 15, 1966, is the date on which grandfather rights accrued under 47 CFR § 74.1107(d). The initial decision of the hearing examiner, issued October 3, 1967, concluded that permanent restrictions on the expansion of respondents' services were unwarranted. *Midwest Television, Inc.*, 11 Pike & Fischer Radio Reg. 2d 273. The Commission has declined to terminate its interim restrictions pending consideration by the Commission of the examiner's decision. *Midwest Television, Inc., id.*, at 721.

Stat. 1064, 47 U.S.C. § 151, to issue such an order.[6] 378 F. 2d 118. We granted certiorari to consider this important question of regulatory authority.[7] 389 U.S. 911. For reasons that follow, we reverse.

I.

CATV systems receive the signals of television broadcasting stations, amplify them, transmit them by cable or microwave, and ultimately distribute them by wire to the receivers of their subscribers.[8] CATV systems characteristically do not produce their own programming,[9] and do not recompense producers or broadcasters for use of the programming which they receive and redistribute.[10] Unlike ordinary broadcasting stations, CATV systems commonly charge their subscribers installation and other fees.[11]

The CATV industry has grown rapidly since the establishment of the first commercial system in 1950.[12] In the late 1950's, some 50 new systems were

[6]The opinion of the Court of Appeals could be understood to hold either that the Commission may not, under the Communications Act, regulate CATV, or, more narrowly, that it may not issue the prohibitory order involved here. We take the court's opinion, in fact, to have encompassed both positions.

[7]We note that the Court of Appeals for the District of Columbia Circuit has concluded that the Communications Act permits the regulation of CATV systems. See *Buckeye Cablevision, Inc.* v. *F.C.C.*, 128 U.S. App. D.C. 262, 387 F. 2d 220.

[8]CATV systems are defined by the Commission for purposes of its rules as "any facility which ... receives directly or indirectly over the air and amplifies or otherwise modifies the signals transmitting programs broadcast by one or more television stations and distributes such signals by wire or cable to subscribing members of the public who pay for such service, but such term shall not include (1) any such facility which serves fewer than 50 subscribers, or (2) any such facility which serves only the residents of one or more apartment dwellings under common ownership, control, or management, and commercial establishments located on the premises of such an apartment house." 47 CFR § 74.1101(a).

[9]There is, however, no technical reason why they may not. See Note, The Wire Mire: The FCC and CATV, 79 Harv. L. Rev. 366, 367. Indeed, the examiner was informed in this case that respondent Mission Cable TV "intends to commence program origination in the near future." *Midwest Television, Inc., supra*, at 283.

[10]The question whether a CATV system infringes the copyright of a broadcasting station by its reception and retransmission of the station's signals is presented in *Fortnightly Corp.* v. *United Artists TV, Inc.*, No. 618, now pending before the Court.

[11]The installation costs for CATV systems in 16 Connecticut communities were, for example, found to range from $31 to $147 per home. M. Seiden, An Economic Analysis of Community Antenna Television Systems and the Television Broadcasting Industry 24 (1965).

[12]CATV systems were evidently first established on a noncommercial basis in 1949. H.R. Rep. No. 1635, 89th Cong., 2d Sess., 5.

established each year; by 1959, there were 550 "nationally known and identified" systems serving a total audience of 1,500,000 to 2,000,000 persons.[13] It has been more recently estimated that "new systems are being founded at the rate of more than one per day, and . . . subscribers . . . signed on at the rate of 15,000 per month."[14] By late 1965, it was reported that there were 1,847 operating CATV systems, that 758 others were franchised but not yet in operation, and that there were 938 applications for additional franchises.[15] The statistical evidence is incomplete, but, as the Commission has observed, "whatever the estimate, CATV growth is clearly explosive in nature." Second Report and Order, 2 F.C.C. 2d 725, 738, n. 15.

CATV systems perform either or both of two functions. First, they may supplement broadcasting by facilitating satisfactory reception of local stations in adjacent areas in which such reception would not otherwise be possible; and second, they may transmit to subscribers the signals of distant stations entirely beyond the range of local antennae. As the number and size of CATV systems have increased, their principal function has more frequently become the importation of distant signals.[16] In 1959, only 50 systems employed microwave relays, and the maximum distance over which signals were transmitted was 300 miles; by 1964, 250 systems used microwave, and the transmission distances sometimes exceeded 665 miles. First Report and Order, 38 F.C.C. 683, 709. There are evidently now plans "to carry the programing of New York City independent stations by cable to . . . upstate New York, to Philadelphia, and even as far as Dayton."[17] And see *Channel 9 Syracuse, Inc.* v. *F.C.C.*, 128 U.S. App. D.C. 187, 385 F. 2d 969; *Hubbard Broadcasting, Inc.* v. *F.C.C.*, 128 U.S. App. D.C. 197, 385 F. 2d 979. Thus, "while the CATV industry originated in sparsely settled areas and areas of adverse terrain . . . it is now spreading to metropolitan centers . . ." First Report and Order, *supra*, at 709. CATV systems, formerly no more than local auxiliaries to broadcasting, promise for the future to provide a national communications system, in which signals from selected broadcasting centers would be transmitted to metropolitan areas throughout the country.[18]

[13]CATV and TV Repeater Services, 26 F.C.C. 403, 408; Note, The Wire Mire: The FCC and CATV, *supra*, at 368.

[14]Note, The Wire Mire: The FCC and CATV, *supra*, at 368.

[15]Second Report and Order, 2 F.C.C. 2d 725, 738. The franchises are granted by state or local regulatory agencies. It was reported in 1965 that two States, Connecticut and Nevada, regulate CATV systems, and that some 86% of the systems are subject at least to some local regulation. Seiden, *supra*, at 44-47. See Conn. Gen. Stat. Rev., Tit. 16, c. 289 (1958); Nev. Stat. 1967, c. 458.

[16]The term "distant signal" has been given a specialized definition by the Commission, as a signal "which is extended or received beyond the Grade B contour of that station." 47 CFR § 74.1101 (i). The Grade B contour is a line along which good reception may be expected 90% of the time at 50% of the locations. See 47 CFR § 73.683(a).

[17]Note, The Wire Mire: The FCC and CATV, *supra*, at 368 (notes omitted).

[18]It has thus been suggested that "a nationwide grid of wired CATV systems, inter-connected by microwave frequencies and financed by subscriber fees, may one day offer a

The Commission has on various occasions attempted to assess the relationship between community antenna television systems and its conceded regulatory functions. In 1959, it completed an extended investigation of several auxiliary broadcasting services, including CATV. CATV and TV Repeater Services, 26 F.C.C. 403. Although it found that CATV is "related to interstate transmission," the Commission reasoned that CATV systems are neither common carriers nor broadcasters, and therefore are within neither of the principal regulatory categories created by the Communications Act. *Id.*, at 427-428. The Commission declared that it had not been given plenary authority over "any and all enterprises which happen to be connected with one of the many aspects of communications." *Id.*, at 429. It refused to premise regulation of CATV upon assertedly adverse consequences for broadcasting, because it could not "determine where the impact takes effect, although we recognize that it may well exist." *Id.*, at 431.

The Commission instead declared that it would forthwith seek appropriate legislation "to clarify the situation." *Id.*, at 438. Such legislation was introduced in the Senate in 1959,[19] favorably reported,[20] and debated on the Senate floor.[21] The bill was, however, ultimately returned to committee.[22]

Despite its inability to obtain amendatory legislation, the Commission has, since 1960, gradually asserted jurisdiction over CATV. It first placed restrictions upon the activities of common carrier microwave facilities that serve CATV systems. See *Carter Mountain Transmission Corp.*, 32 F.C.C. 459, aff'd, 321 F. 2d 359. Finally, the Commission in 1962 conducted a rule-making proceeding in which it re-evaluated the significance of CATV for its regulatory responsibilities. First Report and Order, *supra*. The proceeding was explicitly restricted to those systems that are served by microwave, but the Commission's conclusions plainly were more widely relevant. The Commission found that "the likelihood or probability of [CATV's] adverse impact upon potential and existing service has become too substantial to be dismissed." *Id.*, at 713-714. It reasoned that the importation of distant signals into the service areas of local stations necessarily creates "substantial competition" for local broadcasting. *Id.*, at 707. The Commission acknowledged that it could not "measure precisely the degree of . . . impact," but found that "CATV competition can have a substantial negative effect upon station audience and revenues . . ." *Id.*, at 710-711.

The Commission attempted to "accommodat[e]" the interests of CATV and of local broadcasting by the imposition of two rules. *Id.*, at 713. First,

---

viable economic alternative to the advertiser-supported broadcast service." Levin, New Technology and the Old Regulation in Radio Spectrum Management, 56 Am. Econ. Rev. 339, 341 (Proceedings, May 1966).

[19] See S. 2653, 86th Cong., 1st Sess.

[20] S. Rep. No. 923, 86th Cong., 1st Sess.

[21] See 106 Cong. Rec. 10416-10436, 10520-10548.

[22] *Id.*, at 10547. The Commission in 1966 made additional efforts to obtain suitable modifications in the Communications Act. See n. 30, *infra*.

CATV systems were required to transmit to their subscribers the signals of any station into whose service area they have brought competing signals.[23] Second, CATV systems were forbidden to duplicate the programming of such local stations for periods of 15 days before and after a local broadcast. See generally First Report and Order, *supra*, at 719-730. These carriage and nonduplication rules were expected to "insur[e] many stations' ability to maintain themselves as their areas' outlets for highly popular network and other programs . . ." *Id.*, at 715.

The Commission in 1965 issued additional notices of inquiry and proposed rule-making, by which it sought to determine whether all forms of CATV, including those served only by cable, could properly be regulated under the Communications Act. 1 F.C.C. 2d 453. After further hearings, the Commission held that the Act confers adequate regulatory authority over all CATV systems. Second Report and Order, *supra*, at 728-734. It promulgated revised rules, applicable both to cable and to microwave CATV systems, to govern the carriage of local signals and the nonduplication of local programming. Further, the Commission forbade the importation by CATV of distant signals into the 100 largest television markets, except insofar as such service was offered on February 15, 1966, unless the Commission has previously found that it "would be consistent with the public interest," *id.*, at 782; see generally *id.*, at 781-785, "particularly the establishment and healthy maintenance of television broadcast service in the area," 47 CFR § 74.1107(c). Finally, the Commission created "summary, nonhearing procedures" for the disposition of applications for separate or additional relief. 2 F.C.C. 2d, at 764; 47 CFR § 74.1109. Thirteen days after the Commission's adoption of the Second Report, Midwest initiated these proceedings by the submission of its petition for special relief.

II.

We must first emphasize that questions as to the validity of the specific rules promulgated by the Commission for the regulation of CATV are not now before

---

[23] See generally First Report and Order, *supra*, at 716-719. The Commission held that a CATV system must, within the limits of its channel capacity, carry the signals of stations that place signals over the community served by the system. The stations are to be given priority according to the strength of the signal available in the community, with the strongest signals given first priority. Exceptions are made for situations in which there would be substantial duplication or in which an independent or noncommercial station would be excluded. *Id.*, at 717.

the Court. The issues in these cases are only two: whether the Commission has authority under the Communications Act to regulate CATV systems, and, if it has, whether it has, in addition, authority to issue the prohibitory order here in question.[24]

The Commission's authority to regulate broadcasting and other communications is derived from the Communications Act of 1934, as amended. The Act's provisions are explicitly applicable to "all interstate and foreign communication by wire or radio . . ." 47 U.S.C. § 152(a). The Commission's responsibilities are no more narrow: it is required to endeavor to "make available . . . to all the people of the United States a rapid, efficient, Nation-wide, and world-wide wire and radio communication service . . ." 47 U.S.C. § 151. The Commission was expected to serve as the "single Government agency"[25] with "unified jurisdiction"[26] and "regulatory power over all forms of electrical communication, whether by telephone, telegraph, cable, or radio."[27] It was for this purpose given "broad authority."[28] As this Court emphasized in an earlier case, the Act's terms, purposes, and history all indicate that Congress "formulated a unified and comprehensive regulatory system for the [broadcasting] industry." *F.C.C.* v. *Pottsville Broadcasting Co.*, 309 U.S. 134, 137.

Respondents do not suggest that CATV systems are not within the term "communication by wire or radio." Indeed, such communications are defined by the Act so as to encompass "the transmission of . . . signals, pictures, and sounds of all kinds," whether by radio or cable, "including all instrumentalities, facilities, apparatus, and services (among other things, the receipt, forwarding, and delivery of communications) incidental to such transmission." 47 U.S.C. § § 153(a), (b). These very general terms amply suffice to reach respondents' activities.

Nor can we doubt that CATV systems are engaged in interstate communication, even where, as here, the intercepted signals emanate from

---

[24]It must also be noted that the CATV systems involved in these cases evidently do not employ microwave. We intimate no views on what differences, if any, there might be in the scope of the Commission's authority over microwave and nonmicrowave systems.

[25]The phrase is taken from the message to Congress from President Roosevelt, dated February 26, 1934, in which he recommended the Commission's creation. See H. R. Rep. No. 1850, 73d Cong., 2d Sess., 1.

[26]S. Rep. No. 781, 73d Cong., 2d Sess., 1.

[27]*Ibid.* The Committee also indicated that there was a "vital need" for such a commission, with jurisdiction "over all of these methods of communication." *Ibid.*

[28]The phrase is taken from President Roosevelt's message to Congress. H. R. Rep. No. 1850, *supra*, at 1. The House Committee added that "the primary purpose of this bill [is] to create such a commission armed with adequate statutory powers to regulate all forms of communication . . ." *Id.*, at 3.

stations located within the same State in which the CATV system operates. [29] We may take notice that television broadcasting consists in very large part of programming devised for, and distributed to, national audiences; respondents thus are ordinarily employed in the simultaneous retransmission of communications that have very often originated in other States. The stream of communication is essentially uninterrupted and properly indivisible. To categorize respondents' activities as intrastate would disregard the character of the television industry, and serve merely to prevent the national regulation that "is not only appropriate but essential to the efficient use of radio facilities." *Federal Radio Comm'n* v. *Nelson Bros. Co.*, 289 U.S. 266, 279.

Nonetheless, respondents urge that the Communications Act, properly understood, does not permit the regulation of CATV systems. First, they emphasize that the Commission in 1959 and again in 1966[30] sought legislation that would have explicitly authorized such regulation, and that its efforts were unsuccessful. In the circumstances here, however, this cannot be dispositive. The Commission's requests for legislation evidently reflected in each instance both its uncertainty as to the proper width of its authority and its understandable preference for more detailed policy guidance than the Communications Act now provides. [31] We have recognized that administrative agencies should, in such situations, be encouraged to seek from Congress clarification of the pertinent statutory provisions. *Wong Yang Sung* v. *McGrath*, 339 U.S. 33, 47.

Nor can we obtain significant assistance from the various expressions of congressional opinion that followed the Commission's requests. In the first

[29] Respondents assert only that this "is subject to considerable question." Brief for Respondent Southwestern Cable Co. 24, n. 25. They rely chiefly upon the language of § 152(b), which provides that nothing in the Act shall give the Commission jurisdiction over "carriers" that are engaged in interstate communication solely through physical connection, or connection by wire or radio, with the facilities of another carrier, if they are not directly or indirectly controlled by such other carrier. The terms and history of this provision, however, indicate that it was "merely a perfecting amendment" intended to "obviate any possible technical argument that the Commission may attempt to assert common-carrier jurisdiction over point-to-point communication by radio between two points within a single State . . ." S. Rep. No. 1090, 83d Cong., 2d Sess., 1. See also H. R. Rep. No. 910, 83d Cong., 1st Sess. The Commission and the respondents are agreed, we think properly, that these CATV systems are not common carriers within the meaning of the Act. See 47 U.S.C. § 153(h); *Frontier Broadcasting Co.* v. *Collier*, 24 F.C.C. 251; *Philadelphia Television Broadcasting Co.* v. *F.C.C.*, 123 U.S. App. D.C. 298, 359 F. 2d 282; CATV and TV Repeater Services, *supra*, at 427-428.

[30] See H. R. 13286, 89th Cong., 2d Sess. The bill was favorably reported by the House Committee on Interstate and Foreign Commerce, H. R. Rep. No. 1635, 89th Cong., 2d Sess., but failed to reach the floor for debate.

[31] See, for the legislation proposed in 1959, CATV and TV Repeater Services, *supra*, at 427-431, 438-439. The Commission in 1966 explicitly stated in its explanation of its proposed amendments to the Act that "we believe it highly desirable that Congress . . . confirm [the Commission's] jurisdiction and . . . establish such basic national policy as it deems appropriate." H. R. Rep. No. 1635, *supra*, at 16.

place, the views of one Congress as to the construction of a statute adopted many years before by another Congress have "very little, if any, significance." *Rainwater* v. *United States*, 356 U.S. 590, 593; *United States* v. *Price*, 361 U.S. 304, 313; *Haynes* v. *United States*, 390 U.S. 85, 87, n. 4. Further, it is far from clear that Congress believed, as it considered these requests for legislation, that the Commission did not already possess regulatory authority over CATV. In 1959, the proposed legislation was preceded by the Commission's declarations that it "did not intend to regulate CATV," and that it preferred to recommend the adoption of legislation that would impose specified requirements upon CATV systems.[32]   Congress may well have been more troubled by the Commission's unwillingness to regulate than by any fears that it was unable to regulate.[33]   In 1966, the Commission informed Congress that it desired legislation in order to "confirm [its] jurisdiction and to establish such basic national policy as [Congress] deems appropriate." H. R. Rep. No. 1635, 89th Cong., 2d Sess., 16. In response, the House Committee on Interstate and Foreign Commerce said merely that it did not "either agree or disagree" with the jurisdictional conclusions of the Second Report, and that "the question of whether or not . . . the Commission has authority under present law to regulate CATV systems is for the courts to decide . . ." *Id.*, at 9. In these circumstances, we cannot derive from the Commission's requests for legislation anything of significant bearing on the construction question now before us.

Second, respondents urge that § 152(a)[34] does not independently confer regulatory authority upon the Commission, but instead merely prescribes the forms of communication to which the Act's other provisions may separately be made applicable. Respondents emphasize that the Commission does not contend either that CATV systems are common carriers, and thus within Title II of the Act, or that they are broadcasters, and thus within Title III. They conclude that CATV, with certain of the characteristics both of broadcasting and of common carriers, but with all of the characteristics of neither, eludes altogether the Act's grasp.

[32]See S. Rep. No. 923, 86th Cong., 1st Sess., 5-6.

[33]Thus, the Senate Committee on Interstate and Foreign Commerce observed in its 1959 Report that although the Commission's staff had recommended that authority be asserted over CATV, the Commission had "long hesitated," and had only recently made clear "that it did not intend to regulate CATV systems in any way whatsoever." S. Rep. No. 923, *supra*, at 5. Nonetheless, it must be acknowledged that the debate on the Senate floor centered on the broad question whether the Commission should have authority to regulate CATV. See, *e.g.*, 106 Cong. Rec. 10426.

[34]47 U.S.C. § 152(a) provides that "[t]he provisions of this chapter shall apply to all interstate and foreign communication by wire or radio and all interstate and foreign transmission of energy by radio, which originates and/or is received within the United States, and to all persons engaged within the United States in such communication or such transmission of energy by radio, and to the licensing and regulating of all radio stations as hereinafter provided; but it shall not apply to persons engaged in wire or radio communication or transmission in the Canal Zone, or to wire or radio communication or transmission wholly within the Canal Zone."

We cannot construe the Act so restrictively. Nothing in the language of §
152(a), in the surrounding language, or in the Act's history or purposes limits
the Commission's authority to those activities and forms of communication that
are specifically described by the Act's other provisions. The section itself states
merely that the "provisions of [the Act] shall apply to all interstate and foreign
communication by wire or radio . . ." Similarly, the legislative history indicates
that the Commission was given "regulatory power over all forms of electrical
communication . . ." S. Rep. No. 781, 73d Cong., 2d Sess., 1. Certainly Congress
could not in 1934 have foreseen the development of community antenna
television systems, but it seems to us that it was precisely because Congress
wished "to maintain, through appropriate administrative control, a grip on the
dynamic aspects of radio transmission," *F.C.C.* v. *Pottsville Broadcasting Co.,
supra*, at 138, that it conferred upon the Commission a "unified jurisdiction"[35]
and "broad authority."[36] Thus, "[u]nderlying the whole [Communications
Act] is recognition of the rapidly fluctuating factors characteristic of the
evolution of broadcasting and of the corresponding requirement that the
administrative process possess sufficient flexibility to adjust itself to these
factors." *F.C.C.* v. *Pottsville Broadcasting Co., supra*, at 138. Congress in 1934
acted in a field that was demonstrably "both new and dynamic," and it
therefore gave the Commission "a comprehensive mandate," with "not niggardly
but expansive powers." *National Broadcasting Co.* v. *United States*, 319 U.S.
190, 219. We have found no reason to believe that § 152 does not, as its terms
suggest, confer regulatory authority over "all interstate . . . communication by
wire or radio."[37]

Moreover, the Commission has reasonably concluded that regulatory
authority over CATV is imperative if it is to perform with appropriate
effectiveness certain of its other responsibilities. Congress has imposed upon the
Commission the "obligation of providing a widely dispersed radio and television
service,"[38] with a "fair, efficient, and equitable distribution" of service among

[35] S. Rep. No. 781, *supra*, at 1.

[36] H. R. Rep. No. 1850, *supra*, at 1.

[37] Respondents argue, and the Court of Appeals evidently concluded, that the opinion of the
Court in *Regents* v. *Carroll,* 338 U.S. 586, supports the inference that the Commission's
authority is limited to licensees, carriers, and others specifically reached by the Act's
other provisions. We find this unpersuasive. The Court in *Carroll* considered the very
general contention that the Commission had been given authority "to determine the
validity of contracts between licensees and others." *Id.*, at 602. It was concerned, not
with the limits of the Commission's authority over a form of communication by wire or
radio, but with efforts to enforce a contract that had been repudiated upon the demand
of the Commission. The Court's discussion of the Commission's authority under § 303(r),
see *id.*, at 600, must be read in that context, and as thus read it cannot be controlling
here.

[38] S. Rep. No. 923, *supra*, at 7. The Committee added that "Congress and the people" have
no particular interest in the success of any given broadcaster, but if the failure of a station
"leaves a community with inferior service," this becomes "a matter of real and immediate
public concern." *Ibid.*

the "several States and communities." 47 U.S.C. § 307(b). The Commission has, for this and other purposes, been granted authority to allocate broadcasting zones or areas, and to provide regulations "as it may deem necessary" to prevent interference among the various stations. 47 U.S.C. §§ 303(f), (h). The Commission has concluded, and Congress has agreed, that these obligations require for their satisfaction the creation of a system of local broadcasting stations, such that "all communities of appreciable size [will] have at least one television station as an outlet for local self-expression."[39]   In turn, the Commission has held that an appropriate system of local broadcasting may be created only if two subsidiary goals are realized. First, significantly wider use must be made of the available ultra-high frequency channels.[40]   Second, communities must be encouraged "to launch sound and adequate programs to utilize the television channels now reserved for educational purposes."[41] These subsidiary goals have received the endorsement of Congress.[42]

The Commission has reasonably found that the achievement of each of these purposes is "placed in jeopardy by the unregulated explosive growth of CATV." H. R. Rep. No. 1635, 89th Cong., 2d Sess., 7. Although CATV may in some circumstances make possible "the realization of some of the [Com-

[39] H. R. Rep. No. 1559, 87th Cong., 2d Sess., 3; Sixth Report and Order, 17 Fed. Reg. 3905. And see Staff of the Senate Comm. on Interstate and Foreign Commerce, 85th Cong., 2d Sess., The Television Inquiry: The Problem of Television Service for Smaller Communities 3-4 (Comm. Print 1959). The Senate Committee has elsewhere stated that "[t]here should be no weakening of the Commission's announced goal of local service." S. Rep. No. 923, *supra*, at 7.

[40] The Commission has allocated 82 channels for television broadcasting, of which 70 are in the UHF portion of the radio spectrum. This permits a total of 681 VHF stations and 1,544 UHF stations. H. R. Rep. No. 1559, *supra*, at 2. In December 1964, 454 VHF stations were on the air, 25 permittees were not operating, and 11 applications were awaiting Commission action, leaving 63 unreserved VHF allocations available. Seiden, *supra*, 162, n. 11, at 10. At the same time, 90 UHF stations were operating, 66 were assigned but not operating, 52 applications were pending before the Commission, and 1,108 allocations were still available. *Ibid.* The Commission has concluded that, in these circumstances, "an adequate national television system can be achieved" only if more of the available UHF channels are utilized. H. R. Rep. No. 1559, *supra*, at 4.

[41] S. Rep. No. 67, 87th Cong., 1st Sess., 8-9. The Committee indicated that it was "of utmost importance to the Nation that a reasonable opportunity be afforded educational institutions to use television as a noncommercial educational medium." *Id.*, at 3. Similarly, the House Committee on Interstate and Foreign Commerce has concluded that educational television will "provide a much needed source of cultural and informational programing for all audiences . . ." H. R. Rep. No. 1559, *supra*, at 3. It is thus an essential element of "an adequate national television system." *Id.*, at 4. See also H. R. Rep. No. 572, 90th Cong., 1st Sess.; S. Rep. No. 222, 90th Cong., 1st Sess.

[42] Legislation was adopted in 1962 to amend the Communications Act in order to require that all television receivers thereafter shipped in interstate commerce for sale or resale to the public be capable of receiving both UHF and VHF frequencies. 76 Stat. 150. The legislation was plainly intended to assist the growth of UHF broadcasting. See H. R. Rep. No. 1559, *supra*. Moreover, legislation has been adopted to provide construction grants and other assistance to educational television systems. 76 Stat. 68, 81 Stat. 365.

mission's] most important goals," First Report and Order, *supra*, at 699, its importation of distant signals into the service areas of local stations may also "destroy or seriously degrade the service offered by a television broadcaster," *id.*, at 700, and thus ultimately deprive the public of the various benefits of a system of local broadcasting stations.[43] In particular, the Commission feared that CATV might, by dividing the available audiences and revenues, significantly magnify the characteristically serious financial difficulties of UHF and educational television broadcasters.[44] The Commission acknowledged that it could not predict with certainty the consequences of unregulated CATV, but reasoned that its statutory responsibilities demand that it "plan in advance of foreseeable events, instead of waiting to react to them." *Id.*, at 701. We are aware that these consequences have been variously estimated,[45] but must conclude that there is

[43] See generally Second Report and Order, *supra*, at 736-745. It is pertinent that the Senate Committee on Interstate and Foreign Commerce feared even in 1959 that the unrestricted growth of CATV would eliminate local broadcasting, and that, in turn, this would have four undesirable consequences: (1) the local community "would be left without the local service which is necessary if the public is to receive the maximum benefits from the television medium"; (2) the "suburban and rural areas surrounding the central community may be deprived not only of local service but of any service at all"; (3) even "the resident of the central community may be deprived of all service if he cannot afford the connection charge and monthly service fees of the CATV system"; (4) "[u]nrestrained CATV, booster, or translator operation might eventually result in large regions, or even entire States, being deprived of all local television service – or being left, at best, with nothing more than a highly limited satellite service." S. Rep. No. 923, *supra*, at 7-8. The Committee concluded that CATV competition "does have an effect on the orderly development of television." *Id.*, at 8.

[44] The Commission has found that "we are in a critical period with respect to UHF development. Most of the new UHF stations will face considerable financial obstacles." First Report and Order, *supra*, at 712. It concluded that "one general factor giving cause for serious concern," *ibid.*, was that there is "likely" to be a "severe" impact between new local stations, particularly UHF stations, and CATV systems. *Id.*, at 713. Further, the Commission believed that there was danger that CATV systems would "siphon off sufficient local financial support" for educational television, with the result that such stations would fail or not be established at all. It feared that "the loss would be keenly felt by the public." Second Report and Order, *supra*, at 761. The Commission concluded that the hazards to educational television were "sufficiently strong to warrant some special protection . . ." *Id.*, at 762. Similarly, a recent study has found that CATV systems may have a substantial impact upon station revenues, that many stations, particularly in small markets, cannot readily afford such competition, and that in consequence a "substantial percentage of potential new station entrants, particularly UHF, are likely to be discouraged . . ." Fisher & Ferrall, Community Antenna Television Systems and Local Television Station Audience, 80 Q. J. Econ. 227, 250.

[45] Compare the following. Seiden, *supra,* at 69-90; Note, The Federal Communications Commission and Regulation of CATV, 43 N.Y.U. L. Rev. 117, 133-139; Note, The Wire Mire: The FCC and CATV, *supra* at 376-383; Fisher & Ferrall, *supra*. We note, in addition, that the dispute here is in part whether local, advertiser-supported stations are an appropriate foundation for a national system of television broadcasting. See generally Coase, The Economics of Broadcasting and Government Policy, 56 Am. Econ. Rev. 440 (May 1966); Greenberg, Wire Television and the FCC's Second Report and Order on CATV Systems, 10 J. Law & Econ. 181.

substantial evidence that the Commission cannot "discharge its overall responsibilities without authority over this important aspect of television service." Staff of Senate Comm. on Interstate and Foreign Commerce, 85th Cong., 2d Sess., The Television Inquiry: The Problem of Television Service for Smaller Communities 19 (Comm. Print 1959).

The Commission has been charged with broad responsibilities for the orderly development of an appropriate system of local television broadcasting. The significance of its efforts can scarcely be exaggerated, for broadcasting is demonstrably a principal source of information and entertainment for a great part of the Nation's population. The Commission has reasonably found that the successful performance of these duties demands prompt and efficacious regulation of community antenna television systems. We have elsewhere held that we may not, "in the absence of compelling evidence that such was Congress' intention . . . prohibit administrative action imperative for the achievement of an agency's ultimate purposes." *Permian Basin Area Rate Cases*, 390 U.S. 747, 780. Compare *National Broadcasting Co.* v. *United States, supra,* at 219-220; *American Trucking Assns.* v. *United States*, 344 U.S. 298, 311. There is no such evidence here, and we therefore hold that the Commission's authority over "all interstate . . . communication by wire or radio" permits the regulation of CATV systems.

There is no need here to determine in detail the limits of the Commission's authority to regulate CATV. It is enough to emphasize that the authority which we recognize today under § 152(a) is restricted to that reasonably ancillary to the effective performance of the Commission's various responsibilities for the regulation of television broadcasting. The Commission may, for these purposes, issue "such rules and regulations and prescribe such restrictions and conditions, not inconsistent with law," as "public convenience, interest, or necessity requires." 47 U.S.C. § 303(r). We express no views as to the Commission's authority, if any, to regulate CATV under any other circumstances or for any other purposes.

III.

We must next determine whether the Commission has authority under the Communications Act to issue the particular prohibitory order in question in these proceedings. In its Second Report and Order, *supra*, the Commission concluded that it should provide summary procedures for the disposition both of requests for special relief and of "complaints or disputes." *Id.*, at 764. It feared that if evidentiary hearings were in every situation mandatory they would prove "time consuming and burdensome" to the CATV systems and broadcasting stations involved. *Ibid.* The Commission considered that appropriate notice and opportunities for comment or objection must be given, and it declared that "additional procedures, such as oral argument, evidentiary hearing, or further written submissions" would be permitted "if they appear necessary or appropriate . . ." *Ibid.* See 47 CFR § 74.1109(f). It was under the authority of these provisions that Midwest sought, and the Commission granted, temporary relief.

The Commission, after examination of various responsive pleadings but without prior hearings, ordered that respondents generally restrict their carriage of Los Angeles signals to areas served by them on February 15, 1966, pending hearings to determine whether the carriage of such signals into San Diego contravenes the public interest. The order does not prohibit the addition of new subscribers within areas served by respondents on February 15, 1966; it does not prevent service to other subscribers who began receiving service or who submitted an "accepted subscription request" between February 15, 1966, and the date of the Commission's order; and it does not preclude the carriage of San Diego and Tijuana, Mexico, signals to subscribers in new areas of service. 4 F.C.C. 2d 612, 624-625. The order is thus designed simply to preserve the situation as it existed at the moment of its issuance.

Respondents urge that the Commission may issue prohibitory orders only under the authority of § 312(b), by which the Commission is empowered to issue cease-and-desist orders. We shall assume that, consistent with the requirements of § 312(c), cease-and-desist orders are proper only after hearing or waiver of the right to hearing. Nonetheless, the requirement does not invalidate the order issued in this case, for we have concluded that the provisions of §§ 312(b), (c) are inapplicable here. Section 312(b) provides that a cease-and-desist order may issue only if the respondent "has violated or failed to observe" a provision of the Communications Act or a rule or regulation promulgated by the Commission under the Act's authority. Respondents here were not found to have violated or to have failed to observe any such restriction; the question before the Commission was instead only whether an existing situation should be preserved pending a determination "whether respondents' present or planned CATV operations are consistent with the public interest and what, if any, action should be taken by the Commission." 4 F.C.C. 2d, at 626. The Commission's order was thus not, in form or function, a cease-and-desist order that must issue under §§ 312(b), (c).[46]

The Commission has acknowledged that, in this area of rapid and significant change, there may be situations in which its generalized regulations are inadequate, and special or additional forms of relief are imperative. It has

---

[46] Respondents urge that the legislative history of § 312(b) indicates that the Commission may issue prohibitory orders only under, and in conformity with, that section. We find this unpersuasive. Nothing in that history suggests that the Commission was deprived of its authority, granted elsewhere in the Act, to issue orders "necessary in the execution of its functions." 47 U.S.C. § 154(i). See also 47 U.S.C. § 303(r).

found that the present case may prove to be such a situation, and that the public interest demands "interim relief ... limiting further expansion," pending hearings to determine appropriate Commission action. Such orders do not exceed the Commission's authority. This Court has recognized that "the administrative process [must] possess sufficient flexibility to adjust itself" to the "dynamic aspects of radio transmission," *F.C.C.* v. *Pottsville Broadcasting Co., supra,* at 138, and that it was precisely for that reason that Congress declined to "stereotyp[e] the powers of the Commission to specific details ..." *National Broadcasting Co.* v. *United States, supra,* at 219. And compare *American Trucking Assns.* v. *United States,* 344 U.S. 298, 311; *R. A. Holman & Co.* v. *S.E.C.,* 112 U.S. App. D.C. 43, 47-48, 299 F. 2d 127, 131-132. Thus, the Commission has been explicitly authorized to issue "such orders, not inconsistent with this [Act], as may be necessary in the execution of its functions." 47 U.S.C. § 154(i). See also 47 U.S.C. § 303(r). In these circumstances, we hold that the Commission's order limiting further expansion of respondents' service pending appropriate hearings did not exceed or abuse its authority under the Communications Act. And there is no claim that its procedure in this respect is in any way constitutionally infirm.

The judgments of the Court of Appeals are reversed, and the cases are remanded for further proceedings consistent with this opinion.

It is so ordered.

Mr. Justice Douglas and Mr. Justice Marshall took no part in the consideration or decision of these cases.

6

CATV AND COPYRIGHT

Fortnightly Corp. v.
United Artists Television, Inc.
    392 U.S. 390
    June 17, 1968

In addition to the question of FCC jurisdiction over CATV, the matter of cable television's liability under existing copyright law remained unresolved until 1968. The Copyright Act of 1909, like the Communications Act of 1934, neither contemplated nor provided for CATV.

Decided only a week after the *Southwestern* case, the Supreme Court's 5-1 *Fortnightly* decision holds CATV immune from copyright infringement action when cable systems merely relay TV station signals to subscribers' homes. CATV systems are held fully liable under law for copyrighted materials they originate, i.e., "cablecast."

The second sentence of footnote 17 of the Court's opinion remains current as of 1973, for Congress has not yet been able to fashion a new copyright law sufficiently harmonious with the conflicting interests of the many concerned parties to warrant enactment.

Mr. Justice Stewart delivered the opinion of the Court.

The petitioner, Fortnightly Corporation, owns and operates community antenna television (CATV) systems in Clarksburg and Fairmont, West Virginia.[1] There were no local television broadcasting stations in that immediate area until 1957. Now there are two, but, because of hilly terrain, most residents of the area cannot receive the broadcasts of any additional stations by ordinary rooftop

---

[1] For a discussion of CATV systems generally, see *United States* v. *Southwestern Cable Co., ante,* . . .

antennas. Some of the residents have joined in erecting larger cooperative antennas in order to receive more distant stations, but a majority of the householders in both communities have solved the problem by becoming customers of the petitioner's CATV service.[2]

The petitioner's systems consist of antennas located on hills above each city, with connecting coaxial cables, strung on utility poles, to carry the signals received by the antennas to the home television sets of individual subscribers. The systems contain equipment to amplify and modulate the signals received, and to convert them to different frequencies, in order to transmit the signals efficiently while maintaining and improving their strength.[3]

During 1960, when this proceeding began, the petitioner's systems provided customers with signals of five television broadcasting stations, three located in Pittsburgh, Pennsylvania; one in Steubenville, Ohio; and one in Wheeling, West Virginia.[4] The distance between those cities and Clarksburg and Fairmont ranges from 52 to 82 miles.[5] The systems carried all the programming of each of the five stations, and a customer could choose any of the five programs he wished to view by simply turning the knob on his own television set. The petitioner neither edited the programs received nor originated any programs of its own.[6] The petitioner's customers were charged a flat monthly rate regardless of the amount of time that their television sets were in use.[7]

The respondent, United Artists Television, Inc., holds copyrights on several motion pictures. During the period in suit, the respondent (or its predecessor) granted various licenses to each of the five television stations in question to broadcast certain of these copyrighted motion pictures. Broadcasts made under these licenses were received by the petitioner's Clarksburg and Fairmont CATV systems and carried to its customers. At no time did the petitioner (or its predecessors) obtain a license under the copyrights from the respondent or from any of the five television stations. The licenses granted by the respondent to the five stations did not authorize carriage of the broadcasts by CATV systems, and in several instances the licenses specifically prohibited such carriage.

---

[2]In 1960, out of 11,442 occupied housing units in the Clarksburg area, about 7,900 subscribed to the petitioner's CATV service; out of 9,079 units in Fairmont, about 5,100 subscribed.

[3]The petitioner's systems utilized modulating equipment only during the period 1958-1964.

[4]Since 1960, some changes have been made in the stations carried by each of the petitioner's systems. As of May 1, 1964, the Clarksburg system was carrying the two local stations and three of the more distant stations, and the Fairmont system was carrying one local station and four of the more distant stations.

[5]Clarksburg and Fairmont are 18 miles apart.

[6]Some CATV systems, about 10%, originate some of their own programs. We do not deal with such systems in this opinion.

[7]The monthly rate ranged from $3.75 to $5, and customers were also charged an installation fee. Increased charges were levied for additional television sets and for commercial establishments.

The respondent sued the petitioner for copyright infringement in a federal court, asking damages and injunctive relief. The issue of infringement was separately tried, and the court ruled in favor of the respondent. 255 F. Supp. 177. On interlocutory appeal under 28 U.S.C. § 1292(b), the Court of Appeals for the Second Circuit affirmed. 377 F. 2d 872. We granted certiorari, 389 U.S. 969, to consider an important question under the Copyright Act of 1909, 35 Stat. 1075, as amended, 17 U.S.C. § 1 *et seq.*

The Copyright Act does not give a copyright holder control over all uses of his copyrighted work.[8] Instead, § 1 of the Act enumerates several "rights" that are made "exclusive" to the holder of the copyright.[9] If a person, without authorization from the copyright holder, puts a copyrighted work to a use within the scope of one of these "exclusive rights," he infringes the copyright. If

---

[8] See, *e.g., Fawcett Publications* v. *Elliot Publishing Co.*, 46 F. Supp. 717; *Hayden* v. *Chalfant Press, Inc.*, 281 F. 2d 543, 547-548.

"The fundamental [is] that 'use' is not the same thing as 'infringement,' that use short of infringement is to be encouraged . . ." B. Kaplan, An Unhurried View of Copyright 57 (1967).

[9] "Any person entitled thereto, upon complying with the provisions of this title, shall have the exclusive right:

"(a) To print, reprint, publish, copy, and vend the copyrighted work;

"(b) To translate the copyrighted work into other languages or dialects, or make any other version thereof, if it be a literary work; to dramatize it if it be a nondramatic work; to convert it into a novel or other nondramatic work if it be a drama; to arrange or adapt it if it be a musical work; to complete, execute, and finish it if it be a model or design for a work of art;

"(c) To deliver, authorize the delivery of, read, or present the copyrighted work in public for profit if it be a lecture, sermon, address or similar production, or other nondramatic literary work; to make or procure the making of any transcription or record thereof by or from which, in whole or in part, it may in any manner or by any method be exhibited, delivered, presented, produced, or reproduced; and to play or perform it in public for profit, and to exhibit, represent, produce, or reproduce it in any manner or by any method whatsoever. The damages for the infringement by broadcast of any work referred to in this subsection shall not exceed the sum of $100 where the infringing broadcaster shows that he was not aware that he was infringing and that such infringement could not have been reasonably foreseen; and

"(d) To perform or represent the copyrighted work publicly if it be a drama or, if it be a dramatic work and not reproduced in copies for sale, to vend any manuscript or any record whatsoever thereof; to make or to procure the making of any transcription or record thereof by or from which, in whole or in part, it may in any manner or by any method be exhibited, performed, represented, produced, or reproduced; and to exhibit, perform, represent, produce, or reproduce it in any manner or by any method whatsoever; and

"(e) To perform the copyrighted work publicly for profit if it be a musical composition; and for the purpose of public performance for profit, and for the purposes set forth in subsection (a) hereof, to make any arrangement or setting of it or of the melody of it in any system of notation or any form of record in which the thought of an author may be recorded and from which it may be read or reproduced . . ." 17 U.S.C. § 1.

he puts the work to a use not enumerated in § 1, he does not infringe.[10] The respondent's contention is that the petitioner's CATV systems infringed the respondent's § 1(c) exclusive right to "perform . . . in public for profit" (nondramatic literary works)[11] and its § 1(d) exclusive right to "perform . . . publicly" (dramatic works).[12] The petitioner maintains that its CATV systems did not "perform" the copyrighted works at all.[13]

At the outset it is clear that the petitioner's systems did not "perform" the respondent's copyrighted works in any conventional sense of that term,[14] or in any manner envisaged by the Congress that enacted the law in 1909.[15] But our inquiry cannot be limited to ordinary meaning and legislative history, for this is a statute that was drafted long before the development of the electronic phenomena with which we deal here.[16] In 1909 radio itself was in its infancy, and television had not been invented. We must read the statutory language of 60 years ago in the light of drastic technological change.[17]

---

[10]The Copyright Act does not contain a definition of infringement as such. Rather infringement is delineated in a negative fashion by the § 1 enumeration of rights exclusive to the copyright holder. See M. Nimmer, Copyright § 100 (1968).

[11]See n. 9, *supra*. We do not reach the petitioner's claim that the respondent's animated cartoons are not "literary works."

[12]See n. 9, *supra*.

[13]The petitioner also contends that if it did "perform" the copyrighted works, it did not do so "in public."

[14]Cf. *White-Smith Music Co.* v. *Apollo Co.*, 209 U.S. 1.

[15]The legislative history shows that the attention of Congress was directed to the situation where the dialogue of a play is transcribed by a member of the audience, and thereafter the play is produced by another party with the aid of the transcript. H. R. Rep. No. 2222, 60th Cong., 2d Sess., 4 (1909).

[16]"While statutes should not be stretched to apply to new situations not fairly within their scope, they should not be so narrowly construed as to permit their evasion because of changing habits due to new inventions and discoveries." *Jerome H. Remick & Co.* v. *American Automobile Accessories Co.*, 5 F. 2d 411.

[17]A revision of the 1909 Act was begun in 1955 when Congress authorized a program of studies by the Copyright Office. Progress has not been rapid. The Copyright Office issued its report in 1961. Register of Copyrights, Report on the General Revision of the U.S. Copyright Law, House Judiciary Committee Print, 87th Cong., 1st Sess. (1961). Revision bills were introduced in the House in the Eighty-eighth Congress and in both the House and the Senate in the Eighty-ninth Congress. See H. R. 11947, 88th Cong., 2d Sess.; Hearings on H. R. 4347, 5680, 6831, 6835 before Subcommittee No. 3 of the House Judiciary Committee, 89th Cong., 1st Sess. (1965); Hearings on S. 1006 before the Subcommittee on Patents, Trademarks, and Copyrights of the Senate Judiciary Committee, 89th Cong., 2d Sess. (1966). H. R. 4347 was reported favorably by the House Judiciary Committee, H. R. Rep. No. 2237, 89th Cong. 2d Sess. (1966), but not enacted. In the Ninetieth Congress revision bills were again introduced in both the House (H. R. 2512) and the Senate (S. 597). The House bill was again reported favorably, H. R. Rep. No. 83, 90th Cong., 1st Sess. (1967), and this time, after amendment, passed by the full House. 113 Cong. Rec. 9021. The bill as reported contained a provision dealing with CATV, but the provision was struck from the bill on the House floor prior to enactment. See n. 33, *infra*. The House and Senate bills are currently pending before the Senate Subcommittee on Patents, Trademarks, and Copyrights.

The Court of Appeals thought that the controlling question in deciding whether the petitioner's CATV systems "performed" the copyrighted works was: "[H]ow much did the [petitioner] do to bring about the viewing and hearing of a copyrighted work?" 377 F. 2d, at 877. Applying this test, the court found that the petitioner did "perform" the programs carried by its systems.[18] But mere quantitative contribution cannot be the proper test to determine copyright liability in the context of television broadcasting. If it were, many people who make large contributions to television viewing might find themselves liable for copyright infringement — not only the apartment house owner who erects a common antenna for his tenants, but the shopkeeper who sells or rents television sets, and, indeed, every television set manufacturer. Rather, resolution of the issue before us depends upon a determination of the function that CATV plays in the total process of television broadcasting and reception.

Television viewing results from combined activity by broadcasters and viewers. Both play active and indispensable roles in the process; neither is wholly passive. The broadcaster selects and procures the program to be viewed. He may produce it himself, whether "live" or with film or tape, or he may obtain it from a network or some other source. He then converts the visible images and audible sounds of the program into electronic signals,[19] and broadcasts the signals at radio frequency for public reception.[20] Members of the public, by means of television sets and antennas that they themselves provide, receive the broadcaster's signals and reconvert them into the visible images and audible sounds of the program. The effective range of the broadcast is determined by the combined contribution of the equipment employed by the broadcaster and that supplied by the viewer. [21]

The television broadcaster in one sense does less than the exhibitor of a motion picture or stage play; he supplies his audience not with visible images but only with electronic signals. The viewer conversely does more than a member of a theater audience; he provides the equipment to convert electronic signals into audible sound and visible images. Despite these deviations from the conventional

---

[18]The court formulated and applied this test in the light of this Court's decision in *Buck* v. *Jewell-LaSalle Realty Co.*, 283 U.S. 191. See also *Society of European Stage Authors & Composers* v. *New York Hotel Statler Co.*, 19 F. Supp. 1. But in *Jewell-LaSalle*, a hotel received on a master radio set an unauthorized broadcast of a copyrighted work and transmitted that broadcast to all the public and private rooms of the hotel by means of speakers installed by the hotel in each room. The Court held the hotel liable for infringement but noted that the result might have differed if, as in this case, the original broadcast had been authorized by the copyright holder. 283 U.S., at 199, n. 5. The *Jewell-LaSalle* decision must be understood as limited to its own facts. See n. 30, *infra*.

[19]If the broadcaster obtains his program from a network, he receives the electronic signals directly by means of telephone lines or microwave.

[20]Broadcasting is defined under the Communications Act of 1934 as "the dissemination of radio communications intended to be received by the public . . ." 47 U.S.C. § 153(o).

[21] See Hearings on H. R. 4347, 5680, 6831, 6835 before Subcommittee No. 3 of the House Judiciary Committee, 89th Cong., 1st Sess., at 1312-1318 (1965).

situation contemplated by the framers of the Copyright Act,[22] broadcasters have been judicially treated as exhibitors, and viewers as members of a theater audience. Broadcasters perform.[23] Viewers do not perform.[24] Thus, while both broadcaster and viewer play crucial roles in the total television process, a line is drawn between them. One is treated as active performer; the other, as passive beneficiary.

When CATV is considered in this framework, we conclude that it falls on the viewer's side of the line.[25] Essentially, a CATV system no more than enhances the viewer's capacity to receive the broadcaster's signals; it provides a well-located antenna with an efficient connection to the viewer's television set.[26] It is true that a CATV system plays an "active" role in making reception possible in a given area, but so do ordinary television sets and antennas. CATV equipment is powerful and sophisticated, but the basic function the equipment serves is little different from that served by the equipment generally furnished by a television viewer.[27] If an individual erected an antenna on a hill, strung a

[22] See n. 15, *supra.*

[23] *Jerome H. Remick & Co.* v. *American Automobile Accessories Co.*, 5 F. 2d 411 (radio broadcast); *Associated Music Publishers* v. *Debs Memorial Radio Fund*, 141 F. 2d 852 (radio broadcast of recorded program); *Select Theatres Corp.* v. *Ronzoni Macaroni Co.*, 59 U.S.P.Q. 288 (D.C.S.D.N.Y.) (radio broadcast of program received from network). Congress in effect validated these decisions in 1952 when it added to § 1(c) a special damages provision for "infringement by broadcast." 66 Stat. 752.

[24] "One who manually or by human agency merely actuates electrical instrumentalities, whereby inaudible elements that are omnipresent in the air are made audible to persons who are within hearing, does not 'perform' within the meaning of the Copyright Law." *Buck* v. *Debaum*, 40 F. 2d 734, 735.

"[T]hose who listen do not perform . . ." *Jerome H. Remick & Co.* v. *General Electric Co.*, 16 F. 2d 829.

[25] While we speak in this opinion generally of CATV, we necessarily do so with reference to the facts of this case.

[26] Cf. *Lilly* v. *United States*, 238 F. 2d 584, 587:

"[T]his community antenna service was a mere adjunct of the television receiving sets with which it was connected . . ."

[27] The District Court's decision was based in large part upon its analysis of the technical aspects of the petitioner's systems. The systems have contained at one time or another sophisticated equipment to amplify, modulate, and convert to different frequencies the signals received — operations which all require the introduction of local energy into the system. The court concluded that the signal delivered to subscribers was not the same signal as that initially received off the air. 255 F. Supp., at 190-195. The Court of Appeals refused to attach significance to the particular technology of the petitioner's systems, 377 F. 2d, at 879, and we agree. The electronic operations performed by the petitioner's systems are those necessary to transmit the received signal the length of the cable efficiently and deliver a signal of adequate strength. Most of the same operations are performed by individual television sets and antennas. See Hearings on H. R. 4347 before Subcommittee No. 3 of the House Judiciary Committee, *supra*, at 1312-1318. Whether or not the signals received and delivered are the "same," the entire process is virtually instantaneous, and electronic "information" received and delivered is identical. 255 F. Supp., at 192.

cable to his house, and installed the necessary amplifying equipment, he would not be "performing" the programs he received on his television set. The result would be no different if several people combined to erect a cooperative antenna for the same purpose. The only difference in the case of CATV is that the antenna system is erected and owned not by its users but by an entrepreneur.

The function of CATV systems has little in common with the function of broadcasters.[28] CATV systems do not in fact broadcast or rebroadcast.[29] Broadcasters select the programs to be viewed; CATV systems simply carry, without editing, whatever programs they receive. Broadcasters procure programs and propagate them to the public; CATV systems receive programs that have been released to the public and carry them by private channels to additional viewers. We hold that CATV operators, like viewers and unlike broadcasters, do not perform the programs that they receive and carry. [30]

We have been invited by the Solicitor General in an *amicus curiae* brief to render a compromise decision in this case that would, it is said, accommodate various competing considerations of copyright, communications, and antitrust policy.[31] We decline the invitation.[32] That job is for Congress.[33] We take the

---

[28]Cf. *Intermountain Broadcasting & Television Corp.* v. *Idaho Microwave, Inc.*, 196 F. Supp. 315, 325:

"[Broadcasters] and [CATV systems] are not engaged in the same kind of business. They operate in different ways for different purposes.

"[Broadcasters] are in the business of selling their broadcasting time and facilities to the sponsors to whom they look for their profits. They do not and cannot charge the public for their broadcasts which are beamed directly, indiscriminately and without charge through the air to any and all reception sets of the public as may be equipped to receive them.

"[CATV systems], on the other hand, having nothing to do with sponsors, program content or arrangement. They sell community antenna service to a segment of the public for which [broadcasters'] programs were intended but which is not able, because of location or topographical condition, to receive them without rebroadcast or other relay service by community antennae. . . ."

[29]*Cable Vision, Inc.* v. *KUTV, Inc.*, 211 F. Supp. 47, vacated on other grounds, 335 F. 2d 348; *Report and Order on CATV and TV Repeater Services*, 26 F.C.C. 403, 429-430.

[30]It is said in dissent that, "Our major object . . . should be to do as little damage as possible to traditional copyright principles and to business relationships, until the Congress legislates . . ." *Post*, . . . But existing "business relationships" would hardly be preserved by extending a questionable 35-year-old decision that in actual practice has not been applied outside its own factual context, *post*, . . . so as retroactively to impose copyright liability where it has never been acknowledged to exist before. See n. 18, *supra*.

[31]Compare, *e.g.*, Note, CATV and Copyright Liability, 80 Harv. L. Rev. 1514 (1967); Note, CATV and Copyright Liability: On a Clear Day You Can See Forever, 52 Va. L. Rev. 1505 (1966); B. Kaplan, An Unhurried View of Copyright 104-106 (1967); Statement of then Acting Assistant Attorney General (Antitrust Division) Zimmerman, Hearings on S. 1006 before the Subcommittee on Patents, Trademarks, and Copyrights of the Senate Judiciary Committee, 89th Cong., 2d Sess., at 211-219 (1966).

[32]The Solicitor General would have us hold that CATV systems do perform the programs they carry, but he would have us "imply" a license for the CATV "performances." This

Copyright Act of 1909 as we find it. With due regard to changing technology, we hold that the petitioner did not under that law "perform" the respondent's copyrighted works.

The judgment of the Court of Appeals is *Reversed.*

Mr. Justice Douglas and Mr. Justice Marshall took no part in the consideration or decision of this case.

Mr. Justice Harlan took no part in the decision of this case.

Mr. Justice Fortas, dissenting.

This case calls not for the judgment of Solomon but for the dexterity of Houdini. We are here asked to consider whether and how a technical, complex, and specific Act of Congress, the Copyright Act, which was enacted in 1909, applies to one of the recent products of scientific and promotional genius, CATV. The operations of CATV systems are based upon the use of other people's property. The issue here is whether, for this use, the owner of copyrighted material should be compensated. From a technical standpoint the

---

"implied in law" license would not cover all CATV activity but only those instances in which a CATV system operates within the "Grade B Contour" of the broadcasting station whose signal it carries. The Grade B contour is a theoretical FCC concept defined as the outer line along which reception of acceptable quality can be expected at least 90% of the time at the best 50% of locations. Sixth Report and Order, 17 Fed. Reg. 3905, 3915. Since we hold that the petitioner's systems did not perform copyrighted works, we do not reach the question of implied license.

[33]The copyright revision bill recently passed by the House, see n. 17, *supra*, originally contained a detailed and somewhat complex provision covering CATV. H. R. 2512, 90th Cong., 1st Sess., § 111. Congressman Poff described the bill in terms of its effect on the District Court's decision in the present case:

"By, in effect, repealing the court decision which would impose full copyright liability on all CATV's in all situations, the committee recommends H. R. 2512, which would exempt them in some situations, make them fully liable in some, and provide limited liability in others." 113 Cong. Rec. 8588.

See H. R. Rep. No. 83, 90th Cong., 1st Sess., 6-7, 48-59 (1967). On the House floor the CATV provision was deleted in order to refer the matter to the Interstate and Foreign Commerce Committee, which has jurisdiction over communications. 113 Cong. Rec. 8598-8601, 8611-8613, 8618-8622, 8990-8992. In urging deletion of the CATV provision, Congressman Moore said:

"[W]hat we seek to do in this legislation is control CATV by copyright. I say that is wrong. I feel if there is to be supervision of this fast growing area of news media and communications media, it should legitimately come to this body from the legislative committee that has direct jurisdiction over the same.

"... This bill and the devices used to effect communications policy are not proper functions of copyright ..." 113 Cong. Rec. 8599.

question — or at least one important question — is whether the use constitutes a "performance" of the copyrighted material within the meaning of § 1(c) of the Copyright Act, 17 U.S.C. § 1(c). But it is an understatement to say that the Copyright Act, including the concept of a "performance," was not created with the development of CATV in mind. The novelty of the use, incident to the novelty of the new technology, results in a baffling problem. Applying the normal jurisprudential tools — the words of the Act, legislative history, and precedent — to the facts of the case is like trying to repair a television set with a mallet. And no aid may be derived from the recent attempts of Congress to formulate special copyright rules for CATV — for Congress has vacillated in its approach.[1]

At the same time, the implications of any decision we may reach as to the copyright liability of CATV are very great. On the one hand, it is darkly predicted that the imposition of full liability upon all CATV operations could result in the demise of this new, important instrument of mass communications; or in its becoming a tool of the powerful networks which hold a substantial number of copyrights on materials used in the television industry. On the other hand, it is foreseen that a decision to the effect that CATV systems never infringe the copyrights of the programs they carry would permit such systems to overpower local broadcasting stations which must pay, directly or indirectly, for copyright licenses and with which CATV is in increasing competition.[2]

The vastness of the competing considerations, the complexity of any conceivable equitable solution to the problems posed, and the obvious desirability of ultimately leaving the solution to Congress induced the Solicitor General, in a memorandum filed prior to oral argument in this case, to recommend "that the Court should stay its hand because, in our view, the matter is not susceptible of definitive resolution in judicial proceedings and plenary consideration here is likely to delay and prejudice the ultimate legislative solution."

That is a splendid thought, but unhappily it will not do. I agree with the majority that we must pass on the instant case. An important legal issue is involved. Important economic values are at stake, and it would be hazardous to assume that Congress will act promptly, comprehensively, and retroactively. But the fact that the Copyright Act was written in a different day, for different factual situations, should lead us to tread cautiously here. Our major object, I suggest, should be to do as little damage as possible to traditional copyright principles and to business relationships, until the Congress legislates and relieves the embarrassment which we and the interested parties face.

[1] See B. Kaplan, An Unhurried View of Copyright 105-106, 127-128 (1967).
[2] The Solicitor General, in his brief on the merits, recommends that we adopt a compromise approach — finding a license implied in law with respect to some CATV operations, but not with respect to others. Regardless of the advisability of such an approach from the standpoint of communications, antitrust, and other relevant policies, I do not believe it is open to us, in construing the Copyright Act, to accept the Solicitor General's proposal.

The opinion of the majority, in my judgment, does not heed this admonition. In an attempt to foster the development of CATV, the Court today abandons the teachings of precedent, including a precedent of this Court (see *Buck* v. *Jewell-LaSalle Realty Corp.*, 283 U.S. 191 (1931); *Society of European Stage Authors and Composers* v. *New York Hotel Statler Co.*, 19 F. Supp. 1 (1937)), as to the meaning of the term "perform" in the Copyright Act. It is not our general practice to reverse ourselves, without compelling reasons to do so, on matters of statutory construction, especially on a construction of many years' standing under which an entire industry has operated.[3] Yet today's decision might not be objectionable, if the majority replaced what it considers an outmoded interpretation of the term "perform" with a new, equally clear, and workable interpretation. It does not, however, do this. It removes from copyright law an interpretation which, though perhaps not altogether satisfactory as an analytical matter,[4] has at least been settled for nearly 40 years; and it substitutes for that discarded interpretation a rule which I do not believe is an intelligible guide for the construction of the Copyright Act. Moreover, the new rule may well have disruptive consequences outside the area of CATV.

The approach manifested in the opinion of the Court is disarmingly simple. The Court merely identifies two groups in the general field of television, one of which it believes may clearly be liable, and the other clearly not liable, for copyright infringement on a "performance" theory: "Broadcasters perform. Viewers do not perform." From this premise, the Court goes on to hold that CATV "falls on the viewer's side of the line. Essentially, a CATV system no more than enhances the viewer's capacity to receive the broadcaster's signals; it provides a well-located antenna with an efficient connection to the viewer's set. . . . CATV equipment is powerful and sophisticated, but the basic function the equipment serves is little different from that served by the equipment generally furnished by a television viewer." *Ante*, . . .

The decision in *Buck* v. *Jewell-LaSalle*, must, the Court says today, "be understood as limited to its own facts." *Ante*, at . . . n. 18. In *Buck*, the Court, speaking unanimously through Mr. Justice Brandeis, held that a hotel which received a broadcast on a master radio set and piped the broadcast to all public and private rooms of the hotel had "performed" the material that had been broadcast. As I understand the case, the holding was that the use of mechanical equipment to extend a broadcast to a significantly wider public than the broadcast would otherwise enjoy constitutes a "performance" of the material

---

[3]Nimmer, a leading authority in the copyright field, states that although "the two major performing right societies, ASCAP and BMI, do not choose to enforce the Jewell-LaSalle doctrine to its logical extreme in that they do not demand performing licenses from commercial establishments such as bars and restaurants which operate radio or television sets for the amusement of their customers, . . . such demands are made of hotels which operate in the manner of the LaSalle Hotel." M. Nimmer, Copyright § 107.41, n. 204 (1968).

[4]See M. Nimmer, Copyright § 107.41 (1968).

originally broadcast. I believe this decision stands squarely in the path of the route which the majority today traverses. If a CATV system performs a function "little different from that served by the equipment generally furnished by a television viewer," and if that is to be the test, then it seems to me that a master radio set attached by wire to numerous other sets in various rooms of a hotel cannot be distinguished.[5]

The vague "functional" test of the meaning of the term "perform" is, moreover, unsatisfactory. Just as a CATV system performs (on the majority's analysis) the same function as the antenna of the individual viewer, so a television camera recording a live drama performs the same function as the eye of a spectator who is present in the theater. Both the CATV and the television camera "receive programs that have been released to the public and carry them by private channels to additional viewers." *Ante, . . .* Moreover, the Court has indulged in an oversimplification of the "function" of CATV. It may be, indeed, that insofar as CATV operations are limited to the geographical area which the licensed broadcaster (whose signals the CATV has picked up and carried) has the power to cover, a CATV is little more than a "cooperative antenna" employed in order to ameliorate the image on television screens at home or to bring the image to homes which, because of obstacles other than mere distance, could not receive them. But such a description will not suffice for the case in which a CATV has picked up the signals of a licensed broadcaster and carried them beyond the area — however that area be defined — which the broadcaster normally serves. In such a case the CATV *is* performing a function different from a simple antenna for, by hypothesis, the antenna could not pick up the signals of the licensed broadcaster and enable CATV patrons to receive them in their homes.

Buck v. *Jewell-LaSalle* may not be an altogether ideal gloss on the word "perform," but it has at least the merit of being settled law. I would not overrule that decision in order to take care of this case or the needs of CATV. This Court may be wrong. The task of caring for CATV is one for the Congress. Our ax, being a rule of law, must cut straight, sharp, and deep; and perhaps this is a situation that calls for the compromise of theory and for the architectural improvisation which only legislation can accomplish.

I see no alternative to following *Buck* and to holding that a CATV system does "perform" the material it picks up and carries. I would, accordingly, affirm the decision below.

---

[5]The majority attempts to diminish the compelling authority of *Buck* v. *Jewell-LaSalle*, by referring to a vague footnote in that opinion to the effect that the Court might not have found a "performance" if the original broadcast, which was picked up by the hotel and brought to its various rooms, had been authorized by the copyright holder — as it was not. I cannot understand the point. Whatever might be the case in a contributory infringement action (which this is not), the interpretation of the term "perform" cannot logically turn on the question whether the material that is used is licensed or not licensed.

7

THE MIDWEST CASE

United States et al. v.
Midwest Video Corp.
406 U.S. 649
June 7, 1972

Following the two 1968 Supreme Court CATV decisions the FCC issued more rules affecting several aspects of cable operation (20 FCC 2d 201 (1969)). One of the rules required substantial amounts of local program origination by CATV systems having 3,500 or more subscribers.

The 1972 *Midwest* decision finds the Supreme Court continuing to uphold the Commission, but by the barest of margins. It remains to be seen how much further the FCC can proceed to regulate CATV in the absence of clearer authority from Congress without being reversed by the High Court.

During the pendency of *Midwest* the Commission enacted a burgeoning collection of CATV rules: see 23 FCC 2d 816 (1970); 23 FCC 2d 825 (1970); 32 FCC 2d 13 (1971); 32 FCC 2d 923 (1971); and, most significantly, 36 FCC 2d 141 (1972).

Mr. Justice Brennan announced the judgment of the Court and an opinion in which Mr. Justice White, Mr. Justice Marshall, and Mr. Justice Blackmun join.

Community antenna television (CATV) was developed long after the enactment of the Communications Act of 1934, 48 Stat. 1064, as amended, 47 U.S.C. § 151 *et sec.*, as an auxiliary to broadcasting through the retransmission by wire of radio signals to viewers otherwise unable to receive them because of distance or local terrain.[1] In *United States* v. *Southwestern Cable Co.*, 392 U.S. 157 (1968), where we sustained the jurisdiction of the Federal Communications Commission to regulate the new industry at least to the extent "reasonably ancillary to the effective performance of the Commission's various responsibilities for the regulation of television broadcasting," *id.*, at 178, we observed that the growth of CATV since the establishment of the first commercial system in 1950 has been nothing less than " 'explosive.' " *Id.*, at 163.[2] The potential of the new industry to augment communication services now available is equally phenomenal.[3] As we said in *Southwestern, id.*, at 164, CATV "[promises] for the future to provide a national communications system, in which signals from selected broadcasting centers would be transmitted to metropolitan areas throughout the country." Moreover, as the Commission has noted, "the expanding multichannel capacity of cable systems could be utilized to provide a variety of new communications services to homes and businesses within a community," such as facsimile reproduction of documents, electronic mail delivery, and information retrieval. Notice of Proposed Rulemaking and Notice of Inquiry, 15 F.C.C. 2d 417, 419-420 (1968). Perhaps more important, CATV systems can themselves originate programs, or "cablecast" — which means, the Commission has found, that CATV can "[increase] the number of local outlets for community self-expression and [augment] the public's choice of programs and types of services, without use of broadcast spectrum . . ." *Id.*, at 421.

Recognizing this potential, the Commission, shortly after our decision in *Southwestern*, initiated a general inquiry "to explore the broad question of how best to obtain, consistent with the public interest standard of the Communications Act, the full benefits of developing communications technology for the public, with particular immediate reference to CATV technology . . ." *Id.*, at 417. In particular, the Commission tentatively concluded, as part of a more expansive program for the regulation of CATV,[4] "that, for now and in general,

[1]"CATV systems receive the signals of television broadcasting stations, amplify them, transmit them by cable or microwave, and ultimately distribute them by wire to the receivers of their subscribers." *United States* v. *Southwestern Cable Co.*, 392 U.S. 157, 161 (1968). They "perform either or both of two functions. First, they may supplement broadcasting by facilitating satisfactory reception of local stations in adjacent areas in which such reception would not otherwise be possible; and second, they may transmit to subscribers the signals of distant stations entirely beyond the range of local antennae." *Id.*, at 163.

[2]There are now 2,678 CATV systems in operation, 1,916 CATV franchises outstanding for systems not yet in current operation, and 2,804 franchise applications pending. Weekly CATV Activity Addenda, 12 Television Digest 9 (Feb. 28, 1972).

[3]For this reason the Commission has recently adopted the term "cable television" in place of CATV. See Report and Order on Cable Television Service; Cable Television Relay Service, 37 Fed. Reg. 3252 n. 9 (1972) (hereinafter cited as Report and Order on Cable Television Service).

[4]The early regulatory history of CATV, canvassed in *Southwestern*, need not be repeated here, other than to note that in 1966 the Commission adopted rules, applicable to both microwave and non-microwave CATV systems, to regulate the carriage of local signals, the

CATV program origination is in the public interest," *id.*, at 421, and sought comments on a proposal "to condition the carriage of television broadcast signals (local or distant) upon a requirement that the CATV system also operate to a significant extent as a local outlet by originating." *Id.*, at 422. As for its authority to impose such a requirement, the Commission stated that its "concern with CATV carriage of broadcast signals is not just a matter of avoidance of adverse effects, but extends also to requiring CATV affirmatively to further statutory policies." *Ibid.*

On the basis of comments received, the Commission on October 24, 1969, adopted a rule providing that "no CATV system having 3,500 or more subscribers shall carry the signal of any television broadcast station unless the system also operates to a significant extent[5] as a local outlet by cablecasting [6] and has available facilities for local production and presentation of programs

---

duplication of local programing, and the importation of distant signals into the 100 largest television markets. . . . The Commission's 1968 notice of proposed rulemaking addressed, in addition to the program origination requirement at issue here, whether advertising should be permitted on cablecasts and whether the broadcast doctrines of "equal time," "fairness," and sponsorship identification should apply to them. Other areas of inquiry included the use of CATV facilities to provide common carrier service; federal licensing and local regulation of CATV; cross-ownership of television stations and CATV systems; reporting and technical standards; and importation of distant signals into major markets. The notice offered concrete proposals in some of these areas, which were acted on in the Commission's First Report and Order, 20 F.C.C. 2d 201 (1969) (hereinafter cited as First Report and Order), and Report and Order on Cable Television Service. See also Memorandum Opinion and Order, 23 F.C.C. 2d 825 (1970) (hereinafter cited as Memorandum Opinion and Order). None of these regulations, aside from the cablecasting requirement, is now before us, see n. 14, *infra*, and we, of course, intimate no view on their validity.

5 "By significant extent [the Commission indicated] we mean something more than the origination of automated services (such as time and weather, news ticker, stock ticker, etc.) and aural services (such as music and announcements). Since one of the purposes of the origination requirement is to insure that cablecasting equipment will be available for use by others originating on common carrier channels, 'operation to a significant extent as a local outlet' in essence necessitates that the CATV operator have some kind of video cablecasting system for the production of local live and delayed programing (*e.g.*, a camera and a video tape recorder, etc.)." First Report and Order 214.

6 "Cablecasting" was defined as "programming distributed on a CATV system which has been originated by the CATV operator or by another entity, exclusive of broadcast signals carried on the system." 47 CFR § 74.1101(j). As this definition makes clear, cablecasting may include not only programs produced by the CATV operator, but "films and tapes produced by others, and CATV network programing." First Report and Order 214. See also *id.*, at 203. The definition has been altered to conform to changes in the regulation, see n. 7, *infra*, and now appears at 47 CFR § 76.5(w). See Report and Order on Cable Television Service 3279. Although the definition now refers to programing "subject to the exclusive control of the cable operator," this is apparently not meant to effect a change in substance or to preclude the operator from cablecasting programs produced by others. See *id.*, at 3271.

other than automated services." 47 CFR § 74.1111(a).[7] In a report accompanying this regulation, the Commission stated that the tentative conclusions of its
earlier notice of proposed rulemaking:

recognize the great potential of the cable technology to further the
achievement of long-estatablished regulatory goals in the field of television
broadcasting by increasing the number of outlets for community self-expression
and augmenting the public's choice of programs and types of services . . . They
also reflect our view that a multi-purpose CATV operation combining carriage of
broadcast signals with program origination and common carrier services,[8] might
best exploit cable channel capacity to the advantage of the public and promote
the basic purpose for which this Commission was created: "regulating interstate
and foreign commerce in communication by wire and radio so as to make
available, so far as possible, to all people of the United States a rapid, efficient,
nationwide, and worldwide wire and radio communication service with adequate
facilities at reasonable charges . . ." (sec. 1 of the Communications Act).[9] After
full consideration of the comments filed by the parties, we adhere to the view
that program origination on CATV is in the public interest. [10]   First Report and
Order, 20 F.C.C. 2d 201, 202 (1969).

[7]This requirement, applicable to both microwave and non-microwave CATV systems
without any "grandfathering" provision, was originally scheduled to go into effect on
January 1, 1971. See First Report and Order 223. On petitions for reconsideration,
however, the effective date was delayed until April 1, 1971, see Memorandum Opinion and
Order 827, 830, and then, after the Court of Appeals decision below, suspended pending
final judgment here. See 36 Fed. Reg. 10876 (1971). Meanwhile, the regulation has been
revised and now appears at 47 CFR § 76.201(a). The revision has no significance for this
case. See Memorandum Opinion and Order 827, 830 (revision effective Aug. 14, 1970);
Report and Order on Cable Television Service 3271, 3277, 3287 (revision effective March
31, 1972).

[8]Although the Commission did not impose common carrier obligations on CATV systems in
its 1969 report, it did note that "the origination requirement will help ensure that
origination facilities are available for use by others originating on leased channels." First
Report and Order 209. Public access requirements were introduced in the Commission's
Report and Order on Cable Television Service, although not directly under the heading of
common carrier service. See Report and Order on Cable Television Service 3277.

[9]Section 1 of the Act, 48 Stat. 1064, as amended, 47 U.S.C. § 151, states:
     "For the purpose of regulating interstate and foreign commerce in communication
by wire and radio so as to make available, so far as possible, to all the people of the United
States a rapid, efficient, Nation-wide, and world-wide wire and radio communication
service with adequate facilities at reasonable charges, for the purpose of the national
defense, for the purpose of promoting safety of life and property through the use of wire
and radio communication, and for the purpose of securing a more effective execution of
this policy by centralizing authority heretofore granted by law to several agencies and by
granting additional authority with respect to interstate and foreign commerce in wire and
radio communication, there is created a commission to be known as the 'Federal
Communications Commission,' which shall be constituted as hereinafter provided, and
which shall execute and enforce the provisions of this chapter."

[10]In so concluding, the Commission rejected the contention that a prohibition on CATV
originations was "necessary to prevent potential fractionalization of the audience for

The Commission further stated, *id.*, at 208-209:

The use of broadcast signals has enabled CATV to finance the construction of high capacity cable facilities. In requiring in return for these uses of radio that CATV devote a portion of the facilities to providing needed origination service, we are furthering our statutory responsibility to "encourage the larger and more effective use of radio in the public interest" (sec. 303(g)).[11] The requirement will also facilitate the more effective performance of the Commission's duty to provide a fair, efficient, and equitable distribution of television service to each of the several States and communities (sec. 307(b)),[12] in areas where we have been unable to accomplish this through broadcast media.[13]

---

broadcast services and a siphoning off of program material and advertising revenue now available to the broadcast service." First Report and Order 202. "[B]roadcasters and CATV originators . . . ," the Commission reasoned, "stand on the same footing in acquiring the program material with which they compete." *Id.*, at 203. Moreover, "a loss of audience or advertising revenue to a television station is not in itself a matter of moment to the public interest unless the result is a net loss of television service," *ibid.* – an impact that the Commission found had no support in the record and that, in any event, it would undertake to prevent should the need arise. See *id.*, at 203-204. See also Memorandum Opinion and Order 826 n. 3, 828-829.

[11] Section 303(g), 48 Stat. 1082, 47 U.S.C. § 303, states that "[e]xcept as otherwise provided in this chapter, the Commission from time to time, as public convenience, interest, or necessity requires, shall" "(g)[s]tudy new uses for radio, provide for experimental uses of frequencies, and generally encourage the larger and more effective use of radio in the public interest . . ."

[12] Section 307(b), 48 Stat. 1084, as amended, 47 U.S.C. § 307(b), states:

"In considering applications for licenses [for the transmission of energy, communications, or signals by radio], and modifications and renewals thereof, when and insofar as there is demand for the same, the Commission shall make such distribution of licenses, frequencies, hours of operation, and of power among the several States and communities as to provide a fair, efficient, and equitable distribution of radio service to each of the same."

[13] The Commission added: "[I]n authorizing the receipt, forwarding, and delivery of broadcast signals, the Commission is in effect authorizing CATV to engage in radio communication, and may condition this authorization upon reasonable requirements governing activities which are closely related to such radio communication and facilities." First Report and Order 209 (citing, *inter alia*, § 301 of the Communications Act, 48 Stat. 1081, 47 U.S.C. § 301 (generally requiring licenses for the use or operation of any apparatus for the interstate or foreign transmission of energy, communications, or signals by radio)). Since, as we hold, *infra*, the authority of the Commission recognized in *Southwestern* is sufficient to sustain the cablecasting requirement at issue here, we need not, and do not, pass upon the extent of the Commission's jurisdiction over CATV under § 301. See, *e.g., FCC v. Pottsville Broadcasting Co.*, 309 U.S. 134, 138 (1940); *General Telephone Co. of Cal.* v. *FCC*, 134 U.S. App. D.C. 116, 130-131, 413 F. 2d 390, 404-405 (1969); *Philadelphia Television Broadcasting Co.* v. *FCC*, 123 U.S. App. D.C. 298, 300, 359 F. 2d 282, 284 (1966): "In a statutory scheme in which Congress has given an agency various bases of jurisdiction and various tools with which to protect the public interest, the agency is entitled to some leeway in choosing which jurisdictional base and which regulatory tools will be most effective in advancing the Congressional objective."

Upon the challenge of respondent Midwest Video Corporation, an operator of CATV systems subject to the new cablecasting requirement, the United States Court of Appeals for the Eighth Circuit set aside the regulation on the ground that the Commission "is without authority to impose" it. 441 F. 2d 1322, 1328 (1971).[14] "The Commission's power [over CATV] . . .," the court explained, "must be based on the Commission's right to adopt rules that are reasonably ancillary to its responsibilities in the broadcasting field," *id.*, at 1326 — a standard that the court thought the Commission's regulation "goes far beyond." *Id.*, at 1327.[15] The court's opinion may also be understood to hold the regulation invalid as not supported by substantial evidence that it would serve the public interest. "The Commission report itself shows," the court said, "that upon the basis of the record made, it is highly speculative whether there is sufficient expertise or information available to support a finding that the origination rule will further the public interest." *Id.*, at 1328. "Entering into the program origination field involves very substantial expenditures," *id.*, at 1327, and "[a] high probability exists that cablecasting will not be self-supporting," that there will be a "substantial increase" in CATV subscription fees, and that "in some instances" CATV operators will be driven out of business. *Ibid.*[16] We granted certiorari. 404 U.S. 1014 (1972). We reverse.

[14] Although this holding was specifically limited to "existing cable television operators," the court's reasoning extended more broadly to all CATV systems, and, indeed, its judgment set aside the regulation in all its applications. See 441 F. 2d, at 1328.

Respondent also challenged other regulations, promulgated in the Commission's First Report and Order and Memorandum Opinion and Order, dealing with advertising, "equal time," "fairness," sponsorship identification, and per-program or per-channel charges on cablecasts. The Court of Appeals, however, did not "[pass] on the power of the FCC ... to prescribe reasonable rules for such CATV operators who voluntarily choose to originate programs," *id.*, at 1326, since respondent acknowledged that it did not want to cablecast and hence lacked standing to attack those rules. See *id.*, at 1328.

[15] The court held, in addition, that the Commission may not require CATV operators "as a condition of [their] right to use ... captured [broadcast] signals in their existing franchise operation to engage in the entirely new and different business of originating programs." *Id.*, at 1327. This holding presents no separate question from the "reasonably ancillary" issue that need be considered here. See n. 22, *infra.*

[16] Concurring in the result in a similar vein, Judge Gibson concluded that although "the FCC has authority over CATV systems," "the order under review is confiscatory and hence arbitrary," 441 F. 2d, at 1328, for the regulation "would be extremely burdensome and perhaps remove from the CATV field many entrepreneurs who do not have the resources, talent and ability to enter the broadcasting field." *Id.*, at 1329. If this is to suggest that the regulation is invalid merely because it burdens CATV operators or may even force some of them out of business, the argument is plainly incorrect. See n. 31, *infra.* The question would still remain whether the Commission reasonably found on substantial evidence that the regulation on balance would promote policy objectives committed to its jurisdiction under the Communications Act, which, for the reasons given *infra*, we hold that it did.

I

In 1966 the Commission promulgated regulations that, in general, required CATV systems (1) to carry, upon request and in a specified order of priority within the limits of their channel capacity, the signals of broadcast stations into whose service area they brought competing signals; (2) to avoid, upon request, the duplication on the same day of local station programing; and (3) to refrain from bringing new distant signals into the 100 largest television markets except upon a prior showing that that service would be consistent with the public interest. See Second Report and Order, 2 F.C.C. 2d 725 (1966). In assessing the Commission's jurisdiction over CATV against the backdrop of these regulations,[17] we focused in *Southwestern* chiefly on § 2(a) of the Communications Act, 48 Stat. 1064, as amended, 47 U.S.C. § 152(a), which provides in pertinent part: "The provisions of this [Act] shall apply to all interstate and foreign communication by wire or radio . . ., which originates and/or is received within the United States, and to all persons engaged within the United States in such communication . . ." In view of the Act's definitions of "communication by wire" and "communication by radio,"[18] the interstate character of CATV services,[19] and the evidence of congressional intent that "[t]he Commission was expected to serve as the 'single Government agency' with 'unified jurisdiction' and 'regulatory power over all forms of electrical communication, whether by telephone, telegraph, cable, or radio,' " 392 U.S., at 167-168 (footnotes omitted), we held that § 2(a) amply covers CATV systems and operations. We also held that § 2(a) is itself a grant of regulatory power and not merely a

[17]*Southwestern* reviewed, but did not specifically pass upon the validity of, the regulations. See 392 U.S., at 167. Their validity was, however, subsequently and correctly upheld by courts of appeals as within the guidelines of that decision. See, *e.g., Black Hills Video Corp.* v. *FCC*, 399 F. 2d 65 (CA8 1968).

[18]Sections 3(a), (b), 48 Stat. 1065, 47 U.S.C. §§ 153(a), (b), define these terms to mean "the transmission" "of writing, signs, signals, pictures, and sounds of all kinds," whether by cable or radio, "including all instrumentalities, facilities, apparatus, and services (among other things, the receipt, forwarding, and delivery of communications) incidental to such transmission."

[19]"Nor can we doubt that CATV systems are engaged in interstate communication, even where . . . the intercepted signals emanate from stations located within the same State in which the CATV system operates. We may take notice that television broadcasting consists in very large part of programming devised for, and distributed to, national audiences; [CATV operators] thus are ordinarily employed in the simultaneous retransmission of communications that have very often originated in other States. The stream of communication is essentially uninterrupted and properly indivisible. To categorize [CATV] activities as intrastate would disregard the character of the television industry, and serve merely to prevent the national regulation that 'is not only appropriate but essential to the efficient use of radio facilities.' *Federal Radio Comm'n* v. *Nelson Bros. Co.*, 289 U.S. 266, 279." 392 U.S., at 168-169.

prescription of the forms of communication to which the Act's other provisions governing common carriers and broadcasters apply:

> We cannot [we said] construe the Act so restrictively. Nothing in the language of § [2(a)], in the surrounding language, or in the Act's history or purposes limits the Commission's authority to those activities and forms of communication that are specifically described by the Act's other provisions. . . . Certainly Congress could not in 1934 have foreseen the development of community antenna television systems, but it seems to us that it was precisely because Congress wished "to maintain, through appropriate administrative control, a grip on the dynamic aspects of radio transmission," *F.C.C.* v. *Pottsville Broadcasting Co.*, [309 U.S.], at 138, that it conferred upon the Commission a "unified jurisdiction" and "broad authority." Thus, "[u]nderlying the whole [Communications Act] is recognition of the rapidly fluctuating factors characteristic of the evolution of broadcasting and of the corresponding requirement that the administrative process possess sufficient flexibility to adjust itself to these factors." [*Ibid.*] Congress in 1934 acted in a field that was demonstrably "both new and dynamic," and it therefore gave the Commission "a comprehensive mandate," with "not niggardly but expansive powers." *National Broadcasting Co.* v. *United States*, 319 U.S. 190, 219. We have found no reason to believe that § [2] does not, as its terms suggest, confer regulatory authority over "all interstate . . . communication by wire or radio." *Id.*, at 172-173 (footnotes omitted).

This conclusion, however, did not end the analysis, for § 2(a) does not in and of itself prescribe any objectives for which the Commission's regulatory power over CATV might properly be exercised. We accordingly went on to evaluate the reasons for which the Commission had asserted jurisdiction and found that "the Commission has reasonably concluded that regulatory authority over CATV is imperative if it is to perform with appropriate effectiveness certain of its other responsibilities." *Id.*, at 173. In particular, we found that the Commission had reasonably determined that " 'the unregulated explosive growth of CATV,' " especially through "its importation of distant signals into the service areas of local stations" and the resulting division of audiences and revenues, threatened to "deprive the public of the various benefits of [the] system of local broadcasting stations" that the Commission was charged with developing and overseeing under § 307(b) of the Act.[20] *Id.*, at 175. We therefore concluded, without expressing any view "as to the Commission's authority, if any, to regulate CATV under any other circumstances or for any other purposes," that the Commission does have jurisdiction over CATV "reasonably ancillary to the

[20] See n. 12, *supra*. See also § § 303(f), (h), 48 Stat. 1082, 47 U.S.C. § § 303(f), (h) (authorizing the Commission to prevent interference among stations and to establish areas to be served by them respectively). "In particular, the Commission feared that CATV might . . . significantly magnify the characteristically serious financial difficulties of UHF and educational television broadcasters." 392 U.S., at 175-176.

effective performance of [its] various responsibilities for the regulation of television broadcasting . . . [and] may, for these purposes, issue 'such rules and regulations and prescribe such restrictions and conditions, not inconsistent with law,' as 'public convenience, interest, or necessity requires.' " *Id.*, at 178 (quoting § 303(r) of the Act, 50 Stat. 191, 47 U.S.C. § 303(r)).

The parties now before us do not dispute that in light of *Southwestern* CATV transmissions are subject to the Commission's jurisdiction as "interstate . . . communication by radio or wire" within the meaning of § 2(a) even insofar as they are local cablecasts.[21] The controversy instead centers on whether the Commission's program-origination rule is "reasonably ancillary to the effective performance of [its] various responsibilities for the regulation of television broadcasting."[22] We hold that it is.

[21] This, however, is contested by the State of Illinois as *amicus curiae*. It is, nevertheless, clear that cablecasts constitute communication by wire (or radio if microwave transmission is involved), as well as interstate communication if the transmission itself has moved interstate, as the Commission has authorized and encouraged. See First Report and Order 207-208 (regional and national interconnections) and n. 6, *supra*. The capacity for interstate nonbroadcast programing may in itself be sufficient to bring cablecasts within the compass of § 2(a). In *Southwestern* we declined to carve CATV broadcast transmissions, for the purpose of determining the extent of the Commission's regulatory authority, into interstate and intrastate components. See n. 19, *supra*. This result was justified by the extent of interstate broadcast programing, the interdependencies between the two components, and the need to preserve the " 'unified and comprehensive regulatory system for the [broadcasting] industry.' " 392 U.S., at 168 (quoting *FCC v. Pottsville Broadcasting Co.*, n. 13, *supra*, at 137). A similar rationale may apply here, despite the lesser "interstate content" of cablecasts at present.

But we need not now decide that question because, in any event, CATV operators have, by virtue of their carriage of broadcast signals, necessarily subjected themselves to the Commission's comprehensive jurisdiction. As Mr. Chief Justice (then Judge) Burger has stated in a related context:

"The Petitioners [telephone companies providing CATV channel distribution facilities] have, by choice, inserted themselves as links in this indivisible stream and have become an integral part of interstate broadcast transmission. They cannot have the economic benefits of such carriage as they perform and be free of the necessarily pervasive jurisdiction of the Commission." *General Telephone Co. of Cal. v. FCC*, n. 13, *supra*, at 127, 413 F. 2d at 401.

The devotion of CATV systems to broadcast transmission – together with the interdependencies between that service and cablecasts, and the necessity for unified regulation – plainly suffices to bring cablecasts within the Commission's § 2(a) jurisdiction. See generally Barnett, State, Federal, and Local Regulation of Cable Television, 47 Notre Dame L. 685, 721-723, 726-734 (1972).

[22] Since "[t]he function of CATV systems has little in common with the function of broadcasters," *Fortnightly Corp. v. United Artists Television, Inc.*, 392 U.S. 390, 400 (1968), and since "[t]he fact that . . . property is devoted to a public use on certain terms does not justify . . . the imposition of restrictions that are not reasonably concerned with the proper conduct of the business according to the undertaking which the [owner] has expressly or impliedly assumed," *Nor. Pac. Ry. v. North Dakota*, 236 U.S. 585, 595 (1915), respondent also argues that CATV operators may not be required to cablecast as a

At the outset we must note that the Commission's legitimate concern in the regulation of CATV is not limited to controlling the competitive impact CATV may have on broadcast services. *Southwestern* refers to the Commission's "various responsibilities for the regulation of television broadcasting." These are considerably more numerous than simply assuring that broadcast stations operating in the public interest do not go out of business. Moreover, we must agree with the Commission that its "concern with CATV carriage of broadcast signals is not just a matter of avoidance of adverse effects, but extends also to requiring CATV affirmatively to further statutory policies." ... Since the avoidance of adverse effects is itself the furtherance of statutory policies, no sensible distinction even in theory can be drawn along those lines. More important, CATV systems, no less than broadcast stations, see, *e.g., Federal Radio Comm'n* v. *Nelson Bros. Co.*, 289 U.S. 266 (1933) (deletion of a station), may enhance as well as impair the appropriate provision of broadcast services. Consequently, to define the Commission's power in terms of the protection, as opposed to the advancement, of broadcasting objectives would artificially constrict the Commission in the achievement of its statutory purposes and be inconsistent with our recognition in *Southwestern* "that it was precisely because Congress wished 'to maintain, through appropriate administrative control, a grip on the dynamic aspects of radio transmission,' ... that it conferred upon the Commission a 'unified jurisdiction' and 'broad authority.' " ...[23]

---

condition for their customary service of carrying broadcast signals. This conclusion might follow only if the program origination requirement is not reasonably ancillary to the Commission's jurisdiction over broadcasting. For, as we held in *Southwestern*, CATV operators *are*, at least to that extent, engaged in a business subject to the Commission's regulation. Our holding on the "reasonably ancillary" issue is therefore dispositive of respondent's additional claim. See *infra* ...

It should be added that *Fortnightly Corp.* v. *United Artists Television, Inc., supra*, has no bearing on the "reasonably ancillary" question. That case merely held that CATV operators who retransmit, but do not themselves originate copyrighted works do not "perform" them within the meaning of the Copyright Act, 61 Stat. 652, as amended, 17 U.S.C. § 1, since "[e]ssentially, [that kind of] a CATV system no more than enhances the viewer's capacity to receive the broadcaster's signals . . ." 392 U.S., at 399. The analogy thus drawn between CATV operations and broadcast viewing for copyright purposes obviously does not dictate the extent of the Commission's authority to regulate CATV under the Communications Act. Indeed, *Southwestern*, handed down only a week before *Fortnightly*, expressly held that CATV systems are not merely receivers, but transmitters of interstate communication subject to the Commission's jurisdiction under that Act. See 392 U.S., at 168.

[23] See also *General Telephone Co. of Cal.* v. *FCC*, n. 13, *supra*, at 124, 413 F. 2d, at 398:

"Over the years, the Commission has been required to meet new problems concerning CATV and as cases have reached the courts the scope of the Act has been defined, as Congress contemplated would be done, so as to avoid a continuing process of statutory revision. To do otherwise in regulating a dynamic public service function such as broadcasting would place an intolerable regulatory burden on the Congress – one which it sought to escape by delegating administrative functions to the Commission."

The very regulations that formed the backdrop for our decision in *Southwestern* demonstrate this point. Those regulations were, of course, avowedly designed to guard broadcast services from being undermined by unregulated CATV growth. At the same time, the Commission recognized that "CATV systems ... have arisen in response to public need and demand for improved television service and perform valuable public services in this respect." Second Report and Order, 2 F.C.C. 2d 725, 745 (1966).[24] Accordingly, the Commission's express purpose was not:

to deprive the public of these important benefits or to restrict the enriched programing selection which CATV makes available. Rather, our goal here is to integrate the CATV service into the national television structure in such a way as to promote maximum television service to all people of the United States (secs. 1 and 303(g) of the act [nn. 9 and 11, *supra*]), both those who are cable viewers and those dependent on off-the-air service. The new rules ... are the minimum measures we believe to be essential to insure that CATV continues to perform its valuable supplementary role without unduly damaging or impeding the growth of television broadcast service. *Id.*, at 745-746.[25]

In implementation of this approach CATV systems were required to carry local broadcast station signals to encourage diversified programing suitable to the community's needs as well as to prevent a diversion of audiences and advertising revenues.[26] The duplication of local station programing was also forbidden for the latter purpose, but only on the same day as the local broadcast so as "to preserve, to the extent practicable, the valuable public contribution of CATV in providing wider access to nationwide programing and a wider selection of

---

[24]The Commission elaborated:
"CATV ... has made a significant contribution to meeting the public demand for television service in areas too small in population to support a local station or too remote in distance or isolated by terrain to receive regular or good off-the-air reception. It has also contributed to meeting the public's demand for good reception of multiple program choices, particularly the three full network services. In thus contributing to the realization of some of the most important goals which have governed our allocations planning, CATV has clearly served the public interest 'in the larger and more effective use of radio.' And, even in the major market, where there may be no dearth of service ... , CATV may ... increase viewing opportunities, either by bringing in programing not otherwise available or, what is more likely, bringing in programing locally available but at times different from those presented by the local stations." Second Report and Order, 2 F.C.C. 2d 725, 781 (1966). See also *id.*, at 745.

[25]This statement, made with reference only to the local carriage and non-duplication requirements, was no less true of the distant importation rule. See *id.*, at 781-782.

[26]The regulation, for example, retained the provision of the Commission's earlier rule governing CATV microwave systems under which a local signal was not required to be carried "if (1) it substantially duplicates the network programing of a signal of a higher grade, and (2) carrying it would – because of limited channel capacity – prevent the system from carrying a nonnetwork signal, which would contribute to the diversity of its

programs on any particular day." *Id.*, at 747. Finally, the distant importation rule was adopted to enable the Commission to reach a public-interest determination weighing the advantages and disadvantages of the proposed service on the facts of each individual case. See *id.*, at 776, 781-782. In short, the regulatory authority asserted by the Commission in 1966 and generally sustained by this Court in *Southwestern* was authority to regulate CATV with a view not merely to protect but to promote the objectives for which the Commission had been assigned jurisdiction over broadcasting.

In this light the critical question in this case is whether the Commission has reasonably determined that its origination rule will "further the achievement of long-established regulatory goals in the field of television broadcasting by increasing the number of outlets for community self-expression and augmenting the public's choice of programs and types of services . . ." . . . We find that it has.

The goals specified are plainly within the Commission's mandate for the regulation of television broadcasting.[27] In *National Broadcasting Co.* v. *United States*, 319 U.S. 190 (1943), for example, we sustained Commission regulations governing relations between broadcast stations and network organizations for the purpose of preserving the stations' ability to serve the public interest through their programing. Noting that "[t]he facilities of radio are not large enough to accommodate all who wish to use them," *id.*, at 216, we held that the Communications "Act does not restrict the Commission merely to supervision of [radio] traffic. It puts upon the Commission the burden of determining the composition of that traffic." *Id.*, at 215-216. We then upheld the Commission's judgment that:

---

service." First Report and Order, 38 F.C.C. 683, 717 (1965). See Second Report and Order, n. 24, *supra*, at 752-753. Moreover, CATV operators were warned that, in reviewing their discretionary choice of stations to carry among those of equal priority in certain circumstances, the Commission would "give particular consideration to any allegation that the station not carried is one with closer community ties." Second Report and Order, *supra*, at 755. In addition, operators were required to carry the signals of local satellite stations even if they also carried the signals of the satellites' parents; otherwise, "the satellite [might] lose audience for which it may be originating some local programing and [find] its incentive to originate programs [reduced]." *Id.*, at 755-756. Finally, the Commission indicated that, in considering waivers of the regulation, it would "[accord] substantial weight" to such considerations as whether "the programing of stations located within the State would be of greater interest than those of nearer, but out-of-State stations [otherwise required to be given priority in carriage] – e.g., covering of political elections and other public affairs of statewide concern." *Id.*, at 753.

[27] As the Commission stated, "it has long been a basic tenet of national communications policy that 'the widest possible dissemination of information from diverse and antagonistic sources is essential to the welfare of the public.' *Associated Press* v. *United States*, 326 U.S. 1, 20; *Red Lion Broadcasting Co., Inc.* v. *Federal Communications Commission*, 395 U.S. 367 . . ." First Report and Order 205.

"[w]ith the number of radio channels limited by natural factors, the public interest demands that those who are entrusted with the available channels shall make the fullest and most effective use of them." *Id.*, at 218.

"A station licensee must retain sufficient freedom of action to supply the program . . . needs of the local community. Local program service is a vital part of community life. A station should be ready, able, and willing to serve the needs of the local community by broadcasting such outstanding local events as community concerts, civic meetings, local sports events, and other programs of local consumer and social interest." *Id.*, at 203.

Equally plainly the broadcasting polices the Commission has specified are served by the program origination rule under review. To be sure, the cablecasts required may be transmitted without use of the broadcast spectrum. But the regulation is not the less, for that reason, reasonably ancillary to the Commission's jurisdiction over broadcast services. The effect of the regulation, after all, is to assure that in the retransmission of broadcast signals viewers are provided suitably diversified programing — the same objective underlying regulations sustained in *National Broadcasting Co.* v. *United States, supra,* as well as the local carriage rule reviewed in *Southwestern* and subsequently upheld. See . . . nn. 17 and 26, *supra.* In essence the regulation is no different from Commission rules governing the technological quality of CATV broadcast carriage. In the one case, of course, the concern is with the strength of the picture and voice received by the subscriber, while in the other it is with the content of the programing offered. But in both cases the rules serve the policies of § § 1 and 303(g) of the Communications Act on which the cablecasting regulation is specifically premised, . . . *supra,*[28] and also, in the Commission's words, "facilitate the more effective performance of [its] duty to provide a fair, efficient, and equitable distribution of television service to each of the several States and communities" under § 307(b). . . .[29] In sum, the regulation preserves and enhances the integrity of broadcast signals and therefore is "reasonably ancillary to the effective performance of the Commission's various responsibilities for the regulation of television broadcasting."

[28] Respondent apparently does not dispute this, but contends instead that § § 1 and 303(g) merely state objectives without granting power for their implementation. See Brief for Midwest Video Corp. 24. The cablecasting requirement, however, is founded on those provisions for the policies they state and not for any regulatory power they might confer. The regulatory power itself may be found, as in *Southwestern,* see *supra* . . . in 47 U.S.C. § § 152(a), 303(r).

[29] Respondent asserts that "it is difficult to see how a mandatory [origination] requirement . . . can be said to aid the Commission in preserving the availability of broadcast stations to the several states and communities." Brief for Midwest Video Corp. 24. Respondent ignores that the provision of additional programing outlets by CATV necessarily affects the fairness, efficiency, and equity of the distribution of television services. We have no basis, it may be added, for overturning the Commission's judgment that the effect in this regard will be favorable. See *supra,* . . . and n. 10.

Respondent, nevertheless, maintains that just as the Commission is powerless to require the provision of television broadcast services where there are no applicants for station licenses no matter how important or desirable those services may be, so, too, it cannot require CATV operators unwillingly to engage in cablecasting. In our view, the analogy respondent thus draws between entry into broadcasting and entry into cablecasting is misconceived. The Commission is not attempting to compel wire service where there has been no commitment to undertake it. CATV operators to whom the cablecasting rule applies have voluntarily engaged themselves in providing that service, and the Commission seeks only to ensure that it satisfactorily meets community needs within the context of their undertaking.

For these reasons we conclude that the program-origination rule is within the Commission's authority recognized in *Southwestern.*

II

The question remains whether the regulation is supported by substantial evidence that it will promote the public interest. We read the opinion of the Court of Appeals as holding that substantial evidence to that effect is lacking because the regulation creates the risk that the added burden of cablecasting will result in increased subscription rates and even the termination of CATV services. That holding is patently incorrect in light of the record.

In first proposing the cablecasting requirement, the Commission noted that "[t]here may . . . be practical limitations [for compliance] stemming from the size of some CATV systems" and accordingly sought comments "as to a reasonable cutoff point [for application of the regulation] in light of the cost of the equipment and personnel minimally necessary for local originations." Notice of Proposed Rulemaking and Notice of Inquiry, 15 F.C.C. 2d 417, 422 (1968). The comments filed in response to this request included detailed data indicating, for example, that a basic monochrome system for cablecasting could be obtained and operated for less than an annual cost of $21,000 and a color system, for less than $56,000. See First Report and Order, 20 F.C.C. 2d 201, 210 (1969). This data, however, provided only a sampling of the experience of the CATV systems already engaged in program origination. Consequently, the Commission:

decided not to prescribe a permanent minimum cutoff point for required origination on the basis of the record now before us. The Commission intends to obtain more information from originating systems about their experience, equipment, and the nature of the origination effort. . . . In the meantime, we will prescribe a very liberal standard for required origination, with a view toward lowering this floor in . . . further proceedings, should the data obtained in such proceedings establish the appropriateness and desirability of such action. *Id.*, at 213.

On this basis the Commission chose to apply the regulation to systems with 3,500 or more subscribers, effective January 1, 1971.

This standard [the Commission explained] appears more than reasonable in light of the [data filed], our decision to permit advertising at natural breaks . . ., and the 1-year grace period. Moreover, it appears that approximately 70 percent of the systems now originating have fewer than 3,500 subscribers; indeed, about half of the systems now originating have fewer than 2,000 subscribers. . . . [T]he 3,500 standard will encompass only a very small percentage of existing systems at present subscriber levels, less than 10 percent. *Ibid.*

On petitions for reconsideration the Commission observed that it had "been given no data tending to demonstrate that systems with 3,500 subscribers cannot cablecast without impairing their financial stability, raising rates or reducing the quality of service." Memorandum Opinion and Order, 23 F.C.C. 2d 825, 826 (1970). The Commission repeated that "[t]he rule adopted is minimal in the light of the potentials of cablecasting,"[30] but, nonetheless, on its own motion postponed the effective date of the regulation to April 1, 1971, "to afford additional preparation time." *Id.*, at 827.

This was still not the Commission's final effort to tailor the regulation to the financial capacity of CATV operators. In denying respondent's motion for a stay of the effective date of the rule, the Commission reiterated that "there has been no showing made to support the view that compliance . . . would be an unsustainable burden." Memorandum Opinion and Order, 27 F.C.C. 2d 778, 779 (1971). On the other hand, the Commission recognized that new information suggested that CATV systems of 10,000 ultimate subscribers would operate at a loss for at least four years if required to cablecast. That information, however, was based on capital expenditure and annual operating cost figures "appreciably higher" than those first projected by the Commission. *Ibid.* The Commission concluded:

While we do not consider that an adequate showing has been made to justify general change, we see no public benefit in risking injury to CATV systems in providing local origination. Accordingly, if CATV operators with fewer than 10,000 subscribers request *ad hoc* waiver of [the regulation], they will not be required to originate pending action on their waiver requests. . . . Systems of more than 10,000 subscribers may also request waivers, but they will not be excused from compliance unless the Commission grants a requested waiver . . . [The] benefit [of cablecasting] to the public would be delayed if the . . . stay [requested by respondent] is granted, and the stay would, therefore, do injury to the public's interest. *Ibid.*

---

[30] Commissioner Bartley, however, dissented on the ground that the regulation should apply only to systems with over 7,500 subscribers. Memorandum Opinion and Order 831.

This history speaks for itself. The cablecasting requirement thus applied is plainly supported by substantial evidence that it will promote the public interest.[31] Indeed, respondent does not appear to argue to the contrary. See Tr. of Oral Arg., at 43-44. It was, of course, beyond the competence of the Court of Appeals itself to assess the relative risks and benefits of cablecasting. As we said in *National Broadcasting Co.* v. *United States*, 319 U.S. 190, 224 (1943):

> Our duty is at an end when we find that the action of the Commission was based upon findings supported by evidence, and was made pursuant to authority granted by Congress. It is not for us to say that the "public interest" will [in fact] be furthered or retarded by the . . . [regulation].

See also, *e.g.*, *United States* v. *Storer Broadcasting Co.*, 351 U.S. 192, 203 (1956); *General Telephone Co. of Southwest* v. *United States*, 449 F. 2d 846, 858-859, 862-863 (CA5 1971).

Reversed.

Mr. Chief Justice Burger, concurring in the result.

This case presents questions of extraordinary difficulty and sensitivity in the communications field as the opinions of the divided Court of Appeals and our own divisions reflect. As Mr. Justice Brennan has noted, Congress could not

---

[31] Nor is the regulation infirm for its failure to grant "grandfather" rights, see n. 7, *supra*, as the Commission warned would be the case in its Notice of Proposed Rulemaking and Notice of Inquiry, 15 F.C.C. 2d 417, 424 (1968). See, *e.g.*, *Federal Radio Comm'n* v. *Nelson Bros. Co.*, 289 U.S. 266, 282 (1933) ("the power of Congress in the regulation of interstate commerce is not fettered by the necessity of maintaining existing arrangements which would conflict with the execution of its policy"). Judge Tuttle has elaborated, *General Telephone Co. of Southwest* v. *United States*, 449 F. 2d 846, 863-864 (CA5 1971):

"In a complex and dynamic industry such as the communications field, it cannot be expected that the agency charged with its regulation will have perfect clairvoyance. Indeed as Justice Cardozo once said, 'Hardship must at times result from postponement of the rule of action till a time when action is complete. It is one of the consequences of the limitations of the human intellect and of the denial to legislators and judges of infinite prevision.' Cardozo, The Nature of the Judicial Process 145 (1921). The Commission, thus, must be afforded some leeway in developing policies and rules to fit the exigencies of the burgeoning CATV industry. Where the on-rushing course of events have outpaced the regulatory process, the Commission should be enabled to remedy the [problem] . . . by retroactive adjustments, provided they are reasonable. . . .

"Admittedly the rule here at issue has an effect on activities embarked upon prior to the issuance of the Commission's Final Order and Report. Nonetheless the announcement of a new policy will inevitably have retroactive consequences. . . . The property of regulated industries is held subject to such limitations as may reasonably be imposed upon it in the public interest and the courts have frequently recognized that new rules may abolish or modify pre-existing interests."

With regard to federal infringement of franchise rights, see generally Barnett, n. 21, *supra*, at 703-705 and n. 116.

anticipate the advent of CATV when it enacted the regulatory scheme nearly 40 years ago. Yet that statutory scheme plainly anticipated the need for comprehensive regulation as pervasive as the reach of the instrumentalities of broadcasting.

In the four decades spanning the life of the Communications Act, the courts have consistently construed the Act as granting pervasive jurisdiction to the Commission to meet the expansion and development of broadcasting. That approach was broad enough to embrace the advent of CATV, as indicated in the plurality opinion. CATV is dependent totally on broadcast signals and is a significant link in the system as a whole and therefore must be seen as within the jurisdiction of the Act.

Concededly the Communications Act did not explicitly contemplate either CATV or the jurisdiction the Commission has now asserted. However Congress was well aware in the 1930's that broadcasting was a dynamic instrumentality, that its future could not be predicted, that scientific developments would inevitably enlarge the role and scope of broadcasting and that in consequence regulatory schemes must be flexible and virtually open-ended.

Candor requires acknowledgment, for me at least, that the Commission's position strains the outer limits of even the open-ended and pervasive jurisdiction that has evolved by decisions of the Commission and the courts. The almost explosive development of CATV suggests the need of a comprehensive re-examination of the statutory scheme as it relates to this new development, so that the basic policies are considered by Congress and not left entirely to the Commission and the courts.

I agree with the plurality's rejection of any meaningful analogy between requiring CATV operators to develop programing and the concept of commandeering someone to engage in broadcasting. Those who exploit the existing broadcast signals for private commercial surface transmission by CATV – to which they make no contribution – are not exactly strangers to the stream of broadcasting. The essence of the matter is that when they interrupt the signal and put it to their own use for profit, they take on burdens, one of which is regulation by the Commission.

I am not fully persuaded that the Commission has made the correct decision in this case and the thoughtful opinions in the Court of Appeals and the dissenting opinion here reflect some of my reservations. But the scope of our review is limited and does not permit me to resolve this issue as perhaps I would were I a member of the Federal Communications Commission. That I might take a different position as a member of the Commission gives me no license to do so here. Congress has created its instrumentality to regulate broadcasting, has given it pervasive powers, and the Commission has generations of experience and "feel" for the problem. I therefore conclude that until Congress acts, the Commission should be allowed wide latitude and I therefore concur in the result reached by this Court.

Mr. Justice Douglas, with whom Mr. Justice Stewart, Mr. Justice Powell, and Mr. Justice Rehnquist concur, dissenting.

The policies reflected in the plurality opinion may be wise ones. But whether CATV systems should be required to originate programs is a decision that we certainly are not competent to make and in my judgment the Commission is not authorized to make. Congress is the agency to make the decision and Congress has not acted.

CATV captures TV and radio signals, converts the signals, and carries them by microwave relay transmission or by coaxial cables into communities unable to receive the signals directly. In *United States* v. *Southwestern Cable Co.*, 392 U.S. 157, we upheld the power of the Commission to regulate the transmission of signals. As we said in that case:

CATV systems perform either or both of two functions. First, they may supplement broadcasting by facilitating satisfactory reception of local stations in adjacent areas in which such reception would not otherwise be possible; and second, they may transmit to subscribers the signals of distant stations entirely beyond the range of local antennae. As the number and size of CATV systems have increased, their principal function has more frequently become the importation of distant signals. *Id.*, at 163.

CATV evolved after the Communications Act of 1934, 48 Stat. 1064 was passed. But we held that the reach of the Act which extends "to all interstate and foreign communication by wire or radio," 47 U.S.C. § 152(a), was not limited to the precise methods of communication then known. 392 U.S., at 173.

Compulsory origination of programs is, however, a far cry from the regulation of communications approved in *Southwestern Cable*. Origination requires new investment and new and different equipment, and an entirely different cast of personnel.[1] See 20 F.C.C. 2d 201, 210-211. We marked the difference between communication and origination in *Fortnightly Corp.* v. *United Artists*, 392 U.S. 390, and made clear how foreign the origination of programs is to CATV's traditional transmission of signals. In that case, CATV was sought to be held liable for infringement of copyrights of movies licensed to broadcasters and carried by CATV. We held CATV not liable, saying:

Essentially, a CATV system no more than enhances the viewer's capacity to receive the broadcaster's signals; it provides a well-located antenna with an efficient connection to the viewer's television set. It is true that a CATV system plays an "active" role in making reception possible in a given area, but so do ordinary television sets and antennas. CATV equipment is powerful and sophisticated, but the basic function the equipment serves is little different from

[1] In light of the striking difference between origination and communication, the suggestion that "the regulation is no different from Commission rules governing the technical quality of CATV broadcast carriage," *ante*, . . . appears misconceived.

that served by the equipment generally furnished by a television viewer. If an individual erected an antenna on a hill, strung a cable to his house, and installed the necessary amplifying equipment, he would not be "performing" the programs he received on his television set. The result would be no different if several people combined to erect a cooperative antenna for the same purpose. The only difference in the case of CATV is that the antenna system is erected and owned not by its users but by an entrepreneur.

The function of CATV systems has little in common with the function of broadcasters. CATV systems do not in fact broadcast or rebroadcast. Broadcasters select the programs to be viewed; CATV systems simply carry, without editing, whatever programs they receive. Broadcasters procure programs and propagate them to the public; CATV systems receive programs that have been released to the public and carry them by private channels to additional viewers. We hold that CATV operators, like viewers and unlike broadcasters, do not perform the programs that they receive and carry. *Id.*, at 399-401.

The Act forbids any person from operating a broadcast station without first obtaining a license from the Commission. 47 U.S.C. § 301. Only qualified persons may obtain licenses and they must operate in the public interest. 47 U.S.C. § § 308, 309. But nowhere in the Act is there the slightest suggestion that a person may be compelled to enter the broadcasting or cablecasting field. Rather, the Act extends "to all interstate and foreign communication by wire or radio ... which *originates and/or is received* within the United States." 47 U.S.C. § 152(a) (emphasis added). When the Commission jurisdiction is so limited, it strains logic to hold that this jurisdiction may be expanded by requiring someone to "originate" or "receive."

The Act, when dealing with broadcasters, speaks of "applicants," "applications for licenses," see 47 U.S.C. § § 307, 308, and "whether the public interest, convenience and necessity will be served by the granting of such application." 47 U.S.C. § 309(a). The emphasis in the Committee Reports was on "original applications" and "application for the renewal of a license." H. R. Rep. No. 1918, 73d Cong., 2d Sess., p. 48; S. Rep. No. 781, 73d Cong., 2d Sess., pp. 7, 9. The idea that a carrier or any other person can be drafted against his will to become a broadcaster is completely foreign to the history of the Act, as I read it.

CATV is simply a carrier having no more control over the message content than does a telephone company. A carrier may of course seek a broadcaster's license; but there is not the slightest suggestion in the Act or in its history that a carrier can be bludgeoned into becoming a broadcaster while all other broadcasters live under more lenient rules. There is not the slightest cue in the Act that CATV carriers can be compulsorily converted into broadcasters.

The plurality opinion performs the legerdemain by saying that the requirement of CATV origination is "reasonably ancillary" to the Commission's power to regulate television broadcasting.[2] That requires a brand new amendment to the broadcasting provisions of the Act which only the Congress can effect. The Commission is not given *carte blanche* to initiate broadcasting stations; it cannot force people into the business. It cannot say to one who applies for a broadcast outlet in city A that the need is greater in city B and he will be licensed there. The fact that the Commission has authority to regulate origination of programs if CATV decides to enter the field does not mean that it can compel CATV to originate programs. The fact that the Act directs the Commission to encourage the larger and more effective use of radio in the public interest, 47 U.S.C. § 303(g), relates to the objectives of the Act and does not grant power to compel people to become broadcasters any more than it grants the power to compel broadcasters to become CATV operators.

The upshot of today's decision is to make the Commission's authority over activities "ancillary" to its responsibilities greater than its authority over any broadcast licensee. Of course, the Commission can regulate a CATV that transmits broadcast signals. But to entrust the Commission with the power to force some, a few, or all CATV operators into the broadcast business is to give it a forbidding authority. Congress may decide to do so. But the step is a legislative measure so extreme that we should not find it interstitially authorized in the vague language of the Act.

I would affirm the Court of Appeals.

---

[2]The separate opinion of The Chief Justice reaches the same result by saying "CATV is dependent totally on broadcast signals and is a significant link in the system as a whole and therefore must be seen as within the jurisdiction of the Act." *Ante*, ... The difficulty is that this analysis knows no limits short of complete domination of the field of communications by the Commission. This reasoning — divorced as it is from any specific statutory basis — could as well apply to the manufacturers of radio and television broadcasting and receiving equipment.

8

SUBSCRIPTION TELEVISION

National Association of Theatre Owners v.
Federal Communications Commission*
420 F.2d 194 (D.C. Cir.)
September 30, 1969

Pay-TV (or "Subscription Television") was technically feasible two decades ago. It involves the transmission of programming, either by wire or over-the-air, to subscribers who are charged fees on the basis of what they choose to view.

Various wired Pay-TV experiments were initiated in America during the 1950s and '60s, but all failed. Audience support was inadequate to sustain operations in the smaller experimental communities, and the massive California "STV" attempt was aborted when voters outlawed Pay-TV in a public referendum that was subsequently judged to be unconstitutional. The 1960s' experiment in Hartford, Connecticut, demonstrated the technical (but not the economic) feasibility of over-the-air Pay-TV.

Broadcasters and movie theatre owners, among others, have generally opposed Pay-TV because of the obvious competitive threat it poses to their economic interests. This Court of Appeals decision sustains the FCC's authorization of over-the-air Pay-TV in the face of the objections of movie exhibitors. The Supreme Court declined to entertain an appeal from this decision (397 U.S. 922 (1970)). Nevertheless, because of the restrictive terms under which the Commission's rules permit Pay-TV operations, it seems improbable that this mode of pay-as-you-see transmission could achieve substantial national penetration unless it were associated with cable TV or domestic satellite distribution.

*Reprinted with the permission of West Publishing Company © 1970.

Tamm, Circuit Judge:

Today we are faced with a question of national importance, *id est*, whether the Federal Communications Commission possesses the requisite power to authorize nationwide over-the-air subscription television[1] (commonly referred to as "pay TV") on a permanent basis. For the reasons hereinafter stated, we hold that the Commission can authorize such a service under the authority conferred upon it by the Communications Act of 1934, 48 Stat. 1064, as amended, 47 U.S.C. §§ 301-397 (1964), and that the Commission acted properly in prescribing rules for the development of this new service.

I. PROCEDURAL HISTORY

The history of the Commission's involvement with subscription television (hereinafter STV) is indeed lengthy. Nearly two decades ago, on February 25, 1952, the Zenith Radio Corporation filed a petition with the Federal Communications Commission requesting authority to institute a subscription television service.[2] On February 10, 1955, the Commission issued a Notice of Proposed Rulemaking, 20 Fed. Reg. 988, in which it requested comments from interested parties on the question of whether the Commission had the statutory power to authorize such operations. After voluminous responses to this inquiry were filed, the Commission released a Notice of Further Proceedings, 22 Fed. Reg. 3758 (1957), in which it announced that trial demonstrations of STV would be necessary before a final decision could be made. Shortly thereafter, on October 17, 1957, the Commission issued its *First Report* on subscription television, 23 F.C.C. 532, which concluded that the Commission could authorize pay television, but that trial operations should be conducted first. At this point Congress began to take notice of the problem, and the House Committee on Interstate and Foreign Commerce conducted hearings on the subject. Upon conclusion of these hearings, the Committee passed a resolution requesting the Commission to defer authorization of any STV operations. *See* 16 P&F Radio Reg. 1539-1540 (1958). The Commission then issued its *Second Report*[3] on pay

---

[1] Over-the-air subscription television differs from conventional broadcasting in the nature of the signal that is transmitted; a subscription station broadcasts a "scrambled" signal that can be converted to intelligible form by special equipment which also assesses charges for the subscription programs viewed. CATV systems with direct cable links to subscribers' television sets are also technically capable of using similar devices to offer subscription services. The Federal Communications Commission investigated the possibility of authorizing subscription services on CATV networks, and concluded that the most efficient means of establishing pay television at present was through broadcasting stations. *See* Fourth Report and Order on Subscription Television, 15 F.C.C. 2d 466, 579-587 (1968) [hereinafter *Fourth Report*].

[2] 20 Fed. Reg. 988 n.1 (1955).

[3] 16 P&F Radio Reg. 1539 (1958).

television which suspended the processing of all STV applications until the expiration of the 85th Congress; this delay was subsequently extended through the 86th Congress.

In 1959 the Commission issued its *Third Report* on subscription television, 26 F.C.C. 265, 16 P&F Radio Reg. 1540a, in which it reasserted the conditions for trial operations set out in the *First Report*. In addition, the *Third Report* stated that as soon as the trial operations provided sufficient data, public hearings would be held to determine whether STV should be authorized on a permanent basis. Pursuant to the *Third Report*, three applications were filed for trial STV operations; only one such station ever commenced operations, however.[4] This station, which was operated by Zenith Radio Corporation and its licensee Teco, Inc.,[5] intervenors in this action, began broadcasting over UHF station WHCT in Hartford, Connecticut during 1962. This operation was initially licensed for three years, but the license was subsequently extended for an additional three years in 1965; in 1968 it was again extended for three years, or until such time as the Commission authorized STV on a permanent basis. The Commission's authority to license the trial operation was approved by this court in Connecticut Committee Against Pay TV v. FCC, 112 U.S. App. D.C. 248, 301 F. 2d 835, cert. denied, 371 U.S. 816, 83 S.Ct. 28, 9 L.Ed. 2d 57 (1962).

In 1965 Zenith and Teco jointly filed a petition for further rulemaking to establish permanent nationwide STV on the basis of the data derived from their trial operation in Hartford. The Commission then issued, in 1966, a Further Notice of Proposed Rulemaking and Notice of Inquiry, 31 Fed. Reg. 5136, 7 P&F Radio Reg. 2d 1501, which, in essence, requested further comments on the feasibility of nationwide STV. Subsequently, in 1967, the FCC's Subscription Television Committee submitted to the Commission a *Proposed Fourth Report*, 10 P&F Radio Reg. 2d 1617 (1967); the FCC, *en banc*, invited comments and held oral argument on the proposed report.

After the issuance of the *Proposed Fourth Report*, which concluded that the Federal Communications Commission did have statutory power to authorize permanent nationwide STV, the Communications and Power Subcommittee of the House Interstate and Foreign Commerce Committee conducted hearings on the subject of STV during the week of October 9, 1967. Upon conclusion of these hearings the full Committee recommended that the Commission refrain from taking any action for one year or until the Communications Act of 1934 was amended to authorize subscription television. *See* 15 F.C.C. 2d at 466, 470. On September 3, 1968, the Commission, through Chairman Hyde, sent a letter to Chairman Staggers of the House Committee on Interstate and Foreign Commerce indicating that the Commission could not delay any further in

---

[4] One of the three applications was denied; of the two which were granted, one station relinquished its license before commencing operations. Fourth Report, 15 F.C.C. 2d at 467.

[5] Zenith has patented "Phonevision," a system for over-the-air subscription television, and has licensed Teco to enfranchise local Phonevision operations. Brief for the Intervenors at 2 n.1.

resolving the important question of STV authorization.[6] The Commerce Committee responded on September 11, 1968, by adopting a resolution announcing that it was "the sense of the Committee" that the Commission should delay action on STV "until the end of the first session of the 91st Congress" or until "completion of action on legislation if by the end of said first session legislation pertaining to . . . [STV] is under consideration." The resolution went on to state that "it is the further sense of this committee that to avoid any further delay . . . hearings . . . should be scheduled by the end of May 1969." 15 F.C.C. 2d at 471.

Finally, on December 12, 1968, the Commission issued its *Fourth Report* on subscription television, 15 F.C.C. 2d 466, in which it reaffirmed its earlier conclusion that it possessed the power to authorize a permanent nationwide system of STV and established rules governing the operation of that system. The National Association of Theatre Owners and the Joint Committee Against Toll TV, participants in the Commission proceedings, filed a petition for review in this court pursuant to section 402 of the Communications Act, 47 U.S.C. § 402 (1964), alleging statutory and constitutional errors in the Commission's determinations.

II.   THE FOURTH REPORT

The Commission's *Fourth Report and Order* is a lengthy (144 pages) and carefully reasoned document which surveys the potential advantages and disadvantages of subscription television in light of the Hartford experiment and the contentions of various parties interested in pay television. On the basis of its seventeen-year inquiry into STV, the Commission concluded that subscription television would provide a "beneficial supplement" to conventional "free" broadcasts[7] in the sense that STV broadcasting "is not duplicative of the programming of free TV and that [it] is desired or needed by at least a portion of the viewing public." 15 F.C.C. 2d at 473 n. 20; *see also id.* at 483-488. In considering the critical question of whether STV would have substantial adverse impact on free television, the Commission placed primary emphasis on the possibility that programs, audiences, and talent would be diverted ("siphoned")

---

[6]Fourth Report, 15 F.C.C. 2d at 470-471.

[7]There is some question whether the term "free TV" is a misnomer; in the Fourth Report, for example, the Commission stated: "[F]ree TV is not really free. The advertising costs which support free TV are eventually passed on to the public, and a profit is made by the licensee or others from the use of the public's channels." 15 F.C.C. 2d at 548; *but cf. id.* at 548 n.51; Brief for Petitioners at 39: "[E]conomists have contended that free television is indeed 'free' because, as more and more units of a particular commodity are sold, the purchase price goes down and the advertising costs are borne not by the public, but by the results of mass production."

from free television to STV. Because the Commission recognized that the public's "tremendous investment . . . in television receivers based on the expectation of free service ought to be protected and the millions of viewers who rely on that service for free entertainment should be permitted to do so," it imposed a number of restrictions on STV operations. In brief, the Commission provided that STV stations could be established only in communities located entirely within the Grade A contours of five or more commercial broadcast stations, and that only one STV station could be located in each such community; that each STV station must broadcast at least twenty-eight hours per week of free programming; and that STV stations must observe detailed restrictions on the kind and quantity of subscription programs broadcast in order to prevent "siphoning." See 15 F.C.C. 2d at 494-495, 515-523, 595, 597, 598; see also pt. IVB, infra. Rules were also established governing the technical specifications and modus operandi of STV stations; see 15 F.C.C. 2d at 544-548, 595-598. In promulgating these restrictions, the Commission attempted to strike a balance between the danger of allowing STV operations to acquire enough economic power to destroy free broadcasting, and the risk of hedging the new service with so many restrictions that it would "smother" before it ever got started. Thus, the Commission rejected the suggestion, urged by petitioners and others, that direct regulation of the rates charged by STV stations was necessary in order to prevent "gouging" of the public; instead, it concluded that the available evidence rendered this possibility remote, and that free market forces would be a sufficient check on the prices charged for STV services. (Id. at 526, 548.) We hold that the Commission acted reasonably and within the scope of its authority, both in making its initial decision to authorize permanent nationwide STV and in imposing specific regulations governing subscription television.

III. THE COMMISSION'S POWER TO AUTHORIZE SUBSCRIPTION TELEViSION

The petitioners advance three arguments in support of their contention that the Commission exceeded the proper bounds of its power in authorizing nationwide subscription television. First, they assert that the Communications Act contains no explicit grant empowering the Commission to allow direct charges on the public for broadcast services, and that no such power can be inferred from the language or history of the Act (Brief for Petitioners at 17-21). Second, petitioners contend that the Commission lacks authority to regulate the rates charged for broadcast services, and that the absence of such authority is persuasive evidence of Congress' intent to preclude establishment of direct-charge broadcast operations such as STV (Brief for Petitioners at 21-24). Finally, petitioners claim that even if the Commission did have the necessary authority to establish pay television, its failure to regulate rates or to decide the question of whether it possessed rate-making power constituted an arbitrary and capricious exercise of this authority (Brief for Petitioners at 35-43). We shall consider each of these contentions separately.

A.   The language and history of the Communications Act.

Our inquiry into the scope of the Commission's authority begins with section 303 of the Communications Act of 1934, 48 Stat. 1082, as amended, 47 U.S.C. § 303 (1964), which sets forth the Commission's general powers and duties in regulating radio broadcasting. In pertinent part, this section directs the Commission, "as [the] public convenience, interest, or necessity requires," to:

    (a)   Classify radio stations;

    (b)   Prescribe the nature of the service to be rendered by each class of licensed stations . . .;

*   *   *

    (e)   Regulate the kind of apparatus to be used with respect to its external effects and the purity and sharpness of the emissions from each station . . . ;

*   *   *

    (g)   Study new uses for radio, provide for experimental uses of frequencies, and generally encourage the larger and more effective use of radio in the public interest.

In addition, section 307(a) of the Act, 47 U.S.C. § 307(a) (1964), provides that "[t]he Commission, if public convenience, interest, or necessity will be served thereby, subject to the limitations of this chapter, shall grant to any applicant therefor a station license . . ."

We find it unnecessary to determine the precise significance as precedent of our ruling in Connecticut Committee Against Pay TV v. FCC, 112 U.S. App. D.C. 248, 301 F. 2d 835, cert. denied, 371 U.S. 816, 83 S.Ct. 28 (1962). *Connecticut Committee*, which arose out of the same series of proceedings as this litigation,[8] dealt with the propriety of Commission authorization for a *trial* STV operation, and our opinion placed considerable emphasis upon the experimental nature of the undertaking.[9] Thus, although *Connecticut*

---

[8] *See* part I, *supra*.

[9] In his opinion for the court, Judge (now Chief Justice) Burger pointed out that "Congress specifically commanded the Commission by Sec. 303(g) of the Communications Act, to 'study *new uses* for radio, *provide for experimental uses of frequencies*, and generally encourage the larger and more effective use of radio in the public interest.'" (Emphasis in original.) In addition, he concluded that "[t]he distinguishing characteristic of the Federal Communications Commission's authorization of subscription television in this case is the experimental or trial basis upon which the system is to operate for the duration of its three years authority." 112 U.S. App. D.C. at 250, 301 F. 2d at 837.

Committee can provide assistance in our present inquiry, we feel it appropriate to give fresh consideration to the question of whether the Federal Communications Commission has authority to license STV for an indefinite period.

The basic structure of title III of the Communications Act, from which the foregoing sections are quoted, is a broad grant of general licensing authority to the Commission, subject to a number of specific exceptions and limitations. (*See e.g.*, 47 U.S.C. § § 310, 312, 313(b) (1964).) This plan is consistent with the dynamic and rapidly-changing nature of the statute's subject matter, radio broadcasting, and the courts have consistently recognized that Congress intended to vest expansive powers in the Commission in order to avoid the necessity of repetitive legislation.[10] The classic affirmation of the broad scope of the Commission's authority was enunciated nearly thirty years ago by the Supreme Court in National Broadcasting Company v. United States:

In the context of the developing problems to which it was directed, the Act gave the Commission not niggardly but expansive powers. It was given a comprehensive mandate to "encourage the larger and more effective use of radio in the public interest"...

... While Congress did not give the Commission unfettered discretion to regulate all phases of the radio industry, it did not frustrate the purposes for which the Communications Act of 1934 was brought into being by attempting an itemized catalogue of the specific manifestations of the general problems for the solution of which it was establishing a regulatory agency. That would have stereotyped the powers of the Commission to specific details in regulating a field of enterprise the dominant characteristic of which was the rapid pace of its unfolding.[11]

This continuing imperative need for an expansive interpretation of the Commission's jurisdiction was recently reaffirmed by the Supreme Court in United States v. Southwestern Cable Co., 392 U.S. 157, 167-178, 88 S.Ct. 1994, 20 L.Ed. 2d 1001 (1968), and has been observed repeatedly by this court.[12] Moreover, the Commission has devoted long and careful scrutiny to the question

[10]*See* General Telephone Company of California v. FCC, 134 U.S. App. D.C. 116, at 124, 413 F. 2d 390, at 398 (1969):
> Over the years, the Commission has been required to meet new problems ... and as cases have reached the courts the scope of the Act has been defined, as Congress contemplated would be done, so as to avoid a continuing process of statutory revision. To do otherwise in regulating a dynamic public service function such as broadcasting would place an intolerable regulatory burden on the Congress — one which it sought to escape by delegating administrative functions to the Commission.

[11]319 U.S. 190, 219, 63 S.Ct. 997, 1011, 87 L.Ed. 1344 (1943); *see also* FCC v. Pottsville Broadcasting Co., 309 U.S. 134, 137-138, 60 S.Ct. 437, 84 L.Ed. 656 (1940).

[12]*See, e.g.*, Paducah Newspapers, Inc. v. FCC, 134 U.S. App. D.C. 287, 414 F. 2d 1183 (1969); General Telephone Company of California v. FCC, 134 U.S. App. D.C. 116, 413 F. 2d 390 (1969); Buckeye Cablevision, Inc. v. FCC, 128 U.S. App. D.C. 262, 387 F. 2d 220 (1967).

of whether it possesses authority to license STV operations, and has reached the conclusion that its jurisdiction under the Act is sufficient.[13] In this situation, we are bound to observe the "venerable principle that the construction of a statute by those charged with its execution should be followed unless there are compelling indications that it is wrong." Red Lion Broadcasting Co. v. FCC, 395 U.S. 367, 381, 89 S.Ct. 1794, 1802, 23 L.Ed. 2d 371 (1969); see also General Telephone Company of California v. FCC, 134 U.S. App. D.C. 116 at 127, 413 F. 2d 390, 401 (1969).

Notwithstanding this impressive body of authority, the petitioners contend that STV is clearly beyond the contemplation of the Communications Act. In essence, they assert that "over-the-air pay television represents a fundamental change in the nature of American Broadcasting" (Brief for the Petitioners at 13) and that therefore the power to license pay television cannot be inferred from the Act. Direct charges for broadcasting services are not wholly unprecedented in this country, however; testimony to this fact may be found in Functional Music, Inc. v. FCC, 107 U.S. App. D.C. 34, 274 F. 2d 543 (1958), cert. denied, 361 U.S. 813, 80 S.Ct. 50, 4 L.Ed. 2d 81 (1959), and Muzak Corp., 8 F.C.C. 581 (1941). Indeed, we referred to these cases in *Connecticut Committee* as instances in which subscription services "have been found perfectly acceptable by both [the] Commission and the courts." 112 U.S. App. D.C. at 520 n. 2, 301 F. 2d at 837 n. 2. Since the matter now before us is basically a question of first impression,[14] however, we have examined the legislative history of the Communications Act in order to evaluate petitioners' claim that subscription television is "the most fundamental change in broadcasting that has occurred since the adoption of the original Communications Act in 1927" (Brief for the Petitioners at 20).

The present statute governing the Commission's authority over broadcasting services is derived in large part from the Radio Act of 1927, 44 Stat. 1162.[15] Five years before the Radio Act was adopted, the problem of how radio broadcasts would be financed was still very much an open question. Proposals included endowment of stations by public-spirited citizens, municipal or state financing, donations from the listening public, and taxes on the sale of radio receivers; some variants of these schemes were attempted with limited success in

[13]*See* Fourth Report, 15 F.C.C. 2d at 469-473; First Report on Subscription Television, 23 F.C.C. 532, 535-542 (1957).

[14]Aside from *Connecticut Committee*, the *Functional Music* case parallels the facts of the instant controversy more closely than any other case which we have been able to discover. In *Functional Music*, however, we did not deal with the specific question of the FCC's authority to license direct-charge broadcasting services. The major issues in that case were whether this court possessed jurisdiction to review the Commission's action, and whether the Commission had erred in determining that functional broadcasting was point-to-point communication rather than broadcasting under the Act.

[15]For a brief description of the early federal statutes governing broadcasting, *see* National Broadcasting Co. v. United States, 319 U.S. 190, 210-214, 63 S.Ct. 997 (1943).

the years preceding the Radio Act's passage.[16] The concept of advertiser-financed programs apparently was first developed on a systematic basis[17] by the American Telephone and Telegraph Company in 1922, as part of a plan which the company called "toll broadcasting";[18] initial public reaction to this system has been described as "lukewarm, and in some cases indignant."[19] Various forms of advertising soon became a commonplace adjunct of radio programs, [20] however, and in spite of occasional public and official attacks on the practice [21] it had become a well-established – but hardly universal – [22] method of financing radio programs by 1927 when congested air waves led Congress to establish detailed federal regulation of broadcasting.

Given this rather chaotic background, it is not surprising that the legislative history of the Radio Act casts little light on the precise question presented by this case. An early version of the Act, which was passed by the Senate, gave the regulatory body power to "regulate radio stations where a charge is made to listeners,"[23] but this provision was subsequently deleted in conference without explanation.[24] The problem of authority to license direct-charge broadcasting was mentioned only briefly on several occasions during the floor debates on the Radio Act. The most extensive discussion of the

---

[16] See E. Barnouw, A Tower in Babel: A History of Broadcasting in the United States 154-157 (1966) [hereinafter Barnouw]; G. Archer, History of Radio to 1926, at 252-254 (1938) [hereinafter Archer].

[17] Apparently some sporadic efforts at radio advertising were made in the early 1920's when individual phonograph record merchants who supplied complimentary phonograph records for broadcasts began insisting on radio acknowledgment. See Archer 199.

[18] See Barnouw 106-107; Archer 275-277.

[19] Barnouw 106-107. Cf. C. Siepmann, Radio, Television, and Society 7 (1950) [hereinafter Siepmann]: "We are today so accustomed to the dominant role of the advertiser in broadcasting that we tend to forget that, initially, the idea of advertising on the air was not even contemplated and met with widespread indignation when it was first tried."

[20] See generally Barnouw 131-134, 157-160.

[21] Archer 285-286, 361, 363; Barnouw 177-178; Siepmann 10-11.

[22] At the time the Radio Act was passed, "time-selling stations were still a minority; the climax of a struggle between commercial and noncommercial interests lay ahead." Barnouw 200; see also id. at 202-203; Siepmann 10 ("[I]n 1929 the National Association of Broadcasters adopted 'Standards of Commercial Practice,' which specifically barred commercial announcements from the air between the hours of seven and eleven in the evening.").

[23] S. Rep. No. 772, 69th Cong., 1st Sess. 3 (1926).

[24] The portion of the Conference Report which deals with the relevant section of the bill states:

The jurisdiction conferred in this paragraph is substantially the same as the jurisdiction conferred upon the commission by section 1(c) of the Senate amendment. The important change from the provision of the Senate amendment is that while under the Senate bill this original jurisdiction was vested permanently in the commission, the jurisdiction is by this compromise . . . limited to one year in time.

H. Rep. No. 1886, 69th Cong., 2d Sess. 17 (1927); S. Doc. 200, 69th Cong., 2d Sess. 17 (1927).

question was offered by Senator Dill, sponsor of the Senate bill and Chairman of the Conference Committee:

Mr. *Walsh* of Massachusetts.   A Representative from New York has introduced in the House a bill to prevent a radio-broadcaster from charging the public for listening in. It is claimed that the possible result of this legislation may be the charging of a fee to listeners . . . Is there any provision in this bill that permits that to be done?

Mr. *Dill.*   . . . [T]he commission would have the power to permit or prohibit the use of such apparatus if it so desired, but . . . in my judgment, Congress should not pass a law that would prevent a broadcasting station from so equipping itself that people could not listen to its programs unless they had a certain kind of receiving set.

*   *   *

. . . [H]ere in the United States we have built up a free system of broadcasting and reception, and it has thrived . . . I do not believe, with the condition[s] existing, that any broadcasting station can hope to prosper if it attempts to set up a method by which it would charge the listener in; but I know of no reason why the Congress should interfere with that kind of private business any more than it should interfere with any other kind of private business.

(68 Cong. Rec. 2880-81 (1927).) The bill prohibiting direct charges was never passed, and further references to pay broadcasting during the debates were sparse and inconclusive; in most of these discussions, the principal concern seems to be the possibility that large chain broadcasting organizations would obtain monopoly power, through patent licensing agreements or other devices, and use pay broadcasting schemes to extract monopoly profits from the public. *See generally* 68 Cong. Rec. 2576-2577, 2580, 3033-3034, 4149 (1927). In the years intervening between the passage of the Radio Act of 1927 and the issuance of the Commission's *Fourth Report* on subscription television, Congress has, on occasion, been confronted with the suggestion that the present Act authorizes the Commission to license direct-charge broadcasting services,[25] but no

---

[25]*See, e.g.,* Fourth Report, 15 F.C.C. 2d at 598-599; Second Report on Subscription Television, 16 P&F Radio Reg. 1539 (1957); 98 Cong. Rec. 9032-9033 (1952). The proceedings leading up to the instant case reflect Congress' inability to agree on limitations of the Commission's power in this area. On September 12, 1968, the day after the House Committee on Interstate and Foreign Commerce passed its resolution urging the Commission to defer action on STV (*see* Part I, *supra*), nine members of the Commerce Committee sent a letter to the Commission which stated, in part, that the resolution "represents the thinking of the barest majority of those present at the Commerce Committee hearing" and "does not represent a mandate to the Commission." The letter concluded: "In our opinion, the failure of the FCC to act promptly to decide the 13-year-old rulemaking proceeding on subscription television would be inconsistent with your responsibilities imposed by the Administrative Procedure Act and contrary to the public interest . . ." Fourth Report, 15 F.C.C. 2d at 471-472.

legislation restricting the broad mandate of the original Act has been forthcoming.

Thus, we are unable to agree that the Communications Act absolutely precludes the Commission from approving a system of direct charges to the public as a means of financing broadcasting services. Rather, the Act seems designed to foster diversity in the financial organization and *modus operandi* of broadcasting stations as well as in the content of programs, and we feel that the Commission did not exceed its authority in concluding that subscription television is entirely consistent with these goals.

B. Rate regulation and licensing power

Petitioners seek to negate the broad sweep of the Communications Act by asserting that the Commission lacks the authority to regulate the rates charged by STV operators, and that the absence of such authority reflects Congress' intent to prevent the Federal Communications Commission from authorizing direct-charge broadcasting. The contention that the Commission lacks rate-making authority for over-the-air STV is predicated on the structure of the statute: the Communications Act distinguishes between communications "common carriers" and "broadcasting" operators, providing the Commission with explicit authority to establish tariffs for the former but not for the latter. *See* 47 U.S.C. §§ 201, 203 (1964). However, we need not reach the difficult question of whether Commission power to establish rates for broadcasting services is implicit in some provisions of title III, since we are unable to agree with petitioners' interpretation of the role which rate-making authority plays in the Communications Act.

Federal control over telephone and telegraph evolved earlier than did regulation of radio broadcasting, and, in its early forms, it encompassed supervision of the rates charged by companies providing service.[26] Yet, with this model of common carrier treatment for a communications service available in 1927, Congress elected to establish a less rigorous system of federal control for broadcasting. The significance of this differential treatment was noted by this court in Pulitzer Publishing Co. v. FCC, 68 App. D.C. 124, 126, 94 F. 2d 249, 251 (1937):

[W]e have never said that a radio broadcasting station is a public utility in the sense in which a railroad is a public utility. Generally speaking, that term comprehends any facility employed in rendering quasi public service such as waterworks, gas works, railroads, telephones, telegraphs, etc. The use and enjoyment of such facilities the public has the legal right to demand; but its right to the use and enjoyment of the facilities of a privately owned radio station is of a much more limited character.

[26]*See* 36 Stat. 539, 544-546 (1910).

... [T]he power of Congress has not yet been extended to the point of fixing and regulating the rates to be charged by the licensee or the establishment of rules requiring it to serve alike the entire public in the use of its facilities.

See also FCC v. Sanders Brothers Radio Station, 309 U.S. 470, 60 S. Ct. 693, 84 L.Ed. 869 (1940). In short, we think that it is fair to infer that the differential treatment accorded to communications common carriers and radio broadcasters in the Communications Act reflects Congress' belief that commercial broadcasting is not a natural monopoly which creates the same kinds of risks that a telephone system does. Rather, Congress apparently believed that once the clear dangers of combinations in restraint of trade were removed, competition among those providing broadcasting services in a given area would best protect the public interest. It is also significant that in both the Radio Act of 1927[27] and the present version of the Communications Act,[28] the principal method which Congress provided for combatting anticompetitive practices is regulation through the licensing process — a method which the Commission deemed sufficient to prevent any abuses of economic power by STV operators. *See* Fourth Report, 15 F.C.C. 2d at 548, 596-597.

We approve the Commission's conclusion that it was not called upon to decide whether, or in what circumstances, its licensing regulatory functions might include surveillance or control over rates charged for services. The need for such control would presumably be rooted in developments in the market which demonstrated that STV had been granted a monopolistic or "quasi-monopolistic" position, in which the competition of ordinary TV or other services was not effective to prevent abuse. On the basis of the rates charged in the Hartford experiment, the FCC concluded there was no likelihood of rate abuse. Appellants claim that these rates were kept artificially low in order to obtain a good climate for general approval of STV. Perhaps so, but the Commission was entitled to take into account the facts as they now exist, without ranging into such speculation. If and when the premises of its regulatory approach change, the Commission can and should consider the issues involved. American Airlines, Inc. v. CAB, 123 U.S. App. D.C. 310, 359 F. 2d 624, 633 (*en banc*), cert. denied, 385 U.S. 843, 87 S.Ct. 73, 17 L.Ed. 2d 75 (1966). Its predictions as to the probable course of rates and existence of meaningful competition are certainly not unreasonable; and it is equally certain that the FCC was not required to stake out at this time the techniques and methods it might desire to use in future circumstances that have not yet and may not ever take shape. "In a statutory scheme in which Congress has given an agency various bases of jurisdiction and various tools with which to protect the public interest, the agency is entitled to some leeway in choosing which jurisdictional base and which regulatory tools will be most effective in advancing the

[27]*See* 44 Stat. 1162, 1168-1169 (1927).
[28]*See* 47 U.S.C. § § 313, 314 (1964).

Congressional objective." Philadelphia Television Broadcasting Co. v. FCC, 123 U.S. App. D.C. 298, 300, 359 F. 2d 282, 284 (1966).

C.   The question of arbitrariness

Petitioners advance a separate but related challenge to the Commission's treatment of the rate regulation question. Petitioners contend that, even if the authorization of STV was within the scope of the Commission's power, its action in the *Fourth Report* was arbitrary and capricious because the Commission failed to set forth adequate reasons for its decisions to employ regulatory measures less drastic than rate-making, and to avoid detailed inquiry into the question of whether it possesses the authority to establish rates.

In essence, petitioners' argument rests on the premise that STV operations will be monopolies similar to the public utilities which have traditionally been subject to rate regulation (Brief for Petitioners at 41). In turn, this postulate apparently rests on the assumption that the relevant product market is the television *station*, and that a finding of any other product market would be so unreasonable as to be capricious.[29] The question of market definition is hardly that simple. Within the confines of the *Fourth Report*, there are statements by various parties suggesting a number of other possible product markets affecting STV: all entertainment available in a given area; all television programming available in the area; all programs or performances of a given type, such as motion pictures or sporting events, which could be seen in live performances and other media; subcategories within program types, such as films less than two years old or athletic events featuring home town teams; and unique individual programs. *See generally* 15 F.C.C. 2d at 474-478, 494-509. Obviously, entertainment is an industry in which antitrust concepts such as product market and cross-elasticity of demand[30] are exceptionally difficult to apply; the inquiry is further complicated by the fact that the copyright law operates to create some permissible monopolies within the general area.

In light of the extensive discussion devoted to these topics in the *Fourth Report* and the considerations enumerated in the preceding section, we are not

[29]Brief for Petitioners at 41 (emphasis in original):
The Commission urges that rate regulation is unnecessary since: "We believe that the market place will regulate charges that are paid . . ." Yet, it can fairly be asked: What market place? The Commission has limited pay television to *only one station* in each city with five television allocations. Under these conditions, it is simply fallacious to argue that a "market place" exists, the operation of which would protect the public. There is no "market place" when there is a government-authorized monopoly.

[30]*See, e.g.*, United States v. Columbia Pictures Corporation, 189 F.Supp. 153, 183-192 (S.D.N.Y. 1960); Section of Antitrust Law of the American Bar Association, Antitrust Developments 1955-1968 at 66-70 (1968).

prepared to hold that the Commission was arbitrary and capricious in determining that a substantial amount of economic competition would exist between STV and the other forms of entertainment and enlightenment available in the community.[31]   Courts should be very reluctant, we think, to declare that free market forces must be supplanted by rate regulation when neither Congress nor the agency administering the area has found that such regulation is essential.

IV.   THE FIRST AMENDMENT AND EQUAL PROTECTION ISSUES

Petitioners also challenge the propriety of the Commission's actions on the grounds that the authorization of STV constitutes an invidious discrimination against indigent persons who will be unable to afford STV equipment or fees and that the program restrictions imposed upon STV operations constitute an impermissible restraint on free speech violative of section 326 of the Communications Act[32] and the first amendment to the Constitution. At the outset, there is some doubt whether petitioners possess the requisite standing to raise these issues. We note, for example, that in the proceedings before the Commission petitioner Joint Committee Against Toll TV proposed and urged adoption of program restrictions which were quite similar to the ones which they now attack (J.A. 19-24), and that organizations vitally interested in free speech supported approval of STV as a means of promoting diversity of expression (*see* part IVB, *infra*). Similarly, it is significant that the Commission concluded from the Hartford experiment that in at least one instance STV subscribers were able to observe a major sporting event in their homes at a per capita cost which was substantially less than the prices being charged for viewing the same event on closed circuit television in neighborhood theaters (15 F.C.C. 2d at 485). At the same time, we are familiar with the line of authority cited by petitioners which supports an expansive interpretation of the standing require-

---

[31] The Commission devoted considerable attention to the likelihood that STV will compete not only with free television, but also with motion picture theatres and other "box office" attractions. *See* 15 F.C.C. 2d at 474-488, 497, 508-509.

[32] 47 U.S.C. § 326 (1964):

> Nothing in this chapter shall be understood or construed to give the Commission the power of censorship over the radio communications or signals transmitted by any radio station, and no regulation or condition shall be promulgated or fixed by the Commission which shall interfere with the right of free speech by means of radio communication.

A logical extension of petitioners' constitutional arguments could well render any form of direct-charge broadcasting unconstitutional. Thus, it could be argued that rules against siphoning of programs, talent, and audiences are required in order to prevent STV from damaging free television and imposing impermissible hardship on poor people; but any rules against siphoning would violate the first amendment, and thus the Commission and Congress are without power to approve direct-charge broadcasting.

ment when challenges to the legality of administrative action are made;[33] moreover, we think that petitioners' long and vociferous opposition to the establishment of STV, both here and before the Commission, is evidentiary of "concrete adverseness which sharpens the presentation of issues upon which the court so largely depends for illumination of difficult constitutional questions." Baker v. Carr, 369 U.S. 186, 204, 82 S.Ct. 691, 7 L.Ed. 2d 663 (1962); *see also* Flast v. Cohen, 392 U.S. 83, 99, 88 S.Ct. 1942, 20 L.Ed. 2d 947 (1968). Finally, since we have determined that petitioners' constitutional claims must fail on the merits, we shall assume without deciding that they possess the requisite standing.

A. Discrimination against the poor

Petitioners rely on several findings in the *Fourth Report* to support their contention that the Commission's authorization of nationwide STV will result in unconstitutional discrimination against people in low income groups. Specifically, they point to data from the Hartford experiment which showed that less than two percent of all subscribers had incomes in the range of $0-$3,999 (15 F.C.C. 2d at 493), while nearly thirty percent of the national population in 1964 had incomes of less than $4,000; thus, they conclude that the authorization of STV is "systematic discrimination" against thirty percent of our citizens.[34] We need not reach the question of whether the concepts of equal protection applicable to the federal government by implication from the due process clause of the fifth amendment (*cf.* Bolling v. Sharpe, 347 U.S. 497, 74 S.Ct. 693, 98 L.Ed. 884 (1954)) are any different from the concepts of equal protection applicable to the states under the fourteenth amendment; by any accepted standard of equal protection, we find the petitioners' claim insubstantial.

---

[33]The leading case is FCC v. Sanders Brothers Radio Station, 309 U.S. 470, 477, 60 S.Ct. 693 (1940), where the Supreme Court stated that in enacting the standing provisions of the Communications Act, 47 U.S.C. § 402 (1964), Congress "may have been of the opinion that one likely to be financially injured by the issue of a license would be the only person having a sufficient interest to bring to the attention of the appellate court errors of law in the action of the Commission . . ." The Court held that the standing thus conferred encompassed "any relevant question of law in respect of the order of the Commission." *See also* Office of Communication of the United Church of Christ v. FCC, No. 19,409 (D.C. Cir., June 20, 1969); National Association of Securities Dealers, Inc. v. SEC, 136 U.S. App. D.C.___, at___, 420 F. 2d 83, 95-101 (1969) (Chief Judge Bazelon concurring).

[34]As a matter of statistical technique, we have some doubts about the reliability of figures obtained by comparing data taken from the Hartford area to data taken from the whole nation; in theory, it is possible that the Hartford area contains a substantially smaller proportion of people in the low income levels than does the nation as a whole, and that as a result the two percent figure is misleading. For present purposes, however, we shall disregard this potential discrepancy.

Since the Commission promulgated a number of rules designed to protect free television from economic incursions by STV — rules which we think are reasonable and amply supported by the record — we must confine our inquiry to the proposition that any form of pay broadcasting would, by itself, be discriminatory against the indigent. We must also assume that the charges imposed by STV operators will not be exorbitant, since we have affirmed the Commission's determination that rate regulation is not presently needed to prevent monopoly profits. Thus, unless there is some factor which serves to distinguish broadcasting from other endeavors which are subject to federal regulation, we are being asked to render a decision which would go far toward establishing the rule that every service provided by a regulated industry must be made available to all citizens on the basis of their ability to pay. Such a result would clearly be a constitutional innovation that we are unwilling to make; and we are not convinced that the subject of television broadcasting has unique features distinguishing it from comparable regulated industries.

The equal protection cases cited by petitioners bear scant resemblance on their facts to this controversy; rather the cases involve poll taxes (Harper v. Virginia Board of Elections, 383 U.S. 663, 86 S.Ct. 1079, 16 L.Ed. 2d 169 (1966)) and the administration of criminal justice (Griffin v. Illinois, 351 U.S. 12, 76 S.Ct. 585, 100 L.Ed. 891 (1956)). Petitioners attempt to relate these cases and their progeny to subscription television by arguing that "in order to fulfill their citizenship requirements, or, indeed, to effectively achieve their rights, the poor must have access to the mass media" (Brief for Petitioners at 46). We think that this doctrinal bridge is far too insubstantial to bear the weight of petitioners' argument, and that their analysis fails to take account of the realities which the Commission considered in authorizing STV.

The public's access to the broadcast media has never been wholly free; at minimum, it has been necessary to procure and maintain the necessary apparatus for receiving broadcasts, and this burden necessarily weighs heaviest on those with least resources. Moreover, any "deprivation" of access to the broadcast frequencies which may result from the Commission's approval of STV will almost certainly be slight. At most, one out of five stations serving a given community will be devoted to STV under the rules promulgated by the Commission; this station will be required to carry at least twenty-eight hours of free programming per week. The Commission also adopted detailed programming restrictions which are designed to prevent the more popular kinds of free programs from migrating to subscription television. At the same time, the Commission found that the authorization of STV may create benefits for all citizens which could well offset any deprivation. Thus, in some communities approval of STV operations could result in the opening of a new station rather than the conversion of an existing free station; in this situation, there would be a net gain in the amount of free broadcasts because of the STV operators' obligation to provide free programs (15 F.C.C. 2d at 494). Similar considerations will be present when an existing station that is in serious financial difficulties manages to survive by converting to subscription operations (*Id.*). Subscription television may also make available to a larger viewing public entertainment which would otherwise be unavailable for reasons of distance, lack of seating space, the desire of promoters to protect their gate receipts, or because the per capita cost of STV viewing is less than attendance at a "live" event. *Cf.* 15 F.C.C. 2d at 484-485. Finally, there is also the possibility that competition from STV will spur the free broadcasting networks and stations to make substantial improvements in their services, resulting in an overall gain in the quality of television programming (15 F.C.C. 2d at 505). In short, we believe that the Commission gave full and fair consideration to the potential impact of STV on poor people and free television, and that its findings, conclusions, and rules on these issues were reasonable.

B.   The program restrictions and the First Amendment

Petitioners' final contention is that the program restrictions which the Commission established in order to prevent STV from siphoning programs, talent, and audiences from free broadcasting are repugnant to section 326 of the Communications Act and the first amendment of the Constitution as a prior restraint on free speech. In general, these program restrictions provided that: (1) no advertising could be broadcast during subscription operations, except for announcements promoting STV programs; (2) feature films could not be offered which had been generally released more than two years prior to the broadcast date, with several exceptions; (3) sports events which had been regularly broadcast live on free television in the two years preceding their subscription broadcast could not be shown on STV; (4) no series program with interconnected plots or substantially the same cast of characters could be offered on a subscription basis; (5) not more than ninety percent of the total STV broadcasting hours could consist of feature films and sports events combined. 15 F.C.C. 2d at 597-598.

At the outset, it is appropriate to note the extreme difficulty and delicacy of the tasks which the first amendment imposes on the Federal Communications Commission. The Commission is charged with administering a scarce communications resource, the broadcast spectrum, in such a manner that the great objectives incorporated into the first amendment are realized and debate on public issues is "uninhibited, robust, and wide-open." New York Times Co. v. Sullivan, 376 U.S. 254, 270, 84 S.Ct. 710, 11 L.Ed. 2d 686 (1964). Thus the Commission must seek to assure that the listening and viewing public will be exposed to a wide variety of "social, political, esthetic, moral, and other ideas and experiences." Red Lion Broadcasting Co. v. FCC, 395 U.S. 367, 390, 89 S.Ct. 1794, 1795 (1969). In seeking to provide the broadcasting media with the diversity demanded by the first amendment, however, the Commission must avoid the perils of both inaction and overzealousness — of abdication which would allow those possessing the most economic power to dictate what may be heard, and of censorship which would allow the government to control the ideas communicated to the public. The need to make choices of this kind requires the Commission to take some cognizance of the kind and content of programs being offered to the public.[35] Further, the Commission must be cautious in the manner in which it acts; regulations which are vague and overbroad create a risk of chilling free speech, while rules which are too finely drawn will arouse judicial suspicion that they are designed to suppress uncongenial ideas. *Cf.* Red Lion Broadcasting Co. v. FCC, 395 U.S. 367, 395-396, 89 S.Ct. 1794 (1969). We are convinced that the Commission acted within these limits in promulgating its rules for subscription television.

In Banzhaf v. FCC, 132 U.S. App. D.C. 14, 33-35, 405 F. 2d 1082, 1101-1103 (1968), we established several tests which can aid in determining whether Commission rulings and orders are in conflict with the first amendment. The first consideration mentioned in *Banzhaf* is whether the rulings ban speech, and, as the petitioners point out, the STV restrictions prevent subscription licenses from broadcasting certain kinds of programs. This characterization of the STV rules ignores their context and purpose, however; it seems obvious that the Commission sought only to insure the continuing economic vitality of free television and not to affect the ideas which could be presented on either free or subscription television. Thus, when the net effect of the program restrictions is considered, it seems quite likely that the public in STV areas will receive more rather than less diversity of expression in its television programming. It is significant that the American Civil Liberties Union and the Americans for Democratic Action urged the Commission to approve STV as a means of opening new avenues of speech, and suggested regulations which were similar in some respects to those ultimately adopted in the *Fourth Report* in order to assure that existing economic forces were directed toward achieving maximum diversity of expression. *See generally* 15 F.C.C. 2d at 516, 526, 546-547, 554-555, 575. Here, as in *Banzhaf*, the likely result of the Commission's action is to provide the public with additional information and ideas rather than repressing existing sources. *See* 405 F. 2d at 1103.

In addition, we note that the restrictions now being challenged deal with categories of speech which are, if anything, farther from the central concerns of the first amendment than those at issue when comparable rulings have been upheld by the courts. In *Red Lion*, the Supreme Court upheld against first amendment attack the "fairness doctrine," which restricted broadcasting stations' control over political statements — speech which is certainly the core of

---

[35]*See, e.g.*, Black Hills Video Corp. v. FCC, 399 F. 2d 65 (8th Cir. 1968); Buckley-Jaeger Broadcasting Corp. of California v. FCC, 130 U.S. App. D.C. 90, 397 F. 2d 651 (1968); Buckeye Cablevision, Inc. v. FCC, 128 U.S. App. D.C. 262, 387 F. 2d 220 (1967); Bay State Beacon, Inc. v. FCC, 84 U.S. App. D.C. 216, 171 F. 2d 826 (1948).

the first amendment guaranty. Similarly, our opinion in *Banzhaf* upheld restrictions which required broadcasters to allocate time for opponents of cigarette advertising, a matter which was characterized as a public health issue. We think that the STV rules create far less risk of diminishing the debate on vital public issues. Finally, the Commission found that STV would be a beneficial supplement to present television offerings, provided that neither service could acquire sufficient economic power to drive the other from the marketplace. The program restrictions are designed to preserve this balance and to insure against programming duplication; thus it can be said here, as in *Banzhaf*, that "[e]ven if some valued speech is inhibited by the ruling, the First Amendment gain is greater than the loss." 405 F. 2d at 1102.

Since our review of the petitioners' contentions reveals no error in the Commission's determinations, the *Fourth Report and Order* must be

Affirmed.

RELATED READING

Anderson, James A., Robert L. Coe., and James G. Saunders. "Economic Issues Relating to the FCC's Proposed 'One-to-a-Customer' Rule." *Journal of Broadcasting* 13 (Summer 1969), 241-252.

Archer, Gleason L. *Big Business and Radio.* New York: American Historical Company, 1939 (reprinted New York: Arno Press, 1971).

Barber, Oren G. "Competition, Free Speech, and FCC Radio Network Regulations." *George Washington Law Review* 12 (December 1943), 34-53.

Barnett, Stephen R. "The FCC's Nonbattle Against Media Monopoly." *Columbia Journalism Review*, January/February 1973, 43-50.

Barrow, Roscoe L. "Regulation at Its Best Encourages Competition." *Educational Broadcasting Review* 3:2 (April 1969), 8-12.

Borchardt, Kurt. *Structure and Performance of the U.S. Communications Industry.* Boston: Division of Research, Harvard Business School, 1970.

Brown, S. M., and J. W. Reed. "Regulation of Radio Broadcasting: Competitive Enterprise or Public Utility?" *Cornell Law Quarterly* 27 (February 1942), 249-266.

Brown, Nicholas K. "The Subscription Television Controversy: A Continuing Symptom of Federal Communication[s] Commission Ills." *Federal Communications Bar Journal* 24 (1970-71), 259-282.

"The Cable Fable." *Yale Review of Law and Social Action* 2 (Spring 1972), 193-297 (entire issue).

Chazen, Leonard, and Leonard Ross. "Federal Regulation of Cable Television: The Visible Hand." *Harvard Law Review* 83 (1970), 1820-1841.

Cherington, Paul W., Leon V. Hirsch, and Robert Brandwein, eds. *Television Station Ownership: A Case Study of Federal Agency Regulation.* New York: Hastings House, 1971.

Coase, R. H. "The Federal Communications Commission." *Journal of Law and Economics* 2 (October 1959), 1-40.

Cole, John P., Jr. "Community Antenna Television, The Broadcaster Establishment, and the Federal Regulator." *American University Law Review* 16 (June 1965), 124-145.

Comanor, William S., and Bridger M. Mitchell. "The Costs of Planning: The FCC and Cable Television." *Journal of Law and Economics* 15 (April 1972), 177-206.

Conrad, Edwin. "Economic Aspects of Radio Regulation." *Virginia Law Review* 34 (April 1948), 283-304.

Crandall, Robert W. "The Economic Effect of Television Network Program 'Ownership.' " *Journal of Law and Economics* 14 (October 1971), 385-412.

Doerfer, John C. "Community Antenna Television Systems." *Federal Communications Bar Journal* 14 (1955), 4-14.

Federal Communications Commission. *An Economic Study of Standard Broadcasting.* Washington: Government Printing Office, 1947. (Mimeographed.)

_____. *Report on Chain Broadcasting.* Washington: Government Printing Office, 1941.

_____. *Report* [to the Broadcast Division of the FCC] *on Social and Economic Data Pursuant to the Informal Hearing on Broadcasting, Docket 4063, Beginning October 5, 1936.* Washington: Government Printing Office, 1938.

Ford, Frederick W. "Economic Considerations in Licensing of Radio Broadcast Stations." *Federal Communications Bar Journal* 17 (1961), 191-198.

Herman W. Land Associates, Inc. *Television and the Wired City.* Washington: National Association of Broadcasters, 1968.

Hettinger, Herman S. "The Economic Factor in Radio Regulation." *Air Law Review* 9 (April 1938), 115-128.

Horton, Robert W. *To Pay or Not to Pay: A Report on Subscription Television.* Santa Barbara, Cal.: Center for the Study of Democratic Institutions, 1960.

Jaffe, Louis L. "WHDH: The FCC and Broadcasting License Renewals." *Harvard Law Review* 82 (1969), 1693-1702.

Johnson, Leland L. *Cable Television and the Question of Protecting Local Broadcasting.* Santa Monica, Cal.: Rand Corporation, 1970.

_____. *The Future of Cable Television: Some Problems of Federal Regulation.* Santa Monica, Cal.: Rand Corporation, 1970.

Jome, Hiram L. *Economics of the Radio Industry.* Chicago: A. W. Shaw, 1925 (reprinted New York: Arno Press, 1971).

Jones, William K. *Regulation of Cable Television by the State of New York.* Albany: New York State Public Service Commission, 1970.

Kahn, Frank J. "Economic Injury and the Public Interest." *Federal Communications Bar Journal* 23 (1969), 182-201.

_____. "Economic Regulation of Broadcasting as a Utility." *Journal of Broadcasting* 7 (Spring 1963), 97-112.

_____. "Regulation of Intramedium 'Economic Injury' by the FCC." *Journal of Broadcasting* 13 (Summer 1969), 221-240.

Kern, Edward. "A Good Revolution Goes on Sale: Cassette TV Lets the Viewer Pick His Own Show." *Life*, October 16, 1970, 46-53.

Le Duc, Don R. "The Cable Question: Evolution or Revolution in Electronic Mass Communications." *The Annals of the American Academy of Political and Social Science* 400 (March 1972), 127-139.

_____. "The FCC v. CATV et al.: A Theory of Regulatory Reflex Action." *Federal Communications Bar Journal* 23 (1969), 93-109.

_____. "A Selective Bibliography on the Evolution of CATV, 1950-1970." *Journal of Broadcasting* 15 (Spring 1971), 195-234.

Levin, Harvey J. *Broadcast Regulation and Joint Ownership of Media.* New York: New York University Press, 1960.

_____ "Competition Among the Mass Media and the Public Interest." *Public Opinion Quarterly* 18 (Spring 1954), 62-79.

_____. *The Invisible Resource: Use and Regulation of the Radio Spectrum.* Baltimore: Johns Hopkins Press, 1971.

MacAvoy, Paul W., ed. *The Crisis of the Regulatory Commissions.* New York: Norton, 1970.

Martin, James. *Future Developments in Telecommunications.* Englewood Cliffs, N.J.: Prentice-Hall, 1971.

Minasian, Jora R. "The Political Economy of Broadcasting in the 1920's." *Journal of Law and Economics* 12 (October 1969), 391-403.

Newman, Joseph. *Wiring the World: The Explosion in Communications.* Washington: U.S. News & World Report, 1971.

Palmer, John C., Jr., James R. Smith, and Edwin L. Wade. "Note: Community Antenna Television: Survey of a Regulatory Problem." *Georgetown Law Journal* 52 (Fall 1963), 136-176.

Park, Rolla Edward. "Cable Television, UHF Broadcasting, and FCC Regulatory Policy." *Journal of Law and Economics* 15 (April 1972), 207-231.

_____. "Future Growth of Cable Television." *Journal of Broadcasting* 15 (Summer 1971), 253-264.

Phillips, Mary Alice Mayer. *CATV: A History of Community Antenna Television.* Evanston, Ill.: Northwestern University Press, 1972.

Posner, Richard A. *Cable Television: The Problem of Local Monopoly.* Santa Monica, Cal.: Rand Corporation, 1970.

Robinson, Thomas P. *Radio Networks and the Federal Government.* New York: Columbia University Press, 1943.

Rucker, Bryce W. *The First Freedom.* Carbondale: Southern Illinois University Press, 1968.

Schiller, Herbert I. *Mass Communications and American Empire.* New York: Augustus M. Kelley, 1969.

Schwartz, Bernard. "Comparative Television and the Chancellor's Foot." *Georgetown Law Review* 47 (Summer 1959), 655-699.

Seiden, Martin H. *An Economic Analysis of Community Antenna Television Systems and the Television Broadcasting Industry.* Washington: Government Printing Office, 1965.

_____. *Cable Television U.S.A.: An Analysis of Government Policy.* New York: Praeger, 1972.

Sloan Commission on Cable Communications. *On the Cable: The Television of Abundance.* New York: McGraw-Hill, 1971.

Smith, Ralph Lee. "The Wired Nation." *The Nation,* May 18, 1970, 582-606.

Sucherman, Stuart P. "Cable TV: The Endangered Revolution." *Columbia Journalism Review,* May-June 1971, 13-20.

Taylor, Reese H., Jr. "The Case for State Regulation of CATV Distribution Systems." *Federal Communications Bar Journal* 23 (1969), 110-121.

United States Congress, House, Committee on Interstate and Foreign Commerce. *Regulation of Community Antenna Television.* Hearings before Subcommittee on Communications and Power, 89th Congress, 1st Session, on H.R. 7715, May 28-June 4, 1965. Washington: Government Printing Office, 1965.

_____. *Regulation of Community Antenna Television.* Hearings before Committee, 89th Congress, 2d Session, on H.R. 12914, H.R. 13286, and H.R.

14201, March 22-April 7, 1966. Washington: Government Printing Office, 1966.

————. *Subscription Television — 1969.* Hearings before Subcommittee on Communications and Power, 91st Congress, 1st Session, on H.R. 420 (and related bills), November 18-December 12, 1969. Washington: Government Printing Office, 1969.

United States Congress, Senate, Committee on Interstate and Foreign Commerce. *VHF Booster and Community Antenna Legislation.* Hearings before Communications Subcommittee, 86th Congress, 1st Session, on S. 1739, S. 1741, S. 1801, S. 1886, and S. 2303, Part I, June 30-July 16, 1959; Part II on S. 2653, October 27-December 16, 1959. Washington: Government Printing Office, 1959, 1960.

"Will the Mighty Inherit the CATV Earth?" *Broadcasting,* March 20, 1972, 21-22.

PART FIVE

THE PUBLIC'S INTEREST

The last decade has been a turbulent one. It was a period of civil rights crises, anti-war protests, the "generation gap," Women's Lib, ecological concern, and consumer activism. Never in memory had the public cried out so loudly and fragmentedly in its own behalf. Sometimes exuberance overcame liberalness of outlook, and social schism accompanied attempts to achieve social progress. Often the public and the government it elected to serve it seemed to be adversaries.

Broadcasting tends to reflect the society of which it is a part, and social turmoil leaves no stone unturned. Thus, it was no accident that it was only during the last ten years that a public, yearning for signs of responsive government, first turned to a federal agency and the courts as it sought a greater participatory role in broadcasting.

Throughout its history the FCC had received comments and complaints from the public. These were dutifully filed away and rarely was anything done about them. Although the Commission required its licensees actively to seek out conflicting views on controversial issues of public importance, the agency itself seldom actively sought out the views of the public with respect to the radio and television services they were receiving. The FCC, like other federal regulatory bodies, gradually came to represent the interests of the industry it was established to regulate. It was as if the Commission believed that the public was an entity whose interests could best be served by ignoring them.

Public dissatisfaction with the mass media was hardly confined to broadcasting. The underground newspaper and film signalled a search for alternative media to give voice and image to ideas and modes of expression the establishment media eschewed. Segments of the public were seeking and gaining access to the instrumentation of the mass media, and if their output seemed to be more "minicom" than "masscom," the significance of this movement could not be minimized: increasing numbers of people were rebelling against the accepted patterns of mass communication. They wanted a voice in determining what they saw and heard. They wanted access to the marketplace of ideas, not just as message recipients, but as message senders as well.

In the case of broadcasting this trend has manifested itself in the form of citizens groups contesting license renewals (and sometimes filing competing applications) in instances where they think station performance has been insufficiently attuned to their needs and interests. The right of the public to intervene was hard-won, as the documents that follow illustrate. The burden of proof on public intervenors is a heavy one, and the financial costs of participating in an administrative proceeding are high. This decade will provide an important test of an innocent enough statement contained in the FCC's 1946 "Blue Book": "With them [the public] rather than with the Commission rests much of the hope for improved broadcasting quality."

1

UNITED CHURCH OF CHRIST I

Office of Communication of the United Church of Christ v.
Federal Communications Commission*
359 F.2d 994 (D.C. Cir.)
March 25, 1966

This key Court of Appeals decision establishes the right of representatives of the public to intervene in license renewal proceedings before the Federal Communications Commission. Prior to Judge Burger's decision, only other licensees alleging economic injury or electrical interference were granted standing to intervene in FCC licensing determinations. *UCC I*, then, is a Magna Carta (but not a *carte blanche*) for active public participation in broadcast regulation.

Burger, Circuit Judge:

This is an appeal from a decision of the Federal Communications Commission granting to the Intervenor a one-year renewal of its license to operate television station WLBT in Jackson, Mississippi. Appellants filed with the Commission a timely petition to intervene to present evidence and arguments opposing the renewal application. The Commission dismissed Appellants' petition and, without a hearing, took the unusual step of granting a restricted and conditional renewal of the license. Instead of granting the usual three-year renewal, it limited the license to one year from June 1, 1965, and imposed what it characterizes here as "strict conditions" on WLBT's operations in that one-year probationary period.

The questions presented are (a) whether Appellants, or any of them, have standing before the Federal Communications Commission as parties in interest under Section 309(d) of the Federal Communications Act[1] to contest the

---

*Reprinted with the permission of West Publishing Company © 1966.
[1] 74 Stat. 890 (1960), 47 U.S.C. § 309(d) (1964).

renewal of a broadcast license; and (b) whether the Commission was required by Section 309(e)[2] to conduct an evidentiary hearing on the claims of the Appellants prior to acting on renewal of the license.

Because the question whether representatives of the listening public have standing to intervene in a license renewal proceeding is one of first impression, we have given particularly close attention to the background of these issues and to the Commission's reasons for denying standing to Appellants.

BACKGROUND

The complaints against Intervenor embrace charges of discrimination on racial and religious grounds and of excessive commercials. As the Commission's order indicates, the first complaints go back to 1955 when it was claimed that WLBT had deliberately cut off a network program about race relations problems on which the General Counsel of the NAACP was appearing and had flashed on the viewers' screens a "Sorry, Cable Trouble" sign. In 1957 another complaint was made to the Commission that WLBT had presented a program urging the maintenance of racial segregation and had refused requests for time to present the opposing viewpoint. Since then numerous other complaints have been made.

When WLBT sought a renewal of its license in 1958, the Commission at first deferred action because of complaints of this character but eventually granted the usual three-year renewal because it found that, while there had been failures to comply with the Fairness Doctrine, the failures were isolated instances of improper behavior and did not warrant denial of WLBT's renewal application.

Shortly after the outbreak of prolonged civil disturbances centering in large part around the University of Mississippi in September 1962, the Commission again received complaints that various Mississippi radio and television stations, including WLBT, had presented programs concerning racial integration in which only one viewpoint was aired. In 1963 the Commission investigated and requested the stations to submit detailed factual reports on their programs dealing with racial issues. On March 3, 1964, while the Commission was considering WLBT's responses, WLBT filed the license renewal application presently under review.

To block license renewal, Appellants filed a petition in the Commission urging denial of WLBT's application and asking to intervene in their own behalf and as representatives of "all other television viewers in the State of Mississippi." The petition[3] stated that the Office of Communication of the United Church of

---

[2] 78 Stat. 193 (1964), 47 U.S.C. § 309(e) (1964).
[3] By "petition," we refer to both the original petition and the reply to WLBT's opposition to the initial petition.

Christ is an instrumentality of the United Church of Christ, a national denomination with substantial membership within WLBT's prime service area. It listed Appellants Henry and Smith as individual residents of Mississippi, and asserted that both owned television sets and that one lived within the prime service area of WLBT; both are described as leaders in Mississippi civic and civil rights groups. Dr. Henry is president of the Mississippi NAACP; both have been politically active. Each has had a number of controversies with WLBT over allotment of time to present views in opposition to those expressed by WLBT editorials and programs. Appellant United Church of Christ at Tougaloo is a congregation of the United Church of Christ within WLBT's area.

The petition claimed that WLBT failed to serve the general public because it provided a disproportionate amount of commercials and entertainment and did not give a fair and balanced presentation of controversial issues, especially those concerning Negroes, who comprise almost forty-five per cent of the total population within its prime service area;[4] it also claimed discrimination against local activities of the Catholic Church.

Appellants claim standing before the Commission on the grounds that:

(1)   They are individuals and organizations who were denied a reasonable opportunity to answer their critics, a violation of the Fairness Doctrine.

(2)   These individuals and organizations represent the nearly one half of WLBT's potential listening audience who were denied an opportunity to their side of controversial issues presented, equally a violation of the Fairness Doctrine, and who were more generally ignored and discriminated against in WLBT's programs.

(3)   These individuals and organizations represent the total audience, not merely one part of it, and they assert the right of all listeners, regardless of race or religion, to hear and see balanced programming on significant public questions as required by the Fairness Doctrine[5] and also their broad interest that the station be operated in the public interest in all respects.

---

[4] The specific complaints of discrimination were that Negro individuals and institutions are given very much less television exposure than others are given and that programs are generally disrespectful toward Negroes. The allegations were particularized and accompanied by a detailed presentation of the results of Appellants' monitoring of a typical week's programming.

[5] In promulgating the Fairness Doctrine in 1949 the Commission emphasized the "right of the public to be informed, rather than any right on the part of the Government, any broadcast licensee or any individual member of the public to broadcast his own particular views on any matter . . ." The Commission characterized this as "the foundation stone of the American system of broadcasting." *Editorializing by Broadcast Licensees*, 13 F.C.C. 1246, 1249 (1949). This policy received Congressional approval in the 1959 amendment of Section 315 which speaks in terms of "the obligation imposed upon [licensees] under this Act to operate in the public interest and to afford reasonable opportunity for the discussion of conflicting views on issues of public importance." 73 Stat. 557 (1959), 47 U.S.C. § 315(a) (1964).

The Commission denied the petition to intervene on the ground that standing is predicated upon the invasion of a legally protected interest or an injury which is direct and substantial and that "petitioners . . . can assert no greater interest or claim of injury than members of the general public." The Commission stated in its denial, however, that as a general practice it "does consider the contentions advanced in circumstances such as these, irrespective of any questions of standing or related matters," and argues that it did so in this proceeding.

Upon considering Petitioners' claims and WLBT's answers to them on this basis, the Commission concluded that

serious issues are presented whether the licensee's operations have fully met the public interest standard. Indeed, it is a close question whether to designate for hearing these applications for renewal of license.

Nevertheless, the Commission conducted no hearing but granted a license renewal, asserting a belief that renewal would be in the public interest since broadcast stations were in a position to make worthwhile contributions to the resolution of pressing racial problems, this contribution was "needed immediately" in the Jackson area, and WLBT, if operated properly,[6] could make such a contribution. Indeed the renewal period was explicitly made a test of WLBT's qualifications in this respect.

We are granting a renewal of license, so that the licensee can demonstrate and carry out its stated willingness to serve fully and fairly the needs and interests of its entire area — so that it can, in short, meet and resolve the questions raised.

The one-year renewal was on conditions which plainly put WLBT on notice that the renewal was in the nature of a probationary grant; the conditions were stated as follows:

(a)   "That the licensee comply strictly with the established requirements of the fairness doctrine."

(b)   ". . . [T]hat the licensee observe strictly its representations to the Commission in this [fairness] area . . ."

(c)   "That, in the light of the substantial questions raised by the United Church petition, the licensee immediately have discussions with community leaders, including those active in the civil rights movement (such as petitioners), as to whether its programming is fully meeting the needs and interests of its area."

(d)   "That the licensee immediately cease discriminatory programming patterns."

(e)   That "the licensee will be required to make a detailed report as to its efforts in the above four respects . . ."

---

[6]". . . we cannot stress too strongly that the licensee must operate in complete conformity with its representations and the conditions laid down."

Appellants contend that, against the background of complaints since 1955 and the Commission's conclusion that WLBT was in fact guilty of "discriminatory programming," the Commission could not properly renew the license even for one year without a hearing to resolve factual issues raised by their petition and vitally important to the public. The Commission argues, however, that it in effect accepted Petitioners' view of the facts, took all necessary steps to insure that the practices complained of would cease, and for this reason granted a short-term renewal as an exercise by the Commission of what it describes as a "'political' decision, 'in the higher sense of that abused term,' which is peculiarly entrusted to the agency."[7] The Commission seems to have based its "political decision" on a blend of what the Appellants alleged, what its own investigation revealed, its hope that WLBT would improve, and its view that the station was needed.

STANDING OF APPELLANTS[8]

The Commission's denial of standing to Appellants was based on the theory that, absent a potential direct, substantial injury or adverse effect from the administrative action under consideration, a petitioner has no standing before the Commission and that the only types of effects sufficient to support standing are economic injury and electrical interference. It asserted its traditional position that members of the listening public do not suffer any injury peculiar to them and that allowing them standing would pose great administrative burdens.[9]

Up to this time, the courts have granted standing to intervene only to those alleging electrical interference, NBC v. FCC (KOA), 76 U.S. App. D.C. 238, 132 F. 2d 545 (1942), aff'd, 319 U.S. 239, 63 S.Ct. 1035, 87 L.Ed. 1374 (1943), or alleging some economic injury, e.g., FCC v. Sanders Bros. Radio

---

[7]Intervenor and the Commission depart from the record to argue that WLBT has fully complied with the conditions and that the Commission's hope that WLBT would make a valuable contribution to the problems of race relations is being fulfilled. Appellants respond that WLBT has not adequately corrected unbalanced programming. We do not consider these claims as to the alleged success of the Commission's effort to permit WLBT to purge itself of misconduct relevant either to the question of standing or to the correctness of the grant of a renewal without a hearing. We confine ourselves to the record as made before the Commission.

[8]All parties seem to consider that the same standards are applicable to determining standing before the Commission and standing to appeal a Commission order to this court. See Philco Corp. v. FCC, 103 U.S. App. D.C. 278, 257 F. 2d 656 (1958), cert. denied, 358 U.S. 946, 79 S.Ct. 350, 3 L.Ed. 2d 352 (1959); Metropolitan Television Co. v. FCC, 95 U.S. App. D.C. 326, 221 F. 2d 879 (1955). We have, therefore, used the cases dealing with standing in the two tribunals interchangeably.

[9]See Northern Pacific Radio Corp., 23 P & F Rad. Reg. 186 (1962); Gordon Broadcasting of San Francisco, Inc., 22 P & F Rad. Reg. 236 (1962).

Station, 309 U.S. 470, 60 S.Ct. 693, 84 L.Ed. 869 (1940). It is interesting to note, however, that the Commission's traditionally narrow view of standing initially led it to deny standing to the very categories it now asserts are the only ones entitled thereto. In *Sanders* the Commission argued that economic injury was not a basis for standing,[10] and in *KOA* that electrical interference was insufficient. This history indicates that neither administrative nor judicial concepts of standing have been static.

What the Commission apparently fails to see in the present case is that the courts have resolved questions of standing as they arose and have at no time manifested an intent to make economic interest and electrical interference the exclusive grounds for standing. *Sanders*, for instance, granted standing to those economically injured on the theory that such persons might well be the only ones sufficiently interested to contest a Commission action. 309 U.S. 470, 477, 60 S.Ct. 693. In *KOA* we noted the anomalous result that, if standing were restricted to those with an economic interest, educational and non-profit radio stations, a prime source of public-interest broadcasting, would be defaulted. Because such a rule would hardly promote the statutory goal of public-interest broadcasting, we concluded that non-profit stations must be heard without a showing of economic injury and held that all broadcast licensees could have standing by showing injury other than financial (there, electrical interference). Our statement that *Sanders* did not limit standing to those suffering direct economic injury was not disturbed by the Supreme Court when it affirmed *KOA*. 319 U.S. 239, 63 S.Ct. 1035 (1943).

It is important to remember that the cases allowing standing to those falling within either of the two established categories have emphasized that standing is accorded to persons not for the protection of their private interest but only to vindicate the public interest.

"The Communications Act of 1934 did not create new private rights. The purpose of the Act was to protect the public interest in communications. By § 402(b)(2), Congress gave the right of appeal to persons 'aggrieved or whose interests are adversely affected' by Commission action. . . . But *these private litigants have standing only as representatives of the public interest.* Federal Communications Commission v. Sanders Radio Station, 309 U.S. 470, 477, 642, 60 S.Ct. 693, 698, 84 L.Ed. 869, 1037." Associated Industries of New York State, Inc. v. Ickes, 134 F. 2d 694, 703 (2d Cir. 1943), vacated as moot, 320 U.S. 707, 64 S.Ct. 74, 88 L.Ed. 414 (1943), quoting Scripps-Howard Radio, Inc. v. FCC, 316 U.S. 4, 14, 62 S.Ct. 875, 86 L.Ed. 1229 (1942).

On the other hand, some Congressional reports have expressed apprehensions, possibly representing the views of both administrative agencies and

---

[10] It argued that, since economic injury was not a ground for refusing a license, it could not be a basis of standing. See generally Chicago Junction Case, 264 U.S. 258, 44 S.Ct. 317, 68 L.Ed. 667 (1924).

broadcasters, that standing should not be accorded lightly so as to make possible intervention into proceedings "by a host of parties who have no legitimate interest but solely with the purpose of delaying license grants which properly should be made."[11] But the recurring theme in the legislative reports is not so much fear of a plethora of parties in interest as apprehension that standing might be abused by persons with no *legitimate* interest in the proceedings but with a desire only to delay the granting of a license for some private selfish reason.[12] The Congressional Committee which voiced the apprehension of a "host of parties" seemingly was willing to allow standing to anyone who could show economic injury or electrical interference. Yet these criteria are no guarantee of the legitimacy of the claim sought to be advanced, for, as another Congressional Committee later lamented, "In many of these cases the protests are based on grounds which have little or no relationship to the public interest."[13]

We see no reason to believe, therefore, that Congress through its committees had any thought that electrical interference and economic injury were to be the exclusive grounds for standing or that it intended to limit participation of the listening public to writing letters to the Complaints Division of the Commission. Instead, the Congressional reports seem to recognize that the issue of standing was to be left to the courts.[14]

The Commission's rigid adherence to a requirement of direct economic injury in the commercial sense operates to give standing to an electronics manufacturer who competes with the owner of a radio-television station only in the sale of appliances,[15] while it denies standing to spokesmen for the listeners, who are most directly concerned with and intimately affected by the performance of a licensee. Since the concept of standing is a practical and functional one designed to insure that only those with a genuine and legitimate interest can participate in a proceeding, we can see no reason to exclude those with such an obvious and acute concern as the listening audience. This much seems essential to insure that the holders of broadcasting licenses be responsive to the needs of the audience, without which the broadcaster could not exist.

There is nothing unusual or novel in granting the consuming public standing to challenge administrative actions. In Associated Industries of New York State, Inc. v. Ickes, 134 F. 2d 694 (2d Cir. 1943), vacated as moot, 320 U.S. 707, 64 S.Ct. 74, 88 L.Ed. 414 (1943), coal consumers were found to have

[11] S. Rep. No. 44, 82d Cong., 1st Sess. 8 (1951).
[12] See, *e.g., ibid.*; S. Rep. No. 1231, 84th Cong., 1st Sess. 1-3 (1955); H.R. Rep. No. 1051, 84th Cong., 1st Sess. 2-3 (1955); H.R. Rep. No. 1800, 86th Cong., 2d Sess. 9-10, U.S. Code Cong. & Admin. News 1960, p. 3516 (1960).
[13] H.R. Rep. No. 1051, 84th Cong., 1st Sess. 3 (1955).
[14] Perhaps the mention in these reports of economic and electrical injury arose out of preoccupation with problems surrounding initial licensing procedures, as distinguished from those involved in renewal proceedings. See . . . *infra.*
[15] Philco Corp. v. FCC, 103 U.S. App. D.C. 278, 257, F. 2d 656 (1958); cert. denied, 358 U.S. 946, 79 S.Ct. 350, 3 L.Ed. 2d 35 (1959).

standing to review a minimum price order. In United States v. Public Utilities Commission, 80 U.S. App. D.C. 227, 151 F. 2d 609 (1945), we held that a consumer of electricity was affected by the rates charged and could appeal an order setting them. Similarly in Bebchick v. Public Utilities Commission, 109 U.S. App. D.C. 298, 287 F. 2d 337 (1961), we had no difficulty in concluding that a public transit rider had standing to appeal a rate increase. A direct economic injury, even if small as to each user, is involved in the rate cases, but standing has also been granted to a passenger to contest the legality of Interstate Commerce Commission rules allowing racial segregation in railroad dining cars. Henderson v. United States, 339 U.S. 816, 70 S.Ct. 843, 94 L.Ed. 1302 (1950). Moreover, in Reade v. Ewing, 205 F. 2d 630 (2d Cir. 1953), a consumer of oleomargarine was held to have standing to challenge orders affecting the ingredients thereof.[16]

These "consumer" cases were not decided under the Federal Communications Act, but all of them have in common with the case under review the interpretation of language granting standing to persons "affected" or "aggrieved." The Commission fails to suggest how we are to distinguish these cases from those involving standing of broadcast "consumers" to oppose license renewals in the Federal Communications Commission. The total number of potential individual suitors who are consumers of oleomargarine or public transit passengers would seem to be greater than the number of responsible representatives of the listening public who are potential intervenors in a proceeding affecting a single broadcast reception area. Furthermore, assuming we look only to the commercial economic aspects and ignore vital public interest, we cannot believe that the economic stake of the consumers of electricity or public transit riders is more significant than that of listeners who collectively have a huge aggregate investment in receiving equipment. [17]

The argument that a broadcaster is not a public utility is beside the point. True it is not a public utility in the same sense as strictly regulated common carriers or purveyors of power, but neither is it a purely private enterprise like a newspaper or an automobile agency. A broadcaster has much in common with a newspaper publisher, but he is not in the same category in terms of public obligations imposed by law. A broadcaster seeks and is granted the free and exclusive use of a limited and valuable part of the public domain; when he accepts that franchise it is burdened by enforceable public obligations. A

---

[16] In the most recent case on the subject, the Second Circuit, relying on cases under the Federal Communications Act, held that non-profit conservation associations have standing to protect the aesthetic, conservational, and recreational aspects of power development. Scenic Hudson Preservation Conference v. FPC, 354 F. 2d 608 (2d Cir. 1965).

[17] According to Robert Sarnoff of NBC the total investment in television, by American viewers is 40 billion dollars, a figure perhaps twenty times as large as the total investment of broadcasters. FCC, *Television Network Program Procurement*, H.R. Rep. No. 281, 88th Cong., 1st Sess. 57 (1963). Forty billion dollars would seem to afford at least one substantial brick in a foundation for standing.

newspaper can be operated at the whim or caprice of its owners; a broadcast station cannot. After nearly five decades of operation the broadcast industry does not seem to have grasped the simple fact that a broadcast license is a public trust subject to termination for breach of duty.

Nor does the fact that the Commission itself is directed by Congress to protect the public interest constitute adequate reason to preclude the listening public from assisting in that task. *Cf.* UAW v. Scofield, 382 U.S. 205, 86 S.Ct. 335, 15 L.Ed. 2d 304 (1965). The Commission of course represents and indeed is the prime arbiter of the public interest, but its duties and jurisdiction are vast, and it acknowledges that it cannot begin to monitor or oversee the performance of every one of thousands of licensees. Moreover, the Commission has always viewed its regulatory duties as guided if not limited by our national tradition that public response is the most reliable test of ideas and performance in broadcasting as in most areas of life. The Commission view is that we have traditionally depended on this public reaction rather than on some form of governmental supervision or "censorship" mechanisms.

[I]t is the public in individual communities throughout the length and breadth of our country who must bear final responsibility for the quality and adequacy of television service — whether it be originated by local stations or by national networks. Under our system, the interests of the public are dominant. The commercial needs of licensed broadcasters and advertisers must be integrated into those of the public. *Hence, individual citizens and the communities they compose owe a duty to themselves and their peers to take an active interest in the scope and quality of the television service* which stations and networks provide and which, undoubtedly, has a *vast impact on their lives and the lives of their children.* Nor need the public feel that in taking a hand in broadcasting they are unduly interfering in the private business affairs of others. On the contrary, *their interest in television programming is direct* and their responsibilities important. *They are the owners* of the channels of television — indeed, of all broadcasting.
FCC, *Television Network Program Procurement*, H.R. Rep. No. 281, 88th Cong., 1st Sess. 20 (1963). (Emphasis added.)

Taking advantage of this "active interest in the . . . quality" of broadcasting rather than depending on governmental initiative is also desirable in that it tends to cast governmental power, at least in the first instance, in the more detached role of arbiter rather than accuser.

The theory that the Commission can always effectively represent the listener interests in a renewal proceeding without the aid and participation of legitimate listener representatives fulfilling the role of private attorneys general is one of those assumptions we collectively try to work with so long as they are reasonably adequate. When it becomes clear, as it does to us now, that it is no longer a valid assumption which stands up under the realities of actual experience, neither we nor the Commission can continue to rely on it. The gradual expansion and evolution of concepts of standing in administrative law attests that experience rather than logic or fixed rules has been accepted as the guide.

The Commission's attitude in this case is ambivalent in the precise sense of that term. While attracted by the potential contribution of widespread public interest and participation in improving the quality of broadcasting, the Commission rejects effective public participation by invoking the oft-expressed fear that a "host of parties" will descend upon it and render its dockets "clogged" and "unworkable." The Commission resolves this ambivalence for itself by contending that in this renewal proceeding the viewpoint of the public was adequately represented since it fully considered the claims presented by Appellants even though denying them standing. It also points to the general procedures for public participation that are already available, such as the filing of complaints with the Commission,[18] the practice of having local hearings,[19] and the ability of people who are not parties in interest to appear at hearings as witnesses.[20] In light of the Commission's procedure in this case and its stated willingness to hear witnesses having complaints, it is difficult to see how a grant of formal standing would pose undue or insoluble problems for the Commission.

We cannot believe that the Congressional mandate of public participation which the Commission says it seeks to fulfill[21] was meant to be limited to writing letters to the Commission, to inspection of records, to the Commission's grace in considering listener claims, or to mere non-participating appearance at hearings. We cannot fail to note that the long history of complaints against WLBT beginning in 1955 had left the Commission virtually unmoved in the subsequent renewal proceedings, and it seems not unlikely that the 1964 renewal application might well have been routinely granted except for the determined and sustained efforts of Appellants at no small expense to themselves.[22] Such beneficial contribution as these Appellants, or some of them, can make must not be left to the grace of the Commission.

Public participation is especially important in a renewal proceeding, since the public will have been exposed for at least three years to the licensee's performance, as cannot be the case when the Commission considers an initial grant, unless the applicant has a prior record as a licensee. In a renewal proceeding, furthermore, public spokesmen, such as Appellants here, may be the only objectors. In a community served by only one outlet, the public interest focus is perhaps sharper and the need for airing complaints often greater than where, for example, several channels exist. Yet if there is only one outlet, there

[18] 47 C.F.R. § 1.587 (1965).
[19] 74 Stat. 892 (1960), 47 U.S.C. § 311 (1964).
[20] 47 C.F.R. § 1.225 (1965).
[21] See 30 Fed. Reg. 4543 (1965).
[22] We recognize, of course, the existence of strong tides of public opinion and other forces at work outside the listening area of the Licensee which may not have been without some effect on the Commission.

are no rivals at hand to assert the public interest, and reliance on opposing applicants to challenge the existing licensee for the channel would be fortuitous at best. Even when there are multiple competing stations in a locality, various factors may operate to inhibit the other broadcasters from opposing a renewal application. An imperfect rival may be thought a desirable rival, or there may be a "gentleman's agreement" of deference to a fellow broadcaster in the hope he will reciprocate on a propitious occasion.

Thus we are brought around by analogy to the Supreme Court's reasoning in *Sanders*; unless the listeners — the broadcast consumers — can be heard, there may be no one to bring programming deficiencies or offensive overcommercialization to the attention of the Commission in an effective manner. By process of elimination those "consumers" willing to shoulder the burdensome and costly processes of intervention in a Commission proceeding are likely to be the only ones "having a sufficient interest" to challenge a renewal application. The late Edmond Cahn addressed himself to this problem in its broadest aspects when he said, "Some consumers need bread; others need Shakespeare; others need their rightful place in the national society — what they all need is processors of law who will consider the people's needs more significant than administrative convenience." *Law in the Consumer Perspective,* 112 U.Pa.L.Rev. 1, 13 (1963).

Unless the Commission is to be given staff and resources to perform the enormously complex and prohibitively expensive task of maintaining constant surveillance over every licensee, some mechanism must be developed so that the *legitimate* interests of listeners can be made a part of the record which the Commission evaluates. An initial applicant frequently floods the Commission with testimonials from a host of representative community groups as to the relative merit of their champion, and the Commission places considerable reliance on these vouchers; on a renewal application the "campaign pledges" of applicants must be open to comparison with "performance in office" aided by a limited number of responsible representatives of the listening public when such representatives seek participation.

We recognize the risks alluded to by Judge Madden in his cogent dissent in *Philco*;[23] regulatory agencies, the Federal Communications Commission in particular, would ill serve the public interest if the courts imposed such heavy burdens on them as to overtax their capacities. The competing consideration is that experience demonstrates consumers are generally among the best vindicators of the public interest. In order to safeguard the public interest in broadcasting, therefore, we hold that some "audience participation" must be allowed in license renewal proceedings. We recognize this will create problems for the Commission but it does not necessarily follow that "hosts" of protestors must be granted standing to challenge a renewal application or that the Commission need allow the administrative processes to be obstructed or

---

[23]103 U.S. App. D.C. at 281, 257 F. 2d at 659 (1958), cert. denied, 358 U.S. 946, 79 S.Ct. 350, 3 L.Ed. 2d 352 (1959).

overwhelmed by captious or purely obstructive protests. The Commission can avoid such results by developing appropriate regulations by statutory rule-making. Although it denied Appellants standing, it employed *ad hoc* criteria in determining that these Appellants were responsible spokesmen for representative groups having significant roots in the listening community. These criteria can afford a basis for developing formalized standards to regulate and limit public intervention to spokesmen who can be helpful. A petition for such intervention must "contain specific allegations of fact sufficient to show that the petitioner is a party in interest and that a grant of the application would be prima facie inconsistent" with the public interest. 74 Stat. 891 (1960), 47 U.S.C. 309(d) (1) (1964).

The responsible and representative groups eligible to intervene cannot here be enumerated or categorized specifically; such community organizations as civic associations, professional societies, unions, churches, and educational institutions or associations might well be helpful to the Commission. These groups are found in every community; they usually concern themselves with a wide range of community problems and tend to be representatives of broad as distinguished from narrow interests, public as distinguished from private or commercial interests.

The Commission should be accorded broad discretion in establishing and applying rules for such public participation, including rules for determining which community representatives are to be allowed to participate and how many are reasonably required to give the Commission the assistance it needs in vindicating the public interest.[24] The usefulness of any particular petitioner for intervention must be judged in relation to other petitioners and the nature of the claims it asserts as basis for standing. Moreover it is no novelty in the administrative process to require consolidation of petitions and briefs to avoid multiplicity of parties and duplication of effort.

The fears of regulatory agencies that their processes will be inundated by expansion of standing criteria are rarely borne out. Always a restraining factor is the expense of participation in the administrative process, an economic reality which will operate to limit the number of those who will seek participation; legal and related expenses of administrative proceedings are such that even those with large economic interests find the costs burdensome. Moreover, the listening

---

[24]Professor Jaffe concedes there are strong reasons to reject public or listener standing but he believes "it does have much to commend it" in certain areas if put in terms of "jurisdiction subject to judicial discretion to be exercised with due regard for the character of the interests and the issues involved in each case." Jaffe, *Standing to Secure Judicial Review: Private Actions*, 75 Harv. L. Rev. 255, 282 (1961). "There are many persons . . . who feel that neither the industry nor the FCC can be trusted to protect the listener interest. If this is so, the public action is appropriate. But a frank recognition that the action is a public action and not a private remedy would allow us to introduce the notion of discretion at both the administrative and judicial levels." *Id.* at 284.

public seeking intervention in a license renewal proceeding cannot attract lawyers to represent their cause by the prospect of lucrative contingent fees, as can be done, for example, in rate cases.

We are aware that there may be efforts to exploit the enlargement of intervention, including spurious petitions from private interests not concerned with the quality of broadcast programming, since such private interests may sometimes cloak themselves with a semblance of public interest advocates. But this problem, as we have noted, can be dealt with by the Commission under its inherent powers and by rulemaking.

In line with this analysis, we do not now hold that all of the Appellants have standing to challenge WLBT's renewal. We do not reach that question. As to these Appellants we limit ourselves to holding that the Commission must allow standing to one or more of them as responsible representatives to assert and prove the claims they have urged in their petition.

It is difficult to anticipate the range of claims which may be raised or sought to be raised by future petitioners asserting representation of the public interest. It is neither possible nor desirable for us to try to chart the precise scope or patterns for the future. The need sought to be met is to provide a means for reflection of listener appraisal of a licensee's performance as the performance meets or fails to meet the licensee's statutory obligation to operate the facility in the public interest. The matter now before us is one in which the alleged conduct adverse to the public interest rests primarily on claims of racial discrimination, some elements of religious discrimination, oppressive over-commercialization by advertising announcements, and violation of the Fairness Doctrine. Future cases may involve other areas of conduct and programming adverse to the public interest; at this point we can only emphasize that intervention on behalf of the public is not allowed to press private interests but only to vindicate the broad public interest relating to a licensee's performance of the public trust inherent in every license.

HEARING

We hold further that in the circumstances shown by this record an evidentiary hearing was required in order to resolve the public interest issue. Under Section 309(e) the Commission must set a renewal application for hearing where "a substantial and material question of fact is presented *or* the Commission for any reason is unable to make the finding" that the public interest, convenience, and necessity will be served by the license renewal. (Emphasis supplied.)

The Commission argues in this Court that it accepted all Appellants' allegations of WLBT's misconduct and that for this reason no hearing was necessary.[25] Yet the Commission recognized that WLBT's past behavior, as described by Appellants, would preclude the statutory finding of public interest necessary for license renewal;[26] hence its grant of the one-year license on the policy ground that there was an urgent need at the time for a properly run station in Jackson must have been predicated on a belief that the need was so great as to warrant the risk that WLBT might continue its improper conduct.

We agree that a history of programming misconduct of the kind alleged would preclude, as a matter of law, the required finding that renewal of the license would serve the public interest. It is important to bear in mind, moreover, that although in granting an initial license the Commission must of necessity engage in some degree of forecasting future performance, in a renewal proceeding past performance is its best criterion. When past performance is in conflict with the public interest, a very heavy burden rests on the renewal applicant to show how a renewal can be reconciled with the public interest. Like public officials charged with a public trust, a renewal applicant, as we noted in our discussion of standing, must literally "run on his record."

The Commission in effect sought to justify its grant of the one-year license, in the face of accepted facts irreconcilable with a public interest finding, on the ground that as a matter of policy the immediate need warranted the risks involved, and that the "strict conditions" it imposed on the grant would improve *future* operations. However the conditions which the Commission made explicit in the one-year license are implicit in every grant. The Commission's opinion reveals how it labored to justify the result it thought was dictated by the urgency of the situation.[27] The majority considered the question of setting the

---

[25] The Commission also argues that Appellants do not have standing in this Court as persons aggrieved or adversely affected under 66 Stat. 718 (1952), as amended, 47 U.S.C. § 402(b) (1964), because all their allegations were accepted as true. However, denial of the relief they sought rendered them persons aggrieved.

[26] In the 1959 renewal proceedings the Commission conceded that WLBT's misconduct then shown would preclude a grant except that there were only "isolated instances."

[27] "24. The discussion in B and C, above, establishes that serious issues are presented whether the licensee's operations have fully met the public interest standard. Indeed, it is a close question whether to designate for hearing these applications for renewal of license. In making its judgment, the Commission has taken into account that this particular area is entering a critical period in race relations, and that the broadcast stations, such as here involved, can make a most worthwhile contribution to the resolution of problems arising in this respect. That contribution is needed now − and should not be put off for the future. We believe that the licensee, operating in strict accordance with the representations made and other conditions specified herein, can make that needed contribution, and thus that its renewal would be in the public interest.

25. But we cannot stress too strongly that the licensee must operate in complete conformity with its representations and the conditions laid down. In the last *two* renewal periods, questions have been raised whether the licensee has complied with the requirements of the fairness doctrine; in the last renewal period, substantial public interest questions have been raised by the petition filed by most responsible community leaders.

application for hearing a "close" one; Chairman Henry and Commissioner Cox would have granted a hearing to Appellants as a matter of right.

The Commission's "policy" decision is not a reflection of some long standing or accepted proposition but represents an *ad hoc* determination in the context of Jackson's contemporary problem. Granted the basis for a Commission "policy" recognizing the value of properly run broadcast facilities to the resolution of community problems, if indeed this truism rises to the level of a policy, it is a determination valid in the abstract but calling for explanation in its application.

Assuming *arguendo* that the Commission's acceptance of Appellants' allegations would satisfy one ground for dispensing with a hearing, *i.e.*, absence of a question of fact, Section 309(e) also commands that in order to avoid a hearing the Commission must make an affirmative finding that renewal will serve the public interest. Yet the only finding on this crucial factor is a qualified statement that the public interest would be served, provided WLBT thereafter complied strictly with the specified conditions. Not surprisingly, having asserted that it accepted Petitioners' allegations, the Commission thus considered itself unable to make a categorical determination that on WLBT's record of performance it was an appropriate entity to receive the license. It found only that *if* WLBT changed its ways, something which the Commission did not and, of course, could not guarantee, the licensing would be proper. The statutory public interest finding cannot be inferred from a statement of the obvious truth that a properly operated station will serve the public interest.

We view as particularly significant the Commission's summary:

We are granting a renewal of license, so that the licensee can demonstrate and carry out its stated willingness to serve fully and fairly the needs and interests of its entire area — so that it can, in short, meet and resolve the questions raised.

The only "stated willingness to serve fully and fairly" which we can glean from the record is WLBT's protestation that it had always fully performed its public obligations. As we read it the Commission's statement is a strained and strange substitute for a public interest finding.

We recognize that the Commission was confronted with a difficult problem and difficult choices, but it would perhaps not go too far to say it elected to post the Wolf to guard the Sheep in the hope that the Wolf would mend his ways because some protection was needed at once and none but the Wolf was handy. This is not a case, however, where the Wolf had either promised or demonstrated any capacity and willingness to change, for WLBT had stoutly

---

We are granting a renewal of license, so that the licensee can demonstrate and carry out its stated willingness to serve fully and fairly the needs and interests of its entire area — so that it can, in short, meet and resolve the questions raised. Further, in line with the basic policy determination set out in par. 24, the licensee's efforts in this respect must be made now, and continue throughout the license period."

denied Appellants' charges of programming misconduct and violations.[28] In these circumstances a pious hope on the Commission's part for better things from WLBT is not a substitute for evidence and findings. *Cf.* Interstate Broadcasting Co. v. FCC, 116 U.S. App. D.C. 327, 323 F. 2d 797 (1963).

Even if the embodiment of the Commission's hope be conceded *arguendo* to be a finding, there was not sufficient evidence in the record to justify a "policy determination" that the need for a properly run station in Jackson was so pressing as to justify the risk that WLBT might well continue with an inadequate performance. The issues which should have been considered could be resolved only in an evidentiary hearing in which all aspects of its qualifications and performance could be explored.

It is open to question whether the public interest would not be as well, if not better served with one TV outlet acutely conscious that adherence to the Fairness Doctrine is a *sine qua non* of every licensee. Even putting aside the salutary warning effect of a license denial, there are other reasons why one station in Jackson might be better than two for an interim period. For instance, in a letter to the Commission, Appellant Smith alleged that the other television station in Jackson had agreed to sell him time only if WLBT did so.[29] It is arguable that the pressures on the other station might be reduced if WLBT were in other hands — or off the air. The need which the Commission thought urgent might well be satisfied by refusing to renew the license of WLBT and opening the channel to new applicants under the special temporary authorization procedures available to the Commission on the theory that another, and better suited, operator could be found to broadcast on the channel with brief, if any, interruption of service. The Commission's opinion reflects no consideration of these or other alternatives.

We hold that the grant of a renewal of WLBT's license for one year was erroneous. The Commission is directed to conduct hearings on WLBT's renewal application, allowing public intervention pursuant to this holding. Since the Commission has already decided that Appellants are responsible representatives of the listening public of the Jackson area, we see no obstacle to a prompt determination granting standing to Appellants or some of them. Whether WLBT should be able to benefit from a showing of good performance, if such is the case, since June 1965 we do not undertake to decide. The Commission has had no occasion to pass on this issue and we therefore refrain from doing so.[30]

---

[28]The Commission should have discretion to experiment and even to take calculated risks on renewals where a licensee confesses the error of its ways; this is not such a case.

[29]Letter to Commission from Rev. Robert L. T. Smith, received Jan. 17, 1962, Record, p. 1.

[30]In light of our holding, the special form of license granted here is not unlike a special temporary authorization. Under the Commission's position in Community Broadcasting Co., Inc. v. FCC, 107 U.S. App. D.C. 95, 274 F. 2d 753 (1960), it may be that the Commission will conclude that good performance under this conditional or probationary license should not weigh in favor of WLBT.

The record is remanded to the Commission for further proceedings consistent with this opinion; jurisdiction is retained in this court.

Reversed and remanded.

2

UNITED CHURCH OF CHRIST II

**Office of Communication of the United Church of Christ v.
Federal Communications Commission***
      425 F.2d 543 (D.C. Cir.)
      June 20, 1969

Following *UCC I*, the FCC went ahead with the hearing mandated by the court, placing the major burden of proof on the public intervenors rather than on the renewal applicant. The Commission affirmed the Hearing Examiner's tendency to give little weight or credence to the matters revealed by the intervenors during the hearing, and renewed WLBT's license.

    UCC II reverses the FCC in terms that cannot be mistaken; this decision constitutes as stern a rebuke to the Commission as any court has administered. That this was Judge Burger's last opinion for the Court of Appeals before he assumed the post of Chief Justice of the United States Supreme Court hardly served to lessen the sting.

      Burger, Circuit Judge:

This case returns to the Court again after hearings held pursuant to an earlier opinion of this Court in which we directed that intervenors representing segments of the licensee's listening public were to be permitted to intervene and participate.[1] No additional intervenors thereafter sought to take part in the Commission proceedings.[2]

---

*Reprinted with the permission of West Publishing Company © 1970.

[1] Office of Communication of the United Church of Christ v. FCC, 123 U.S. App. D.C. 328, 359 F. 2d 994 (1966).

[2] The fact that no additional intervenors brought their case to the Commission substantiates our earlier observation that:

      The fears of regulatory agencies that their process will be inundated by expansion of standing criteria are rarely borne out. Always a restraining factor is the expense of

The action of this Court in remanding for hearings with listening-public intervenors taking part followed the Commission's 1965 action which granted the licensee a "probationary" one year license.[3] This unusual Commission action underscored that in the proceedings involving the application for a three-year renewal (from 1964 to 1967) the Commission had not been able to conclude that the licensee met the burden of showing that renewal of its license for three years was in the public interest.

Following various complaints filed with it, in 1962 the Commission had initiated its own field investigation into the programming operations of certain Mississippi broadcast stations, including WLBT. This investigation precipitated a July 25, 1963, letter from the Commission requesting the licensee's comments on listed questions as to its programming policies and set forth some of the specific findings of the field investigation on these matters. The Commission's consideration of WLBT's reply was pending when the licensee filed an application for renewal of its license for the June 1, 1964 to June 1, 1967 period.

In reviewing these responses prior to its award of the one-year probationary grant, the Commission noted, *inter alia*:

The question is rather whether the licensee complied with the requirements of the fairness doctrine — i.e., whether, having presented one side of a controversial issue of public importance, it sought affirmatively to encourage and implement the presentation of contrasting viewpoints. *The licensee's response is not fully satisfactory in this respect.*

*　　　*　　　*

In short, when a fairness complaint is made, a licensee relying upon network programs to balance local broadcasts has the burden of demonstrating that the network shows carried by it did present contrasting viewpoints to those expressed in the local broadcasts. *That showing has not been made here.*

Lamar Life Broadcasting Co., *supra* note 3 at 1146, 1147-1148 (emphasis added).

Moreover, in setting forth the specific conditions attached to its one-year probationary award, the Commission provided:

(iv) *That the licensee immediately cease discriminatory programming patterns.* Thus, it is up to the licensee to make the programming judgment

---

participation in the administrative process, an economic reality which will operate to limit the number of those who will seek participation; legal and related expenses of administrative proceedings are such that even those with large economic interests find the cost burdensome. Moreover, the listening public seeking intervention in a license renewal proceeding cannot attract lawyers to represent their cause by the prospect of lucrative contingent fees, as can be done, for example, in rate cases.

Church of Christ, *supra* note 1 at 340, 359 F. 2d at 1006.

[3] Lamar Life Broadcasting Co., 38 F.C.C. 1143 (1965).

whether or not to have a daily 1-minute devotional program at noon, in which appearances are rotated among the area churches in the area on the basis of race. Such a practice is obviously inconsistent with the public interest; indeed, we note that the licensee does not try to defend it.

Id. at 1154 (emphasis added).

In discussing the Commission's action we noted that the Commission had found that the licensee's prior conduct prevented the grant of a full term license.[4]

When the matter was again before the Commission on our remand, therefore, it was in a posture that the licensee had yet to demonstrate that it was in the public interest for the license to be renewed. This was a less favorable posture for the licensee than would have been the case absent the "probationary license" grant. This is important, but its significance seems to have eluded the hearing Examiner and the Commission as well; we emphasize this now to remove any lingering doubts as to our evaluation of a "probationary" grant — a grant which by its nature assumes that the renewal-licensee has been unable to persuade the Commission that it is presently in the public interest to grant a three-year renewal. That the Examiner failed to grasp this fact is reflected throughout his report and noticeably in his statement that

the evidentiary hearing . . . presented [Appellants] ample and sufficient opportunity to come forward and *sustain their serious allegations* that they had made against the applicant. They have woefully failed to do so . . .

Lamar Life Broadcasting Co., 14 F.C.C. 2d 495, 549 (1967) (emphasis added).

Since the Commission itself had previously found that some of these "serious allegations" were sufficient to withhold the grant of the traditional three-year license, the Examiner's approach, and its subsequent adoption by the Commission, signifies an attitude considerably at odds with the Commission's earlier action in refusing a three-year license. The Examiner seems to have regarded Appellants as "plaintiffs" and the licensee as "defendant," with burdens of proof allocated accordingly. This tack, though possibly fostered by the Commission's own action,[5] was a grave misreading of our holding on this

---

[4] At that time we observed:

> The Commission in this Court argues that it accepted all Appellant's allegations of WLBT's misconduct and that for this reason no hearing was necessary. Yet the Commission recognized that WLBT's past behavior, as described by Appellants, would preclude the statutory finding of public interest necessary for license renewal; hence its grant of the one-year license on the policy ground that there was an urgent need at the time for a properly run station in Jackson must have been predicated on a belief that the need was so great as to warrant the risk that WLBT might continue its improper conduct.

Church of Christ, *supra* note 1 at 341, 359 F. 2d at 1007.

[5] In setting the hearing following our remand, the Commission, on May 26, 1966, designated the hearing issues to be:

> (a) Whether station WLBT has afforded reasonable opportunity for the discussion of conflicting views on issues of public importance;

question.[6] We did not intend that intervenors representing a public interest be treated as interlopers. Rather, if analogues can be useful, a "Public Intervenor" who is seeking no license or private right is, in this context, more nearly like a complaining witness who presents evidence to police or a prosecutor whose duty it is to conduct an affirmative and objective investigation of all the facts and to pursue his prosecutorial or regulatory function if there is probable cause to believe a violation has occurred.

This was all the more true here because prior to the efforts of the actively participating intervenors, the Commission itself had long since found the licensee wanting.[7] It was not the correct role of the Examiner or the Commission to sit back and simply provide a forum for the intervenors; the Commission's duties did not end by allowing Appellants to intervene; its duties began at that stage.

(b) Whether station WLBT has afforded reasonable opportunity for the use of its broadcasting facilities by the significant groups comprising the community of its service area;

(c) Whether station WLBT has acted in good faith with respect to the presentation of programs dealing with the issue of racial discrimination, and, particularly, whether it has misrepresented to the public or the Commission with respect to the presentation of such programming.

(d) Whether in light of all the evidence a grant of the application for renewal of license of Station WLBT would serve the public interest, convenience, or necessity.
In the designation Order, the Commission explained:
10. Pursuant to the rule announced in *D & E Broadcasting Company,* 1 FCC 2d 78 (1965), and in accordance with the statutory mandate of Section 309(e), the burden of proof as to issues (a) and (b) shall be upon the intervenors, the burden of proof as to issue (c) shall be upon the Broadcast Bureau, and the burden of proof as to issue (d) shall be upon the applicant.
Lamar Life Broadcasting Co., 3 F.C.C.2d 784 (1966).

[6]Prior to the initiation of the evidentiary hearing we denied Appellants' motion for clarification of our earlier opinion; however, in a memorandum statement accompanying the denial we noted:
In our view it should not be necessary, and certainly is not desirable, for this court to supervise the details of conduct of hearings before the Commission by the device of periodic revision of the language used in opinions. Only the most extraordinary circumstances would warrant our intervention by this means; such circumstances do not exist here inasmuch as, in respect of paragraphs 9 and 10, respectively, of the Commission's order released May 25, 1966, *we assume that* (1) the Commission's concept of evidence of past performance which, in its words, "is not unduly remote in time" is commensurate with what was, in our words, "a history of programming misconduct of the kind alleged" occasioning our remand, and (2) *the Commission's reference to "the burden of proof" in respect of issues (a), (b), and (c) is intended to mean only the burden of going forward with evidence in the first instance.*
Church of Christ, No. 19,409 (D.C. Cir., Filed November 18, 1966) (emphasis added).

[7]In connection with WLBT's 1959 renewal applications, the Commission had found specific failures to comply with the demands of the Fairness Doctrine, but did not withhold a renewal on the grounds that they were "isolated violations." See Lamar Life Broadcasting Co., *supra* note 3 at 1145.

A curious neutrality-in-favor-of-the-licensee seems to have guided the Examiner in his conduct of the evidentiary hearing. An example of this is found in his reaction to evidence of a monitoring study conducted by Appellants for about one week in 1964 and which was the subject of two days of testimony at the hearing. The Examiner's conclusion was that the play-back had "virtually no meaning for the simple reason that it was not . . . fair and equitable. [It] is worthless and therefore *completely discounted* for any consideration by the hearing examiner." 14 F.C.C. 2d at 543 (emphasis added). In context or out, this reaction is difficult to comprehend.[8] The Commission has often complained — and no doubt justifiably so — that it cannot monitor licensees in any

---

[8]The following excerpts from the hearing transcript illustrate the licensee's success in placing an unrealistic burden on the Intervenors. Mrs. Elizabeth Ewing, who prepared the monitoring study exhibits on behalf of Appellants, was the witness:

Q.   Could you tell from the tape whether the news of, well say, Dick Sanders, whether he was reading from United Press International wirecopy? Do you know what that is?

A.   Yes.

Q.   Could you tell whether he was reading from UPI wirecopy or from a transcript that he, himself, had prepared?

A.   No.

Q.   Did you make any identifications where the source of information was coming from?

A.   No.

*   *   *

Q.   Have you ever lived in Jackson, Mississippi?

A.   No, I have not.

Q.   Did you receive any instructions as to what would be of interest to the people in Jackson, Mississippi?

A.   No.

Q.   Did you study any documents or books or papers to find out what would be of interest to the people in Jackson, Mississippi?

A.   No.

Q.   Did you read Jackson newspapers during this period in March 1964?

A.   No.

*   *   *

Q.   Do you know whether or not Dick Sanders was quoting a press release from the Department of Justice?

A.   No.

Q.   Do you know whether he was quoting directly from the wire service?

A.   No, I don't.

Joint Appendix 172, 183-184, 187 [hereinafter J.A.].

This witness had already produced evidence of the contents of the monitored broadcasts, yet she was pursued to ascertain the *source* of these programs — the type of information particularly in the control and at the disposal of a broadcast licensee. In evaluating Mrs. Ewing's testimony, the Examiner pursued the same tack, discrediting the study and the testimonial evidence to support it without ever placing on the licensee the affirmative burden of producing evidence to establish either the true source of the programming materials or, as compared to that of Mrs. Ewing, its own sensitivity to the needs and interests of portions of its listening audience.

meaningful way; here a 7-day monitoring, made at no public expense, was presented by a public interest intervenor and was dismissed as "worthless" by the Commission.

Concerning the cutting off of a network program relied on by Intervenors as showing violations of the Fairness Doctrine the Examiner found: "There is not one iota of evidence in the record that supports any such allegation." Yet in the transcript of proceedings we find testimony identifying the program which was admittedly cut off. The record shows the following:

Q.   Did you recognize the lunch counter?

A.   I recognized the Woolworth Counter where the demonstration occurred here and the picture immediately disappeared. I picked up the telephone and immediately called WLBT —

Q.   With whom did you speak?

A.   The man refused to identify himself. I did not identify myself. I said, "Did you cut that off because that showed those Negroes sitting in at Woolworth's in Jackson?" *The man said, "Yes."*

Mr. George: *I object. I may be anticipating but I will object to any statement as to the reply.*

Presiding Examiner: *That is correct. We will sustain that portion of it. You can't quote some undisclosed person.*

The portion of the answer is stricken where he was quoting some unidentified person which is sheer hearsay.[9]

J.A. 720-21 (emphasis added).

On allegations that at least two of the licensee's commentators used disparaging terms with reference to Negroes there was testimony of listeners who said they heard these episodes; in his initial decision the Examiner noted that "[a]t least three of the [Appellants'] witnesses" so testified. Nevertheless, the Examiner chose to belittle this evidence:

Because of the conflicting testimony respecting Ellis [one of WLBT's commentators], there is no finding made as whether he did nor did not use the word "nigger" or "negra." But the evidence is undisputed that Alon Bee did use the expressions "negra" or "nigger" at some indefinite time in the past while broadcasting over station WLBT. *A glaring weakness of the intervenors' evidence here is that, as in many of their allegations, they did not pinpoint specific times when certain events supposedly occurred, thereby unfairly depriving the applicant of an opportunity properly to rebut such allegations.*

[9]Conceivably a licensee might be justified, in some circumstances, to decline to carry a program it regarded as inflammatory because of current tensions; if placed on that basis and reasonable exercise of such discretion presumably would be sustained by the Commission.

14 F.C.C. 2d at 510 (emphasis added).

It is not our function to determine whether this would have supported a finding that the licensee had violated the Fairness Doctrine but the Examiner's erroneous concept of the burden of proof shows a failure to grasp the distinction between "allegations" and testimonial evidence, and prevented the development of a satisfactory record.

The infinite potential of broadcasting to influence American life renders somewhat irrelevant the semantics of whether broadcasting is or is not to be described as a public utility. By whatever name or classification, broadcasters are temporary permittees — fiduciaries — of a great public resource and they must meet the highest standards which are embraced in the public interest concept. The Fairness Doctrine plays a very large role in assuring that the public resource granted to licensees at no cost will be used in the public interest. In short, we do not determine how the factors we have discussed should have been weighed by the Commission but only that they had some probative value and should have been considered. To borrow a phrase from the Examiner, his response manifests a "glaring weakness" in his grasp of the function and purpose of the hearing and the public duties of the Commission.

We need not continue recitals from the record or examples of similar situations which shed light on the nature of the hearings; in our view the entire hearing was permeated by similar treatment of the efforts of the intervenors, and the pervasive impatience — if not hostility — of the Examiner is a constant factor which made fair and impartial consideration impossible. The Commission and the Examiners have an affirmative duty to assist in the development of a meaningful record which can serve as the basis for the evaluation of the licensee's performance of his duty to serve the public interest. The Public Intervenors, who were performing a public service under a mandate of this court, were entitled to a more hospitable reception in the performance of that function. As we view the record the Examiner tended to impede the exploration of the very issues which we would reasonably expect the Commission itself would have initiated; an ally was regarded as an opponent.

The Commission, except as modified on some minor points, adopted the Examiner's Initial Decision: "[W]e are in agreement with the examiner's conclusions that the intervenors failed to corroborate or substantiate virtually all of their allegations upon which the hearing was predicated . . ." Lamar Life Broadcasting Co., 14 F.C.C. 2d 431, 433 (1968). In a footnote to this resolution, the Commission notes:

8. Since our decision is based on the preponderance of evidence adduced at the hearing, we are of the opinion that the intervenors' argument that they only had the burden of going forward with evidence in the first instance on hearing issues (a) and (b), that the Broadcast Bureau only had the burden of going forward on issue (c), and that the station had the actual burden of proof on those issues, is mooted.

In this respect, we think it important to set forth what the trial Examiner understood the burdens of proof to be, for his understanding on this point profoundly affected his crediting or dismissing what was in essence *testimonial evidence* although he constantly characterized the evidence as "allegations":

> Mr. Moore [Counsel for appellants]:   . . . I just want to state for the record that as I understand the burden of proof, the burden of proof on all issues is on the station and the only burden on the applicant [sic; should be intervenors] and the Bureau is the burden of going forward.
>
> That is my understanding of the interpretation which has been placed on the Commission's order by the Court of Appeals.
>
> Presiding Examiner: No, that is not my interpretation. My interpretation is, by the Commission action, *is that the burden of proof is primarily upon the intervenors* on issues A and B, on the Broadcast Bureau on C and on the applicant on D, and you can't by waving the magic wand, shift the burden of proof to this applicant or to the Bureau.

J.A. 304-305 (emphasis added).
That this concept of the allocation of the burden of proof permeated the Commission's final resolution can be seen in its constant references to the Public Intervenor's failure to "prove" its "charges." As the Commission noted in closing: "We only conclude that the intervenors have failed to prove their charges and that the preponderance of the evidence before us establishes that WLBT has afforded reasonable opportunity for the use of its facilities by the significant community groups comprising its service area." 14 F.C.C. 2d at 437-438. Once again we see the pervasiveness of the original error in confusing mere "allegations" and testimonial evidence — evidence which if not contradicted by the licensee's evidence, or on its face incredible, was entitled to carry the day in terms of establishing the point to which it was directed.

The Examiner and the Commission appear to have overlooked the 1965 Memorandum Opinion and Order of the Commission which contains much to the contrary to its present position;[10] moreover, the practical effect of the Commission's action was to place on the Public Intervenors the entire burden of showing that the licensee was not qualified to be granted a renewal. The Examiner and the Commission exhibited at best a reluctant tolerance of this court's mandate[11] and at worst a profound hostility to the participation of the Public Intervenors and their efforts.[12]

---

[10] *See* note 4 *supra.*

[11] *See* note 6 *supra.*

[12] Two members of the Commission seemed to read the record much as we read it now. In a further statement filed by Commissioners Cox and Johnson in response to the majority's "further statement" in response to the original dissent, the dissenting Commissioners noted:
   We remain perplexed by our colleagues' interpretation of the burden of proof issue, notwithstanding their attempt to further elucidate this problem in the further statement. As we noted in our dissenting opinion, the court of appeals clearly expressed its expectation that the Commission would resolve the problem

The record now before us leaves us with a profound concern over the entire handling of this case following the remand to the Commission. The impatience with the Public Intervenors, the hostility toward their efforts to satisfy a surprisingly strict standard of proof, plain errors in rulings and findings lead us, albeit reluctantly, to the conclusion that it will serve no useful purpose to ask the Commission to reconsider the Examiner's actions and its own Decision and Order under a correct allocation of the burden of proof. The administrative conduct reflected in this record is beyond repair.

The Commission itself, with more specific documentation of the licensee's shortcomings than it had in 1965 has now found virtues in the licensee which it was unable to perceive in 1965 and now finds the grant of a full three-year license to be in the public interest.

We are compelled to hold, on the whole record, that the Commission's conclusion is not supported by substantial evidence. For this reason the grant of a license must be vacated forthwith and the Commission is directed to invite applications to be filed for the license. We do refrain, however, from holding that the licensee be declared disqualified from filing a new application; the conduct of the hearing was not primarily the licensee's responsibility, although as the applicant it had the burden of proof. Moreover, the Commission necessarily did not address itself to the precise question of WLBT's qualifications to be an applicant in the new proceeding now ordered, and we hesitate to pass on this subject not considered by the Commission.

The Commission is directed to consider a plan for interim operation pending completion of its hearings; if it finds it in the public interest to permit the present licensee to carry on interim operations that alternative is available. The Commission is free to consider whether net earnings of the licensee should be impounded by the Commission pending final disposition of this license application. [13]

Reversed and remanded for further proceedings in accordance with this opinion.

---

by placing upon petitioners [Public Interest Intervenors] "only the burden of going forward with evidence in the first instance." By the strictures of the Communications Act of 1934, it is the licensee who is obligated to prove that renewal of his license is in the public interest, convenience, or necessity.

Our colleagues maintain that, "neither the burden of going forward with the evidence nor the burden of nonpersuasion [is] ... discharged by the party on whom it may fall by the simple making of charges and/or allegations." Needless to say, we have not suggested that "simple charges and/or allegations" are adequate. However, under their construction, it almost seems that presumptions favoring the licensee arise as to each of the issues contained in the pleadings; and, thus, as to the ultimate issue of public interest. This rule of procedure is plainly unjust and flatly contradictory of the court's memorandum respecting the burden of proof questions, a fact noted in our dissent and not disputed by the further statement. Lamar Life Broadcasting Co., 14 F.C.C. 2d 431, 487 (1968).

[13]We are aware that in the ordinary course the license granted by the Commission would expire on June 1, 1970.

3

THE CITIZENS COMMUNICATIONS

CENTER CASE

Citizens Communications Center et al. v.
Federal Communications Commission and United States of America*
447 F.2d 1201 (D.C. Cir.)
June 11, 1971

The two *United Church of Christ* decisions coupled with the
FCC's surprising application of the 1965 *Comparative Broadcast
Hearings* criteria to WHDH-TV (a somewhat atypical licensee
seeking renewal) caused broadcasters to experience alarm
approaching panic proportions during 1969. Fearful that a rash of
license challengers (or "strike applicants") would force the FCC
to favor new applicants over incumbent licensees with absentee
ownership and other media holdings, the broadcasting industry
urged Congress to enact protective legislation. S. 2004 (the
"Pastore bill") was never passed, and the FCC issued a renewal
policy statement in 1970 that the industry found reassuring.

But citizens groups and the Court of Appeals found
otherwise. In overturning the Commission's policy statement,
Judge Wright's decision centers on due process in administrative
proceedings and focuses attention on the distinction to be made
by the FCC between "substantial" and "superior" licensee
performance in cases of contested renewals. That license challengers are not to be denied their legal rights before the
Commission is amply demonstrated in *Citizens Communications
Center.*

*Reprinted with the permission of West Publishing Company ©1972.

665

J. Skelly Wright, Circuit Judge:

Appellants and petitioners[1] in these consolidated cases[2] challenge the legality of the "Policy Statement on Comparative Hearings Involving Regular Renewal Applicants," 22 F.C.C. 2d 424, released by the Federal Communications Commission on January 15, 1970, and by its terms made applicable to pending proceedings. Briefly stated, the disputed Commission policy is that, in a hearing between an incumbent applying for renewal of his radio or television license and a mutually exclusive applicant, the incumbent shall obtain a controlling preference by demonstrating substantial past performance without serious deficiencies.[3] Thus if the incumbent prevails on the threshold issue of

---

[1] Hereinafter "petitioners."

[2] Case No. 24,471 is brought by the Citizens Communications Center (CCC) and Black Efforts for Soul in Television (BEST), two nonprofit organizations organized "for the purposes of improving radio and TV service, of promoting the responsiveness of broadcast media to their local communities, of improving the position of minority groups in media ownership, access and coverage, and of generally presenting a public voice in proceedings before the FCC." They have appeared and are appearing in numerous proceedings before the Commission and in other appeals in this court from Commission rulings. These parties filed a petition pursuant to 47 U.S.C. § 402(a) and 28 U.S.C. § 2342 seeking review of (1) the Commission's Policy Statement Concerning Comparative Hearings Involving Regular Renewal Applicants, 22 F.C.C. 2d 424 (1970); (2) a memorandum opinion and order by the Commission dismissing a request of CCC and BEST that it institute rule making proceedings to codify standards for all comparative proceedings, 21 F.C.C. 2d 355 (1970); and (3) a memorandum opinion and order denying reconsideration of the 1970 Policy Statement and refusing to institute rule making proceedings, 24 F.C.C. 2d 383 (1970).

Case No. 24,491 is a petition for review filed by Hampton Roads Television Corporation and Community Broadcasting of Boston, Inc., two applicants for television channels who have filed in competition with renewal applicants in Norfolk, Virginia and Boston, Massachusetts. They also seek review pursuant to 47 U.S.C. § 402(a) and 28 U.S.C. § 2342 of the Commission's memorandum opinion and order denying reconsideration of the 1970 Policy Statement and refusing to institute rule making proceedings.

Case No. 24,221 is an appeal filed pursuant to 28 U.S.C. § 1291 from an order of the United States District Court for the District of Columbia dismissing a complaint for permanent and preliminary injunction, Civil Action No. 42-70, for lack of jurisdiction. In their complaint filed January 7, 1970, CCC and BEST sought to enjoin the chairman and members of the Commission from "promulgating any policy, rule or interpretation or making any other change" in the standards applicable to comparative broadcast license renewal proceedings without first giving all interested parties notice and an opportunity to be heard pursuant to § 4 of the Administrative Procedure Act, 5 U.S.C. § 553. A temporary restraining order was denied on January 7, 1970, and following a suggestion of lack of jurisdiction made by the Commission, the District Court on January 23, 1970 dismissed the action. In light of our disposition of Cases 24,471 and 24,491, *supra*, this case is moot.

RKO General, Inc. and WTAR Radio TV Corporation have both intervened in this controversy and have filed briefs defending the Policy Statement and subsequent Commission actions.

[3] The Policy Statement declares:

"... Promotion of [the public interest], with respect to competing challenges to renewal applicants, calls for the balancing of two obvious considerations. The first is that the public receive the benefits of the statutory spur inherent in the fact that there

the substantiality of his past record, all other applications are to be dismissed without a hearing on their own merits.

Petitioners contend that this policy is unlawful under Section 309(e) of the Communications Act of 1934[4] and the doctrine of Ashbacker Radio Corp. v. F.C.C., 326 U.S. 327, 66 S.Ct. 148, 90 L.Ed. 108 (1945). The 1970 Policy Statement is also attacked by petitioners on grounds that it was adopted in disregard of the Administrative Procedure Act and that it restricts and chills the exercise of rights protected by the First Amendment.

Respondents urge the court to refrain from considering these arguments at this time because the 1970 Policy Statement is neither a final order nor yet ripe for review. In the alternative, respondents take the position that the Policy Statement is a lawful exercise of the Commission's authority.

---

can be a challenge, and indeed, where the public interest so requires, that the new applicant be preferred. The second is that the comparative hearing policy in this area must not undermine predictability and stability of broadcast operation.

*   *   *

"We believe that these two considerations call for the following policy – namely, that if the applicant for renewal of license shows in a hearing with a competing applicant that its program service during the preceding license term has been substantially attuned to meeting the needs and interests of its area, and that the operation of the station has not otherwise been characterized by serious deficiencies, he will be preferred over the newcomer and his application for renewal will be granted. His operation is not based merely upon promises to serve solidly the public interest. He has done so. Since the basic purpose of the act – substantial service to the public – is being met, it follows that the considerations of predictability and stability, which also contribute vitally to that basic purpose, call for renewal."

22 F.C.C. 2d at 424-425. (Footnote omitted.)

[4] 47 U.S.C. § 309. Section 309 was amended in 1952, 1960 and 1964. As summarized in a Staff Study for the Special Subcommittee on Investigations of the Committee on Interstate and Foreign Commerce. House of Representatives, 91st Cong., 2d Sess., November 1970 (hereinafter cited as Staff Study), "The Act's Legislative History reveals that the amendments dealt primarily with procedure and did not limit the hearing right of Section 309(a) discussed in Ashbacker. The 1952 amendment moved the hearing provision from subsection (a) to subsection (b). The 1960 amendment moved it to subsection (e)." Subsection (e) of § 309 today reads in pertinent part as follows:

"If, in the case of any application to which subsection (a) of this section applies, . . . the Commission for any reason is unable to make the finding specified in such subsection, it shall formally designate the application for hearing on the ground or reasons then obtaining . . . Any hearing subsequently held upon such application shall be a full hearing in which the applicant and all other parties in interest shall be permitted to participate . . ."

Subsection (a) of § 309 reads:

"Subject to the provisions of this section, the Commission shall determine, in the case of each application filed with it to which section 308 of this title applies, whether the public interest, convenience, and necessity will be served by the granting of such application, and, if the Commission, upon examination of such application and upon consideration of such other matters as the Commission may officially notice, shall find that public interest, convenience, and necessity would be served by the granting thereof, it shall grant such application."

We find that the judicial review sought by petitioners is appropriate at this time. Without reaching petitioners' other grounds for complaint,[5] we hold that the 1970 Policy Statement violates the Federal Communications Act of 1934, as interpreted by both the Supreme Court and this court.

I

Petitioners argue that the 1970 Policy Statement is "final" in the primary sense of the term because no further proceedings concerning the Policy Statement are

[5]Petitioners' complaint charging a violation of the APA is based on the Commission's failure to proceed by rule making rather than by issuing a policy statement. One of the purposes of rule making procedures, of course, is to make an administrative agency more aware of the wishes of the public on whose behalf it must regulate. Although it is not necessary for this court, in disposing of this case, to decide whether the Commission violated the letter of the APA in issuing the 1970 Policy Statement without first holding a public hearing, a serious question does arise as to the propriety of the Commission's action.

In order to avoid conflict with Ashbacker Radio Corp. v. F.C.C., 326 U.S. 327, 66 S.Ct. 148, 90 L.Ed. 108 (1945), the Commission characterizes *Ashbacker* as dealing only with "procedure," and distinguishes the Policy Statement as being in effect substantive. Then, caught between Scylla and Charybdis, the Commission turns around and calls the Policy Statement "procedural rather than . . . substantive" in order to avoid conflict with § 4 of the APA. The APA requires the Commission to follow certain procedures (notification, opportunity to file comments, etc.) in all cases of administrative "rule making." Section 2(c) of the APA, 5 U.S.C. § 551(4), defines a "rule" as "the whole or a part of an agency statement of general or particular applicability and future effect designed to implement, interpret, or prescribe law or policy or describing the organization, procedure, or practice requirements of an agency." Section 4(a) of the APA, 5 U.S.C. § 553(a) (3) (A), however, exempts from rule making "interpretative rules, general statements of policy, or rules of agency organization, procedure, or practice." The Commission argues that the January 15, 1970 Policy Statement is an exempted "general statement of policy" under § 4(a) and that it did not therefore have to be developed under the procedural safeguards described in § 4. As was said in Columbia Broadcasting System v. United States, 316 U.S. 407, 416, 62 S.Ct. 1194, 86 L.Ed. 1563 (1942), however, it is not the label placed upon such procedures by the Commission which dictates the procedures to be followed, but rather "the substance of what the Commission has purported to do and has done which is decisive." The issue here turns on whether the January 15, 1970 Policy Statement effected a substantive change in the Commission's comparative renewal standards. And the Commission seems to have decided this issue, *sub silentio* at least, when it

"reimbursed Voice of Los Angeles, Inc., for costs incurred during the initial portions of a comparative challenge to the license of KNBC, Los Angeles, essentially on the ground that [the Commission's] January 15, 1970 Policy Statement came as an unannounced surprise to Voice, and that given the change in policy it would be inequitable not to permit them to withdraw. National Broadcasting Co., Inc. (NBC), FCC 70-691 (Docket No. 18602) (released July 7, 1970). . . ."

In Re Petitions Filed by BEST, CCC, and Others for Rulemaking To Clarify Standards in all Comparative Broadcast Proceedings, 24 F.C.C. 2d 383, 388 (1970) (dissenting opinion of Commissioner Johnson). In any event, the Commission's suggestion that under the APA it can do without notice and hearing in a policy statement what Congress failed to do when the Pastore bill (*see* text . . . *infra*) died in the last Congress is, to say the least, remarkable.

contemplated by the Commission or provided for by the Commission's rules. Respondents' position is that neither the Policy Statement nor the order denying the petitions for reconsideration are final orders within the statutory meaning of 28 U.S.C. § 2342(1) and 47 U.S.C. § 402(a). They argue that the Policy Statement sets only general guidelines to be applied in future adjudicatory proceedings where applicable. We find it unnecessary to resolve this particular disagreement because, even if the Policy Statement is characterized as interlocutory, it is still reviewable at this time. Since the Policy Statement is alleged to deprive petitioners in No. 24,491 of their statutory right to a full comparative hearing under the *Ashbacker* doctrine, the Commission's action in issuing the Policy Statement is reviewable now. Chicago & Southern Air Lines, Inc. v. Waterman Steamship Corp., 333 U.S. 103, 113, 68 S.Ct. 431, 92 L.Ed. 568 (1948); Delta Air Lines v. C.A.B., 97 U.S. App. D.C. 46, 228 F. 2d 17 (1955). As this court stated in summarizing the holding of *Delta Air Lines* in a subsequent case, "when the Commission adopts a procedure which precludes a true comparative hearing of conflicting applications, review may be sought here without awaiting a grant of one of the applications." Midwestern Gas Transmission Co. v. F.P.C., 103 U.S. App. D.C. 360, 336, 258 F. 2d 660, 666 (1958).

Petitioners contend that the same line of cases holding an interlocutory order denying a party an *Ashbacker* hearing to be final for purposes of review necessarily supports the proposition that such an order is also ripe for review before completion of the contemplated hearing. Without deciding whether this proposition holds in every case, we agree that the Policy Statement is ripe for review under the test laid out in Abbott Laboratories v. Gardner, 387 U.S. 136, 87 S.Ct. 1507, 18 L.Ed. 2d 681 (1967). According to the Supreme Court in *Abbott Laboratories*, the ripeness of a controversy depends upon both "the fitness of the issues for judicial decision and the hardship to the parties of withholding court consideration." *Id.* at 149, 87 S.Ct. at 1515. The Policy Statement controversy is ripe under both halves of this test. Here the Policy Statement has been administratively considered and reconsidered by the Commission. The issues before us are "purely legal."[6] *Ibid.* Whether the Policy Statement denies a competing applicant the full comparative hearing to which he is entitled is strictly a matter of statutory interpretation involving a comparison of the hearing procedures spelled out in the Policy Statement with the requirements of 47 U.S.C. § 309(e) and *Ashbacker*. Likewise, the other issues raised by petitioners and enumerated in the introduction of this opinion are also purely legal and will not be focused or clarified by further proceedings in particular cases before the Commission.

[6]As this court stated in Environmental Defense Fund, Inc. v. Hardin, 138 U.S. App. D.C. 391, 396, 428 F. 2d 1093, 1098 (1970): "The doctrines of ripeness and finality are designed to prevent premature judicial intervention in the administrative process, before the administrative action has been fully considered, and before the legal dispute has been brought into focus."

Moreover, it would work a severe hardship on petitioners for the court to withhold consideration of their appeal. The substantial financial expense[7] to which Hampton Roads and Community Broadcasting will have been put if review of their alleged denial of procedural rights is delayed is a hardship which the court may properly take into account in finding this case ripe for review. *Abbott Laboratories, supra*, 387 U.S. at 153-154, 87 S.Ct. 1507; City of Chicago v. Atchison, Topeka & Santa Fe R. Co., 357 U.S. 77, 84, 78 S.Ct. 1063, 2 L.Ed. 2d 1174 (1958). Even more important perhaps is the deadening effect the Policy Statement has had since its institution upon renewal challenges generally. By depriving competing applicants of their right to a full comparative hearing on the merits of their own applications, and by severely limiting the importance of other comparative criteria, the Commission has made the cost of processing a competing application prohibitive when measured by the challengers' very minimal chances of success. That the Policy Statement is in this sense self-executing[8] and that it has in fact served to deter the filing of a single competing application for a television renewal in over a year[9] is perhaps the most compelling factor in the court's decision to review this dispute at this time.

II

In order to clarify not only the legal issues but also the related substantive policy considerations involved in these consolidated cases, the court will first attempt to put the present controversy in its historical context. The national effort at comprehensive regulation of broadcasting began in 1927 with the Federal Radio Act.[10] This Act was intended to insure that "the broadcasting privilege will not be a right of selfishness" but would rather "rest upon an assurance of public interest to be served."[11] To achieve this purpose the Act provided for expiration of licenses, and consequent renewal hearings, every three years.[12] At both initial and renewal licensing, applicants were to be tested by the basic standard of "public interest,

---

[7] The expense of preparing and presenting an application is substantial, rising to as much as $250,000 for a station in a top market area. Inside the FCC: The Renewal Branch, Television Age, August 25, 1969, at 72.

[8] *See* 3 K. Davis, Administrative Law Treatise § § 22.01 and 22.03 (1958).

[9] *See* text . . . *infra.*

[10] 44 Stat. 1162. The Radio Act of 1927, with its several amendments, was later included under Title III in the Communications Act of 1934. S. Rep. No. 681, 73rd Cong., 2d Sess., at 6 (1934). According to F.C.C. v. Pottsville Broadcasting Co., 309 U.S. 134, 137, 60 S.Ct. 437, 84 L.Ed. 656 (1940), the objectives of governmental regulation remained substantially the same.

[11] 67 Cong. Rec. 5479 (1926) (Representative White, House floor manager).

[12] Federal Radio Act, § 9, 44 Stat. 1166 (1926).

convenience, or necessity,"[13] which was defined by the Federal Radio Commission in 1928 as

a matter of *comparative* and not an absolute standard when applied to broadcasting stations. Since the number of channels is limited and the number of persons desiring to broadcast is far greater than can be accommodated, the Commission *must determine from among the applicants before it which of them will, if licensed, best serve the public.*[14]

Although the Federal Communications Act does not itself establish any specific licensing criteria, the Supreme Court has noted that "[s]ince the very inception of federal regulation [of] radio, comparative considerations as to the services to be rendered have governed the application of the standard of 'public interest, convenience, or necessity.'" National Broadcasting Co. v. United States, 319 U.S. 190, 217, 63 S.Ct. 997, 1009, 87 L.Ed. 1344 (1943). With the great expansion of the broadcast media after World War II, the Commission was under heavy pressure to develop specific criteria for choosing among competitors seeking licenses for the quickly diminishing number of unallocated frequencies. The criteria were developed through a series of comparative hearing decisions and were reviewed and given final statement in the Commission's 1965 Policy Statement on Comparative Broadcast Hearings, 1 F.C.C. 2d 393. The 1965 Policy Statement defines the purpose of the comparative hearing as choosing the applicant who will provide the "best practicable service to the public" and who will insure the "maximum diffusion of control of the media of mass communications." The basic criteria relating to the determination of which applicant will provide the best service to the public are listed as fulltime participation in station operation by owners, proposed program service, past broadcast record, efficient use of frequency, and character. Diversification of control of the media of mass communication is elevated in the 1965 Policy Statement to a factor of primary significance; and in an effort to resolve the inherent contradiction between the goal of diversification and its tradition of according an advantage to initial applicants with past broadcasting experience,

---

[13]*Id.* § § 9, 11, 44 Stat. 1166, 1167. The applicability of the public interest, convenience and necessity standard to license renewal was made explicit in the Communications Act of 1934, § 307(d), which amended § 11 of the 1927 Act by adding:

"but action of the Commission with reference to the granting of such application for the renewal of a license shall be limited to and governed by the same considerations and practice which affect the granting of original applications."

48 Stat. 1084 (1934). Perhaps to guard against the inference that an incumbent's past broadcast record could not be considered at all at renewal time, Congress in 1952 deleted the provision subjecting renewal applications to "the same considerations and practice" as original applications, substituting the provision of the 1927 Act which subjected renewal and original applications alike to the standard of "public interest, convenience and necessity."

[14]Federal Radio Commission, Second Annual Report to Congress 169 (October 1, 1928). (Emphasis added.)

the Commission states that it will not consider a past broadcast record which is "within the bounds of average performance." Only records which demonstrate "unusual attention to the public's needs and interests" are to be given favorable consideration, since average performance is expected of all licensees.

Although the 1965 Policy Statement explicitly refrains from reaching the "somewhat different problems raised where an applicant is contesting with a licensee seeking renewal,"[15] the Communications Act itself places the incumbent in the same position as an initial applicant. Under the 1952 amendment to the Act, both initial and renewal applicants must demonstrate that the grant or continuation of a license will serve the "public interest, convenience, and necessity." The Communications Act itself says nothing about a presumption in favor of incumbent licensees at renewal hearings; nor is an inability to displace operating broadcasters inherent in government management, as is established by the fact that in its early years of regulation the Federal Radio Commission often refused to renew licenses.[16]

Nonetheless, the history of Commission decision and of the decisions of this court reflected until recently an operational bias in favor of incumbent licensees;[17] despite Commissioner Hyde's observation in his dissent to the 1965

[15] 1 F.C.C. 2d at 393 n. 1. *But see* Note 23, *infra.*

[16] Under the Radio Act, 150 AM broadcasters out of the 732 operating prior to 1927 surrendered their licenses. Even then, however, the refusal was less a result of the competition of a new applicant than of the desire to reduce the absolute number of broadcasters and the concomitant electrical interference. *See* H. Levin, Broadcast Regulation and Joint Ownership of Media 186, 198 (1960), and cases cited therein.

[17] For criticism of the Commission's "rubber stamp" policy on renewals prior to its decision in WHDH, Inc., 16 F.C.C. 2d 1 (1969), affirmed, *sub nom.* Greater Boston Television Corp. v. F.C.C. [WHDH] , – U.S. App. D.C. –, 444 F. 2d 841 (1970), *see* Cox & Johnson, Broadcasting in America and the FCC's License Renewal Process: An Oklahoma Case Study, 14 F.C.C. 2d 1 (1968); *and* Commissioner Johnson's dissent to group renewal granted to broadcasters in Iowa and Missouri, 11 F.C.C. 2d 810 (1968).

In Chicago Federation of Labor v. Federal Radio Com'n, 59 App. D.C. 333, 41 F. 2d 422 (1930), this court affirmed a Federal Radio Commission refusal to change the broadcast frequency of Station WCFL since the change would displace existing licenses. The court said:

> "It is not consistent with true public convenience, interest, or necessity, that meritorious stations ... should be deprived of broadcasting privileges when once granted to them ... unless clear and sound reasons of public policy demand such action. ..."

50 App. D.C. at 334, 41 F. 2d at 423. Cases such as this one established a presumption in favor of license renewals when their past broadcast record was satisfactory, and led some observers to contend, despite clear language in the Act itself requiring that a licensee expressly waive any claim to use of a frequency predicated on prior use, 47 U.S.C. § 301, that "legal rights or equities flow from a license and must be considered by the Commission in the exercise of its jurisdiction." H. Warner, Radio and Television Law 720 (1949). *See also* Journal Co. v. F.R.C., 60 App. D.C. 92, 48 F. 2d 461 (1931); WOKO, Inc. v. F.C.C., 80 U.S. App. D.C. 333, 153 F. 2d 623, reversed on other grounds, 329 U.S. 223, 67 S.Ct. 213, 91 L.Ed. 204 (1946). Recently, however, and before the Commission's WHDH decision, this circuit has begun to take a hard look at the presumption in favor of renewals. *See* Note 23, *infra.*

Policy Statement that there was no rational or legal basis for its purported nonapplicability to comparative hearings involving renewals,[18] it was commonly assumed that renewal decisions would continue to be governed by policy established in the well-known *Hearst* [19] and *Wabash Valley* [20] cases. These two cases, which began with the unassailable premise that the past performance of a broadcaster is the most reliable indicator of his future performance, were typical of the Commission's past renewal rulings in that their actual effect was to give the incumbent a virtually insuperable advantage on the basis of his past broadcast record *per se.* In *Hearst* the Commission ruled that the incumbent's unexceptional record of past programming performance, coupled with the unavoidable uncertainty whether the challenger would be able to carry out its program proposals, was sufficient to overcome the incumbent's demerits on other comparative criteria. And in *Wabash Valley* the Commission held that a newcomer seeking to oust an incumbent must make a showing of superior service and must have some preference on other comparative criteria.

Then, in the very controversial *WHDH* [21] case, the Commission for the first time in its history, in applying comparative criteria in a renewal proceeding, deposed the incumbent and awarded the frequency to a challenger. Indicating a swing away from *Hearst* and *Wabash Valley*, in practical if not theoretical terms, the Commission stated its intention to insure that "the foundations for determining the best practicable service, as between a renewal and a new applicant, are more nearly equal at their outset."[22] Finding that because the incumbent's programming service had been "within the bounds of the average" it was entitled to no preference, and that the incumbent was inferior on the comparative criteria of diversification and integration, the Commission awarded the license to one of the challengers.

The *WHDH* decision became the immediate subject of fierce attack, provoking criticism from those who feared that it represented a radical departure from previous law [23] and that it threatened the stability of the broadcast

---

[18] 1 F.C.C. 2d at 403.

[19] Hearst Radio, Inc. (WBAL), 15 F.C.C. 1149 (1951).

[20] Wabash Valley Broadcasting Corp. (WTHI-TV), 35 F.C.C. 677 (1963).

[21] *See* Note 17, *supra.*

[22] 16 F.C.C. 2d at 10.

[23] Despite the warning in the 1965 Policy Statement that it was not applicable to the "somewhat different problems" involved in renewal hearings, there were ample indications before the *WHDH* decision that the criteria relevant to original licensing hearings (if not the weight assigned to each such criterion) would be relevant at renewal hearings as well. In Seven (7) League Productions, Inc. (WIII), 1 F.C.C. 2d 1597 (1965), for example, the Commission had decided to apply the 1965 Policy Statement to the introduction of evidence in renewal cases and to give all parties in such cases an opportunity to present arguments as to the relative weight to be accorded the various criteria. At the same time, our own court, which had in earlier cases routinely approved the renewal of incumbent licensees, expressed a concern in two cases that a renewal applicant not receive an unfair advantage by the mere fact of his prior operation of the station. *See* South Florida Television Corp. v. F.C.C., 121 U.S. App. D.C. 293, 349 F. 2d

industry by undermining large financial investments made by prominent broadcasters in reliance upon the assumption that licenses once granted would be routinely renewed. [24] While the Commission's decision was still on appeal to this court, ultimately to be affirmed, the broadcast industry sought to obtain from Congress the elimination or drastic revision of the renewal hearing

---

971 (1965), cert. denied, 382 U.S. 987, 86 S.Ct. 541, 15 L.Ed. 2d 475 (1966), *and* Community Broadcasting Corp. v. F.C.C., 124 U.S. App. D.C. 230, 363 F. 2d 717 (1966).

Although this court affirmed the Commission's *WHDH* decision on the ground that WHDH was in a "special and unique category" because of its past history of inroads made upon the Commission's rules governing fair and orderly adjudication and consequent grant of a four-month temporary license to operate, we also noted:

"... Although the 1965 Policy Statement did not purport to deal with the problems raised by renewal applications the Commission concluded in the same year that the policy statement properly governed the nature and scope of evidence contemplated for renewal proceedings. Seven (7) League Productions, Inc. (WIII), 1 F.C.C. 2d 1597, 1598 (1965). Each applicant was aware that its task was to make the best case possible on the basis of program offering, integration, diversification, past performance and any other matters the parties asked the Commission to consider as pertaining to licensee fitness. As the Hearing Examiner noted, all the applicants were given the fullest opportunity to display their advantages. It is certainly not uncommon for a contender to be called on to put forward all the factors he deems favorable though he cannot be confident what absolute or relative weights will be accorded by those charged with appraisal and judgment."

— U.S. App. D.C. at —, 444 F.2d at 857.

The appropriateness of these decisions is underscored by explicit language in the Communications Act to the effect that no automatic preferential rights are intended to be extended to the renewal applicant. The Act provides, *inter alia*, that "no ... license shall be construed to create any right beyond the terms, conditions, and periods of the license" (47 U.S.C. § 301); that an applicant waives any claim to a frequency "because of the previous use of the same" (47 U.S.C. § 304); that a renewal license may be granted for "a term of not to exceed three years" (47 U.S.C. § 307(d)); and that a license does "not vest in the licensee any right ... in the use of the frequencies ... beyond the term thereof" (47 U.S.C. § 309(h)). *See also* F.C.C. v. Sanders Bros. Radio Station, 309 U.S. 470, 475, 60 S.Ct. 693, 697, 84 L.Ed. 869 (1940):

"The policy of the Act is clear that no person is to have anything in the nature of a property right as a result of the granting of a license. Licenses are limited to a maximum of three years' duration, may be revoked, and need not be renewed. Thus the channels presently occupied remain free for a new assignment to another licensee in the interest of the listening public.

"Plainly it is not the purpose of the Act to protect a licensee against competition but to protect the public. ...."

And see F.C.C. v. Pottsville Broadcasting Co., *supra* Note 10, 309 U.S. at 138, 60 S.Ct. 437; Ashbacker Radio Corp. v. F.C.C., *supra* Note 5; Transcontinental Television Corp. v. F.C.C., 113 U.S. App. D.C. 384, 386-387, 308 F. 2d 339, 341-342 (1962). "[The Federal Communications Act] does not reflect the same concern for 'security of certificate' that appears in other laws." *WHDH, supra* Note 17, — U.S. App. D.C. at —, 444 F. 2d at 854.

[24] *See, e.g.*, $3 Billion in Stations Down the Drain in *Broadcasting*, February 3, 1969, at 19; Jaffe, WHDH: The FCC and Broadcasting License Renewals, 82 Harv. L. Rev. 1693 (1969).

procedure. A bill introduced by Senator Pastore, Chairman of the Communications Subcommittee of the Senate Commerce Committee,[25] proposed to require a two-stage hearing wherein the renewal issue would be determined prior to and exclusive of any evaluation of challengers' applications. The bill provided that if the Commission finds the past record of the licensee to be in the public interest, it shall grant renewal. Competing applications would be permitted to be filed only if the incumbent's license is not renewed. Although more than 100 congressmen and 23 senators quickly announced their support, the bill was bitterly attacked in the Senate hearings by a number of citizens groups testifying, *inter alia*, that the bill was racist, that it would exclude minorities from access to media ownership in most large communities, and that it was inimical to community efforts at improving television programming.[26]

The impact of such citizen opposition measurably slowed the progress of S. 2004. Then, without any formal rule making proceedings,[27] the Commission suddenly issued its own January 15, 1970 Policy Statement, and the Senate bill was thereafter deferred in favor of the Commission's "compromise." The 1970 Policy Statement retains the single hearing approach but provides that the renewal issue must be determined first in a proceeding in which challengers are permitted to appear only for the limited purpose of calling attention to the incumbent's failings.[28] The Policy Statement sets forth that a licensee with a record of "substantial" service to the community, without serious deficiencies, will be entitled to renewal notwithstanding promise of superior performance by a challenger. Only upon a refusal to renew because of the incumbent's past failure to provide substantial service would full comparative hearings be held. Thus, in effect, the Policy Statement administratively "enacts" what the Pastore bill sought to do. The Statement's test for renewal, "substantial service," seems little more than a semantic substitute for the bill's test, "public interest," and

---

[25] S. 2004, 91st Cong., 1st Sess. (1969).

[26] See Hearings on S. 2004 Before the Subcommittee on Communications of the Senate Committee on Commerce, 91st Cong., 1st Sess. (December 1, 1969). A New York Times article entitled "F.C.C. License Renewals: A Policy Emerges" (April 27, 1969), suggested that an analogous change in election laws would mean that no one could run for office until the incumbent had been impeached.

For a critical scholarly analysis of S. 2004, *see* Comment, The Aftermath of WHDH: Regulation by Competition or Protection of Mediocrity? 118 U. Pa. L. Rev. 368, 401-402 (1970): "[T]he Pastore Bill, in its endeavor to promote security in the broadcasting industry and to avoid irrational decision-making, would have the effect of protecting licensees rendering mediocre service and eliminating the most powerful available incentive for better broadcasting."

[27] *See* Note 5 *supra.*

[28] The Commission has in effect abolished the comparative hearing mandated by § 309(a) and (e) and converted the comparative hearing into a petition to deny proceeding. The petition to deny proceeding is separately provided for in the Act under § 309(d), but this section is intended to cover only those situations in which the petitioner does not seek the license himself but seeks only to prevent its award again to the incumbent.

the bill's two-stage hearing, the second stage being dependent on the incumbent's failing the test, is not significantly different from the Statement's summary judgment approach. The "summary judgment" concept of the 1970 Policy Statement, however, runs smack against both statute and case law, as the next section of this opinion will show.

III

Superimposed full length over the preceding historical analysis of the "full hearing" requirement of Section 309(e) of the Communications Act [29] is the towering shadow of *Ashbacker, supra*, and its progeny, perhaps the most important series of cases in American administrative law. *Ashbacker* holds that under Section 309(e), where two or more applications for permits or licenses are mutually exclusive, the Commission must conduct one full comparative hearing of the applications. [30] Although *Ashbacker* involved two original applications, no one has seriously suggested that its principle does not apply to renewal

---

[29] *See* Note 4, *supra.*

[30] The primary question in *Ashbacker* was whether an applicant for a construction permit under the Federal Communications Act is granted the hearing to which he is entitled by the Act where the Commission, having before it two applications which are mutually exclusive, grants one without a hearing and sets the other for hearing. Faced with two "actually exclusive" applications, the Commission had granted that of the Fetzer Broadcasting Company. At the same time, the Commission had designated the Ashbacker Radio Corporation application for hearing. The Commission took the position that at this hearing Ashbacker would have ample opportunity to show that its operation would better serve the public interest than would the grant of the Fetzer application and that the Fetzer grant did not preclude the Commission, at a later date, from taking any action which it found would better serve the public interest. Construing the Act, the Supreme Court stated:

"... We do not think it is enough to say that the power of the Commission to issue a license on a finding of public interest, convenience or necessity supports its grant of one of two mutually exclusive applications without a hearing of the other. For if the grant of one effectively precludes the other, the statutory right to a hearing which Congress has accorded applicants before denial of their applications becomes an empty thing. We think that is the case here.

"... [The procedure adopted by the Commission] is in effect to make [Ashbacker's] hearing a rehearing on the grant of the competitor's license rather than a hearing on the merits of its own application. That may satisfy the strict letter of the law but certainly not its spirit or intent.

         *   *   *

"... We only hold that where two *bona fide* applications are mutually exclusive the grant of one without a hearing to both deprives the loser of the opportunity which Congress chose to give him."

326 U.S. at 330-333, 66 S.Ct. at 150. (Footnote omitted.)

proceedings as well. This court's opinions have uniformly so held, as have decisions of the Commission itself.[31]

It is not surprising, therefore, that the Commission's 1970 Policy Statement implicitly accepts *Ashbacker* as applicable to renewal proceedings. To circumvent the *Ashbacker* strictures, however, it adds a twist: the Policy Statement would limit the "comparative" hearing to a single issue — whether the incumbent licensee had rendered "substantial" past performance without serious deficiencies. If the examiner finds that the licensee has rendered such service, the "comparative" hearing is at an end and, barring successful appeal, the renewal application must be granted. Challenging applicants would thus receive no hearing at all on their own applications, contrary to the express provision of Section 309(e) which requires a "full hearing."

In *Ashbacker* the Commission had promised the challenging applicant a hearing on his application after the rival application was granted. The Supreme Court in *Ashbacker* said that such a promise was "an empty thing." At least the Commission here must be given credit for honesty. It does not make any empty promises. It simply denies the competing applicants the "full hearing" promised them by Section 309(e) of the Act. Unless the renewal applicant's past performance is found to be insubstantial or marred by serious deficiencies,[32] the competing applications get no hearing at all. The proposition that the 1970 Policy Statement violates Section 309(e), as interpreted in *Ashbacker*, is so obvious it need not be labored.[33]

In support of its 1970 Policy Statement the Commission is reduced to reciting the usual litany that "[t]he task of choosing between various claimants for the privilege of using the air waves is essentially an administrative one" consigned by Congress to the Commission. Brief for the Commission at 30. But Congress did not give the Commission *carte blanche*. To protect the public it

---

[31] *See* Note 33, *infra.*

[32] "such as rigged quizzes, violations of the Fairness Doctrine, overcommercialization, broadcast of lotteries, violation of racial discrimination rules, or fraudulent practices as to advertising." 22 F.C.C. 2d at 426.

[33] Although the broadcast industry was perhaps less satisfied with the substantive *result* in *WHDH* than it had been with the results in *Hearst* and *Wabash Valley*, it should be clear from our earlier historical review that the *procedure* by which the Commission came to its decision was precisely the same in all three of these cases. It is true that the 1965 Policy Statement on Comparative Broadcast Hearings specifically refrained from reaching the "somewhat different problems" raised by renewal applications. But the Commission itself concluded within the same year, and consistently with its own past practice, that the same comparative criteria set out in the Statement (if not the weight assigned to each such criterion) must also be considered in renewal hearings. Seven (7) League Productions, Inc. (WIII), *supra* Note 23. Thus, without impinging at all upon the Commission's substantive discretion in weighing factors and granting licenses, our holding today merely requires the Commission to adhere to the comparative hearing procedure which it has followed without fail since *Ashbacker* and which has rightly come to be accepted by observers as a part of the due process owed to all mutually exclusive applications.

limited its mandate with the Section 309(e) "full hearing" requirement. Unless the limitation is observed, any putative exercise of the mandate is a nullity.

Early after *Ashbacker* this court indicated what a "full hearing" entailed. In Johnston Broadcasting Co. v. F.C.C., 85 U.S. App. D.C. 40, 45-46, 175 F.2d 351, 356-357 (1949), we explained that the statutory right to a full hearing included a decision upon all relevant criteria:

> A choice between two applicants involves more than the bare quali-fications of each applicant. It involves a comparison of characteristics. Both A and B may be qualified, but if a choice must be made, the question is which is the better qualified. . . .
> . . . Comparative qualities and not mere positive characteristics must then be considered.

*   *   *

> . . . The Commission cannot ignore a material difference between two applicants and make findings in respect to selected characteristics only. . . . It must take into account all the characteristics which indicate differences, and reach an over-all relative determination upon an evaluation of all factors, conflicting in many cases. . . .

We, as well as the Commission,[34] have consistently applied the teaching of *Johnston Broadcasting* to renewal proceedings. *See* South Florida Television Corp. v. F.C.C., 121 U.S. App. D.C. 293, 349 F. 2d 971 (1965); Community Broadcasting Corp. v. F.C.C., 124 U.S. App. D.C. 230, 363 F. 2d 717 (1966). Particularly since the 1965 Policy Statement, in a comparative hearing involving a renewal application each applicant has been aware that its task is "to make the best case possible on the basis of program offering, integration, diversification, past performance and any other matters the parties asked the Commission to consider as pertaining to licensee fitness." *WHDH, supra*, – U.S. App. D.C. at –, 444 F. 2d at 857.

We do not dispute, of course, that incumbent licensees should be judged primarily on their records of past performance. Insubstantial past performance should preclude renewal of a license. The licensee, having been given the chance and having failed, should be through. *Compare WHDH, supra.* At the same time,

---

[34] There are several cases cited by respondents to the effect that *no hearing* need be held where an application fails to measure up to the Commission's rules and does not indicate waiver, or where one of several mutually exclusive applicants is basically unqualified. United States v. Storer Broadcasting Co., 351 U.S. 192, 76 S.Ct. 763, 100 L.Ed. 1081 (1956); Guinan v. F.C.C., 111 U.S. App. D.C. 371, 297 F. 2d 782 (1961); Simmons v. F.C.C., 79 U.S. App. D.C. 264, 145 F. 2d 578 (1944). Contrary to the suggestion of respondents, however, these cases in no way undercut our holding of today. Whatever the power of the Commission to set basic qualifications in the public interest and to deny hearings to *unqualified* applicants, the cases cited above cannot be read as authorizing the Commission to deny *qualified* applicants their statutory right to a *full hearing* on their own merits.

superior performance should be a plus of major significance in renewal proceedings.[35] Indeed, as *Ashbacker* recognizes, in a renewal proceeding, a new applicant is under a greater burden to "make the comparative showing necessary to displace an established licensee." 326 U.S. at 332, 66 S.Ct. at 151. But under Section 309(e) he must be given a chance. How can he ever show his application is comparatively better if he does not get a hearing on it? The Commission's 1970 Policy Statement's summary procedure would deny him that hearing.[36]

[35]The court recognizes that the public itself will suffer if incumbent licensees cannot reasonably expect renewal when they have rendered superior service. Given the incentive, an incumbent will naturally strive to achieve a level of performance which gives him a clear edge on challengers at renewal time. But if the Commission fails to articulate the standards by which to judge superior performance, and if it is thus impossible for an incumbent to be reasonably confident of renewal when he renders superior performance, then an incumbent will be under an unfortunate temptation to lapse into mediocrity, to seek the protection of the crowd by eschewing the creative and the venturesome in programming and other forms of public service. The Commission in rule making proceedings should strive to clarify in both quantitative and qualitative terms what constitutes superior service. *See* Comment, *supra* Note 26, 118 U. Pa. L. Rev. at 406. Along with elimination of excessive and loud advertising and delivery of quality programs, one test of superior service should certainly be whether and to what extent the incumbent has reinvested the profit on his license to the service of the viewing and listening public. We note with approval that such rule making proceedings may soon be under way. News Notes, 39 U.S. L. Week 2513 (March 16, 1971).

[36]Since one very significant aspect of the "public interest, convenience, and necessity" is the need for diverse and antagonistic sources of information, the Commission simply cannot make a valid public interest determination without considering the extent to which the ownership of the media will be concentrated or diversified by the grant of one or another of the applications before it. Johnston Broadcasting Co. v. F.C.C., 85 U.S. App. D.C. 40, 175 F. 2d 351 (1949); McClatchy Broadcasting Co. v. F.C.C., 99 U.S. App. D.C. 195, 239 F. 2d 15 (1956), cert. denied, 353 U.S. 918, 77 S.Ct. 662, 1 L.Ed. 2d 665 (1957); Scripps-Howard Radio v. F.C.C., 89 U.S. App. D.C. 13, 189 F. 2d 677, cert. denied, 342 U.S. 830, 72 S.Ct. 55, 96 L.Ed. 628 (1951). The Supreme Court itself has on numerous occasions recognized the distinct connection between diversity of ownership of the mass media and the diversity of ideas and expression required by the First Amendment. *See, e.g.*, Associated Press v. United States, 326 U.S. 1, 20, 65 S.Ct. 1416, 89 L.Ed. 2013 (1945); Red Lion Broadcasting Co. v. F.C.C., 395 U.S. 367, 390, 89 S.Ct. 1794, 23 L.Ed. 2d 371 (1969). While it is possible under the "fairness doctrine" approved in *Red Lion Broadcasting Co., supra*, to insure that all stations will give time to more than one side of important and controversial issues, we reiterate the observation of this court in *WHDH, supra* Note 17, that:

"The Commission need not be confined to the technique of exercising regulatory surveillance to assure that licensees will discharge duties imposed on them, perhaps grudgingly and perhaps to the minimum required. It may also seek in the public interest to certify as licensees those who would speak out with fresh voice, would most naturally initiate, encourage and expand diversity of approach and viewpoint."

− U.S. App. D.C. at −, 444 F. 2d at 860. As new interest groups and hitherto silent minorities emerge in our society, they should be given some stake in and chance to broadcast on our radio and television frequencies. According to the uncontested testimony of petitioners, no more than a dozen of 7,500 broadcast licenses issued are owned by racial minorities. The effect of the 1970 Policy Statement, ruled illegal today,

The suggestion that the possibility of nonrenewal, however remote, might chill uninhibited, robust and wide-open speech cannot be taken lightly. But the Commission, of course, may not penalize exercise of First Amendment rights. And the statute does provide for judicial review. Indeed, the failure to promote the full exercise of First Amendment freedoms through the broadcast medium may be a consideration against license renewal. Unlike totalitarian regimes, in a free country there can be no authorized voice of government. Though dependent on government for its license, independence is perhaps the most important asset of the renewal applicant.

The Policy Statement purports to strike a balance between the need for "predictability and stability"[37] and the need for a competitive spur. It does so by providing that the qualifications of challengers, no matter how superior they may be, may not be considered unless the incumbent's past performance is found not to have been "substantially attuned" to the needs and interests of the community. Unfortunately, instead of stability the Policy Statement has produced *rigor mortis*.[38] For over a year now, since the Policy Statement substantially limited a challenger's right to a full comparative hearing on the merits of his own application, not a single renewal challenge has been filed.

Petitioners have come to this court to protest a Commission policy which violates the clear intent of the Communications Act that the award of a broadcasting license should be a "public trust."[39] As a unanimous Supreme Court recently put it, "It is the right of the viewers and listeners, not the right of the broadcasters, which is paramount."[40] Our decision today restores healthy

---

would certainly have been to perpetuate this dismaying situation. While no quota system is being recommended or required, and while the fairness doctrine no doubt does serve to guarantee some minimum diversity of views, we simply note our own approval of the Commission's long-standing and firmly held policy in favor of decentralization of media control. Diversification is a factor properly to be weighed and balanced with other important factors, including the renewal applicant's prior record, at a renewal hearing. For two strong statements by the Commission itself on the importance of diversification, *see* Bamberger Broadcasting Service, Inc., 3 Pike & Fischer R.R. 914, 925 (1946), *and* Policy Statement on Comparative Broadcast Hearings, 1 F.C.C. 2d 393, 394 & n. 4 (1965).

[37]The Commission's fears for the stability of the industry seem groundless in view of the fact that in the year following the *WHDH* opinion — that is, in the period when feared instability was greatest — only eight out of approximately 250 (or three per cent of) television license renewals were challenged. *See* Staff Study, *supra* Note 4, at 18 n. 101.

[38]The recent report of the United States Commission on Civil Rights commented that the kinds of competitive proceedings eliminated under the 1970 Policy Statement are "an effective mechanism for bringing about greater racial and ethnic sensitivity in programming, nondiscriminatory employment practices, and other affirmative changes which otherwise might not take place." U.S. Commission on Civil Rights, Federal Civil Rights Enforcement Effort 283 (1971).

[39]"By whatever name or classification, broadcasters are temporary permittees — fiduciaries — of a great public resource . . ." Office of Communication of United Church of Christ v. F.C.C., 138 U.S. App. D.C. 112, 117, 425 F. 2d 543, 548 (1969).

[40]Red Lion Broadcasting Co. v. F.C.C., *supra* Note 36, 395 U.S. at 390, 89 S.Ct. at 1806.

competition by repudiating a Commission policy which is unreasonably weighted in favor of the licensees it is meant to regulate, to the great detriment of the listening and viewing public.

Wherefore it is ORDERED: (1) that the Policy Statement, being contrary to law, shall not be applied by the Commission in any pending or future comparative renewal hearings; (2) that the Commission's order of July 21, 1970 denying petitioners' petition for reconsideration of the Policy Statement and refusing to institute rule making proceedings is reversed; and (3) that these proceedings are remanded to the Commission with directions to redesignate all comparative renewal hearings to which the Policy Statement was deemed applicable to reflect this court's judgment.

MacKinnon, Circuit Judge.

I concur in the foregoing opinion. While I recognize the desire and need for reasonable stability in obtaining renewal licenses, under the present statute as construed by Ashbacker Radio Corp. v. F.C.C., 326 U.S. 327, 66 S.Ct. 148, 90 L.Ed. 108 (1945), I do not consider it possible to provide administratively that operating licensees who furnish program service "*substantially* attuned to meeting the needs and interests of its area . . . [without] *serious* deficiencies . . . will be preferred over the newcomer and *his* application for renewal will be granted." Such policy would effectively prevent a newcomer applicant from being heard on the merits of his application, no matter how superlative his qualifications. It would also, in effect, substitute a standard of *substantial* service for the *best possible* service to the public and effectively negate the hearing requirements of the statute as interpreted by the Supreme Court. If such change is desired, in my opinion, it must be accomplished by amendment of the statute.

RELATED READING

Broadcasting and Social Action: A Handbook for Station Executives.
Washington: National Association of Educational Broadcasters, 1969.

Cohn, Marcus. "Should the FCC Reward Stations That Do a Good Job?"
Saturday Review, August 14, 1971, 45-47.

Emery, Walter B. "Nervous Tremors in the Broadcasting Industry." *Educational Broadcasting Review* 3:3 (June 1969), 43-51.

Goldin, Hyman H. " 'Spare the Golden Goose' — the Aftermath of WHDH in FCC License Renewal Policy." *Harvard Law Review* 83 (1970), 1014-1036.

Guimary, Donald. "Citizens Broadcast Councils." *Educational Broadcasting Review* 6 (October 1972), 333-338.

Jennings, Ralph M. *How to Protect Citizen Rights in Television and Radio.*
Revised ed. New York: Office of Communication, United Church of Christ, 1969.

Johnson, Nicholas. *How to Talk Back to Your Television Set.* Boston: Atlantic-Little, Brown, 1970.

Kennel, LeRoy E. *Ecology of the Airwaves.* Scottsdale, Pennsylvania: Herald Press, 1971.

Leone, Richard C. "Public Interest Advocacy and the Regulatory Process." *The Annals of the American Academy of Political and Social Science* 400 (March 1972), 46-58.

Lobsenz, Norman M. "Everett Parker's Broadcasting Crusade." *Columbia Journalism Review*, Fall 1969, 30-36.

Mayer, Martin. "The Challengers." *TV Guide*, February 3, 1973, 5-13; February 10, 1973, 33-40; February 17, 1973, 18-21.

"McGraw-Hill Sets Record for Concessions to Minorities." *Broadcasting*, May 15, 1972, 25-26.

Milam, Lorenzo W. *Sex in Broadcasting: A Handbook on Starting Community Radio Stations.* Los Gatos, Cal.: Dildo Press, 1972.

Millard, Steve. "Broadcasting's Pre-emptive Court." *Broadcasting*, August 30, 1971, 17-23.

Mullally, Donald P. "Broadcasting and Social Change." *Quarterly Journal of Speech* 56 (February 1970), 40-44.

Padden, Preston R. "The Emerging Role of Citizens' Groups in Broadcast Regulation." *Federal Communications Bar Journal* 25 (1972), 82-110.

Price, Monroe E., and John Wicklein. *Cable Television: A Guide for Citizen Action.* Philadelphia: Pilgrim Press, 1972.

Prowitt, Marsha O'Bannon. *Guide to Citizen Action in Radio and Television.*
New York: Office of Communication, United Church of Christ, 1971.

Shamberg, Michael. *Guerrilla Television.* New York: Holt, Rinehart and Winston, 1971.

Source Catalog No. 1 — Communications. Chicago: Swallow Press, 1971.

Stavins, Ralph L., ed. *Television Today: The End of Communication and the Death of Community.* Washington: Communication Service Corporation, 1971.

Tate, Charles, ed. *Cable Television in the Cities: Community Control, Public Access, and Minority Ownership.* Washington: Urban Institute, 1972.

Zeidenberg, Leonard. "The Struggle Over Broadcast Access." *Broadcasting*, Part I, September 20, 1971, 32-43; Part II, September 27, 1971, 24-29.

United States Congress, Senate, Committee on Commerce. *Amend Communications Act of 1934.* Hearings before Communications Subcommittee, 91st Congress, 1st Session, on S. 2004, Part I, August 5-7, 1969; Part II, December 1-5, 1969. Washington: Government Printing Office, 1969.

U.
24

Ap.
18

433
359
92

Sewell
Sorbel
Atkinson
Anderson

Andy.
new
apt.

Rayman Ruby
        Raiman
717 W. 7th

①
139
74
42
255

Graßif?

1-119
92
68
279

433
394
340

687
637
44(3)